SOCIOLOGY ON THE MENU

Sociology on the Menu is an accessible introduction to the sociology of food. High-lighting the social and cultural dimensions of the human food system, from production to consumption, it encourages us to consider new ways of thinking about the apparently mundane, everyday act of eating.

This book provides a broad conceptual framework, based on the proposition that the food systems and food consumption patterns of contemporary Western societies are the products of the complex interplay of the social forces of change and innovation on the one hand and, on the other, those which engender stability and continuity. The main areas covered include the origins of human subsistence, the development of the modern food system, food and the family, eating out, diet and health, food risks and food scares, dieting and body image, the meanings of meat, vegetarianism and the role of sweetness in the human diet.

Sociology on the Menu provides a comprehensive overview of the multidisciplinary literature, focusing on key texts and studies to help students identify the main themes. It urges us to reappraise the taken-for-granted and familiar experiences of selecting, preparing and sharing food and to see our own habits and choices, preferences and aversions in their broader cultural context.

Alan Beardsworth is Lecturer in Sociology and **Teresa Keil** is Visiting Fellow, both in the Department of Social Sciences, Loughborough University.

SOCIOLOGY ON THE MENU

An invitation to the study of food and society

Alan Beardsworth and Teresa Keil

London and New York

First published 1997
by Routledge
11 New Fetter Lane, London EC4P 4EE

Simultaneously published in the USA and Canada
by Routledge
29 West 35th Street, New York, NY 10001

Typeset in Baskerville by
Pure Tech India Limited, Pondicherry

Printed and bound in Great Britain by
TJ Press Ltd, Padstow, Cornwall

British Library Cataloguing in Publication Data

A catalogue record for this book is available from the British Library

Library of Congress Cataloging in Publication Data

A catalogue record for this book has been requested

ISBN 0–415–11424–1 (hbk)
ISBN 0–415–11425–X (pbk)

For Helen and Ian

CONTENTS

vii

CONTENTS

FIGURES AND TABLES

FIGURES

TABLES

PREFACE

The origins of this book can be traced back to the mid-1980s when we first became aware of the curious fact that food and eating seemed to be topics for enthusiastic discussion for virtually everyone but the sociologist. This realization led us to begin a search for any sociologically relevant material that could satisfy our curiosity. We then went a step further by initiating our own research into the fascinating subject of vegetarianism, a choice of research area which was made in order to give us access to respondents who had critically examined much of our conventional wisdom about the day-to-day realities of eating. Grappling with the problem of explaining our findings helped us to clarify our understanding of what a sociology of food and eating might look like.

Happily, we were not alone in identifying an area of potentially fruitful expansion in sociology. The amount of research and writing in this field began to increase to such an extent that by the early 1990s we felt confident enough to offer an undergraduate course entitled 'Food and Society: Sociological Perspectives'. It is that course which provided the foundations of this book and helped us to identify the themes which we have sought to develop and illustrate.

Many people have provided assistance, both direct and indirect, in the preparation of this text. In particular, we would like to express our appreciation of the interest shown in our work by Alan Bryman, Nick Norgan and Alan Radley, and of the help provided by Frank Parry of the University's Pilkington Library. Special thanks must also go to those colleagues with whom we have worked in the context of a series of food- and nutrition-related projects, namely, Barbara Dobson, Jackie Goode, Cheryl Haslam, Marie Kennedy, Emma Sherratt and Robert Walker. We have benefited enormously from our discussions with them and from their insight and expertise. However, any shortcomings and inadequacies are entirely our own responsibility. The smooth progress of this whole project has also depended heavily on the invaluable secretarial support provided by Ann Smith, and additionally by Christine Mosley.

Alan Beardsworth and Teresa Keil
Loughborough University
October 1995

INTRODUCTION

FOOD AND EATING: A CASE OF SOCIOLOGICAL NEGLECT?

One of the most effective ways of assessing which topics or issues are generally regarded as fundamental to a given discipline is to survey the contents of that discipline's standard introductory textbooks. In such hallowed volumes are enshrined, if only in their most basic form, those principles, theories and doctrines which are deemed essential for all recruits to master. However, scanning the contents pages of the wide range of introductory sociology texts available leads to an inevitable conclusion: alongside the themes which, in various guises, occur again and again (stratification, work and employment, crime and deviance, ethnicity, gender, the family, etc.) you will not come across food and eating as a specifically identified focus of interest. If such issues are addressed at all, they usually appear on the margins of one or more of the central themes.

In one sense, at least, this marginality is not too surprising. Quite clearly, it is feasible for sociologists with imagination and initiative to create an almost endless list of potentially fruitful sub-headings within their discipline (the sociology of housing, the sociology of sport, the sociology of transport, the sociology of tourism – or, more fancifully, why not the sociology of furniture, or the sociology of children's games?). While such lines of intellectual pursuit may yield all kinds of fascinating insights, they are likely to remain relatively specialized interests, coexisting with each other and developing each along its own lines beneath the broad umbrella of sociology. Much the same might be said of the sociology of food and eating. Here we have a specialized area which deserves attention, but which is never likely to be of central importance. This is a perfectly viable position and one that allows interested teachers and researchers to get on with work in this area to the benefit of themselves, their students and their readers. On the other hand, we might argue that attempts to describe and understand the complex interrelations between food and society deserve special attention, deserve elevation to a position equal to that of the major themes of contemporary sociology. This view becomes eminently plausible if one considers

1

just how fundamental a part of human experience eating really is, given the inexorable and relentless demands of the body for nutrients, and given the potent and multifaceted symbolic charges that food can carry. Moreover, enormous amounts of human energy, ingenuity and co-operative effort are devoted to the processes involved in the production, distribution and preparation of food – processes which are absolutely essential to the long-term survival and continuity of any society. What is more, the human food chain, with its myriad interlinked and interacting human and non-human elements, might justifiably be conceived of as the core sub-system of the social system as a whole, the very foundation of human social organization. With these arguments in mind, and given the high level of popular interest in this area, sociology's relative neglect of such issues and their virtual absence from its intellectual heartlands becomes something of a puzzle. However, this is a puzzle to which one might offer some tentative answers.

For example, it may well be that the very much taken-for-granted nature of eating has rendered this activity, and the complex of other activities and relationships which cluster around it, relatively 'invisible' to sociologists. Of course, for eating to be a mundane activity, for food to be an unproblematical aspect of daily life, one crucial condition must be fulfilled: the food supply itself must be secure. This is certainly the case for the vast majority of people in Western societies (and is especially so for the vast majority of sociologists). In circumstances where the food supply is less secure, food-related concerns will usually be a good deal higher on the agenda. In addition, in developed, industrialized societies, the processes of food production and distribution (if not of food preparation and consumption) are usually largely beyond the view and concern of the urban, middle-class individual that is the typical professional sociologist. It is frequently only within the confines of the specialized area of rural sociology that such issues come under sociological scrutiny. Indeed, this effect is mirrored at the domestic end of the human food chain. The purchasing, preparation and presentation of food (and, indeed, the disposal of leftover food and the more menial tasks of the kitchen) are strongly associated with the mundane, unglamourous labour of housework, the traditional domain of women, and hold little intellectual appeal to the male researchers and theorists who have historically dominated the profession.

There is an additional factor which may well have helped to inhibit the development of sociological interest in this area. In a sense, the study and analysis of food-related issues may have been seen as the intellectual property of other professions and other academic disciplines (for example, on the production side, the property of agronomists, economists and geographers, and, on the consumption side, of nutritionists and dietitians). What is more, since the inception of sociology as a recognized discipline, its practitioners have striven to assert its intellectual autonomy and to demonstrate that social processes exist at their own distinctive level and require their own distinctive explanations. This seems to have encouraged sociologists to be somewhat wary of becoming too closely associated with debates about the significance of the physiological bases of human experience and human existence, possibly out of concern about being seen as guilty of reductionism by their colleagues. Thus, activities where the physiological dimension is clearly salient have, to some extent, been seen as outside the proper theoretical preoccupations and research interests of sociologists.

This coyness in relation to food and eating stands in contrast to the long-standing interest in the area shown by some of sociology's neighbouring disciplines. Historians, for example, have shown a good deal of interest in such issues. This is hardly surprising, given the tremendous impact that basic realities relating to the control of and access to food resources can have upon broader social, economic and political events and processes. Similarly, social anthropologists also seem to have been much more willing to incorporate the analysis of matters alimentary into their work. One can perhaps speculate that this fact is, to some extent, due to the nature of the subject matter of the discipline. Social anthropology's major concern in the twentieth century has been the detailed description, documentation and analysis of the workings of relatively small-scale, traditional social systems which have usually been conceptualized in broadly holistic terms. Looking at a traditional society in this holistic fashion virtually demands that some attention be paid to the processes involved in producing, distributing, preparing and consuming food, since these make up a complex of activities which provides the whole framework of life on a daily and a seasonal basis. What is more, in societies where the food supply is somewhat insecure and unpredictable, food-related matters are likely to be much more .salient in the day-to-day concerns of the researcher's subjects.

However, it is perhaps within the discipline of psychology that an interest in food and eating has been particularly well developed. This interest has covered a wide range of topics, including the sensory, cognitive and emotional dimensions of eating, the processes of nutritional socialization and the causes and manifestations of eating disorders. Again, it is possible to speculate about why psychologists have devoted a good deal more of their attention to dietary issues than have sociologists. It may be that the key to this puzzle lies in the nature of the disciplinary range of psychology itself. Those working towards the physiological end of this range are well placed to investigate the physical processes of eating in their immediate sensory and behavioural contexts. On the other hand, those working towards the social end of this range are in a good position to investigate the complex influences of personality, biography and interpersonal relationships. In fact, the interests of the social psychologist may sometimes overlap with those of the sociologist, as, indeed, may those of the social anthropologist and the historian.

A SURGE IN SOCIOLOGICAL INTEREST

Despite what has been argued above, there can be no doubt that recent years have seen a marked increase in the willingness of some sociologists to direct their attention towards this previously neglected set of topics. Evidence for this rising level of engagement comes from a number of sources. Perhaps the most significant indicator is the increasing numbers of books and journal articles produced by sociologists which are either directly or indirectly addressed to food-related issues. While it would certainly be an unwarranted exaggeration to suggest that what had previously been a trickle of material has become a flood, there can be little doubt that the current of publications (to continue the hydraulic metaphor) is now flowing more strongly than ever before.

Other indicators appear to confirm this overall impression. University courses which can be classified under the broad heading of 'Food and Society' are already widely available in the USA and Canada, and have now gained a foothold in the UK. Recent research developments also support this view. Perhaps the most notable is the research initiative entitled 'The Nation's Diet', set up in 1991 by the UK's Economic and Social Research Council. With a budget of £1.4 million, this six-year programme was divided into two phases. In both phases a substantial number of the projects funded were sociological in orientation or contained a significant sociological component. The increasing inclination of sociologists towards research related to the social and cultural dimensions of food and eating is also indicated by their ever more frequent participation in both national and international conferences devoted to nutritional issues. What is more, there is an increasingly wide range of international organizations and associations dedicated wholly or partly to the study of the relationships between nutritional and social processes from a sociological perspective.

Accounting for this surge of sociological interest is undoubtedly as speculative an exercise as attempting to explain previous neglect. However, one factor that is almost certainly of considerable significance is the occurrence in recent years of a shift in the centre of gravity of sociology itself. A discipline once largely concerned with the analysis of the processes of *production* (in terms of their social organization and their consequences for the social, economic and political dynamics of society) is now increasingly turning its attention to the social organization of *consumption*, and to the ideological foundations of consumerism in its many guises. Such a change serves to push food-related issues up the sociological agenda, given the importance of food items in any household's expenditure patterns.

Another important shift in sociology involves the increasing salience of issues relating to the experiences of women, largely as a result of the initiatives taken by writers and theorists informed by feminist perspectives. Since the purchasing, preparation and presentation of food is still regarded, in many senses, as essentially women's work, such activities have been drawn increasingly into the domain of sociological scrutiny. Indeed, this has been closely associated with an enhanced recognition by sociologists of the significance of domestic work and the domestic sphere in general.

Furthermore, sociological concerns are often indirectly (or even directly) linked to the broader political and policy-oriented issues current in the society

4

in which the discipline is practised. In this sense, sociology's increasing interest in food can be seen as, in part, a reflection of the increasing importance of a range of nutritional issues in the various policy arenas. Pressure groups, professional groups and the state itself are engaged in a whole series of debates about dietary standards, food purity and hygiene, production methods and standards, animal welfare, the links between diet and health, and the nutritional adequacy of food intake patterns of certain vulnerable groups such as low-income households, to name but a few key examples. In this connection, it is also worth bearing in mind that environmental issues are now much higher on the agenda in the developed, industrial societies than ever before. Sociologists have realized, somewhat belatedly, that this area demands their attention, too. However, environmental concerns almost inevitably entail a consideration of the dynamics of human food chains in all their complexity. The ways in which food is produced and distributed have an enormous impact upon particular ecological systems and upon the environment in general. Conversely, environmental changes (for example, habitat degradation, erosion and various forms of pollution) can have significant implications for food supply and food quality. The increasing willingness of sociologists to focus upon such possibilities has also contributed to a rising awareness of food as a topic.

THE INCORPORATION OF FOOD-RELATED ISSUES INTO SOCIOLOGY

There are, perhaps, two basic routes through which the study of food and eating is being incorporated into the mainstream of sociology. The first of these involves the analysis of food production and consumption (and the elaborate social structures and relationships which underpin these) with the specific aim of illuminating existing sociological preoccupations. Thus, the analysis of patterns of food allocation and consumption has been used very effectively to illustrate the ways in which the underlying dimensions of social differentiation (gender, age and class, for example) manifest themselves in the experiences of everyday life. Similarly, the analysis of the processes of food production and distribution has been used to highlight the workings of capital-intensive, highly rationalized economic systems. The second of these two routes involves the reverse of the first. Instead of food-related social processes being investigated as a means to a particular sociological end, food-based topics can become ends in themselves, that is, specific questions can be asked about how we obtain, share, select, prepare and eat our food, and how we allocate meaning to what we are doing. Once these questions have been posed, well-tried sociological methods, perspectives and theories can be applied in order to attempt to understand what is going on. Of course, these two approaches may happily coexist within one piece of work, since the difference between them is essentially one of emphasis. However, if the sociology of food is to establish itself in the mainstream of the discipline, the second of these two approaches deserves attention, since the social and cultural dimensions of food systems raise many unique and fascinating issues, a selection of which it is the purpose of this book to address.

There can, indeed, be no doubt that the complex of human activities and experiences which relates to producing and consuming food is potentially a source of endlessly tantalizing puzzles for the sociologist. While food intake is an inescapable physiological necessity, eating entails far more than its basic physiological dimensions. Quite clearly, the act of eating lies at the point of intersection of a whole series of intricate physiological, psychological, ecological, economic, political, social and cultural processes. Such intersections present the human and social sciences with some of their most intriguing questions and challenges. However, in order to rise to such challenges, sociologists may need to be prepared to think more flexibly about the traditional boundaries of their discipline. Historically, sociologists have laid considerable stress on the idea of a clear dichotomy between the biological and the social, between 'nature' and 'culture', with the intellectual territory of sociology located firmly on the cultural/social side of this deep divide. In the past, this confident demarcation has proved to be highly fruitful, and capable of stimulating brilliant analyses of the social organization and dynamics of modern societies, centred upon such enduring themes as conflict and integration, change and stability, rationalization and industrialization. However, such a clear-cut demarcation may have contributed to the marginalization of such themes as gender, sexuality, the body, health and illness and, of course, food and eating. For many reasons yet to be documented fully we now seem to be witnessing a softening of this previously strictly enforced boundary and an increasing recognition of its essential permeability. Interactions across this boundary are generating more and more sociological interest, thus opening up novel areas of study and moving previously marginal themes towards the centre of interest and into the mainstream of sociological debate.

THE AIMS OF THIS BOOK

A text such as this one has a number of interrelated aims, and it is helpful for the reader to see these set out at this stage in a reasonably systematic fashion:

1   To highlight for the reader the social and cultural dimensions of the human food system, from production to consumption.
2   To achieve this by providing accounts of key texts and studies which are to be found in the diverse and rather widely dispersed literature which exists in this area.
3   To focus the reader's attention on the main themes which have been addressed in the literature (these themes being reflected in the sequence of chapters which makes up the structure of the book).
4   To draw out the interconnections between these themes and to attempt to set them within a broad conceptual framework, which will be discussed in more

detail in Chapter 3. This framework is based upon the proposition that the food systems and food consumption patterns of contemporary Western societies are the products of the complex interplay of, on the one hand, social forces and processes inducing instability, change and innovation, and, on the other, social forces and mechanisms engendering stability and continuity.

5 To encourage professional social scientists (particularly sociologists) to develop an interest in this area, and, even more importantly, to begin to take up some of the intellectual challenges it presents.
6 To encourage the reader to consider new ways of thinking about the apparently mundane, everyday act of eating, and to see his or her own habits and choices, preferences and aversions in their broader cultural and social contexts.
7 To achieve these admittedly rather grandiose aims by presenting ideas and information in an accessible, although not necessarily undemanding, fashion.
8 Finally, if at all feasible, to entertain and engage the reader with some of the intriguing insights which are on offer.

The approach employed will be a deliberately eclectic one. While sociological sources will provide the bulk of our raw material, the ideas and findings of neighbouring disciplines will also be drawn upon, as and when these can be used in order to support sociological analysis and to extend sociological perspectives. The audience for this book is conceived in similarly broad terms:

1 Students of sociology at all levels, whether in the context of specific food-related courses or in the context of other sociology courses where such topics are relevant.
2 Other social science students, including those studying such diverse disciplines as social policy, psychology, social anthropology and human geography.
3 Students undergoing professional training in the areas of nutrition and dietetics.
4 Students undergoing professional training in the various branches of nursing and medicine.
5 Students undergoing training on food-related vocational courses.
6 Established professionals in areas related to nutrition, health or social policy.
7 The general reader who is attracted to a sociological approach to the contemplation of food and eating.

Quite clearly, with such a diverse readership in mind, the avowed aim of producing a text which is accessible to the non-sociologist but at the same time can provide the stimulus for the sociologically oriented reader to follow up the issues in more depth, is by no means a straightforward one to fulfil.

THE ORGANIZATION OF THIS BOOK

The text is organized into four main parts, each with its distinctive subject matter.

Part I seeks to set the scene by looking briefly at selected aspects of the prehistory and history of human food systems (Chapter 1). Chapter 2 deals with the far-reaching changes in human social organization which have produced a whole series of crucial transformations, culminating in the emergence of the modern food system in all its global complexity. Chapter 3 then goes on to lay down a basic framework for the sociological analysis of the food system and to examine the various sociological perspectives which have been, or might be, employed to carry out such analysis. This chapter also deals with complementary approaches from neighbouring disciplines which have influenced or informed the work of sociologists.

Part II sets out to examine a number of aspects of the social organization of eating. Chapter 4 looks at the processes of social differentiation within the family (for example, by age and gender) that influence the ways in which food is prepared and distributed within the household. The ways in which food consumption patterns can be seen to highlight class differences and reinforce family identity are also considered. Since an increasing proportion of food intake takes place outside the family or household setting, Chapter 5 focuses on the phenomenon of eating out, in its many guises.

Part III attempts to provide an insight into the very broad area of food, health and well-being by focusing on a series of issues which have emerged as important themes in the available literature. Thus, Chapter 6 describes changing conceptions of the linkages between dietary patterns, on the one hand, and health and disease outcomes on the other. Such conceptions, it will be argued, have undergone a fundamental process of rationalization in modern societies. Chapter 7 focuses on the interrelated phenomena of deep-seated chronic food anxieties and acute 'food scares'. Both these phenomena can exert a potent influence on food choices and consumption patterns, and their underlying causes will be analysed. Chapter 8 moves on to consider another characteristic set of anxieties frequently related to food intake. Unease in relation to body image and concern about the acquisition of body fat can reach obsessional levels in certain circumstances, and the cultural and social roots of these effects will be discussed.

Part IV looks at selected examples of patterns of food preferences and, on the other side of the coin, at food prohibitions or avoidances. The subject matter of Chapter 9 is the convoluted and sometimes contradictory symbolism of meat, simultaneously one of the most widely prized components of the human diet and one of the most ambivalent. Meat rejection and meat avoidance figure in Chapter 10, which sets out to describe the origins and multifaceted manifestations of vegetarianism as an increasingly popular dietary option. Chapter 11 takes as its topic the role of sweetness in the human diet, the importance of the production and consumption of sugar for the global food system and the symbolism of confectionery.

In a sense, each of the chapters described here is designed to provide a self-contained introduction to its chosen subject matter. However, the social processes under discussion are themselves frequently shaped by a set of underlying ideological trends and structural transformations in human food systems. As has been indicated above, these trends and structures, which form the framework for the everyday practices of food production and consumption, will be analysed in · Chapter 3, along with the various sociological perspectives which can be drawn upon. As a prelude to this, however, Chapters 1 and 2 set out to sketch the background to the emergence of the modern food system, the system which is the basic object of analysis of this book.

Perhaps at this stage the authors can be forgiven for succumbing to the temptation to use a nutritional metaphor in expressing the hope that readers will enjoy selecting from the menu of ideas displayed here and will find that their appetite for more has been whetted!

Part I

THE SOCIAL DIMENSIONS OF THE FOOD SYSTEM

1

THE ORIGINS OF HUMAN SUBSISTENCE

Any attempt to make sense of the contemporary realities of food and eating from a sociological viewpoint must involve some consideration of the past. If we wish to try to understand the food production systems upon which we depend and the food consumption patterns in which we participate, then a familiarity with certain crucial historical themes is essential. Indeed, it is also necessary to push beyond the boundaries of recorded history into the even more speculative and hazy realms of prehistory. The aim of this first chapter is to begin to provide that background. Of course, in this context, such a background cannot be provided in any great detail, since the history and prehistory of food is a vast subject in itself, covering broad sweeps of human activity and experience. Rather, the intention is to draw attention to a number of key ideas which can enhance our comprehension of the foundations of human foodways, foundations which, by their very nature, usually remain unexamined.

Our starting point will be a consideration of the diet of early humans, a contentious and complex question, but one which can lead to insights whose implications are as important now as they were in the early stages of human evolution. The issue of the basic forms of human subsistence will then be raised, along with a discussion of what is arguably one of the most important transitions in human social organization, the shift from an ancient, long-standing dependence on hunting and gathering to food production based on the techniques of agriculture. However, it will be argued that conventional views of this transition may require reconsideration and revision. Finally, we will go on to examine the enormous implications of this transition for human social relations and arrangements, not least of which was the facilitation of the emergence of increasingly complex and large-scale social systems.

THE EARLY HUMAN DIET

Perhaps the most basic nutritional question of all relates to the nature of the 'original' human diet. In other words, we need to ask how our evolutionary history as a species has shaped, or been shaped by, our dietary patterns. Attempting to build up a detailed picture of the foods which our distant

13

forebears ate and the relative importance of the various items which figured in ancestral diets, is a task beset with enormous difficulties. Foodstuffs are, by and large, relatively perishable, and thus traces of them rarely survive over long periods of time to provide the archaeologist with direct evidence about dietary practices and subsistence strategies. Thus, all too often, investigators are compelled to rely upon the indirect evidence provided by more durable artefacts like tools, or upon the animal bones which are assumed to be the remains of ancient meals. However, such evidence can be controversial and subject to conflicting interpretation. As Binford (1992) has pointed out, the fact that animal bones and stone tools are found together in particular caves and rock shelters does not in itself demonstrate that the hominids who occupied those sites were hunters, or were solely responsible for these accumulations, since carnivores like wolves, leopards and hyenas also occupied such sites and also created accumulations of prey animals' bones.

There are, however, alternative ways of addressing these questions, and one of these involves not only looking at evidence about the diet of early hominids, but also comparing human dietary patterns with those of modern non-human primates. This is the approach adopted by Leonard and Robertson (1994), who re-examine a range of nutritional and physiological data relating to humans and their primate relatives. They point out that among primates in general there exists a consistent negative correlation between body size and diet quality. That is, large primates (such as gorillas and orang-utans) depend upon diets which consist of large amounts of bulky, hard-to-digest foods which are relatively low in nutrients per unit of weight (for example, plant parts like leaves, stems and bark). In contrast, smaller primates' diets consist of much higher quality foods, in the sense that such foods are much more densely packed with nutrients and contain far lower proportions of indigestible bulk. Their diets include the reproductive parts of plants, like seeds, nuts, fruits, bulbs and tubers, and a wide range of small animals. The authors give the example of the pygmy marmoset, which tends to focus its feeding behaviour on protein-rich insects and energy-rich plant gums and saps.

The explanation for this relationship between body size and diet quality appears to be related to metabolism, that is, the sum total of the chemical processes which drive and maintain a living body. Smaller animals have higher metabolic costs and energy needs per unit of body weight than larger animals. Although the latter have higher *total* energy needs, they need less per unit of weight, and can, therefore, make a successful living out of consuming large quantities of low-quality but relatively abundant foods. However, what is striking about humans is that they do not fit neatly into this broad overall picture. The authors examine data on the dietary intakes of a number of peoples dependent on foraging (i.e., the exploitation of wild animals and plants) for subsistence. These groups show a far higher level of dietary quality (as measured by a composite index) than would have been expected for primates of their size. They also consume a far higher proportion of animal material (material defined as high-quality in terms of nutrient density) than comparably sized primates (e.g., anthropoid apes). What is more, when the authors looked at data from agricultural societies, where much lower quantities of animal products like meat are consumed, the diet quality is still significantly higher than would have been predicted for primates in general in that size range, since the grains and cereals eaten by these human consumers are much richer in calories than are fibrous leaves and stems.

We are therefore faced with a puzzle, in that humans eat a diet which is of much greater quality than would be predicted by their body size. Indeed, Leonard and Robertson (1994) also demonstrate that this quality is higher than might be expected from humans' resting metabolic rate, a baseline which expresses the amount of energy required for metabolism when the body is at rest. In fact, the authors go on to argue that the key to this puzzle is the size of the human brain. The human brain is, of course, relatively large in relation to body weight compared with other primates, and for that reason its energy demands are proportionately higher. They calculate that humans spend around three to four times more on brain metabolism than do other primates. Thus, in humans 20–25 per cent of the energy expenditure making up the resting metabolic rate goes to the brain, as opposed to an average of 8–9 per cent for our non-human primate relatives. There seems to be a close association between the possession of a large brain with a high energy requirement and the consumption of a high-quality, nutrient-rich diet.

Switching their attention to the archaeological data, Leonard and Robertson (1994) note that early members of our own genus *Homo*, specifically *Homo habilis* and *Homo erectus*, seem to show signs of this characteristically human relationship between brain size, body size and resting metabolic rate. Archaeological evidence also indicates that these species ate higher-quality diets (in that they contained a higher proportion of animal material) than did, for example, the ancient ape-like primates belonging to the genus *Australopithecus*. All this would appear to indicate that in the course of hominid evolution, increasing brain size (with a concomitant increase in the brain's energy demands) would have had to be associated with a shift towards an increasingly nutrient-rich diet. While these authors, quite explicitly, do not argue that somehow dietary factors caused changes in human brain evolution, they do seem to demonstrate that a move towards a higher-quality diet would have been a necessary condition for sustaining an evolutionary trend towards a larger and more powerful brain.

If we accept the arguments of these two biologists, we are led to a striking conclusion: the very basis of our human distinctiveness, our large and uniquely sophisticated brain, appears to demand that we maintain a high-quality, energy-rich diet. This appears to be confirmed by the fact that the human digestive tract is relatively short compared to most other primates, indicating its adaptation to high-energy, easy-to-digest foods. All these factors add up to what are, in effect, the nutritional 'facts of life' for human beings, facts rooted in our evolutionary past and our actual physiology. However, to state this is not to argue for a form of biological determinism. Our humanness imposes certain nutritional imperatives upon us, making us ominivores with a need for a high-quality diet, but these imperatives do not determine human nutritional endeavours and choices, rather they set a framework within which they are played out. Within that framework there is the scope for enormous variation, since human ingenuity is capable of generating an apparently infinite variety of solutions within an impressive range of cultural and ecological settings.

HUNTING AND GATHERING

However, varied as these solutions may be, attuned as they are to the mix of opportunities and constraints presented by their own unique circumstances, they can be placed into more general categories. Quite clearly, if we wish to consider the earliest forms of human subsistence, then we will need to focus our attention upon that broad category of activities that are often referred to as 'foraging'. In this sense, the term is used to describe the exploitation for food of plants and animals over which the user has little or no control (in other words, organisms which can be seen as 'wild'). When the organisms in question are animals that have sufficient agility and alertness to require active pursuit or stalking, the term 'hunting' is used. When the organisms consumed are plants, or animals with little or no mobility, the term 'gathering' is conventionally applied. (Trapping can be seen as an intermediate category, since certain forms of it permit the capture of active animals without the need for pursuit.) The combination of hunting and gathering has provided our species with its sustenance for most of its evolutionary history.

It is intriguing to note, however, that from the early days of scientific debate concerning ancestral patterns of human subsistence, far more stress has been placed upon the hunting component of the hunter/gatherer lifestyle than on the gathering component. Hunting has conventionally been seen as having exerted a potent formative influence upon human social and physiological evolution. Perhaps the clearest and most explicit academic expressions of the role of hunting in the development of human social, cultural and physical characteristics can be found in papers which emerged from a highly influential symposium entitled 'Man the Hunter', held at the University of Chicago in 1966. Thus, Washburn and Lancaster (1968) argue that human hunting (an activity almost entirely the preserve of males) represents a form of subsistence and a way of life that has provided the common factors which have dominated human evolution for over 99 per cent of its course. They point to key physiological and social adaptations which they see as closely associated with hunting: the development of a large brain, the use of tools and weapons which demand high levels of skill in their production and use, a sexual division of labour with females concentrating on food gathering and child rearing while being supplied with meat by males, and the development of complex forms of communication and co-operation between males to facilitate hunting success. From this list, it is apparent that this view of hunting sees it as the root of human features as diverse as skill in the creation of artefacts, the male-dominated family and the emergence of that most sophisticated of communication devices, language.

This hunting-centred view is presented even more emphatically by Laughlin, who goes as far as to assert that, 'Hunting is the master behaviour pattern of the human species' (Laughlin 1968: 304). He maintains that the fact that the human species achieved worldwide distribution while dependent on hunting for subsistence demonstrates the universality of this particular adaptation. What is more, he also suggests that an impressive range of human physical attributes arises directly from our hunting past. These include muscular strength and a high load-carrying capacity, sustained endurance at running speed, a high level of agility and manual dexterity, excellent colour vision, good hearing and a remarkably tough and durable outer skin. These features provide a degree of physiological flexibility sufficient to enable humans to colonize habitats far more diverse than those available to any other comparable animal. When these features are combined with a high-capacity memory, superior learning ability, the use of tools and language, and the development of complex forms of co-operation (these features also being seen as emerging out of the demands of a hunting way of life), the recipe for human success as a species appears to be complete. Indeed, so compelling is this view of human development that it has strongly influenced popular views of human origins and human nature.

THE EMERGENCE OF AGRICULTURE

However, while what has been termed the 'Hunting Hypothesis' does provide us with a number of fascinating possibilities concerning the links between human subsistence strategies and dietary patterns on the one hand, and human evolution on the other, it does exhibit some significant limitations. We will return to these limitations later in this chapter, although before doing this it is necessary to confront a fundamental conundrum which has been puzzling scholars for several generations: if the hunting and gathering approach to subsistence is such a successful one, and if it is so closely integrated with human evolutionary developments, why does there eventually occur a radical shift towards a very different form of subsistence? This novel approach to providing food involves deliberately and systematically *producing* food, rather than capturing food animals or gathering food plants which exist independently of human activities and interventions.

The timing of this shift is, in geological terms, comparatively recent. The end of the Pleistocene, some 14,000 years ago, saw the retreat of the glacial ice in the northern hemisphere, accompanied by dramatic climate changes. Tundra and grasslands were, in many areas, replaced by forests, and humans were compelled to adapt their hunting and gathering patterns accordingly. Foraging strategies appear to have become more diversified, since vast herds of large herbivorous mammals inhabiting wide, open plains were no longer available to the same extent in the northern temperate zones to provide human hunters with an

17

abundant food supply. Shortly after these far-reaching environmental changes occurred, the emergence of agriculture began, spanning a period dating from between 9,000 and 12,000 years ago. As Hole (1992) points out, the shift to agriculture appears to have begun in the warmer latitudes and spread later to temperate regions. The process was dependent upon the domestication of a range of plant species, domestication itself being conventionally viewed as the replacement of the pressures of natural selection with artificial selection carried out by human beings. Artificial selection is seen as enabling humans to modify food plants in ways which make them more productive (in terms of yield per unit of land area), which make them more palatable, easier to harvest, store or process, and even aesthetically more pleasing.

The emergence of agriculture can be dated to approximately 10,000 years ago in southwest Asia (Palestine) and approximately 8,000 years ago in Central and South America. However, as Hole (1992) notes, although agriculture took hold in several other locations, the dating of these events is less certain. Nevertheless, it is clear that by 4,000 years ago all the basic agricultural techniques, such as ploughing and irrigation, had been developed. At each location in which agriculture was established, it was based upon a characteristic mix of domesticated plants which Hole documents in some detail. For example, the so-called 'fertile crescent' of southwest Asia is associated with wheat, barley, various legumes, grapes, melons, dates and almonds, while the area around the northern Mediterranean is characterized by olives, grapes, figs and cereals. Tropical West Africa embraced such crops as yams and oil-palm, whereas the eastern sub-Saharan zone is associated with millet and sorghum. The complex of domesticated plants originating in Southeast Asia includes such species as taro, yam, breadfruit, sago-palm, coconut and banana, although Hole notes that the origins of the current staple food of much of Asia, rice, are poorly understood. The region that is now Central America gave rise to such major domesticated species as maize, beans, squash and tomatoes. White potatoes originated in the Andean mountains of South America, and the Amazon basin saw the domestication of manioc and sweet potatoes. Of course, in the intervening millenniums, many of these crops have spread throughout the world, to become staples in areas far removed from their region of origin.

Hand in hand with the domestication of plant species went the domestication of animals. Domesticated animals, of course, did more than provide readily available sources of food products like meat, and non-food products like hides, hair and bone that might otherwise have been obtained from wild animals. Certain species also provided a source of muscle power far in excess of that achievable by human beings, muscle power which could be harnessed directly to agricultural activities (e.g., ploughing) and which could also be used for transportation purposes. The domestication of animals has had an enormous impact on human foodways, dietary patterns and social organization, yet our understanding of exactly how this process occurred is largely based upon supposition (Reed 1984: 2). Nevertheless, it is possible to identify certain key attributes which, in effect, render a given species suitable for domestication (Clutton-Brock 1987: 15–16). These include the ability of the young to survive removal from the mother and to adapt to a novel diet and environment, plus the possession of a set of behavioural patterns which facilitate the animal's incorporation into human society. Specifically, this requires a social animal, whose behaviour is based upon a dominance hierarchy, which will adopt a submissive role *vis-à-vis* its human companions. In addition, the species must be able to adapt to confinement and must be capable of breeding freely under such constrained conditions. All these features require an innate gregariousness on the part of the animal in question, as well as a relatively placid temperament that will tolerate human proximity and human interventions without exhibiting excessive signs of stress.

Domestication in mammals, for example, is usually accompanied by a number of characteristic physiological changes (Clutton-Brock 1987: 22–4). In the early stages of the process, there is often a reduction in body size as compared with the wild ancestor (although this may be reversed later). In addition, domestic mammals tend to carry a higher burden of fat beneath the skin and distributed through muscle tissue. Perhaps most strikingly, the brain becomes much smaller in relation to body size, and sense organs are also reduced. What is more, in the skull, the facial region and the jaws may become much shorter and more compressed, which may in effect involve the retention of juvenile characteristics.

Animal domestication occurred in a number of locations around the world (Clutton-Brock 1992). In western Asia, around 9,000 years ago, there is archaeological evidence for the domestication of sheep and goats, although they appear to have been domesticated later than the dog, whose domestication is usually estimated at approximately 12,000 years ago. Domestic cattle and pigs appear to originate in western Asia roughly 8,000 years ago (although in the case of the pig, its progenitor, the wild boar, is so widespread there may have been several separate centres of domestication). The domestic horse originated in central Asia 6,000 years ago, about the same time that the donkey (descended from the wild ass) appeared in Arabia and North Africa. The domestic chicken (descended from the jungle fowl) can be traced to southern Asia approximately 4,000 years ago. The New World has contributed such species as the llama and the alpaca (domesticated in South America, roughly 7,000 years ago) and, more importantly in a global sense, the turkey (North America, 1,500 years ago). As we have already noted, the causes of the shift to agriculture, based on the domestication of key species of plants and animals, remain a puzzle. As might be expected, however, there has been much speculation about these causes. For example, Hole (1992) argues that a series of interconnected changes in global temperatures, sea levels and the distributions of plants and animals generated a range of human responses, one of which was a move towards agriculture and direct food production. This author suggests that, in a sense, the ecological and social limits of the hunting and gathering lifestyle had been reached. This idea is echoed by Van der Merve (1992), who argues that archaeological evidence suggests that agriculture may have developed in response to situations in which the rates of food extraction by hunter-gatherers had begun to exceed the carrying capacity of the environments in which they were active.

However difficult it may be to identify the actual causes of these transformations in the ways in human beings obtained their food, there can be no mistaking the enormous and far-reaching consequences of these changes. Indeed, these consequences have proved so momentous that the shift from foraging to food production is often referred to as the agricultural or neolithic 'revolution', despite the fact that this was a revolution which took some thousands of years to run its course. Perhaps the most obvious consequence was a dramatic increase in the impact upon the natural environment of human subsistence-related activities. Of course, hunter-gatherers can have a significant impact upon the habitats in which they live. In intensely foraged areas, the whole balance of flora and fauna may be modified by human activities. In addition, hunters may use fire as a means of driving prey towards ambush or as a way of generating new plant growth to attract quarry species into the group's territory. The habitual burning of vegetation can produce extensive environmental changes if repeated over long periods of time. However, once agriculture takes hold, the rate and extent of environmental impact increases rapidly. Early agriculture took place on a shifting basis, involving, as Hole (1992: 374) puts it, 'a cycle of use, abuse, abandonment and re-use'. The clearance of forests (by burning and felling) and the ploughing of relatively unstable or fragile soils could result in severe erosion and the wholesale degradation of the landscape. Such effects would also be exacerbated by the cumulative impact of heavy grazing and browsing by domesticated herbivores. In regions of settled agricultural activity, the progressive depletion of the surrounding habitat would be an ever-present hazard.

So extensive has been the impact of agriculture upon the natural world that in the regions of the globe in which it has been practised for several millenniums, it is now difficult to identify many areas which can in any sense be seen as 'natural' in the sense of being completely untouched by human intervention and manipulation. Indeed, the whole thrust of this great revolution has been to replace the diversity of natural ecological systems with a much narrower range of plants and animals linked to human beings through the nexus of domestication.

As well as transforming the interactions between humans and the natural world, this agricultural revolution was inevitably associated with fundamental changes in the organization of human social relationships. Relatively settled agriculture facilitated the building up of stocks of food (in the form, for example, of relatively durable grains, or livestock 'on the hoof'). Such stocks, quite clearly, might be built up as an insurance against future shortages or famines, but in social terms they could represent very much more than that. The power over others that flows from the control of food stocks means that the whole concept of *ownership* becomes crucial in such societies. Stocks of wealth in the form of stored food surpluses could be used, within an appropriate system of barter and exchange, to command the labour, obedience or political allegiance of others.

Gifts of food or the use of food animals in religious sacrificial rites could also be employed to gain status and enhance political influence. In short, the initiation of a system of agricultural production greatly facilitates the extension and elaboration of patterns of social differentiation and inequality. Privileged groups or elites could now emerge and be supported by the sustained efforts of their subordinates. There is clear archaeological evidence that such elite groups typically enjoyed higher nutritional standards than those lower in the social order. For example, in the Sumerian civilization in Mesopotamia, detailed records of the food rations allocated to the various strata in that society indicate that the highest groups enjoyed a rich and varied diet, while the diet of the lower orders was heavily dependent on a single staple, barley (Gordon 1987: 28). For such subordinates, subsistence-related activities became ever more unlike those of hunters and gatherers.

There is a good deal of evidence to suggest that hunters and gatherers, on average, need to spend only relatively short periods of time actually engaged in catching or searching for food items in order to meet their nutritional needs (Sahlins 1974: 14–27). What is more, the nutritional standards of early human hunter-gatherers in the Paleolithic appear to have been good, even compared with modern Western standards (Gordon 1987: 30), given the typically diversified and balanced nature of their diets. The relatively low levels of effort, and the abundance of leisure time, has led Sahlins (1974: 1–39) to refer to the hunting gathering lifestyle as 'the original affluent society'. In contrast, however, farmers find themselves committed to much more onerous, protracted and physically demanding inputs of labour, inputs which may be determined not only by their own subsistence needs, but by the need to generate food surpluses to support the debts and obligations they may owe to individuals who control more resources or wield more power than themselves. Indeed, it is tempting to assert that the actual concept of 'work' is one that could only have come into existence after the advent of agriculture.

Demographic changes were also associated with the spread of agricultural systems. The population densities of hunter-gatherers, depending upon the habitat, may be in the order of one person per square mile. In contrast, the densities of some early farming populations may have exceeded the level of sixty persons per square mile (Hartley 1972). These higher population densities, in turn, created the conditions for increases in overall population levels. Indeed, in certain circumstances population densities would eventually reach unprecedented values. This occurred through the creation of a novel form of human settlement, the city, a complex physical and social structure drawing its food resources from a wide agricultural hinterland (Sjoberg 1960). Thus, between 6,000 and 5,000 years ago there occurred in Mesopotamia, for example, what Roaf (1990) has termed an 'urban explosion'.

The shift towards agriculture was, therefore, clearly associated with a series of social and cultural transformations whose long-term implications were to prove enormous. However, the impact upon human nutritional and health standards

21

was, in fact, often deleterious (Gordon 1987: 30) (although privileged strata may have been protected from such effects to some extent). As has already been noted, agricultural diets are in general much more narrowly based than those of hunter-gatherers, often with a much greater emphasis on the consumption of carbohydrates and with lower intakes of protein. Hole (1992: 378) suggests that relatively poor dietary standards led to higher levels of diseases related to nutritional deficiencies and also of infectious and parasitic diseases, which could spread more readily in the insanitary conditions pertaining in more densely populated, sedentary societies. He also argues that dietary changes may have led to an increased incidence of dental caries.

Van der Merve (1992: 372) presents a striking case study which demonstrates dramatically some of the negative effects of the nutritional changes associated with agriculture. The people of the lower Ilinois Valley (of what is now the central USA) around the year AD 600 were still largely dependent for food upon wild plants and animals (although they obtained some maize by trading with neighbouring agriculturalists). However, by AD 1200 their society had undergone a radical transformation. By this time they had become maize growers in their own right, and their population was concentrated in large villages. However, these changes were accompanied by an increase in weaning deaths among infants and a slowing down in skeletal development, so that maturity was not reached until age 25. In addition, the incidence of the bone disease porotic hyperostosis (caused by iron-deficiency anaemia) had increased to such an extent that it was affecting over half the population. In fact, as the author points out, the increases in population levels associated with agriculture were not the result of improved life expectancy (which remained about the same as for hunter-gatherers) and were apparently accompanied by a heightened incidence of nutritional stress.

What is more, a dependence on agriculture could have other serious disadvantages. Thus, while a settled, food production approach to subsistence could facilitate attempts to even out short-term fluctuations in food supply (i.e., through food storage), more long-term fluctuations, produced by such factors as drought, climatic change and resource depletion, could potentially generate chronic food shortages (Gordon 1987: 30). In the most severe instances such shortages could become full-scale famines. In contrast, hunter-gatherers were much less exposed to chronic food shortages and famines. The diversity of their diets made them less reliant on any one food item, and therefore a failure in the availability of any given food source was not as likely to prove catastrophic. In addition, the geographical mobility associated with foraging lifestyles would have meant that hunter-gatherers were much more capable of moving quickly away from areas of food shortage into areas where food resources were more abundant. The development of agricultural systems also appears to have increased the scale and heightened the intensity of another of the major scourges of humankind, warfare (Harris 1978: 35). With permanent settlements and the ownership of land, crops and livestock comes a much stronger sense of the occupation of an exclusive territory which must be defended from the incursions of others or, indeed, expanded at the expense of others.

Given some of the unwelcome effects of a shift towards agriculture, it is perhaps hardly surprising that we find evidence of hunter-gatherers actively resisting making the switch away from the foraging approach to subsistence (Van der Merve 1992: 370). Sahlins (1974: 27) provides the contemporary example of the Hadza people of Africa, foragers inhabiting a region of abundant wild food supplies, who, until recently, successfully resisted taking up agriculture despite being surrounded by cultivators. Given what we know about the spread of agriculture (for example, from southern Europe into northern Europe), it is tempting to speculate that an emphasis on farming did not replace the exclusive reliance on foraging because the former represented a more appealing and secure lifestyle (which it almost certainly did not). Rather, it may well have been that, once established, agriculturalists, as a result of their greater numbers and more intensive approach to warfare, could readily displace foragers from territory that was suitable for agricultural exploitation and settlement.

HUMAN SUBSISTENCE RECONSIDERED

In the previous section we examined a view of the origins and development of the basic forms of human subsistence which consists of a number of key elements, for example, the idea that the hunting component of the hunting and gathering lifestyle has had a particularly powerful influence on human physical and social evolution, and the notion that environmental changes and pressures eventually led human beings to respond by shifting their subsistence activities towards agriculture. This broad view carries considerable authority and appears to provide a coherent and plausible perspective on the prehistory of human food systems. However, as a perspective, it has its limitations and its critics, and these demand our consideration before we move on to the next stage of the discussion.

The first point which needs to be addressed relates to the conventional view that hunting represents an extremely ancient approach to human subsistence. While it has frequently been assumed that the animal remains associated with early hominid species demonstrate a reliance upon hunting as a food source, this view has frequently been questioned. Reviewing a broad spectrum of evidence, Gordon (1987) suggests that for early hominids, the acquisition of animal protein through scavenging may have been more likely than through actual hunting. It is only in the middle and upper Pleistocene that the clearest evidence exists for sophisticated hunting strategies and for the successful killing of large numbers of game animals. Thus, the claim put forward by advocates of the 'Hunting Hypothesis', that hunting dominated the subsistence activities of the various hominid species for 99 per cent of human prehistory (Washburn and Lancaster 1968: 293; Laughlin 1968: 304) needs to be viewed with some caution. The picture is further complicated if we consider the hunting-gathering cultures of modern humans which have survived to the present day, or at least survived long enough to become the objects of systematic study by anthropologists. While some of these cultures did rely very heavily on meat and other animal products for subsistence (the Innuit of the high Arctic are usually cited as prime example; see Damas 1972), in general food gathering was probably the predominant activity. In most foraging societies, the hunting of game animals, which is the preserve of men, is a sporadic and often unpredictable activity, yielding highly variable returns according not only to the methods employed but to uncontrollable fluctuations in such factors as the weather and the behaviour of quarry species. On the other hand, the activity of gathering (and this includes 'gathering' immobile or slow-moving small animals as well as plant foods), generally the preserve of women, tends to provide the bulk of resources for everyday subsistence. Thus, the meat of game animals, although the single most highly prized category of food in such societies, does not usually constitute the principal source of nutrients.

A particularly interesting reinterpretation of the development of human subsistence patterns is offered by Foley (1988), who invites us to consider the possibility that evolutionary changes have occurred in our species since its first appearance, particularly relating to the ways in which we obtain our food. Examining data concerning the Cro-Magnon populations of the Upper Paleolithic period in Europe (the earliest anatomically modern humans), he notes two striking features. Firstly, the stature and 'robusticity' of these people was much greater than that of later populations. Secondly, the degree of sexual dimorphism (e.g., in terms of the larger size of adult males compared to adult females) was also more pronounced than that found in later populations. Foley puts forward the proposition that the powerful stature of these males was an adaptation which facilitated the hunting of the big game animals that were abundant during this period in this area and may also have been related to competition between males, where size and strength would have conferred clear advantages. The exploitation of abundant big game would then have enabled these males to support dependent females and their offspring.

However, as we have already noted, far-reaching environmental changes were afoot at the end of the Pleistocene (about 10,000 years ago). Foley (1988) points out that at this time there is a reduction in overall body size and a reduction in the degree of sexual dimorphism. He argues that these anatomical changes in humans were associated with the changed subsistence patterns which accompanied the disappearance of the vast herds of big game animals upon which the Upper Paleolithic peoples had depended. A more 'gracile' and less 'robust' anatomy, and reduced differences between male and female, may have reflected the fact that the foraging strategies of the sexes now became much more similar, and indeed, in a sense, more balanced and egalitarian. It is at this point in his argument that he introduces his most interesting contention. The Upper Paleolithic hunters who exploited the rich reserves of game in the late Pleistocene, he suggests, were very different from more recent hunter-gatherers, in that they had more complex social structures, a far heavier dependence on hunting and even a different, more robust, physical appearance. This leads him to argue that 'modern' (i.e., post-Pleistocene) hunting and gathering are not, in any sense, ancestral to agriculture. Rather, the hunter-gatherer lifestyle, examples of which have survived to the present day, was itself an adaptation to post-Pleistocene conditions and involved diversification of foraging strategies and a much increased significance for the gathering activities of women. Thus, recent hunter-gatherer lifestyles on the one hand, and agriculture on the other, are seen as parallel adaptations to the same set of environmental changes.

While such views are, by their very nature, somewhat speculative, they do help to shed some light upon otherwise puzzling facts. For example, it is intriguing that humans appear to have exploited intensively certain plant species for long periods before those species began to show signs of actual domestication (Gordon 1987: 26). Moreover, despite the conventional use of the term 'revolution' to describe the switch to agriculture, this term is more appropriately applied to the eventual consequences of this change than to the timescales involved, which were often protracted. Indeed, many agriculturalists retained an involvement in foraging, particularly hunting, and such activities remained a significant component of their day to day activities (see e.g., Rosman and Rubel 1989; Sponsel 1989).

There is an additional aspect of the debate about the prehistory of human subsistence patterns which also needs to be approached with some caution. Much of the literature appears to be based upon the view that the process of domestication, upon which the development of agriculture inevitably depended, was a process which was quite deliberately and consciously initiated and carried through by human beings. This view of domestication and the emergence of agriculture is, of course, in line with our common-sense ideas about the ambitions and abilities of humans to exercise control over the natural world and to shape it according to human priorities. From this perspective, domestication would be seen as the result of the active selection of particular strains of plants and animals in terms of the desirable characteristics they exhibit. The processes of reproduction are then manipulated and regulated to ensure that these desirable characteristics are passed on to subsequent generations of the domesticated species.

While this might be a reasonably plausible description of the theoretically and scientifically driven forms of plant and animal breeding which have been developed in recent centuries, serious doubt has been cast upon the idea that domestication could actually have been *initiated* in this calculating manner. One of the most detailed challenges to the conventional view is presented by Rindos (1984). In fact, Rindos does not seek to deny that people act consciously and that these actions are oriented towards goals. However, he argues that in the context of plant domestication, for example, people could never have intentionally domesticated a crop, thereby deliberately 'inventing' agriculture. This is because the biological and evolutionary processes involved in domestication cannot be accounted for in solely cultural terms. The long-term effects of deliberate environmental manipulations and attempts at selective breeding are highly unpredictable, and domestication-related changes can only occur within the genetic parameters of the species in question. Thus, human intentions can only play a limited role in the whole process. This is perhaps best illustrated by the existence of weeds. These plants have evolved alongside 'desirable' plants as part of the whole process of the development of agriculture. They are, in a sense, domesticated plants, but they are not wanted by farmers, who expend considerable effort in ultimately unsuccessful attempts to eliminate them.

Thus, Rindos is suspicious of the argument that agriculture developed as a deliberate response to specific environmental stresses in given historical situations. Rather, he argues that domestication arose out of an *interactive* process between plants and humans. Indeed, it would make just as much (or just as little) sense to say these plants 'chose' humans to protect and disseminate them as to say early agriculturalists 'chose' to domesticate them. In fact, Rindos suspects that crops evolved through a natural process, with humans acting as a largely unintentional selective force, the process itself conferring some evolutionary advantages on both the people and plants involved. Thus, Rindos reminds us, although we use the idiom of intention as a kind of literary convention, it is, in effect, a metaphor and not a description of reality. Agriculture, then, according to Rindos, represents a form of co-evolution between humans and certain plant species and is, in effect, a highly developed form of symbiosis. The term 'symbiosis', meaning a situation in which at least two different species interact to their mutual benefit, is also used by Reed (1984) to describe agriculture and domestication. However, he also adds the concept of the 'secondary energy trap'. In a symbiotic relationship, each symbiant represents a reserve of energy other symbionts may be able to draw upon (and thus a way of storing energy outside their own bodies). Agriculture, therefore, represents a complex system of mutual secondary energy traps for the species involved, with plants and animals drawing upon stored human energy for protection and dissemination, and humans drawing upon stored plant energy for food and stored animal energy for food and motive power.

Once we begin to think of agriculturally based food systems in these terms, our whole view of human subsistence necessarily undergoes an important shift. Domestication and agriculture come to be seen as something more than innovations created initially by the intentional application of human ingenuity. The impressive selective advantages which accrue to domesticated plants and animals through their association with humans become much more visible. Domesticated species have, by and large, achieved spectacular increases in their populations (or the sheer volume of 'biomass' which they make up) and in their geographical ranges and the environments they occupy. This has been achieved, in some instances, by species which, prior to domestication, may well have been on the verge of disappearance. For example, the Aurochs, which is now actually extinct in its wild form, is the direct ancestor of domestic cattle, and this animal is now one of the most numerous and widely distributed large mammals on earth.

Furthermore, the impact of these changes on human beings may now be seen from a rather different perspective. Human population densities and overall numbers saw increases far beyond what could have been sustained by foraging lifestyles, although these increases were sometimes associated with an actual deterioration in nutritional standards. Extensive changes in culture and patterns of social relations also associated with the development of agricultural systems, and the move towards an emphasis on food production, saw human communities become increasingly sedentary and spacially restricted, their members (at least in the lower strata) committed to the physically demanding seasonal inputs of agricultural labour.

In seeing the human food system that emerged after the introduction of agriculture as a complex form of symbiosis, we begin to recognize the ways in which the biological and reproductive potential of a complex of domesticated plants and animals came to be organized and articulated through the unique adaptabilities of human intelligence and human culture. If, following the advice of Rindos (1984), we are cautious about using the idea that early farmers 'intended' to domesticate plants and animals, and 'intended' to create agriculture, then we ought also to be cautious about using terms like 'exploitation'. In an agricultural system, who is exploiting whom? Conventionally, we accept the idea that humans are the exploiters, although we base this notion upon the fact that we are at the top of the agricultural food chain (we eat the other members, but they do not eat us). But it would be equally logical to assert that the other members of these systems exploit humans (for dissemination, protection and nurture). In a very real sense, *Homo sapiens* in an agricultural system is also a domesticated animal, subject to the increasing demands and the unforgiving disciplines attached to our species' role in the complicated networks of symbiotic relationships. The human species must exhibit, in these circumstances, such domesticated characteristics as an acceptance of restricted mobility and a tolerance of crowding and close proximity with humans and non-humans.

There can be no doubt that the symbiotic complex that we call agriculture has come to dominate the land surface of large areas of the earth and, indeed, is continuing to extend this domination. At this stage in our argument, doubt must now be cast upon the notion that humans are actually in control of this process. Despite Western culture's deep-seated inclination to emphasize the idea of human control and manipulation of the natural world, it is extremely unlikely that generation upon generation of agriculturalists were really able to foresee in any detail the longer-term outcomes of their activities. This point is reinforced when we take into account the unpredictable nature of climatic and environmental fluctuations and the immensely complex genetic and environmental processes involved in the evolution of domesticated species, and of the diseases, pests and parasites which infest and colonize agricultural systems. Thus, although human agricultural activities are themselves goal-oriented and driven by more or less explicitly recognized intentions, their long-term outcomes may be quite unintentional, and often unforeseeable.

THE EMERGENCE OF THE STATE

It has already been argued that agriculture created the conditions in which increasing levels of population density and degrees of complexity in social organization became possible. These changes were eventually to give rise to forms of social organization which created, for the first time, many of the features of economic, cultural, political and religious life which we now take virtually for granted. In other words, conditions were formed in which the emergence of states was possible. The creation of states was to see a fundamental change away from the situation of human social groupings comprising relatively small mobile bands or relatively small sedentary villages. Where such units maintain their autonomy, levels of individual freedom and control over the pace and nature of daily and seasonal activities is relatively high and access to natural resources is relatively open (although it may be subject to competition). However, increasing social complexity appears to bring in its wake increasing social inequality. Highly privileged political, military and intellectual elites become increasingly distant in outlook and lifestyle from the strata beneath them, made up of castes or classes whose autonomy is severely limited by the power and authority of those they serve. We might legitimately ask how such highly structured relationships of dominance and subordination could come about. This is, clearly, a large question and has absorbed the efforts of generations of scholars of many different persuasions. However, of particular interest from our point of view are the ideas of Harris (1978: 67–82), who puts forward the proposition that the control and redistribution of food resources may have been vital factors in this process.

Harris's specific concern is the issue of how a 'pristine' state can emerge, a pristine state being one which arises spontaneously, not as a result of the influences or effects of other states which have a prior existence. In fact, it is Harris's view that the pristine state can be seen as a consequence of attempts to intensify agricultural production (i.e., to increase agricultural output) in order to provide short-term relief of the pressures generated by a rising population. This contention is hardly a remarkable one, but what is interesting about Harris's analysis is his description of the mechanism through which this intensification may come about. He refers to the phenomenon that social anthropologists term the 'big man' (1978: 70–1). These big men are typically renowned and respected war leaders, but in pre-state societies loyalty can only be maintained if the leader can keep up a constant flow of rewards to his followers. Food, of course, is one of the principal forms such rewards can take. What is more, in order to enhance further their prestige, these ambitious individuals may exhort and cajole their followers and relatives into increasing food output so that a spectacular feast can be held. This feast provides not only an abundance of food for his followers and their dependents, but also enhances the standing in the community of the leader himself and, by implication, that of all his supporters. Thus, we have what Harris terms 'redistributor war chiefs' (1978: 73–6), who

28

have the ability to accumulate large food stocks and then to expend these stocks in such a way as to entrench and extend their own power. Harris actually calls these individuals 'food managers' (1978: 71), given their crucial position at the centre of a web of food production and distribution. It is then but a short step for the chief-manager role to evolve into that of a hereditary ruler with coercive powers, the 'great provider' (1978: 71) who can build up substantial reserves of storable foodstuffs on the basis of his position. As populations become larger and denser, food redistribution systems become larger and more elaborate, and the more powerful becomes the individual at the centre. In effect, the chief becomes a monarch, and what were voluntary contributions become obligatory taxes and tithes.

Thus, a crucially significant reversal takes place. Whereas the chief is dependent on the generosity and allegiance of his followers, the subjects of a monarch come to be seen as dependent on his (or, more rarely, her) generosity and dispensations. Indeed, even access to land and other natural resources comes to be defined in terms of such royal dispensation. The subjects themselves also become increasingly differentiated. Around the monarch there builds up an increasingly elaborate hierarchy of functionaries (military personnel, priests, administrators, artists and craft specialists) all supported and fed from the reserves controlled by the monarchy itself. Members of this network experience a lifestyle and enjoy privileges which set them apart from the strata of agricultural drudges below them. The embryo state is given further impetus towards even greater elaboration by the process that Harris terms 'impaction' (Harris 1978: 78). This effect occurs when fertile land upon which the state relies is in limited supply, being bounded by relatively or largely infertile areas. This means that it is not feasible for outlying groups in the population to escape from demographic pressures and central control by moving outwards. The system is turned in on itself, and the processes of intensification are given further impetus. Harris cites the civilizations which developed in areas of high fertility surrounded by zones of much lower agricultural value, for example, the Nile delta in Egypt, the flood plain of the Tigris and the Euphrates in Mesopotamia, the flood plain of the Indus in what is now Pakistan, and the margins of the Yellow River basin in China.

Once this process of impacted intensification takes off, it appears to engender a self-reinforcing cycle of further intensification through increasing levels of taxation, tribute extraction, labour conscription and food production integration. In addition, relationships with neighbouring societies in terms of warfare, conquest, trade, or all three, also intensify. However, once pristine states have become established, secondary states may begin to emerge. These may develop among peoples seeking to resist conquest by a pristine state that has moved into an expansionist phase or, indeed, among peoples who seek to plunder the riches of a pristine state which is vulnerable to external attack.

Harris (1978) makes it perfectly clear that he regards the formation of a pristine state as an essentially unconscious process, not as an outcome of

29

deliberate planning, manipulation or conspiracy. Over many generations, imperceptible shifts in the balances of power relating to the control and redistribution of resources in general, and food resources in particular, eventually produced social institutions and relationships whose forms and directions could not have been foreseen by those involved. In this sense, we can see a close parallel with our earlier discussion of the changes which led to the establishment of symbiotic links between humans and domesticated species and the emergence of agriculture (an emergence which was a necessary condition for the later emergence of the state itself). These changes, in an important sense, can also be seen as the unforeseen and unintended consequences of incremental adjustments and adaptations in the ways in which humans went about the task of satisfying their nutritional needs.

OVERVIEW

In this brief sketch of the origins of human subsistence patterns attention has been drawn to several crucial insights. Perhaps the most striking of these is the idea that the extraordinarily high energy demands of the brain, arguably the very seat of our human distinctiveness, require us to consume a 'high-quality', energy-rich diet. Our basic physiology simply does not allow us the option of grazing or browsing directly upon the enormous quantities of structural plant material (stems, leaves, bark, etc.) which blanket vast areas of the earth's surface. For most of the history of our species (and of our closely related species) humans have relied upon harvesting wild animals and plants in order to obtain the dietary quality and variety that we need. The development of relationships of domestication with certain key animal and plant species brought about far-reaching changes, not only in human subsistence patterns but also in human social organization. However, the causes and the dynamics of domestication and the move to food production remain obscure, even mysterious. We simply cannot assume that domestication and agriculture were, in the first instances, conscious human inventions or deliberately adopted strategies aimed at coping with reproductive or environmental pressures. These changes may indeed have provided adaptive advantages for all the species that were to become part of the human food system, but that does not prove that humans intended to obtain these advantages any more than it proves that cattle and rice plants, for example, 'intended' to obtain them. As we have seen, when dealing with relationships of symbiosis (of which the human food system is a particularly complex example), references to the intentions of the species involved are essentially metaphorical rather than literal.

With the establishment and development of the first pristine states, all the features that we would recognize as fundamental to agricultural production were in place. These included an extensive range of domesticated plants and animals, the use of the plough, the construction of irrigation systems, the use of natural fertilizers and the use of fallowing to allow land to regain fertility after cropping.

What is more, trading in relatively non-perishable foods (for example, grains) became feasible with the production of food surpluses, and such foods, in turn, were to become the currency of tribute and taxation. The motive power for these agricultural systems came primarily from muscles, animal and human, although renewable sources of inanimate power (wind and water) also played a part.

On the basis of these forms of agricultural production, societies ranging from the limited world of the small village to the dazzling power and complexity of the ancient civilizations could be constructed. We have already referred to the intensification of food systems, but this was an intensification that occurred within the limits set by available technologies and forms of social organization. However, eventually these limits were to be overcome and new waves of much more rapid intensification and integration were set in train, waves which were to lead to what we now conceptualize as the modern food system.

2

THE MAKING OF THE MODERN FOOD SYSTEM

CONTRASTING TRADITIONAL AND MODERN FOOD SYSTEMS

A visit to any supermarket, with its elaborate displays of food from all parts of the world, is a readily available demonstration of the choice and variety available to the modern consumer. The supermarket itself may be considered one of the most successful outcomes of the development of modern systems of food production and distribution, indicating the extent of control over quality and the reliability of supplies. It might be tempting to consider such quality and reliability as unequivocal evidence of progress. However, in trying to understand the developments and beliefs which underpin the modern food system, we are faced with a fascinating paradox. In the past, certainly in the West, ascendancy over the natural world was taken for granted, yet it was not always possible to use that ascendancy to provide constant and reliable supplies of food. However, in modern society, where food supplies are virtually guaranteed, there are now serious doubts about the extent and moral acceptability of our control over the natural environment. In parallel with the technological, engineering and scientific changes which have established control over food production and distribution, serious debate has emerged about the unanticipated consequences of such changes, together with challenges to the allegedly overconfident exploitation of natural resources. Thus, in giving an account of the development of the modern food system, it is important to include some discussion of several issues: the character of the food system itself; the processes which made it possible; the operation of the system; current debates about the system. These issues are the focus of this chapter and all are relevant to understanding the making of the modern food system as we know it today.

The use of the term 'food system' may conjure up an idea of a formally organized set of links between food production, distribution and consumption which is arranged according to some well-thought-out plan or scheme. The issues discussed in Chapter 1 and the studies covered in the following pages will make it clear that such a model is inappropriate and unworkable. However, if we are careful not to assume that there is some underlying plan which informs its organization, the term food system can be a convenient way of drawing attention to the particular character of the complex of interdependent interrelationships associated with the production and distribution of food which have developed to meet the nutritional needs of human populations. (In Chapter 3 we will examine specific examples of the kinds of model which social scientists have devised to provide descriptions of such systems.)

In trying to understand the making of the modern food system, it is necessary to be aware of both continuity and change in the social processes which shape the ways in which food is produced, distributed and consumed. Chapter 1 has identified the physiological need for variety in food, the constant interaction between humans and their environment and the importance of the social and political control of food production and distribution. If we were to choose to emphasize continuity, it could be argued that the modern system is merely the most recent attempt of human societies to come to terms with these perennial problems of providing food, and that the only distinguishing characteristic is the scale of the endeavour. However, it has also been argued that the modern food system is, in many respects, radically different from what has gone before. It is this assertion which we explore and which provides the starting point for the discussion in this chapter.

An emphasis on change and discontinuities draws attention to the main contrasts between the food systems of traditional and modern societies. These are set out in Table 2.1. For ease of discussion, a distinction has been

Table 2.1 Contrasts between traditional and modern food systems

Activity	Traditional systems	Modern systems
Production	Small-scale/limited	Large-scale/highly specialized/industrialized
	Locally based for all but luxury goods	De-localized/global
	High proportion of population involved in agriculture	Majority of population have no links with food production
Distribution	Within local boundaries	International/global
	Exchange governed by kinship and other social networks	Access governed by money and markets
Consumption	Swings between plenty and want dependent on harvests and seasons	Food always available at a price/independent of seasons
	Choice limited and dependent on availability and status	Choice available to all who can pay
	Nutritional inequalities within societies	Nutritional inequalities between and within societies
Beliefs	Humans at the top of the food chain/exploitation of the environment necessary	Debate between those who believe in human domination of the environment and those who challenge such a model

made between the processes of production, distribution and consumption, even though in practice it is not always easy to separate them. In addition, it has been necessary to emphasize the similarities between traditional societies in order to bring out the contrasts with modern societies which are to be discussed. For example, although there is a wide variety of traditional systems, each associated with a particular organization of the interaction between humans and their environment, it is possible to identify some shared characteristics. For a start, traditional food systems are characterized by patterns of local, relatively small-scale production. In addition, the division of labour associated with food production involves a relatively high proportion of the population. Further, both distribution and consumption are linked to established social relationships, in particular, those of status and kinship. Gifts of food are often exchanged between relatives rather than being sold in the market, and social position determines the amount and type of food received. Importantly, choice is often limited for all consumers, whatever their status, and is constrained by the seasonal and local availability of food supplies. As a consequence, swings between times of plenty and those of want, particularly from season to season, are taken for granted. Also, there is little evidence of sharp differences in beliefs about dietary practices, possibly because food supplies are relatively uncertain and unreliable. There is one characteristic, that of nutritional inequalities, which appears in relation to both traditional and modern food systems. However, it can be argued that such inequalities are structured and organized in different ways and are underpinned by quite different assumptions about who may have access to food and the conditions in which it can be acquired.

At the risk of oversimplifying complex processes, the modern food system may be considered to have five key characteristics which differentiate it from those of traditional societies. Firstly, there is a highly specialized, industrial system of food production. This is large in scale, yet involves relatively small numbers of the working population. Indeed, it could be argued that most of the food production for modern societies goes on virtually concealed, not necessarily deliberately, from the mass of consumers. Secondly, distribution is through the commercial market; whatever our status, as long as we have the money, food is readily accessible. Thirdly, as the example which opened this chapter indicates, a visit to any supermarket demonstrates the opportunities for consumption and emphasizes choice and variety, and this is largely true for smaller food outlets as well. Fourthly, since the markets for buying and selling food are international, even global, shortages are rare. However, that is not to say that shortages do not occur in particular places for particular groups, only that these arise from social and political constraints rather than from the issues related to the availability of food. This latter point links with the final characteristic of the modern food system: constant debates about the sustainability of the system itself and the choices to be made about its future development.

THE EMERGENCE OF THE MODERN FOOD SYSTEM

The documentation of the transformation from the traditional to the modern food system has attracted the efforts of social historians, economists and nutritionists using a variety of approaches (Mennell, Murcott and Van Otterloo 1992). They have sometimes focused on one particular feature in explaining the changes observed, such as technology or transport, for example, or have attempted to analyse the entire process. Whatever the focus of any particular contribution to the literature, it is important to bear in mind several points which provide the context for all discussions. The first is that, in comparison with the period of time for which we have evidence of human social organization, writers who focus on the shaping of the modern food system are usually considering relatively recent developments, beginning approximately in the eighteenth and gathering momentum in the nineteenth century. The second point to bear in mind is that, although many writers document changes, they do not necessarily offer explanations of what happened, and, where they do, such explanations are often the focus of disputes about the validity of the evidence. Thirdly, even where writers concentrate on one particular aspect of change, it is important for the reader to recognize the interrelationship between factors of supply, distribution and demand. Each may have been stimulated by the other and, indeed, by yet other social and economic changes which at first sight do not seem to be linked in any way with food. These accounts and debates in the literature are valuable for giving an indication of the complexity of the processes which contributed to the shape of the modern world and provide a context for the sociological analysis in later chapters.

The process of urbanization in the ancient world had already broken the direct links between food production and consumers and had provided the necessary stimulus for developments in food production. However, it was the process of industrialization which altered the scale of urbanization, created an unprecedented demand for food supplies and distanced urban populations yet further from the sources of their food. Britain, as the first industrial nation, is one of the best-documented examples of the ways in which such changes took place and provides an ideal case study of the processes which contributed to the development of the modern food system. The precise turning point for industrial 'take-off' is still a matter of debate (Rostow 1990; Hudson 1992), but there is no doubt that industrialization 'created machines, factories and vast suffocating cities' (Tannahill 1973: 257). Oddy (1990) argues that this rapid urbanization in the eighteenth century was a major contributor to the commercialization of food markets, since urban living, with its pattern of waged work and separation from the agricultural base, prevented greater populations than ever before from being self-sufficient in food. As these urban centres grew, the food demands of such concentrations of population could not be met from local resources, however efficiently organized. This precipitated the rapid growth of trade over longer distances in produce such as livestock and vegetables. For example,

London as a metropolitan market drew on national and not just local or regional sources for its food supplies. The markets at Smithfield for meat, at Covent Garden for fruit and vegetables and at Billingsgate for fish were renowned for the quantity and range of the produce they handled on a daily basis in response to the demand of the growing metropolis (Burnett 1989).

Such a rapid increase in demand created pressures to produce more, giving all those involved in agriculture an incentive to introduce new techniques and to change the scale of food production. For example, horticulture expanded in areas adjacent to the expanding conurbations (Scola 1992). Deliberate and systematic selective breeding of livestock spread rapidly from the middle of the eighteenth century as well as systematic seed selection for increased arable output and the widespread use of specialized agricultural equipment. Possibly one of the most significant changes was the move to the use of chemical rather than natural fertilizers (Sykes 1981). Increased yields and improved stock gave landlords a better return on their investments. Land rents were raised, putting pressure on farmers to change the pattern of land use to make it even more productive. One of the by-products of this transformation was to change the appearance of the landscape from open fields to fenced and hedged farms (Turner 1985).

A key element which ensured that these newly expanded food supplies reached their markets was the parallel expansion of methods of transport (Bagwell 1974). Traditional drove roads, along which animals were herded to market, often over long distances, were augmented by turnpike roads and canals in the later eighteenth century. These enabled agricultural produce to be moved in bulk, where speed mattered less than cheap and reliable delivery. From the middle of the nineteenth century the capacity of internal transport was further augmented by a railway system which was rapid, reliable and flexible in bringing food supplies to distribution centres and markets. By the end of the nineteenth century railways were even able to provide specialized facilities for handling foods such as fresh milk and chilled or frozen meat. At the same time, the rapid transport of fish from trawler catches in the North Sea and the Atlantic was possible. In the case of Britain, this was said to have established one of the most popular meals of the working classes, fish and chips (Walton 1992).

Specialized facilities for handling food resulted from scientific and technological advances in preservation. Traditional preservation methods, such as salting, pickling and drying, continued in use alongside the greater use of sugar as well as chemical additives (Roberts 1989; Muller 1991). As we shall see in Chapter 11, until the late eighteenth century, sugar had been a luxury confined to the use of the rich, but mass-production made it available for use in a very wide range of food processing (Mintz 1985). The metallurgical development of cheap sheet steel, covered with a veneer of tin, made canning an economic process with minimal health risks, whilst refrigeration and other types of temperature control extended the opportunities to abolish seasonal supply problems (Roberts 1989; David 1994). New foodstuffs were literally invented by food scientists (margarine, for example), or manufactured (condensed milk, block chocolate and cornflakes). The life of some foods, such as milk, was extended by pasteurization. Because of improvements in temperature control in transport by sea, bananas became available in Europe for the first time in the 1890s.

By the beginning of the nineteenth century, Britain was a net importer of food and the contribution of overseas supplies to the British larder became of ever greater importance, particularly from the last quarter of the nineteenth century. In the twentieth century, such was the reliance on these overseas food supplies that Britain continued to import food even during two world wars when transport by sea was both dangerous and uncertain. The diminished quantities of these supplies led to wartime food rationing (Burnett 1989).

As a particularly powerful and affluent nation by the standards of the time, Britain was able to draw upon food supplies on a worldwide basis: grain from the Midwestern USA; dairy products from Denmark and Holland; beef from Argentina; lamb from Australia; tea from the Indian sub-continent; coffee from Brazil; cocoa from West Africa; sugar from the West Indies. All this was made possible by emerging international agricultural specialization combined with improved transport over long distances. By 1850, an international economy had been established which had transformed the landscapes and the organization of agriculture in the participating countries (Foreman-Peck 1993). Many of these, for example the tea gardens, the sheep pastures and the cattle ranges, remain and are part of the current global food system. (However, it is important to note that not all prospered and some led to ecological disaster, for example, the 'dust bowl' created in part of the American Midwest by attempts to grow grain.) Trade was often two-way. Countries of the British Empire, together with a number of nations with close economic ties to Britain, such as Argentina, Chile and Uruguay, paid for imports of capital and of manufactured goods from Britain by the export of food (Cain and Hopkins 1993; Saul 1960). Indeed, Tannahill (1973: 257) suggests that 'the quest for empire was partly quest for overseas markets'. Studies of trade in specific foods (Hobhouse 1985; Mintz 1985; Solokov 1991; Visser 1986) have drawn attention to the ways in which such trade has shaped international relations.

Governments were not neutral in the development of the international economy. In Britain, there were parliamentary debates about the most advantageous policies to pursue in relation to trade with particular consequences for food, the most important debate being that focused on the relative merits of 'free trade' versus 'protection'. The publication in 1774 of Adam Smith's *The Wealth of Nations* anticipated by two years the Boston Tea Party, which signalled the determination of the American colonists to have 'no taxation without representation'. Indirect taxes on food levied by the British government have been cited amongst the causes of the American War of Independence (Langford 1989). Once the Americans had secured their victory, British governments moved with hesitating steps towards free trade and the removal of taxes on food and drink. The main opposition came from agricultural interests which wished to retain protection for the cultivation of wheat. The failure of the potato crop in Ireland in 1845, with its terrible consequences of starvation for large numbers of the rural population, convinced the British government of the wisdom of seeking the cheapest food prices on world markets by removing all import taxes on food (Salaman 1985: 289–316).

Governments had always been concerned to maintain standards in the food market, and weights, measures and qualities had long been the subject of legislation and intervention (Ministry of Agriculture, Fisheries and Food 1989). However, intervention in cases of food adulteration, which was alleged to have become much more common in the nineteenth century because of increased demand and unsupervised production, proved difficult. The development of scientific analysis, particularly in chemistry, made it possible to have reliable tests for impurities. In Britain, the prevention of food adulteration was part of the public health movement which culminated in the appointment of medical officers of health after 1848. Legislation specifically concerned with food and drugs followed once the scientific tests were acceptable to the legislature. In Britain the first law to protect consumers from adulterated food took effect in 1875 (Burnett 1989).

During this time there were concurrent developments in the distribution and retailing of food. Consumers in rural society usually had direct contacts with their suppliers at local markets or by regular contact with the dairy or the bakery. Once towns grew beyond a population of a few hundred families the establishment of regular shops became the norm, a process that accelerated with the urbanization which accompanied industrialization. As supplies to shops became both more regular and reliable, consumers lost contact with processes of production. The number of shops and their range of products increased rapidly with the expansion of retail trade in food. For example, the late nineteenth century was the time when greengrocers, confectioners and other specialist outlets came into separate existence (Fraser 1981).

These changes occurred in advanced economies during the nineteenth century. Large-scale production had begun during the eighteenth century with the establishment of larger breweries, such as Guiness in Dublin and Barclay's in London. A similar willingness to invest in technologies on a large scale to meet the demands of the growing market for manufactured foods gave rise to companies making a wide range of products, from custard powder to margarine. In Britain, from the middle of the nineteenth century, the use of brand names became an advantage in reaching consumers through advertising. The national market, by the end of the nineteenth century, covered a wide range of branded food products in most lines of grocery and confectionery (Roberts 1989).

At the same time as brands replaced locally produced foods or wholly new items became available, retailing itself underwent major changes. The reasons for this were not only a consequence of production methods or the supplies of products from overseas, but also the need to reach the greater numbers and variety of consumers in urban centres. Such consumers included those who

wanted value for money and guaranteed quality. In responding to such consumers in the working class, first in the field in Britain was the retail co-operative
movement which had its successful origins in Rochdale in 1844. Within twenty
years most towns had a co-operative society. Co-operative customers had a
widening range of demands and the Co-operative Wholesale Society, established
in 1864, had its own factories and, in due course, even its own tea gardens in the
Indian sub-continent. Competition for these predominantly working-class customers led to the rapid development after 1870 of various retailing chains, for
example, Lipton and Griegs. By the end of the century, there were shops
glorying in their overseas connections, with names such as Home and Colonial
and International (Matthias 1967). The chains of grocers were matched by chains
of butchers. The Dewhurst company, for example, owned its own cattle ranches
in Uruguay and imported meat, frozen, chilled and canned, from its plant in
Montevideo. Interestingly, the middle and upper classes remained the customers
of privately owned and independent shops (Adburgham 1989; Davis, D. 1966).

The mass market in Britain, the United States and in Europe created the
conditions for international companies to emerge. Examples originating in the
United States include the meat packing firms of Armour and Swift, the Heinz
company and General Foods. In Switzerland, Nestlé, which began by selling
condensed milk, was established. However, the response to the mass market was
not one of uninterrupted expansion. The economic problems of the years
between the beginning of the First World War and the middle of the 1950s
limited or prevented many developments as large-scale unemployment diminished demand. Where prosperity continued even during the Depression of the
1930s, some retail chains continued to grow. The expansion of retail chains into
supermarkets came with the prosperity, particularly related to higher incomes, of
the late 1950s onwards. In organizational terms the self-service supermarket
became the hallmark of the most successful retail traders. This self-service
element depended on sophisticated packaging of all kinds of foods and appropriate marketing skills to persuade customers to buy. Large numbers of urban
consumers moved from older style shops to self-service stores. Experiences in the
United States encouraged some retailers in Britain to create supermarkets and
hypermarkets which offered a wide range of products, not only foodstuffs, for
sale. Amongst the first were the French owned Carrefour and the American
ASDA company. Soon British firms, such as Sainsbury, joined in the provision
of newer-style shopping facilities (Williams 1994). The style relied not only upon
most customers using cars but also upon their ownership of refrigerators. By the
1970s domestic freezers became a prerequisite when deep frozen foods were
available for home storage. The middle of the 1980s saw the wider availability of
microwave ovens giving scope for the expansion of sales of ready-prepared
frozen or chilled dishes. Alongside these developments there occurred an increase in the numbers of those employed to prepare food outside the home
(Gabriel 1988). All these processes combined to abolish the constraints of
seasonal supply and made available to the general population foods which had

previously only been available to the wealthy. This also permitted the expression of dietary preferences catered for by specialist, independently owned, shops.

This record of the triumph of technology and the organizaton of food production and distribution should not lead us to imagine there were no differences between consumers. Considerable inequalities remained, particularly in the nineteenth century (Tannahill 1973). Such divisions in society were reflected in differences between the diets of the rich and the poor. The poor, particularly the industrial poor living in housing with low standards of sanitation and lacking pure water, subsisted on a relatively narrow range of foods, for example, bread, tea, potatoes and a little meat (Tannahill 1973: 287). The rich had access to a wider variety and, by the later nineteenth century, were beginning to demand consistent quality and stable prices. In the middle were greater numbers of people earning higher incomes as industrialization proceeded. These artisans and middle-class consumers had an increasing choice and variety of food. They also had access to the newspapers, magazines, cookery books and guides to household organization and cuisine. Perhaps the most famous example is Mrs Beeton's book on household management, first published in 1868, which remained in demand, with revisions, for more than a century. Ironically, the scientific revolution and its application to the manufacture of new foods sometimes worsened rather than improved the diet of the poor, for example, the cheaper brands of condensed milk (which were made with skimmed rather than whole milk and which contained a high proportion of sugar as a preservative) lacked fats and vitamins A and D, and may, in fact, have increased the incidence of rickets (Tannahill 1973: 332). There are parallel arguments about the use of white bread, with its lack of wheatgerm, rather than brown bread (Tannahill 1973: 333).

INTERNATIONAL INEQUALITIES

In the accounts which are focused on the development of the modern food system in the West, there is an emphasis on changes which can be interpreted as progress: the triumph over the difficulties of improving the scale and quality of production; the technological achievements in both preservation and the food distribution network; the extension of consumer choice free from seasonal constraints. However, considered from a global rather than a Western standpoint, a different picture emerges, one which draws attention to the variable consequences of such changes for those not in the 'First World'. For example, Pelto and Pelto (1985) argue that the transformation of world dietary patterns may be characterized using the concept of 'delocalization' in relation to food production and distribution. By delocalization they refer to the processes in which food varieties, methods of production and patterns of consumption are 'disseminated throughout the world in an intensifying and ever-increasing network of socio-economic and political interdependency' (Pelto and Pelto 1985: 309). They acknowledge that the process of delocalization makes it possible for an increased proportion of the daily diet to be drawn from distant places and that it arrives through commercial channels. However, they also draw attention to the fact that the same process of delocalization has quite different consequences in industrialized societies compared with those which are less industrialized.

In industrialized societies, delocalization is associated with an increase in the diversity of foods available and an increase in the quantity of food imports. Initially, access to such foods may have been for those in privileged positions only, but in the twentieth century they become widely available to most of the population, with the exception of the very poorest. In contrast, delocalization has the opposite effect in less industrialized countries. Where people have been traditionally dependent on locally produced supplies and have distributed food outside the commercial network, the delocalization process draws them into the farming of non-traditional plant and animal varieties, into commercial production of cash crops and new kinds of food-processing on an industrial scale, and into migration from rural to urban settings. In consequence, there is not only a deterioration in food diversity locally but also a loss of control over distribution. In other words, these traditional societies are not in the process of 'catching up' with the West but are caught up in a global system which provides food choice and variety for industrialized societies at the expense of economically marginal peoples.

Bennett (1987) takes this argument even further and suggests that the subordination of underdeveloped societies' economies to the production of food and other commodities for the West can be identified as 'The Hunger Machine'. Drawing upon a considerable range of evidence from the Third World in the 1980s, Bennett argues that famines are, in fact, relatively rare and account for only a fraction of hunger-related deaths. It is poverty, and its associated inability to afford an adequate diet (what Bennett terms 'normal' hunger) which kills children in their first year or undermines the health of those who survive into adulthood. In seeking to explain such a state of affairs, Bennett argues it is important to look beyond conventional Western explanations, such as localized food shortages, overpopulation or droughts, and to consider the 'institutions, policies and ideologies which serve to widen the gap between rich and poor' (Bennett 1987: 13). These create the distinctions between the powerful North (that is, industrialized societies) and the subordinate South (that is, non-industrialized societies). Bennett's analysis draws attention to the impact of the pursuit of profits through cash crops which are exported, to the burden of Third World debt and to the use of food as a weapon in the political struggles between colonizers and the colonized. These are the dramatic consequences of the disappearance of the traditional food systems of the Third World which, Bennett argues, were rational, relatively well-balanced adaptations to the local environment.

The differences between the North and the South are not the only inequalities which can be understood in terms of a political analysis of the global food system. It has been suggested that 'The world re-discovered hunger in the mid-1980s' (Warnock 1987: ix), not only in the Third World but also in the cities of the West. Warnock draws attention to the contradictions in the policies of governments, such as those of the United States and the European Union, which either pay farmers not to produce or allow food 'mountains' to accumulate, whilst at the same time some groups in these societies go hungry. All the evidence suggests that there is no shortage of food on a worldwide basis, that food supplies have been increasing and that reserves of several staples, for example, grain, are high. The question then becomes that of why hunger persists in a world of plenty.

For Warnock, the question of who is undernourished and why, draws attention to issues which challenge Western complacency and optimism and are uncomfortable to contemplate from the perspective of the secure middle and upper classes. For example, 'free' trade in food does not necessarily benefit all countries equally and the model of the 'developing' country which suffers temporarily in the transition to fully developed status conceals the structure of political domination from which it is difficult to escape. Even the so-called 'Green Revolution', entailing the use of scientific knowledge to improve Third World agriculture, benefits the elites of the Third World and the general population of the North, to which foods are exported, more than the underdeveloped countries as a whole. These writers make the reader aware that the modern food system is not a neutral organization of food production and distribution but a political system which benefits some nations more than others. The solution to the problems of world hunger and the inequalities within specific societies are, they argue, political. 'The elimination of poverty and hunger comes at a high price' (Warnock 1987: 297). This price includes challenges to the hierarchical structure and lack of democratic control in the institutions of government, including those linked with the production and distribution of food.

REFASHIONING NATURE

The literature outlined in this chapter presents us with contradictory accounts of the making of the modern food system. It first provides a perspective of growth, expansion and rapid change, all of which appeared to be leading to increases in choice and quantity of food for all, and to a food system which has a responsive and sophisticated articulation between production, distribution and consumption. More recently, the note is more cautious, emphasizing the inequalities, particularly in the distribution of food, and indicating that no society, whether of the North or of the South, is exempt from sharp differences in access to food resources and that the modern food system has variable consequences which depend on political power. From the first perspective the future is bright; any problems can be viewed as temporary and resolvable with the application of the knowledge currently and potentially available. From the second perspective, the picture is of food supplies as precarious, or potentially so, and of a food system which cannot be sustained without continued exploitation of some Third World food producers.

One way of accommodating such contradictory analyses is offered by Goodman and Redclift (1991). Focusing on food supply, they argue that the development of the modern food system and its current operation can be seen as the outcome of a series of changes which they sum up as Western societies' attempt at 'refashioning nature'. Their argument is complex and recognizes the importance of taking into account all kinds of changes, not necessarily all closely connected with food in the first instance, and of drawing upon the materials provided by the literatures on agricultural development, technology, food policy and diet. Their argument is designed to encourage the reader to consider the ideological and economic framework within which the food supply is located. The processes of change they identify are, they argue, part of a process which changed not only how we think and behave towards food but also how we see the world and our own place in relation to nature.

Using such a framework of interconnected structures, it is not always easy to disentangle causes and effects. However, Goodman and Redclift group the changes under several major strands. The first identifies the social processes associated with the household which have accompanied the increasing commoditization of food, which they summarize as 'food into freezers; women into factories' (Goodman and Redclift 1991: 1). They focus on British experience during the twentieth century and note the coincidence of the diversification of household consumption with the movement of more women into paid employment. They also note the production of consumer goods for the home, for example, cookers, refrigerators and other 'white goods', which, in turn, is linked with a switch towards a greater emphasis on processed food products. However, these processes have not been taken to their extremes: neither women's work nor food are fully commoditized. The 'naturalness' of food and the work of women in their homes remain valued. None the less, it can be seen that the modern food system represents a new construction of social and economic divisions in the public domain of paid employment and the private domain of the household. Women's increasing involvement in the labour market has inevitable implications for the gendered division of labour in the home and particularly for the gendered division of labour in relation to food work (purchasing, preparation and presentation).

A further strand in the changes which have contributed to the modern food system is the transformation of food production itself. The modern food system requires reliable and stable supplies of food and conditions of social stability in which to bring about increases in production. These have been achieved by what Goodman and Redclift term a 'social contract' (Goodman and Redclift 1991: xiv) between farmers and government in the West which facilitated the integration of agriculture and industrial activities, increasing the investment in, and scale of, farming. Such processes, they argue, reduced resistance to the

implications of refashioning nature on the farm. The industrialization of farming, along with the drive to control nature in controlling agricultural output,
began with farm mechanization and the use of agri-chemicals and is continuing
currently with the use of revolutionary advances in plant and animal genetics.
The latter are being developed for commercial gain by private corporations
which are in competition with each other and are thus 'refashioning nature
according to the logic of the market place' (Goodman and Redclift, 1991: xvi).

Here there is the recognition that not all will benefit from such processes and
that there are contradictions as well as evidence of progress in the modern food
system. The South appears to have benefited from cheap food policies designed
to accelerate industrialization whilst, at the same time, having its peasant
agriculture and self-provisioning weakened and a dependence on imported
food established. In other words, the South is caught up in the contradictions
of the modern food system. The West itself is also becoming aware of the costs of
this system, for example, the loss of sustainability and the destructive effects of
some modern agriculture. Alternative models for refashioning nature have
emerged, providing a counter-culture opposed to the scale of industrialized
agriculture and to its established practices. Opposition focuses on production
processes (for example, protests about the use of pesticides and factory farming)
as well as· on the quality of food (for example, concerns about the use of food
additives and a perceived loss of 'naturalness'). The entire analysis indicates that
the concept of 'refashioning nature' may be the central one for interpreting the
processes which have produced the modern food system. However, the evidence
indicates also that this refashioning is an extremely difficult task and that control
of the process is precarious and controversial.

The issue of control also emerges as a key feature of the argument of Tansey
and Worsley (1995) who focus on the development of the modern food system
since the Second World War. Although the book is intended to be a guide to the
entire food system, discussion concentrates on 'the rich, industrialized world
where the global food system is being developed and promoted' (Tansey and
Worsley 1995: 1). For these authors, the notion of a food system implies links
between three different processes: the biological (including the production of
food); the economic and political (in particular, the power and control exerted
over the components of the food system); the social and cultural (especially those
factors which shape the ways in which people select and use food). The links are
not always necessarily easy to examine and the authors identify part of their task
as drawing the reader's attention to events and developments which can have
unanticipated consequences for the range of food available as well as its quality
and quantity. Indeed, the book is aimed at alerting 'ordinary citizens', as well as
students and professionals, to the balance of power between consumer and
producer and to the ways in which this might relate to the practicalities of
food safety and its availability for various social groups.

The authors provide a wide range of material from official and other surveys
to inform the reader about the biological and ecological basis of food produc-

tion, the structures and processes associated with what they term the 'key actors', such as farmers, distributors and consumers. They emphasize the ways in which science, technology, information and management, as well as the legal framework, can be used to control the production and distribution of food. They argue that the outcome of such interrelationships in the food system is a triumph, in that more people than ever are being fed and, in the industrialized and some developing countries, famine and scarcity no longer occur. However, the system also provides challenges in that some countries still experience malnutrition, or even famine, and long-term sustainability on a worldwide basis is in doubt. The authors identify six major changes that are likely to have an impact on the food system: increasing longevity (with its consequent strain on the ecosystem); increasing urbanization (which will extend the food chain); globalization of the food market (with large companies controlling a larger share and being independent of national boundaries); increasing technological (including biotechnological) change; changes in attitudes and values (consequent upon any shifts in power); and the decline in the traditional 'housekeeping' role of women as they participate more in the labour market and convenience foods are readily available. The authors conclude that if we wish to avoid the development of a system shaped only by the workings of the commercial market, then it is necessary to have clear food policy goals. The authors make clear their own preference for a food system which has the characteristics of being sustainable, secure, safe, sufficient, nutritious and equitable, and aimed at achieving 'a well-fed future for all' (Tansey and Worsley 1995: 232).

OVERVIEW

In this chapter we have sought to map the major contrasts between the traditional and modern food systems, with particular emphasis placed upon the dramatically increased scale and the extensive delocalization of the productive process. Using Britain as our case study, we have employed an historical perspective to outline the key developments in the emergence of the modern food system, with particular reference to the way that industrialization has transformed the nature of agricultural production and ensured the security of food supplies in the developed countries through the application of sophisticated scientific and technological knowledge.

However, at an international level, we have noted the way in which the globalized modern food system provides benefits for some countries by imposing costs on others, with the disadvantaged South seen as subordinated to the privileged North. The evolution of the modern food system, it has been argued, is also closely associated not only with industrialization itself but with far-reaching changes in the nature of the labour market and the division of labour within the household. Such structural changes appear, themselves, to be linked to some of the most deep-seated features of Western culture, particularly in relation to the right and ability of human beings to refashion and exploit the natural world. However, currently we are experiencing controversy and reappraisal in relation to these deeply rooted ideas in the form of the environmentalist challenges to established ideas.

3

SOCIOLOGICAL PERSPECTIVES ON FOOD AND EATING

In the previous chapter we examined the complex set of transformations which gave rise to the modern food system, a system whose characteristic features distinguish it from earlier modes of producing and distributing food in crucial ways. In a sense, the main object of analysis of this book is the modern food system itself, in terms of its multiplicity of aspects, dimensions and relationships. What is more, just as this system emerged out of far-reaching changes, the system itself is subject to continuing change. Thus, we will also be required to try to make sense of these changes, in terms of their causes and their directions. However, alongside change there is also continuity and stability in certain aspects of the system, and the bases of these features also demand attention and explanation.

THE CONCEPT OF THE HUMAN FOOD SYSTEM

Up to this point we have used the concept of the human food system in a general rather than a specific sense. At this stage it is worthwhile attempting to make more explicit its particular features, linkages and relationships. Of course, at its most basic, the modern human food system can be conceptualized as an immensely complicated set of biological relationships between human beings and symbiotically linked domesticated plants and animals, not forgetting the myriads of micro-organisms upon which the system depends and the hosts of pests and parasites which colonize it at all its tropic levels (see e.g., Jeffers 1980). However, for the purposes of this book, the primary focus is not on the biological but on the social and cultural dimensions of the system. As a starting-point we can take the basic scheme put forward by Goody (1982: 37). In Goody's view, providing and transforming food can be conceptualized in terms of five main processes, each process representing a distinct phase and taking place in a characteristic location, as shown in Table 3.1.

Thus the process of 'growing' food (including the rearing of animals) equals the 'production' phase, and is located on farms. The processes of allocating and storing food are identified as the 'distribution' phase, located in, for example, granaries and markets. Cooking, the preparation phase, takes place in the

47

Table 3.1 The features of the food system

Processes	Phases	Locus
Growing	Production	Farm
Allocating/storing	Distribution	Market/granary
Cooking	Preparation	Kitchen
Eating	Consumption	Table
Clearing up	Disposal	Scullery

Source: Adapted from Goody (1982)

kitchen, and eating, the consumption phase, takes place at the table. The fifth process, clearing up (which, Goody rightly points out, is often overlooked) represents the disposal phase, located in what he rather quaintly refers to as the 'scullery'. In fact, Goody's scheme is rather rudimentary, and clearly omits many of the crucial linkages in the modern food system. Yet it does draw our

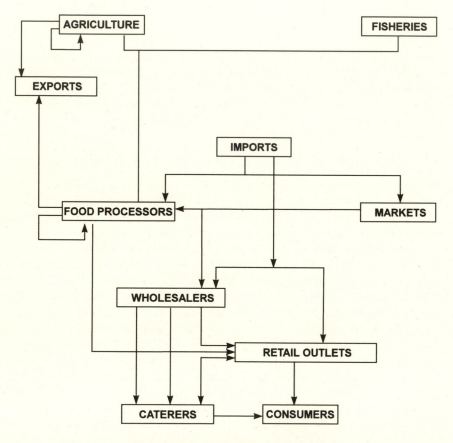

Figure 3.1 A model of the food system
Source: Adapted from Freckleton, Gurr, Richardson, Rolls and Walker (1989)

attention to all the basic processes involved, and it does allow us to begin to conceptualize how we might formulate sociological questions about each of the five phases which make up the system's underlying sequence.

A much more elaborate model of the contemporary food system is offered by Freckleton, Gurr, Richardson, Rolls and Walker (1989), who employ the biological term 'food chain' to refer to their scheme, although the scheme itself is an explicit description of the human, social framework of the system.

As can be seen from Figure 3.1, these authors detail the inputs into the system provided by agriculture (and by fisheries, which still exploit stocks of undomesticated animals) and include the fact that in any 'local' system there are outflows (exports) and inflows (imports). The central role played by food processors is referred to, that is, manufacturing organizations who obtain 'raw' food items from the primary producers (usually through specialist markets) and transform them into marketable products. The model also highlights the role played by wholesalers, who supply products from food processors, or items from specialist markets, to food retailers or to caterers of various kinds, who supply their products direct to the consumer. (For a model describing the food system in terms of factors affecting supply and demand potential see Pierce 1990: 7.)

Examining the multiplicity of flows and linkages in this model, it becomes evident that sociologists (and indeed social scientists in general) can pose a host of fascinating questions about the ways in which each of the components is organized, the ways in which the linkages between the components are actually articulated and the ways in which the system is monitored and regulated (usually by the state). However, even though the whole system is, in principle, susceptible to sociological analysis, there has been a notable tendency to concentrate attention on the consumption end. In effect, in the expanding literature on the sociology of food and eating the practices, preferences, choices, concerns and prejudices of consumers appear to have been allocated priority, although, of course, the beliefs and actions of the food consumer are located by sociologists within broader cultural, ideological and structural frameworks. The production, processing and distribution elements of the system have received, relatively speaking, a good deal less attention. In a sense, this is a curious state of affairs, given that, historically, mainstream sociology has always placed a strong emphasis on the analysis of the processes of production and on the idea that work and work roles play a crucial part in creating individual identity and in locating the individual in the wider social order. It is only comparatively recently that there has been something of a swing away from this production-centred approach towards a greater concern with the dynamics of consumption (Bocock 1993).

In a way, the sociology of food and eating has anticipated this trend, and the contents of this book, of necessity, reflect these priorities. However, there is literature, albeit somewhat fragmentary, on the productive processes of the system, both in domestic and commercial settings, and this literature will be drawn upon to provide context and background. Given the relatively recent arrival of food and eating as objects of analysis within sociology, there are still significant gaps in our knowledge of the human food system. The topics in this book have explicitly been chosen to provide the reader with an introduction to those areas where substantial sociological insights are available.

FROM THE NUTRITIONAL TO THE CULTURAL

In biological and behavioural terms humans can be classed as *omnivores* since they obtain their required nutrients from both animal and plant sources, and do not exhibit the kinds of physiological specializations which identify the dedicated herbivore or the confirmed carnivore. Nutrients can be defined as those chemical components of foods which contribute to one or more of the following vital bodily processes:

1   the production of energy;
2   the growth and repair of body tissue;
3   the regulation and control of energy production and tissue generation.

There are five basic groups of nutrients which we require to fulfil the above functions:

- *carbohydrates* which are primarily sources of energy;
- *fats* which are also, among other things, important energy sources;
- *proteins* which are the sources of the amino acids required for tissue growth, but which can also play a role in the other two functions listed above;
- *minerals* which are inorganic substances which contribute towards tissue growth (e.g., in bones and teeth) and the regulation of bodily processes;
- *vitamins* which constitute a very broad group of substances which function to facilitate the reactions required for the body's nutritional chemistry.

In a sense, water might also be classed as a nutrient, in that this essential compound plays many roles in the human body, e.g., in the breakdown of food into its constituent nutrients (through hydrolysis) and in the transport of those nutrients in the blood. (For introductory discussions of human nutrition, see e.g., Brownsell, Griffith and Jones 1989; Birch, Cameron and Spencer 1986. For a useful reference work see Anderson 1993.)

What is particularly striking about human beings, in nutritional terms, is the sheer diversity of the sources from which they can, and do, obtain the nutrients required to keep the body in existence and to fuel its day-to-day activities. Any attempt to list the whole range of plant and animal products that currently contribute to, or have in the past contributed to, the human diet would be a task of such enormity that it certainly cannot be attempted here. What is the case, however, is that this truly impressive nutritional versatility, probably unequalled by any other omnivore, has been a vital factor in the evolutionary success of our species. *Homo sapiens* has successfully colonized virtually every available habitat type and, along with our domesticated symbionts, we have established effective dominance over a high proportion of the land surface of the earth. None of this would have been feasible for a species with specialized feeding requirements.

However, being an omnivore does involve certain risks in addition to conveying the advantages associated with flexibility and versatility. Investigating and sampling new substances may lead to the discovery of valuable new food resources, and the present diversity of human eating patterns is the result of trial and error exercised over countless generations. But, inevitably, trial and error, as well as providing positive outcomes, can also lead to bad experiences, for example as a result of encountering unpalatable or even dangerously toxic or contaminated items. Thus, we are forced to confront what has been termed the 'omnivore's paradox', the tension between *neophilia*, the drive to seek out novel food items, and *neophobia*, the fear that novel items may be harmful (Rozin 1976; Fischler 1980). Thus, omnivores must successfully balance curiosity and caution, and this is as true for humans as for any other omnivorous animal. This tension is one of several deep-seated conflicts at the very foundation of human eating patterns, conflicts to which we will return in due course.

Of course, for humans, eating is not simply an activity aimed at obtaining required nutrients. There is clearly much more to it than that. This becomes all too obvious when we consider the fact that all cultures are highly selective in what they actually define as food, that is, as items acceptable for human consumption. In fact, Falk (1991) argues that one of the most fundamental distinctions made by human beings is that between *edible* and *inedible*, closely related to more abstract binary oppositions such as *us* and *them, same* and *other, inside* and *outside, good* and *bad, culture* and *nature*. Something edible is something which may be safely taken into the body. However, the cultural sense of inedibility/edibility is not simply a function of some wisdom of the body based upon metabolic processes and nutritional efficiency (Falk 1991: 55). Indeed, any given culture will typically reject as unacceptable a whole range of potentially nutritious items or substances while often including other items of dubious nutritional value, and even items with toxic or irritant properties. For example, the mainstream culinary cultures of the United States and the United Kingdom rule out horses, goats and dogs from the range of mammalian species suitable for inclusion in the human diet, whereas in other cultural contexts all these species have been, or are now, eaten with relish. (Religious beliefs may also play a role in the exclusion of certain items from the diet, obvious examples being the avoidance of pork prescribed by Judaism and Islam, and the avoidance of beef prescribed by Hinduism. We will return to such avoidances in a later chapter.) Conversely, Anglo-American cuisine incorporates large quantities of nutritionally suspect substances like refined sugar, and substances which are actually valued for their irritant properties, like pepper and mustard.

Indeed, when we eat, we are not merely consuming nutrients, we are also consuming gustatory (i.e., taste-related) experiences and, in a very real sense, we are also 'consuming' *meanings* and *symbols*. Every aliment in any given human diet carries a symbolic charge along with its bundle of nutrients. Thus, our view of a particular food item is shaped as much by what that item means to us as by how it tastes or by its ability to satisfy the body's nutritional needs (although, of course, the latter two features may get themselves incorporated into the aliment's charge of meanings). In fact, the symbolic dimensions of the foods we eat are of such central importance to us that in extreme instances we might even envisage starving rather than eat technically eatable substances that our culture defines as prohibited. Perhaps the most dramatic example of this is the near universal taboo on the consumption of human flesh. Instances of the violation of this taboo, e.g., in extreme situations of food deprivation, are regarded with a mixture of abhorrence and morbid curiosity.

Thus, it is no exaggeration to say that when humans eat, they eat with the mind as much as with the mouth. Indeed, the symbolic potential of food and eating is virtually limitless, and food items and food consumption events can be imbued with meanings of great significance and surpassing subtlety, according to the occasion and the context. Particular foods and food combinations, in particular cultures, can be associated with festivity and celebration, with piety, religious observance and sacred ritual, and with the rites of passage which mark crucial status transitions in the life cycle. What is more, gifts of food can be employed as rewards or as demonstrations of affection or approval. In Western cultures confectionery has a particular role to play in this context. Closely connected with this idea of the association between food and reward, is the association between certain foods and hedonism. Some foods may carry powerful meanings which go beyond the actual gustatory satisfaction they offer, being charged with overtones of luxury and self-indulgence. However, it is at this point that the darker side of food symbolism may come to the fore. Luxury and self-indulgence may generate guilt as well as pleasure. Thus, foods such as chocolate may develop ambivalent symbolic charges related to pleasure but also to anxieties concerning the health-related implications of their consumption. Indeed, in a more extreme sense, in specific cultural and historical contexts, particular food items may come to bear a potent negative symbolic charge, carrying meanings associated with the dangers of disease, immorality or ritual pollution. Of course, the reverse is also the case, in so far as other food items may develop associations with health, moral rectitude and spiritual purity. (Some of these issues will be explored further in later chapters.)

Food exchanges between individuals can be used to symbolize their mutual interdependence and reciprocity, whereas the routine provision of food for another, without reciprocity, can express one's dominance over a subordinate. In a domestic context, the preparation and serving of food for a family can express care and concern although, more subtly, the discharging of the responsibility to prepare food for others may also be seen as an expression of the server's effective subordination to the household's provider or 'breadwinner'. Indeed, in more general terms, food represents a powerful symbolic resource for the expression of patterns of social differentiation. If we consider the underlying dimensions of social differentiation which sociologists seek to analyse and understand (class, gender, age and ethnicity), it is clear that food can, and frequently does, play a crucial role in symbolizing and demonstrating social distinctions. Thus, specific foods become associated with a high social class location, with high status or with socially superior aesthetic tastes. Conversely, other foods may symbolize a low social class position, low status or the condition of poverty (economic or aesthetic). There is also no doubt that in many cultures (including modern Western settings) some foods can carry a distinctively masculine or feminine charge. Frequently, this gender charge is centred upon conceptions of strength, with 'strong' foods symbolizing masculinity and the needs of men, and 'weak' foods seen as appropriate to feminine needs and inclinations. Conceptions of this sort may also be implicated in age-related food symbolism. Strong, adult foods are often seen as unsuitable for young children. Similarly, particular foods or food combinations come to be seen as especially well-suited to children's needs and tastes, and these can take on an 'infantile' identity or association. At the opposite end of the age scale, a similar process may occur, with some foods being seen as especially appropriate for the elderly. These associations may also be linked with conceptualizations concerning differences in the appropriate diets of the healthy and the infirm. Of course, the role of food and food preparation conventions in symbolizing ethnic differences is also significant, given the fact that these conventions are such central features of cultural distinctiveness, and can retain their potency among minority groups for several generations after their physical separation from the parent culture.

In the chapters that follow, the theme of food symbolism will occur again and again, and many of the aspects of such symbolism mentioned above will be discussed in more detail in the context of actual empirical studies in which they occur as salient features. However, significant as the idea is that food can be used to *express* social differentiation, it is important not to lose sight of the fact that the food options and choices of specific categories or groups also *reflect* the inequalities inherent in such differentiation. The diet of the poor reflects the economic disadvantages with which they have to cope; the diet of children reflects (to some extent) their subordinate position *vis-à-vis* the adults who wield authority over them.

FOOD, IDENTITY AND SOCIALIZATION

So powerful is the symbolic potential of food that Fischler (1988) argues that it is absolutely central to our sense of identity. However, it is not only true that the eating patterns of a given group assert its collective identity, its position in a wider hierarchy, its organization, etc.. Fischler also points out that food is central to *individual identity*. The crucial process here is that of 'incorporation', the act which involves food crossing the barrier between the 'outside' world and the 'inside' world of the body. But the process, as Fischler points out, is not only conceived as a physiological one. We do not simply think in terms of the incorporation of chemical nutrients into the physical fabric of the body, but also in terms of our beliefs and our collective representations. For example, a widespread feature of human culture is the idea that the absorption of a given food, particularly when occurring repeatedly, can have the effect of transferring certain symbolic properties of that food into the very being of the eater. Fischler cites as a positive example the idea that red meat, with its high blood content, confers strength. (Later in the book we will examine beliefs which are very different from this view.) As a negative example, he cites the belief among French eaters that consuming turnips induces 'spinelessness' or, literally, 'turnip blood' (Fischler 1988: 279–80). Thus, for Fischler, the German aphorism *man ist was man isst* (you are what you eat) has both biological and symbolic dimensions. What is more, not only are the properties of food seen as being incorporated into the eater, but, by a symmetrical process, the very absorption of given foods is seen as incorporating the eater into a culinary system and into the group which practises it.

Both in terms of the formation of individual identity and the transmission of culture from generation to generation, the process of socialization is of central importance, that is, the process through which we internalize the norms and values of society, and learn now to perform the social roles in which we find ourselves. Socialization begins in infancy through the primary agencies of the family and the school, but is not confined to childhood, and represents a continuous process throughout the life cycle, with many other agencies taking a hand. What is more, socialization is not merely a passive process. The individual is also active in socializing himself or herself, and we should beware of accepting an 'oversocialized' view of the human individual, since there is always leeway for a degree of choice, deviance or innovation, and there may be conflicting pressures from different agencies. The socialization of an individual into the foodways of the culture into which he or she has been born effectively begins at weaning. At this stage the infant is encouraged to sample what is, at first, a relatively narrow range of solid foods. This range is progressively widened as the child is introduced to more of the food items and preparations regarded as suitable for the young. Crucially, at these early stages, the child will be taught, and will learn by experience, how to distinguish between foods and non-foods. Young children typically place a variety of objects in the mouth in order to use its elaborate sensory apparatus to investigate their physical properties. Children may also attempt to eat substances which are not actually eatable, and to drink liquids which are not actually potable. Even a small sample of parents could provide an interesting inventory of such substances, ranging from relatively harmless ones like garden soil, to highly toxic ones like domestic bleach.

Thus, a crucial feature of nutritional socialization involves learning how to reduce the risk of introducing hazardous substances into the body, although such hazards may be symbolic as well as physiological. Thus, equally importantly from a sociological point of view, the child must learn how to recognize *food* from among a plethora of potentially edible items with which he or she may be surrounded. As we have already noted, in all cultures, whatever the form of subsistence upon which they are based, humans exploit for food only a relatively small proportion of the available plant and animal species around them. However, in Western society, for example, young children, while unsupervised, may sample such perfectly eatable items as earthworms or pet food, and find them good. The horrified reactions of parents, siblings or peers, nevertheless, may soon convince them that such delicacies are, most emphatically, not appropriate for human consumption. In other words, a central part of learning to be human involves learning what humans, as opposed to non-humans, eat.

A whole range of strategies and verbal devices may be employed by parents to exert control over the child's eating patterns and to encourage, cajole or coerce him or her into the consumption of what is seen as a suitable diet (Widdowson 1981). These strategies may include the offer of rewards if the child consumes what the parents regard as desirable foods and the threat or application of punishments if such foods are persistently refused. Indeed, these threats may be accompanied by the invocation of supernatural agencies who are portrayed as ready to intervene to reinforce parental authority in the face of an offspring's persistent nutritional defiance. A particularly graphic example of such a device is provided by Widdowson, who describes the character of the Crust Man, a figure in Newfoundland folklore. Portrayed as taking the form of a large, ugly man, he was said to patrol the community ensuring that children ate their bread crusts. Those who refused to do so were likely to be carried off in the night by this awesome being!

As the individual's nutritional socialization proceeds, in Western cultures an ever-widening range of agencies, including advertisers, the mass media in general, various professional groups, state institutions and ideological or religious movements, can come to play a role. The individual goes on to learn not only how to distinguish foods from non-foods (fit only for animals or foreigners), but how to recognize appropriate preparation techniques, appropriate combinations of food items, and the conventions which govern where and when one eats, and with whom. Furthermore, socialization involves the familiarization of the individual with the food categorization system of his or her culture. Thus, Jelliffe (1967) describes a range of general categories which underlie the food classification schemes of most cultures. These categories are: *cultural superfoods*, the main staples of the society in question; *prestige foods*, whose consumption is limited to special occasions or to high-status groups; *body-image* foods, which are seen as directly promoting health and bodily well-being; *sympathetic magic* foods, which are believed to have desirable properties which can be acquired by those who eat them; and, finally, *physiologic group* foods, which are seen as suitable for specific categories of individuals defined, for example, in terms of gender, age and bodily condition related to health, pregnancy, etc. (For a discussion of this, and other food classification schemes, see Fieldhouse 1986: 45–54.)

As such conventions and categories are mastered, the satisfaction of the body's nutritional requirements is given its shape as a complex *social* activity, as opposed to a mere set of internally driven behavioural responses to the need for nutrients.

55

In this way, as Mennell (1985: 20–1) points out, the physiological and psychological phenomenon of *hunger* is transformed into the sociological phenomenon of *appetite*. However, appetite, preferences and food symbolism are not necessarily static entities, fixed once and for all in the mind of the individual by the socialization process. Individuals may undergo significant changes in their socially formulated appetites or may experience important transformations in the meanings which they attach to specific food items or, indeed, to the whole process of eating. Thus, in a sense, an individual can be seen as having what can be termed a 'nutritional career'. This career is closely related to the life cycle, as the individual moves through childhood, adulthood and old age, and his or her nutritional practices and preferences change according to changing bodily needs and cultural expectations. In addition, individuals may deliberately initiate changes in their dietary patterns, for a whole range of reasons which they may or may not be capable of comprehending and articulating.

Indeed, modern Western societies can be seen as providing particularly suitable conditions for nutritional careers which commonly include substantial changes. While the nutritional culture of such societies may be characterized by relative stability, continuity and conservatism in some areas of diet (e.g., in relation to cultural superfoods), there is typically a willingness, often an eagerness, to promote and accept change in other areas (say, in relation to body-image foods and physiologic group foods). Indeed, in highly developed, affluent societies the appetite for gustatory and nutritional novelty is actively encouraged (often by commercial interests) and food-related 'sensation-seeking' activities are seen as a normal and accepted part of society's nutritional practices. What is more, in such settings, many agencies (including the state, professional bodies and pressure groups) may deliberately seek to modify the public's food consumption patterns either generally or in relation to particular target groups in the population. Thus, individuals may be undergoing sporadic episodes of resocialization in respect of food choices, practices and beliefs. Such a state of flux has far-reaching implications for many of the topics discussed in this book, and the theme of change will recur frequently in subsequent chapters.

THEORIZING THE FOOD SYSTEM

The question now arises as to what theoretical resources have been brought to bear by sociologists in order to analyse food systems in terms of their symbolic properties and in terms of the intricate webs of social relationships and social processes which articulate them. In this section we wish to offer a broad overview of the various approaches which have been employed. Of course, any scheme for classifying these approaches should be seen simply as an heuristic device. It can only be offered as a summarizing framework to give the reader a sense of the broad picture, a sense of the main theoretical lines which have been pursued by sociologists in the area of food and eating, and can make no claim to be an authoritative description of reality *per se*. What is more, it is important to bear in mind a point made by Goody (1982: 8) concerning the very nature of sociological theories themselves. He draws a clear contrast between theoretical innovations in the natural sciences, which may well produce revolutionary paradigm shifts (Kuhn 1964), and theoretical innovations in sociology (and its sister discipline, social anthropology). In sociology, such innovations are not the cues for the total reorientation of the discipline's research activities and intellectual efforts. Rather, they indicate shifts of emphasis between possibilities which are always present in the act of sociological analysis. Such possibilities may be conceived of in terms of binary oppositions, for example: a focus on the subjective world of the social actor versus a holistic focus on social structure; a focus on qualitative versus quantitative methods; a focus on synchronic versus diachronic analysis; a focus on surface structure versus a focus on deep structure, and so on. All this implies that changes in sociological theory are, in effect, 'repetitive', involving cycles of changing emphasis in relation to the underlying, recurring themes of the discipline. Thus, when we examine a specific area of sociological analysis and research like food and eating we might logically expect it to reflect the changing fashionability of the approaches. Furthermore, particular studies will also reflect these changes, although we should not be surprised to discover that such studies may actually be quite difficult to classify according to any broad scheme, given that they may involve the hybridization of two or more approaches.

Goody's (1982) own classificatory scheme identifies three main approaches: the *functional*, the *structural* and the *cultural*. Having discussed these three, he then goes on to examine approaches which introduce historical and comparative data, although he does not actually provide these approaches with their own distinctive label. Writing somewhat later, Mennell, Murcott and Van Otterloo (1992) put forward a very similar scheme, suggesting that the three main headings under which studies of food and eating can be conveniently classified are *functionalism, structuralism* and *developmentalism* (although the authors do point out that many studies in this area have been empiricist in style or largely policy-oriented, and hence difficult to classify in terms of theoretical approach). Combining these two schemes would provide us with a four-category classification of approaches: functional, structural, cultural and developmental (the latter heading actually being implicit in Goody's own discussion). However, the cultural will be omitted as a separate heading, as Goody's argument does not actually establish the need for this as a category in itself, since it is a concept so fundamental to the other three approaches. We can now examine each of these in turn, analysing its underlying logic and the kinds of questions it poses, and looking at representative examples of its use.

I The functionalist approach

Functionalist perspectives have exercised a powerful formative influence on sociology and on its sister discipline social anthropology. Functionalism is based upon an analogy between a society and an organic system, like a living body. Just as a body is seen as made up of a set of specialized organs, each playing its own unique and indispensable role in the maintenance and continuity of the living system, society is seen as made up of a set of features and institutions which make their own contribution to the cohesion and continuity of the social system. Thus, society is seen in holistic terms and as having emergent properties which spring from the complex interrelationships and interdependency of its component parts. Functionalist analysis consists essentially of examining particular institutions with a view to describing their functional significance. For example, the institution of marriage might be analysed in order to understand its contribution to the long-term viability and continuity of a given social formation. Functionalist theory makes an important distinction between the *manifest* function of some feature (i.e., the function explicitly recognized by members of the society in question) and that feature's *latent* function (i.e., a function that a feature may fulfil, but which may not be recognized or admitted by society's members). Functionalist theory also recognizes that a social system may exhibit *dysfunctional* features which disrupt that system and lead to states which are analogous to pathology in a living body, i.e., to 'social pathology'. Some of the leading figures in sociology have made contributions of central importance to the development of functionalist perspectives, for example, Davis (1966), Durkheim (1984), Merton (1957) and Parsons (1951).

However, the whole funtionalist approach has attracted a barrage of criticism. It has been accused, for example, of being an essentially static view of human social organization, overemphasizing stability and integration, and poorly equipped to explain the presence of conflict and change in social systems. What is more, the approach has also been criticized for failing to account causally for the origins of particular institutions or features in society, assuming that describing a particular institution's alleged role or effects is, in itself, an adequate explanation for its presence. Perhaps even more problematic is the assumption that we can specify the functional needs of a social system in the same way that we might specify the physiological needs of a living body. Given that social systems have the ability to undergo far-reaching structural changes, the notion of a set of immutable and unavoidable functional needs is somewhat implausible.

As a result of such criticisms, functionalism is now out of fashion within the discipline of sociology, although certain aspects of the critique may have been overstated (for example, functionalist perspectives are not totally incapable of coming to terms with conflict and change in a social system). However, functionalist interpretations remain at the core of much sociological analysis, albeit in an implicit form.

It is possible to conceive of a range of questions which could be asked about food and eating from a broadly functionalist perspective. For example:

- How are the food production, distribution and consumption subsystems organized and how do they contribute to the continuity of the social system as a functioning whole? (In posing such questions, the organic analogy upon which functionalism is based is very much to the fore, in that society might be viewed as analogous to an enormous superorganism, feeding itself and distributing nutrients around its 'body'.)

- What are the social (i.e., non-nutritional) functions of patterns of food allocation and consumption? For example, how do allocation and consumption conventions act to express and reinforce the social relationships upon which the stability of the whole system is supposed to depend? One expression of such an issue might be the idea that food-related practices may reinforce gender divisions, such divisions being seen as functional for the system in that they could be regarded as forming the basis of the conventional nuclear family, the institution which organizes reproduction and primary socialization.

- Can we identify, in food systems, dysfunctional features, alongside the kinds of latent functions discussed above? How do such dysfunctional elements arise? What are their consequences for the social system as a whole? (In this connection, for example, we might analyse eating patterns which appear adversely to affect the health of the population, or the mechanisms which generate disruptive food-related anxieties and scares.)

Significantly, perhaps, those studies which can most clearly be identified as adopting a functionalist approach to food and eating are to be found within social anthropology. More specifically, they are to be found within the British school of social anthropology, a branch of the discipline which, in its formative years, was dedicated to the functionalist, holistic analysis of traditional social systems. Thus, one of the founders of this school, Bronislaw Malinowski, provided a highly detailed ethnographic account of food production and allocation systems in the Trobriand Islands, and of the complex patterns of belief and social reciprocity which articulated these systems (Malinowski 1935). One of Malinowski's own students, Audrey Richards, set out to analyse, from a functionalist perspective, the ways in which the production, the preparation and particularly the consumption of food among the Bantu were linked to the life cycle, to group structures and to the social linkages which constituted them (Richards 1932). In a later study of the Bemba (Richards 1939), she attempted to place the nutritional culture of a traditional people into its broader economic setting. A recurring theme in Richard's study was the symbolic significance of food and of nutritional practices, a symbolism which served to express, for example, vital ties of kinship, obligation and reciprocity.

The functional significance of food and foodways was also highlighted by social anthropologists writing more general monographs on traditional peoples. For example, in his discussion of the Andaman Islanders, Radcliffe-Brown (1922) had sought to demonstrate the way in which food-related rituals and taboos were used, not only to impress upon the young the social value of food but also as devices for dramatizing the collective sentiments of the community, hence facilitating the individual's socialization. What is more, the co-operative production of food, and its sharing within the community, were activities which served to emphasize a sense of mutual obligation and interdependence, and hence to reinforce the integration of Andaman society (Radcliffe-Brown 1922: 270–1). In what is undoubtedly one of the classic texts of the British school of social anthropology, Evans-Pritchard (1967) set out to document the political and ecological dimensions of Nuer society. He described in detail the relationship between kinship systems and spatial organization, and demonstrated the extent to which the food system of this pastoralist people was based upon, in his memorable phrase, a form of 'symbiosis with cattle'. In a sense, in a study like Evans-Pritchard's, the functional linkages in a food system are far more visible than in a modern system, where such linkages do not have the same immediate proximity to everyday life. However, for the Nuer, the realities and exigencies of food production, and the seasonal migrations they entail, are integral features of every individual's experience.

The studies discussed above were carried out several decades ago under the aegis of a theoretical approach which has more recently been relegated to the margins of sociology. However, functionalist ideas have proved quite resilient, either as explicit neo-functionalist arguments or as an implicit set of assumptions. As we will see later in this book, functionalist or quasi-functionalist perspectives lie behind some of the questions which we continue to ask about the non-nutritional role of food in society and in everyday life. These questions may not be framed in terms of what might be called 'grand theory' functionalism, but they do attest to the continuing significance of this organic analogy, albeit in a partially concealed form.

II The structuralist approach

Structuralist analyses of social phenomena differ from the functionalist approach in a particularly important respect. Whereas functionalism seeks to theorize the ways in which the various components of the system interrelate with each other to form a coherent whole, structuralism claims to look below these 'surface' linkages into the 'deep structures' which are alleged to underpin them. Thus, structuralism claims to analyse the very structure of human thought, even of the mind itself (Goody 1982: 17). Of greatest interest to the present discussion is the structuralism of the French anthropologist Lévi-Strauss (1963, 1966a, 1970). Lévi-Strauss, unlike the functionalists, is not primarily concerned with producing holistic descriptions of particular traditional societies. Rather, he sets out to examine a wide range of anthropological material and ethnographic data (notably in relation to myth) on the assumption that the examination of these surface features can lead to the recognition of universal, underlying patterns. These patterns are the deep structures, structures which represent the unvarying foundations of the enormous diversity of surface cultural forms which we can observe. There is assumed to be an affinity between the deep structures of the human mind and the deep structures of human society. Just as functionalism is based upon an analogy between society and a living organism, so structuralism also rests on an analogy. In this instance, the analogy is a linguistic one, with cultural surface features seen as generated in the same way that everyday speech is seen as produced by an underlying system of rules (Saussure 1960).

Thus, the questions posed about food and eating from a structuralist perspective have a different emphasis as compared with those posed from a functionalist viewpoint. Rather than focusing upon the practicalities and the social processes involved in producing, allocating and consuming food, the structuralist gaze is directed towards the rules and conventions that govern the ways in which food items are classified, prepared and combined with each other. The assumption is that these surface rules of cuisine are themselves manifestations of deeper, underlying structures. These rules are almost like a language which, if we can decipher it, will tell us much about the organization of the human mind and human society.

Lévi-Strauss uses this analogy directly by referring to the constituent elements of cuisine as 'gustemes', deriving this term from the linguistic concept of the phoneme. His argument is that such gustemes can be analysed in terms of certain binary oppositions. These are endogenous/exogenous (local versus exotic), central/peripheral (staple versus garnish or accompaniment) and marked/not marked (strong flavour versus bland flavour). He actually sets out to analyse the differences between English and French cuisine using this scheme, suggesting that in English cooking the endogenous/exogenous and central/peripheral distinctions are highly pertinent, whereas the marked/not marked opposition is not. In contrast, in French cuisine, the endogenous/exogenous and central/peripheral oppositions are not so pertinent, whereas the marked/not marked opposition is emphasized (Lévi-Strauss 1963).

However, certainly the best known and most widely quoted example of Lévi-Strauss's structuralist approach to cuisine is his analysis of the transformations involved in the actual cooking of food. Cooking is seen as a crucial operation, given that Lévi-Strauss argues that a universal feature of human thought involves linking the distinction between raw ingredients and cooked food with the fundamental distinction between nature and culture (Lévi-Strauss 1966b). Thus, in the sphere of eating, cooking is what transforms nature (raw ingredients) into culture (acceptable food for humans).

Lévi-Strauss formulates these ideas in terms of his so-called 'culinary triangle' (Figure 3.2), which lays out in diagrammatic form the transitions between nature and culture which are associated with food.

Thus, raw food, at the apex of the triangle, becomes cooked food through a cultural transformation. However, cooked food may be reclaimed by nature through the natural transformation of rotting. Of course, raw (fresh) food can itself be transformed from one natural state into another natural state through the process of rotting, as the triangle indicates. Lévi-Strauss takes the position that the transformational operations of cooking can be seen as a kind of

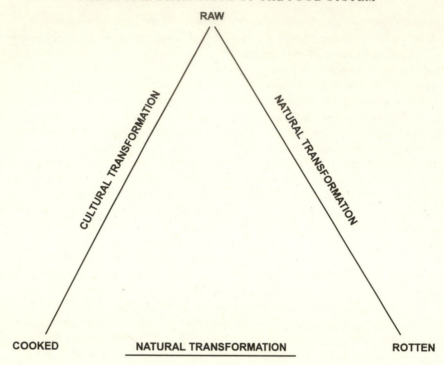

Figure 3.2 The culinary triangle
Source: Adapted from Lévi-Strauss (1966b)

language, in the same way that he regards marriage regulations and kinship systems as a kind of language for establishing and regulating linkages and communication between social groups in traditional societies (Goody 1982: 21).

Developing the basic culinary triangle, Lévi-Strauss then puts forward a more elaborate triangle of recipes, arguing, for example, that roasting is a cooking technique which is closer to the 'raw' apex (since it is seen by him as producing relatively little change in meat, for example). On the other hand, he sees smoking as a technique as closer to culture, since it transforms meat into a durable commodity. He asserts that boiling, which is mediated by water, produces results which are closer to the 'rotten' corner of the basic triangle. As Lévi-Strauss elaborates his arguments, the justifications for his assertions appear to become ever more idiosyncratic and even fanciful. This has led some authors to raise doubts about the actual analytical and heuristic usefulness of such a scheme. For example, Mennell (1985: 9) points out that when Lévi-Strauss attempts to explain the foodways of European societies, his celebrated triangles are of comparatively little use and, in effect, he falls back on common-sense arguments. What is more, Goody (1982: 31) suggests that there is a certain circularity in arguing that by analysing surface structures (like culinary practices) we can deduce the deep structures of the mind or of society, and that these deep structures are what 'generate' the surface effects we observe.

Another social anthropologist, Mary Douglas, also has close links with the structuralist approach to food and eating, but in an important sense her concerns are less arcane and less obscure than those of Lévi-Strauss, and more clearly rooted in a less exotic, more familiar everyday world. She bases her analysis on the structuralist idea that food can be treated as a code, and the messages that it encodes are messages about social events and about social relations like 'hierarchy, inclusion and exclusion, boundaries and transactions across boundaries' (Douglas 1975: 61). Douglas employs the scheme devised by Halliday (1961) who puts forward a framework of categories for the description of eating. The uppermost category is the daily menu, below this is the meal, below this is the course, below this the helping and at the base of the structure is the mouthful, which he regards as the equivalent of the gastronomic morpheme. He then goes on to show how these categories can be elaborated in terms of primary and secondary structures so that a complete description of all the elements of a daily menu could be produced using a grammatical format. In fact, Halliday's purpose in offering such a scheme was to cast light on the problems of grammatical categorization, but Douglas takes up the basic idea and applies it to the analysis of the eating patterns of her own family. In so doing, she is able to provide a fascinating insight into the way in which the same structure appears to underly most meals in English cuisine, and the ways in which this structure repeats itself over a whole range of meal occasions, from the most mundane to the most festive. (In a later chapter we will examine Douglas's analysis of family meal structures and their broader social significance in much more detail.) Certainly, the strength of Douglas's use of structuralist perspectives is that she never loses sight of the fact that, while food may be seen as a metaphor, a symbol or a vehicle of communication, it is, above all, a life-giving substance, and a meal is a physical as well as a social event (Douglas 1984).

In any discussion of the structuralist approach to food and eating reference must also be made to the work of the French author, Roland Barthes. Barthes (1979) firmly locates himself within the structuralist framework, as his terminology clearly testifies. For him, an item of food constitutes an item of information. All foods are seen as signs in a system of communication. Thus, in theory, the conceptual units for describing food can be used to construct 'syntaxes' (or 'menus') and 'styles' (or 'diets') in a semantic rather than an empirical fashion. Hence, it becomes possible to ask to what these food significations refer. Looking at food advertising as an example, Barthes identifies one theme in which specific foods are used to signify continuity with tradition and the past. A second major theme embodies the distinction between masculinity and femininity, and involves an element of sublimated sexuality. A third theme revolves around the concept of health, in the rather specific sense of 'conditioning' the body via appropriate foods with associations like 'energy', 'alertness' or 'relaxation' (Barthes 1979: 171). For Barthes, in the developed countries there has emerged a nutritional consciousness which is 'mythically directed' towards adapting human beings to the modern world, and at the same time an increasingly diverse range of behaviours is expressed through food (for example, work, sport, effort, leisure and celebration). Mennell (1985) is critical of Barthes' lack of any systematic historical perspective and of his tendency to draw upon the resources of his own common-sense views of historical knowledge. However, despite these criticisms, the food-related themes Barthes identifies are striking ones (and will recur at various points in this book), even though he cannot actually deliver a fully elaborated 'grammar of food'.

As a perspective, structuralism has been subjected to numerous critical attacks and reappraisals. While this is not the place to discuss this critique in any detail, some of the criticisms which have been levelled at the application of these ideas to food-related issues do need to be reiterated and made explicit at this point. Certainly, by focusing attention on the idea of food as communication, structuralism effectively rules out the analysis of the crucial interconnections which articulate the human food system as a whole. The links between food production and consumption and the wider economic order tend to fade from view, as does the consideration of the significance of the hierarchical organization of human societies and any potential influences of biological or climatological factors (Goody 1982: 28–9). What is more, the structuralist analysis of foodways and food consumption patterns has had little to say about the origins of such patterns, that is, about the specific social and historical conditions which give rise to them. However, despite these shortcomings, the structuralist approach, with its use of a linguistic metaphor, has succeeded in highlighting some key themes. These themes, as we will see, continue to inform the sociological analysis of food and eating. This is despite the fact that structuralism (like functionalism), in its various guises and phases, has now largely passed into unfashionability, and also that the grandiose promise of unlocking the underlying grammar of food has remained largely unfulfilled.

Perhaps the most telling criticism of the structuralist analysis of food is highlighted by Mennell (1985: 13–14). He refers to the point made by Elias (1978a) that structuralism is based upon an assumption fundamental to Western thought, namely, the idea that underlying the surface changes of the everyday world there are deep-seated relationships which are themselves unchanging. The tendency to allocate overriding significance to such hypothetical underlying entities is referred to by Elias as 'process-reduction'. In fact, Mennell implies, this process-reduction assumption seriously undermines attempts to get to grips with the nature and origins of the significant changes under way in human food systems. It is for this reason that he lays such emphasis on what he terms the 'developmental' approach, in which the analysis of change is placed centre stage.

III The developmental approach

The developmental approach to which Mennell (1985) refers directly, and to which Goody (1982: 33–7) refers in a more indirect fashion, does not really represent an explicit perspective and a coherent body of theory in the same sense as functionalism and structuralism do. Rather, it is something of a residual category into which can be placed a range of approaches which exhibit some common features and preoccupations. The most fundamental of these common features is the assumption that any worthwhile attempt to understand contemporary cultural forms or patterns of social relations must take into account the ways in which these are related to past forms. Thus, social change becomes a primary focus, in terms of its directions, its processes and its origins. Once change is given primacy in this fashion, the presence of conflicts and contradictions in social systems may also become a much more important strand in sociological analysis.

Mennell's own principal contribution to the sociology of food, a comparative study of eating and taste in England and France (Mennell 1985), fits very neatly into the developmental category. This study draws its theoretical underpinnings from the work of Elias (1978b, 1982), whose broad developmental theory ranged from the processes of state formation to the formation of individual personality and conduct. One of the central contentions of Elias's work was the view that an extensive and protracted civilizing process has been at work in Western societies for several centuries. One of the notable effects of this process has been a progressive shift from the exercise of external constraints upon individuals towards the development of internalized constraints which, in effect, individuals exercise upon themselves. This switch from external to internal constraints affects many areas of social life, including eating. It leads to what Mennell (1985: 20–39) terms the 'civilizing of appetite', a concept which has considerable explanatory power in relation to nutrition-related phenomena as diverse as anorexia nervosa and vegetarianism. In fact, Mennell's work represents an ambitious attempt to apply Elias's figurational or sociogenic approach to understanding the contrasts and similarities of two developing systems of cuisine. How 'figurations', or sets of social, cultural, economic or political arrangements, change over time in the context of the ebb and flow of competing ideas and interests is the key question. Mennell's study is arguably one of the best and most fully worked out examples of the developmental approach, and his ideas will be examined in more depth in Chapter 4.

Goody, too, can be located unequivocally in the developmentalist camp. His major study of food and eating (Goody 1982) focuses much of its attention on the cuisine and foodways of two ethnic groups in northern Ghana. However, Goody's book is not simply a narrowly conceived anthropological monograph. He makes a concerted attempt to analyse the changes going on in the groups he studies in terms of the development of what is, in effect, an increasingly globalized food system. Thus, he argues, for example, that the African peoples he studied have not given up their traditional cuisine. However, just as they now employ the English language in areas like politics, religion and education (as a result of the impact of colonialism), they also use English cooking techniques and conventions in certain formal contexts (Goody 1982: 184). Significant changes in a particular set of foodways are shown to be the result of processes of change which are literally occurring on a global scale. Thus, an important part of Goody's analysis is an examination of the development of what he terms 'industrial food', with all the complexities of processing, preservation (through techniques like canning and freezing), mechanized distribution and large-scale retailing. Indeed, the global perspective which forms a background to Goody's analysis provides the central theme of the fascinating study by Mintz of the crucial role of sugar in the nutritional practices and preferences of the Western industrial working class. Mintz (1985) sets out to demonstrate how dramatic rises in sugar consumption were linked to political and economic processes acting at a global level. Mintz's convincing and comprehensive analysis will be discussed further in Chapter 11.

A particularly significant contribution to the sociological and social anthropological analysis of food and eating has been made by Harris (1986). Harris's approach, which he describes as a form of cultural materialism, is not easy to classify under the three broad headings, although Mennell, Murcott and Van Otterloo (1992) opt to locate him under the developmental umbrella, if only because his stance is assertively anti-structuralist. Harris is highly critical of the notion that the symbolic dimensions of food and eating are the overriding ones and that these dimensions can be analysed independently of the nutritional, ecological and economic realities of human life. Harris's own study consists of a series of essays in which he looks at a number of food prohibitions or taboos which appear to have an essentially symbolic, moral or religious basis (e.g., the prohibition on beef associated with Hinduism, the prohibition on pork associated with Judaism and Islam). He sets out to demonstrate that such ideas, and the nutritional practices derived from them, may well have a strong practical logic behind them, a logic which springs out of a society's attempts to adapt to its physical environment and exploit available resources effectively. Mennell and his co-authors see this line of thinking as consistent with the developmental approach, in so far as Harris is seeking to describe the specific conditions and processes which have given rise to a particular feature of a food system or a nutritional culture. However, it is probably fair to say that Harris's form of explanation also has marked affinities with the functionalist approach discussed earlier. We will return to examine some of Harris's distinctive ideas in more detail in Chapter 9.

Mennell, Murcott and Van Otterloo (1992) place the work of the French sociologist Claude Fischler in the structuralist category, while noting that his position is decidedly critical of the limitations of structuralism and shows significant linkages with the developmental approach. Certainly, from the point of view of the present book, it is the developmental aspects of Fischler's concerns that are of particular interest. A crucial thesis put forward by Fischler is the idea that the traditional rules, norms and meanings which structure human food intake (which he labels collectively as the rules of 'gastronomy', the word being used in its literal sense) are increasingly being subjected to 'disaggregation'

(Fischler 1980: 947). This disaggregation involves a breakdown of these long-established rules, and this crisis in gastronomy leads to a state that Fischler terms 'gastro-anomy' (a concept closely linked with Durkheim's concept of anomie). Fischler suggests that this situation arises out of a proliferation of contradictory and inconsistent pressures acting upon the contemporary food consumer (e.g., from the food industry, advertising and the state). What is more, the uncertainties and anxieties created by gastro-anomy and the expansion of agro-industry and industrialized food production are seen as generating disturbances in those processes through which culinary culture helps to create and sustain the individual's very identity (Fischler 1988: 288–90). Fischler's acute and sometimes disturbing analysis will be spelled out in more detail in Chapter 7, when we will examine the interrelated phenomena of food risks, food anxieties and food scares.

The picture of the cultural dimensions of the modern food system painted by Fischler, is, in some senses, a decidedly pessimistic one. However, he does point out that there are likely to be individual and collective attempts to restore order to eating practices and food meanings. Thus, individuals may adopt dietary regimes (weight-loss diets, vegetarianism, etc.) in an attempt to restore some 'normative logic' into their eating (Fischler 1988: 290–1). This idea leads on to the work of the present authors, whose theoretical orientation can also be located beneath the broad umbrella of the developmental approach. The starting point of this analysis is the concept of the aliment, that is, any basic item recognized as edible within a given nutritional culture. The term 'aliment' is employed in preference to the term 'gusteme' which is used by Lévi-Strauss, since it is a more general notion and does not carry the structuralist implications of the gusteme concept (Beardsworth and Keil 1992a: 287–9). Hence, the *alimentary totality* of a society is made up of the whole range of aliments available during a particular time period. At this point the central concept of the 'menu' can be introduced. This term is used in a more abstract and general sense than its employment in everyday speech. It refers to those sets of principles which guide the selection of aliments from the available totality. Clearly, these menu principles can take a multiplicity of forms, and a range of examples can serve to illustrate the possibilities. Thus, *traditional menus* draw their recommendations and rules of food choice and combination from customary practice. Such customary practices, and their supporting beliefs, are built up over many generations and derive their authority and their legitimacy from their long-established status. The prescriptions and prohibitions of traditional menus have a taken-for-granted nature for those socialized into their acceptance, so taken for granted that the rules appear natural and immutable. Violations of these rules are likely to induce consternation, contempt or disgust, as are the rules of other cultures, which, if encountered, may be seen as barbarous or perverse.

In contrast, *rational menus* involve selection criteria which are designed explicitly to achieve some specified goal. These goals may include weight loss, weight gain, improvement of physical or mental performance, the avoidance of particular diseases or the generalized promotion of good health. Such rational menus are commonly based upon scientific or quasi-scientific principles and often involve the elements of deliberate measurement and calculation. Closely related to rational menus, we might identify *convenience menus*, where the overriding goal is the minimization of the time and effort required for acquiring, preparing and presenting food. Another sub-type of the rational menu group is represented by *economy menus* where the prime consideration is to keep food costs within a strict budget. In a similar vein, a whole group of *hedonistic menus* can be identified, based on the goal of maximizing gustatory pleasure. In contrast to these types of menu, a group that can be termed *moral menus* can be identified, where the predominant food selection criteria are derived from ethical considerations (related, for example, to political or ecological issues, or to issues relating to animal welfare or animal rights).

In any given society, we might expect to observe a degree of *menu differentiation*, that is, different categories of individuals within the population (defined in terms of gender, age, class, caste, etc.) would be expected or compelled to make characteristically different choices from the aliments made available within a given menu. The developmental thrust of this whole scheme becomes clear when we note that in traditional societies, characterized by relatively low rates of social change, there may be, in effect, one traditional master menu, which coincides with the boundaries of the alimentary totality. In contrast, in modern and modernizing societies, with more rapid rates of social change, the exercise of choice between a whole range of contrasting and competing menu principles becomes increasingly possible. Thus, individuals will find it ever more feasible to construct their own personal *diets* by making more or less deliberate choices between alternative menus, possibly adjusting their menu choices to suit their mood, economic circumstances or the setting in which the eating event is taking place. This situation can be described as one of *menu pluralism*, that is, a situation in which many alternative schemes to structure food choice and eating patterns are on offer. This pluralism is, in an important sense, a product of the very processes which have combined to create the modern food system with its globalization of food supply, its industrialization of production and distribution. As we have seen, Fischler sees these processes as leading to a breakdown in the rules of gastronomy and a rise in gastro-anomy, with all its negative consequences. He does, however, hold out the possibility that these effects are being countered. Indeed, it may well be that the uncertainties of gastro-anomy are but symptoms of the strains involved in the emergence of a new, more open, flexible and pluralistic nutritional order (Beardsworth and Keil 1992b). These issues will re-emerge several times later in this book, particularly in Chapters 7, 9 and 10.

This vision of menu pluralism can be seen as having some connections with the concept of postmodernity which has gained considerable ground in sociology and other related disciplines within the last decade or so. As it has come to be used in sociology, this term refers to a phase in the development of capitalism where, it is argued, the location of individuals in the social order, and the formation of personal identity, are less and less a matter of class position and work roles. Instead, an ever-increasing emphasis is placed upon consumption patterns as ways of demonstrating an individual's position and expressing personality and individuality (Bocock 1993: 77–9). Thus, it is clear that, within a setting of menu pluralism, the dietary choices made by each person within the context of an increasing variety of menu principles on offer become ever more important devices for establishing a sense of personal identity and for expressing personal distinctiveness. However, we need to exercise some caution in applying the broad concept of the ideology of consumerism (whether in its 'mass-consumption' or its 'postmodern' form) to the activity of eating. For example, Baudrillard (1988) takes up the idea that 'wants' are unlimited, an idea deeply rooted in modern Western thought. He argues, in effect, that there are no limits to consumption, since in modern and postmodern societies consumption is essentially the consumption of signs and symbols. It does not literally involve 'devouring' and absorbing the objects themselves. In effect, we consume with the mind, and the mind is potentially insatiable. This argument may sound convincing for goods and services like cars, video machines, audio equipment, domestic appliances, clothes, holidays, entertainment, etc. However, it is only partially applicable to food items. While we have already argued very strongly that the symbolic dimensions of food and eating are crucial for the sociologist, the fact remains, of course, that when an individual eats, he or she consumes not only the symbolic ingredients of that item but also its physical components and nutrients. These nutrients can and do produce actual physiological satiety (through ingestion and absorption) in a way that other commodities cannot. Hence, there are always physical limits on the socially constructed demands of appetite. Even if a particular food item (oysters, for example) were seen as conferring high social status and a strong sense of self worth, an individual could eat these only in limited quantities and with limited frequency before the body itself exercised the sanctions of nausea or even physical expulsion. Thus, while it may be important to understand the changes taking place in the broader areas of consumption and consumerist ideology, we must always bear in mind the unique features of eating.

OVERVIEW

In this chapter we have begun to consider food and eating at a number of different levels: initially at the system level, as a complex framework of productive and distributional relationships, and subsequently at the cultural level, as a highly elaborate corpus of ideas, symbols and meanings. The personal level has also been introduced, as issues concerning nutritional socialization and the significance of food symbolism for personal identity have been raised.

As has already been emphasized, any attempt to provide a tidy classification of sociological approaches to food and eating is bound to lead to a somewhat arbitrary outcome. However, the exercise is worthwhile, if only because it highlights certain conclusions which are worth bearing in mind. While we have, so far, placed a deserved emphasis on the symbolic dimensions of food and eating, the relative lack of success of the structuralist approach in delivering convincing explanations of food-related practices and beliefs in purely symbolic terms should give pause for thought. We clearly also need to consider the linkages and interrelationships between the various components of food systems, and the ways in which these are articulated by actual social and economic relationships. What is more, we must also consider the connections between the food system and other subsystems of society (e.g., domestic, political, medical, hierarchical, etc.). However, a static view of these connections is not sufficient in itself. The emphasis given in this chapter to developmental approaches reflects the importance of trying to describe and explain the ways in which the features of the food systems of contemporary Western societies are themselves the products of long-term processes of social change. Of course, current processes of change, as well as those which occurred in the past, also demand our attention. The present stage of development of the sociology of food and eating means that there are still many gaps in our understanding. The chapters that follow have been designed to provide the reader with an overview of those areas where substantial bodies of knowledge do exist.

While the focus of this chapter, and indeed of the whole book, is upon sociological perspectives, this does not imply that the contributions of related disciplines will be ignored. We have already drawn upon the ideas of sociology's sister discipline of social anthropology, and in subsequent chapters findings and insights from outside sociology will be borrowed quite explicitly where these can be put to a sociological purpose. The work of psychologists, nutritional anthropologists and economic and social historians can be mined to enrich the sociological analysis of food-related issues. Feminist perspectives in various forms have also made significant contributions to the development of our understanding of certain key questions in the area of food and eating, and such perspectives will figure prominently in Chapter 8 and will also put in an appearance in Chapters 5, 9 and 10. The whole gamut of methods will be encountered: the exploitation of historical sources and secondary data, surveys, semi-structured interviews and participant observation. In short, most of the familiar weapons in the armoury of the social scientist will appear, plus, on occasions, specialized techniques like the dietary diary.

Each topic is of intrinsic interest in itself, but our hope is that the whole will prove to be more than sum of its parts. As we proceed through diverse subject matter and varied sources, the intention will be to draw out the underlying foundations of continuity and the significant currents of change which coexist in contemporary food systems.

Part II

THE SOCIAL ORGANIZATION OF EATING

4

FOOD, FAMILY AND COMMUNITY

In this chapter, the emphasis is upon the significance of food and eating within the private sphere of the family. Of course, adopting such a perspective does not imply that the private sphere is some kind of hermetically sealed microcosm that can be examined in isolation. The domestic world of the family is inextricably linked to the structures of the wider social system, and this is no less true of eating than of any other aspect of family life. In a sense, the sociological analysis of the family is pervaded by two apparently opposing themes. On the one hand, the family is seen in essentially positive terms, as an intimate, supportive institution. It is seen, at one level, as contributing to the continuity and stability of society as a whole, and at another level as providing the individual with a secure refuge from a demanding world. On the other hand, the family has been viewed in more sinister terms, as a locus of conflict, oppression and even overt violence, with the power differences between men and women, and parents and children, seen as particularly important. Both of these views will be reflected in the material discussed in this chapter, although we might sensibly regard them as two sides of the same coin, rather than mutually exclusive claims to absolute truth. Whatever the viewpoint adopted, however, there can be no doubting the family's continuing importance as a unit of consumption and the powerful formative influences it continues to assert over its members.

Before our discussion proceeds, a simple but basic terminological point is worth making. The terms 'family' and 'household' are not synonymous. The nuclear family (parents and children) may or may not make up a household (which is a group of people sharing accommodation and, to varying degrees, pooling their resources). The intact nuclear family is only one type of household, and is characteristic of a particular stage of the life cycle. There are, of course, many other types of household, and nuclear families may be part of wider extended family systems. These rather obvious distinctions do have important implications for the issues raised in this chapter, as we examine the ways in which food can be used to mark and forge links across family boundaries, the ways in which food is implicated in differentiation within families and between families, and the long-term processes of change in domestic foodways which appear to be under way.

73

MARKING THE BOUNDARIES OF THE FAMILY

In the section dealing with structuralist approaches in Chapter 3 we have already encountered the work of Mary Douglas, who has suggested that food-ways can be seen as a kind of language encoding patterns of social relations, particularly those connected with social boundaries and with processes of inclusion and exclusion (Douglas 1975). We can now look at Douglas's ideas in rather more detail. In order to examine this food language and its messages she adopts the somewhat unusual methodological strategy of analysing the food-related ideas, categories and practices in use in her own home. Her first point is to argue that there is a crucial distinction between *drinks* and *meals*. Meals are sequenced through the day and their elements are linked together in pre-determined combinations and successions of courses. Drinks, on the other hand, are not so highly organized. Douglas then goes on to describe the key features of meals as consumed within her own family:

- Meals require a table with a seating order, and entail the restriction of movement. Thus, a meal 'frames the gathering' and effectively rules out certain simultaneous activities.
- Meals incorporate significant contrasts like hot/cold, bland/spiced and liquid (or semi-liquid)/solid.
- Meals incorporate a broad range of nutrient sources (cereals, vegetables, animal proteins and fats, etc.).

(Douglas 1975: 65–6)

Douglas also observes that these meals have a characteristic 'tripartite' structure, consisting of one 'stressed' or main element accompanied by two 'unstressed' or supporting elements. She describes this structure with the simple algebraic expression $A + 2B$. What is more, she sees meals as arranged in a hierarchy according to their importance and symbolic significance. For her family, at the bottom of this hierarchy is the routine weekday lunch, with just one course. This single course (A) itself exhibits the tripartite structure $a + 2b$. Further up the hierarchy is the Sunday lunch, consisting of two substantial courses (main and dessert). Such a meal is described as $2A$, with each A having the $a + 2b$ structure. At the top of the hierarchy for her family come celebratory meals (Christmas, birthdays, etc.). Here the whole meal can be described as $A + 2B$, with a main course and two supporting courses. Each of the three courses is, as usual, structured in terms of $a + 2b$.

In effect, Douglas is arguing that this repeating $A + 2B$ pattern means that every meal carries within it something of the structure and meaning of all other meals. What is more, participation in this repetitive, structured sequence of meals is one of the key ways of expressing and experiencing family membership. The sharing of meals is drawing the boundaries of the family's symbolic and emotional existence, and only certain very specific categories of non-family are permitted to cross these boundaries. In contrast, drinks can be shared much more widely. As Douglas herself puts it:

Drinks are for strangers, acquaintances, workmen and family. Meals are for family, close friends, honoured guests.

(Douglas 1975: 66)

Of course, Douglas's analysis does have its limitations. It refers to the practices of just one upper-middle-class English family and so we must be very cautious about attempting to generalize its arguments. A study based on participant observation of four English industrial working-class families (Nicod 1980) found that the four families in question each had rather different ways of drawing the boundaries of the family unit in nutritional terms. Looking at three staple food items (potato, bread and biscuit), the relationship between intimacy and the foods shared varied considerably from family to family. These findings suggest that while families do draw boundaries with food; there is considerable leeway for each to establish its own ways of expressing inclusion and exclusion. More-over, as Lalonde (1992) points out, Douglas's structuralist analysis, by its very nature, is concerned primarily with describing the structure of the meal-as-object. However, he reminds us that it is not simply the meal's *structure* which expresses its symbolic significance. The meal-as-event (as he calls it) is a lived experience which draws its meanings from a complex array of sensory and cognitive factors, factors which a structuralist account tends to neglect.

Of course, while food consumption patterns can be seen as highlighting the boundaries of the nuclear family, food and eating can also act as linkages between the nuclear family and the extended family and, indeed, between the nuclear family and the wider community. The use of food to articulate such linkages is neatly demonstrated by an intensive study of two Italian-American families in an industrial suburb of Philadelphia (Theopano and Curtis 1991). Through the use of participant observation techniques the researchers were able to uncover the ways in which elements of Italian and American cuisine were combined in this close-knit community, which they referred to by the pseud-onym 'Maryton'. Their findings make it very clear that women bear the main responsibility for sustaining domestic and social life and maintaining social networks. This is borne out by the fact that, although over 80 per cent of the women observed were in full- or part-time employment, they essentially held 'jobs' rather than pursued 'careers', and their main preoccupations were still marriage, maternity and domestic responsibilities. The authors set out to show the ways in which the bonds of family and community are expressed through food exchange by focusing attention on two particular women, whom they refer to as 'Marcella' and 'Anne'.

Marcella's social life revolves around an extensive network of relatives and friends. She exchanges food and hospitality with, for example, her two sisters and her brother (and his wife), with her three daughters and with certain intimate friends. The authors describe a series of exchange events, including a buffet dinner for thirty people, the invitation of her daughter's fiancé to dinner, the shared preparation of dishes with her sisters and, on Easter Sunday, the serving of breakfast to daughters, grandson, daughter's fiancé and the serving of dinner to nine people. Anne's social network is described as more limited than Marcella's, with a strong emphasis on ties with her two sisters, her two sons (one married) and her one daughter. She is also a close friend of Marcella. Examples of food exchanges documented include participating in a celebratory meal at her cousin's home, taking dinner at her daughter-in-law's home, eating out (dinner) with Marcella and inviting twelve people to her own home for Sunday dinner, including her son and his family, two friends (Marcella and Andrea) and her daughter's boyfriend (plus the two participating and observing researchers, with one spouse and one child).

The authors describe the various forms of exchange which are being employed in such settings:

- the exchange of hospitality (inviting guests and being invited);
- the sharing of non-mealtime eating (snacks, etc.);
- the exchange of raw foodstuffs or cooked dishes (e.g., desserts);
- payment for services with food, often in the form of the 'specialities' of the giver;
- co-operative provisioning and preparation of family dinners, celebratory meals, etc.

The reciprocity involved in these exchanges varies according to whether the relationship is symmetrical (between social equals and members of the same generation) or asymmetrical (where there are differences in status or generation) and according to the relationship's level of intimacy. It is also affected by the nature of the occasion, i.e., whether it is a 'recurrent' event (festivals, birthdays, etc.) or a 'milestone' event (weddings, graduations, etc.). According to the combination of these factors, the expectation may be for immediate reciprocity, long-term reciprocity or there may actually be no expectation of reciprocity at all (see Figure 4.1).

The sheer volume of food exchange taking place in such close-knit communities is illustrated by the fact that, in the course of the two-month period of

CATEGORY OF RELATIONSHIP	CATEGORY OF OCCASION	
	Recurrent	*Milestone*
High intimacy		
symmetrical	immediate	immediate
asymmetrical	no expectation	long duration
Low intimacy		
symmetrical	immediate	long duration
asymmetrical	immediate	no expectation

High intimacy = immediate/extended family, friendship network (frequent contact)
Low intimacy = workmates, friendship network (infrequent contact)

Figure 4.1 Expectations for reciprocity
Source: Adapted from Theopano and Curtis (1991)

observation, guests were present at food events on more than 100 occasions in Marcella's household. Over the same period, Anne participated in sixteen food exchanges and had guests for thirty food events. All this took place within a system of cuisine that was far from rigid, since what the authors term 'menu negotiation' produced variation from family to family and from year to year. Thus, even in a community with a relatively distinctive cultural identity, reciprocity based on food exchange does not necessarily rely entirely upon the persistence of a conservative, ethnically marked cuisine. Even in the face of change and variability food exchange can play a crucial articulating role. As the authors themselves put it:

> Through the food system, women express and maintain their social positions in the community... Exchanging food in Maryton is a token of social bonding and integral to all social interaction.
>
> (Theopano and Curtis 1991: 171)

FOOD AND DIFFERENTIATION WITHIN THE FAMILY

The quotation which rounded off the preceding section emphasizes the positive aspects of women's relationships to food provision and food exchange in domestic settings. There is, however, a more pessimistic view of such relationships, which suggests that gender differentiation within the family in respect of food preparation responsibilities and food consumption patterns can work to the disadvantage of women. Indeed, it has been argued that in traditional societies there may exist significant nutritional inequalities related to gender (and to age). An example of such inequality is provided by a study of the foodways of the traditional peasant family in rural France by Delphy (1979). Men, the author points out, customarily held a privileged position in relation to scarce food resources, this applying particularly to male heads of households. Thus, butcher's meat, a relatively rare item on this traditional menu, was largely reserved for men or, if it was shared, men were allocated the choice cuts. Indeed, traditional peasant culture characterized adult men as 'needing' such meat in a direct, physiological sense. In contrast women (plus the young and the elderly) were not seen as having this need in the same way. What is more, men were typically seen as requiring larger quantities of food than women, and one of the ways in which this idea was justified was in terms of differences in energy expenditure. However, as Delphy demonstrates, this notion did not rest on realistic calculations of energy expended in different types of work but was, rather, related to the gendered nature of particular tasks. Thus, carrying water (a task for women) was defined as 'light work', whereas carrying manure (a task for men) was classed as 'heavy work'. Interestingly, such attitudes were also applied to alcohol consumption. Red wine was seen as making men strong, whereas a woman who drank this beverage in quantity would be regarded with contempt (hence the saying, *femme de vin, femme de rien*).

77

These inequalities were woven into the very fabric of the rural culture. Thus, the young were socialized into internalizing a whole range of food prohibitions and deprivations, such socialization being backed up by a range of repressive measures and sanctions. Indeed, it was a widespread cultural assumption that a chronic feeling of hunger was normal for children and adolescents. Similarly, women were socialized into accepting the idea that they should consume only meagre portions of the dishes they prepared, and into accepting that they had a duty to provide the best food for others. Delphy contends that differentiation of this sort may have produced significant nutritional deficiencies (especially of protein) in the diets of the elderly and the very young, with consequent implications for general health. The impact on adult women may have been compounded by the added burdens of pregnancy, and heightened rates of infant and maternal mortality in rural areas appeared to support this contention (Delphy 1979: 223).

The picture painted by Delphy is a bleak one, although she emphasizes that the conditions she is analysing are specific to a particular historical period and a specific cultural and economic setting. However, the question inevitably arises as to whether such inequalities might be observed in more contemporary settings. Some significant insights into this issue are provided by a comprehensive study of food and families carried out in the north of England (Charles and Kerr 1988; Kerr and Charles 1986). The research project in question was based upon a survey involving 200 women with pre-school children, and employed semi-structured interviews and entailed the completion of detailed food and drink diaries for a two-week period. The study's aim was to examine a range of issues relating to food practices, but most importantly to examine nutritional differentiation within the family based on gender and age. As might be expected in this type of household (most were intact nuclear families with both parents, and all had young children) the women had the main responsibility for buying, preparing and serving food. Indeed, after the arrival of their first child, many had given up work to devote their time to domestic tasks, and cooking skills, for example, were seen as crucial by these respondents.

A central finding of Charles and Kerr's study is the importance of the concept of the 'proper meal'. The proper meal, based upon freshly cooked meat supported by potatoes and vegetables, was construed as fundamental to the identity of the family and to its well-being. Indeed, the authors argue, the provision of proper meals (in their everyday or more elaborate festive forms) was viewed by respondents as a key indicator of a 'proper family'. This underlying symbolic significance of the proper meal (readily described in terms of Douglas's $A + 2B$ formula) appeared to hold across social class divisions in the sample. Significantly, in terms of our earlier discussion of Delphy's arguments, Charles and Kerr's respondents reported that men's tastes and preferences took priority over those of women and children. The provision of proper meals, in line with the relatively conservative tastes of the husband, was seen by wives as a way of showing affection, and as a device for retaining the husband as a breadwinner and keeping him working. Thus, these wives were portraying themselves as food servers, 'refuelling' an active male breadwinner (even though many of the men were in occupations which did not demand high levels of physical exertion) to whom they were subordinate and on whom they were economically dependent. The authors conclude that such women are, in effect, in a position of responsibility without authority in relation to food, given their husbands' economic dominance and priority of preference. What is more, they conclude that the men in these households actually did eat what the authors define as 'high-status' foods more frequently than women (and children) and they also consumed alcohol more frequently. They argue that these differences reflect the essentially patriarchal structure of the nuclear family, and their findings appear to support the view that the gender- and age-based nutritional inequalities characteristic of many traditional rural settings may find echoes in the contemporary urban milieu.

In Table 4.1 some of their most interesting results are laid out. The data shown consist of the average frequency of consumption of selected food items over the two-week period covered by the dietary diaries. The researchers did not actually ask to have recorded the quantities of food consumed, only frequencies,

Table 4.1 Average frequency of consumption of selected items over a two-week period

Item	Women	Men	Children
High-status meat	4.5	4.9	3.1
Medium-status meat	6.8	9.0	5.3
Low-status meat	5.1	6.8	5.2
Whole fish	1.7	1.9	0.9
Low-status fish	1.6	1.5	1.7
Eggs	4.4	5.1	3.5
Cheese	5.6	5.8	3.8
Green leafy vegetables (cooked)	2.9	2.8	2.1
Other vegetables (cooked)	7.9	8.2	6.8
Fresh fruit	5.9	5.2	7.3
Potatoes (boiled/roast)	6.4	6.6	6.3
Chips	7.0	7.0	7.0
Bread	19.0	21.6	17.4
Breakfast cereal	5.2	5.3	10.4
Cakes	6.7	7.3	4.9
Biscuits	8.0	6.4	11.3
Puddings	7.0	7.0	9.3
Sweets	3.5	2.6	8.1
Soft drinks	2.7	2.0	22.5
Baked beans, etc.	1.9	2.0	2.9
Milk	6.0	6.3	21.5
Tea/coffee	58.0	54.3	13.4
Alcohol	2.7	4.4	0.2

Source: Adapted from Charles and Kerr (1988)

hence these results may somewhat understate differences, as men are claimed to consume larger portions.

One immediately striking finding is that men do indeed eat meat more often than do women and children. This applies to 'high-status' meat (which the authors define as red meat in joints, chops, etc.), 'medium-status' meat (white meat like chicken) and 'low-status' meat (e.g., processed products like sausages and hamburgers). What is more, children eat medium- and low-status meat more frequently than high-status meat and adults eat medium-status food like cheese and eggs more often than do children. Children eat fresh fruit (which the authors classify as a low-status food) more often than do adults, and women and children eat biscuits (low status) more frequently than do men. Not surprisingly, children are reported as consuming sweets and soft drinks far more frequently than adults, and the same also applies to milk. The various differences visible in this table are taken by the authors to be reflections of the status and power hierarchy within the patriarchal nuclear family, with men at the top, women in the middle and children at the bottom.

While this conclusion may be basically plausible, we should note a number of reservations. For example, the women frequently reported that they found it difficult to get children to eat 'proper meals', hence children's consumption of 'low-status' foods may actually be a reflection of their own tastes. What is more, children's more frequent consumption of such items as fresh fruit and milk, which the authors do not see as high-status items, would conventionally be construed as conferring a nutritional advantage. The male/female differences in meat consumption also appear somewhat marginal, and may be partly accounted for by the reported practice of giving men leftover cold meat in sandwiches. Further, the whole picture is complicated by the decidedly ambivalent attitudes to food reported by the study's women respondents. Concern with slimness and body image was frequently mentioned, coupled with attempts to restrict food intake (no less than 34 per cent of respondents were actually dieting at the time of the study). The authors note that for many women:

> the questions on dieting seemed to release a flood of dissatisfaction and guilt, not only with their bodies and their weight but with their whole social situation.
>
> (Charles and Kerr 1988: 143)

Charles and Kerr suggest that, in a sense, for women food is 'the enemy'. This concern with the desire to restrict food intake in the face of a readily available supply is a very different predicament from the potential threat of malnutrition for women described by Delphy. (We will return to these complex and contentious issues in Chapter 8.)

A later study carried out in Manchester (Warde and Hetherington 1994) based upon questionnaires returned by 323 households, produced results broadly similar to those of Charles and Kerr, but with some important differences. The gender division of labour in respect of food-related tasks comes out

Table 4.2 Persons last doing specific food-related tasks in households containing a couple

Task	Man (%)	Woman (%)	Other (%)	Shared (%)	N
Cake baking	5	61	31	4	243
Jam making	6	63	28	3	68
Cooking meals	11	79	5	5	271
Bread making	9	57	27	7	89
Preparing packed lunches	13	64	20	3	234
Main shopping	14	54	2	30	272
Doing the dishes	23	46	20	10	274
Take-away meals	42	21	26	10	242
Beer or wine making	64	12	11	14	94
Cooked barbecue	59	9	22	11	153

Source: Adapted from Warde and Hetherington (1994)

clearly in Warde and Hetherington's findings, which document which person or persons last performed specific tasks (see Table 4.2).

As might be expected, women predominate in the key activity of preparing meals, whereas men predominate in more marginal areas of foodwork like collecting take-away meals, beer or wine making and barbecue cooking. Significantly, however, in 30 per cent of households containing a couple, main shopping was a shared activity. What is more, Warde and Hetherington's results highlight a limitation of Charles and Kerr's study which has been pointed out by a number of commentators (Beardsworth and Keil 1990; Prout 1991). Because Charles and Kerr deliberately chose to look at households with at least one pre-school child, the focus is very much upon one particular stage of the life course. On the other hand, the households in Warde and Hetherington's study were rather more 'mature', and 81 per cent of the women in the sample were in paid employment, compared to 40 per cent in Charles and Kerr's study. Warde and Hetherington note that the woman's being in full-time employment was the most important factor in inducing men to cook family meals. Thus, they argue, Charles and Kerr's findings cannot necessarily be generalized as applicable to all adult men, since the very nature of their study design tended to exclude those men (with wives in full-time employment) who were most likely to be involved in food preparation (Warde and Hetherington 1994: 765). What is more, a class factor appeared to be at work here. For example, in households where the woman was in a salaried occupation or self-employed, the man was more likely to have cooked the last family meal. In contrast, in households where both partners were working class, there were no cases where the man had cooked the last meal. (These issues of social class will be discussed in more detail later in this chapter.)

The wider international applicability of the conclusions drawn by Charles and Kerr and Warde and Hetherington in relation to families in England is indicated by the fact that similar studies in the USA (DeVault 1991) and Sweden (Ekström 1991) appear to have produced broadly similar findings. DeVault's study was based upon interviews in thirty households located within the city or suburbs of Chicago, selected to ensure ethnic and social diversity. She interviewed the individual who bore the main responsibility for what she terms 'feeding work' within the family. Unsurprisingly, the overwhelming majority of these were women, 50 per cent of whom also worked outside the home. What emerges very clearly from the interview material is the primary role which women continue to play in the planning, provision and preparation of meals, and the extent to which this role is perceived as an onerous one. Fascinatingly, she notes that a concept analogous to Charles and Kerr's notion of the proper meal also exists here (although the nature and content of such meals, as we might expect, shows significant cultural variations). In effect, DeVault argues, women's work of feeding the family, of creating and staging the family-meal-as-event, can be seen as counteracting the centrifugal forces which push apart the activities of the individual family members, each with his or her own schedules, commitments, interests and priorities. In this sense, she maintains feeding literally *produces* 'family'. However, this work of socially constructing the family through feeding is largely invisible, so much so that women respondents often appeared to experience some difficulty in explaining their taken-for-granted deference to their husband's tastes and preferences. In fact, DeVault sees women's apparent autonomy in the organization and execution of domestic routines as masking the fact that they are essentially making choices to please and accommodate others, and suggests that these responsibilities effectively contribute to their oppression.

Ekström's analysis of food provision and cooking in Sweden provides a useful quantitative insight into the extent to which these tasks continue to be associated with women in contemporary urban settings. Her study was based on a simple random sample of 348 families with children, and employed the usual data-gathering devices (a questionnaire and a food diary, supplemented by qualitative interviews with selected respondents) The results of the study are presented under four headings (Ekström 1991: 151):

- planning meals;
- shopping for food;
- the preparation of breakfast;
- the preparation of dinner.

The results for the 292 families in the sample where both parents were present are clear cut, as can be seen in Table 4.3.

In relation to the activity of planning, the categories 'mother alone' and 'both, mother most part' clearly predominate. It is very rare for fathers to take much responsibility in this area. There appears to be underparticipation in the activity of shopping, although the modal category is the joint one, in which mothers take main responsibility. The provision of breakfast shows some interesting diversity, fathers clearly taking responsibility more frequently. In a significant number of

Table 4.3   The division of labour in two-parent families

Agent(s)	Planning %	Shopping %	Breakfast %	Dinner %
Mother alone	44	16	34	59
Father alone	1	1	13	2
Both, mother most part	34	49	0	0
Both, father most part	2	6	0	0
Adults	8	16	24	29
Adults and child	10	9	5	5
Child/children	0	0	1	0
Each individual	–	–	14	0
Others	1	2	8	5
Total (N = 292)	100	99	99	100

Source: Adapted from Ekström (1991)

households (24 per cent) breakfast is the generalized responsibility of all the adults in the household and in 14 per cent individuals cater for themselves. For the main meal of the day (dinner) 59 per cent of households rely entirely on the mother, with individual fathers figuring very rarely. However, interestingly, in 29 per cent of cases responsibility for this meal is shared among all the adults in the household. What is more, a familiar picture emerges from Ekströms's qualitative interviews, with women placing a strong emphasis on pleasing their husband and providing a good service in relation to food preparation and presentation, an emphasis which they see as a feature of a mutual but unconscious contract between couples based on the explicit or implicit subordination of women.

Perhaps one of the neatest demonstrations of this process of subordination through the imposition of culinary and nutritional responsibilities on women is provided by Murcott's influential analysis of the significance of the 'cooked dinner' in a community in South Wales (Murcott 1982). Murcott's research consisted of unstructured tape-recorded interviews with thirty-seven expectant mothers between the ages of 16 and 40, and her aim was to document what she terms 'folk models' and the 'properties of domestic eating' (Murcott 1982: 678). The finding which dominates her results is the central importance of the 'cooked dinner' for her respondents. This dish was seen as the centrepiece, indeed, the defining feature, of a 'proper meal', and its provision on a regular basis (say three to four times a week) was seen as vital for the health and welfare of family members, and therefore as one of a woman's most crucial obligations. The features of the cooked dinner, as an expression of the traditional menu of British culinary culture, can readily be specified in detail:

- Its focal point, or stressed element, must consist of the flesh of a warm-blooded animal (beef, lamb, pork, chicken, turkey at Christmas). Ideally, the meat should be fresh not frozen.
- The preferred method of cooking this meat is roasting or grilling.
- Potatoes must be served (boiled, mashed or roasted).

- Vegetables must be served. If there is only one vegetable, ideally this should be green). Again, these should be fresh.
- The components of the dish must be arranged in neat piles on a single plate.
- The components must be moistened and co-ordinated with gravy, but not submerged or disguised by it.
- Portions must be large.
- The dish must be eaten with knife and fork.

Such dishes clearly take a highly conventionalized form, offering little scope for innovation, and were seen by respondents as geared to their husband's tastes and perceived nutritional needs. In other words, it is the husband's preferences which dictate the choices made within this rigid culinary framework. What is more, the elaborate nature of this dish requires the attention of the cook over relatively long periods of time, in terms of preparing as well as actually cooking the ingredients. The fresh ingredients themselves demand regular shopping and cannot be bought in advance and stored for long periods. The cooking techniques and skills employed are those passed on from mother to daughter over several generations, emphasizing the continuity of women's domestic obligations. On the basis of these features, Murcott argues that the cooked dinner has important social (as opposed to purely nutritional) functions. In effect, the provision of a cooked dinner for her family demonstrates that a wife has been spending her time in an activity appropriate to her status and gender. The extended time commitment and the protracted labour involved can be seen as devices for tying the wife into the domestic setting, enforcing and expressing her femininity and her domesticity. Thus, the cooked dinner is seen as exerting a form of control (Murcott 1983: 88) as well as constituting a symbol of the inequality which segregates the gender roles of wife and husband.

There is a good deal of evidence to suggest that, in some family settings, the failure of a wife to fulfil her husband's expectations concerning the carrying out of domestic tasks may lead to violent retaliation. Ellis (1983) draws upon her own research into violent families (and that of other authors like Dobash and Dobash (1980)) to demonstrate that physical attacks by husbands on their wives are frequently triggered by some aspect of a husband's dissatisfaction with his wife's culinary performance. Ellis cites the expectation in British working-class households that a wife should have a hot meal ready for her husband as soon as he returns from work. Case material examples are cited where failure to provide this meal provoked an attack. In even more extreme instances, violent men might expect a meal to be provided at any time when they arrived in the household (even if this were unexpectedly in the early hours of the morning after a drinking bout). Physical force (or the direct threat of it) might then be used to compel the wife's compliance. Similarly, when men's expectations concerning the quality of cooked meals or the range of food choice were not fulfilled, violence might well be the result. It is Ellis's contention that the tendency to see such phenomena as indicating that violence can be provoked by 'trivial'

incidents is somewhat misguided. The fundamental significance of food preparation and serving obligations for female gender roles means that non-compliance
may be regarded as a particularly serious dereliction of female 'duty'. In
certain households, actual physical assaults, of varying levels of seriousness,
may be the habitual response, although Ellis sees this food-related violence as
simply the most explicit manifestation of a more general pattern of patriarchal
domination.

Significantly, the study of divorce and remarriage carried out by Burgoyne
and Clarke (1983) with forty remarried couples in Sheffield found that tensions
in marriage frequently centred upon food and mealtimes. For example, the
Sunday dinner, supposedly a focus of family integration and harmony, could
become the occasion for the more or less overt expression of intra-familial
conflicts and interpersonal jealousies. What is more, where women were perceived by their spouse as having failed in their wifely duties with respect to the
provision of meals, the authors came across evidence of violent responses by
husbands similar to the incidents described by Ellis (Burgoyne and Clarke 1983:
154–5). However, the authors also provide some fascinating evidence concerning the responses of divorced fathers who were allocated custody of their
children. In some cases, such men (who were somewhat over-represented in
this study) went to considerable lengths to maintain conventional eating patterns
in order to sustain a sense of domestic security and continuity for their children,
even to the extent of taking on the preparation of Sunday dinners (Burgoyne and
Clarke 1983: 157–8). In describing the process of finding a replacement partner,
respondents noted the difficulties that could be involved in establishing new and
mutually acceptable domestic arrangements with respect to food preparation
and mealtimes, describing in some detail the problems of adapting and accommodating to each other's established habits and preferences. Certainly, the
emphasis placed on food by these respondents demonstrates a number of
important points. Not only are food and food-related domestic arrangements
central features of family functioning, they may also play a crucial role in family
breakdown. What is more, attempts by divorced individuals to reconstitute the
family through remarriage may be dependent on the successful re-establishment
of a domestic food provision routine acceptable to the various parties concerned.
Food may, therefore, play a role in the continuity, the breakdown and the
reconstitution of the nuclear family.

The evidence we have been discussing appears to paint a fairly consistent
picture. Within the family women are seen as essentially subordinate to men and
are required to assume responsibility for preparing and serving food while
actually exercising relatively little control over the underlying patterns of provisioning and food selection, in which areas men's tastes and preferences are the
authoritative ones. Such perspectives lead McIntosh and Zey (1989) to adopt a
highly critical approach towards earlier views of women's relationships to food
and the family which suggested that women wield considerable power in this
area. For example, it has long been assumed that women act as 'gatekeepers',

controlling the flow of goods (food in particular) into the household and controlling the channels through which food reaches the table. However, McIntosh and Zey cite a range of studies (e.g., Burt and Hertzler 1978) which support the contention that, within families, the father's tastes take precedence. They also demonstrate that this precedence is usually linked to the husband's economic predominance within the household; the higher his earnings, in general, the greater his power (McIntosh and Zey 1989: 323). Raising doubts about the gatekeeper model which, as the authors point out, has long been relied upon by nutritionists and those concerned with nutritional policy, has a number of implications beyond purely sociological ones. For example, targeting nutritional education information at women in order to engineer what are seen as health-promoting dietary changes within families could be largely ineffectual in the light of what may be women's relative powerlessness in this area.

The studies which we have examined in this section are predominantly guided by feminist perspectives on the complex interactions between food, gender and domestic life. Two basic themes run through such perspectives: firstly, the idea that women's food-related roles in effect *express* and *reflect* their subordination and, secondly, the idea that the food-related obligations and duties imposed upon women actually serve to *enforce* their subordination. This enforcement is seen as being achieved through the fact that responsibility for domestic 'feeding work' is deeply embedded within the core of the whole concept of femininity, through the socialization of women into the acceptance of such obligations as natural and through the sanctioning of women who fail or refuse to fulfil these obligations. When the processes we have been examining are formulated in this way, the affinity between such views and functionalist forms of explanation becomes apparent, in that one of the 'functions' of gendered feeding work is seen as the maintenance of patriarchal family configurations.

The consistency of the results of the various studies across national and cultural boundaries is striking (although, in fairness, it should be noted that this may be due in part to some of the shared theoretical perspectives and expectations of the researchers). There is, however, one important limitation common to most of these studies which should be recognized. With the exceptions of Burgoyne and Clarke (1983) and Warde and Hetherington (1994), they rely almost exclusively upon adult female respondents. Men's ideas, viewpoints and accounts are rarely, if ever, heard at first hand, and where they do figure they are often reported at second hand by women. The same can also be said of children's accounts and preferences. Whether the picture which emerges would have been significantly different if men's and children's ideas had been given equal weight is an open question, and one which could be resolved only by suitably designed empirical research. Of course, the emphasis on women's accounts is not determined solely by theoretical and ideological factors; it also emerges out of practical considerations. The empirical studies from which our insights are derived by and large focus their attention on the individual in the household who bears the main responsibility for feeding work.

This understandable methodological strategy necessarily generates predominantly female response groups.

FOOD AND DIFFERENTIATION BY SOCIAL CLASS

Having considered the ways in which food-related differentiation operates within families, attention can now be turned to differences and inequalities which separate individuals, families and households along the broader lines of social class. We do not need to look too far back into Europe's historical past, for example, to find instances where class-based nutritional inequalities were literally a matter of life and death. Disastrous famines (often resulting from crop failures) continued to occur in Europe well into the eighteenth century (Mennell 1985: 24–7). An individual's risk of dying of starvation or of experiencing protracted hunger and damaging malnutrition was very much a function of his or her position in the economic and social hierarchy. As late as the latter part of the nineteenth century, the poor in England, for example, subsisted on a chronically inadequate diet, as classic studies of poverty like that of Rowntree (1901) clearly demonstrate. The consequences of such deprivations included endemic deficiency diseases like rickets, high urban infant mortality rates and poor levels of physical development in those who survived to maturity (Burnett 1989: 61). Clearly, in developed Western societies at least, the economic inequalities of social class no longer generate nutritional inequalities in such extreme forms, although they may now have subtler and less dramatic manifestations. Of greater relevance and interest for the contemporary sociologist are the cultural, economic and ideological differences between social class groupings in relation to food, and the ways in which these differences produce characteristic patterns of food preference and facilitate or constrain food choice.

A useful starting-point for the discussion of such differences can be found in the work of Bourdieu (1984). Bourdieu sets out to analyse the ways in which upper- and lower-class tastes are generated and reproduced in relation to the realities of social class in contemporary France, although his analysis is not confined to food, covering areas as diverse as art, literature, cinema, dress, interior decoration and hairstyles. Bourdieu stresses the competitive dimension of taste, seeking to demonstrate the ways in which conceptions of taste, and actual consumption practices, are used to create and sustain distinctions between social classes and to maintain the elevated status of those groups at the upper levels of the class hierarchy. However, Bourdieu sees eating and drinking as one of the few areas where working-class ideas challenge what he terms the 'new ethic of sobriety and slimness' (Bourdieu 1984: 179). The tastes in food of high-status individuals like professionals and senior executives tend towards 'the light, the refined and the delicate', which serves to set them apart from popular, working-class tastes for the 'heavy, the fat and the coarse' (Bourdieu 1984: 185). The middle and upper classes, largely freed from economic constraints on food consumption, actually come to lay increasing stress upon slimness and refined eating, and become increasingly censorious of coarseness and fatness. Middle-class groups like teachers, rich in what Bourdieu terms 'cultural capital' if not in economic capital, are seen as maintaining distinctiveness by cultivating tastes for exotic and foreign foods. In contrast, members of the working class put a greater emphasis on indulgence, spend a higher proportion of their income on food, and consume larger quantities of bread, and fat-rich foods like pork, milk and cheese.

Bourdieu sees these differences in dietary preference as also related to differences in each class's perception of the body and of the effects of food on the body. Of central significance in this respect is the working-class emphasis on the importance of the strength of the male body, hence an emphasis on cheap and nutritious food to build and fuel such a physique. This stands in sharp contrast to what Bourdieu regards as the professional classes' emphasis on tasty, health-promoting, light and non-fattening foods. These ideas are closely bound up with working-class conceptions of masculinity in relation to the actual act of eating. Men are seen as larger, needing more food and as eating in gulps and mouthfuls, and hence foods which require picking and nibbling (e.g., fish) are seen as unmanly, as essentially feminine and suited to the needs and inclinations of women (Bourdieu 1984: 190–2).

Of course, differences in eating patterns related to social class are not static, they change over time. Such changes may be driven by cultural processes, as higher social groupings develop new tastes and preferences in order to maintain their distinctiveness from the strata below them, but they are also a function of fundamental political and economic changes. A useful case study of class-based nutritional change is provided by Nelson (1993), who examines long-term trends in British diet over the period 1860 to 1980. Nelson bases his analysis on household data drawn from budget surveys. While he acknowledges the limitations of such data, he is able to outline the broad features of the changes in class differentials which have been under way. For example, he demonstrates that in the latter part of the nineteenth century the dietary differences between the highest and the lowest strata in Britain were extreme ones, with the poorest in the population living barely above subsistence level on a meagre diet of bread, potatoes and limited amounts of fats (usually butter or dripping), and small amounts of meat (usually pork or bacon). These low-income diets were low in energy, protein, fat, calcium and vitamins A and C, but high in carbohydrate and fibre. In contrast, the diets of families in the middle and upper ranges of the class structure contained more eggs, fish, meat, sugar and fat and were richer in calcium and vitamins (Nelson 1993: 103–4).

However, the twentieth century has seen a series of significant shifts in this overall picture. Government food policies during the First World War produced some temporary narrowing of class differentials in nutrition, and during the 1920s and the 1930s there was a gradual narrowing of differences. However, the most dramatic changes occurred during the Second World War, when government rationing policies, which were introduced in response to food shortages, effectively lowered the intake of many food items among upper-income groups and increased the intakes of lower-income groups, producing striking convergences. What is more, after the Second World War and the end of rationing, this narrowing of class differentials was maintained, due largely to rising real incomes and to the state's welfare policies. Indeed, not only were narrowed differentials maintained but, in the case of certain foodstuffs, there was actually an inversion of the previous relationship, with items once consumed in greater quantities by higher-income groups now being consumed at higher rates by lower-income groups and vice versa.

These changes can be illustrated by looking at specific examples. In the case of bread, flour and grains, consumption of this group of foodstuffs has been in chronic decline in lower-income families throughout the twentieth century (except for a brief rise during the years of the First World War). In higher-income groups consumption actually rose, but then began to decline in the 1930s. In 1980 the high-income group in Nelson's data consumed approximately 2 lb per person per week, and the low-income group approximately 2.5 lb. The figures for 1900 were approximately 3.3 lb and 5.6 lb, respectively. In 1860, middle-class families consumed mainly white bread, whereas lower income groups ate mainly brown or wholemeal. However, due to innovations in milling, by 1900 cheap white bread had become a working-class staple. Since 1970, the amounts of brown and wholemeal bread consumed have once more increased, but with an inverted class relationship. In 1980 the highest of Nelson's income groups ate 6.85 oz per person per week, compared with 4.25 oz per person in the lowest group (Nelson 1993: 105–6).

Meat and meat products show a dramatic convergence pattern. In 1900 the high-income group as defined by Nelson consumed an estimated 54 oz of meat and meat products per person per week, as compared to a figure of 20 oz for the low-income group. But by the early 1940s these two figures were virtually identical at around 25–6 oz per week. After the Second World War both increased, but hardly diverged, to give 1980 figures of roughly 42 oz (high-income group) and 38 ounces (low-income group) per person per week. Fish and eggs show the same convergence of inequalities in consumption, to the point where an inversion occurred for both foodstuffs in the 1960s and 1970s, with consumption in the low-income group overtaking that in the high-income groups. Convergence from a position of inequality of consumption also occurred in the 1940s in the case of fats and of sugar, syrup, treacle and jam. By the 1960s low-income group consumption of sugar, syrup, treacle and jam actually exceeded that of the high-income group, and by the 1970s the low-income group had overtaken the high-income group in fat consumption. These shifts are clearly reflected in Nelson's data for overall average per capita energy intake. In 1900 the energy intake for the high-income group is estimated by Nelson to have been around 2,750 kilocalories per person per day, substantially higher than the low-income group at around 1,650 kilocalories. Virtual convergence was achieved in the 1940s, and the 1980 data show both groups at just over

2,000 kilocalories, with the low-income group's figure actually marginally the higher of the two. Thus, the evidence presented by Nelson (which also covers nutrients like vitamins and minerals) appears to suggest that gross nutritional inequalities between classes in developed economies like the UK have been largely removed, although some especially vulnerable groups or individuals may still experience nutritional deprivation.

However, while overall convergence can be demonstrated in terms of broad estimates of nutrient intake, the question inevitably arises as to whether there remain significant ideological and cultural differences between classes in relation to food, as Bourdieu's analysis would predict. To throw some light upon this issue we can turn to the work carried out by Calnan and Cant (1990), which consisted of an exploratory qualitative study based upon households made up of married couples or couples living as married, with at least one partner in paid employment. Their response group consisted of twenty-one households which can be termed 'middle class' (drawn from what the authors refer to as social classes I & II) and sixteen households which can be termed 'working class' (drawn from what the authors refer to as social classes IV and V). Households were sampled on the basis of a community survey carried out in a local district in southeast England. The study does indicate that there are a number of underlying similarities between middle-class and working-class families with respect to food and eating. For example, the two groups appeared to have similar shopping patterns and, in both classes, women were primarily responsible for food shopping and cooking. What is more, it was largely upon wives that the responsibility for 'healthy eating' appeared to fall, although the authors note that women in both class groups faced considerable difficulties in introducing 'healthier' foods into the household, due to resistance from other family members (Calnan and Cant 1990: 59).

However, some significant differences between the two groups did emerge. For example, in connection with views concerning healthy eating, far more middle-class than working-class women had purchased 'healthy diet' items, such as margarine high in polyunsaturated fats, wholemeal bread and semi-skimmed or skimmed milk, in the week before the interview. What is more, when respondents were encouraged to discuss the issue of the link between diet and health, working-class women tended to refer to the specific health problems of particular members of their family. On the other hand, middle-class women were more likely to refer to a more generalized form of health knowledge consisting of ideas drawn from sources like books and the medical press. Interestingly, however, concern with weight loss, dieting and calorie counting was mentioned more frequently by working-class than middle-class women.

As might be expected when comparing two groups in significantly different positions in the socioeconomic hierarchy, there are clear contrasts in food-related spending patterns. For example, the middle-class families spent a markedly lower proportion of their disposable income on food (an average of 20 per cent) than did working-class families. The latter spent, on average, 30 per cent of their disposable income on food, a disposable income which was itself on average only about 60 per cent of the middle-class figure. While all the working-class women reported careful budgeting of food expenditure (with some flexibility for treats or money shortages), this was not the case for the middle-class women. In general, they did not work on the basis of a fixed food budget, and felt that if they overspent they could readily have access to further funds. Interestingly, however, although working-class women appeared to be more price conscious, neither group was particularly enthusiastic about the practice of 'shopping around' to take advantage of bargain food prices, as this was seen as excessively time-consuming. Not surprisingly, the price consciousness and strict budgets of working-class women meant that they put a greater emphasis on cost as a factor affecting food choice than did the middle-class respondents, who tended to stress food quality as the main selection criterion. Some striking differences emerged when respondents were asked what foods they would like to purchase but could not actually afford. Working-class women tended to mention 'high-status' meat (red meat in the form of joints, steak, etc.), whereas middle-class women were more likely to mention what they regarded as luxury items, including exotic foods and elaborate prepared dishes.

There also appeared to be an important difference between the two groups in relation to the processes of food choice and food-related decision-making. Calnan and Cant's results suggest that the middle-class husbands were much more directly involved in food selection and food purchasing decisions than were the husbands in the working-class group. In the middle-class families this was more likely to be a joint process, whereas in working-class families the husband's influence was more indirect, it being more or less tacitly assumed that the wife was responsible for buying food and preparing meals which suited her partner's tastes. Attitudes to cooking also exhibited a significant class-related difference, despite the fact that in both groups it was seen as essentially women's work, with men usually involved in cooking only in specific circumstances (e.g., at the weekend or when the wife was ill), rather than taking it on as a routine responsibility. In fact, working-class women were much more likely to express the view that cooking was an important skill for a woman to possess. Among the middle-class women this view was much more rarely expressed, even by respondents who rated themselves as good cooks.

Calnan and Cant's study (1990), despite its admittedly small scale and its essentially qualitative nature, does strongly suggest that in urban communities in contemporary developed societies class continues to exert an important influence upon patterns of eating and upon nutritional beliefs and practices. The proportion of income spent on food, the financial management of food expenditure, attitudes to 'healthy eating' options, the nature of household decision-making and views on women's feeding work skills are all apparently sensitive to variations in social class. Broadly speaking, the working-class families in the sample seem to have remained closer to what might be regarded as 'traditional' or relatively long-standing ideas concerning the linkages between food, health, status and gender.

Consideration of class-based differences in nutritional attitudes and practices inevitably raises a further question. How do those at the bottom of the socio-economic hierarchy of contemporary society fare? What are the effects on these beliefs and practices when choices and possibilities are tightly constrained by poverty? A number of studies, British and American, are available to provide us with some direct empirical evidence on the implications of low income for food choices and eating patterns. For example, Charles and Kerr, whose major study of food and families has already been discussed above, in the course of their main survey, came across seventeen families who were living on state benefit and whose incomes were, by contemporary British standards, very low. The authors subjected this sub-sample to detailed scrutiny and published these results in a separate paper (Charles and Kerr 1986a). Of these seventeen low-income house-holds (all of which contained at least one pre-school child, given the design of the main study), ten were headed by a female single parent, six were made up of women living with an unemployed male partner and one was headed by a woman whose husband was in prison at the time of the interview. On average, these families were spending approximately one-third of all the income coming into the household on food (a figure marginally higher than the 30 per cent estimate made by Calnan and Cant (1990) for the food expenditure of their working-class response group). Although, in a sense, food expenditure was seen as a protected, priority area, with economies being made first in such areas of expenditure as heating and clothing, respondents reported reductions in the consumption of items such as fresh fruit, take-away meals, milk and desserts.

However, the area of economy and reduced consumption which was most frequently mentioned, and which appeared to generate most concern for these women, was meat. This was a specific form of meat: the joints, steaks and chops which qualify as the centre-piece of a 'proper meal'. Alternatives like mince, liver and belly pork had been taken up, but these were seen as less desirable substitutes. Like the rest of the sample, these low-income respondents subscribed strongly to what appears to be one of the cornerstones of the dominant British food ideology, the idea that the 'proper meal' represents the foundation of sound nutrition for the family. Hence, a strong sense of deprivation was reported by respondents who could not provide 'proper meals' on the regular basis they deemed necessary. Significantly, however, where a male partner was present in the household, there was a much higher frequency of proper meals (or 'cooked dinners' in Murcott's terminology). This was the case, even though it might well mean that as a result less money was available for food items like fresh fruit, milk and cereals. Charles and Kerr report that women saw the presence of a man as creating a 'proper family', and hence the need for 'proper meals'. In fact, the authors argue, in nutritional terms, women tended to privilege men at their own and their children's expense (Charles and Kerr 1986a: 245). Overall, because of their low income, these families found it extremely difficult to maintain adherence to the dominant food ideology's insistence on the proper meal. In a very real sense, they found themselves in a position where 'they could not live up to the social and cultural standards which are an accepted part of family life within British Society' (Charles and Kerr 1986a: 427). Thus, it becomes clear that the food-related penalties of living on a low income in contemporary developed economies are as much a question of social and cultural deprivations as nutritional ones.

Quite clearly, the insights offered by Charles and Kerr are based upon a relatively small group of low-income respondents who happened to come to the researchers' attention in the course of a larger-scale, more general study. However, information concerning the food-related ideas and choices of low-income families is also available from such studies as that conducted by Dobson, Beardsworth, Keil and Walker (1994), which take such issues as the main focus of attention. Dobson and her co-workers carried out a qualitative analysis of the nutritional practices and ideas of a group of forty-eight low-income families, using a combination of individual interviews, expenditure diaries, food consumption diaries and, where feasible, combined family interviews. Their response group was made up of a mix of families with children. Some were families which had just begun to receive state benefits (income support). Some were families who were long-term recipients of such benefits (that is, had been in receipt of income support for more than twelve months) and others were low-income families who were not receiving such benefits. The study itself was carried out in a large industrial city in the British Midlands.

One of the study's main findings was that the families who had been living on state benefit for longer periods had effectively adapted their expenditure patterns and lifestyles to their restricted circumstances, and were less likely to experience financial crises than new benefit recipients. What is more, food expenditure proved to be one of the few areas where many of these families had any elasticity or flexibility in their budget. In some weeks their already minimal expenditure on food would be reduced in order to meet a pressing bill or some unanticipated expense. Coping with financial adversity was achieved through extremely strict budgeting, which was carried out largely by women, who also were mainly responsible for food shopping and preparation in all these families (as one might expect). What is more, these women adopted a number of strategies to deal with the problem of their limited resources. For example, the researchers noted that the less money a family had to spend on food, the more frequent was food shopping. Thus, in extreme cases, food shopping was carried out on a daily basis, on the principle that, if more than one day's supply of food was in the house, the extra was likely to be eaten, creating a shortage on subsequent days. Food shopping patterns were also heavily biased towards local discount stores, as opposed to the more desirable large supermarkets with their wider range of more prestigious food products. In addition, many women reported using the strategy of doing the food shopping alone, in order to keep strict control of expenditure and to avoid arguments over what should be bought and impulse purchases by other family members. Processed and frozen food products were often bought, as these were calculated to be cheaper overall than preparing dishes from fresh ingredients.

Also strategically significant was the maintenance of relatively conservative eating patterns. The logic behind this stance was a simple but compelling one: women often would not risk trying to introduce unfamiliar foods or dishes into their family's diet (either for health reasons or as an economy measure), since if the novel item was rejected, this would involve a substantial element of wastage which could seriously disrupt an extremely tight food budget. Interestingly, DeVault's Chicago study also noted this reluctance on the part of poor families to experiment with unfamiliar food items. This arose out of a fear that the results would be unpalatable and hence lead to unacceptable wastage, although in this instance reference was being made to dubious bargain items of suspect quality (DeVault 1991: 178–9). Coupled with this nutritional conservatism was a form of enforced commensality that many families adopted, since they could not afford to cater for the differing tastes and divergent needs of individual family members. Having the whole family eat the same meal at the same time was an important economy measure in itself.

The relatively conservative approach to eating indicated above, however, has wider implications than its function as a means of avoiding waste. It was clear from the interview material presented by Dobson and her colleagues that for these families it was of paramount importance to maintain conventional eating patterns as far as possible. By and large, they were not willing to introduce far-reaching changes into their diets in a radical attempt to obtain sufficient nutrients at a drastically reduced cost. As we have argued elsewhere (Beardsworth and Keil 1993b) even though it is feasible to derive all one's nutritional requirements from an extremely simple, low-cost diet, to subsist on such a diet would involve being, in effect, a kind of nutritional deviant, a violator of basic Western cultural assumptions about the contents and combinations that go to make up orthodox meals. For these low-income families, the effort expended in order to maintain conventional eating patterns was worthwhile, in so far as it helped them to maintain a sense that they were still in touch with the mainstream of consumer culture. This desire manifested itself most clearly in relation to children. For example, although they could rarely if ever afford to provide food for others outside the family (e.g., by inviting guests), many mothers sought to avoid their children's becoming isolated from their peers by being unable to accept and reciprocate invitations to eat at friends' homes. Thus, special planning and savings would be undertaken so that invited friends could be offered a conventional array of snack foods and branded products. In one particularly poignant case, a mother described how she usually poured low-cost cola into a Coca-Cola bottle before serving this to her son's friends, to avoid his being teased by his brand-conscious young guests. In a similar vein, mothers regarded it as important that their children should be able to take conventional snacks and packed lunches to school, in order to avoid the public stigma of poverty.

The food-related deprivations suffered by these families were primarily those associated with a lack of access to preferred, higher-status foods. What is more, particular strains were imposed upon women, whose task it was to cope and to adapt, and to try to protect other family members from the consequences of economic privation. For women, food shopping became a tiring and demoralizing chore, and large amounts of time were spent seeking competitively priced items. The very act of food shopping appeared to serve as a constant reminder of their poverty, of the desired items they could not afford. Shopping, one of the key leisure activities of consumer culture, could not be enjoyed but only endured. Similarly, many women reported that the constant worry over food budgeting and economizing actually meant that they derived little pleasure from eating. For the family as a whole, having to eat together could be a source of tension and a reminder that the household did not have the resources to provide the individual choice and flexibility that are seen as becoming the norm in more affluent households. However, in a sense, these families are examples of relatively successful adaptations to the constraints of feeding a household on a very restricted budget, and it was not uncommon for respondents to express some pride in their ability successfully to manage the feeding of the family in such circumstances. Indeed Sharman (1991: 180) notes a similar pride in feeding and nurturing the family in deprived conditions in her study of low-income households in a large city in the northeastern United States, based upon the analysis of life histories.

The above discussion of the impact of low income on food consumption and nutritional practice is essentially based on data derived from families located in urban households. There is a temptation to assume that low-income families in rural settings, families with close connections to the processes of food production, might be in a relatively advantageous position, possibly benefiting from direct access to agricultural produce of various kinds. However, as an image of the position of agricultural workers and their families in a modern, developed society, this may be a somewhat misleading picture. Indeed, Newby (1983) demonstrates that in certain circumstances such families may actually be at a disadvantage compared with their urban counterparts. Newby's study is based upon participant observation carried out while living with a farmworker's family in Suffolk, in eastern England. What Newby is able to show is that farmworkers employed by large commercialized food production units are just as effectively alienated from the fruits of their labour as is the typical factory worker. This family had no privileged access to produce and its situation was very far from anything like self-sufficiency. Despite the fact that the family did grow some vegetables and kept two goats for milking, its actual eating patterns were essentially the same as those of an equivalent low-income urban family. There was the same repetitive and conservative pattern of food consumption, the same obligatory commensality, the same gender division of labour and the same assumption that adult men require larger portions (an assumption more obviously appropriate in this setting, given the nature of farmworkers' energy

95

expenditure). In other words, there was nothing distinctly rural about this diet (Newby 1983: 33).

However, what was distinctly rural about this family's predicament was the cost penalty it bore in relation to food purchasing. The nearest shops were in a town 2 miles away and since the family could not afford to run a car, these had to be reached by bicycle, apart from a monthly 'stocking-up' visit, when bus transport was used. Food prices in this small town were significantly higher than those in large supermarkets. However, the nearest of these was in Ipswich, and reaching it by bus involved so time-consuming and expensive a journey that the family was unable to take advantage of the lower prices. The family was thus aware of a puzzling contradiction. Although their 'breadwinner' was deeply involved on a day-to-day basis in the production of food, the family actually paid considerably more for their food than did the urban dweller, who lived far removed from the toils and vicissitudes of agriculture. In fact, Newby's respondents admitted that they were baffled by this contradiction, which the author explains with reference to the fact that they could see only the two ends of the commercial food chain at first hand (initial production and eventual retailing of processed and packaged food items). What they could not see, and therefore could not comprehend, was the monolithic and increasingly vertically integrated structure of modern agri-business. As we have already noted when considering the making of the modern food system, the manufacturing, distribution and retailing of food have been increasingly concentrated into the hands of a relatively small number of very large firms. Since the aggregate added value of these processes greatly exceeds that generated by production itself, these firms have achieved a high level of dominance in a marketplace which emphasizes diversity of choice, convenience and attractive packaging. In such a marketplace, low-income families, rural as well as urban, find themselves marginalized, often clinging tenuously to the mainstream of nutritional culture.

OVERVIEW

With the diverse material discussed in this chapter we have sought to demonstrate the complex ways in which nutritional activities and family life interact. Thus, while eating patterns reflect family processes, at the same time, family relationships and family boundaries are expressed and reinforced by the day-to-day routines of provisioning, preparation and consumption. Similarly, the division of labour with respect to feeding work reflects gender inequalities and male dominance within the family. At the same time, the obligations imposed upon, and by and large accepted by, women to take primary responsibility for such work have been seen as serving to perpetuate their effective subordination, a subordination which has been characterized by some of the writers whose work we have considered as having fundamentally oppressive or even violent undertones.

Clearly, food choices and eating patterns are influenced by broader social class inequalities, with those at the lower end of the socioeconomic hierarchy struggling with financial deprivations and experiencing severely restricted access to the wide range of food items and dietary options on offer to the rest of the population. However, as we have seen from the ideas of writers like Bourdieu, nutritional differences between social classes are not only reflections or manifestations of their economic and cultural inequalities. Such differences, in the form of refined tastes and cultivated preferences, become vehicles for maintaining the distinctions between the layers of the social hierarchy. What is more, these distinctions are reproduced from generation to generation as the processes of nutritional socialization shape the individual's exposure to and experience of the dishes, food items and food ideologies characteristic of his or her location in the wider social order.

Some of the limitations of the studies discussed in this chapter have already been mentioned, for example, the strong tendency on the part of investigators to rely heavily (and often exclusively) on the evidence provided by women respondents when attempting to build up a picture of food-related beliefs and activities within the family setting. In many instances, this tendency reflects an explicit intention to give priority to women's views and women's experiences, on the grounds that in the past these have been all too often neglected by social scientists. Furthermore, since it is a consistently observed fact of life that women bear most of the responsibility for feeding work in the domestic sphere, in terms of economy of effort it clearly makes sense for the researcher to use women as informants. Yet there is a distinct possibility that significant bias can be introduced in this fashion, when conclusions are drawn and generalizations put forward concerning the dynamics of an entire household on the basis of the accounts of just one of its members. The accounts of husbands or partners, and of younger and older children, must become the focus of increased research attention if our view of food and the family is to become a more rounded and complete one.

When sociological attention is being focused on eating in the private domain (as opposed to eating out in the public domain), there is a widespread assumption that this essentially involves examining the dynamics of the nuclear family, conventionally composed of parents and their children. The bulk of the research carried out in this area is founded on this assumption, and this in turn is reflected in the contents of this chapter. However, this basic assumption is one whose relevance to future research in this area needs to be subjected to critical questioning. The nuclear family represents specific phases in the life cycle of any given individual. Admittedly, these phases are of crucial importance (for example, he or she will be undergoing primary socialization and also may be responsible for the primary socialization of his or her offspring). However, many other household types exist. For example, households containing a single person, households made up of an adult couple (married or not, different sex or same sex), households made up of a nuclear family plus other relatives, households made up of extended kinship groups and households made up of groups of individuals not related by kinship at all. In fact, there are numerous possible combinations, and each combination is likely to exhibit a variety of food selection, preparation and consumption patterns which may cut across conventional assumptions concerning gender differentiation and class differentiation, for example. Thus, in households consisting of an adult couple, both of whom are in full-time employment, might we expect traditional assumptions concerning the gendered nature of feeding work to be less binding and less closely adhered to? In households consisting of unrelated adults (students, for example) we might ask how shopping, cooking and eating are organized – whether collectively or individually – and how such groups negotiate their feeding arrangements and their household division of labour.

It also needs to be recognized that the distribution of household types has been changing consistently in recent decades. Thus, in the UK in 1979, 31 per cent of all households consisted of the classic nuclear family, that is, a married couple with dependent children (Thomas, Goddard, Hickman and Hunter 1994: 21). Overall, in that year, 49 per cent of the total population of the UK lived in such households. However, by 1992, such households had declined to 24 per cent of the total, and contained only 40 per cent of the population. In contrast, single-person households over the same period rose from 23 per cent (containing 9 per cent of the population) to 27 per cent (containing 11 per cent of the population). Other household types also showing increases over this period are those containing a lone parent with dependent children and those containing couples with no children. The picture is a similar one in the USA. Between 1980 and 1992 the proportion of households made up of married couples with children under 18 declined from 31 per cent to 26 per cent, to a point where they contained just 41 per cent of the total population (a figure virtually identical to that in the UK). Over the same time period, the number of households made up of lone women with children under 18 went up by 29 per cent, and those consisting of lone men with children under 18 rose by 108 per cent. Single male households rose by 41 per cent, and single female households by 29 per cent (U.S. Bureau of the Census 1993). These far-reaching shifts in household composition seem to represent underlying trends which are likely to persist. The implication must be that if we wish to develop a more complete sociological insight into domestic nutritional activities, the whole spectrum of household types will need the attention of researchers.

Even within the nuclear family household itself changes are clearly under way. The increasing involvement of women in the labour market has resulted in a steady increase in the demand for, and the supply of, convenience foods. The use of such products, the components of what we have already termed the 'convenience menu', has the potential to produce fundamental alterations in the nature of feeding work within the family, especially when linked to innovations in food manufacturing and food preparation (the increasing domestic use of microwave ovens being an obvious example of the latter). Such possible changes include a shift towards a more co-operative and less gender-differentiated mode of allocating feeding work, and towards much more personalized patterns of eating, where individual family members increasingly make their own idiosyncratic food choices and time their eating to co-ordinate with their own personal schedules and priorities. If such possibilities really do represent the future development of eating within the domestic sphere, then the eclipse of more traditional notions of commensality and the symbolic significance of proper meals could be seen as holding the promise of lightening what has been seen as the oppressive burden of feeding responsibilities borne by women. What is more, such changes would also imply the gradual breakdown of the allegedly conservative influence of the dominance of the husband's tastes within the setting of the family. This, in turn, would imply an enhancement of the permeability of the boundary between the family and the outside world, which would render it increasingly susceptible to the influences of such agencies as advertisers, health educators and food propagandists of various kinds.

Of course, the above discussion is, of necessity, a somewhat speculative one. Future developments will depend upon the outcome of the complex interplay of two opposing sets of forces. On the one hand, there is the braking effect of customary food ideologies and long-established nutritional practices which can command habitual, almost taken-for-granted obedience. On the other hand, there are the change-inducing effects of underlying demographic, economic and cultural trends. Describing and explaining this interplay, and monitoring its outcomes, will represent a major task for sociologists working in this area over the next few decades.

5

EATING OUT

The restaurant is the tank in the warfare of cookery because it has always been a major instrument for smashing old eating habits. Take-away food is the guerrilla of cooking.

(Zeldin 1983: 147).

Such dramatic assertions raise expectations that the analysis of some, if not all, kinds of eating out will present major contrasts with the patterns of eating at home considered in the previous chapter. For the most part, studies of the household emphasize the important contribution of patterns of food preparation and serving in maintaining traditions, particularly stability of food choice, in setting reassuring boundaries between members of the household and others, and providing a means of social communication and identity and a constant reaffirmation of the existing divisions of labour and power hierarchies within the family. However, before it is possible to make any assessments as to whether eating away from home is different from eating at home, and the extent to which Zeldin's assertions are justified, it is necessary to consider information about a series of relevant issues. For example, it is important to clarify what is meant by 'eating out', how and why opportunities for eating away from home emerged, became established, were organized and staffed and, perhaps the most intriguing issue, what we know of how such opportunities are used, perceived and experienced by consumers.

From the point of view of the late twentieth century, it is easy to imagine all the activities which might take us away from home, and which might entail our being compelled or choosing to find something to eat. We could consume anything ranging from a snack to a full meal, and it could be eaten with friends or family in their homes. However, even if we did not have any social contacts, we could still eat. In most situations in our society, access to a wide range of food would be readily available, providing, of course, that we were able to afford it. It is the kind of food made available for money, from commercial outlets such as shops, take-aways, fast-food and other restaurants, that has been identified as a twentieth-century 'revolution' in our eating habits (Gabriel 1988: 7). The identification of these commercial food outlets also draws our attention to the fact that the food sold is eaten in public rather than in private and that it is likely to be eaten alongside, but not with, strangers.

Comparisons with the past suggest that there are differences of degree as well as of kind in the balance between public and private eating. It would not be possible to argue that there was no market for food outside the home before modern times, but it was a relatively undeveloped market and most food would have been provided within a framework of social obligation rather than as a commercial transaction. In all the social anthropological and historical accounts of traditional societies there is strong emphasis on the importance of hospitality. Such hospitality would be extended to travellers (many societies had particularly strong culturally defined obligations to welcome strangers). Neighbours too, often identified in terms of lineage and kinship, would be invited to share food, often on the occasions of feasts. Some of the meals recorded in the anthropological literature were spectacularly generous, involving the preparation of foods which took time and were scarce and therefore valuable. One of the most dramatic and well-recorded examples is the 'potlatch' held by American Indians who lived along the northwestern Pacific coast from Oregon to Southern Alaska. The potlatch host not only provided a feast for other members of the group but also gifts of food and other goods which were distributed to the visitors when the feast was over. Indeed, gifts and feasts were often closely interconnected and indicated the ways in which the welcome to neighbour and stranger was embedded in a framework of social relationships. The potlatch was a regular occurrence and, without any formal or explicit calculation, there would be an approximately equal balance of gifts and feasts between those involved. In other words, the feast locked members of the society into a pattern of reciprocal obligations. Social anthropologists have identified the latent and manifest functions of such obligations, amongst them the sharing of current food surpluses (particularly of perishable foods) and the provision of a virtual guarantee that they, in turn, would benefit from feasts with others when their own supplies were short (Farb and Armelagos 1980: 176–90). The network of social relationships within which such feasts were set brought many social and economic benefits, but ruled out as totally inappropriate any calculation or payment at the time when they occurred. Of course, the importance of food as a means of expressing social solidarity continues to be recognized in modern societies. 'Sharing food is held to signify "togetherness", an equivalence among a group that defines and reaffirms insiders as socially similar' (Mennell, Murcott and Van Otterloo 1992: 115). The bond created by eating and drinking together operates in a wide range of social contexts. There are formal dinners, even feasts, to mark political agreements and, linking private lives with the transition to new social statuses, there are wedding 'breakfasts' and celebrations which involve food for birthdays and other occasions of symbolic significance. As in traditional societies, there is no explicit calculation of cost or notion of payment, but there is a recognition of reciprocal obligation.

101

EATING WITH OTHERS: THE DEVELOPMENT OF TABLE MANNERS

The evidence of the continued importance of kinship connections when away from home suggests that the first experience of eating away from home was likely to have been as the guest of others in their homes. Visser (1993) turns her attention to the 'rituals of dinner' and focuses on how we eat and why we eat as we do. She argues that, given all the effort of acquiring food, eating it should be the easiest part but we 'cloak the proceedings with a system of rules about places and times to eat, specific equipment, decoration, sequence, limitations of movement, bodily propriety' which are not a biological necessity but a 'carefully cultured phenomenon' (Visser 1993: ix). Paying particular attention to the European and American tradition, she analyses current and historical material to consider why rules were established and how rules are taught. She draws attention to the ways in which table manners force us into ever stricter control of our bodies and the implements for serving and eating food, and illustrates the process by discussing all the stages associated with eating out at the invitation of others in their home. Visser's underlying theme is to argue that such controls are necessary because eating together, and sharing such a valuable resource as food, is potentially dangerous. Violence could erupt at any time and table manners are social agreements devised to defuse such a possibility. Just as weapons are not brought to meals in traditional societies, modern societies have rules about cutting and the style and placement of knives which reassure us, at however deep a level, that we are in safe company. However, at the same time, it is recognized that table etiquette relies on both training and knowledge so that table manners may be used to serve a class system and to reinforce snobbery. Visser acknowledges and documents the fact that the presentation of food and associated table manners change, and gives as an example the shift, which began in the eighteenth century and was virtually completed by the end of the nineteenth, the change from service à la française to service à la russe. The social consequences of this shift were considerable. Service à la française was a meal pattern which involved two servings of a large range of food (before and after the 'remove'). Such display was a feast for the eyes of guests as well as nourishment, and good manners demanded that they helped themselves and others (by directing servants) to any of the dishes on display. She suggests that this pattern, where the guest must be active in choosing, remains in buffet meals and in airline food (Visser 1993: 197). Service à la russe was a meal pattern which involved a succession of dishes with lots of courses. Guests are helpless and passive and are always served. In contrast with the earlier pattern of selection, the same food is offered to all. There is less display of food and more emphasis on the equipment for service – platters, place settings and table decorations. Visser's account makes it quite clear that each pattern had important consequences for the behaviour of hosts and guests.

The direction of such changes was examined by Elias (1978a), one of the first to attempt to analyse the social significance of something as 'everyday' as table manners. Elias sees the history of manners as part of the 'civilizing process'. Central to the study is the identification of modes of behaviour considered typical of Western 'civilized' man in the twentieth century. If such a person could be transported to the past, say to the fourteenth century, it is certain that he would recognize the prevailing behaviour as quite different and more unrestrained than our own. He might find it repulsive or attractive, but would definitely notice a difference. Elias sets out to investigate what changed and how the change occured or, in Elias's terms, how Western Europe became 'civilized'. Elias makes a specific study of the transformation of behaviour in relation to manners through the study of texts (beginning with that of Erasmus in the fifteenth century, which was dedicated to the son of a prince) written for the instruction of high-born boys on 'outward bodily propriety'. The guidelines are highly specific: for example, do not stare at others and take care over dress. Readers are also advised to wipe their noses, to use clean knives for food, not to make belching or other noises, not to slurp food, to consider others, and so on. Facial expressions are argued to be the expression of the inner person and should be controlled to indicate appropriate attitudes. Changes in the focus of such texts indicate 'gradual civilization' through changes in feelings of shame and delicacy as society demands and prohibits different manners. There is a move from unrestrained and spontaneous behaviour towards socially instilled displeasure and fear. We become increasingly self-conscious and less impulsive, always concerned about how we appear to others. Elias argues that these changes reflect broader changes in the links between society and the individual, together with a process of distancing between adults, and between adults and children. In psychological terms, Elias argues that these changes indicate the formation of the superego. Explanations of the historical changes which encouraged the development of such civility towards others, and the civilizing process itself, are, Elias argues, associated with state formation and centralization as well as with the state's monopolization of force which began in the fourteenth century and continues into the twentieth.

The important lesson to be learned from these writers for the analysis of eating out is that the changes they describe continue to the present day to influence our table manners and behaviour with others. We learn to handle cutlery and other equipment, together with ways of being considerate to others, which vary according to whether we are hosts or guests. We have moved from the situation where food is not a topic of conversation because we eat food appropriate to status and respectability to a context where food is always a topic of conversation as we seek to select that which displays taste, respectability, knowledge and a 'search for marginal differentiation' (Mennell, Murcott and Van Otterloo 1992: 4). We learn to control the way we sit, talk and eat at table. In addition, just as in the times described by Elias and Visser, if we are uncertain about how to conduct ourselves, we can consult books on social etiquette.

THE BEGINNINGS OF COMMERCIAL PROVISION OF EATING FACILITIES

In the context of well-established patterns of mutual obligation which persist even in the most modern societies, the question arises as to why it was necessary for a market in the provision of food to arise. Part of the answer appears to lie in the process of modernization itself, in particular, the gradual breakdown of the importance of kinship and social obligations based on status ascription, combined with the process of urbanization. When individuals and groups, no longer tied to their local regions, were free to travel throughout large geographical areas or to be away from their homes in an urbanized context and when there was, as a consequence, no longer any guarantee of being able to link with kin, we see the beginnings of eating out on a commercial rather than a reciprocal basis. There are examples from widely different societies and historical periods. The Romans, for example, had a highly developed system for selling food and drink on a commercial basis in their cities. There were also hostelries along the roads of the empire to provide food and lodging for any traveller who could afford the charges. In another imperial setting, China, the earliest records show there were inns providing both food and accommodation for travellers, often officials on imperial business, as well as stalls selling food to those who worked away from home in the larger towns and cities. There are even records, from the T'ang dynasty which reigned over the Chinese empire from AD 618 to 907, of the existence of restaurants offering meals as part of the enjoyment of leisure rather than as mere necessity (Farb and Armelagos 1980: 232). The records also show that in many societies there were food sellers of every sort, who set up on the occasions of markets and fairs or wherever large numbers of people gathered. All these are 'modern' in the sense that they catered for all who could pay (and operated in a cash economy) rather than for those who had some call on the resources of their kin, however distant, when away from home. For most people, however they did not form a major part of the experience of eating.

Apart from the sales of food at markets and fairs and the sale of ale at inns, commercial eating out in Europe developed relatively slowly. Until the end of the feudal period, a high proportion of the population was tied to the land and had no opportunity to travel. Travel for the sake of it was rare and those who did travel, often on official business of one kind or another, were able to claim hospitality from the kin of their masters at their manors, or they stayed at inns. Other travellers, such as pilgrims, were provided for by the religious houses on the routes to shrines and other centres of worship. It is interesting to note that although there was a Christian duty to be charitable, such charity was aimed at the poor, so that staying at religious houses was not necessarily at no cost. Pilgrims were supposed to be self-supporting and to make contributions for their keep. Except for members of the nobility, who might be offered more privacy, both food and accommodation at these religious houses were very simple and offered little choice. With minor variations, all shared the food available that season or from store. Merchants and others who needed to move from place to place often stayed at religious houses too, and some houses, located in important centres of pilgrimage or trade, eventually separated the care of travellers from their day-to-day activities by establishing inns run on commercial lines. Indeed, Medlik (1961) goes so far as to argue that the dissolution of the monasteries in England in 1539 set in train changes which encouraged more rapid development in the range and quality of provision, in that it was part of the break-up of the feudal system and encouraged movement to the towns.

With the breakdown of feudalism and the growth of towns, many more were free to travel either locally or over large distances. Such changes precipitated the development of existing provision and the establishment of new types. Whilst the grandest travellers still looked to their kin to house and feed them on their journeys, those without such contacts would stay with local households willing to take lodgers overnight, or in inns. In both cases, travellers would share whatever food and accommodation were available. Inns and lodging houses increased in number and size as demand rose. However, it was in the cities that entirely new opportunities for eating away from home for pleasure, as much as necessity, developed. One of the earlier examples which is relatively well-documented is the establishment of the coffee house in the seventeenth century. Coffee had been introduced to Europe in the early seventeenth century but took some time to become popular. However, according to Visser, 'The birth of cafés in the late seventeenth century in Europe was one of the prerequisites for the growth of modern city life' (Visser 1993: 123). Their contribution, she argues, was in providing a non-hierarchical, or even anti-hierarchical, location for meeting and discussion where those present could not be 'placed' in a social sense. In both Paris and London special coffee shops opened near theatres as places for conversation (Leclant 1979). However, they developed in each society in rather different ways. In France, the café continued as one of the most popular locations for food and drink and continued to be open to all, whereas in England the coffee house became associated with work as well as leisure, a place where men could drink coffee, read newspapers (at that time too expensive for individual purchase) and transact some kinds of business. For example, Lloyds coffee house was where insurers met, particularly those involved in marine insurance, and the organization of Lloyds 'names' remains to the present day. In England, particular coffee houses became so exclusive that they eventually became gentlemen's clubs. The term 'café' was also used and, to some extent, paralleled the development in France as a place open to all levels of society. However, there were exceptions, for example, very grand establishments such as the Café Royal were frequented by the very rich and, at the other end of the social scale, cafés attracted the working classes (and became more likely to serve tea than coffee). Interestingly, the term 'coffee house' was used by the temperance movement in the second half of the nineteenth century for the eating places provided for the working classes as an alternative to public houses where alcohol was sold (Harrison 1971). Possibly because they tried to 'improve' as well as feed their customers, they were not very successful and did not last much beyond the 1890s. However, the new style coffee houses did something which public houses of the time rarely did: provide a wide range of food, from full meals to what we would now call snacks. Girouard (1984) argues that, as a consequence, they reinforced the pattern of eating out amongst the working class and contributed to the success of cafés, which were 'straightforward, unambitious and useful' and did not try to improve their customers. He also argues that they precipitated change in public houses which, in the face of such competition, were forced to provide food as well as drink. Some, like their twentieth-century counterparts, even started to serve coffee (Girouard 1984: 205–6).

The provision of commercial facilities for eating out accelerated during the nineteenth century. Freeman (1989) provides a vivid historical account of the Victorians and their food. She describes the food sold at markets and at fairs and by street-sellers. For example, in London, street-sellers sold food to take home or eat on the spot: hot eels, pea soup, fried fish, pickled whelks, nuts, apples, cakes, potatoes, roast chestnuts and, later, ice-cream. Cows were kept in St James's Park and milked to order. Fresh food in season, for example, fruit, was brought in from the countryside. However, more formal eating out did not develop to any great extent until well into Victoria's reign, largely because

> [since] eating out was looked on as a matter of necessity rather than pleasure, most establishments were utility rather than luxurious, and fashionable restaurants in the modern sense did not exist – fashionable dining being a matter of eating in (in the sense of in private houses) rather than out.
>
> (Freeman 1989: 179)

In addition, opportunities for eating out were radically different for men compared with women. Middle- and upper-class men could dine at their clubs, which were the nearest equivalent to restaurants, or at a handful of relatively high-class taverns. Freeman (1989) gives examples of one at Greenwich which specialized in serving fish and one in the City which was so famous for its turtle soup that customers could visit the basement and view the live turtles before eating. Taverns were noisy places, where waiters called out what was on offer and shouted the orders to the kitchen. It was not acceptable for ladies of standing to visit such places; the only public places where they could dine respectably were at inns and hotels, and even then they probably followed the custom, which earlier had been the rule for both sexes, of taking their meals in private rooms. For the growing middle classes working in the cities, the cheapest eating places were initially the coffee houses, which were perceived as 'worthy and conservative' (Freeman 1989: 273) eating places for those whose work kept them from home. Coffee houses offered some of the earliest 'take-aways' in that people at work could send out to a local coffee shop for food to be delivered to them. The development of railways and linked suburban housing meant that commuters were able to travel considerable distances to work. The distance travelled, and the time workers spent away from home, gave yet further impetus to the development of places to eat lunch at all social levels and all prices.

Change and expansion also came with the development of the tourist as well as the commuter trade. Larger and smarter hotels were built, often associated with and near railway stations. Simmons (1984), in his study of the development of the Victorian hotel, argues that the new London hotels built in the 1850s and later were quite different from the inns of earlier periods for several reasons. Firstly, they offered choice and a fixed tariff of prices. Even more importantly for their subsequent development, they offered opportunities for respectable women to dine in public and be seen in the public parts of the hotel (in ways which had always been available to men) rather than in the 'purdah of private-sitting rooms' (Simmons 1984: 10). Indeed, he comments that 'Hitherto the whole world of inns and hotels, still more of eating-rooms, in London had been a man's world' (Simmons 1984: 9). Interestingly, these new hotels, in London and elsewhere, checked rather than encouraged the development of independent restaurants, because guests were expected to eat in the hotel as well as to stay there. Particular hotels became associated with famous chefs (for example, Escoffier and the Savoy hotel) and reinforced them as centres for prestigious eating out. Such hotels also prevented the development of the type of hotel already common in the rest of Europe, offering just rooms or rooms with breakfast only. It was argued that, since the English insisted on elaborate cooked breakfasts, hotels must employ kitchens and staff and these could only be profitable if they were used to prepare other meals, too (Simmons 1984: 20).

Mennell, Murcott and Van Otterloo (1992: 81–3) argue that the restaurant as a social institution was, to some degree, a product of the French Revolution. Eating places open to the public existed in Paris before the Revolution. However, the social upheaval and its consequences for the collapse of the French aristocracy increased the availability of skilled professional cooks, who had formerly worked only for specific aristocratic houses. They opened dining rooms where they continued to prepare food to the highest standards (*haute cuisine*), this time for those who could pay. At its most elaborate, these chefs produced food of a range and quality which would have been impossible in private homes without a great deal of money to spend on ingredients and a large kitchen staff. However, Aron (1975) documents the development of a range of restaurants to suit all levels of expenditure. The restaurants which gave the middle and upper classes some insight into the quality and style of aristocratic dining are viewed by Mennell (1985) as part of a process of the democratization of luxury and an attack on privilege, with the restaurateur as someone who made accessible to the lower orders secrets from superior classes. Since 'Britain forgot how to cook at the time of the Enclosures and the Industrial Revolution' (Driver 1980: 170), it was French cuisine which set the standard all over the Western world, though Driver (1983: 89) adds the rider that the preference might have been as much for its expense and exclusiveness as for its taste. The social groups who were willing to pay for *haute cuisine*, Driver argues, were also the people who bought various guides to good food when eating out.

Driver emphasizes that styles of public eating vary and restaurants flourish for a range of reasons. 'In France, the public restaurant was a by-product of the Revolution; in mid twentieth-century Britain, of imperial decline' (Driver 1980: 178). Driver writes about the rise of immigrant cuisines as the 'collision of food worlds' (1980: 73) and suggests that they can be considered as either a triumph or a tragedy: as a triumph because they offered cooks and eaters access to many major culinary civilizations (Chinese, Indian and Middle Eastern, and later Italian), and as a tragedy because of the contempt which could be shown between 'native and newcomer'. Driver makes the comment that interest in these new cuisines did not initially arise from foreign travel (it is sometimes argued that many British people abroad insist on traditional foods), but from the opportunity to eat cheaply in ethnic restaurants (which also offer informality and extended opening hours). Such ethnic restaurants, together with other types which also offer informal modes of dining (for example, vegetarian), can provide a 'tentacle of taste, extended laterally to global foodways that lie outside the British tradition' (Driver 1980: 176).

Mennell (1985) argues that these changes carried with them a shift in the balance of power in favour of chefs and against the paying customer. Some chefs achieved fame and fortune not only through their restaurants but through their writing on cooking and cuisine. Often these books became regarded as the classic statements on French cookery and guides for subsequent training of new chefs. Examples are Careme and Escoffier in nineteenth-century France and Soyer, whose career was mostly spent in England but who was French-trained. Mennell also argues that these chefs shaped the menus and practice of the twentieth century, which rested on a wide range of ingredients, a large kitchen with a high degree of specialization and a standard of presentation which would be virtually impossible for the amateur cook. In due course, there were reactions to the dominance of this model of the restaurant, for example, the enthusiasm for country recipes and provincial styles of presentation. In the twentieth century, perhaps the most spectacular challenge came from *nouvelle cuisine*, associated with the name of Paul Bocuse. The emphasis on fresh ingredients (determined by what was available at market that day), the minimum of cooking and awareness of health considerations, made for meals which could not be planned in advance or produced on a large scale. Significantly, the practitioners of *nouvelle cuisine* were mostly chef-proprietors who created dishes in a highly individualistic manner. Wood (1991) describes the development of the *nouvelle cuisine* restaurant in terms of the 'shock of the new' and argues that this cuisine is a type of cooking of increased refinement, where the 'producer' continues to dominate. However, the fact that there are barriers to routinizing and incorporating *nouvelle cuisine* suggests that it is not the last word in the refinement of taste. For Wood, *nouvelle cuisine*:

is a social construct rather than a culinary one, reflecting the narrow concerns of, and changes within, the middle-class. Nouvelle cuisine is the fish and chips, hamburger, pizza and pancake of the middle-classes. It may become an integral part of the culinary scene but it will always be on the periphery of 'serious' food and eating, remaining far more interesting for its sociological, rather than gastronomic, significance.

(Wood 1991: 337)

The nineteenth century is associated with the development of one of the most popular street foods: fish and chips. Walton (1992) provides a detailed account of the trade's economic, social and political relevance. Walton acknowledges that little is known of the origins of the fish and chips, which became established in the form we know today before the end of the last century. Ironically, Walton concludes that this 'great and quintessentially British institution' (Walton 1992: 1) probably arose from ethnic diversity, when Jewish migrants to the East End of London fried the fish left over from fresh fish vending, for sale in the street to eat immediately or take home. Walton also argues that fish and chips, whether eaten in the street or taken home, was initially and continues to be, for the most part, food for the working classes. Buying fish and chips to eat out was always seen as rather 'common'; it had little appeal to the middle classes because of the smells, dubious hygiene and rough behaviour said to be associated with it. Walton also suggests that this may be part of the reason why the industry was neglected by historians. He shows that the growth of fish and chip retail outlets, particularly as they emerged from their down-market, backstreet origins to respectable locations with improved hygiene and strict controls on their operations, stimulated considerable capital investment. Such expansion introduced sophisticated technology and became an important component of the national fish trade and the demand for potatoes. There is also evidence to suggest that fish and chips was an important element in the regular diet of a large proportion of working-class families and that there was a constant debate amongst those concerned with the nutritional standards of the poor as to whether the dish was a healthy contribution to working-class diets, or part of secondary poverty induced by incompetent use of limited resources. The supporters of fish and chips, who included some medical practitioners, argued that the dish offered good food value at low cost. As part of the food eaten at home, it was one of the earliest convenience foods for working wives: easily accessible, highly palatable and time-saving. In addition, the food did not demand investment in expensive domestic technology. Not all working-class people considered it respectable to eat fish and chips in the street from newspaper, although the dish was a popular street food for people coming out of cinemas and public houses. In the 1940s researchers for the Mass Observation organization noted that sales of fish and chips fluctuated with the closing times of pubs (Mass Observation 1987).

Walton (1992) also draws attention to the social functions of the fish and chip shops. They were centres of gossip and sociability and, in contrast to many of their higher-status equivalents, welcomed women and children. In the interwar period, when many shops were refurbished, they were associated with warmth and comfort. They were also associated with courting, particularly for adolescents, where calling for fish and chips marked the end of an evening out. The lack of general appeal to the middle classes is highlighted by accounts of the exception: Harry Ramsden's. Harry Ramsden built his fish and chip 'palace' in the Yorkshire countryside in the 1930s, complete with seating for 200 in a restaurant which was carpeted and lit by chandeliers. He succeed in attracting large numbers of the middle classes who could afford to travel to his restaurant by car. However, his success rested on having the custom of both the 'upmarket' trade and the regular daily orders from the local mill workers. As incomes rose, other restaurants, for example those in department stores, hoped to attract the skilled working classes to their stores and to the experience of eating out in restaurants. To complaints from the independent fish fryers, who resented the competition, the stores' restaurants began to do this by including the ever popular fish and chips on their menus. Fish and chips also became available in works canteens.

Studies from the United States argue that there the development of commercial facilities for eating away from home was similar but more rapid than in the UK. The essentially rural character of much of the country meant that commercial developments were concentrated in the cities and on the coast. For example, Pillsbury (1990: 13) asserts that 'Most colonial Americans never dined in a restaurant even once'. Their experience of eating away from home would have been at non-commercial social gatherings or in the homes of others at weddings and funerals. Travel for pleasure was rare and was seen as the prerogative of the very rich; travel for business would involve staying at taverns, inns or boarding houses where facilities were basic and there was little or no choice of food or accommodation. There were restaurants (specializing in selling food for consumption on the premises) at the beginning of the nineteenth century and it was these, together with the coffee houses already established in the larger cities, which expanded to meet the demands of the 'mercantile age'. For Pillsbury, it was the industrial revolution of the late nineteenth century that brought about 'a new set of operational assumptions and parameters' (1990: 33) to meet the demands of the growing urban centres with their 'unparalleled need to feed the multi-shift factory workers at all times of the day and night' (1990: 37). The boarding houses and taverns, with their fixed times of eating, were insufficiently flexible and the need was met by street vendors and then by 'diners' (wagons where patrons could sit whilst eating) which became more and more sophisticated in their design and provisions. From the 1870s onwards, demand was met by 'new restaurants for a factory age' (Pillsbury 1990: 48) which included lunchrooms, cafeterias and diners, often supplied with quality foodstuffs by the fast and efficient railways.

It was at this time that the hamburger became part of the basic menu offered (with the first reference to a 'hamburger steak' as early as 1834, although the first hamburger sandwich was recorded much later in 1916). The first quarter of the

twentieth century saw the rapid growth of all kinds of catering and the establishment of chains, both regional and national, and the development of franchising.
Eating away from home from choice during leisure time became popular
amongst the middle and working classes at this period, particularly when car
ownership became more widespread. The 'drive-in' concept was developed in
the 1920s and along with all catering outlets in residential neighbourhoods
(where they were associated with pleasure rather than work). 'These new stores
targeted the discretionary food dollar, not the work dollar. They represented
pleasure not a necessary evil' (Pillsbury 1990: 77). Pillsbury attempts to make
sense of a situation where the choice of eating out facilities was so great that
'chaos rules our palate' (1990: 3) by drawing a distinction between body food (to
fuel the body) and soul food (to serve the inner person). Each is a matter of time,
money and intent and, in the late twentieth century, it is possible to have the
choice. 'The restaurant is simply a place where, for a fee, one may dine away
from home; a modest concept which has taken on literally thousands of expressions in the world around us' (Pillsbury 1990: 225). In sum, he sees the restaurant as a mirror of its society. This echoes the concluding comments of Farb and
Armelagos (1980: 266), who noted that, in responding to the new rituals of
eating based on automobiles, television, technology and efficiency (which cut
across previous religious affiliations, ethnic loyalties and class allegiances), we
make choices which are cultural statements, and that our eating patterns are
reflections of contemporary social formations.

Levenstein (1988) identifies a special factor in the expansion of commercial
facilities for eating out in the United States: the prohibition on the public sale of
alcohol in 1920. This destroyed the ascendancy of French cuisine in the highest-
status restaurants (because it was virtually impossible to cook many of the dishes
without wine or to enjoy them without an accompanying wine). It also undermined such restaurants economically, in that many of them had relied on the
profits from their alcohol sales to subsidize the provision of high-quality food.
However, the catering industry expanded at other levels, providing for the
growing numbers of men and women of the middle classes who worked and
ate a midday meal away from home. The new lunchrooms, tearooms and self-
service cafeterias provided low-cost food served quickly. They also offered
respectable places for women workers and shoppers to eat, something which
had not been available in the era of the dominance of restaurants and hotels.
Women's food preferences for light snacks and salads also shaped the menus
offered to workers, whilst American rather than French cuisine featured in the
restaurants more geared to the leisure trade. Levenstein (1988: 192) argues that
these changes had a considerable impact on the pattern of employment in that
'most food preparation could be accomplished by unskilled, barely trained,
cheap, male labor'.

The period of dramatic expansion, particularly of chains and franchise outlets, is documented by Carlioro (1994) in tracing the 'odyssey' of eating out over
the seventy-five years up to 1994. Whilst many of the chains whose histories he

describes are great business success stories and have become household names, Carlioro also identifies the risks and uncertainties of the commercial sector of catering provision. Following the financial and organizational strategies of earlier successes does not necessarily guarantee further success. There is evidence of both spectacular failures and a continued enthusiasm on the part of new entrepreneurs for trying to meet the demands of a public whose willingness to spend cannot always be evaluated – entrepreneurs who may be faced with unexpected costs such as health care for their employees (Carlioro 1994: 190). Although, as Carlioro points out, in spite of economic depression, world wars and the unpredictability of the dining public, the history of the restaurant industry in America is one of resilience and expansion.

'BEHIND THE SCENES': EMPLOYMENT IN THE CATERING INDUSTRY

In his study, Walton (1992) also addressed the issue of the fish and chip shop as a small business. The pattern varied over time, but Walton argues that owners were usually located at the margin of the lower middle and upper working classes, recruited from skilled and supervisory labour. The shop was sometimes a supplementary source of income where one or more wage earners worked outside the home. Typically, the shop was a small family business rather than part of a chain. Husband and wife often worked together with heavy dependence on child labour. In contrast to some of their more modern competitors, they remained small-scale, labour-intensive operations.

Clearly, the provision of food for those at work or at leisure makes work, and there has been a series of attempts to analyse the work of those 'behind the scenes' (Mennell, Murcott and Van Otterloo 1992: 85). The literature available varies according to the work undertaken. For example, cooks and chefs as a group are under-researched although there is a range of literature about cooking and waiting occupations. Such literature varies in its focus from analyses of tensions within the kitchen from a management perspective (Whyte 1948) to the study of catering as an example of routine, semi-skilled work (Gabriel 1988). In addition, Wood (1992) reviews this and other literature in his study of the 'hospitality industry' of hotel and catering work. In contrast, and more recently, Adkins (1995) has discussed the special character of service work, particularly its gendered organization. There is also literature about food workers, particularly waiters, as part of the illegal economy (Mars 1982). All agree that many jobs in catering are stressful and poorly paid, with little training and low expectations amongst workers, and often with high turnover of staff. There is often little mutual understanding between cook, waiter and customer, which Driver (1980: 153–5) puts down to the complacency of large commercial organizations which claim that they rarely receive complaints. Even the highest-status personnel, chefs and cooks, have a long training with relatively poor pay and see themselves as artists unappreciated by their patrons (Mennell, Murcott and Van Otterloo 1992).

Gabriel's (1988) study is an attempt to make up for some of the gaps in our knowledge about working lives in catering. The preface states that 10 per cent of British workers are catering employees and are part of the service sector, which accounts for 62 per cent of all jobs. Yet the area has been described as the 'stepchild of economic research' (Gabriel 1988: 6). He argues that the expansion in catering jobs reflects changes in eating and drinking habits over the past twenty to thirty years in terms of what is eaten and where and how it is prepared. The central features of change are the growth of consumer interest in take-away meals, fast food, health food, ethnic restaurants, cafés, wine bars, and *haute cuisine* restaurants. In the past it has been acknowledged that these enterprises are, by their nature, labour-intensive. However, the trend is towards the industrialization of service and the substitution of labour by machinery and technology. Such changes have come through the availability of frozen foods and routinized production so that cooks become 'material handlers' and waiters become 'interface workers'. With fascinating prescience, Gabriel even writes (1988: 4) of the 'McDonaldization of the Economy' but does not pursue the social consequences of such a process.

Gabriel's own field research covers a range of situations in which food is prepared: a traditional mass catering unit in a hospital, the modern frozen food unit in a community centre, a fast food chain, a traditional fish and chip restaurant, a kebab house and a gentlemen's club, using interviews to reveal the diversities and similarities of the working lives which are described. The chapter headings ('Home cooking for thousands', 'The cooking factory', 'The fun food machine', 'Craft cooking for gentlemen', 'The small independent restaurant or café: the price of independence') touch on the analysis of gendered work in the service sector, but the chief focus is indicated by the title of the concluding chapter, 'Conclusions: keeping the lid on', which emphasizes the similarities, not differences, between these workers and other workers. In the context of economic depression and fear of unemployment, these workers are argued to be trapped in jobs with poor pay, variable job satisfaction (with the cooks and private dining room workers having highest and the others very little) and little economic power as workers. These themes are echoed and developed by Wood (1992) in his account of work in hotels and catering. Drawing upon a considerable literature about the hospitality industry, he confirms the lack of empirical data but argues that there is sufficient in what exists to support the general agreement about the low level of rewards for work which is often both insecure and carried out in unpleasant conditions. Wood discusses the problems of high levels of labour turnover, the frequent lack of collective organization in regard to pay and conditions, de-skilling and the demand for flexibility from the work-force, and the lack of appreciation from the customer for services provided. In his concluding observations, Wood (1992: 163–5) considers the possibility of a future where the exploitative relationships of work in hotels and catering will produce a hospitality industry in which most employees will work for a brief time only, as one phase in their movement towards a career in some other part of the economy.

Mars (1982) includes hotel workers amongst his potential 'cheats at work' in that they operate in a work setting which provides them with motives and opportunities for 'fiddling'. His analysis of 'covert reward systems' covers four job categories (designated 'hawks', 'donkeys', 'wolves' or 'vultures'), each with structural characteristics in common and broadly similar opportunities to rob, cheat, short-change and 'fiddle' in transactions with customers, employers, subordinates and the state. Waiters are placed amongst the vultures, in that they need the support of a group but act on their own 'at the feast'. They are linked to the common base, depending on support and information from colleagues, but still being competitive and acting in isolation. The waiter gets formal rewards (basic pay) with informal rewards ('free' meals, accommodation, tips) and potentially illegal 'alternative' rewards in the 'black economy', through access, for example, to pilfered food and opportunities to short-change customers.

Adkins (1995) raises more directly the links between the public and the private domains and the special character of service work. She focuses on the gendering of the contemporary labour market, in particular the processes through which power relations between men and women in employment are constituted, specifically in paid work in the service sector associated with leisure. The nature of service work is discussed and, in particular, how and in what way service work differs from other forms of wage-labour relations. Adkins argues that, unlike other kinds of work, service work cannot be understood in terms of economic rationality alone. She agrees that the imperatives of management are economic rationalization and standardization. However, some autonomy must be allowed to the service provider to ensure that the specific requirements or situations of customers can be accommodated. Such autonomy is not *ad hoc* but has the important social function of the maintenance of 'normal conditions' (Adkins 1995: 6), since service work is not just fixed outcomes and rigid controls but also the (re)production of the social structure. The processes of mediation and normalizing are central to understanding the dynamics of service work, including employment relations. Where there is spatial and temporal proximity between production and consumption, services for customers/clients/guests have to be delivered in the same place and at the same time as produced. In other words, Adkins argues, in service work the quality of the social interaction between the provider and the consumer of the service becomes part of the product. As a consequence, the cultural expectations of consumers regarding service provision have particular significance in structuring the form of service delivery, and hence employment relations, because consumers are buying a particular kind of social experience. Thus, the social composition of 'front-line/high-contact' workers becomes part of what is sold. Race, age, gender all become relevant in recruitment and employers intervene in areas of dress, speech, behaviour and training. In other words, it is recognized that service employment may involve carrying out what Adkins identifies as 'emotion work' in relation to customers. Even though it is difficult to get accurate data because service workers are often working in non-standard kinds of employment (for example, part-time, casual or temporary), estimates support the view that front-line consumer service work is typically carried out by women. In 1991, 81 per cent of all employed women worked in service occupations and in 1990 70 per cent of the total hotel and catering work-force was female.

Adkins's field work was undertaken to explore the gendered dynamics of service employment in the context of a leisure park and amongst hotel and catering managers. Data were collected on the gendered structure of employment, the construction of work relations and the significance of sexuality. The analysis suggests that these service workers, particularly the women, were operating in a more complex framework than other workers (Adkins 1995: 144). Far from existing outside the domain of employment, both family and sexual relations played a significant role in structuring gendered work relations within the labour market. In the case of management in hotel and catering, work relations (or relations of production) within the occupation were shown frequently to be organized by the patriarchal relations of the family. For example, husband and wife were hired as a 'team', yet the husband directly controlled the wife's occupational work, to the benefit of employers, even though the wife had no wage-labour agreement or contract. The wives worked under the marriage contract in a family mode of production, organized in a patriarchal way. In the leisure park, there was patriarchal structuring of waged-labour. To get a job, most women (regardless of occupation) were required to fulfil conditions which related to the production of an 'attractive' female work-force, which included expecting and dealing with forms of 'sexual objectification from men customers and men co-workers' (Adkins 1995: 145). It is emphasized that only women had to carry out such 'sexual work' in order to have the opportunity to exchange labour in the marketplace. 'Men and women were constituted as different kinds of workers within these workplaces, even when they were located in the same jobs' (Adkins 1995: 147). To be workers, women had to be 'attractive' and carry out forms of sexualized work, whereas men did not have to do this. Women not only had to take orders, serve food and drinks and clear tables, they also had to provide what Adkins sees as 'sexual services' for men, both customers and co-workers (for example, by smiling, looking flattered, entering into jokes, etc.). It is acknowledged that such interaction was not always unpleasant. However there were cases of dismissal where women had resisted conventional asumptions about their behaviour. Adkins' analysis challenges and invites a reinterpretation of a range of studies of restaurant work and of the selection and training of workers in various types of food outlets.

CONTEMPORARY PATTERNS OF EATING OUT

The USA is often used as an indicator of what is likely to become the pattern in the UK. McCarthy and Strauss (1992) report on a survey about the 'Tastes of America 1992'. After a drop in 1990, the amount spent per week on eating out continued to increase. However, although spending was up, the frequency of dining out had declined. 'Customers often see eating out as a treat – and, as the survey shows, they expect the service they receive to live up to that perception' (McCarthy and Strauss 1992: 25). For example, 70 per cent were reported as eating at 'full service' restaurants to celebrate a special occasion. The survey polled 4,000 households and 2,502 responded. Almost all (98 per cent) had eaten out during the previous month. Typically, households ate out 9.42 times a week with adult males eating out 4.68 times a week on average, compared with 3.76 for an adult female and 4.16 for 'child/teen'. Married couples with two incomes and at least one child spent most per household, with singles under 30 spending the most per capita. Healthy eating, such as ordering salads, was often offset by also ordering french fries, although the evidence indicates an increase in orders for grilled rather than fried chicken.

Although not directly comparable with the American material, a useful overview of the pattern of eating out in the UK is provided by Payne and Payne (1993). Since the authors are writing for the business community, they are concerned to highlight the features of the market, consumer attitudes and the prospects for the 1990s. They emphasize the growth of the market, calculating that the consumer catering market (excluding institutional catering but including drinks consumed with meals) was worth £16.6 billions in 1992, an increase of 69 per cent on the figure for 1986. Even taking into consideration the recession, they argue that the long-term trend is for real spending on eating out to increase (and for it to increase as a proportion of consumer spending overall). Compared with 109,471 in 1980, they identify 124,900 catering businesses in the UK in 1990. The great majority of these businesses (120,168) operated in the consumer catering sector and the number of actual outlets was around double that figure. Public houses were the most common type, with around 70,000 outlets (two-thirds of them serving snacks and meals at the bar and 40 per cent having a restaurant). Change has occurred with franchising increasing in importance and a nationwide network of outlets being built up by catering chains. In addition, in-store restaurants have changed as shopping centres grow in number and with them food courts, offering a range of food from a number of counters.

Payne and Payne (1993) draw upon the National Food Survey to show that in 1990 the average number of meals taken outside the home totalled 195 per person, of which 100 were consumed at lunchtime. People with higher incomes, and Londoners, were the most likely to eat out. They also report on the Economist Intelligence Unit survey of consumer attitudes to and patterns of eating out of a sample of 1,000 people aged 16 and over (see Table 5.1)

A detailed analysis of the results showed that: people aged 55 and over and those in the 'DE' socioeconomic groups were considerably less likely than others to have eaten out in the previous 12 months. Pubs, hotels and fish and chip shops showed a broad-based popularity; other 'English' restaurants, Indian restaurants, French restaurants and roadside diners showed a strong male bias; ethnic restaurants were preferred by those in the younger age groups, while pizza houses, French restaurants and vegetarian restaurants displayed a strong

Table 5.1 Types of restaurant meals eaten during the
last twelve months (1991)

Type of outlet	Respondents (all adults) (%)
Pub	60
Hotel	31
Chinese	29
Roadside diner	28
Pizza	24
Indian	24
Fish and chip restaurant	23
Steakhouse	21
Other 'English' restaurant	16
American style	16
Italian	16
Wine bar	8
French	7
Greek	7
Vegetarian	4
Other	6
None of these/don't know	13

Source: Adapted from Payne and Payne (1993: iii)

upmarket bias. Regional results varied greatly but Londoners were far less likely to have eaten in a pub and considerably more likely to have eaten in ethnic restaurants (Payne and Payne 1993: iii).

Respondents were also asked their main reasons for choosing a restaurant. In descending order of importance they were quality of food, value for money, range of menu, attentiveness of service, overall atmosphere, the welcoming of families, availability of parking and convenience of location. The first two factors were considerably more important than any other. For an ordinary meal most people aimed to spend less than £10 per head, for a special meal they would spend between £10 and £40.

On the basis of their study, Payne and Payne predict that there will be the further spread of systems catering (i.e., chains with a standardized menu and format), food courts and themed restaurants. Two significant factors – convenience and health – will also continue to be influential, with convenience expressed in terms of the growth in home delivery (and intense competition between suppliers) and the health influence reflected 'in an increased offering of salads, low fat food, vegetarian meals and, perhaps, fresh and healthy ingredients' (Payne and Payne 1993: iv). They also predict that ethnic food will become more popular, with more ethnic restaurants and an increase in non-ethnic restaurants offering some of the most popular ethnic dishes. Writing about Britain, Jones (1985) also predicts intense competition amongst fast food companies, with a small number of large operators continuing to dominate the sector. Farb and Armelagos (1980: 197) argue that, on the one hand, national cuisines are basically conservative and that successful developments (for example, the expansion of fast food outlets with limited menus which give the assurance of familiarity) support this view. On the other hand, they also recognize that new foods are constantly being added and suggest that national cuisines can be flexible in exploiting novel cultural and environmental resources.

SOCIOLOGICAL ANALYSES OF CONTEMPORARY EATING OUT

Wood (1992) draws attention to the fact that, typically, sociological concern has been on 'domestic dining' rather than on dining out, even though dining out is experienced and enjoyed by all except the poorest members of society. Drawing upon a range of studies, Wood estimates that there are about 231,750 'commercial catering outlets' in Britain (including hotels, restaurants, public houses, commercial travel catering, major fast food chains, cafés and take-aways, and club, leisure and entertainment catering). In addition, there are 72,610 outlets in non-commercial catering (including staff canteens, health care catering, education and public service catering). He alerts readers to the fact that the term 'eating out' can be misleading in that a substantial proportion (about two-thirds) of the meals served in the cafés and take-aways, which represent 18 per cent of meals served in the commercial sector, are consumed on a take-away basis and may well be eaten at home. He also draws attention to the fact that dining out as an ancillary activity (for example, food eaten when out shopping) may have a different symbolic significance from that of dining out as a leisure activity in itself. Wood identifies these issues as part of an agenda for sociological research. He also advocates the further exploration of the family and gender dimensions of food choice as experienced in the public domain.

Mazurkiewicz (1983) had already identified the relevance of gender and argued that not all food outlets are equally accessible to men and women, although more research is need to document these differences in detail. She focuses on women's access to and use of the facilities and services in the commercial sector of the hotel and catering industry in the context of reports concerned with the failure of this sector to cater for female customers, particularly female business travellers. In contrast to those who see the problem as one of inadequate marketing, Mazurkiewicz makes the case that there are social barriers to women's use of hotel and eating out facilities. Women's defined location in the private sphere of the home, their prescribed roles and expected behaviour patterns, and male domination and control of women in the public areas of life, combine to generate social barriers which exclude unaccompanied women from public places. These patterns are reinforced by the managerial strategies of hotels and public houses which respond to female customers in terms of such stereotypes.

Finkelstein (1989) offers an analysis of dining out as 'a sociology of modern manners'. The focus is on the 'ordinary'. Dining out, she argues, is very popular and it has been estimated that by the close of the twentieth century two-thirds of all meals in the United States will be purchased and consumed outside the home. Finkelstein's study is an attempt to examine dining out for the presuppositions and concealed values it contains. The starting-point is the popularity of restaurants and the ways in which their use might reflect changing family patterns and, in particular, changes in the functions of the nuclear family. However, it is not possible to argue that restaurants are used because they save time during the working week, because restaurants are actually busier at weekends. Nor can it be argued to be a question of physiological pleasure from consumption because there is sometimes distress from overindulgence and also a willingness to eat junk foods when out. So there is a need to explain why people derive such pleasure from eating in the public domain. Clearly this is more complex than mere eating and represents a range of meaningful activity. Finkelstein suggests several possibilities: pleasure in the sense of occasion; an opportunity to demonstrate our knowledge of how to behave; participation in a form of entertainment and spectacle through visual images and imagined atmosphere. In sum, these are all aspects of 'bourgeois sensibility' of self – the opinions of others, the appearance of wealth and being in control. Dining out may be viewed as the convergence of the private and the personal with the public and social. There are even different restaurants for different moods (for example, McDonald's for family unity, a bistro for romance) as well as 'waves of style' in fashions of dining out (Finkelstein 1989: 3).

However, Finkelstein argues against the popular view that dining out is an expression of individuality, choice, spontaneity and that we select restaurants for food and price in ways which demonstrate our discrimination and what we value and desire. On the contrary, dining out has the capacity to transform emotions into commodities which are made available to the individual as if they were consumer items. The styles of interaction encouraged in the restaurant produce an 'uncivilized sociality'; the restaurant makes dining out a mannered exercise, disciplined by customs in a framework of prefigured actions. We act in imitation of others, in accord with images, in response to fashions, out of habit, without need or thought for self-scrutiny. Far from being in control, we are relieved of the responsibility of shaping our relationships with others. For Finkelstein (1989: 8), this provides an extension of Elias's analysis, in that, for her, civility refers to exchanges between individuals who are equally self-conscious and attentive to each other, who avoid power differentials, and do not mediate exchanges through status and prestige. Civility is not unthinking obedience to habit and custom but intentional exchange (even if it is sometimes difficult, conflictual, raucous). It is reflected in the degree of engagement required of those who interact. It follows that if people are being used to serve self-interest, then there cannot be civility. For example, the business lunch is not the setting for civilized exchange, even if the hidden agenda is known; it is merely a pretence of cordiality.

Finkelstein comes to the thought-provoking conclusion that restaurants have structural characteristics which make the social exchange there inherently uncivilized. There is artifice and pretence, diners are under close surveillance from waiters, they are guided through the menu so that the waiter is between food and eater, wine waiters subdue the diners and establish boundaries and hierarchies and assure diner discomfort. The restaurant owner greets and guides in ways which enhance control. Dining out is mediated through money and engenders callous and calculative orientations. Finkelstein is aware that this is not the way diners perceive the dining out experience. They may well view it as a pleasure, highly convenient and entertaining, with social formulae which make it easier to act without thinking. However, she wants us to be aware that the underlying processes she describes are linked to the rise of modern bourgeois culture and the 'democratization of luxury' argued by Mennell (1985). Dining out gives license to take pleasure where there is no sense of accountability or personal history, since it takes place amongst strangers. It is democratic and open to all with money, so remote from the everyday that it permits the confident presentation of self. The restaurant is part of the entertainment industry in Westernized societies and is concerned with the marketing of emotions, desires, states of mind. Finkelstein (1989) identifies a paradox: as with all leisure activities in modern society, dining out weakens participation in the social area even as it appears to increase such participation. By offering social formulae for relationships with others, it prevents the development of what Finkelstein (1989: 5) terms 'the examined life' expressed as a civilized awareness of others.

From a somewhat different theoretical starting point, Ritzer (1993) analyses what is perhaps the most characteristic type of eating out in the second half of the twentieth century: 'fast food', which can be either eaten in a restaurant or taken away. There are many outlets and chains currently, each competing to become a household name. Ritzer (1993: 30) gives an account of the first fast food restaurant opened by the two McDonald brothers in 1937 in Pasadena, California. Their established restaurant had experienced high demand at specific times (for example, workers' lunchtimes) and they responded with a circumscribed menu (burgers) and were able to serve large numbers at high speed and low price. The assembly line procedures, with food preparation and serving made into simple repetitive tasks, combined with a specialized division of labour for each stage, have been recognized as constituting the first 'fast food factory'. In 1954 the brothers moved and followed the same pattern in San Bernardino, California. They continued to prosper but were merely a local sensation until visited by Ray Kroc, an enthusiast for scientific management. It was he who suggested the idea of franchising which led, eventually, to expansion world-wide. The particular franchise package used retained centralized control, maintained conformity throughout the system and gave the company a return on all sales. Such rationalization of the fast food business through uniformity in production, a standardized menu and systematic staff training provided customers with a guarantee of a familiar setting and the same quality of food prepared in the same way wherever they ate at McDonalds. The demand in the USA and internationally for such eating out seems insatiable and, as Ritzer says, 'the rest is history'. He argues that developments in fast food were possible because of the processes of formal rationality already in place, such as scientific management, assembly-line work, the mass-production of cars and homes and the development of centres for shopping, parts of which became 'amusement parks for food', where both the setting and the food on offer were guaranteed to be familiar and unchanging. In addition, families, particularly those with children, could eat without anxieties about cutlery, tableware and the disapproval of other customers. Interestingly, in terms of Elias's notions of civility, this is an example of 'uncivilized' behaviour. However, Ritzer also makes us aware that such efficiency, predictability and control extends to control over the customer. Fast food is served so that the customer is encouraged to leave and make room for the next person. There is little choice and the food served has been criticized by nutritionists for being high in calories, fat, salt and sugar.

Ritzer goes on to argue that rationalization (or what he terms 'McDonaldization') is not only characteristic of fast food but also of society in general and is becoming an all-embracing feature of life. He makes a case for education, commerce, industry and medicine all being influenced by the push towards higher profits and lower costs. Such pressures can only be countered by individual subversion or by circumstances in which post-Fordism has lead to greater diversity of provision and hence more choice. Ritzer makes it plain that he wishes to encourage such responses. For example, he mentions the importance of eating seasonally and, along with others (for example Driver 1980), advocates 'slow' rather than 'fast' food (Ritzer 1993: 184).

OVERVIEW

The foregoing discussion has indicated some of the ways in which eating occasions are situated in a complex social space. Eating events can clearly be seen to be located at points upon a number of dimensions. For example, we might identify a dimension which has eating events shaped by personal social obligations and relationships at one end and, at the other, eating events articulated by a commercial nexus between a consumer and a service provider. We can also recognize a dimension which ranges from informal eating situations only loosely constrained by culture and convention to formalized, highly structured eating events. Finally, this chapter and the previous chapter have indicated that, in an important sense, there is also a continuum linking domestic food events at one end and public food events at the other, and that there is not necessarily a simple dichotomy between 'eating in' and 'eating out'.

The studies discussed in this chapter indicate the changes which have occurred and the continuities which have remained. The commercialization of eating out was a consequence of the breakdown of traditional social relationships, particularly those of feudalism, and the growth of towns and cities. Such changes, which accelerated after the industrial revolution and the separation of home from work, had far-reaching consequences for the organization of both employment and domestic life. Economic resources and socioeconomic position continue to exert a powerful influence upon patterns of dining out. However, despite the somewhat pessimistic assumptions of authors like Finkelstein and Ritzer, at whatever level one eats out there has been a significant expansion in the range of choice. Depending on the context and cuisine chosen, eating out may be either similar or radically different from eating at home. The very diversity of contemporary opportunities for eating out challenges conventional ideas about resistance to change being at its strongest in relation to what we eat.

Part III

FOOD, HEALTH AND WELL-BEING

6

CHANGING CONCEPTIONS OF DIET AND HEALTH

The linkage between diet and health is an inescapable fact of life. However, in some senses this linkage can be a complex and subtle one, and clear causal pathways may be very difficult to establish, whether by time-honoured intuitive techniques or by the sophisticated, systematic methods of modern science. Thus, while this link is widely recognized in human culture, there are seemingly endless variations in the ways in which it is conceptualized and in the ways in which such conceptualizations are translated into actual beliefs and practices. However, as a starting-point it is useful to see conceptualizations of the relationship between diet and health as having two opposed aspects: positive and negative. The positive aspect is based upon the idea that certain food items, combinations of food items or diets can produce beneficial health outcomes. These beneficial outcomes may be viewed, by those who accept such ideas, as generalized and unspecific. That is, certain dietary choices are seen as maintaining, or actually enhancing, an individual's resistance to disease or as promoting the efficiency or durability of the body. However, such ideas can be much more specific. For example, particular dietary options or particular foodstuffs may be seen as capable of preventing a particular disease. Similarly, certain food items, or a given dietary regime, may be seen as suitable for treating a disease or for managing a disease and relieving its symptoms.

Many of the negative aspects of the linkage between diet and health are self-evident. Most obviously, a grossly inadequate food intake will lead to weight loss and eventually to death (either through starvation or the onset of a related disease). However, nutrient deficiencies which fall short of the absolute deprivation of starvation can result from low food intake, an unbalanced diet or poor assimilation. Thus, dietary protein deficiency in infants after weaning can result in the disease known as kwashiorkor. A deficiency of vitamin D can cause rickets, a disease which mainly affects children and is characterized by the softening of developing bone (resulting in bow legs). The disease scurvy results from a lack of vitamin C, and produces anaemia, spongy gums, and, in infants, is associated with malformations of bones and teeth. Furthermore, inevitably, food intake can act as a channel for the introduction of harmful agents into the body. These may be toxins (whether organic or inorganic, naturally occurring or

125

synthetic) or any of a vast array of disease-inducing organisms. What is more, in many cultures such agents may be conceptualized in ways which modern Western rationality would regard as supernatural or mystical.

The purpose of this chapter is to focus attention upon such cultural constructions of the connections, or supposed connections, between what an individual eats and that individual's state of health. Of course, such ideas, particularly in the context of Western societies, are not static. They change, sometimes radically, over time. Thus, this dynamic perspective is essential, as we look firstly at examples of traditional forms of belief and practice in relation to diet and health and then at the gradual rise to dominance in Western culture of more systematic and rationalized perspectives. The dominance of such perspectives, however, is by no means complete, as will become evident when contemporary common-sense ideas and 'alternative' dietary ideologies are examined.

TRADITIONAL PERSPECTIVES ON THE LINKS BETWEEN DIET AND HEALTH

Traditional forms of understanding and practice clearly cover an impressive array of activities, including hunting, fishing, agriculture, the manufacture of tools, weapons and other artefacts, healing, divination, and so on. Such traditional forms of understanding, often termed 'folk knowledge' or 'pre-scientific knowledge', are usually based upon the accumulation of often highly detailed empirical information. Accumulation typically takes place over many generations, as concepts and techniques are refined through a repetitive, if somewhat haphazard, process of trial and error. Change in such knowledge is usually slow, although the patient exercise of everyday curiosity plus the occasional fortuitous insight or discovery can lead to effective and sophisticated ways of controlling and manipulating the world. However, it should be borne in mind that traditional knowledge frequently incorporates conceptualizations of cause and effect which modern scientific perspectives would see as essentially irrational, assuming causal mechanisms which would not stand up to rigorous examination. The term 'magic' is conventionally used to refer to such ideas, usually somewhat dismissively and disparagingly. Nevertheless, in traditional societies magical techniques and their associated rituals are employed in many areas of everyday life, particularly where there is uncertainty and unpredictability. What is more, accumulated empirical knowledge and magical formulations of cause and effect become enmeshed with one another, the one difficult to distinguish from the other in any absolute sense, forming a single holistic system of thought. Thus, while the hard lessons of trial and error may eventually be incorporated into practice, where there is ambiguity and ambivalence 'supernatural' forms of explanation have a flexibility which allows them to adapt and survive apparent refutation. We can now turn to actual examples of such traditional ideas in the area of food and health.

Perhaps the most widespread of these traditional conceptualizations of the ways in which diet and health interact are those which are based upon classification according to a hot–cold dimension. In this sense, hot and cold do not refer to the actual physical temperature of the food, but to a more elusive (and in rational terms possibly a more illusory) property of food. In addition, herbs, beverages, medicines, illnesses and even people may be classified in this way in many such belief systems. As Manderson (1987) points out, hot–cold concepts can be found in cultures in Latin America, Asia and Africa. These ideas also appear to have an affinity with ancient traditions of humoral medicine that have existed in Europe, in the Islamic world and in China and India. However, ethnographic evidence indicates that such belief systems are often very variable and are characterized by inconsistencies and disagreements (Manderson 1987: 329). In other words, they exhibit the typical flexibility and elasticity of traditional modes of thought. In certain circumstances, as we will see, these properties enable hot–cold conceptions to survive, and adapt to, the impact of modernization.

Malaya provides an example of a society whose people's beliefs place a strong emphasis on the link between diet and health. In that country, hot–cold categorization remains an important feature of folk medicinal systems and of the practices of the folk healers who are the custodians of these systems. Manderson provides us with a general description of Malay hot–cold ideas, indicating the way in which these are sometimes related to a concept of balance. Thus, food classified as hot may be taken to alleviate 'chilling', but consuming hot foods to excess may result in such unwelcome complaints as rashes, fevers and constipation. These complaints can be relieved by the consumption of foods classified as cold (and such foods are also seen as beneficial for the young, whose bodies by their very nature, are hot). However, an excess of cold foods is seen as leading to weakness and lethargy, and to arthritis and rheumatism in the aged. In Malay communities, some illnesses are also classified as hot or cold. For example, measles, smallpox and chickenpox are hot infections and the patient should avoid hot foods until after recovery. Conversely, chills, arthritis, rheumatism and neuralgia are cold ailments and their symptoms can be relieved by reducing the consumption of cold foods and increasing the consumption of hot foods and medicines (Manderson 1987: 330). In some cultural groups, individuals may be seen as varying in terms of hot and cold (for example, the old may be seen as colder than the young, and men as hotter than women), and there may even be a personal dimension (what is hot for one individual being cool or neutral for another). Even within Malaya there is considerable variation in these beliefs, and hot–cold is often seen more in terms of a subtle continuum than as a simple binary opposition. However, broadly speaking, foods which are spicy or which are higher in fats, calories or protein (e.g., animal products) are located towards the hot end of the continuum, and foods higher in water content (fruits, vegetables, etc.) towards the cold end.

A more detailed ethnographic account is provided by Wilson's participant observation study carried out in a fishing village on the east coast of the Malay

Peninsula. In fact, this study detected a considerable amount of variation in individuals' opinions concerning exactly how particular items should be classified. However, there was broad agreement that such foods as chicken, beef, goat, eggs, manioc, yeast, chilli peppers and spices are hot, and that fruits and vegetables are cold. Rice and fish, the two basic ingredients of Malay cuisine, were regarded as neutral (Wilson 1981: 391). What is more, certain foods were seen as having direct health implications over and above the hot–cold dimension. For example, rice was seen as endowed with an innate vital force which generates strength-giving, curative powers, and there was no condition for which it was regarded as a forbidden food. Garlic was seen as good for the relief of stomach ache, ginger as relieving fatigue, and young coconuts were said to be good for general health. Conversely, some foods could present health hazards. Papaya was said to give small children worms, and prawn paste could give rise to headaches (Wilson 1981: 394–5). Food substances might also be used externally by these villagers for medicinal purposes, for example, in the form of poultices to treat headache, toothache, boils, chills, fever and dizziness. Thrush in a newborn infant was treated by placing the cut end of a young coconut, covered with powdered medicinal leaves, on the infant's stomach. By and large, these can be regarded as essentially magical treatments, although Wilson does admit that in some instances the plant substances employed may have active pharmacological properties.

In fact, these Malay villagers recognize a whole range of diseases which could be seen as having a magical or supernatural causation, and response to such ailments frequently involves food prescriptions or proscriptions. Thus 'seduan', an upper respiratory disease, was believed to be caused by an evil spirit and, if neglected, as likely to lead to serious damage. Treatment entailed the use of incantations and root medicines and the avoidance of soy sauce, groundnuts, duck, prawns and most kinds of fish. In addition, ailments which were not seen as having supernatural causes might also require the avoidance of certain foods. Thus, 'medu', a condition involving breathing difficulties and pain throughout the body, was seen as caused by constipation, and such cold foods as okra, eggplant, pumpkin and papaya were regarded as harmful for sufferers.

As well as employing self-diagnosis and self-treatment, Malays consult both traditional healers and doctors trained in modern medicine, according to the nature of the illness concerned. Western medicines are incorporated into the traditional conceptual scheme, in so far as such substances (whether in liquid or solid form) are classified as hot, and thus eating hot foods while taking them is prohibited. In fact, certain foods like eggs may become *bisa* (toxic) when taking Western medicines like pills. The flexibility and adaptability of hot–cold beliefs in Malay culture is further illustrated by the fact that novel food items, introduced as a result of the modernization of some aspects of Malay society, have been absorbed into the system. These include bread, flour, refined sugar, icecream, soft drinks and foreign fruits and vegetables which have been assimilated into the categories used for local produce. While Wilson suggests that traditional food prohibitions may, in certain circumstances, adversely affect the nutrient intakes of women subject to the high physiological demands of reproduction, she recognizes the extent to which these ideas form a coherent, integrated and reassuring body of belief and practice. In fact, as Manderson (1987: 330) notes, the power of such ideas resides in their ability to provide plausible and intelligible explanations for (and accessible responses to) otherwise incomprehensible processes of affliction and recovery.

Some valuable insights into the cognitive foundations of hot–cold classification systems are provided by Messer (1987). Focusing her attention on hot–cold beliefs in indigenous Mesoamerican thought, she notes the essential syncretism between European versions of the 'humoral' medical framework (introduced by the Spanish) and the deeply rooted concepts based on a hot–cold continuum found, for example, in Aztec and Mayan culture. In fact, Aztec hot–cold beliefs were not limited to such areas as food, health and medicine. Indeed, this basic duality appears to have been seen as encompassing the entire cosmos and was applied to plants, animals, minerals, stars and supernatural beings. Among the Aztecs, in food terms, dark-coloured substances, piquant flavours and sweet fruits were regarded as hot, whereas wild animals, sour fruits and thick-skinned fruits were regarded as cold. The Mitla Zapotec people (like the Aztec, indigenous to Mexico) classify foods according to digestibility. 'Hard to digest' foods are classified as hot or cold according to whether the individual regards his or her body to be hot or cold at the time of eating (Messer 1987: 341–2). Thus, care must be taken, since a hot–cold imbalance may cause illness or aggravate an existing condition.

What Messer attempts is a general description of the underlying logic of such hot–cold classifications. Taking the classification of herbs as an example, she suggests that three types of attribute may be taken into consideration by those operating hot–cold ideas. The first of these types she terms 'perceptible' attributes (those which can be seen, tasted, etc.). These perceptible attributes may be intrinsic (e.g., red colouring is often associated with hot) or extrinsic (e.g., plants which require sunny conditions may be regarded as hot). Secondly, 'functional' attributes may be referred to, again split between intrinsic and extrinsic. As an example of an intrinsic functional attribute, Messer cites the belief that certain herbs may act to 'cook' uncooked foods in the stomach, and are therefore hot. An example of an extrinsic functional attribute is the idea that a given herb is hot because it can be applied externally to treat a 'cold' headache. Finally, 'affective' attributes operate in terms of good and bad. Hot herbs may be regarded as bad if they produce an excess of hot over cold in the eater and thereby result in illness. Messer suggests that children learn these principles through a gradual process of socialization, although the vagueness and essential flexibility of the system allows for competing and sometimes flatly contradictory classifications to be arrived at by different individuals apparently operating the same classificatory criteria.

It is Messer's contention that the hot–cold duality may represent an opposition which is as primordial and as universal as the fundamental opposition between male and female. Such an opposition, being 'good to think' (Messer 1987: 344), is therefore good for classification. Hot–cold beliefs, deeply embedded in the epistemological foundations of many traditional cultures, can provide a potent conceptual framework for articulating the complex linkages between diet and health. While the linkages and mechanisms proposed by such ideas may seem eccentric or implausible according to the criteria of Western scientific, medical and nutritional discourses, they do provide their adherents with a framework of everyday understanding and practical action. Indeed, built up over many centuries and elaborated by dedicated specialists, such beliefs may evolve into highly complex systems of thought. Perhaps one of the most highly developed of these systems, in which food items can be construed as having important medicinal properties, is represented by Chinese traditional medicine (see, e.g., Read 1982).

RATIONALIZATION AND MODERN VIEWS OF DIET AND HEALTH

The process of rationalization represents a powerful driving force in modern societies, placing strong emphasis on measurement, calculation, prediction and systematic organization. The analysis of this process has been one of sociology's central and most enduring themes, a theme which has already been confronted at least twice in this book (in Chapter 2 in relation to the emergence of the modern food system and in Chapter 5 in relation to Ritzer's (1993) 'McDonald-ization' thesis). However, the principles of rational calculability have been extended beyond the spheres of food production, distribution and marketing, and have been applied to diet itself. Turner (1982: 255) draws a parallel between earlier religious asceticism and modern medical regimens, both of which seek to discipline the body by the imposition of rules, and both of which commonly use diet as a focus for such discipline. Turner points out that the development of formal rationality and its application to an ever-widening range of human activities is a process which in turn generates a broad spectrum of specialist professional groups, whose specific collective interests are closely bound up with the process itself. What is more, the rationalization of diet, and the production of rational scientific conceptions of the links between diet and health, required the creation of a new metaphor for the body. That metaphor emerged as the Cartesian concept of the body as machine, a machine whose functioning, inputs and outputs could all be subjected to precise measurements and quantification (Turner 1982: 258–9).

In order to illustrate the emergence of rational medical views of diet and health, Turner examines the career and ideas of George Cheyne, an influential Scottish physician born in 1671 or 1673 in Aberdeenshire. Having studied medicine at Edinburgh University under Archibald Pitcairne, a proponent of the application of mathematics to medicine, by the 1720s Cheyne had become a highly successful medical practitioner in London, with many individuals from England's aristocracy and political and literary elites among his patients. He also published a series of books on his medical ideas and treatments, which were translated into several European languages. In a very real sense, Cheyne's approach to the issue of the link between diet and health was directly connected to his experience of a crisis in his own health. As a result of a prodigious appetite for food and drink, Cheyne's weight rose to a grotesque 448 lb. He experienced considerable difficulty in walking and, understandably, lapsed into a state of deep depression. However, after a period of experimentation, Cheyne devised a treatment scheme for himself based upon a diet of milk and vegetables, regular exercise on horseback, strictly limited alcohol intake and regular periods of sleep. This self-imposed discipline proved highly successful, in that his weight was significantly reduced and he survived to the age of 70.

Cheyne's therapeutic system was based upon a specific and explicitly ratio-nalistic view of the nature of the human body. This was conceptualized by Cheyne as a hydraulic machine, a complicated interlocking system made up of pumps, pipes and canals around which circulated a vital liquor. This machine could only function satisfactorily with the correct inputs of foods and liquids, and the qualities and quantities of these foods and liquids were seen as crucial for proper digestion. In turn, proper digestion and evacuation, and suitable levels of exercise, were seen as the foundations of good health, the role of medical practitioners being conceived as essentially a secondary, facilitating one. In fact, what the body machine required was the careful monitoring of its inputs and outputs, an approach which Cheyne termed 'Diaetetick Management'. In his view, threats to the smooth functioning of the body machine came from a number of sources. First among these were dietary changes in the eighteenth century which had particularly affected the more affluent sections of English society. The expansion of trade had brought numerous rich and exotic foods and wines within reach of the upper strata, and it was overindulgence in such delicacies, coupled with an inactive lifestyle, that was seen by Cheyne as the root cause of most of the illnesses which afflicted his privileged clients. Of particular concern for Cheyne was the consumption by the rich of strong wines and potent spirits, which had the lethal potential to dry up the body machine's vital juices. However, he also laid considerable emphasis on wider environmen-tal factors. Not least of these was another of the consequences of economic success and the advance of civilization, the increasing levels of overcrowding in expanding urban areas like London. Insanitary conditions and poor air quality could create a reservoir of diseases which could threaten the most affluent as well as the most impoverished.

Given the central importance of digestion to Cheyne's views on health and illness, it is not surprising that, as part of his system of Diaetetick Management, he set out to classify foods according to their 'digestibility'. White flesh and dry, fibrous and mild-tasting foods were deemed easy to digest, whereas red flesh and

Table 6.1 Cheyne's classification of foods according
to digestibility

Easy to digest	Less easy to digest
Spring vegetables	Pears
Asparagus	Apples
Strawberries	Peaches
	Nectarines
Poultry	Cows
Hares	Horse
Sheep	Asses
Kids	
Rabbets (sic)	
Whiting	Salmon
Perch	Eel
Trout	Turbot
Haddock	Carp
Pullet	Duck
Turkey	Geese
Pheasant	Woodcock
	Snipe
Veal	Red deer
Lamb	Fallow deer

Source: Adapted from Turner (1982)

fatty and strong-tasting or spicy foods were deemed hard to digest. Turner (1982: 263) provides a schematic representation of Cheyne's classification based upon these principles, as is shown in Table 6.1.

Furthermore, Cheyne favoured 'natural' foods, uncomplicated by exotic preparation techniques and ingredients, which could inflame 'unnatural' appetites. Cheyne's approach led him to devise a whole series of dietary regimens, each one appropriate to a given age group and lifestyle.

Many of Cheyne's ideas may seem eccentric to the modern reader, and the classification scheme laid out in Table 6.1 has an appealing quaintness about it, appearing to have a closer affinity with traditional beliefs about food than with current dietary ideas. Yet, on the other hand, other features of Cheyne's perspectives appear strikingly familiar, from his hydraulic metaphor of the body to his insistence on the importance of 'natural', minimally processed plain foods, moderation in alcohol consumption and regular exercise. His warnings concerning the negative effects of overcrowded, urban living also strike a familiar note. In fact, his ideas are prototypically modern, emphasizing as they do the rational, instrumental use of dietary regimens to enhance health and avoid disease. There is a clear linkage between Cheyne's conception of the nutritionally disciplined, healthy body and the ideas of Elias on the internalization of restraint which we encountered in Chapter 5.

As we have seen, Cheyne's system was aimed specifically at 'a class of people that was professional, sedentary, urban and engaged in mental activity' (Turner 1982: 265). This was essentially a discipline for the elite, overindulged body, in many ways irrelevant to the demands imposed upon the labouring body, a body all too often on the verge of malnutrition, or even starvation, in the eighteenth century. However, by the late nineteenth and early twentieth century this rational gaze was to be turned upon the problem of managing and modifying the diets of the lower strata of society. Turner's analysis of the grounds for this shift in focus rests upon the argument that a number of major issues came together to concentrate the concerns of the elite upon the health and dietary standards of the masses. Such issues included the fear that the insanitary and overcrowded conditions of the working class could always pose an indirect threat to the middle and upper classes through the spread of contagious diseases, and there was also an unwillingness to bear the burden of taxation involved in maintaining an extensive system of relief for the destitute and malnourished. But, underlying such concerns, Turner identifies deeper anxieties among the elite concerning the state of the working classes. Not only could an undisciplined work-force be seen as a threat to the stability of a civilized capitalist state, but also unhealthy and undernourished working classes could present a threat to society's very continuity and long-term survival. Thus, Turner argues that the findings of Rowntree's influential study of urban poverty (Rowntree 1901), pointing out the significant undernourishment of the bulk of the industrial population who carried out the heaviest manual labour, are symptomatic of a rising awareness that the nutritional status of the working classes is, in some senses, the responsibility of the state.

In fact, from the latter part of the nineteenth century onwards, the government of the United Kingdom was increasingly to involve itself in attempts to monitor, regulate and improve the dietary standards of the mass of the population. This increasingly interventionist stance on the part of the state went hand in hand with the development of an ever more sophisticated and rationalistic intellectual apparatus whose theories and methods could be applied to measuring the extent of these problems and devising suitable responses and solutions. Thus, scientific and statistical disciplines like demography, dietetics and biology could be harnessed to the attempt to apply a form of social engineering to the British diet (Turner 1982: 267).

Yet it is, perhaps, a tragic irony that the most powerful single impetus which drove the British government towards ever more ambitious attempts to improve the population's health by improving its dietary standards was in response to the demands of modern mass warfare. In fact, at least one historian has suggested that the disclosures of social reformers like Rowntree concerning the poor state of nutrition of lower sections of the working classes initially had relatively little impact on the thinking of those in power (Burnett 1989: 243). The piece of information which appears to have attracted the attention of the government was a finding by the Director General of the Army Medical Service during the

Boer War in which the United Kingdom was engaged towards the end of the nineteenth century. No less than 38 per cent of the men who volunteered for military service were rejected on grounds of ill health, including heart disease, defective vision, defective hearing and decayed teeth (Burnett 1989: 243). The concern generated by this finding caused the government to set up the Inter-departmental Committee on Physical Deterioration and, in 1906, to pass an Act of Parliament providing free school meals for deprived children. The govern-ment also began to provide grants for infant welfare centres, set up to advise mothers on child-rearing practices. However, it was to be the food crises created by the First World War which were to push the state gradually towards a more interventionist stance. Initially, the government was reluctant to intervene in food markets, but by 1916 food supplies had been severely disrupted by the German submarine campaign. In 1916 the Ministry of Food was established, and a Committee of the Royal Society was asked to draw up minimum food requirements for the population. Measures introduced included, in 1917, a subsidy for bread and the fixing of milk prices. Early in 1918, rationing for key foodstuffs like meat and butter was introduced. Burnett, in assessing the success of the government's food measures, points out that Britain was far better fed than her enemies, with average intakes remaining over 3,300 kilocalories per day (Burnett 1989: 249). However, that there remained an enormous legacy of the consequences of earlier poor nutritional standards in Britain is indicated by the fact that of 2,500,000 men medically examined in 1917–18 as a prelude to conscription, 41 per cent were graded as C3 and unfit for military service (Burnett: 1989: 254). Such findings meant that national nutritional and health standards, and the state's responsibility for these, were becoming an increasingly important political issue in the United Kingdom (Tannahill 1988: 334).

The interwar years saw a general rise in dietary standards in Britain, although on the basis of 1933 data it has been estimated that some 30 per cent of the population were still technically 'undernourished', according to standards laid down by the British Medical Association for a basic minimum diet devoid of obvious deficiencies (Burnett 1989: 271). On the basis of data gathered in 1936–7 it was calculated that over 17 per cent of the population, nearly eight million people, were spending less on food than the minimum necessary total set by the BMA. However, state interest in such results was rising, and an increasing amount of work on nutritional standards and related health issues was being carried out by such agencies as the Medical Research Council, the Food Investigation Board and local Medical Officers of Health. It is Burnett's conten-tion that by 1939 the government had begun to acknowledge that nutritional policy would have to form an integral part of any system of health services, and that professional dieticians, armed with ever more sophisticated nutritional knowledge, were pressing for the state to take on an enhanced role in this area.

It was, however, the outbreak of the Second World War which pushed the British government into far-reaching intervention. Food price controls and a detailed system of food rationing were rapidly introduced and effectively implemented in response to the threats to Britain's food supply posed by the hostilities, threats all the more serious given the United Kingdom's continued reliance on food imports. Improving levels of knowledge concerning nutritional needs allowed rationing to be placed on a much more precise scientific basis. In addition, the nutritionist, Professor J. C. Drummond, in his role as Chief Scientific Adviser to the Ministry of Food, was able to use his position of power and influence to see that food controls were used to raise overall dietary standards, especially those of the poorest sections of the population (Burnett 1989: 290). Schemes were introduced to provide additional proteins, vitamins and minerals to vulnerable groups like pre-school children and pregnant and nursing mothers. On the other hand, for the general population, animal proteins and fats, for example, were strictly rationed, whereas carbohydrate-rich foods like bread and potatoes were freely available at controlled prices. Government measures, including the provision of communal eating facilities in factory and school canteens, did eventually produce actual improvements in nutritional standards in Britain over the war period. Thus, Burnett notes that by 1944, the pre-war average intake of 3,000 kilocalories per head per day had risen to 3,010 and total protein intake had risen by 6 per cent above its pre-war level. What is more, there were also improvements in the intake of minerals like calcium and iron and also of riboflavin, vitamin B and vitamin C. Overall, these improvements appear to have played a significant role in a fall in infant mortality and a rise in the birth rate in Britain over the war years. In stark contrast, over the same period Germany saw a decline in the birth rate and a rise in infant mortality.

Burnett's analysis demonstrates just how successful was the British government's attempt to regulate the food system and to protect the nutritional welfare of the population, despite the demands placed upon the state by the conduct of warfare on a global scale. While much of the bureaucratic apparatus of regulation was eventually to be dismantled (although it was some years after the end of the Second World War that the last food rationing measures were abolished), the ideological apparatus of intervention, once created, proved to be more enduring. However, in the intervening decades, the logic of intervention has undergone a number of very significant changes. For example, once direct state control could no longer be justified on the grounds of national emergency, more subtle forms of indirect intervention gradually came into play. In the post-war period an increasing emphasis has been placed upon the individual's responsibility to protect his or her own health through adopting the eating patterns and dietary choices congruent with current scientific orthodoxies concerning the links between diet and health. Hence, regulation and rationing have, in the longer term, been replaced by education and exhortation. What is more, dietary threats to health have been fundamentally reconceptualized. Food deprivation and serious nutritional deficiencies, historically two of the most widespread threats to human well-being, have been banished to the margins of public concern in most modern, developed societies. Currently, concern has become focused squarely upon the nutritional problems associated with affluence and over indulgence.

By 1983 professional and official consensus concerning the most pressing issues relating to diet and health had developed to a sufficient degree to permit the publication of specific dietary targets for the UK population. In that year the National Advisory Committee on Nutrition Education (NACNE) under the aegis of the Health Education Council, put forward proposals for a set of explicit nutritional guidelines. The Committee was particularly concerned with the effects on health, not only of actual obesity, but also of relatively mild levels of overweight, especially in relation to such ailments as coronary heart disease, high blood pressure, diabetes mellitus and gall bladder disease. Lack of exercise was cited as a contributory factor to the diseases associated with being over-weight, and recommendations concerning slimming diets and the control of food intake were also made (National Advisory Committee on Nutrition Education 1983: 10–14). The targets set by the Committee were detailed and explicitly quantified. They included recommended reductions in fat intake, in saturated fatty acid intake, in sucrose intake, in salt intake and in alcohol consumption, plus a rise in the intake of dietary fibre (see Figure 6.1).

---

i.   Fat intake should be reduced to an average 30% of total energy intake.

ii.   Saturated fatty acid intake should be reduced to an average 10% of total energy intake.

iii. Average sucrose intakes should be reduced to 20 kg per head per year.

iv. Salt intake should fall on average by 3g per head per day.

v.   Alcohol intake should decline to 4% of the total energy intake.

vi. Protein intake should not be altered, but a higher proportion of vegetable proteins is appropriate.

vii. Fibre intake should increase on average from 20g per head per day to 30g per head per day.

Figure 6.1 Selected long-term dietary aims for the UK population proposed by the National Commitee on Nutrition Education (NACNE)

Source: Adapted from National Advisoty Committee on Nutrition Education (1983)

The Committee went on to discuss a whole series of measures that would be involved in achieving such targets. These included not only education-based attempts to encourage individuals to modify their own diet, but also the selective breeding of leaner food animals, the reduction of fat content in meat products and the labelling of food products with energy, sugar and fat content.

Some eight years later, an independent, multidisciplinary committee noted that obesity in Britain was, in fact, increasing (Jacobson, Smith and Whitehead 1991: 44). The report reiterated the kinds of dietary targets that had been set by the Committee on Medical Aspects of Food Policy (COMA) which, in turn, were closely related to those proposed by NACNE (Jacobson, Smith and Whitehead 1991: 249). COMA's advice at that stage included a reduction of the amount of energy from total fats to 35 per cent or less of energy intake, reductions in sugar and salt consumption, and the replacement of fatty and sugary foods with cereals and starchy foods. The need to increase levels of exercise was also stressed, particularly in relation to what was seen as the role of exercise in the prevention of coronary heart disease and the maintenance of general health. *The Health of the Nation* white paper also recommended the setting up of the Nutrition Task Force, and this recommendation was carried out in 1992. Two years later the Nutrition Task Force itself published a detailed action plan to achieve the targets which had been set out (Department of Health 1994). The components of this action plan included proposals for schematic dietary models for conveying information to the public (e.g., in the form of plates or pyramids), liaison with the advertising industry in the promotion of approved dietary patterns, and extending the role of the educational system in disseminating official conceptions of healthy diets. The action plan also included proposals to recruit the support of the catering industry in achieving nutritional targets (e.g., hospital and school caterers, restaurants and fast food outlets). Indeed, the production, manufacturing and retailing sectors of the food industry were also to be drawn into the process, particularly in terms of undertaking an industry-wide 'fat audit' to examine the possibilities for reducing fat content across the whole product range. This whole strategy, it was suggested, should be supported by enhanced training for health professionals, nutritionists and dieticians, and by improved research into the relationship between nutritional factors and clinical outcomes.

This ambitious and far-reaching programme of nutritional intervention and persuasion provides a graphic demonstration of the extent to which the state has taken on a central role in shaping national dietary patterns with a view to improving overall health standards. However, what is arguably the most distinctive aspect of this process is the striking family resemblance between eighteenth-century conceptions of diet and health and the medically and scientifically informed targets and guidelines which form the basis of current thinking. The dietary prescriptions and proscriptions are decidedly similar, as are the emphases on the deleterious effects of excessive weight and low levels of physical exercise. However, as we have seen, Cheyne's criticisms, admonitions and treatments were aimed at high-status and relatively sedentary elite groups, and in his day had little relevance to the broader population. The emergence of the modern food system, and fundamental changes in work organization and activity levels, have been construed as requiring the degree of dietary restraint and control on the part of the whole population that was formerly seen as appropriate only to the privileged and overindulgent few. The mantle of George Cheyne, successful nutritional and medical moral entrepreneur, has been assumed by an expanding army of professionals, bureaucrats and politicians, who increasingly claim ownership of what can be regarded as nutritional wisdom and acceptable dietary practice. However, whereas Cheyne was a physician, in direct contact with his patients and tailoring his therapeutic recommendations to what he perceived to be their specific needs, the current role of the state is an essentially impersonal one. Quantified nutritional objectives have been established for the entire population, yet the translation of such objectives into dietary choices and practices at the individual level remains problematic. For example, while it may make sense to recommend that no more than 35 per cent of energy should be derived from fats as a long-term aim for the population as a whole, such a recommendation is of little relevance to the day-to-day decisions of the individual consumer, who is not equipped to monitor food intake in this quantified fashion. There are clearly limits to the application of rational, systematic conceptualization of the links between diet and health to the mundane routines of everyday life.

Further dimensions are added to our understanding of the modern rationalization of diet by Levenstein's account of the evolution of nutritional theory and nutritional policy in the USA. In the last two decades of the nineteenth century, for example, an ambitious attempt was made to rationalize the eating patterns of the poor in order to improve their nutritional standards while actually reducing the amount spent on food. A Boston businessman, Edward Atkinson, taking up recent developments in scientific knowledge concerning the nature of human nutritional requirements propounded by the chemist Wilbur Atwater, put forward the argument that those on low incomes could achieve greater 'nutritional efficiency' by avoiding the consumption of expensive food items selected merely on the basis of taste or prestige. Instead, he argued, they should consume cheaper items (e.g., less expensive cuts of meat) which, though less prestigious, nevertheless provided an equivalent input of nutrients for the body (Levenstein 1988: 45–8). In co-operation with a nutritionist and a chemist (both women) Atkinson was instrumental in setting up public kitchens to demonstrate to the working classes the benefits of selecting foods on the grounds of nutrient content and value for money, and of preparing these foods in a fuel-saving, slow-cooking oven of his own invention. However, despite some initial success in Boston and New York, the quaintly named 'New England Kitchen' culinary regime had little impact on the eating patterns of the American working classes, which was probably just as well, given its heavy emphasis on the consumption of animal fat, and its serious vitamin deficiencies, the significance of which was not understood at the time (Levenstein 1988: 57–8).

In fact, the proponents of the New England Kitchen concept were soon to shift their attention towards the middle and upper classes, on the assumption that good nutritional practices, once entrenched in the upper reaches of society, would eventually 'trickle down' to the lower orders. At the same time, 'home economics' and 'domestic science' were undergoing a process of professionalization, involving their inclusion in programmes at the University of Wisconsin in 1895 and subsequently at the University of Illinois. What is more, the teaching of these subjects in schools shifted away from an exclusive emphasis on cooking skills towards the physiology and chemistry of food and eating. Thus, by the early twentieth century large numbers of young American women who had graduated from the public school system had absorbed at the least the rudiments of the rational scientific view of human nutrition (Levenstein 1988: 79–80). It is Levenstein's contention that American middle-class women were able to use these ideas to rationalize and simplify domestic cuisine in order to reduce the burden of food-related work in a situation in which domestic servants were becoming increasingly difficult to acquire and retain.

As in Britain, but to a lesser extent, the First World War acted as a catalyst which stimulated government intervention in the food system of the United States. Food prices, already on an upward trend, rose sharply in 1916, partly due to the demands of the Allies actually involved in the war, and there were foot riots in some eastern cities (Levenstein 1988: 109). With America's entry into the war imminent, the Food Administration was set up (headed by Herbert Hoover). Its task was to seek to regulate the food supply and to encourage Americans to reduce food wastage and to cut down on their consumption of meat, white wheat flour, sugar and butter, substituting more readily available items like beans, pulses, cornmeal, oats, lard and vegetable oil. Levenstein notes the similarity between these ideas of substitution and those of the nutritionists who had already sought to rationalize the diets of the poor. The Food Administration harnessed the ideas of the home economists and embraced the scientific approach to nutrition as a means of putting the American diet on a war footing. While it seems clear that these exhortations had little effect on the mass of the American population (for example, beef consumption actually rose in 1917 to above pre-war levels) the more affluent classes did appear to have reduced their food consumption. What is more, in the interests of sound nutrition and the avoidance of waste, the War Department, in 1916, issued a new manual for army cooks based upon the new nutritional principles, and dieticians were recruited to oversee food provision in army hospitals. In this way, Levenstein argues, through the experience of military service, large numbers of American men were exposed to rationalized and simplified diets (Levenstein 1988: 145–6).

However, in the decades after the First World War, discoveries in the new science of nutrition led to an increasing emphasis on the role of vitamins and minerals in the diet. These innovations in nutritional knowledge were enthusiastically taken up by large food processing firms eager to promote their products using the latest scientific ideas, aiming at a public ever more susceptible to rationalized conceptions of food quality and suitability (Levenstein 1988: 152–3). The impact of the Second World War also appears to have been a significant one. Levenstein points out that dieticians played an even greater part in the rationalization of the feeding of the armed forces than in the First World War. The Institute of Medicine's Food and Nutrition Board created generous dietary standards for the population, and food shortages, while never as severe as had been expected, were managed through direct state intervention in the form of rationing and price controls. The standards set down by the Food and Nutrition

Board were first established in 1941, and took the form of Recommended Dietary Allowances (RDAs), these being defined as the level of intake of essential nutrients adequate to meet the nutritional needs of healthy individuals, as currently understood. The first edition of these standards was published in 1943, and by 1989 the publication had reached its tenth edition, these regular revisions reflecting the constant elaboration and extension of scientific nutritional knowledge in the intervening decades. Drawing upon a truly impressive range of scientific research, the tenth edition lays down detailed, updated recommendations concerning energy intake, protein allowances, and the intake of such vitamins as K, C, B_6 and B_{12}. It also covers changes in the RDAs for such minerals as calcium, magnesium, iron, zinc and selenium, and changes in scientific views on estimated safe and adequate intakes of such substances as copper, manganese and molybdenum. The central role played by the RDA concept in the scientific and medical rationalization of nutritional ideas and practices is demonstrated by an extract from the tenth edition itself:

> Over the years, RDAs have become widely known and applied. They are typically used for planning and procuring food supplies for population subgroups, for interpreting food consumption records of individuals and populations, for establishing standards for food assistance programs, for evaluating the adequacy of food supplies in meeting national nutritional needs, for designing nutrition education programs, and for developing new products in industry.
>
> (National Research Council 1989: 8)

In addition to the RDAs, the Food and Nutrition Board has also set out a series of dietary guidelines or targets for the American population. These are broadly comparable to those which have been laid down for the population of the UK and reflect similar scientific and medical views concerning the links between diet and health, and the prevention of specific illnesses. These targets (expressed in terms of individual diets) include the reduction of total fat intake to 30 per cent or less of total calories consumed, the daily consumption of five or more servings of fruit and vegetables, the moderation of protein intake levels, the balancing of food intake with physical activity level, the limiting of sodium intake and the maintenance of adequate calcium consumption (see Figure 6.2 and compare Figure 6.1).

As well as setting these targets, the Food and Nutrition Board provides a highly detailed set of recommendations about how they might be attained in everyday settings by real individuals making real food choices. The advice provided ranges from the selection of low-fat meat to the use of lemon juice and salt-free seasonings to reduce sodium consumption (Thomas 1991: 84–109).

As has been suggested earlier in this chapter, there can be no doubt that the rationalization of conceptions of diet and health has been associated with the professionalization of nutritional science and dietetics. Riska (1993), in outlining

140

i. Reduce total fat intake to 30% or less of calories. Reduce saturated fatty acid intake to less than 10% of calories and the intake of cholesterol to less than 300 mg daily.
ii. Eat five or more daily servings of a combination of vegetables and fruits. Also, more daily servings of a combination of breads, cereals and legumes. Increase carbohydrate intake to more than 55% of total energy.
iii. Maintain protein intake at moderate levels.
iv. Balance food intake and physical activity to maintain appropriate body weight.
v. Limit alcohol consumption to the equivalent of less than one ounce of pure alcohol per day.
vi. Maintain adequate calcium intake.
vii. Avoid taking dietary supplements in excess of the RDAs in any one day.
viii. Maintain an optimal intake of fluoride.

Figure 6.2   Dietary guidelines for North Americans from age 2
Source: Adapted from Thomas (1991)

this process of professionalization in the USA, shows how women largely succeeded in capturing this area for their own. She points out the central role played by women in the health reform movement in the latter part of the nineteenth century, with its strong emphasis on hygiene and a nutritious diet. At the same time, middle-class women in America were increasingly infiltrating the sciences and the professions, although they were mainly channelled into 'female' areas like home economics and domestic science, and women physicians were concerned primarily with the care of women and children. This form of professional separatism, Riska argues, led to the development of separate institutions, and the American Dietetic Association founded in 1917 was dominated by women. However, from the Second World War onwards, nutritional science as an area of study has been largely male dominated (see e.g., Copping 1985). On the other hand, women have retained their dominance in the dietetics profession, which has been incorporated into the health care system. The professionalization of dietetics was enhanced when in 1969 the American Dietetic Association instituted the credential 'registered dietician', and this licence is currently held by approximately 60,000 practitioners (Riska 1993: 175). The processes of social closure and collective upward mobility promoted by professionalization have also been enhanced by a drive towards increased specialization within dietetics itself. However, the profession as a whole remains one of relatively low status and remuneration, largely subordinate within the health care system to a medical establishment which is still male-dominated. Indeed, Riska highlights a fundamental dilemma for dieticians. In stressing the medical importance of diet, that is, in 'medicalizing' food choice and nutritional practice, dieticians reinforce their own claims to professional status. At the same time, however, this strategy seems to guarantee continuing subordination to the medical profession, which jealously guards its exclusive title to medical diagnosis and treatment.

In this section we have seen how the rationalization, and indeed the medicalization, of diet was initially a process aimed at a relatively inactive and 'overfed' elite. Eventually, however, the political and social establishment in both Britain and America chose to concern itself more and more with the nutritional standards of the poor and the underprivileged. In both countries, reformers, nutritional moral entrepreneurs and the state itself, employing the increasingly sophisticated knowledge made available by a rapidly developing science of nutrition, sought to lay down adequate nutritional standards and to intervene in the dietary affairs of groups perceived as disadvantaged and nutritionally vulnerable. Such intervention took many forms, from attempts at exhortation and education to rationing, subsidies and the provision of free foods and supplements. In recent decades, a distinct shift of emphasis has become obvious, as concern has switched away from a preoccupation with nutritional deficiencies to a preoccupation with the implications of the overconsumption of certain nutrients and food items. Thus, contemporary official guidelines and targets are not so much aimed at bringing standards up to specified levels as at encouraging the reduction of the intake of specific nutrients to below what are seen as desirable upper limits. Thus, in a sense, the controls on food intake that characterized George Cheyne's recipes for the dietary chastening of the privileged have been generalized for whole populations, for whom overindulgence rather than deprivation is seen as the main problem.

Of course, the whole process of rationalization has been facilitated by key professions, not only medical practitioners and physicians, but also scientists, nutritionists and dieticians. In a sociological sense, it is perhaps not surprising that dietetics as an occupation has developed as an essentially feminine profession, which can be seen as an extension of customary assumptions about women's domestic duties, obligations and competences into the public domain.

CONTEMPORARY COMMON-SENSE IDEAS AND ALTERNATIVE IDEOLOGIES

There can be little doubt that rationalized and medicalized models of the links between diet and health have come to exert enormous influence over public perceptions. However, although public awareness of official dietary guidelines is increasing, such awareness is sometimes confused and lacking in clarity, for example, in relation to fat, a group of nutrients which has certainly figured particularly prominently in current nutritional messages (Thomas 1991: 48–9). Indeed, guidelines and targets expressed in scientific and quantitative terms may be extremely difficult for members of the public to interpret, and even more difficult to translate into informed choices and everyday decisions at the supermarket or in the kitchen. In effect, rationalized views of diet may lack some of the intuitive comprehensibility of more traditional ideas, and thus it is hardly surprising that common-sense notions survive and continue to shape nutritional ideologies and practices in modern Western societies. These notions come in many guises and range from claims that excessive sugar consumption causes diabetes, that red meat causes aggressiveness and that eating fried food causes acne, to beliefs in the medicinal properties of substances like honey and garlic. Some of these ideas do appear to find some support from current medical and scientific knowledge, whereas others are inconsistent with, or actually contradict, orthodox scientific views (Rinzler 1991). Happily, there exist several sociological studies which can provide us with direct insights into the contents and logic of such common-sense ideas and their relationship in everyday life to more rationalized and systematic forms of knowledge.

Inevitably, there is likely to be a good deal of variation from individual to individual and from household to household in exposure to and reliance upon rationalized conceptions of diet as opposed to 'folk' or lay conceptions. Pill (1983) set out to examine working-class mothers' views on food and health by studying a sample of forty-one women from South Wales, all aged between 30 and 35, living with their husband and at least one primary-school-age child. In fact, Pill uncovered a clear distinction between what she termed the 'lifestyle' group and the 'fatalist' group. The former tended to see illness as caused by environmental and lifestyle factors. Thus, by implication, health and resistance to disease could be enhanced by making the correct lifestyle choices. On the other hand, the fatalists tended to see illness as caused by factors over which the individual had little or no control, and resistance to disease as an unchangeable personal characteristic, determined largely by heredity. Not surprisingly, these two groups held sharply contrasting views on the relationship between diet and health. Members of the lifestyle group were much more likely to mention foods that they avoided for health reasons (e.g., foods with a high sugar content) and foods they deliberately selected for health reasons (e.g., wholemeal bread). These mothers also appeared to be attempting to plan and control their family's diet explicitly in order to improve its members resistance to disease. In contrast, the fatalist mothers were much less likely to mention specific health-oriented avoidances and selections. While both groups emphasized the value of fresh food, the fatalists stressed taste as the main advantage whereas the lifestyle mothers tended to mention the importance of vitamin content and the perceived health dangers of processed foods. However, the defining characteristic of the fatalist mothers' view on food and health was the emphasis they placed upon the traditional 'cooked dinner' as the epitome of good food and the source of nutritional well-being. The customary combination of roast meat, gravy, potatoes and vegetables clearly retained a powerful symbolic significance for this group of respondents (Pill 1983: 122–4).

It is a plausible hypothesis that adherence to the concept of the 'cooked dinner' as a basis for good health is related to respondents' age. It would seem likely that older respondents would be more attached to long-established common-sense views of diet and health than would their younger counterparts.

Some supporting evidence for this contention is to be found in a study of fifty-eight three-generation families carried out in a Scottish city (Blaxter and Paterson 1983). Amongst the two generations of working-class women studied, the authors did indeed uncover a powerfully nostalgic attachment on the part of the older women to the 'good' food of the past. For them 'goodness' was equated with simple and natural foods, prepared in basic, uncomplicated ways (boiling or baking, for example). Meat and vegetables were seen as essentials, and slow cooking (boiling meat and vegetables together) was seen as a process which could, in effect, distil the very essence of goodness (Blaxter and Paterson 1983: 97). The very opposite of 'good' food was food which has been manufactured or processed, food which replaced 'proper' meals: snacks, sweets and biscuits. Indeed, almost any food item, except fruit, eaten outside the context of the proper meal, was classed as 'rubbish' in health terms. In contrast, the younger generation of women was actually less likely than the older to mention food when asked, for example, about how children's health could be protected. Fewer mentioned the proper meal as the basis of healthy eating, and those who did were noticeably less enthusiastic than their elders.

The importance of such symbolic considerations in common-sense conceptions of diet and health is demonstrated even more clearly by a study which included an analysis of French mothers' views concerning children's health and nutritional needs (Fischler 1986). The study was based upon semi-structured interviews with a sample of 161 mothers with children aged from 4 to 14, drawn from six socioeconomic categories and various regions of France. Fischler concludes that, for these mothers, the feeding of children is, in fact, a highly 'medicalized' issue. In the course of interviews, respondents were at pains to exhibit their knowledge of the technical terminology of nutritional science and, indeed, a rudimentary familiarity with the basics of rationalized concepts of health and nutrition was perceived by these interviewees as an indispensable requirement for the responsible and competent mother (Fischler 1986: 948). However, Fischler, despite the fact that he finds the medicalization of lay discourses on diet and health unsurprising, goes on to pose a crucial question: 'Just what do these mothers know about the science of nutrition, and just what are the contents of their own ideas?' In fact, what Fischler uncovers is a series of themes, but these are sometimes not quite what they seem. For example, the desire to limit children's sugar intake appeared to be as much about preventing the child from subverting the parent's dietary authority by 'nibbling', as about preventing tooth decay. Starches were seen by many as implicated in obesity (Fischler 1986: 953) and therefore to be limited in children's diets, and fats invoked a good deal of disapproval, but for reasons little connected with nutritional science.

Yet, the most striking aspect of these mothers' views on children's nutritional needs is the concept that was mentioned more frequently than any other: the notion of 'balance'. The idea of a balanced diet was clearly gleaned from professional discourses on nutrition, but many of the respondents' nutritional ideas showed significant discrepancies in relation to current medical views. As suggested above, starch was given largely negative connotations (a contradiction of contemporary medical evaluations) and ideas relating to fat and fat intake did not necessarily coincide with the current medical orthodoxy. In fact, Fischler claims, the concept of dietary balance, although often discussed by respondents in nutritional terms, is a pre-scientific as well as a scientific concept. The idea of achieving an 'equilibrium' in terms of food intake is a feature of many forms of traditional medicine, and has an ancient pedigree. What is more, balance is an open-ended, self-justifying concept, and can mean quite different things to different respondents. In common-sense thought, it goes beyond merely technical considerations. As Fischler puts it:

> However, for the greater number of respondents, a true dietetic balance seemed to result from equilibria of another nature, i.e., as it were, of a moral order. Balance, in more than one way, could indeed be viewed as an almost ethical requirement. What must be balanced, the interviewees believed, was pleasure and health, gratification and duty, appetite and reason.
>
> (Fischler 1986: 961)

Thus, the need for balance in contemporary common-sense thought is seen as deeply rooted in traditional ideas and as expressing the fusion of what Fischler sees as 'modern' and 'archaic' symbolic demands. Evidence for the universal appeal of this concept of balance is provided by a study carried out in a context very different from that discussed by Fischler. In the course of a long-term analysis of African-American folk beliefs concerning health and illness, Snow (1993) notes a recurring theme of balance and moderation in food intake as a means of preventing ill health. Snow's respondents also laid stress on the idea that not only could overindulgence and eating the 'wrong' foods induce illness, but that even 'good' foods could be hazardous if eaten in the 'wrong' context. For example, foods suitable for fit adults might be too 'strong' for children, invalids and the elderly. What is more, good foods might pose a threat to health if eaten in the wrong combinations. The author came across respondents living in Michigan who reiterated traditional beliefs from the South, such as the idea that eating fish and drinking milk at the same meal is dangerous, and that one should never consume whisky and watermelon together for fear of a potentially fatal toxic reaction (Snow 1993: 78). What is more, there is also evidence for the survival of beliefs concerning sorcery and witchcraft in relation to food, with one respondent describing the way in which magically doctored food could pose a very real hazard to the intended victim (Snow 1993: 79). However, certainly the central theme running through these beliefs is the idea that diet influences health through the effects that it has on the blood. The basis of good health is seen as 'good blood' (Snow 1993: 95–113). A balanced food intake is viewed as crucial, in that certain foods are seen as having the effect of changing the actual composition of the blood, making it too 'thick', too 'thin' or too 'acid'. Thus, it is vital for the individual always to be aware that one's dietary choices will have a direct impact upon the blood and hence upon one's state of health.

Folk beliefs of this kind can often form a backdrop to the mundane routines of everyday life and act as a set of taken-for-granted assumptions about the relationship between food intake and bodily well-being. As such, they may require deliberate probing by the social scientist to bring them to light and to render them intelligible. On the other hand, lay or non-medical perspectives on the links between diet and health can also develop into much more elaborate and explicit conceptualizations, which are not simply the vestiges of a folk tradition but which enter into the public domain and attract public attention in their own right. Perhaps the best example of such conceptualizations are the ideas behind what are widely known as 'health foods'. From the point of view of the sociologist, one of the problems involved in explaining such ideas is their very diversity. However, a study by Kandel and Pelto (1980) of what they term the 'health food movement' in the USA provides a clear and convincing analysis of the underlying features which underpin the surface variations in the contents of these beliefs. Kandel and Pelto carried out their study in the Boston area and at a rural university centre, using a battery of techniques including survey methods, 24-hour recall diet histories and participant observation.

On the basis of their results, the authors conclude that the beliefs and practices they studied had two significant aspects. The first of these is what they term 'social revitalization', a process through which a cult or movement provides its followers with the means radically to restructure their cultural affiliations and ideological postures in order to lead a more satisfying way of life. The ideologies of these revitalization cults may include metaphysical as well as dietary tenets (Kandel and Pelto 1980: 337). Secondly, these beliefs may constitute what the authors call an 'alternative health maintenance system', a system which is seen by its adherents as a viable alternative to modern medicine, which may be characterized as fragmented and unable to adopt a holistic approach to the individual, and preoccupied with the treatment of disease rather than its prevention. The alternative view of health maintenance sees food choice as one of the most direct and practical ways an individual can influence his or her health standing. In fact, the authors identify three recurring themes which run through the dietary ideologies of these alternative systems. The *vitamin motif* often uses a terminology similar to that employed in the technical discourses of nutritionists, but participants may believe certain nutrients are required in very large amounts (e.g. massive supplementary doses of certain vitamins or minerals daily). The *organic motif* places a high value on what are seen as the health-giving properties of 'organic' or 'natural' foods, which have been subjected to a minimum of human interference and processing. Stress is laid upon what are perceived as the harmful effects ascribed to 'synthetic' foods, whose production may involve, for example, artificial fertilizers, additives, colourings and preservatives. Finally, the *mystical motif* represents food selection according to the symbolic rather than the nutritional properties of foods. For example, 'life

146

energy' may be seen as inherent in raw vegetable foods, or foods may be selected explicitly to achieve a mystical balance, as in the balancing of positive and negative forces (*yin* and *yang*) in the macrobiotic dietary system.

The authors go on to describe the complex social networks which make up the broad health food movement, with their different cults and their different levels of participation, including the largely independent followers, the peripheral social members and the committed full 'joiners' (Kandel and Pelto 1980: 339). In addition to these fluid categories of membership, there are many styles of leadership and many channels of communication (ranging from books, articles and television to face-to-face channels like lecture tours and word of mouth spread through friendship networks, health food outlets, etc.).

The clear implication of the arguments put forward by Kandel and Pelto is that the potent symbolism inherent in the very idea of health foods represents a challenge to more orthodox modes of conceptualizing human health, and, indeed, the relationship between the 'cultural' and the 'natural'. This notion is taken up and developed by Atkinson (1980), who points out that health food use often takes place in the context of broader 'alternative' and unorthodox movements and ideologies (particularly alternative views of science and medicine). In the health sphere, such ideologies may include acupuncture, herbalism, faith healing, popularized forms of psychotherapy, and so on. These forms of belief frequently depend upon challenges to conventional divisions like mind/body and human/non human. A crucial feature of such thinking is the ubiquitous emphasis on 'naturalness' also noted by Kandel and Pelto. Modern life is seen as antithetical to 'balance', and modern foods are seen as overprocessed, contaminated and nutrient-deficient. In contrast, health foods offer naturalness, and explicitly appeal to tradition and folk wisdom. The emphasis laid upon avoiding foods which have undergone elaborate transformations and manufacturing represents a desire to benefit from the perceived virtues of 'pure' food. By implication, pure and natural foods offer a counterbalance to what are seen as the destructive, stressful and unhealthy features of modern lifestyles. Atkinson argues quite explicitly that such ideas are closely related to pre-scientific modes of thought, and summarizes the symbolic significance of health foods in the following terms:

> They convey the message that ills are created by the particular characteristics of modern living, specifically by virtue of a fracture between the realms of Nature and Culture. Hence health foods provide a concrete resolution of this separation. Therein lies their symbolic power.
>
> (Atkinson 1980: 87)

However, despite the fact that health foods promise benefits by putting the consumer back into contact with a more 'natural' way of life, there can be a subtle irony at work here. For example, in an earlier paper Atkinson provides a fascinating account of the way in which certain features of the folk medicine of rural Vermont were taken up and propounded in the 1960s by a medical practitioner, D. C. Jarvis (Atkinson 1979). Jarvis was concerned to promote the alleged health-giving properties of a traditional blend of honey and vinegar. Despite a negative reaction in several medical journals and an investigation by the Food and Drugs Administration, both Jarvis's books, and the commercial version of this preparation (under the brand name 'Honegar'), sold well. In effect, Atkinson demonstrates how folk beliefs can be rediscovered and packaged for sale to a public eager to benefit from customary wisdom. What is more, commercial appropriation of concepts of 'naturalness' and 'tradition' in relation to foodstuffs, and their health implications, can take place on a large scale. Thus, health foods themselves are increasingly mass-produced while still being marketed on the basis of an appeal to naturalness. What is more, in the marketing of a much broader range of foods (and, particularly in the UK, beverages like beer) manufacturers and retailers increasingly use the rhetoric of tradition and of rural life to enhance the appeal of their merchandise (Atkinson 1983: 15–16). Attached to food products, such terms as 'farmhouse', 'granary', old-fashioned', 'dairy', 'heritage', 'natural' and 'traditional', all serve to evoke a connection with what is seen as an older and less synthetic way of life. Yet, the irony is that elements of common-sense beliefs concerning food and health have been taken over and recycled in the pursuit of profitability by a highly rationalized and industrialized commercial food production and distribution system.

In fact, Belasco (1993) makes the bold claim that, from the 1960s onwards in the USA, the health food movement, as a form of radical consumerism, represented a kind of 'counter-cuisine'. He sees the challenge that it presented to the orthodox food system, dominated by the great food producing, processing and retailing corporations, as central to the broader challenge mounted by the 'counter-culture' to some of American society's most basic assumptions and institutions. Yet, what had begun as a challenge to the commercial food system turned out to be a golden marketing opportunity. Through a process of 'nutrification' (Belasco 1993: 218) food manufacturers could add back the nutrients lost through processing and charge a premium for the new product. Yet, despite this process of incorporation and attempts by the food industry to contradict the claims of the 'counter-cuisine', Belasco contends that it has had a significant impact on American attitudes to food and health.

OVERVIEW

As we have sought to demonstrate in this chapter, the intimate and intricate connections between one's eating patterns and one's state of health are an enduring focus of human concern. Modern societies have witnessed a fundamental and far-reaching transformation in the ways in which these concerns are conceptualized. Traditional beliefs, while rich in detail and highly ingenious and imaginative in the causal mechanisms they postulate, are essentially straightforward in their underlying logical structure. They offer plausible ways of explaining events and experiences relating to health and illness which might otherwise be perceived as driven by arbitrary and capricious forces, largely beyond the reach of human intervention. What is more, these explanations can be readily understood by any competent adult because of the nature of their basic structure. Although specialist healers (individuals perceived as gifted with special powers and insights) may be consulted, by and large the patient will be conversant with the reasoning behind the treatments being used. The manipulation of diet represents a response to illness (or the threat of potential illness) which is clearly within the realm of the individual's own control. Whatever else they offer, traditional conceptions of diet and health can provide a reassuring sense that the individual has access to remedies which are, in both a practical and an intellectual sense, readily within his or her own reach.

However, the rationalization and medicalization of diet and health issues has brought about a significant change in this connection. There can be no doubt that, in a technical sense, modern scientific formulations of the physiological mechanisms which articulate the links between diet and health, offer great explanatory power and theoretical sophistication. But, by their very nature, such formulations have become the intellectual property of specialized and highly trained professionals: medical practitioners and researchers, physiologists, nutritionists and dieticians. As such, they are not readily within the reach of the average member of the public, whose grasp of them will be at best partial and selective and at worst confused. Yet the rationalization of diet has seen professional groups, and the state itself, progressively claim ever more authority over nutritional knowledge and over dietary choices, in so far as these affect both short- and long-term health outcomes. Recommendations concerning the restraint of the appetite for certain foodstuffs, originally relevant only to the eating habits of a privileged minority, have now been generalized to entire populations in societies like the USA. and the UK.

Yet the public's response to the nutritional pronouncements of the 'authorities' (in the widest sense of that term) has often been uneven and inconsistent. Common-sense conceptions clearly continue to play a central role in the public's views on diet and health. What is more, as we have seen, 'alternative' frameworks of explanation, in the form of what might loosely be termed the 'health food movement', have emerged and established themselves as offering versions of the 'rational menu' which, within a climate of menu pluralism, can attempt to compete with or complement orthodox perspectives. Certainly, a good measure of the appeal of the health food approach is related to a characteristic it shares with traditional modes of belief: its promise to provide individuals with a sense that they can influence their own health for the better by means of choices and practices which they feel they personally can control and comprehend.

149

7

FOOD RISKS, ANXIETIES AND SCARES

The risks and anxieties associated with eating in modern Western societies need to be placed both in economic and historical context. Quite clearly, for large numbers of people in the contemporary world the overriding anxiety relating to food emerges out of a concern that now or in the future one simply will not be able to get enough food to remain healthy and active or, for that matter, alive. Similarly, even in Europe, we do not need to reach very far back into history to come across situations in which food shortages affected the lives of millions of individuals. The Second World War, for example, saw widespread food shortages in continental Europe, although they were often unevenly distributed in geographical and social terms. Indeed, in some instances, large numbers starved, or were starved, to death. As we have already seen, low nutritional standards and inadequate food intake were common in the lower orders of British society in the nineteenth century. Indeed, Mennell (1985: 27) argues that centuries of recurrent famine have left their mark upon the European mind, with such themes as starvation and cannibalism woven into the very fabric of European folklore.

Risks other than shortage have long threatened the food consumer. The contamination of food with naturally occurring micro-organisms and toxins has always posed threats to human health, all the more disturbing when the underlying mechanisms were not understood. Perhaps one of the most chilling and bizarre manifestations of such contamination is the illness known as ergotism. Ergot is a fungal disease which affects cereals, the grain becoming infested with the spore-bearing bodies of the fungus. Rye is particularly susceptible to this fungus, and if the grain is badly affected cooking may not neutralize the toxic effects, rendering bread baked with the affected flour highly dangerous. The symptoms of ergotism include either burning pains and gangrene in the limbs, or itching skin and convulsions, hence the names 'Holy Fire' or 'St Anthony's Fire' given to the disease. An outbreak in the Rhine valley in AD 857 is thought to have caused literally thousands of deaths (Tannahill 1988: 101). The disease occurred all over Europe throughout the Middle Ages, causing intense suffering, insanity and death. Its actual cause was not discovered until 1670, when a French country physician, a Dr Thuillier, after years of patient study of the affliction, deduced its connection with the rye bread which was the staple of rural peasant families (Carefoot and Sprott 1969: 19–21). However, it was not until 1853 that the fungus parasite itself was identified and its connection with disease finally proven.

Yet, if in the past the presence of natural contaminants and infections could pose a threat to the food consumer's well-being and peace of mind, so too could the presence of deliberately introduced substances in food placed there for fraudulent purposes. As Burnett (1989: 86) reminds us, food adulteration has a long history, but the increasing industrialization and urbanization of society meant that from the late eighteenth century onwards food adulteration became increasingly feasible, profitable and widespread. The work of the chemist Frederick Accum, published in 1820, revealed the diversity and the seriousness of the abuses taking place, including the use of copper to colour pickles green, the use of sulphuric acid to 'age' beer, the use of verdigris to give a green bloom to dried hedgerow leaves passed off as tea, and the use of red lead to colour the rind of cheese. Such adulterations were not only an assault on the consumer's purse, but on his or her long term health. Later in the nineteeth century a voluminous treatise running to nearly 900 pages (Hassall 1876) detailed the adulteration, often with hazardous substances, of a wide range of everyday foodstuffs, including tea, coffee, cocoa, sugar, honey, bread, flour, milk, butter, cheese, lard, potted meat, preserves, mustard, vinegar and spices.

Currently, of course, the kinds of food hazard discussed above no longer appear to menace the consumer in quite such a direct way. Life-threatening food shortage or starvation are pressing concerns for few, if any, individuals in most modern societies. Advances in medicine and the biological sciences have provided the means to comprehend and avoid the deleterious effects of microbial contamination. In relation to deliberate adulteration, the state has increasingly taken upon itself the task of creating a legislative framework to ensure the purity of food (Paulus 1974). Indeed, there now exist substantial bodies of legislation in countries like the UK and the USA governing such aspects of food processing as additives, contaminants, packaging, labelling and hygiene (Jukes 1993). Yet, perhaps ironically, despite these undoubted advances in food safety, food-related anxieties persist, sometimes in a decidedly disturbing form. It may even be the case that once many of the traditionally most threatening food risks have retreated into the background, other, subtler anxieties, perhaps previously masked and relatively low in visibility, have become more prominent and have thereby gained more public attention. The aim of this chapter is to analyse such anxieties and to attempt to uncover some of the mechanisms which generate and sustain them. In order to achieve this aim, we will first need to consider the fact that the very act of eating can be charged with ambivalence, and then go on to examine customary modes of coping with the anxieties such ambivalence may produce. It will then be argued that these customary modes of managing food-related anxieties may be breaking down, a breakdown which has given rise to both acute and chronic effects on consumers' food choices and attitudes. Whether new modes of sustaining food confidence and alleviating anxiety are, in fact, emerging is a question which will also be addressed.

THE DIMENSIONS OF FOOD AMBIVALENCE AND THEIR ASSOCIATED ANXIETIES

In Chapter 3 we encountered the concept of the omnivore's paradox. This paradox, it will be recalled, emerges out of the fact that all omnivores (and this includes, of course, the human omnivore) experience the opposing pulls of *neophilia* (the inclination to sample novel food items) and *neophobia* (caution when confronted with novel items, based on the possibility that they may be harmful). All omnivores must find ways of coping with this paradoxical juxtaposition of attraction and repulsion. Thus, for the omnivore, eating is a profoundly ambivalent activity, as is the individual's relationship to food itself. However, for the human omnivore, eating with the mind as much as with the mouth, immersed in the symbolic nuances of food, this ambivalence has many more dimensions than the basic tension between neophilia and neophobia. In a study of vegetarianism, the present authors identified three additional paradoxes which can be seen as generating ambivalence for the food consumer (Beardsworth and Keil 1992a), and these can be used as examples in order to develop the argument. Each of the three paradoxes consists of an opposition between a positively valued and a negatively valued feature of food (see Table 7.1).

Table 7.1   The paradoxical nature of food

Positive	Negative
1. Food provides gustatory pleasure, satiety, etc.	Food can produce gustatory displeasure, dyspepsia, nausea, vomiting.
2. Food is required for vigour, energy and health.	Food can introduce illness or disease.
3. Food is required for the continuation of life.	Food entails the death of the organisms consumed.

Source: Adapted from Beardsworth and Keil (1992a)

Paradox 1 (what might be termed the pleasure/displeasure paradox) refers to the fact that while food can provide gustatory gratification and a welcome sense of fullness and satisfaction, it can also produce sensations and reactions ranging from mildly unpleasant to severely distressing. The anxieties associated with these negative possibilities are largely self-evident. For example, there is the fear of encountering unpalatable flavours or textures, as well as the fear of experiencing digestive distress, in the form of sensations of 'bloatedness' or nausea. Concerns about such unwelcome effects are likely to be particularly prominent when the individual encounters a novel food item, and such concerns represent an important component of neophobia. Indeed, disgust when encountering novel food items may, in certain circumstances, represent an important safeguard against biological hazards, even though its origins may be largely cultural (Fischler 1988: 282–4). In addition to these anxieties about effects which may be felt by the eater himself or herself, there may be fears about potential effects of food intake which may be disapproved of by others (for example, short-term effects like flatulence and belching, and long-term effects like weight gain, regarded as cosmetically undesirable).

Paradox 2 (the health/illness paradox) is based upon the fact that, while food is the source of physical energy and can be conceived of as the foundation of vitality and health, it is also recognized as having the potential to introduce disease-inducing substances or organisms into the body. As has been argued in the previous chapter, the issue of the ways in which the connections between diet and health are conceptualized is a complex one. However, it is clear that this paradox can give rise to anxieties about acute effects (e.g., rapidly acting toxins and infections) and chronic effects (e.g., slow-acting toxins, disease-causing agents or long-term nutrient deficiencies).

Paradox 3 (the life/death paradox) emerges out of the fact that, while the consumption of food is absolutely essential for the maintenance of life, the act of eating usually entails the death and dissolution of other organisms. There are, of course, some qualified exceptions to this general rule. Fruits can be consumed without the destruction of the donor plant, and cereals are derived from plants that in any case have an annual life cycle. Nevertheless, fruits, seeds and vegetables are living organisms. There are also some animal secretions which can be used for food without necessarily entailing the killing of the donor animal itself. Two significant examples are milk and honey. Some pastoralist peoples also use blood from their livestock as a source of nutrients, opening a blood vessel to draw off the required quantity, thus obviating the need to slaughter the animal. However, although the use of such animal products does not directly involve the taking of life, it is usually based upon a regime of husbandry of which this is an integral part. For example, aged or unproductive dairy cows are slaughtered and eaten, as are the male offspring of dairy herds.

Typically, the consumption of plants and plant products gives rise to little or no concern, since plants are generally not regarded as sentient organisms. Animals, however, are an altogether different matter, and paradox 3 may generate a whole range of anxieties related to ethical concerns about inflicting suffering and death upon food animals. This is not to argue that all animals are likely to stimulate the same level of ethical interest, since there is clearly a distinct 'hierarchy of sympathy'. Invertebrates of all kinds are obviously very near the bottom of this hierarchy, with 'cold-blooded' vertebrates a step up the ladder. At the top of the hierarchy are 'warm-blooded' vertebrates, particularly large mammals, with their perceived proximity to the human species.

TRADITIONAL MODES OF COPING WITH FOOD AMBIVALENCE AND ANXIETY

Coping with or managing the anxieties generated by the kinds of food paradox discussed in the previous section is not a process which goes on merely at the individual level. Rather, solutions and coping strategies must emerge and be sustained at the cultural level, and thus be available as ready-made social constructs upon which the individual can rely to make sense of his or her experiences and to produce a feeling of ease and confidence. In traditional societies with relatively low rates of social change, long-established customs, beliefs and rituals provided a taken-for-granted frame of reference within which food-related anxieties could be submerged or neutralized. It is, of course, difficult to sustain hard and fast generalizations concerning the nature of traditional societies given the fact that they have exhibited such tremendous variety in culture and institutional forms. However, it is possible to identify a number of common features of premodern social systems which contributed to the process of anxiety neutralization.

A prime factor in the neutralization of paradox 1 (pleasure/displeasure) anxieties is undoubtedly the long-term stability of what we have termed the 'alimentary totality' of traditional societies, that is, the sum total of all the items defined as food suitable for humans. Changes in the alimentary totality are rare and gradual, with the result that familiarity with staple foods breeds in individuals a largely unquestioning confidence that they understand the implications and conditions which cluster around the consumption of a particular item. What is more, long-established rules of cuisine also work to sustain a sense of familiarity and confidence. Rozin and Rozin (1981) note that many traditional cuisines, that is, bodies of rules and recipes governing the preparation of food, have at their foundations distinctive 'flavour principles'. Such flavour principles actually consist of specific combinations of flavouring elements which provide each cuisine system with its own characteristic gustatory identity. The authors point out that the principles operated by major 'cuisine groups' like those found in India, China and Mexico, have remained relatively stable over long periods of time. Thus, in traditional societies, not only does the sum total of food items remain relatively unchanging, but so do the modes of cooking, combining and flavouring these items. Indeed, Rozin (1976) argues that established flavour principles can also mitigate the effects of neophobia. Unfamiliar or novel food items can be rendered less threatening by being suffused with familiar flavours, flavours which the author suggests can reduce the 'tensions of ingestion' which are necessarily inherent in omnivorous eating patterns (Rozin 1976: 66–7). In fact, the entire traditional culinary culture, based upon a set of flavour principles, can operate to sustain confidence and reassurance. Taken-for-granted rules concerning the structure and timing of meals, the appropriateness of given foods in relation to the gender, age and rank of the individual, and the division of labour in respect of food production and preparation, all serve to maintain an overarching framework of familiarity.

Digestive distress produced by overeating, which is also one of the anxieties associated with paradox 1, may be of somewhat different significance in traditional societies. For all but the most privileged, opportunities for overindulgence are likely to be rare, with food shortage being a more likely possibility. Chronic insecurity in the food supply can give rise to a characteristic oscillation between fasting and feasting, with occasional gorging (often associated with particular rituals or observances) providing a periodic release from fears of food deprivation and starvation (Mennell 1985: 23). Anxiety concerning the experience of embarrassment due to the effects of eating and digesting (also related to paradox 1) is likely to be much less salient in traditional societies. For example, medieval Europeans seem to have been largely uninhibited about the physiological processes of digestion, and the sounds and odours they can produce (Elias 1978a: 129–43). Embarrassment in relation to these effects seems to be a product of the civilizing of appetite discussed in Chapter 5. Indeed, in some traditional cultures, manifestations which would be seen by modern Westerners as dreadful lapses in good manners may be required expressions of politeness. For example, Grimble (1952: 35–6) noted that, among the people of the Gilbert Islands in the Western Pacific, a guest who had been provided with food was expected to belch loudly after eating to show his or her appreciation.

In Chapter 6 we have already come across some of the ways in which beliefs and practices in traditional societies can act to neutralize paradox 2 (health/illness) anxieties. We have noted the way in which the combination of tried and tested empirical knowledge and flexible magical beliefs can cope well with threatening aspects of daily life. In relation to food and illness, such a combination can provide intelligible and plausible explanations for disease. In addition, however, traditional cultures provide ways of responding to such misfortunes. Afflicted individuals have, within their realm of common-sense knowledge, criteria for the selection or avoidance of specific foods or food combinations, as well as remedies which are within their own grasp and under their own control. The very fact that traditional knowledge and ethnomedical practices evolve slowly, without frequent or obvious disjunctures in their continuity, provides them with the power to reassure. Their taken-for-granted nature is, perhaps, the best guarantee of the suppression or masking of paradox 2 anxieties. To a degree, this guarantee can operate independently of the actual technical efficiency of the particular avoidances, dietary regimes and treatments that a given traditional culture prescribes. Given the flexibility of common-sense knowledge and magical beliefs, apparent failures can be accommodated or explained away without their presenting a damning challenge to the whole system. Thus, the very resilience of these ideas, along with their apparent immutability, is a powerful factor behind the maintenance of a sense of confidence in the face of the threat of ingesting harmful as well as nutritious substances in the course of day-to-day eating.

As we have already noted, most animal-derived foods (although not all) directly entail the killing of the donor animal, although the extent to which this fact gives rise to ethical concern on the part of the human consumer is likely

155

to vary markedly from species to species. Thus, the probability of the emergence of anxieties related to paradox 3 will itself vary according to the species being eaten. As a broad generalization, warm-blooded animals seem to elicit most concern, especially mammals. Indeed, the larger the mammal the more intense is likely to be the moral unease associated with dining upon it. However, inside paradox 3 is yet another paradox, for the flesh of large mammals, in Western culture at least, is traditionally accorded high status and credited with great potency. This is demonstrated, for example, in its role as the focal or 'stressed' element in the 'cooked dinner' or 'proper meal' which is such an important feature of British culinary culture. (The multiple significances of meat will be dealt with in detail in Chapters 9 and 10.) Within the cultures of many traditional societies are to be found deeply rooted beliefs and customs which serve to legitimize the use of animals for food and to allay any qualms the individual might entertain concerning the morality of eating meat.

Such beliefs and customs are particularly clear and explicit in cultures which derive a significant proportion of their protein resources from the hunting of large game animals. These ideas can take many forms, including ritual apologies to the slain animal and the notion that the purpose of the prey animal's existence is to provide for the needs of the hunters and their dependants. For example, in the past the Akoa pygmies of West Africa would chant a formal incantation of apology to each elephant they killed, absolving the hunter of blame for the animal's death and exhorting the creature's spirit not to return and take revenge upon them. The Mbuti pygmies of the same region also carried out elaborate rites over the body of a freshly killed elephant to appease its affronted spirit (Coon 1976: 140–4). A rather different approach to the explicit rituals of the Akoa and the Mbuti is found in the culture of the Chipewyan, a people of the boreal forests of Canada. In Chipewyan thought, animals are seen as exhibiting features which locate them both in the realm of the natural and of the supernatural, mystically renewing themselves to become rejuvenated each spring. Such beings, reason the Chipewyan, can only be killed with their own consent, voluntarily giving themselves up to the hunter they deem worthy of their sacrifice (Sharp 1988: 187). Indeed, the Chipewyan believe that respect must be shown for game animals at all times, since offending or insulting them could lead them to withdraw their consent to be preyed upon, with disastrous consequences for a people traditionally dependent on the resources of the wilderness for their subsistence. The Bushman hunters of the African Kalahari desert protect themselves from moral qualms by emphasizing the 'otherness' of the animals upon which they prey, rather than seeing them as surrogate humans (Guenther 1988: 198–9). Thus, although these people express affection, respect and aesthetic appreciation in connection with their quarry animals, they see them as sufficiently distinct and distant from themselves to render them legitimate sources of food.

If the hunting of wild mammals presents ethical problems, so too does the slaughter of domesticated mammals. Among pastoralist and agricultural peoples the belief is often found that humans have been granted permission by a creator or supreme being to exploit and subjugate the natural world for their own benefit. Within this context, the use of domesticated animals for food is seen as a divinely licensed practice. This idea is, for example, deeply rooted in Judaism, Christianity and Islam, and in each of these three religions it is seen as based upon the consent given by God to Noah to consume flesh. However, within Judaism, privileges such as this are hedged around with a complex set of food prohibitions, including detailed specifications of those animals which are 'clean' and therefore can be eaten, and those which are 'unclean' and therefore forbidden. A taboo is also placed upon the consumption of an animal's blood, since this is regarded as the medium which contains its vitality (Lowenberg, Todhunter, Wilson, Savage and Lubowski 1974: 207). Thus, slaughter must be carried out in a ritually prescribed fashion, to ensure that all the blood is drained from the animal so that its spirit can flow into the earth (Farb and Amelagos 1980: 23–4). Islam, too, specifies animals which are clean and unclean, and forbids, for example, the consumption of animals that die by strangulation or are beaten to death (Lowenberg, Todhunter, Wilson, Savage and Lubowski 1974: 216).

Even in the context of religions which explicitly forbid the killing of animals, customary practices and beliefs can emerge which legitimize such killing or purge the agent of any culpability. For example, although practising Buddhists are prohibited by their religious beliefs from slaughtering animals or even witnessing slaughter, they are permitted to consume meat as long as they did not participate directly in the taking of the animal's life (Harris 1986: 23–4). In fact, blame may be transferred down the social hierarchy or to pariah groups which specialize in slaughter (Simoons 1961: 11–12). In Buddhist Thailand, villagers usually sell pigs to Chinese dealers to be slaughtered and sold. Similarly, Thai villagers, for whom fish is an important addition to their rice-based diet, argue that they do not actually kill the fish, but merely remove them from the water (Lowenberg, Todhunter, Wilson, Savage and Lubowski 1974: 226). Despite the apparently rigid ban on the killing of cattle in India, Harris (1986: 60–1) points out that Hindu farmers can circumvent this prohibition in a fashion which obviates any sense of guilt. They simply sell surplus animals to Muslim traders, and the resulting meat is consumed by Muslims, Christians and even lower-caste Hindus. This conscience-easing accommodation is supported by the common practice of referring to such meat euphemistically as 'mutton'.

THE EROSION OF TRADITIONAL MODES OF MANAGING AMBIVALENCE AND ANXIETY

In the above section we have examined examples of the ways in which the kinds of anxieties associated with the three paradoxes detailed in Table 7.1 have been managed within the settings of traditional cultures, ranging from hunting-gathering peoples to long-established civilizations like those of the Middle East and India. However, a whole series of factors has been working to erode these reassuring beliefs and practices along with the high level of nutritional confidence (in relation to our three paradoxes) that comes with participation in a world-view which provides effective protection from anxiety and guilt. In broad terms, the factors associated with this erosion are linked to more general processes behind the emergence of the modern food system that were outlined in Chapter 2. The intensification and industrialization of food production and processing, and the globalization of food supply, have led to a veritable explosion in food choice. Coupled with rising affluence and purchasing power in Western economies, this has meant that food consumption patterns have been freed from many of the traditional constraints of locality and season, constraints which would once have generated a framework of familiarity and a sense of cyclical participation in the annual rhythms of agriculture. Indeed, the industrialization of the food system means that food production and processing increasingly take place beyond the view of the average food consumer, involving techniques that he or she is only vaguely aware of or simply does not understand. Thus, many of the food items routinely purchased may be perceived as having unknown features or unknown ingredients, with a consequent loss of the consumer's confidence. This effect is reinforced by the fact that modern food manufacturing techniques, including the use of synthesized substances and flavourings, can imitate or conceal 'natural' textures or tastes, leaving the consumer effectively unable to trust the sensory messages given off by any given food product as a reliable guide to its actual nature (Fischler 1988: 289).

Many of the cultural features of late capitalist societies also appear to contribute to the erosion of the traditional bases of nutritional confidence. The whole ideology of consumerism, driven by an emphasis on a ceaseless search for novel consumption experiences, is essentially antithetical to the maintenance of long-term stability in eating patterns. This hunger for novelty is, in turn, fostered and extended by the mass media, most obviously through explicit advertising and less obviously through the assumptions built into the content of the messages which are conveyed to the various audiences being targeted. Coupled with the globalization of the food supply and the expansion of the alimentary totality of each developed society, virtually open-ended wants can become a salient factor in the affluent consumer's views on food. However, it is not simply that a somewhat bewildering level of choice emerges in relation to food items as such. Even underlying flavour principles, which once served mainly to mark the identity of a particular cuisine and thereby could help sustain confidence and familiarity, have now been effectively uncoupled from the regions and cultures which gave birth to them. In effect, flavour principles themselves have become commodities, options on a kind of meta-menu which consumers with sufficient resources can select from at will. The result is that the long-standing features of the consumer's own native set of flavour combinations become submerged in the sheer variety of principles on offer, with the consequence that they may tend to lose the authority which once made them so reassuring.

If traditional flavour principles can be seen to be losing their central place in the experience of eating, then the changes in the actual patterns of eating that have already been discussed in earlier chapters can also play a role in the erosion of food confidence. Given the changing role of women in the labour market, the modern household (or indeed, the 'postmodern' household) has been characterized as one where the multiple and often conflicting activities and priorities of its members mean that the familiar patterns of commensality, with their confidence-enhancing rituals and habits, have begun to break down. A greater reliance on pre-prepared convenience foods, for example, has led to a situation in which the family meal is far less significant as an occasion for expressing time-honoured assumptions about age, gender and status which serve to locate each individual within the taken-for-granted order of everyday social life (Gofton 1990: 92).

In the previous section, it was suggested that religious beliefs can play a part in the alleviation of food-related anxieties, particularly those pertaining to the moral concerns arising out of the killing of animals for food. However, with the extensive secularization of contemporary Western society, the theological and philosophical supports for the use of animals as food sources have themselves been weakened. More generally, accompanying the broad processes of secularization has been the extensive and impressive development of the scientific world-view, which has transformed the ways in which humans seek to understand and explain the natural world. As we saw in Chapter 6, despite the fact that common-sense ideas and 'alternative' views on food manage to persist, it is the professionally accredited voice of the nutritionist, the dietician, the physician, the microbiologist, the toxicologist and the physiologist which speak with the greatest authority on matters nutritional. Yet, professional scientific discourses on diet are by no means necessarily reassuring ones in relation to our three paradoxes. By its very nature, scientific knowledge is always provisional, subject to controversy, challenge, refutation and replacement. In this sense, it is very unlike common-sense knowledge and traditional empirical/ magical thinking, whose elastic and slowly evolving nature makes them appear both homely and proverbial. Scientific knowledge can be subject to disturbing and bewildering changes of revolutionary significance, and its ideas are often largely inaccessible, except in the broadest terms, to those outside a specific discipline. Thus, scientific discourses on food and nutrition do not necessarily produce reassurance and confidence in the public mind.

Indeed, the possibility exists that such discourses may also actively generate public anxiety. This possibility arises out of the fact that science continually and inevitably raises what are, in effect, 'trans-scientific' questions. Weinberg (1972) defines trans-scientific questions as those which scientists can pose quite rationally and reasonably on the basis of widely held views within a given discipline, but to which science itself cannot actually provide satisfactory or unambiguous responses. Questions which appear to require no more than a recourse to suitable facts or data to settle them once and for all can turn out to be highly intractable, with little prospect of clear solutions in the medium or even the long term. There can be a whole range of reasons behind such intractability. For example, there may be compelling ethical barriers which prevent the necessary experimentation on human subjects. Cause and effect linkages may be extremely difficult to detect if they are embedded in a complex matrix of interacting variables which are difficult or impossible to control. Some effects may be long-term or delayed and may need decades of study to detect, and others may be so complex as to require enormous resources for thorough investigation. In fact, Tracey (1977) argues that some aspects of human nutritional needs and requirements have these trans-scientific dimensions. Indeed, it has been suggested that many of the current issues relating to links between diet and health do appear to exhibit trans-scientific aspects, which may mean that scientists may not be able to provide clear-cut answers to seemingly straightforward questions (Beardsworth 1990). Two striking examples of such questions are whether the consumption of beef from cattle infected with bovine spongiform encephalopathy (BSE) can produce an analogous disease in humans, and the nature of any long-term effects of chronic exposure to pesticide residues in food. Both these questions can be posed in such a way as to alert public attention to possible risks, but both raise extremely complex scientific issues and have generated considerable professional debate and controversy. However, the doubt and uncertainty surrounding such questions in scientific circles, and the controversies they create, may not be well understood by the general public.

Indeed, many members of the public at large lack the basic mathematical skills and insights to assess the practical significance of risks to their health which are pointed out by scientists but are expressed in quantitative or statistical terms. As a result, many individuals may experience exaggerated levels of anxiety and even demand guarantees of freedom from risk which would be virtually impossible to implement (Paulos 1988). It is, perhaps, rather ironic that scientific pronouncements and warnings may act to stimulate food-related anxiety at precisely the time when greatly expanded scientific knowledge has produced significant advances in food hygiene and food safety generally.

SOME CONSEQUENCES OF THE EROSION OF FOOD CONFIDENCE

The thrust of the argument being put forward here is that many of the structural and ideological features of modern food systems have the effect of raising the visibility of the paradoxical nature of food and eating. The resulting anxieties and sense of insecurity about food are characterized by Fischler (1988: 288–90) as, in effect, a significant 'disturbance of modern identity'. In fact, as was noted in Chapter 3, Fischler goes so far as to argue that modern societies are witnessing a crisis in gastronomy which involves the breakdown of regulating and reassuring rules, producing a state of *gastro-anomy* (Fischler 1980: 947–48). It is Fischler's contention that modern individuals, less than ever integrated into

160

supportive networks of family and community, increasingly have to make their nutritional decisions in a kind of cultural vacuum, unrestrained by the limitations of season and locality. This nutritional normlessness is, in itself, an anxiety-generating feature of modern society. It clearly goes hand in hand with the erosion of the traditional modes of anxiety management that we have already been discussing. These interlinked phenomena clearly interact with each other, compounding their negative effects upon the confidence and the peace of mind of the contemporary food consumer.

Warde (1991) summarizes this situation by highlighting the three principal competing forces at play in the modern food system, all of which can be seen as pulling in conflicting directions. The first of these forces is made up of the professional nutritional discourse and the official health-oriented dietary advice which were discussed in the previous chapter. The second consists of the customary practices and beliefs which survive in modern societies from traditional culinary culture (which contain the protective elements outlined above). The third force Warde identifies as the taste for novelty, which is a characteristic of the consumption patterns of modern societies in general (and, in a sense, might be seen as an exaggerated manifestation of nutritional neophilia). Each of these three forces is seen as exercising its own potent influence over public attitudes and practices, and the contradictions between them are seen as giving rise to what Warde rather dramatically calls 'a mire of uncertainty' (Warde 1991: 9).

The overall consequence of these gastro-anomic effects and conflicting forces at the cultural level of the food system, exacerbated by the erosion of traditional modes of sustaining confidence, has been a general rise in food-related anxieties in the context of all three of our paradoxes. For example, in relation to paradox 1 (pleasure/displeasure) Mennell (1992) seeks to show how in England from the early nineteenth century onwards both professional medical practitioners and members of the public became increasingly obsessed with the uncomfortable or embarrassing aspects of eating and digestion. The practice of attempting to classify foods according to their perceived ability to generate unwelcome effects, like 'indigestion', constipation and flatulence, became increasingly widespread and led to such potentially harmful effects as the increased use of laxatives and the exclusion of an ever-widening range of items from anxious individuals' diets (Mennell 1992: 7–8). In more general terms, it may also be the case that intensified paradox 1 anxieties may be one of the contributing factors behind the modern preoccupation with body fat, body shape and the restriction of food intake through dieting (which issues will be discussed in some detail in the next chapter). These modern concerns with body fat have, of course, both medical and cosmetic dimensions.

Tensions and anxieties related to paradox 2 (health/illness) also seem to have intensified in the modern setting. Indeed, one of the unintended consequences of official nutritional and health education campaigns may have been a rise in public nervousness over health and food issues, which would have to be set alongside the beneficial outcomes such campaigns may be capable of generating. Interestingly, however, there is some evidence that the public's perceptions of food-related health risks may be significantly different from those of professional experts. For example, a study carried out in Sweden suggests that lay opinion actually reverses the rank order of risks as assessed by experts. Thus, experts tended to place dietary fat, sugar and salt high on their list of food hazards, followed by food poisoning, natural poisons, residues and additives. Conversely, consumers appeared to regard poisons as the greatest risk, with concern expressed in relation to such substances as mercury and heavy metals. Then came pesticides, bacteria and mould poisons, with fat, sugar and salt well down the rank order (Sellerberg 1991: 197). A similar finding has been reported from the USA (Schafer, Schafer, Bultena and Hoiberg 1993). A study based on a random sample of 630 adults indicated that respondents perceived the highest food-related risks as coming from chemicals and the lowest risks from bacterial contamination (although, to place this finding in context, respondents rated concerns about food safety lower than concerns about such issues as cost and taste). However, a study of adult Texans which investigated public knowledge concerning the specific risks associated with undercooked meat products (McIntosh, Acuff, Christensen and Hale 1994) found that of the 46 per cent of respondents who identified a risk, the majority of these (52 per cent) cited food poisoning as the most likely hazard. Indeed, the cross-cultural study by Jussaume and Judson (1992), examining public perceptions of food safety in the USA and Japan, indicates that food safety concerns are becoming globalized in modern societies. With particular reference to pesticide residues and additives, the researchers found analagous levels of concern in the US and Japanese samples, with particular anxiety in households in which children under the age of 18 were present (Jussaume and Judson 1992: 246).

A rise in ethical concerns relating to food seems to suggest an intensification of anxieties in connection with paradox 3. Most obviously, these concerns manifest themselves in the context of heightened interest in issues of animal welfare and animal rights. However, they can also find more indirect expression in the attention increasingly being paid by consumers in modern, developed societies to the environmental implications of intensive food production techniques and to the ethical dilemmas raised by the extreme inequalities in nutritional standards which are present in the global food system. These issues will re-emerge as important themes in Chapters 9 and 10.

THE PHENOMENON OF THE FOOD SCARE

The effects that we have been discussing so far are, in a sense, broad and somewhat diffuse ones, representing gradual shifts at the cultural and ideological levels of the food system. On the other hand, it may well be possible to identify phenomena which are related to the changes in nutritional confidence outlined above, but which manifest themselves in a much more dramatic fashion. One such phenomenon is the so-called 'food scare', an acute outbreak of collective nutritional anxiety which can seize hold of public awareness and can give rise to significant short- and long-term consequences. The typical food scare seems to exhibit a fairly consistent pattern, which for the purposes of presentation can be conveniently presented as consisting of a sequence of steps:

1 An initial 'equilibrium' state exists in which the public are largely unaware of or are unconcerned about, a potential food risk factor.
2 The public are initially sensitized to a novel potential food risk factor.
3 Public concern builds up as the risk factor becomes a focus of interest and concern within the various arenas of public debate.
4 Public response to the novel risk factor begins, often consisting of the avoidance of the suspect food item. (This response may be an 'exaggerated' one, apparently not in proportion to the 'actual' risk.)
5 Public concern gradually fades as attention switches away from the issue in question and a new 'equilibrium' state establishes itself. However, chronic low-level anxiety may persist, and can give rise to a resurgence of the issue at a later date.

In recent years a series of such food scares has occurred in Britain (Mitchell and Greatorex 1990). The scares themselves have been centred upon a diverse range of perceived hazards, including the presence of the dangerous organism listeria in pâté, cook-chill foods and soft cheeses, the presence of salmonella in eggs and the risks posed to human health by the outbreak of bovine spongiform encephalopathy (BSE) in British cattle. Alarm has also been generated by revelations concerning the contamination of bottled spring water with benzene, and by acts of 'food terrorism', where food products have been deliberately contaminated with poisonous substances or foreign bodies, usually as a means of blackmailing large retail food companies. From a sociological point of view, there are two major questions to be addressed here. Firstly, 'How do we explain the sudden and dramatic nature of these surges of public concern?' Secondly, 'Why do nutritional issues seem prone to this kind of effect?'

In relation to the first of these questions, both Gofton (1990) and Beardsworth (1990) have suggested that the concept of the 'moral panic' may be a relevant one (although reservations about the application of this concept to food scares have been expressed by Miller and Reilly (1995: 328–9), who point out that the concept originally implied the focusing of public and official concern on specific marginal or deviant groups who could be characterized as posing a threat to social order). The term itself is to be found in the work of Cohen (1971, 1973) who set out to analyse society's reactions to a series of incidents involving violent public disorder in a number of English coastal resorts in the 1960s. His argument is that the sensationalized coverage of these events by the mass media had two effects. Firstly, it sensitized the public at large to what was perceived as a novel and threatening form of deviance. Secondly, it may even have acted to sharpen and solidify the collective identities of the two rival youth factions involved in the clashes, providing the stimulus for subsequent repeat perform-ances. Cohen uses the term 'moral panic' to describe the rapid surge of public concern which commonly accompanies intensive mass media coverage of such phenomena. The workings of this effect have also been analysed by Hall, Critcher, Jefferson, Clarke and Roberts (1978), who examine the emergence of the 'mugging' scare which occurred in Britain in the 1970s. Although no specific crime of 'mugging' exists in law, for example, the authors argue that the term itself was imported from the USA by British newspaper and television journal-ists. The mugging concept was then used as a category into which a whole range of violent street crimes could be reclassified. Thus combined, these crimes could then be presented to the public as a frightening new phenomenon which demanded action from the authorities. In response to rising public concern, the police and judiciary reacted by increasing the severity of penalties for street violence. Examples of such severe penalties were highly newsworthy and were widely reported in the media, as were the pronouncements of senior police officers, judges and members of the establishment. Such reports themselves added more fuel to the public's collective anxiety, and expressions of such anxiety were frequently featured in press reports. In fact, Hall and his co-authors maintain, this intensive media coverage created the impression of a serious crime wave, although it is by no means clear that violent street crime was actually increasing rapidly at this time.

The mechanism which creates these relatively intense but short-lived 'panics' can be seen as a kind of 'news spiral' consisting of a positive feedback loop. Figure 7.1 provides a simplified diagrammatic representation of the workings of this feedback effect.

The stages in this simplified model are virtually self-explanatory. Initially, a novel issue or phenomenon emerges into the public sphere through reporting in the mass media. Next, the public become sensitized to this issue through their exposure to such coverage. Subsequently, the public are likely to react to the issue to which they have been sensitized. Of course, such reactions may be difficult to predict, as mass media audiences are not simply passive recipients of media messages, but actively select and interpret. Audiences' reactions are themselves newsworthy, although not all audience members' voices have an equal probability of being heard, with those in authority and those claiming 'expert' status likely to receive greater attention. The reporting of audience reactions itself increases public awareness of the issue and increases the level of sensitization, thereby closing the feedback loop and allowing a spiralling level of anxiety to build up. This mechanism does appear to be capable of generating acute surges in collective anxiety, and in recent years in the UK such surges have characterized a wide range of issues, including soccer hooliganism, child abuse, dog attacks on humans, and various forms of criminal behaviour and drug abuse.

Of course, the anxiety 'amplification' produced by this feedback effect is bound to be a self-limiting process, and public and media interest in a topic

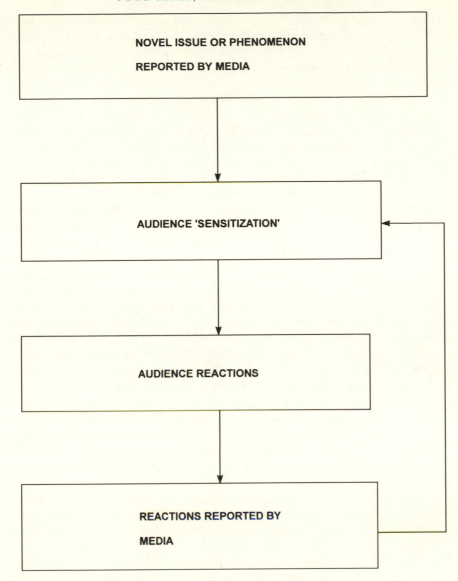

Figure 7.1 A simplified model of the news spiral

will eventually start to decline as that topic goes 'stale' in news terms. This effect is clearly documented by Miller and Reilly (1995: 320–2), who present data showing peaks in the frequencies of items in the British press relating to salmonella and BSE between 1988 and 1994. In effect, public attention can be seen as a kind of scarce resource for which the media have to compete

(Hilgartner and Bosk 1988). The development of a particular topic as a problem or scare will be affected by what Hilgartner and Bosk see as the limited carrying capacity of the public arenas within which issues can be debated and played out by rival authorities, opinions and interest groups. Eventually, a kind of saturation will occur in connection with a given topic, and the media's need to maintain a sense of novelty and dramatic interest will mean a switch to competing issues in order once again to command public attention. However, even though such scares are of limited duration, they may well produce enduring effects. Official policies may be changed, new legislation may be introduced and long-term alterations in the public's activities and attitudes may be produced. What is more, months or even years after a scare episode, an issue may re-emerge and, given the right conditions, generate further surges of acute anxiety.

We have already noted several examples of food scares which seem to have been characterized by this moral panic effect (although, given that the term 'moral panic' was originally coined to describe reactions to social deviance, in the food context the more neutral term 'news spiral' may be rather more appropriate). Nevertheless, such scares, augmented by powerful news spirals, can and do have both short- and long-term effects on consumer choices and food habits. For example, the scare concerning the dangers of salmonella contamination in eggs caused a dramatic and sudden fall in egg consumption in the UK, with the result that large numbers of laying birds were slaughtered and many egg producers were forced out of business. The scare concerning BSE among British cattle caused some local authorities to remove beef products from their school meals menus and moves were made in some European countries to ban the importing of British beef. The scare itself has arguably accelerated the long-term decline in beef consumption in the UK. The revelation of benzene contamination in a well-known brand of mineral water necessitated a temporary withdrawal of the product and the resulting media coverage and public concern is likely to have produced a significant decline in that product's previously dominant market share.

Thus, in the acute phase of a food scare, consumers are likely to respond by switching away from the affected products or brands. Of course, in a market in which there is an abundance of choice, there are likely to be numerous substitutes for suspect products and therefore switching will be relatively easy, involving little or no deprivation for the consumer. This fact in itself is likely to exaggerate the effects of food scares on consumer behaviour. Once the acute phase of the scare is over, there are several possibilities. Demand may stabilize at a lower level, go into chronic decline or recover to the levels which pre-dated the news spiral, depending upon such factors as the appeal of available substitutes and the intensity and durability of the public concern generated. The impact of food scares upon the food industry of a modern economy is, therefore, likely to be somewhat unpredictable. What is more, this impact will vary from sector to sector of the industry. For retailers, product switching by consumers will be relatively easy to accommodate, as purchasing and stocking policies can be modified quickly. Food manufacturers and processors, heavily committed in capital terms to particular products or product areas, may find rapid adaptation difficult. At the level of the agricultural foundations of the food system, food producers may find rapid responses to changes in consumer demand generated by acute scares virtually impossible, given that significant shifts in patterns of production may take years or even decades to accomplish.

Although news spirals touching upon a whole range of issues can be seen as regularly occurring features of the cultural landscape of modern societies, there are several factors which might render food-related topics particularly prone to this effect. Certainly, questions raised about threats to human health are likely to be newsworthy, virtually guaranteed to gain public attention. Threats to health posed by food are likely to be especially newsworthy, since such threats activate those deep-seated anxieties associated with what we have already argued is one of the fundamental paradoxes associated with food: its ability to provide vital nourishment alongside its ability to introduce disease into the body which it feeds. Given that we have proposed that customary ways of submerging or coping with this paradox have been eroded, the cultural ground is fertile for the food scare to take root. Furthermore, as we have seen, the trans-scientific nature of many food and health issues fuels uncertainty and heightens anxiety. Constant debate and dispute between experts, which are essential to the conduct of the natural sciences as professional discourses (Gilbert and Mulkay 1984), when reported through the mass media, can convey to the public a sense of confusion, indecision and even incompetence in the face of what are seen as serious threats to well-being. Indeed, the coverage of such disputes and controversies is often a crucial component of the food scare news spiral. We must add to these factors the recognition that scientific, technological and organizational innovations in food production, processing, storage and transportation have been so successful as to raise public expectations concerning food quality and food safety to unprecedented levels. These high expectations themselves make a direct contribution to the public's susceptibility to food scares.

Significant levels of public anxiety in relation to food, occasionally manifesting themselves as acute scares, indicate how firmly issues relating to the overall acceptability of food have now taken on a prominent place in the arenas of public debate. While it was the case in the UK, for example, that after the Second World War and until a few years ago, decisions pertinent to issues like food quality and food safety were taken within a relatively closed and elitist 'policy community', this is no longer so (Smith 1991). Increasingly in Britain, food-related issues have become politicized, and the original, officially-based policy community can no longer exclude other voices and opinions. Indeed, those agencies which once constituted the closed policy community (both governmental and commercial) may be viewed by the mass media and the public as excessively secretive and potentially untrustworthy (Miller and Reilly 1995: 316–18). Currently, many competing groups seek to influence the public's ideas and to shape food policy. What we now have is an 'issue network' (Smith 1991: 236), with food firmly established on the political agenda and food controversies far more visible to the public at large.

THE RECONSTRUCTION OF FOOD CONFIDENCE

This chapter has been primarily concerned with the idea that traditional modes of shielding the individual from underlying food anxieties have been eroded, leading to a rise in both chronic and acute manifestations of nutritional unease. However, from a sociological point of view, it is important to consider the question of whether a culture is likely, in the longer run, to permit a set of anxiety-provoking dilemmas to remain excessively visible or effectively unresolved. As Sellerberg (1991: 193) observes, humans *need* to trust in the food they eat. Like any other animals, they have to eat to live yet, unlike other animals, they can and do reflect upon the darker symbolic significances of the food items they consume, and they can at times confront in a conscious fashion the risks and hazards that eating can entail. Yet such reflection and confrontation cannot possibly be undertaken at every meal, or with every mouthful. The result would be a kind of nutritional paralysis or alimentary dithering which would be a constant source of distress. As Sellerberg found from her own study of food trust and mistrust, and as we would expect, most people, most of the time, are not experiencing a constant sense of turmoil about the food they eat. Sellerberg tries to identify what she terms 'strategies of confidence' (Sellerberg 1991: 196) which individuals employ to reassure themselves in the face of confusing advice, alarms and reports. Such strategies include emphasizing the choice of foods which are regarded as 'natural' and avoiding those perceived as 'unnatural', and deliberately developing a repertoire of trusted foods and then excluding all others from the diet.

Yet Sellerberg's strategies of confidence are seen as essentially personal and individual. On the other hand, Fischler (1988) advances the proposition that at the social and cultural level there may be forces working to re-establish some kind of equilibrium in the face of modern insecurity and uncertainty in relation to food. As an illustration of this he refers to the increasing demand for what he terms the 're-identification' of foods (Fischler 1988: 290). This re-identification involves ever more detailed labelling of food products with elaborate listings of ingredients, and formalized guarantees of purity and quality, often sponsored by official bodies. Similarly, expanding forms of what Fischler calls 'food sectarianism' are also seen as capable of playing a role in this overall process. For example, in the previous chapter we considered the significance of the health food movement in this context, and in Chapter 10 one of the many aspects of vegetarianism that will be discussed will relate to its anxiety-relieving features. In fact, Fischler argues, the aim of such diverse processes is to attempt to re-introduce a sense of order into everyday eating, to provide it with an intelligible normative logic and a coherent framework.

Indeed, it may well be that the state of gastro-anomy which Fischler (1988) describes is an essentially transitional one, a feature of the strains involved in the breakdown of a more traditional set of foodways and the emergence of a new, more pluralistic nutritional order (Beardsworth and Keil 1992b). This menu pluralism, which we have already suggested is an important emergent feature of contemporary Western food systems, can be seen as providing the setting within which the existence of a multiplicity of menu principles, flavour principles and systems of cuisine is seen as quite normal and essentially unproblematic. Thus, sampling different principles and cuisines, switching from one to the other as mood, context and conscience dictate, can become normal. Traditional, stable and established foodways may be less and less important for the maintenance of nutritional confidence, as long as there exists a relatively stable overall framework within which the choices, whims, fashions and fads of a pluralistic approach to eating can be played out.

There is, perhaps, a certain irony in suggesting that the commercial dynamics of the modern food system are capable of providing such a framework, since capitalism itself has been seen as containing inherently anomic features. Yet there are clearly identifiable aspects of the commercial food system which do act to generate consumer confidence and to counterbalance gastro-anomic forces. One striking example that we have already come across is the commercialization of certain features of the health food movement. The mass-production and mass marketing of health food products and the commercial appropriation of rhetorical devices like 'tradition', 'naturalness', 'wholesomeness', make available to an ever wider public ranges of products which have reassurance as one of their principal ingredients. Broadening the argument to consider the whole field of food marketing, the larger food producers and manufacturers, in particular, make great efforts to establish and maintain high levels of brand loyalty to their products. Such efforts can be extremely costly, in terms of advertising expenditure alone, but clearly can be effective in maintaining or improving market share and profitability. Yet brand loyalty can also provide a form of benefit for the consumer, in that recognized brands provide a sense of familiarity and reassurance in terms of the quality and safety of the products to which they are attached. What is more, capitalist food organizations which own widely recognized and respected brands will make strenuous efforts to protect such commercially valuable assets and to avoid damage to a brand's reputation. Food brands, in fact, provide some of the symbolically most potent and instantly recognizable icons of Western consumer culture. Established brands can thus assume the taken-for-granted acceptability once reserved for the most basic staple foods.

A particular dimension of this brand loyalty effect is related to the phenomenon, discussed in Chapter 5, which Ritzer (1993) terms 'McDonaldization'. The extensive rationalization of fast food catering epitomized by the McDonald's organization is quite clearly geared to control, efficiency and profitability. However, this relentless rationalization of the product range and the methods of handling, preparing and serving the food items on offer also produces an additional crucial feature: predictability. As we have already noted, wherever the outlet, the consumer can feel confident that the food product purchased will be predictably familiar in terms of portion size, texture, taste and ingredients. In the context of the increasing globalization of culture and increasing levels of both social and geographical mobility, standardized branded food items for consumption inside or outside the home provide sources of nutritional confidence which transcend class, cultural and sometimes even national boundaries.

The commercial food system offers products which assuage not just the anxieties generated by our first two paradoxes, but also ease those moral qualms which emerge out of the third paradox. Worries regarding the possible suffering imposed upon food animals in the course of rearing, transportation and slaughter can be tempered by the consumption of food products which offer guarantees or assurances concerning the conditions and treatment to which domesticated animals have been subjected. There is, in the UK, for example, an established market for so-called 'free range' eggs and 'free range' poultry (chickens and turkeys). Some consumers are clearly willing to pay a significant premium for such products, which are not the results of highly intensified 'battery' farming characterized by very high densities of birds in extremely restricted conditions, but purport to be derived from livestock enjoying more 'natural' living conditions. Thus, in certain circumstances, humane production techniques become important saleable features of animal-based food products, with the potential for providing extra peace of mind for the consumer and extra profits for the producer. This principle can also operate in a broader sense, since, as we have already seen, wider moral and ecological anxieties may also be associated with the third paradox. Products advertised as being 'ecologically friendly' also offer the dual benefits of consumer reassurance and premium prices. One example of this effect relates to widespread concerns about the large numbers of dolphins killed annually by becoming entangled in tuna nets. Canned tuna carrying a printed guarantee that it has been produced using techniques and equipment which avoid such undesirable consequences, offers a form of reassurance which can be lifted directly off the supermarket shelf.

Anxiety-reducing or confidence-generating food products can be turned out at all levels of the commercial food system. They may be the stock-in-trade of small, specialized producers, and retailed through specialized outlets and co-operatives catering for highly specific minority tastes and requirements. On the other hand, such items increasingly figure in the product ranges of the giant national and multinational food processing and food retailing corporations, as they move towards the kind of niche marketing necessary to exploit the increasingly pluralistic diversification of tastes, priorities and menu principles.

Of course, it is also the case that a whole range of official agencies and professional bodies is engaged in attempts to influence the public's dietary practices and to shape the public's nutritional beliefs and priorities. By implication, this also represents a form of confidence maintenance, in this context confidence in the officially or professionally sponsored view of what constitutes safe, healthy or ethically acceptable food. Yet these official sources of reassurance are likely to be somewhat ambivalent ones. The guidelines on healthy eating, upon which the state's dietary targets are based, are themselves founded upon the shifting sands of scientific opinion. Even when an orthodoxy has been established which is intelligible to the public at large (for example, in connection with the links between diet and heart disease), that orthodoxy is always open to challenge and is always susceptible to being undermined by the publicity given to evidence which does not fit the prevailing view. There also appear to be circumstances in which official reassurances concerning the safety of specific suspect food items have the opposite effect to that intended. For example, at the height of the BSE scare in the UK, statements by government ministers and by senior medical officers were juxtaposed by the mass media with dire warnings from controversial dissenters from the official line. The official statements were themselves highly newsworthy and effectively added further fuel to an already vigorous news spiral. Once issues of food safety, for example, have escaped the control of a closed, oligarchical policy community and truly entered into the public domain, the official voice becomes only one voice among many, each presenting its own competing account. What is more, the state's ability to sustain confidence and generate reassurance may be further compromised in the UK setting, for example, where the Ministry of Agriculture, Fisheries and Food, one of the main government agencies in this area, is widely perceived, rightly or wrongly, to accord higher priority to the interests of food producers than to the interests of food consumers.

OVERVIEW

The underlying paradox beneath all the issues and debates which have been discussed in this chapter is one which has already been touched upon in several contexts: the fact that food anxieties persist (and even intensify) in modern food systems, despite the advances made in such systems which have improved the reliability and safety of the food supply. As we have seen, this effect is due in part to the fact that those features of traditional cultures and traditional food systems which could sustain nutritional confidence have been eroded or diluted by the processes of modernization. What is more, the very success of modern food systems in delivering to the consumer an abundance of varied, high-quality foodstuffs has in itself led to a cycle of constantly rising expectations on the part of the public. With immediate and obvious threats to nutritional well-being fading into the background, the consumer is able to occupy himself or herself with more arcane and subtle threats and misgivings relating to food. An antici-pation of continually rising standards is established, and members of the public become less and less tolerant of real or supposed food hazards, although the priorities accorded to such hazards may be very different from those calculated by scientists, who may perceive a rather different hierarchy of risks.

Yet there are clearly conflicting forces at work here. On the one hand, we have examined those forces and tendencies which appear to be undermining confidence and generating anxiety. On the other, we have also analysed in some detail the social mechanisms which may be capable of rebuilding and sustaining confidence and assuaging anxiety. It is tempting to speculate which of these two opposing sets of forces is likely to prevail. Should we predict a slide into ever deepening gastro-anomy, or should we anticipate the emergence of a new, stabilized nutritional order? The probability is that neither extreme case is a particularly likely one. Rather, the two tendencies will continue to coexist and interact with each other. If a new form of equilibrium is emerging, it is an equilibrium which is going to remain vulnerable to disturbance.

Perhaps the most plausible scenario is one characterized by periods of calm, during which chronic anxieties remain relatively dormant. However, such periods are likely to be punctuated by episodes of acute anxiety, produced either by the surfacing of underlying worries or by the introduction of novel scares which tap those deep-seated misgivings inherent in our three paradoxes. Indeed, it is possible to envisage potential food scares waiting in the wings for their day in the public eye. For example, the irradiation of food items in order to reduce microbiological contamination, slow down deterioration and extend shelf life, is already technically feasible. Similarly, the use of the hormone bovine somato-tropin (BST) to increase the milk yields (and therefore the profitability) of dairy cows is also a technically feasible option. However, at the time of writing neither of these measures has been fully implemented in the UK, despite their obvious advantages for producers and distributors. This reluctance to sanction the introduction of these types of new high-profile food technologies is almost certainly born of a recognition of the public's enhanced sensitivity to such potentially emotive and anxiety-generating innovations. Such are the implications of a cultural climate in which volatile public reactions to nutritional issues remain an ever-present possibility.

8

DIETING, FAT AND BODY IMAGE

Many sections of this book may be read as something of a celebration of the conquest of food shortage, of the growth in the security of supplies and of the varieties of food available. It is true that there are issues about access to food by the very poor but, for the majority, food resources are readily available. As a consequence, it may seem rather surprising to be introducing debates about the control of eating by dieting amongst some of the most prosperous groups in society and drawing attention to attempts to explain why some eating disorders, notably those which involve reducing food intake, are so severe that they threaten the life of the individuals concerned. However, these are some of the issues to be addressed if we want to understand current patterns of dieting and the powerful fear of fat which is expressed in popular literature about food, health and body shape in modern western societies.

Although there are many established ways in which these issues may be considered, addressing them also involves the sociologist in a relatively novel activity, one which has been absent from mainstream sociology until relatively recently: the analysis of the ways in which our bodies are socially constructed and experienced in modern society. Featherstone, Hepworth and Turner (1991: vii) argue that the sociology of the body is a way of focusing on 'one of the crucial instances of the complex interrelationships of nature, culture and society'. However, it was neglected as an area of study for a range of reasons, in particular because the early sociologists concentrated on questions concerning society, social change and social relations as a denial of the 'natural' as an explication of the social (Turner 1991: 8). Of course, these interests remain in current sociology, expressed in the continued interest in the social relations of production and the use of occupation as a key to understanding individual social position, but they are no longer considered to be the only ways of understanding social organization and social relationships. The new emphasis is on how people present themselves and appear to others. For example, Cash (1990: 52) argues that 'Physical appearance is often the most readily available information about a person and conveys basic information about that person – most obviously, for example, the person's gender, race, approximate age, and possibly even socio-economic status or occupation'. The interest in and development of the sociology of the body can be viewed, according to Turner (1991) as the consequence of several broad social changes. These include the growth of consumer culture in the post-war period, the development of postmodern themes in the arts, the feminist movement and changes in the demographic structure of industrial societies. For example, he argues that the 'erosion of competitive capitalism based on a disciplined labour force and heavy industrial production for a world market' (Turner 1991: 19) has been associated with the growth of the service sector and the development of new lifestyles which emphasize consumption and leisure. Associated with these is 'commercial and consumerist interest in the body' and its representation in art and advertisements together with an emphasis on 'keeping fit, the body beautiful and the postponement of ageing by sport' (Turner 1991: 19). Feminist criticism of the subordinate position of women in society has created a much greater sensitivity to issues of gender, sexuality and biology. The body as a focus of medical control and intervention also becomes important where improvements in standards of living and medicine have increased life expectancy and changed the age distribution to one which is historically unique in that there is a growing proportion of the elderly and the control of disease and of ageing itself are of increasing concern.

An awareness of the reasons why the sociology of the body has become the focus of interest does not necessarily inform us about the specific issues which should be on the sociological agenda. For these we need to consider current writing about dieting, fat and body image, where it is possible to identify at least four major puzzles of interest to the sociologist. The first is the knowledge that, as food supplies become both more secure and more plentiful, a substantial proportion of the population is on a diet with the aim of achieving weight loss and so are trying to avoid eating the range and variety of foods now available. The second is the awareness that, as the average body weight increases in the general population, the preferred (perhaps even the 'ideal') body image as shown in the media and entertainment industry and as demanded by commercial and industrial organizations emphasizes the slim, the slender and the underweight. The third is the fact that the second half of the twentieth century is associated with a rise in eating 'disorders', that is, problems which arise from weight loss which is so extreme as to endanger health and even life (anorexia nervosa) or from a pattern of unrestrained eating (bulimia nervosa) which again threatens the health of the sufferer. The fourth puzzle is highlighted by the data which show that most, if not all, of those involved in dieting and suffering from eating disorders are women, that is, the people who are normally responsible, or will as adults become responsible, for the selection, preparation and serving of food. As Brown and Jasper (1993) argue so cogently, if we are to contribute anything to the analysis of such issues we should find answers to these questions: 'Why weight?' 'Why women?' and 'Why now?'

Anyone interested in these issues has a wide range of sources of information to consider. Much of the writing about dieting, fat and body image appears in popular magazines and other media output. Where these issues emerge in the academic literature, they are discussed by nutritionists, medical researchers, psychologists and also, more recently, by feminists and sociologists. Amongst the multitude of discussions on topics such as body image, dieting and eating disorders, contrasts are often drawn between those who focus on individual experience and those who focus on social constraints. However, it is equally important to be aware of two other contrasting approaches: firstly, those where the underlying purpose is intervention, for example, to help individuals to be slimmer, recover from an eating disorder, adjust to lack of success in dieting. In such writing, the problem may be identified as individual or social in origin; however, the 'solution' is offered at the individual level. The second (and rarer) approach is where the underlying purpose is an analysis of the contemporary cult of slimness, the social pressures to 'shape up' to perceived expectations or the social conditions for the occurrence of eating disorders. Even where these studies give detailed accounts of particular individuals, the analysis remains at the level of the social and does not attempt to offer individual solutions. Although this latter approach may seem unsympathetic to individual sufferers, it may offer useful clues for sociological answers to the questions we have identified.

WHY NOW? THE MAKING OF THE CONTEMPORARY CULT OF SLIMNESS

In her analysis of sociocultural determinants of body image, which she defines as 'the way people perceive themselves and, equally important, the way they think others see them' (Fallon 1990: 80), Fallon emphasizes that the concept of beauty has never been static. She traces Western cultural ideals through time with particular reference to body shape and weight. Drawing upon art as an indicator of the ideals of male and female beauty, she argues that from the fifteenth to the eighteenth centuries fat was considered both erotic and fashionable and the 'beautiful woman was portrayed as a plump matron with full, nurturant breasts' (Fallon 1990: 85). By the nineteenth century there were two contrasting models of the female ideal. They shared small waists (with an 18-inch circumference where possible) but were different in that one was 'a fragile lady who was admired for her moral values, social status, and beauty' and the other was 'a bigger, bustier, hippier, heavy-legged woman found among the lower classes, and actresses and prostitutes' (Fallon 1990: 85). Both these ideals were modified in the twentieth century, initially towards an ideal body that was 'almost boylike' (Fallon 1990: 87). Fallon argues that the rise of the mass media, particularly film, probably contributed to the imposition of more general standards of beauty and fashion in the West. Since the media often focused on high-status groups, it was these groups' standards which became widespread. In the

USA the 1950s saw the glorification of large-breasted women in films and magazines, followed by the return to an emphasis on slimness in the 1960s. Similarly, in Britain in the 1960s a young woman nicknamed 'Twiggy' and weighing only 97 lbs, became one of the most famous fashion models of her generation. Fallon draws attention to data from studies of the winners of the Miss America contest between the years 1959 and 1978 indicating a decline in average weight related to height (that is, successful contestants increased in height and declined in weight over the period) and to a similar trend among the women featured in the centrefolds of Playboy magazine between 1960 and 1978 (Fallon 1990: 89–90). Fallon also reports on studies of the changes in the commercial images of women, from nineteenth-century curvaceousness to the 1980s' 'more muscular, healthy ideal of the female body' (Fallon 1990: 91). She reiterates the point made by other authors that such shapes are neither average nor 'natural' and can only be achieved by those who have the time, the money and the appropriate lifestyle.

Summarizing a wide range of research, Fallon shows that attractiveness is important for the positive evaluation of adults and that slimness is a component of attractiveness. However, many people, particularly women, are dissatisfied with their own weight and shape, with most women preferring to be lighter than their current weight. For example, a study discussed by Fallon (1990) reports that:

> College students judged their current figures to be significantly heavier than their ideal figure. In contrast, male college students (as a group) feel themselves to be close to their ideal in weight. Both men and women in their 40s and 50s share similar dissatisfaction with body shape; both judge their ideal to be significantly thinner than their current shape.
>
> (Fallon 1990: 93)

For those of us who take for granted the desirability of being slim, Fallon's work is an important reminder that ideals of beauty are variable and that the emphasis on slimness is a very recent characteristic and, even today, occurs only in modern western societies. There are other illustrations of the processes Fallon describes. For example, in the medieval period it was said: 'Eating made one handsome. A thin wife brought disgrace to a peasant. But of a plump wife it was said that 'a man will love her and not begrudge the food she eats' (quoted by Mennell 1987: 147). The notion that eating made people handsome was not confined to women, nor to those who worked on the land; there are many portraits of the rich, both men and women, who are shown in 'magnificent amplitude'. This emphasis on the importance of size remained an important theme at least until the end of the nineteenth century. Similarly, in modern non-Westernized societies, the ideal woman is much larger than in the West. For example, Buchanan writes of Tanzania that 'men expect their wives to gain weight once they are married: "If she doesn't get fat, people will think I'm not taking good care of her!" men often say' (Buchanan 1993: 36). In the light of such evidence, it is clear that the task is to identify what it is about modern Western societies which is different from Western societies in the past and non-Western societies of today.

These studies raise an important question: 'If standards of attractiveness and ideals of beauty are highly variable, why is the mid- and late-twentieth century associated with an ideal of slimness?' Fallon suggests that the 'curvy look, associated with motherhood, may have lost much of its value in a world striving for zero population growth' (Fallon 1990: 88). For Mennell (1985) the key lies in changed historical circumstances and, in particular, the increasing security of food supplies. As we have already seen in earlier chapters, he argues that, in the premodern period, fluctuations between fasting and feasting, want and plenty, were taken for granted. Even when supplies increased, the fear of food scarcity remained because of the lack of coordination between the location of needs and supplies of produce. The change towards greater security of supplies was a consequence of other changes, for example, the development of trade and a more specialized division of labour in the context of the development of the nation-state. Mennell (1985) maintains that changes in the regulation of appetite in the quantitative sense paralleled the civilizing process and the development of manners. He distinguishes between hunger and appetite and sees appetite as controlled by the 'appestat'. With the appestat set too high, we eat too much food; with it set too low, we eat too little. The setting of the appestat is influenced, even controlled, by both individual and social factors. For example, in Western society the move is towards greater self-control over appetite, a change encouraged by the growing medical opinion, based on rational medical knowledge, that moderation is healthier than excess and that gluttony was coarse. Over time, these processes have culminated in the twentieth-century fear of fatness. This began with the elite and then moved downwards and was associated with the growing confidence in food supplies and the unlikelihood of dearth. Indeed, Mennell (1987) goes so far as to argue that the fear of fat, and certainly the eating disorders of anorexia nervosa and obesity, are problems of prosperous Western societies. His case is supported by the incidence of anorexia nervosa which is thought to have first occurred amongst high-status families. However, the more general approval of self-control over appetite is now part of the message of all magazines going to every social level where slimness is equated with health and sexual attractiveness.

The issue of control is argued by Turner (1991) to be of particular importance in what he terms the production of 'disciplined' bodies. Featherstone (1991) in the same volume draws attention to the contemporary emphasis on general 'body maintenance' which sometimes culminates in an obsession with the procedures for presenting oneself as youthful, healthy and beautiful, almost regardless of biological age. People are willing to spend large sums of money and to invest time and effort in order to overcome any perceived defects or to improve their appearance. Slimness is part of the demonstration to others of individual success, with fat becoming associated with lack of control ('letting oneself go') and thus with moral failing. This preoccupation with fat, diet and slenderness is viewed by Bordo as 'one of the most powerful "normalizing" strategies of our century, ensuring the production of self-monitoring and self-disciplining "docile bodies"' (Bordo 1990: 85). She points out that this creates a situation in which the individual becomes habituated to self-improvement and self-transformation. For historical reasons, she suggests, women are subjected to this form of control to a greater extent than are men, and the idea that women's divergence from these norms is somehow 'pathological' is a powerful device for the reproduction of conventional gender relations. Such a position leads to a closer consideration of other writers' ideas about the links between gender and a concern with body weight and shape.

WHY WOMEN? THE IMPORTANCE OF GENDER

Meadow and Weiss (1992) write as psychologists who work with women suffering from eating disorders. They argue that their work, together with all that they have read in the popular literature and observed 'in the culture', leads them to the view that food and eating are 'a metaphor for what is required for survival as a woman in today's society' (Meadow and Weiss 1992: ix). They contrast the contemporary situation with the 1950s and 1960s, when eating disorders were rare and almost unheard of, and magazines showed food as a natural part of life with none of the 'romantic, mysterious and forbidden connotations that it has today' (Meadow and Weiss 1992: 60). At that time, the ideal figure was voluptuous. However, it must not be assumed that it was easy to achieve. Women struggled to achieve it in the same way as they try to attain today's ideal of the thin and sinewy body. They argue that women 'have always defined themselves in terms of an external ideal' which 'simply reflects the norms of the times' (Meadow and Weiss 1992: 96). The authors are in no doubt that the norms are set by men and that women tend to be evaluated on the basis of their physical appearance as an indicator of their value in the marriage market. Traditionally, the great majority of women would have been financially as well as emotionally dependent on men, and would have been able to embrace the qualities of caretaking and nurturing as an integral part of the 'female psyche', leading them to place particular value on sexual and social relationships.

However, the current preoccupation with thinness for women has its origins in a series of social changes: the new youth culture of the 1960s with its emphasis on the natural, youthful look; the demands for equality from the women's movement and the move towards a more androgynous body image; reliable contraception; greater access to career opportunities in the labour market where a 'motherly image' would be positively disadvantageous; the fitness movement and ideas about the ways in which exercise could change the look of the body. In sum, 'Through her perfect body, she announces that she can have it all: look like a woman and succeed like a man' (Meadow and Weiss 1992: 99). The preoccupation with thinness is so powerful that 'Fat oppression, the fear and hatred of fat people, remains one of the few "acceptable" prejudices still held by otherwise progressive persons' (Meadow and Weiss 1992: 133).

Meadow and Weiss argue that the tension between the demands of personal relationships and those of the marketplace place women in a situation where there is conflict between the desire for dependence and the need for self-expression, a conflict which manifests itself through food. They argue that the link between food and love begins at birth, and that food can become a source of love, comfort, warmth and security, particularly in a society where high divorce rates offer no guarantees of permanent partners and providers and where women are encouraged to maintain their independence. However, although food offers the advantages of asking nothing from you other than that you enjoy it, and is an area of life where one can put one's own needs ahead of others, it also presents problems in that 'food is a destructive lover, a double-edged sword. At the same time that it offers immediate gratification and comfort, it insidiously builds up a layer of fat that society states is guaranteed to make one unlovable' (Meadow and Weiss 1992: 125). The authors conclude that there is a direct link between eating disorders and the powerful emphasis on slimness as the basis of female beauty. For the authors, the solution to the problem of eating disorders is to challenge the rules by recognizing that it is impossible to attain bodily perfection and that slimness does not automatically deliver love and happiness.

Charles and Kerr (1986b) point out that most empirical studies of women and food focus on women who have some kind of eating disorder and that there is virtually no research exploring women's 'normal' relationship with food. Drawing upon their own sociological research based on interviews with 200 women, research which was discussed in detail in Chapter 4, they argue that virtually all women have a relationship with food which is problematic and that individual responses lie on a continuum with eating disorders at one extreme. Women are caught up in a contradiction: they must be both the guardians of their families' health and see that they are properly fed, whilst at the same time they must be attractive for their husbands by being slim and fashionably dressed. It is slimness which is equated with sexual attractiveness in our society and it is also legitimized by the medical profession as being healthy, yet these views do not fit with the ideologies of maternity and maternal care. There is clearly a tension inherent in being both slim and going through pregnancies and in feeding others and yet remaining slender. A further tension is caused by the fact that sweet foods are used to reward and comfort. It is no surprise that the women in the sample were dissatisfied with their present weight and not happy with their body image. Only twenty-three (11.5 per cent) of the women in the sample claimed never to have dieted nor to have had worries about their weight. Dissatisfaction was reinforced by the negative comments of men, particularly their partners. Except when pregnant, it was virtually impossible to be relaxed about food. Since the women in the sample were no longer in employment, there were tensions because they were constantly in the presence of food, acknowledging it as a source of comfort, yet wanting to avoid eating it. All wished to be a few pounds lighter and successful dieting was reported to give a feeling of well-being, achievement and control, yet it was extremely difficult to manage. Charles and Kerr (1986b) also present the argument that this situation of tension is the consequence of women's position of relative powerlessness in capitalist society, where control is exerted over women by ideologies which define female beauty in terms of unnatural slimness to which, by definition, most women's bodies do not approximate. At its most serious, the body and food are regarded as hated enemies. For example, some women even start smoking in an attempt to suppress appetite or to avoid eating. Charles and Kerr emphasize that these are not the problems of those with identifiable eating disorders; these problems are the product of women's structural position and are a function of their marginal and powerless situation in society.

Cline (1990) draws upon qualitative interviews with women in England and in North America, together with her own experiences in relation to food, to argue a similar case: that women's relationship to food rests on contradictions. However, she goes further and argues that food is yet one more focus for the battle between men and women. The writing is vivid and direct: 'Women's bodies have always been a screen onto which different values, such as receptive sexiness or fecundity, have been projected by men' (Cline 1990: 164). Thus, the ideal might vary over time (for example from rounded to 'razor thinness') but the models are always defined by men, and women strive to achieve each in order to obtain men's approval. When the ideal is to achieve extreme slimness, then women take seriously the latest diet and fear the possibility of getting fat. All this makes food a source of danger for women. In common with Charles and Kerr, Cline emphasizes the widespread character of these concerns and argues that eating disorders have to be seen in this context. As the Western cultural ideal weight continues to decline, all women's eating habits become destabilized, raising the possibility of higher levels of clinical disorders. The author sees it as a tragedy that 'there is hardly a woman in the West between adolescence and old age who does not desire to alter something about her shape or size' (Cline 1990: 187). If they do not achieve the changed shape or weight loss, then women feel themselves to be failures. This is also a tragedy in that women, Cline asserts, are challenging their own biology, a biology which may be geared to maintaining a certain fat level and which may resist attempts to achieve a permanent reduction in that level.

One of the most famous contributions to the general debate about the cult of slimness is *Fat is a Feminist Issue* (Orbach 1988). Originally intended to be a self-help guide to compulsive eaters, the book has subsequently been interpreted as having a more general relevance. Orbach locates the preference for being thin in the structure and organization of patriarchal society of late capitalism where middle-class female socialization offers contradictory expectations: an egalitarian emphasis on educational and work opportunities existing alongside an emphasis on traditional female sexual identity in motherhood. The outcome is confusion, insecurity, low self-esteem and negative body images which are expressed in ambivalence about eating and ambiguities about women's aspirations. The solution offered by Orbach is for women to abandon dieting and to allocate priority to their own interests and their own life. Once fat is no longer a central concern, weight will no longer be a problem, in that a more 'natural' (and lower?) body weight will be achieved. Examples are given from her own and others' experiences. Orbach writes as a 'feminist therapist' with a commitment to help women who suffer from compulsive eating to reduce both their anxieties and their weight. Diamond (1985) contends, however, that it is inappropriate for feminists to engage in discussions about weight and body image, in that involvement in such discussion takes for granted, instead of challenging, the thin/fat opposition and, in particular, the privileging of thin over fat. In Diamond's view, feminists should be concerned to develop, collectively, new arrays of identities and alternative body images.

A collection of contributions from academics and from those involved in therapy and in community education edited by Brown and Jasper (1993) reports on feminist approaches which present challenges to the conventional pressures on women to police their own bodies through habitual dieting. There are women, they argue, who are prepared to accept their bodies as they are and to reject the treadmill of constant nutritional self-denial. The editors indicate their preference for avoiding terms such as 'eating disorders', 'anorexia', and 'bulimia' because they are terms which originated in psychiatric literature and are associated with a medical or disease model, a model which they wish to criticize. However, in the end, they retain the use of such terms because they are everyday terms which are readily comprehensible to a wide readership. Interestingly, whilst they recognize that words like 'obese' and 'overweight' imply deviation from some objective standard, the editors recommend reclaiming the word *fat* by shedding its pejorative overtones and using it simple to refer to a particular body type.

Brown and Jasper's answer to the questions 'Why weight?' 'Why women?' and 'Why now?' is similar to those identified above, in that they see the ideal of the slim body as a product of industrialization, the increasing participation of women in the labour force and the impact of feminism with its pressure for increased social equality.

RECENT TRENDS IN BODY WEIGHT

Alongside feminist analyses of the significance of slimness in the context of the control of women in a patriarchal framework, there does, of course, exist a medical model of the significance of body weight. In contemporary medical discourse slimness is often equated with health and a range of diseases and disorders has been directly linked to obesity. For example, the US Food and Nutrition Board of the Institute of Medicine (Thomas 1991: 102–3) began its discussions on dietary recommendations by noting that body weight and body mass index are increasing in the USA and other Westernized societies and also noted that excess weight is associated with an increased risk of several health disorders, including certain types of diabetes, hypertension and coronary heart disease. The Board also note that, in the USA, disadvantaged groups are more likely than the general population to suffer from diseases associated with obesity. Although some feminists might deplore an argument which equates fatness with pathology, seeing it as part of an oppressive patriarchal ideology, we nevertheless need to confront the question of how weight varies in the populations of countries like the USA and the UK, and whether the patterns are currently undergoing change. Ironically, as the evidence about the links between weight level and health builds up, there is also evidence that an increasing proportion of the population falls into the category of being medically defined as obese. The government-initiated *Health Survey for England 1991* (Office of Population Censuses and Surveys – Social Survey Division 1993: x) summarizes the situation as follows: 'There is a considerable amount of epidemiological evidence that obesity is related to ill health and results in increased risks of a number of diseases including hypertension and CVD [cardiovascular disease].' The report employs the standard measure known as body mass index (BMI), calculated by dividing the weight of the individual in kilograms by the square of his or her height in metres. The BMI, a continuous variable, can be divided into a series of categories and the ones used in the report are those used by the Royal College of Physicians (See Table 8.1).

Table 8.1   Body mass index categories

Level of BMI Index	Description
20 or less	Underweight
over 20 to 25	Desirable
over 25 to 30	Overweight
over 30	Obese

Source: Adapted from Office of Population, Censuses and Surveys 1993

The 1991 data indicated that mean BMI for men was 25.6 and for women 25.4. However, 53 per cent of men and 44 per cent of women were shown to have a BMI of over 25 and, indeed, 13 per cent of men and 16 per cent of women fell into the category over 30 and therefore were defined as obese. The report also identified significant increases in mean BMI for men and women in the 16–64 age group over the previous decade (for men an increase from 24.3 to 25.5 and for women an increase from 24.0 to 25.2). The report also compares the situation in 1991 with that which pertained in 1986/7 and notes a striking increase in the proportion of adults aged 16–64 with a BMI of over 30. For men the figure rose from 7 per cent to 13 per cent and for women from 13 per cent to 15 per cent (OPCS 1993: x).

The association between BMI and such variables as age, social class and education is also discussed. BMI tends to increase with age up to 65 but then tails off. Men in non-manual social class categories tend to have a higher BMI than those in manual categories although, interestingly, the reverse is the case for women, with those in non-manual groups tending to have a lower BMI than those in manual groups (OPCS 1993: x).

These figures suggest yet another paradox within the realm of food and eating. If we accept the contention that Western society places a heavy emphasis on the slender body as a cultural ideal, these data suggest that the average woman (and, indeed, the average man) is actually moving further away from this ideal, and for an increasingly large number this ideal is completely out of reach. This ideal and the divergence from it creates the conditions for the development of a thriving slimming industry. It is an industry with a guaranteed clientele in those who strive for slimness but may actually see their goal constantly retreating before them. This is illustrated dramatically by the estimates given by Meadow and Weiss (1992) in their discussion of the scale of the slimming market in the USA. Over 60 per cent of women are said to be dieting at some point in a year and that number may be increasing. The authors present calculations to show that more than $10 billion a year are spent on 'diet drugs, diet meals, diet books, exercise tapes, weight-loss classes, and fat farms' (Meadow and Weiss 1992: 25). Within this overall figure, they estimate that $800 million are spent on frozen diet dinners and another $200 million on diet pills. There are no directly comparable firgures for the UK. However, there is evidence to suggest that the UK slimming product market is also big business. For example, the market for all types of reduced-calorie foods was estimated at £1.5 billion in 1994 (Economist Intelligence Unit 1994: 48). Within this figure, the market for slimming foods (defined as including meal replacements, very low-calorie diets and appetite suppressants) was valued at more than £69 million. In the previous three years, meal replacements were the fastest-growing sector of the slimming foods market with the market in very low-calorie diets declining and the market in appetitie suppressants remaining a relatively low but stable sector of the market. The authors refer to medical research which indicates that up to 24 per cent of women and 37 per cent of men are 'overweight'. Even so, it is women who are more likely to be involved in slimming. As the association of slimness with health (rather than with responsiveness to social pressures to be slim) becomes established, the authors argue that a more 'unisex image' is likely to develop, with men and women associating slimming with movement towards a more healthy lifestyle. If this happens, the writers argue, the market in slimming foods is likely to change and there may be a blurring of the lines between foods which are marketed as slimming and those which are marketed as being associated with more general healthy eating (Economist Intelligence Unit 1994: 52). There is nothing to suggest that such foods will not also be marketed aggressively in an effort to continue to profit from the manufacture and sale of special foods.

EATING DISORDERS

The paradoxical nature of the situation in which there simultaneously exists a cultural ideal of slimness and a rising trend towards obesity, as we have already noted, is one which potentially creates a certain tension for many individuals in their relationship to food. It is clear that a significant proportion of the population of societies like the UK and USA experience a chronic state of concern about their weight and that conventionally this is seen as a concern which affects women more frequently than men. However, in certain circumstances, disturbances related to eating and weight can be so severe that they are clinically defined as serious eating disorders, which can be very debilitating and, indeed, even life-threatening to the sufferer.

Any discussion of such eating disorders is likely to rely heavily upon studies of those specifically involved in the analysis, treatment and management of anorexia nervosa. This particular disorder has certainly attracted the major share of attention in this area. Amongst such studies is the work of Bruch (1978) who was one of the first to draw attention to the increase in the number of cases amongst young women and to the contradictions and paradoxes associated with the disease. Although focused on a set of case studies from her own therapeutic practice, Bruch sets her analysis in the context of cultural and, indeed, physiological responses to food and uses this context to highlight the underlying and often unrecognized logic of her patients' anorexic behaviour. Bruch's interpretation of her case studies is that these young women from upper-middle- and upper-class homes use their anorexia, consciously or otherwise, to draw attention to themselves, possibly in an exhibitionistic fashion, in order to make sure that others care for them. In a sense, she suggests, their behaviour attracts a degree of awe and even admiration from people for whom self-starvation is a course of action which they would never countenance for themselves. She goes on to argue that the disease gives the girls power through the control of their eating. In contrast to those who argue that women are passive recipients of cultural expectations, Bruch uses her case material to argue that the sufferer is an active participant, rejecting food that is offered and available and becoming resentful of attempts to restore 'normal weight', because this process of starving 'in some strange way...fulfils their urgent desire to be special and outstanding' (1978: 20–1).

Bruch's book is entitled *The Golden Cage*, a title derived from an image used by one of her patients to explain her feeling both of being unworthy of all the privileges and benefits offered by her family and of at the same time being constrained and deprived of freedom of action. The question thus arises as to what kind of home relationships could produce feelings of this kind, so powerful that the outcome was a health-threatening condition. Bruch indicates that many of her patients had in common small family size with a predominance of daughters (two-thirds of the families had daughters only), and older parents. The impression of the harmonious home and the initially compliant behaviour from the child may conceal complex relationships of high expectations and parental lack of awareness concerning the extent to which the child is being controlled and restricted. Bruch argues that their inability to let go and permit the child to develop independently may contribute to and sustain the illness. Her case material seemed to indicate that the illness often manifested itself at a point where the young women were confronted by some new experience, such as going to a new school or to college, where they no longer had the support of the family and where they were anxious about having to cope with relationships outside the family and to perform on the basis of their own merits. In other words, they seemed to be afraid of becoming teenagers with all the independence and femininity implied. In extreme cases, Bruch argues, the patients' weight loss enabled them to return to childhood. Bruch even goes as far as to suggest, perhaps very contentiously, that this behaviour may be interpreted as a means of avoiding the end of 'a secret dream of growing up to be a boy' (Bruch 1978: 69). In addition, dieting could provide an area of control and accomplishment and, paradoxically, patients could even experience a sense of satisfaction in relation to their own self-imposed ill-health. Within this framework, treatment involves the family as well as the specific sufferer and is considered successful when the young women involved both are able to gain sufficient weight so that their health is not endangered and to be recognized within the family as an individual with independent needs. Interestingly, Bruch is one of the few writers on this topic who see the possibility of a decline in the incidence of anorexia nervosa. She notes the way in which, when she first had sufferers referred to her, each of her patients would emphasize her uniqueness. In recent years, not only do patients know of other sufferers but they have also read a great deal about the illness (including Bruch's own contributions to the literature), so Bruch speculates that, if anorexia nervosa becomes sufficiently common, it will, in a sense, become 'commonplace'. Thus, sufferers would no longer gain the same sense of satisfaction at being special through achieving something that others cannot achieve.

One of the most comprehensive reviews of the literature on the characteristics of those suffering from eating disorders is that of Hsu (1990), which was written specifically to provide a summary of current knowledge on the eating disorders of anorexia nervosa and bulimia nervosa. The focus is on attempts to define and identify the disorders in a clinical sense and also to provide information about empirical findings, although there is more information about anorexia nervosa than about bulimia nervosa. Like other writers, he notes that the first use of the term 'anorexia nervosa' (from the Greek term for 'loss of appetite') was relatively recent, even though the condition had been recognized earlier as an illness which occurred infrequently. The term was used first in 1874 by the medical practitioner Sir William Gull to identify the eating problems of some of his young, female patients. The term has remained and is used widely in non-medical contexts, even though Hsu argues that it may, in fact, be a misnomer, since the evidence suggests that many patients have not 'lost' their appetites and often, in fact, wish to eat but are afraid to do so. Many studies show that patients identified as suffering from anorexia nervosa exhibit similar characteristics. However, the boundary between this disorder and 'normal' dieting is recognized as a blurred one and Hsu (1990) raises the question of whether anorexia nervosa is, in fact, an extreme form of the widespread phenomenon of dieting but a form which has run out of control. Having recognized what he sees as a 'behavioural continuum' between dieting and anorexia nervosa, Hsu takes the view that the crucial task is to identify those factors which might push the individual towards the anorexic end of this continuum. Thus, he identifies the central feature of the anorexia nervosa sufferer as a severe distortion of attitudes towards weight, eating and fatness. Hsu notes that the resultant fear of fatness actually intensifies as the individual loses weight, though for sufferers from bulimia nervosa the fear is accompanied by powerful urges to overeat or 'binge' and then to shed the unwanted food through vomiting or the use of laxatives. Since Hsu's task is largely informed by a wish to provide information which could form the basis for the treatment of disorders, he is primarily concerned to analyse the available data in such a way as to reveal crucial interactions between the cultural, psycho-logical and biological processes involved. The survey of empirical investigations of these which Hsu provides is an attempt to examine data on such interactions.

Hsu begins by summarizing the data recorded about sufferers from eating disorders and indicates that those most commonly affected consistently exhibit certain features: they are young (often adolescent), white, female (the ratio of female to male is ten to one), and drawn from families located in the middle or upper social classes. They are also likely to already have been involved in attempts to control weight. Reviewing the clinical data from the available American and British studies, Hsu notes that most cases are presented to the medical practitioner when the sufferer is in her late teens. The case notes which Hsu reviews indicate that approximately 25 per cent of anorexics and about 40 per cent of bulimics were recorded as overweight before the onset of their illness and thus he concludes that attempts to control weight are the initiating phase of both these illnesses, though once there has been some weight loss, the two disorders diverge (Hsu 1990: 14). The anorexic person pursues thinness in spite of escalating weight loss; the bulimic person establishes a pattern of fasting, bingeing and purging with two-thirds using vomiting to control their weight. In ways which are similar to accounts of those who have been forced on to starvation diets because of external factors such as war or imprisonment, suf-ferers from eating disorders also begin to show an increased preoccupation with food and eating and an obsessive interest in recipes and cooking.

At the very point when family, friends and medical advisers are deeply concerned about the pattern of rapid weight loss, the sufferers themselves often deny that they are ill. Some even claim that they feel special or unique because of their thinness and experience despair and panic if they begin to gain weight. Some, indeed, claimed explicitly that their thinness demonstrated their auton-omy. However, few were able to explain their fear of fatness. Those suffering from bulimia nervosa also feared fatness but were less able to control their food intake. Various situations or experiences could trigger binges. There are con-siderable problems involved in obtaining accurate information about the events which may have precipitated these eating disorders. However, the material provided by patients includes a range of possibilities which seem to emphasize the significance of social relationships and potentially stressful events in adolescence. Such events included feelings of being too fat, being teased about size, the occurrence of interpersonal conflicts, separation from the family, personal illness or failure and family crises. In relation to the latter, Hsu draws attention to the importance of recognizing that, in certain circumstances, the illness might prove useful to the family by, for example, stabilizing its relationships by focusing collective concern on the person who is ill.

Anxieties about weight appear to be accentuated amongst higher socio-economic groups where thinness is sought after yet where there is ample food available. The high-status young women described in the case material were particularly aware of the importance of a favourable evaluation from others for the maintenance of their self-esteem. In addition, many of the young women in these groups aspired to combine professional careers with motherhood, that is, non-traditional aspirations informed by new models of women's potential. For some, these tensions about social identity could lead to eating disorders. Indeed, as Hsu asserts, 'Thus it would appear that the feminist movement has so far brought mixed blessings for women' (Hsu 1990: 86).

The range and detail handled by Hsu in his analysis is impressive. However, he is not able to come to any precise conclusions about the causes of eating disorders and sees treatment of them as involving a largely pragmatic selection from a wide range of possible therapeutic responses. None the less, Hsu's account involves more than mere summary. He makes an important argument that, if eating disturbances occur on a behavioural continuum, then the prevalence of eating disorders will increase or decline in proportion to dieting behaviour in the population. Associated with this is his observation that, although eating disorders appear to be linked with dieting behaviour, not everybody who diets moves along the continuum towards an eating disorder. This means that an interesting research issue would be an attempt to identify those influences which moderate eating patterns as well as those which precipitate disordered eating patterns.

Whilst Hsu acknowledges the significance of sociocultural factors, it is not his primary concern to analyse these in detail. However, for other authors such factors provide their central interest. For example, Brumberg (1988) focuses on the cultural context of eating disorders, in particular, anorexia nervosa. In common with other writers, she recognizes that anorexics frequently belong to prosperous families in an affluent social world: 'In other words, the anorexic population has a highly specific social address' (Brumberg 1988: 13). Brumberg sees anorexia nervosa as the outcome of the 'psychopathology' of middle-class life which, for some, generates tensions between a preoccupation with looks, dating rituals and pressures to succeed in both the private and the public domains. In more general terms, she suggests that the idealization of the thin and weak female body is a symptom of the female subordination which is characteristic of capitalism and patriarchy.

MacSween (1993) takes previous studies as her starting-point with the aim of providing a perspective on anorexia nervosa which is both feminist and şocio-logical. She notes the ways in which anorexia nervosa has recently moved from being a relatively unknown psychiatric illness to a position where the term has been incorporated into the popular vocabulary and is increasingly used to label any woman in the public eye who is perceived as underweight. Anorexia nervosa is seen by MacSween as of particular interest for feminists and for sociologists in that its apparent increasing incidence has taken place among middle-class women at precisely the time when feminism is challenging female subordination. MacSween argues that most discussions recognize these issues and make reference to them but few actually attempt to provide a satisfactory sociological analysis. Her own analysis is based upon an examination of anorexic meanings and practices as revealed by interview material from one bulimic and eight anorexic women, together with the results of a postal questionnaire completed by women who had experienced or were experiencing this disorder. MacSween wishes to avoid what she terms an 'added on' sociological perspective which simply argues that, while there are 'social pressures' on young women, it is some shortcoming in the sufferer prior to the onset of anorexia nervosa which explains why one woman rather than another becomes anorexic. On the contrary, she asserts that 'in the anorexic symptom women try to synthesize contradictory elements in their social position through the creation of an "anorexic body"' (MacSween 1993: 2).

In discussing the rejection of such social causation by writers who emphasize the importance of individual psychology in the onset of anorexia nervosa, MacSween (1993) argues that it is important not to assume that social pressures constrain all individuals in similar ways and to recognize that circumstances do not determine behaviour but rather set the framework within which a range of behaviours can occur. In this author's terms, anorexia nervosa is one particular response to the contradictions and pressures experienced by women in a patri-archal and capitalist setting. Anorexia nervosa is one response to the contra-dictions inherent in female identity as constructed in a patriarchal capitalist system which, in effect, survived the onslaught of feminism and continued into the post-feminist era. A further barrier to a fuller understanding of the social construction of conditions like anorexia nervosa and how they are experienced is the emphasis of many writers on therapy and treatment. Psychological analysis, in particular, appears to be based on the assumption that the cause of anorexia nervosa is to be found at the individual level and therefore it should be treated at the individual level. In MacSween's view psychological analysis overemphasizes the idea that the causation of anorexia nervosa can be understood at the individual and interpersonal level and, therefore, puts too much faith in the effectiveness of treatment at the individual level. From this point of view, the emphasis on therapy, with its model of the 'natural', 'whole' person which can be reclaimed through successful treatment, gets in the way of a thorough going analysis of the roots of the problem. According to MacSween, the social construction of bodies in bourgeois society involves gender defined in terms of an opposition between masculine as active and feminine as passive. The problem for women in modern society is to reconcile the contradictory demands of being both active and passive, both assertive and responsive. It is MacSween's contention that this struggle can be manifested at the level of the body, through the production of the classic symptoms of anorexia nervosa.

The strength of MacSween's position as a feminist sociologist is that it encourages us to be aware of the cultural and structural setting which can give rise to such apparently bizarre phenomena as eating disorders. There is, of course, the strong implication in this view that, while an individual 'cure' for an individual case of, for example, anorexia nervosa might be achieved through skilful and dedicated therapy, the underlying conditions and contradictions remain. Not surprisingly, from her sociological perspective, MacSween takes the view that only a transformation guided by feminist principles of the structural conditions which sustain the subordination of women can have any long-term effect on the incidence of eating disorders of the kind we have been discussing in this chapter.

OVERVIEW

There can be little doubt that concern with body image, body fat and dieting is so pervasive within contemporary popular consciousness that it represents one of the more distinctive cultural obsessions of our age. We are faced with an apparent paradox: in the context of an abundant food supply many Western consumers (particularly women) become preoccupied with the desire to restrict food intake. However, in a sense, this apparent paradox is dispelled when we recognize that in a situation where food is not abundant and the food supply is not reliable the restriction of food intake to control body weight is, for the most part, an irrelevance. In this sense, the highly productive nature of the modern food system itself generates the motivation to control the quantity of nutrients absorbed. In fact, we have noted the existence of a more clear-cut paradox: the observation that, at precisely the time when our cultural preference for the slim body has been intensifying, actual body weights and levels of obesity in the population (as measured, for example, by mean BMI) have been rising. The response of commercial interests within a capitalist system has been to focus these anxieties by the provision of special diets, foods and relevant information and to capitalize on them to enhance profits.

The feminist contribution to the whole debate concerning body image and dieting has been a considerable one. It has encouraged social scientists to pay due attention to the patriarchal and capitalist context of the social construction of the feminine body. Similarly, feminist analyses have made a valuable contribution to the enhancement of our understanding of eating disorders by requiring that they be extracted from the narrow confines of a purely clinical setting and placed within a broader context of gender politics. As we have seen, the already complex debate concerning the causation of eating disorders has itself been complicated by a division between those who are primarily concerned to offer treatment at an individual level, and those whose main concern is to offer a sociological analysis which may emphasize structural constraints and contradictions which could only be resolved through collective action or far-reaching social transformations.

Quite clearly, this chapter, in attempting to provide a review of the literature on dieting, body image and eating disorders, inevitably reflects that literature's preoccupation with the predicament of women. However, we must bear in mind the distinct possibility that concern about weight and even the incidence of eating disorders may actually be rising amongst men. To date, this issue has received comparatively little attention from social scientists. If it should prove to be that case that issues of body weight and disordered eating become entangled with masculinity as well as femininity, then currently widely accepted explanatory frameworks, particularly those based on feminist perspectives, would need extensive reappraisal and revision.

Part IV

PATTERNS OF PREFERENCE AND AVOIDANCE

9

THE MYSTERIOUS MEANINGS
OF MEAT

Meat, in its many forms, represents what is probably the most universally valued of foods across the broad spectrum of human cultures. For an omnivorous species like ourselves, it can be construed as a food of particularly high nutritional value, especially as a source of protein. However, this whole book is, of course, based upon the premise that human food consumption is not only a question of satisfying nutritional needs. Certainly, it could be argued that there is much more to meat eating than the ingestion of a conveniently packaged range of important nutrients. For example, meat is arguably one of the most ambivalent of food items in terms of the three paradoxes discussed in Chapter 7. In gustatory terms, in health terms and in moral terms, meat carries particularly potent connotations, both positive and negative.

This chapter is concerned with the fundamental questions of why humans eat meat, and why they endow it with such significance. Are these effects largely a function of its physiological and nutritional relevance to the human diet or is its symbolic potential the more important source of its widespread appeal? We will consider these questions by examining the work of a range of social scientists whose views are sometimes in conflict, but who all acknowledge the singular salience of this particular food. However, initially we will need to consider briefly, by way of background, the nutritional import of meat in the human diet before examining the argument that our appetite for meat is, at root, a physiologically driven imperative which finds expression in many ways and in many guises. The symbolic dimensions of meat will be introduced by reconsidering examples of the taboos and prohibitions which exist, or have existed, in more traditional cultures. This will then lead us to an examination of the complex and often highly ambiguous symbolism associated with meat in contemporary Western culture. Finally, we will assess the view that the underlying meanings of meat in Western thought are undergoing far-reaching changes, associated with broader shifts in ideas about the relationship between humans and the natural world.

MEAT IN THE HUMAN DIET

In order to understand the role of meat in the human diet, a necessary first step is to attempt to clarify just what is meant by this term. In fact, in English the word 'meat' has a very broad meaning and can, indeed, signify literally anything that is edible. However, in its narrower sense, the word has come to denote the flesh of animals in general. Even more narrowly, in everyday parlance, the word 'meat' can be used quite specifically to refer to the flesh of mammals. What is more, the term 'meat' is usually assumed to refer to lean skeletal muscle tissues, that is, muscle tissue attached to the skeleton directly, and thus excluding the muscular tissues of such organs as the heart and the tongue. Indeed, in contemporary British culinary culture these organs are classified as 'offal' and usually regarded as cheap, low-status and not particularly palatable food items. Nevertheless, in the UK food manufacturers and retailers are permitted by law to label quite a wide range of offal as 'meat' on their product packaging. As well as heart and tongue, this category includes kidney, liver and pancreas, but excludes brain tissue and parts of the alimentary canal and reproductive system. It is clear, then, that the word 'meat' is something of a semantic minefield, with its multiple meanings and convoluted connotations. In this chapter we will be using the term in the broader sense of animal flesh in general, as well as in the narrower sense of lean muscle tissue (usually, but not necessarily, derived from a mammal).

Lean meat (i.e., lean muscle tissue) is composed of approximately 70 per cent water and 20 per cent protein before cooking, plus variable amounts of fat, connective tissue, vitamins and minerals. The amount of fat in muscle tissue depends upon a range of factors related to genetics, feeding and activity levels. Wild mammals, for example, have significantly less fat inside their muscle tissues than do domesticated mammals. The actual structure of meat is complex. It is composed of muscle blocks made up of bundles of elongated cells capable of contraction and relaxation to produce movement in limbs and organs. Muscles are bound together with connective tissue containing the proteins elastin and collagen (which yields gelatin on boiling) and are served by an elaborate network of blood vessels and nerves. Well-used muscles are made up of thicker fibres and contain more connective tissues than less-used muscles and therefore produce tougher meat. Meat intended for human consumption is usually cooked in order to neutralize potentially harmful organisms it may contain and to tenderize it. Tougher meat is often subjected to 'moist' cooking methods like boiling and stewing, since these are more effective in breaking down connective tissue than 'dry' methods like grilling and roasting. Hanging meat after slaughter is also a common practice, as this allows rigor mortis to wear off and facilitates the tenderizing effect brought on by complex chemical changes in the tissues themselves.

The nutritional significance of meat for humans is related to our specific needs for certain amino acids. The proteins which are indispensable constituents of the human body (as they are of all living things) are made up of chains of amino acid molecules. Some of the amino acids which make up human proteins can be made by the body itself, and do not need to be supplied in a ready-made form in the diet. However, other amino acids cannot be synthesized by the human body and have to be obtained directly by breaking down proteins that have been ingested. These are termed *essential* amino acids, in the sense that they are essential components of any nutritionally adequate diet. There are eight of these essential amino acids for adults, and ten for children. Quite clearly, dietary proteins whose components most closely match human essential amino acid requirements will be of particular nutritional value. In fact, the closest match is provided by egg protein, and this is often used as a kind of standard against which other proteins can be compared. Proteins which are rich in essential amino acids are conventionally termed 'high biological value' proteins (Brownsell, Griffith and Jones 1989: 40), and as well as eggs include a wide range of meat, fish and other animal products. Those which are deficient in one or more of the essential amino acids are termed 'low biological value' proteins. All plant proteins fall into this category, since no plant proteins contain all the essential amino acids. Of course, the full inventory of essential amino acids can be obtained by consuming a suitable combination of plant-derived foods. However, what is distinctive about animal-derived proteins like meat is that they contain all the essential amino acids in one readily assimilable package. In addition, animal products also provide the crucial vitamin B_{12}, which is not found in vegetable food items. Liver is the richest source of this vitamin, although it is also present in meat, milk, eggs and fish. A deficiency of vitamin B_{12} causes the disease pernicious anaemia, which is associated with such symptoms as spinal cord lesions, weakness, numbness of the arms and legs, and diarrhoea. This disease is usually the result of the body's failure to absorb vitamin B_{12}, but pernicious anaemia among vegans, arising from the total exclusion of animal products from the diet, has been observed (Gaman and Sherrington 1981: 96). Thus, the use of dietary supplements containing synthesized B_{12} is a sensible precaution for anyone following a strictly vegan dietary regime.

As a rough rule of thumb, it has been suggested that the typical adult requires approximately one gram of protein per kilogram of body weight per day, whereas children, with the added demands of growth, require approximately two grams per kilogram of bodyweight per day. Protein requirements rise during pregnancy and lactation, and during illness and convalescence. Various attempts have been made to calculate the sources of protein in the average British diet, and from these we can obtain some idea of the significance of meat in this respect. Thus, Gaman and Sherrington (1981: 80–1) estimate that meat in all forms contributes around 31 per cent of protein intake. Fish contributes approximately 4 per cent (being eaten much less frequently), milk 18 per cent, cheese 5 per cent and eggs 5 per cent. Significant contributions from non-animal products include bread and flour (19 per cent) and other cereal foods, such as rice, pasta and breakfast cereals (7 per cent). Later estimates offered by Brownsell, Griffith and Jones (1989: 45) provide a broadly comparable picture, with meat making a 30 per cent contribution to the protein component of the British diet, fish 4 per cent, milk 18 per cent, eggs 5 per cent and bread 20 per cent. While these figures are only broad approximations, they do indicate the centrality of meat as a protein source, and the overall preponderance of animal products in this respect.

Meat has long held a dominant position in the typical American diet, a dominance which has its origins in the early days of European settlement and the abundance of game species (Thomas 1991: 42). Levenstein (1988: 4–5) also links the centrality of meat in American diets to the long-term influence of British culinary culture, in which meat has traditionally been accorded pride of place. Thus, for example, nineteenth-century American cuisine involved the consumption of large quantities of pork, plus lesser amounts of lamb and poultry. Beef, however, was pre-eminent in terms of the status accorded to it and the symbolic value placed upon it. On the other hand, as Levenstein points out, the early New Englanders held fruit and vegetables in relatively low esteem, consuming them in comparatively small quantities. Indeed until the mid-nineteenth century constipation seems to have been regarded as a widespread national affliction among Americans, due to the large quantities of meat and starch consumed, compared to the modest intake of fruit and vegetables (Levenstein 1988: 5).

However, although meat has historically played a central role in British and American diets, the actual patterns of meat consumption are by no means static. In fact, in the course of the twentieth century a number of significant trends have emerged. For example, if we consider meat consumption patterns in the

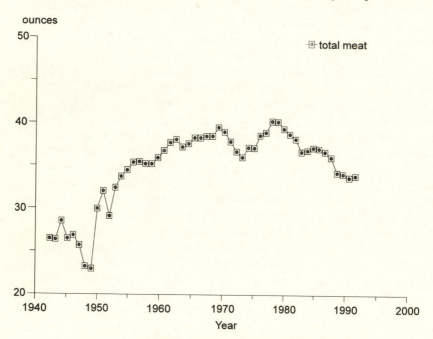

Figure 9.1 Total UK meat consumption (oz per person per week)
Source: Ministry of Agriculture, Fisheries and Food (1991, 1994)

196

UK from the Second World War onwards, we can detect not only changes in overall consumption but also noteworthy shifts in the consumption of specific types of meat and meat products. Figure 9.1 shows the total consumption of meat and meat products in the United Kingdom from 1940 until 1993, expressed in ounces per person per week. This graph has some very clear features. Meat consumption was relatively low during the Second World War as a result of meat rationing, although it dropped even lower during the late 1940s as a result of post-war austerity measures. However, from the early 1950s onwards meat consumption began to rise consistently in response to increased affluence resulting from rising real incomes. After a temporary dip in the 1970s, the figures peaked at 40.27 oz per head in 1979, and then went into decline in the 1980s. Within these broad overall trends, different pictures emerge for different types of meat. Figure 9.2 provides details of consumption trends for beef and veal, mutton and lamb, and poultry, also for the years 1940 to 1993 in oz per person per week. Figure 9.3 shows the same data for pork, bacon and ham, and sausages.

Thus, for example, the consumption of beef and veal, relatively low in the 1940s, rose in the mid-1950s and peaked in 1957 at 10.54 oz per person per week. It then appears to have gone into a rather erratic decline, down to a figure of 4.68 oz by 1993. Mutton and lamb seem to have followed a similar pattern, with consumption peaking at 7.16 ozs in 1956 and declining to 2.33 by 1993. Pork consumption, low in the 1940s, peaked in 1982. Bacon and ham peaked in

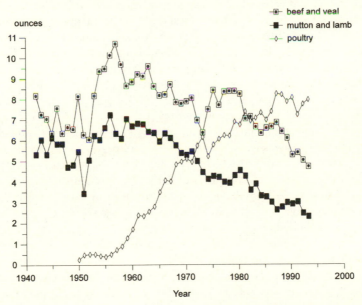

Figure 9.2 UK consumption of beef, lamb and poultry (oz per person per week)
Source: Ministry of Agriculture, Fisheries and Food (1991, 1994)

Figure 9.3 UK consumption of sausages and pork products (oz per person per week)
Source: Ministry of Agriculture, Fisheries and Food (1991, 1994)

1962 and then also declined. Sausages showed their highest level of consumption as early as 1948 and then their popularity began to diminish steadily and consistently. In stark contrast, the data for the consumption of poultry (in the UK this category is made up largely of chicken) exhibits the opposite of the trends we have so far been discussing. From very low levels in the early 1950s (well under 1 oz per person per week on average) consumption climbed steadily to peak at no less than 8.14 oz in 1987. In 1993, poultry was the most popular category of meat in the UK by a wide margin. This trend towards poultry is due in large part to the dramatic drop in its price relative to other meats, a fall which is a result of the progressive intensification of poultry production techniques in a drive to reduce costs and improve profitability. The data indicate a clear pattern, which involves a switch away from meat derived from mammals to meat derived from birds and, broadly speaking, from red meat towards white meat.

A broadly similar picture emerges for the USA when we examine data relating to the quantities of various types of meat available to the public. Such data are not, in themselves, directly comparable to the survey based per capita consumption statistics in Figures 9.1, 9.2, and 9.3, since they are actually attempting to estimate the disappearance of food into both wholesale and retail markets. This is achieved on an annual basis by subtracting exports, year end inventories and non-food uses from production, start of year inventories and imports. Of course, the availability levels will be higher than actual consumption

198

Table 9.1   Quantities of meat available for consumption in the US food supply (lb per capita per annum)

Type of meat	1909–13	1929–33	1944–8	1970–4	1975–9	1987
Beef	53.2	38.2	48.2	83.9	87.8	73.4
Veal	6.3	5.9	9.8	2.0	2.8	1.5
Pork	60.9	63.6	63.9	62.1	55.8	59.2
Lamb & mutton	6.2	5.8	5.4	2.6	1.5	1.3
Chicken	14.9	14.4	19.3	40.5	44.8	62.7
Turkey	1.1	1.6	3.1	8.6	9.1	15.1
Total	142.6	129.5	149.7	199.7	201.8	213.2

Source: Adapted from Thomas (1991: 44–5)

levels, due to wastage in distribution and processing, and in the home (Thomas 1991: 42). Table 9.1 shows the quantities of various types of meat available for consumption in the USA, covering the period 1909 to 1987.

The data for beef show a significant dip in the period 1929–33 and then a dramatic rise to the levels of 1970–4 and 1975–9. This latter period, however, seems to represent a peak, and the figure calculated for the year 1987 shows a significant fall. Veal availability peaks much earlier, in the period 1944–8, and lamb and mutton decline steadily throughout the entire period covered. Interestingly, pork availability seems to remain remarkably stable. In contrast, the availability of chicken rises dramatically, to a level in 1987 which is approximately four times that of 1909–13. The rise of turkey is even more spectacular, to a level in 1987 which is nearly fourteen times higher than the 1909–13 figure. Thus, once again, we observe the stagnation or decline of red meat and a clear trend towards white meat.

However, the trends in meat consumption in countries like the UK and the USA clearly need to be placed in a wider global context. Such a global context is provided by Grigg (1993) who uses the Food Balance Sheets produced by the Food and Agriculture Organization (FAO) as a source of comparative data. For each member country over eighty food items are listed along with the weight available for consumption each year. Items are also converted, for example, into calories per capita per day and grams of protein per capita per day. The data are arrived at by starting with national agricultural production statistics and adding imports and the quantities withdrawn from storage, and then deducting exports, industrial usage and crops retained on the farm. Finally, 10 per cent is deducted to allow for wastage between the production and retailing stages. Although, as we have already noted, actual consumption is lower than availability and, in addition, these statistics can be criticized on several counts, they do provide at least some basis for international comparisons. Perhaps the most useful comparative measure is that which converts food items into calories per capita per day. On this basis, for the years 1986–8, in worldwide terms animal-derived foods provided only 15.7 per cent of per capita calories daily. In fact, meat itself provided only 7.0 per cent of per capita daily calories on a global basis. This figure masks a significant difference between developed and developing countries, however. In the former, on average, individuals derive 30.8 per cent of their daily calories from animal products and 13.1 per cent from meat specifically. In developing countries these figures are only 8.9 per cent and 4.3 per cent respectively (Grigg 1993: 67). Indeed, there appears to be a consistent positive correlation between Gross Domestic Product per capita and livestock-derived calories per capita consumed daily. In short, in worldwide terms, meat eating is clearly associated with wealth. Indeed, the extent of the inequalities in meat consumption becomes even clearer when the data are broken down on a regional basis, as shown in Table 9.2.

Table 9.2   Available meat supply by region expressed as calories per capita per day (1986–88)

Region	All meat	Bovine meat[1]	Sheep meat[2]	Pig meat	Poultry meat	Other meat
Western Europe	476	121	22	269	56	8
Australasia	593	189	168	143	89	4
North America	641	259	1	247	131	3
Eastern Europe & USSR	359	171	13	132	40	3
Latin America	210	113	5	48	42	2
Near East	95	34	42	–	18	1
Far East	30	7	4	12	6	1
Africa	32	23	9	–	–	–
Developed	436	161	15	190	66	4
Developing	100	21	7	60	11	1
World	182	55	9	92	24	2

Note:
1 Cattle and buffalo
2 Includes goat meat
Source: Adapted from Grigg (1993)

There are clearly considerable regional variations in the patterns of meat consumption. For example, the availability of beef-derived calories is particularly high in North America and Australasia, and the same is true for poultry meat. The availability of pig-meat calories is even higher in Western Europe than in North America, and sheep meat is far more common in Australasia than in any other region. Yet the most striking features of Table 9.2 relate to the differences between developed and developing countries, with on average 436 calories per person per day available from meat in the former, and only 100 calories in the latter. Comparing regional inequalities provides even more striking results. The Far East and Africa show only 30 and 32 calories respectively available from meat daily, just about one-twentieth of the level of availability in North America.

Despite the limitations inherent in the statistics Grigg employs, his results clearly demonstrate the extent to which levels of meat consumption vary between the richer and poorer regions. In general, as wealth rises, meat consumption also tends to rise, indicating the extent to which the desirability of this food item is translated into actual demand. Moreover, it should be noted that the comparative data we have considered, given that they are per capita averages, conceal the extensive inequalities which often exist between individuals within a given society or culture, related to status, gender and age, for example. Thus, when we consider the role of meat in the human diet, we must always bear in mind that, while for some individuals this role may be highly significant, for others it may be minimal, and that this state of affairs is as likely to be due to economic constraint as to cultural dictate or personal preference.

THE IDEA OF 'MEAT HUNGER'

In the above section we have noted the nutritional significance of meat in the human diet, in the setting of particular societies like the UK and the USA as well as in a global context. In addition, important changes in meat consumption patterns have been pointed out. Before possible explanations for such changes can be considered in further detail, it is necessary to pose a very fundamental question: 'Why, in fact, do humans go to all the trouble of eating meat?' After all, in its wild form it is often difficult to pursue and hard to catch (Farb and Armelagos 1980: 44). In its domesticated form it is decidedly expensive to obtain. For example, animal protein produced in modern intensive agricultural systems by feeding grain to livestock involves the input of large quantities of vegetable protein. For every kilogram of poultry-meat protein, a chicken needs to be fed 5.9 kilograms of grain protein. For every kilogram of pork protein a pig must be fed 7.7 kilograms of grain protein. Grain-fed beef produced in feedlots is even more demanding, requiring 22 kilograms of grain protein per kilogram of beef protein (Allaby 1977: 20). Thus, in terms of yield per unit of land, livestock products apparently cannot compare in efficiency with vegetable products. Indeed, it has been estimated that every calorie of animal foodstuff produced requires the input of five to eight primary calories (Borgstrom 1972: 31). However, it should be noted that in less intensive agricultural systems, animal husbandry may be a much more obviously efficient use of resources. For example, domesticated food animals can be fed on vegetable by-products and food wastes inappropriate for direct human consumption. Also, areas unsuitable for arable farming (e.g., low-fertility uplands, semi-arid or arid zones) can be used for food production by stocking with grazing or browsing ruminants which can consume high-cellulose plant foods with which the human digestive system cannot cope (Blaxter 1986: 55).

Perhaps the most obvious answer to the question of why humans eat meat (despite the fact that, as already noted, its production can appear inefficient compared to that of vegetable-based foods) relates to the fact that it represents a compact and palatable package rich in nutrients. Some social scientists accept this view as their starting-point for explaining patterns of meat consumption, arguing that the complex symbolic significances which cultures ascribe to meat are, in effect, manifestations or reflections of this underlying nutritional attraction. In contrast, others have argued that the symbolic dimensions of meat, the potent meanings it bears within a given cultural context, provide the principal reasons for its consumption, with nutritional considerations taking second place. Of course, these two views are not, in practice, mutually exclusive, although they do represent an important difference in emphasis, a difference which can lead to very different conclusions. In this chapter we will examine both these views, beginning with what is perhaps the intuitively more obvious one: the idea that humans are drawn to the nutritious properties of meat, and that this is a basic inclination of primary significance.

This idea finds its most direct expression in the work of Harris (1986), who explicitly entitles one of his chapters 'Meat hunger'. Harris bases his argument for the universal appeal of meat for humans on the idea that, although we are not true carnivores, meat provides an especially appropriate source of nutrients for our species. He refers specifically to the profile of essential amino acids which meat contains and to its provision of the vitamin B_{12}, which features were discussed in some detail above, as well as to its provision of essential minerals like iron, zinc, copper and iodine. Indeed, the contention is put forward that the evolutionary background of the human species is at the root of this match between meat and our most basic nutritional needs. The inability of the human digestive system to deal with bulky and fibrous plant tissues rich in cellulose and lignin is seen as associated with our preference for high-energy, high-protein and low-bulk foods, of which animal products represent one of the most desirable categories (Harris 1986: 36–7).

It will be recalled that in Chapter 1 we came across the argument that the human need for a high-quality, high-energy diet is related to the unusually high metabolic demands of the human brain, which typically takes up 20–5 per cent of the energy expended at the resting metabolic rate. Thus, in Harris's terms, meat consumption could be seen as part of a broader set of nutritional needs related to low bulk and high quality. What is more, as Harris (1986: 29–31) and Farb and Armelagos (1980: 43) point out, with the exception of larger species like the gorilla, our close primate relatives are by no means exclusively vegetarian. For example, baboons, although largely dependent upon vegetable foods, will eat insects, reptiles, birds and small mammals. Both baboons and chimpanzees will also engage in the co-operative hunting of small primates and the young of small grazing animals like gazelles. On these grounds, it would appear that the incorporation of meat into the diet as a significant, if not necessarily dominant, component is a common feature of the order of mammals to which our own species belongs. It is in this evolutionary context that authors like Harris, and Farb and Armelagos, locate their argument for an inbuilt meat hunger related to the intrinsic nutritional needs of humans. This position is closely related to the somewhat contentious viewpoint discussed in Chapter 1 which allocates central significance to hunting, not only as the basic mode of subsistence of early humans but also as the key driving force behind the initial development of human co-operative capacities and human culture.

In order to support his contention that meat represents an intrinsically preferred element in the human diet, Harris points out the esteem in which meat is held, not only in Western cultures but also in a wide range of traditional societies. He provides ethnographic evidence relating to traditional cultures where meat is accorded significantly higher status and desirability than plant foods, and points out that the languages of traditional peoples may contain explicit concepts of 'meat hunger', that is, a hunger which is construed as focused specifically upon animal flesh, and one which can be satisfied by no other foodstuff. For examples of the use of such a concept he cites the Canela of Amazonia and the Semai people of Malaysia (Harris 1986: 26–7). Indeed, he argues that meat is so highly valued that there usually exist elaborate rules which govern the way in which the carcass of a game animal or slaughtered domesticated beast is divided up and the parts then distributed through the community. Such rules appear to ensure access to this prized food by a wide range of individuals and also establish and maintain obligations of reciprocity which guarantee future supplies of meat when one's own hunting or husbandry is less productive. (See Coon 1976: 201–4 for examples of meat sharing rules among such hunting peoples as the Tigarans, the Ona, the Birhors and the Mbuti.) As Farb and Armelagos (1980: 48) point out, using the Inuit as an example, such is the value placed on meat in hunting-gathering cultures that the consistently successful hunter is accorded a unique degree of prestige. In contrast, the providers of gathered (e.g., plant) foods are accorded far less prestige, this differential being closely associated, as we might expect, with gender. Indeed, the intense desire for meat, Harris argues, can lead to disputes and quarrels when the supply is reduced and reciprocity gives way to jealousy and resentment. He cites the case of the Yanomamo of Amazonia, whose communities may split and separate as a direct result of the tensions generated by meat shortages which begin to occur when the group's hunters have seriously depleted the stock of game in the immediate locality (Harris 1986: 28).

Such evidence, then, is taken as demonstrating the unique status of meat, placing in its true nutritional and cultural contexts the considerable amount of effort and ingenuity humans expend in order to obtain this particular source of nutrients. Yet, even if we accept, at least in broad principle, Harris's view that there is a powerful physiological factor behind meat eating by humans, this position does not necessarily lead to clear-cut conclusions about the role of meat in the diet of members of affluent, industralized societies. In such societies, a foodstuff traditionally hard to obtain and often in relatively short supply, becomes abundant and accessible. In such circumstances, its nutritional and symbolic significances may undergo fundamental changes.

MEAT TABOOS AND PROHIBITIONS IN TRADITIONAL CULTURES

However, having examined the argument for human 'meat hunger', we need to confront an apparently awkward question: 'If humans have an innate taste for meat, why is this prized food item the object of complicated taboos and prohibitions in many traditional societies and in some of the world's major religions?' Perhaps the best documented and most detailed study of the diverse customs of meat avoidance found around the world is provided by Simoons (1961). In effect, the study is based upon the premise that flesh foods are far more likely to be the subjects of powerful prohibitions supported by punitive sanctions than are vegetable-based foods (Simoons 1961: 108). Such prohibitions, therefore, demand description and explanation, and Simoons examines the patterns of acceptance and avoidance relating to six types of meat: pork, beef, chicken, horse flesh, camel flesh and dog flesh.

In relation to pork, Simoons notes that the pig is a very significant source of meat for a substantial proportion of the world's population. Pork was a favoured food among the Greeks and the Romans, and the pig was introduced as a domesticated animal into Africa south of the Sahara from the fifteenth century onwards. Pig keeping is widespread in South East Asia, in Polynesia and Micronesia, and is particularly important in China, where pork is a highly valued food. Yet, despite the importance of the pig as a domesticated animal, its use for food is totally rejected by adherents to two of the world's major religions, Judaism and Islam, whose doctrines define the animal as unclean and unfit for human consumption. (As we noted in Chapter 7, this rejection of pork is part of wider sets of prohibitions relating to flesh foods contained in the teachings of these two related religions.) What is more, Hindus also regard the pig as unclean, and in India these animals are raised and eaten mainly by aboriginal peoples.

Domesticated cattle, in all their various breeds and forms, constitute the single most numerous large herbivore on earth. Their flesh is consumed with relish in Europe, North and South America, Africa and Australasia, and consumption has also begun to rise in areas like China and Japan, where traditionally it was relatively low. Yet, apparently paradoxically, Hinduism, the major religion of India, a country estimated to contain a fifth of the world's cattle, prohibits the consumption of beef. This prohibition appears to be related to the status of the cow as a sacred animal and to the fact that vegetarianism and the avoidance of flesh foods is associated with the higher ranks of the Indian caste system.

While the prohibitions which relate to the consumption of pork and beef are well known to most Westerners, far less well known in the West are the widespread taboos which exist around the world relating to the eating of chicken and eggs (Simoons 1961: 65). In fact, Simoons describes the rejection of the flesh of domestic fowl by such peoples as the Vedda of Ceylon (Sri Lanka) and provides numerous examples of beliefs which hold that the consumption of chicken or eggs can be positively dangerous (e.g., the belief among the rural Annamese that chicken is toxic for pregnant women). What is more, there is a widespread dislike of chicken among Hindus, which seems to be related to vegetarian preferences and to the belief that because of its eating habits, the chicken is unclean. Similarly, Buddhist beliefs are largely antithetical to the consumption of chicken, again possibly related to distaste for the bird's feeding habits. Thus, in Tibet, chickens are seen as 'sinful' and 'unclean' since they eat worms (Simoons 1961: 70).

In contrast to his discussion of prohibitions which run counter to Western dietary practices, Simoons also describes avoidances and taboos which the average Western consumer would find entirely in line with his or her own nutritional culture. For example, horse flesh is a prohibited food in a wide range of societies and cultural settings, including Europe, where the influence of Christianity gradually eliminated the practice of eating horse, which had strong associations with pagan beliefs (Simoons 1961: 83–4). The teachings of Islam are somewhat ambivalent on the acceptability of horse flesh, and in Hindu India only a few untouchable groups eat horse meat. Camel flesh is widely consumed in the Muslim world, but is a prohibited food among many non-Muslim peoples of the Middle East. Camel meat is also widely avoided in the Far East, and in Mongolia camel milk is drunk but the flesh is rejected as a food item.

Faced with the wide range of prohibitions on flesh foods, of which the above are only illustrative examples, the challenge of explaining their origins and significance is a decidedly daunting one. This is particularly so when neighbouring cultures contain quite different forms of avoidances and taboos. In fact, Simoons offers a number of explanations, each of which is tailored to the taboo in question. By and large, his explanations rest upon the premise that such prohibitions are primarily based upon the symbolic significance of the foods or animals in question, and that the avoidance of particular flesh foods can often be a powerful expressive act in itself. For example, in discussing the range of explanations which has been put forward to explain the Hindu rejection of beef, he gives particular prominence to the view that this rejection had its roots in rivalry between Brahmans and Buddhists. Indeed, one argument maintains that Brahmans gave up cattle sacrifice and beef eating in order to improve their moral and political credibility in the face of Buddhist criticisms of these practices. What is more, Simoons suggests that such a move could have been facilitated by the long established sacred character of cattle in Indian culture (Simoons 1961: 61–3). This line of reasoning concerning the expressive significance of meat rejection is closely related to the view that the rejection of a certain animal as a source of food may be a way of showing disapproval of, or contempt for, those peoples or cultures with which that animal is associated. Thus, for example, the taboo on pork characteristic of Judaism and Islam has been characterized as having its early roots in the pastoralist's disdain for the way of life of the settled agriculturalist. Given that the conditions needed for successful pig rearing can only be achieved by settled farmers, and that pigs are quite unsuited to a nomadic, pastoralist way of life, they came to symbolize, as an animal and a food source, the very antithesis of nomadic culture.

In effect, what is being suggested is that the rejection of a particular flesh food can be a powerful cultural device to reinforce and emphasize a particular group's collective identity, as can the acceptance of a given flesh food. Thus, the acceptability of camel flesh to Muslims may be countered by the rejection of camel flesh by non-Muslim groups wishing to resist Muslim cultural influences (Simoons 1961: 121). Indeed, the prophet who initiates a new religion or cult may lay down a whole series of dietary regulations and avoidances to enable the faithful clearly to distinguish themselves from non-believers. As we have already noted, such symbolic avoidances can be associated with carefully specified rituals concerning the slaughtering of animals and the preparation of flesh foods for human consumption. Flesh not prepared according to the prescribed rituals is likely to be seen as dangerous or polluting. The rejection of such flesh is in itself a clear expression of the individual's continuing commitment to the religion or system of belief in question.

As well as the flesh avoidances which are integral to some of the world's major religions, magical beliefs leading to the avoidance of the flesh of particular animals also appear to be very widespread. Indeed, Simoons provides a wide range of examples of such beliefs, which often take the form of the idea that eating a given animal will magically produce specific undesirable or dangerous effects. One instance of this is the avoidance of venison by warriors and young men among the Dyak of Northwest Borneo, for fear that they would become timid like deer (Simoons 1961: 117). Where totemic beliefs are present in a culture, individuals may be required to honour and protect their totemic animal and forbidden to kill and eat it under threat of dire supernatural sanctions. It has even been suggested by structuralists like Mary Douglas that animals which present taxonomic contradictions within a given culture will be rejected as food sources because of their disturbing symbolic import (Douglas 1966: 54–6).

The argument that meat taboos, generally speaking, have their origins in the diverse symbolic significances and cultural meanings attached to this particular form of food can, as we have seen, be countered with a much more pragmatic view of such prohibitions. In essence, the pragmatic perspective argues that meat prohibitions frequently have a real practical utility and that this utility is the fundamental reason for their existence, any symbolic or expressive attributes being merely reflections or reinforcements. One of the best-known versions of this pragmatic view is the idea that certain forms of meat prohibition have important hygienic aspects. For example, animals which act as scavengers and consume waste products may be seen as sources of health hazards, a view which has often been cited to explain pork avoidance in Judaism and Islam. A similar argument suggests that pork may be avoided in warmer climates because of its supposed susceptibility to rapid decay and spoiling. Perhaps the most sophisticated of these hygienic arguments relates to the disease trichinosis. This serious illness produces nausea, diarrhoea, fever and swelling of the muscles, and is caused by eating undercooked pig muscle tissue infested with the larvae of the parasitic nematode worm *trichinella spiralis*. However, both Harris (1986) and Simoons (1961) are sceptical concerning such arguments, pointing out, for example, that it is only comparatively recently that the aetiology of trichinosis has been fully understood, and that other serious diseases like tapeworm infestation can be contracted from other forms of undercooked meat. Furthermore, since the delay between the ingestion of the larvae and the onset of symptoms is a relatively long one, it is unlikely that traditional cultures could have established the causal link and made it the basis of a prohibition. In fact, hygiene-based explanations may be little more than modern rationalizations of much more ancient and deep-seated taboos and prejudices (Simoons 1961: 16).

A much more convincing example of the attempt to explain meat taboos in pragmatic terms is provided by Harris's analysis of the Hindu prohibition on beef consumption. Harris confronts the apparent irrationality inherent in the fact that India has the largest cattle population of any country on earth (a significant proportion of this population being sick, barren or dry) along with a very large population of humans, many of whom are desperately short of dietary protein. In these circumstances, a taboo on beef eating seems the height of folly, a curious religious observance which wastes precious resources and condemns many to malnutrition. However, Harris seeks to demonstrate that the prohibition on beef consumption may actually have crucial practical advantages, protecting and enhancing the living standards of some of the poorest sections of Indian society. The whole argument hinges upon the nature of the humpbacked Zebu breeds of cattle which are found in India. These breeds are capable of providing the motive power for ploughing, even in extreme conditions of heat and drought, and can survive on very meagre rations of feed and fodder, often consisting of little more than such items as stalks, chaff, leaves and waste left over from human food consumption (Harris 1986: 56). Harris points out that such animals are, in fact, far more cost-efficient than tractors for ploughing purposes, given that most Indian farming units are very small and taking into account the very high initial investment that mechanization demands. Indeed, cows provide the Indian peasant with several valuable products: oxen for ploughing, milk (a precious source of fats and protein even if available only in small amounts) and dung (a clean and effective fuel for cooking in an environment where wood is scarce). In short, Harris argues that the prohibition on killing cows effectively enhances the long-term viability of Indian agriculture. It encourages farmers to resist the temptation to eat temporarily useless animals during periods of food shortage and climatic stress. If they were to succumb to this temptation, their ability to resume the cycle of agricultural production when conditions improved would be seriously compromised, and many of the poorest farmers would be driven off the land and into an even more marginal existence in already overcrowded cities.

As further evidence of what he sees as the underlying pragmatism of Indian attitudes to cattle, Harris cites a number of practices, some of which have already been referred to in Chapter 7. For example, surplus animals are sold off to Muslim traders, and many of these animals are actually destined for slaughter and consumption. Cows which die of natural causes or neglect become available as food to carrion-eating castes, who consume the edible parts and recycle the rest of the carcass. What is more, the sex ratios within the cattle population vary significantly from region to region in India, according to local agricultural requirements and practices. Harris suggests that such differences can only be produced by farmers' favouring calves of the preferred sex and neglecting calves of the non-preferred sex, thereby producing significant differences in mortality rates (Harris 1986: 59–60).

Harris also seeks to find a similarly pragmatic explanation for the avoidance of pork inherent in the teachings of Judaism and Islam. For example, he is highly critical of the view put forward by Douglas (1966) that this pork taboo emerges out of the idea that the pig represents a kind of taxonomic anomaly in terms of the dietary laws of the Old Testament, which require that in order to be acceptable to eat an animal must both chew the cud and be cloven-hoofed. Since the pig only fulfils one of these conditions but not the other (it does not chew the cud), Douglas maintains that it came to be seen as a dangerous abomination and therefore as unclean, unfit for human consumption. Harris (1986) rejects what he sees as the circularity of this kind of structuralist argument, looking instead for a more mundane and practical basis for this prohibition. In effect, his explanation is an ecological one. The deforestation of the Middle East and the degradation of farmland into desert progressively removed the conditions in which pig husbandry could be practised economically. Pigs require shade, water, mud for wallowing and a relatively high-quality diet which in many ways overlaps with that of humans. All these features would militate against their use as food animals in arid conditions. On the other hand, cloven-hoofed, cud-chewing ruminants like cattle, sheep and goats can survive even in near-desert conditions and can subsist on high-bulk, fibrous plant foods like leaves and stems that humans simply cannot digest. Thus, in agricultural and ecological terms, the ruminants were clearly a better option than the pig in the arid Middle East. This inescapable fact of life represents, for Harris, the basis of pork rejection in these cultures.

There can be no doubting the ingenuity and the plausibility of arguments like those of Harris. The value of such arguments is that they remind us that no food system can possibly maintain its continuity in the long term other than within the parameters set by economic, climatic and ecological realities. Yet, within the framework provided by those parameters there is often enormous scope for humans to exploit the multilayered symbolic potential of food for a whole range of expressive and cultural purposes. This is certainly the case when we consider the logic behind meat prohibitions of various types. Such prohibitions certainly carry potent symbolic charges. They are loaded with meanings, some explicit, some more implicit, but they may also carry some direct or indirect pragmatic advantage, at least for some of the parties who subscribe to the taboo. Any attempt to assess the relative weightings of symbolic and practical factors is fraught with difficulty, particularly as the two are inevitably closely, often inextricably, intertwined with each other. Even more difficult is the attempt to allocate priority to one or other. Do pragmatic choices and strategies give rise to prohibitions, which are then enshrined in the symbolic vocabularies of ritual, custom and religion? Or do attempts to create meaning, order and legitimacy at the symbolic level give rise to prohibitions which later have retrospective pragmatic rationalizations attached to them? In the case of meat prohibitions these are unresolved, perhaps unresolvable, questions. This lack of resolution means that we must keep both possibilities in mind when analyzing the role of meat in any nutritional culture.

MEAT SYMBOLISM IN CONTEMPORARY WESTERN CULTURE

Of course, meat prohibitions are not limited to traditional cultures, but also exist in modern Western societies and can exert a significant influence on dietary patterns. For example, while the flesh of wild mammals and birds currently furnishes only a very small proportion of the protein component of Western diets, some species are still hunted for recreational purposes and as seasonally available sources of food. However, in general, only a very narrow range of fish, bird and mammal species is defined (legally and culturally) as 'game', although the actual list does vary somewhat from society to society (North American hunters, for example, regard the grey squirrel as an edible quarry species, whereas in Britain the same animal is regarded either as an inedible pest or as an attractive decorative feature of park or garden, depending on one's point of view). Thus, in effect, all wild species outside the definition 'game' are prohibited flesh for the average Westerner, and eating them would be virtually inconceivable. This taboo upon the eating of wild species is so ingrained in Western culture as to be totally taken for granted by the average individual. Yet it stands in sharp contrast to the dietary practices of our not-too-distant forebears, who were happy to feast upon a veritable menagerie of wild creatures should their status and the occasion permit. For example, the menus of courtly feasts provide ample evidence of the variety of species that were prepared and served, often in highly elaborate dishes. Explaining this near universal Western taboo is by no means easy. It has been suggested that the taboo on eating the flesh of predatory, meat-eating birds and mammals arises out of the idea that, in symbolic terms, they are too 'strong' for human consumption, and we will return this notion below. The prohibition on eating other wild species, which might otherwise be regarded as palatable and nutritious, may be largely the result of the changing orientation of increasingly industrialized and urbanized cultures to the natural environment, and this is also an issue to which we return later in the chapter.

Western meat taboos quite obviously do not apply only to wild animals but also to certain domesticated species. The most notable of these prohibited species is the horse which, despite the fact that it has been used as a food animal in many cultures, has long been taboo in Europe. In ancient Greece and Rome, as in Christian Europe, horse flesh was regarded with aversion, only eaten in times of starvation or desperate need. Despite the efforts of nineteenth-century advocates of the hygienic and dietary advantages of horse flesh like the

Frenchman Geoffroy de Saint-Hilaire to encourage its use, the prohibition on horseflesh remains as powerful as ever for most Westerners (Toussaint-Samat 1992: 98). Similarly, the dog, also a prized source of flesh in a variety of cultures ranging from Polynesia to China, is a taboo species in the West, where the idea of consuming dog flesh would generally be regarded with horror. Indeed, in contemporary Western culture both these animals would be construed as 'pets', although the horse, given its size, is not suited to quite the same level of domestic integration within a human household as a dog. The notion of eating a pet seems self-evidently abhorrent, since such animals can be seen as entering into a social relationship with their human owners. They are given names, credited with personalities and granted quasi-human status in certain limited respects. Anthropomorphism of this kind would thus appear to render the eating of pets, in symbolic terms, almost the equivalent of cannibalism, the focus of the most potent flesh taboo of all.

However, just as he seeks to demonstrate that meat prohibitions in traditional societies may have pragmatic foundations, Harris also suggests that prohibitions on eating horses and dogs may also have sound practical bases, rather than being merely the manifestations of emotional attachment to pets. Indeed, he points out that in New Guinea people frequently become emotionally attached to their pigs, and treat them as pets, but still slaughter and eat them (Harris 1986: 176). Horses, given the nature of their digestive system, are not particularly efficient converters of feed into flesh, and thus rearing them for food does not make economic sense when more efficient species are available. The horse is far more useful for transportation and, particularly more recently, as an aid to recreation. Similarly, dogs in a Western setting make little economic sense as food animals, yet can provide valuable services, notably companionship and security (the latter being particularly pertinent in areas of high crime or for vulnerable individuals or households). In short, domestic animals that are more use alive than dead are likely to be the focus of an eating prohibition, according to Harris.

Yet, despite the force of Harris's arguments, the symbolic potency of meat in contemporary thought is self-evident. How, then, can meat be seen as fitting into the broad framework of meaning which underpins Western culinary and nutritional culture? One attempt to provide such a framework takes the form of a hierarchy of status and potency (Twigg 1979). Twigg locates red meat near the top of this potency hierarchy, with white meat and fish below it, other animal products like eggs and cheese below these and vegetable foods lowest of all. What her scheme represents is her conception of the conventional rankings of animal and plants foods in terms of power, status and desirability (see Figure 9.4)

The feature which places red meat in such a high position, she argues, is its high blood content, the same feature which gives it its characteristic colour. It is the compelling and ambivalent symbolic charge of blood which gives red meat its power and its appeal. Blood is seen as bearing the special essence of the person or the animal, and is associated with virility, strength, aggression and

TOO STRONG: (TABOO)	Uncastrated animals Carnivorous animals Raw meat
DOMINANT CULTURE BOUNDARY	
STRONG: POWERFUL/BLOOD LESS POWERFUL/NON-BLOOD *VEGETARIAN BOUNDARY*	Red meat Chicken Fish
LESS STRONG: *VEGAN BOUNDARY*	Eggs Dairy products
TOO WEAK	Fruit Cereals Root vegetables Leaf vegetables

Figure 9.4   The conventional hierarchy of food status and potency
Source: Adapted from Twigg (1979: 18)

sexuality (Twigg 1979: 17). Yet, at the same time, it is a dangerous and potentially polluting substance. Eating red meat is seen, in a sense, as the ingesting of the very nature of the animal itself, its strength and its aggression. However, in Western culture, there is an element of ambivalence present. There is danger involved in the ingestion of too much power. Thus, as Figure 9.4 indicates, there is a cultural boundary near the top of the food hierarchy, and above that boundary are items which are defined as too potent for humans to eat. Raw meat is seen as too obviously charged with the power of blood; it is therefore taboo and has to undergo deliberately induced transformations (cooking, smoking, curing, etc.) to wrest it from the realm of nature and bring it into the realm of culture, where it can be safely consumed. Similarly, the flesh of animals which are themselves flesh eaters is seen as too powerful for human consumption, even when cooked, and is taboo in Western culture. Even the flesh of uncastrated male domesticated animals like bulls and boars is seen as too strong, as tainted with an excess of virility which renders it unpalatable in a conceptual if not a gustatory sense.

However, below red meat comes white meat like poultry. This is 'bloodless' and therefore seen as less powerful, as is fish, which comes immediately below it in the hierarchy. Both these 'bloodless' forms of flesh, when prepared by boiling or poaching, are seen as suitable for those perceived as having a delicate digestion (e.g., invalids and children). Eggs and dairy products, although of animal origin, are even further from the blood-rich summit of the hierarchy and therefore even less potent. Finally, vegetable foods at the bottom of the hierarchy are commonly regarded as too weak to provide adequate nutrition in themselves, or to furnish the stressed or central element of a conventional meal. (As we will see in the next chapter, vegetarian ideology may actually seek to invert this overall scheme.)

We have already noted in Chapter 5 the central significance of the 'cooked dinner' (Murcott 1982) or the 'proper meal' (Charles and Kerr 1988) in twentieth-century British culinary culture. In such meals, which are conventionally seen by many women as the very foundation of the family's nutritional well-being, meat is the central feature. Its presence, preferably in roasted form is, in effect, the defining element, and all the other elements (which are mainly of vegetable origin) are subordinated to it and are seen as playing an essentially supportive role in the careful composition which appears upon the plate. Given Twigg's hierarchy, red meat can be regarded as the most desirable and the most prestigious form of this dominant element. What is more, the above authors argue that women explicitly relate the importance of the proper meal, arranged around its definitive core of meat, to the tastes and needs of adult men (in the studies in question, usually the respondent's husband). In this sense, then, meat-based meals are seen as associated with masculinity and with the demands which men make upon women on the basis of what is conceptualized as a dominant and nutritionally privileged position. Indeed, the idea that women's purchasing and preparation of red meat is influenced by their husband's perceived views is given some indirect empirical support by a study of intentions to consume beef carried out in the USA. Zey and McIntosh (1992) interviewed by telephone a sample of 400 women in the state of Texas. Their findings suggest that women's intentions to consume beef are not so much influenced by their own attitudes (e.g., concerning its health implications and gustatory features) as by what they believe to be the attitudes and beliefs of their spouse and, to a lesser extent, of their friends. These findings were largely supported by a similar study by Sapp and Harrod (1989), which was carried out after Zey and McIntosh's field work was completed.

However, perhaps the most radical and far-reaching analysis of the association between meat and masculinity in Western culture is put forward by Adams (1990). Her starting-point is the crucial association in patriarchal societies between meat eating and male power. Not only is meat eating seen as an essentially masculine activity, but the consumption of meat is also seen as strongly associated with virility and male physical strength. She mentions, for example, the importance placed upon feeding beef to American soldiers during the Second World War (Adams 1990: 32). Thus, if meat eating is to be symbolically equated with male dominance, men must maintain a privileged access to meat, even though, as Adams points out, women's protein needs may be higher than men's during the crucial periods of pregnancy and lactation. However, she does admit that in times of affluence, gender-related differences in meat consumption may be much less significant than in times of shortage.

Furthermore, class-based differences in meat consumption, she suggests, may be of greater magnitude than the differences between men and women in the same class location.

If meat is effectively a symbol of male dominance, then vegetables, defined as 'women's foods', are seen as inherently less desirable and less potent, as second-class foods fit only for second-class citizens. Adams notes that the word 'meat' has the connotation of 'essence' or 'most important feature' (as in the 'meat of the argument'). On the other hand, 'vegetable' suggests monotony, dullness and inactivity, and the verb 'to vegetate' implies leading a passive, inactive existence. Thus, there emerges a kind of symmetrical symbolism between meat and vegetables, masculine and feminine: men are active and consume foods imbued with power (the power of active animals), and women are passive, and consume foods derived from 'inactive', 'immobile' forms of life (plants) (Adams 1990: 36–7). What is more, the responsibility imposed upon women for the cooking of meat for consumption by men is seen as a further expression of patriarchal power and female subordination. On the other hand, men who refrain from meat eating may be regarded as repudiating or undermining conventional conceptions of masculinity.

The whole argument, however, is taken a crucial step further by Adams, who draws a direct analogy between the oppression of women by men and the oppression of animals by (male) meat eaters. Even more disturbingly, an analogy is also drawn between the killing and dismemberment of women and the slaughter and butchering of animals in the process of converting them into meat (Adams 1990: 45–61). She notes how in everyday speech the equation of the female body with meat involves processes of objectification and fragmentation which facilitate the occurrence of sexual violence towards women-as-objects (Adams 1990: 47). In this sense, she implies, the association between meat consumption and male power reaches its most extreme and potentially most dangerous form of expression.

As we will see in the next chapter, which focuses upon vegetarianism, Adams' exploration of the darker regions of meat symbolism in Western culture also entails a powerful polemic in favour of fundamental changes in Western foodways and the values and ethics which underpin them. Indeed, the argument has been advanced that, in relation to meat eating, such changes may already be under way.

THE MEANING OF MEAT: THE BEGINNINGS OF CHANGE?

If we take the patterns of meat consumption in the UK as our case study, there appear to be a number of clear trends which demand explanation. It will be recalled, for example, that total meat consumption in the UK peaked in 1979, and has since been declining steadily (see Figure 9.1). Even more strikingly, the consumption of red meats has declined quite sharply. As we have seen, the peak year for beef and veal consumption in the post-war period was 1957, and by 1993 consumption had fallen to well under half the peak level. The peak year for mutton and lamb was 1956, and by 1993 British consumers were eating under one-third of the peak level (see Figure 9.2). While significant increases in the consumption of poultry have meant that overall meat consumption has not shown such dramatic falls, it is very clear that there has been a fundamental shift in the demand for red meat. Once wartime and post-war shortages and rationing were over, the amounts of red meat eaten in Britain rose, in line with what would be predicted on the basis of the well-established correlation between levels of affluence and levels of meat consumption. The fact that in Britain the link between rising living standards and rising demand for meat appears to have broken down presents us with a genuine puzzle, particularly in relation to red meat. If we accept the argument that red meat is at the pinnacle of the Western status hierarchy of foods, that it carries a heavy symbolic charge of power, strength, prestige and virility, why does it seem to be falling from favour? What is more, although this phenomenon is particularly marked in Britain, it appears also to be affecting other European countries to some extent. Data produced by the European Commission indicate that, in the European Community, beef and veal's share of total meat consumption fell from 38 per cent in 1961 to 25 per cent in 1991 (Bansback 1993: 2). What is more, between the years 1981 and 1991 per capita consumption of beef and veal declined in eight out of the twelve nations which then made up the community, by amounts ranging from 3 per cent in the Netherlands to 33 per cent in the Irish Republic (Bansback 1993: 3).

Some empirical evidence concerning the reasons for reduced meat consumption in Britain is provided by Woodward (1988). Woodward's study was based upon a sample of 584 respondents drawn from three cities in the north of England. The findings indicated that, overall, around a third of the respondents who were meat eaters (87 per cent of the total sample) felt that they were now eating less meat than they had in the past. This proportion of meat reducers was fairly consistent across social class groups (Woodward 1988: 102). When questioned concerning their motives for reduced meat eating, 51per cent indicated health reasons, 46 per cent referred to cost, 22 per cent referred to the increased availability of acceptable alternatives and 19 per cent indicated that it was a question of taste. Misgivings concerning production methods were indicated by 16 per cent, and 12 per cent and 11 per cent respectively voiced misgivings about the use of growth hormones and antibiotics. Issues relating to animal welfare were highlighted by 12 per cent of the meat reducing respondents (Woodward 1988: 103). These results seem to support the contention that the decision to reduce meat consumption is an essentially instrumental and pragmatic one, dictated largely by economic considerations and by some consumers' acceptance of health education messages which have consistently encouraged the reduction of red meat intake in particular. This interpretation receives further support from attitude survey data published in the United Kingdom.

Questioned in 1986, only 66 per cent of respondents classified beef, pork and lamb as 'good for people', and 3 per cent actually characterized them specifically as 'bad for people'. A follow-up survey in 1989 found that the proportion classifying these three meats as 'good for people' had fallen to 57 per cent, and the proportion classifying them as specifically 'bad' had risen to 6 per cent (Jowell, Witherspoon and Brook 1990: 148). The authors also report that health concerns were commonly cited by respondents as reasons for eating less beef, pork and lamb (Jowell, Witherspoon and Brook 1990: 156).

However, we must also consider the possibility that trends in meat consumption in Britain, particularly the observed decline in the eating of red meat, are not driven purely by pragmatic factors. Is it also possible that the very meaning of meat is changing, and changing in line with much more fundamental shifts in the very foundations of British culture? This proposition is at the centre of the analysis of the significance of meat as a 'natural symbol' which is put forward by Fiddes (1991). The starting-point of his argument is the claim that 'meat's pre-eminence in our food system derives primarily from its tangibly representing to us the principle of human power over nature' (Fiddes 1991: 225–6). The human need to dominate the natural world and to control the environment is seen as deeply rooted in human history and prehistory, in terms of a desire to mitigate the threats posed by unpredictable natural processes and to maximize security (especially of the food supply). This means that animal flesh, in Fiddes' view, is prized so highly as food, not in spite of the exploitation of animals which it entails but precisely because of that exploitation. Despite the fact that individuals may experience unease, meat eating is approved and encouraged at the cultural level because it effectively demonstrates and symbolizes power over nature. Indeed, as we noted in Chapter 7, individual anxieties connected with such exploitation can be accommodated within a suitably protective cultural framework. It is Fiddes' contention that the significance of meat, both in terms of the quantities consumed and the symbolic charge it carried, began to increase markedly from the seventeenth-century onwards. This was precisely the period in which the rationalist scientific world-view was placing greater and greater emphasis on the human domination of nature. In such circumstances, where such dominance can be construed as a moral as well as a practical imperative, meat eating could be seen as an even more compelling expression of overriding human authority in relation to the natural order.

However, Fiddes maintains that this long-established orthodoxy, celebrating and legitimizing the extension of human power, is in decline, and that powerful ideological currents are now flowing in the opposite direction (Fiddes 1991: 116). The human domination of nature is now seen by many as having gone too far, with the threat of dire ecological consequences. There has emerged a whole range of environmentalist movements and factions dedicated to slowing, or even reversing, this process. Indeed, as Thomas (1983) has pointed out, misgivings concerning the anthropocentric world-view, which saw nature as ripe for human exploitation, were present in embryonic form on the English cultural scene by

215

the late seventeenth century. Such ideas, Fiddes argues, have now assumed a much more prominent position and are leading to a more generalized acceptance of the view that the relationship of humans to the natural world should be one of sensitivity and stewardship rather than unrestrained power. It is in this context that the meaning of meat (and that of red meat in particular) is seen as undergoing an important transformation. Its consumption is no longer seen as a reassuring and assertive expression of human dominance, but as a potentially disturbing reminder of a more 'barbarous' and insensitive past. Thus, we become more squeamish in relation to meat and meat products, requiring them to be prepared and presented to us in a disguised and sanitized form. There is a parallel here between Fiddes's argument and that advanced by Elias (1978a: 120–2), even though the two authors actually operate with rather different conceptualizations of civilization and the civilizing process. In fact, Elias contends that the civilizing process itself entails, among other things, the cultivation of increasingly delicate sensibilities, which in turn generate what he terms an advancing 'threshold of repugnance' (1978a: 120). As an example of this advancing threshold he cites the gradual decline of the practice of carving whole animals (or large sections of animals) within sight of those who were to dine upon them, as diners became progressively less willing directly to contemplate the actual origins of their meal.

Thus, for Fiddes, increasing squeamishness, the decline of red meat consumption, the ever more widespread acceptance of the view that red meat is 'unhealthy', the rise of environmentalist movements and the increasing salience of animal rights issues are all interlinked phenomena. They are each, in their own way, manifestations of far-reaching changes in an entire world-view. Indeed, he goes as far as to suggest that eventually meat eating may come to be seen in the same light as smoking and drug addition: as an anti-social and damaging practice attracting general disapproval. Thus, 'the turbulently declining reputation of meat . . . may be a harbinger of the evolution of new values' (Fiddes 1991: 233).

OVERVIEW

In this chapter we have encountered what appear to be, at first sight, two fundamentally opposed views of the role of meat in the human diet. On the one hand, meat's appeal for its human consumers is seen as rooted in its nutritional properties, particularly in its ability to provide a comprehensive range of nutrients. On the other hand, meat's significance is said to reside in its symbolic charge, in the complex meanings relating to power, status, strength and gender which it can be used to convey. Clearly, stated in this stark and uncompromising way, this opposition is a false one. Meat is quite capable of delivering both a nutritional reward and a symbolic message simultaneously. Thus, sociological and other analyses of the role of meat will, in effect, vary largely in terms of the emphasis they place on these two aspects of the issue.

However, this does not prevent some authors from quite deliberately and openly overstating their case, for example, in relation to the priority of symbolism over nutrition, in order to press home what they regard as an important and otherwise neglected point (Fiddes 1991: ix). In truth, the nutritional and symbolic properties of meat are inextricably interlinked, the one, metaphorically at least, feeding off the other.

When we consider the changes in the patterns in meat consumption which have been taking place (in the UK and in other advanced Western societies), we are faced with a range of possible explanations. For example, the shift away from red meat might be explained in economic terms, with rising affluence producing an initial increase, and then a decline as an ever wider choice of substitutes and alternatives becomes available. There may also be an instrumental or pragmatic factor at work, as individuals become sensitized to current health education messages and make what they regard as rational choices to improve health or to avoid disease. Finally, as Fiddes claims, this particular trend may be an indication that Western culture's whole conceptualization of its relationship to the natural world is undergoing changes which will transform the entire human food system. Of course, it may well be that only a culture in which the food supply is secure and which can provide good nutritional standards and an extensive range of food choices for the majority of its members could ever afford to develop the kinds of sensibilities which might ultimately transform the meaning of meat from delicacy to anathema. However, at this point we may need to exercise a degree of caution concerning Fiddes's overall argument. Powerful as the imagery and symbolism of red meat may be, we should, perhaps, be wary of loading too much significance onto trends in its consumption as indicators of broader changes in ecological awareness and environmental sensitivity. After all, other forms of consumption which might have an equal or greater claim to symbolize the human domination of nature, continue to be embraced with undiminished enthusiasm.

Speculating about future trends in the consumption of this most ambivalent of foodstuffs, with its heavy symbolic baggage of contradictory and sometimes disturbing connotations, poses considerable difficulties. It might seem reasonable to assume that current trends away from red meat will continue, and that some other Western countries may even begin to follow the trend evident in the UK, with an overall decline in total per capita meat consumption. If this were to happen, the implications for the agricultural, processing and distribution sectors of the food system would be considerable. The deep-seated, 10,000-year-old symbiosis between humans, domesticated plants and domesticated animals would be transformed as the animal participants in this convoluted web of interrelations were progressively removed from the system. Whether such a transformation is actually feasible, given the close interweaving of the relationships that make up the system, is a matter for debate. What is certain is that the unravelling of these relationships would have social, economic and ecological consequences which might be quite unforeseen.

10

THE VEGETARIAN OPTION

The speculations which concluded the previous chapter concerning the long-term consequences of a possible decline in meat eating generally, or in the consumption of particular types of meat, lead inevitably to our next major topic: vegetarianism. For, if meat eating is replete with symbolism, then the deliberate rejection of meat as a foodstuff must also carry a compelling symbolism of its own. However, as we also noted in the previous chapter (Table 9.1), in many developing countries meat consumption appears to be very low indeed, particularly in the Far East and Africa. Indeed, even when we take into account the whole range of animal products consumed by humans (including offal, fats, milk products, eggs and fish) the number of calories consumed per capita per day from all livestock products in Africa is 111 and in the Far East 151. This compares with 1,255 in Western Europe and 1206 in North America (Grigg 1993: 69). Given that within these averages there is a wide range of individual variation, it becomes clear that large numbers of people in the developing world are effectively vegetarian. This vegetarianism, however, is generally not a matter of choice, and the individuals concerned would usually consume more animal products had they the means to do so.

The real challenge for the social scientist, in fact, is the explanation not of involuntary but of voluntary vegetarianism. In other words, the pertinent question is: 'What are the conditions in which vegetarianism can emerge as a viable and attractive option and what cultural forces and individual motivations encourage its adoption?' Any attempt to answer such questions, however, is complicated by the fact that vegetarianism itself is by no means a clear-cut concept and, indeed, the term itself is of relatively recent origin. Individuals who define themselves as 'vegetarian' may have widely differing dietary patterns. Perhaps the most straightforward way of coming to terms with this variation is to conceptualize it in terms of a simple linear scale relating to the strictness of the exclusions involved. At the left-hand, or least strict, end of the scale will be those self-defined vegetarians who may consume eggs, dairy products, fish (or shellfish) and even meat (especially white meat) on rare occasions. Moving to the right, we find those who exclude all meat and fish, but still consume eggs and dairy products. Further to the right are those who exclude one or other of these latter categories and individuals who consume only rennet-free cheese, for example. Further still to the right we arrive at the boundary of veganism, which requires abstention from all animal products. However, even veganism is scaled according to strictness. There may be controversy among vegans about whether honey should be consumed and whether non-food animal-derived products should be used (for example, leather shoes and certain drugs). At the extreme right of the scale is the fruitarian, who will consume only vegetable products which do not entail killing the donor plant.

Quite clearly, then, vegetarianism is a complex set of interrelated foodways, and in this chapter we look briefly at its historical background as well as at current trends, at the arguments which have been advanced to support it and at the insights into its contemporary manifestations which can be derived from recent empirical studies by social scientists.

THE HISTORICAL AND CULTURAL BACKGROUND

In Chapter 1 we looked in some detail at the origins of human subsistence patterns and noted how the versatility of the human hunter-gatherer, exploiting perhaps the widest range of food sources of any single species, can be regarded as one of the most important factors behind the evolutionary success of the human species and its progressive colonization of an enormous diversity of terrestrial habitats. Of course, survival in demanding conditions necessarily entails making the most of the available food resources, with diversity providing invaluable insurance against the shortages of particular food items which are bound to occur due to natural fluctuations. In these circumstances, it seems highly unlikely that humans would have chosen quite deliberately to exclude a whole class of nutrient sources (i.e., animal products generally, or meat specifically); such voluntary abstention would simply have been too risky for an omnivore to adopt. Of course, this is not to suggest that from the early stages of the development of culture humans did not practice particular avoidances or recognize particular taboos in relation to specific food items. Yet, the decision completely to forego the consumption of all forms of meat, for example, is one which could only have been taken in the context of access to an assured food supply which could provide the required nutritional inputs. This in turn implies that voluntary meat rejection is probably most likely to have occurred first in the context of settled agricultural societies, among individuals or groups in a nutritionally privileged and secure position. Such a rejection would almost certainly have carried a powerful symbolic message, possibly one of dissent from prevailing cultural assumptions.

What little we know about meat rejection in the early stages of the evolution of civilization appears to be consistent with this proposition. For example, the Greek philosopher and mathematician Pythagoras (born in approximately 580 BC) propounded the doctrine that the soul was immortal and could migrate into other living creatures. Thus, the killing and eating of any living creature

219

could be construed as murder, since the transmigration of souls implied a kindred and common fate for all animals. The teachings of Pythagoras seem to be a fusion of ideas derived from Egypt, Babylon and possibly even from Hinduism and Zoroastrianism (Spencer 1993: 59), and imposed upon his immediate followers a strict vegetarianism. Although the actual details of Pythagoras' life are very sparse, he and his inner circle of devotees appeared to have subsisted on a diet of bread, honey, cereals, fruits and some vegetables (Spencer 1993: 46). In a sense, this meatless diet, and the doctrine upon which it was based, can be recognized as, in part, a reaction against the emphasis placed by Greek culture on the consumption of large amounts of meat and the linking of such gorging with Herculean strength and athletic prowess (Spencer 1993: 38). What is more, Pythagorean teaching also embodied what would now be construed as environmentalist elements, and Pythagoras' opposition to some of the mainstream elements of his society's *status quo* is indicated by the fact that his devotees were essentially outsiders, deliberately seeking solitude and separation (Dombrowski 1985: 50).

Among the intellectual elite of the Hellenistic era and of the Roman world, certain key figures stand out for their vegetarianism, developing and extending the arguments advanced in previous centuries. The Roman Seneca argued for vegetarianism on moral grounds, although the fact that this stance probably led him to become politically suspect meant that his public advocacy was relatively muted (Dombrowski 1985: 81). The poet Ovid's advocacy of vegetarianism was also morally based, his position on the sufferings of animals being traceable back to the earlier arguments of the Pythagoreans. The Greek biographer and philosopher Plutarch (born around AD 46) wrote a treatise specifically on the issue of meat eating and the moral and philosophical grounds for abstention from this practice. Interestingly, Plutarch argued emphatically that meat eating was a grossly unnatural act for human beings. He sought to demonstrate this proposition by suggesting that those who wished to eat meat should try killing the animal themselves, unaided by any tools or weapons, as carnivorous animals do, and then consume the flesh raw (Dombrowski 1985: 93). The average human's inability, or unwillingness, to perform such directly carnivorous acts was taken as an indication of the inappropriateness of meat in the human diet. The only other philosopher of the ancient world that we know to have devoted an entire work to the debates surrounding vegetarianism was Porphyry, who was born in Tyre in AD 232. His great treatise, divided into four books, is remarkable in so far as it examines in great detail not only the arguments in favour of vegetarianism, but also the arguments, both philosophical and popular, against vegetarianism, in order to refute them. However, as Spencer (1993: 107) points out, Porphyry died in AD 306, just a few years before Christianity was recognized as the official religion of the Roman world in AD 313 by Emperor Constantine. The Christian doctrine of human supremacy in relation to the natural world became the dominant one, and the Pythagorean tradition of which Porphyry was, in a sense, the heir, with its rejection of the killing of animals for food, was to be effectively suppressed for many centuries to come.

In the Greek and Roman worlds vegetarianism among the elite and the learned was, in effect, a kind of critique of orthodox moral and cultural assumptions. In contrast, in India, vegetarianism developed as a set of ideas and dietary strictures which eventually came to be located at the very core of religious and ethical beliefs. Hinduism's central doctrine of the transmigration of the soul through a perpetual cycle of death and rebirth, holds the promise of release from this cycle only through progressive purification until the soul itself can be reunited with Brahman (or Brahma), the divine life force of the universe from which all being originates and to which it ultimately returns. This doctrine, which embodies the notion of the sacredness of the cow, as we noted in Chapter 9, effectively entails vegetarianism, given the presence of a soul in all living things. What is more, the principle of karma dictates that the act of killing itself will be punished in one's next reincarnation by demotion down the scale of life forms (which has devil at the bottom and cow just one place below human). These Hindu doctrines, of which vegetarianism is an integral part, are very ancient, their origins dating back to teachings which existed in written form as early as 800 BC (Spencer 1993: 77).

Buddhism, founded by the nobleman Gautama Siddhartha, who is believed to have been born around 566 BC in northern India, also embraces the doctrine of transmigration. Nirvana, the final release from the cycle of reincarnation and the attainment of absolute blessedness, is only to be achieved through the extinction of all desires and earthly preoccupations. Gautama (known as Buddha or the enlightened one) preached compassion to all living creatures and the avoidance of violence. However, the incorporation of explicit vegetarianism into Buddhist doctrine appears to have come rather later and is laid out most clearly in a text translated into Chinese in AD 430 (Spencer 1993: 84). Buddhism was to spread widely outside India (for example, into China, Tibet and Japan). By way of contrast, Jainism, also founded in the sub-continent (by Mahavira, born in 599 BC), with its requirement of total non-violence and strict vegetarianism, has remained largely restricted to western India.

While an impulsion towards vegetarianism or abstention from flesh foods is inherent in Hinduism, Buddhism and Jainism, this is certainly not the case in Judaism and Christianity. In fact, the elaborate list of clean and unclean creatures to be found in Leviticus and Deuteronomy implies that the orthodox will indeed consume the flesh of those creatures whom God has decreed fitting. What is more, given the influence of Mosaic dietary laws on Christian beliefs, and the doctrine that God has granted humans dominion over the natural world, vegetarianism and Christianity appear somewhat at odds with one another. Thus, Spencer (1993: 127) points out that in the early Christian Church it was only possible totally to renounce meat eating as an aid to achieving a higher degree of asceticism and spirituality. Indeed, the rejection of meat eating came to be associated with radical heresies which challenged the authority of the Catholic Church. Two notable sects which included vegetarianism in their heresies were the Bogomils, who emerged in Bulgaria in the tenth century, and the Cathars, who flourished first in northern Italy and later in France from the eleventh century to the fourteenth century. Paradoxically, perhaps, the centrality of meat in the Christian's diet was confirmed by ecclesiastical rules which required abstention from this prized food on specific days or in the context of specific religious festivals (Montanari 1994: 78). These temporary abstentions could act as clear demonstrations of penitential self-denial.

However, by the time of the Renaissance the ideas of the classical thinkers had once again become influential. Criticisms of the cruelties inflicted upon animals by humans appeared in the works of the Dutch scholar Erasmus and the English statesman Sir Thomas More (Spencer 1993: 185–6), as well as in those of the French humanist Michel de Montaigne (Barkas 1975: 75–6). The man who is perhaps the leading figure of the Renaissance, retrospectively viewed as its very embodiment, Leonardo da Vinci, was a dedicated vegetarian. However, it has been argued that there is a deep and unresolved contradiction between Leonardo's vegetarianism and compassion for animals on the one hand, and his enthusiastic involvement in the arts of war and the design of weapons on the other (Barkas 1975: 72).

In 1558, at the age of 83, an Italian nobleman, Luigi Cornaro, published the first of a series of essays extolling the hygienic and health-giving properties of a meatless diet. Barkas (1975: 73–5) regards Cornaro (who lived to be 100 years old) as the first modern exponent of the idea of vegetarianism as a device for promoting health and longevity. In the next century an Englishman, Thomas Tryon, wrote a series of books, including *The Way to Health*, in which he argued vehemently against flesh eating on both moral and health grounds, and passionately argued the virtues of a vegetarian diet. However, Tryon and other advocates of vegetarianism around this time (who included the physician George Cheyne, whom we encountered in Chapter 6), were relatively isolated voices in a general climate within which meat eating was becoming more popular, and in which Henry More could claim in 1653 that cattle and sheep had only been granted life to keep their flesh fresh until it was needed for human consumption (Spencer 1993: 213). However, Spencer argues, with the rise of humanism and increasing questioning of the Christian world-view, vegetarianism was able to win over an increasing number of high-profile converts, one of the most eminent and controversial of whom was the poet Shelley, as well as the co-founder of Methodism, John Wesley, and the prison reformer John Howard.

Perhaps the single most important event in the development of vegetarianism as a coherent movement as well as a set of ideas and arguments, took place on 30 September 1847, at Northwood Villa, Ramsgate, Kent. From this meeting emerged the Vegetarian Society, and the term 'vegetarian' was officially adopted. (Although, for convenience, we have used the term vegetarian so far in this chapter to refer to meatless diets in general, the word did not achieve currency until the 1840s, and previously such terms as 'Pythagoreans' and 'vegetable regimen' had been used to refer to vegetarians and vegetarianism respectively.) With the founding of the Vegetarian Society, a wide range of individuals practising meatless diets, for whatever reasons, now had a focus for their beliefs and a forum for debate (Barkas 1975: 85). As a direct result of the founding of the British Vegetarian Society, an American Vegetarian Convention assembled in New York in 1850, and in 1867 the German Vegetarian Society was founded, maintaining close links with the British and American movements (Spencer 1993: 274). What is more, the international visibility of vegetarianism was further advanced by its espousal by such pre-eminent literary figures as Tolstoy and George Bernard Shaw (although the latter was always careful to point out that his vegetarianism was related to health and economic issues, not to a rejection in principle of the killing of animals). For Spencer, however, it is no coincidence that a coherent vegetarian movement emerged first in England, in the nineteenth century. Urbanization itself brought together vegetarians and concentrated them, while at the same time separating and insulating them from the harsher realities of rural life. Moreover, throughout the nineteenth century and into the twentieth vegetarianism maintained its long-standing links with radicalism and dissent, developing in association with such kindred movements as socialism, animal welfare and pacifism (Spencer 1993: 294).

ESTIMATING THE EXTENT OF CONTEMPORARY VEGETARIANISM

In our discussion of the historical roots of vegetarianism it is difficult to avoid the conclusion that this particular set of dietary beliefs and practices has characteristically been an option selected by exceptional or unusual individuals. In a sense, the decision to reject the consumption of meat could be seen as a stance which accentuated and dramatized that individual's distinctiveness, even superiority, in a moral or intellectual sense, in relation to the rest of humankind. However, this association between vegetarianism and the exceptional individual (the intellectual, the artist, the philosopher, the visionary) has, in recent decades, undergone some significant changes. In some Western societies, vegetarianism appears to have broadened its appeal beyond relatively small circles of devotees, to a point where its adherents would no longer be counted in handfuls but in millions. Quite clearly, such a striking change in the popularity of a once obscure and arcane dietary option demands an attempt at explanation, and later in this chapter we will review the kinds of explanations which have been advanced. However, if we are asserting that vegetarianism has now become a 'mass' phenomenon, we do need to have some idea about the numbers involved and the percentage of the population of a country like the UK, for example, that can be regarded as vegetarian. There are considerable difficulties involved in finding answers to such questions. As we have already seen, vegetarianism is by no means a straightforward concept, and it has many varieties which shade into one another. The researcher inevitably faces the problem of whether to generate a set of objective definitions of varieties of vegetarianism, and work in terms of these or, alternatively, to work with the subjective self-definitions of respondents, which may be somewhat variable and even positively idiosyncratic.

In fact, the data available for countries like the UK and the USA are sparse and rather fragmentary. Perhaps the most consistent set of results for the UK comes from a series of surveys carried out for the Realeat Company between 1984 and 1993 by Gallup (Realeat Survey Office 1993). Over this decade the proportion of respondents reporting themselves as vegetarian or vegan rose steadily, from 2.1 per cent in 1984 to 4.3 per cent in 1993. Over the same period, the proportion of respondents reporting avoidance of red meat rose from 1.9 per cent to 6.5 per cent, and the proportion reporting reduced overall meat consumption rose from 30 per cent to 40 per cent. The next survey in this series was carried out in 1995, using a similar methodology of a sample of 4,237 interviewees aged 16 and over, stratified by region and town size (Realeat Survey Office 1995). This yielded an estimate of 4.5 per cent as the proportion of vegetarians in the adult population. Interestingly, the results also appear to suggest that overall some 12 per cent of the adult population might be regarded as non-meat-eaters (i.e., as vegetarian, vegan, or as no longer eating red or white meat). The 1995 survey results also appear to indicate that those respondents moving away from meat consumption tended to stress health concerns when questioned about their motivations. The significance of gender also emerges clearly in these data, with women (at 5.8 per cent) showing twice the rate of vegetarianism as men. The influence of age as a contributory factor is indicated by the fact that the highest proportion of vegetarians in the 1995 survey was found in the category which covered women aged 16 to 24, the figure being 12.4 per cent. Indeed, the survey found that no less than 25 per cent of its young female respondents in this age group reported abstinence from meat consumption. The survey also highlighted a distinctive social class gradient in vegetarianism, with the highest rates being indicated by respondents in the 'AB' category (6.2 per cent).

A slightly different picture emerges from a single survey carried out for the Vegetarian Society by researchers from the University of Bradford (Vegetarian Society 1991). The study was based upon a quota sample (designed in terms of age, sex, socioeconomic group and region) consisting of 942 adults (aged over 18) and 2,651 young people aged between 11 and 18 years. Among the 11–18 year olds, 8 per cent of the respondents claimed to be vegetarian, the figure for the sample as a whole being 7 per cent. Among the adults in the sample, women indicated a significantly higher rate of vegetarianism than men (10 per cent as compared to 4 per cent). Interestingly, however, the study did not reveal the kind of class gradient in adherence to vegetarian dietary patterns suggested by the Realeat surveys. In fact, the highest rates of vegetarianism were reported by respondents in the 'C1' and 'C2' categories. What is more, although the Realeat surveys identified health issues as the prime motivations behind a switch to vegetarianism, the Bradford data suggest that, among adults, concerns relating to the treatment of food animals rank equally with concerns about human

224

health. Indeed, in the 11–18 age group, concern about the treatment of domesticated food animals outranks concern with health as the prime motivation behind a switch to vegetarianism.

Although there are some noticeable differences between the findings produced by these two sources, it does seem reasonable, on the basis of these results, to estimate the proportion of self-defined vegetarians in the UK population (excluding young children) at between 4 per cent and 7 per cent, and to conclude that this proportion is rising steadily. Indeed, an indirect indication of the increasing popularity of vegetarianism in Britain is provided by the membership statistics of the Vegetarian Society itself, which more than doubled from 1980 to 1995 (from approximately 7,500 to 18,550). Of course, such an increase cannot be taken as direct evidence of the rise of vegetarianism (as we will see later in this chapter, research indicates that there is a significant difference between 'joiners' and 'non-joiners' among vegetarians). However, what this increase does highlight is the enhanced visibility of vegetarianism and the complex issues which surround it.

There have been various attempts to estimate the number of vegetarians in the USA. Citing the ASPCA as their source, Delahoyde and Desperich (1994: 135) offer a figure of approximately 15 million. Stahler (1994) cites a 1977–8 US Department of Agriculture nation-wide food consumption survey in which 1.2 per cent of the 37,135 respondents reported themselves vegetarian, and suggests that more recent estimates have ranged between 3 per cent and 7 per cent. More interestingly, however, Stahler describes the results obtained from a question on animal products in the diet which was included in a Roper poll carried out in 1994. This poll was based upon home interviews with 1,978 respondents aged 18 and over, the sample being designed to be representative of the adult population of the continental USA. The question posed did not rely upon the self-definitions of interviewees, but asked them to indicate which animal products they *never* ate, the list they were offered being made up of the following categories: meat, poultry, fish/seafood, dairy products, eggs, honey. On the basis of the results obtained, Stahler (1994: 6–9) argues that there is a 95 per cent probability that the proportion of vegetarians/vegans in the US population falls in the interval 0.3 per cent to 1 per cent. This, of course, is a much lower figure than that typically obtained when a more straightforward self-definition approach is used. Such findings provide some empirical support for the proposition that many individuals may regard themselves as vegetarian while still consuming (if only occasionally) animal products other than dairy products and eggs.

We have already noted that vegetarianism and veganism cover a broad spectrum of dietary choices and avoidances. Thus we must always bear in mind the fact that an individual's actual eating patterns and his or her conceptualization of those eating patterns as a dietary stance or lifestyle may not always fit neatly with each other. In sociological terms, the conceptualizations must be as worthy of attention and analysis as the observed or reported patterns.

Thus, in effect, self-defined vegetarianism and veganism are the principal objects of analysis in this chapter.

MOTIVES AND RHETORIC

The data we have considered are, admittedly, relatively sparse, but they do appear to indicate that in Western societies like the UK and the USA, self-defined vegetarians can be numbered in millions. Accounting for the emergence of vegetarianism as a large-scale phenomenon is a process which must operate on at least two levels. Firstly, we must consider the issue of the motives behind individual decisions to adopt some form of vegetarianism. Secondly, we must attempt to describe the broader social and cultural processes or conditions which can facilitate such a shift towards meat avoidance or the avoidance of animal products in general. In this section we will examine the kinds of motives which adherents of vegetarianism describe. However, in such a context, it is not necessarily easy to distinguish between the considerations which may impel an individual to make a particular choice and the arguments that individual may employ retrospectively to justify that choice or, indeed, to encourage others to make the same choice. In a sense, then, the themes discussed here refer both to motivations and to what Maurer (1995: 146–7) refers to as the 'rhetorical idioms' which can be employed in the advocacy of vegetarianism. Of course, the thematic headings used below, in some instances, overlap one with another and it should be borne in mind that they are not being offered as mutually exclusive categories.

The moral theme

We have already seen how a moral concern in relation to any animal suffering entailed in obtaining meat was a central feature in the thinking of those classical philosophers who advocated vegetarianism. This same moral concern featured strongly in the arguments of later advocates, and has been developed and discussed in considerable detail by a number of contemporary philosophers. Singer (1976), for example, presents an ethical argument for vegetarianism on the basis of a rejection of 'speciesism', a form of discrimination against non-human creatures which he sees as paralleling racism and sexism in the context of human relationships. The capacity of animals to experience suffering and enjoyment implies that they have interests that should not be violated and that they are not simply Cartesian automata, oblivious to pain and beyond the boundary of moral consideration. Thus, the fundamental utilitarian principle of the minimizing of suffering is seen as demanding the adoption of a vegetarian diet. Other philosophers, like Midgley (1983), also reject the view, deeply embedded in the religious and philosophical traditions of Western thought, that animals can legitimately be excluded from moral consideration and can, therefore, be freely exploited as food sources and for other purposes. Indeed,

Midgley explicitly argues that the boundaries of moral consideration have, historically, been advancing continually, and that we must recognize that they can now breach the species barrier to embrace certain non-human creatures.

However, reservations about the problems involved in attempting to use utilitarian concepts to discuss animal rights (as suggested by Singer 1976) lead other philosophers to adopt alternative lines of reasoning to provide a moral basis for vegetarianism. For example, Regan (1984) argues that, even if we accept that animals cannot be moral agents, certain categories of animals can be regarded as moral patients and as therefore having inherent value which demands our respect. This respect principle effectively rules out their use for food. Similar arguments are used by Clark (1984), who lays considerable emphasis on the idea that humans, by their very nature as intelligent beings, bear a special responsibility of stewardship towards the creatures with whom they form a complex community of living things, such stewardship entailing the rejection of the exploitation of animals that is involved in meat eating.

What, in effect, the detailed and sometimes convoluted discourses developed by philosophers like these represent are attempts to elaborate and make explicit deep-seated anxieties and misgivings concerning the use of animals for food (anxieties which were set in a broader context in Chapter 7).

The food production theme

This theme is based upon the premise (discussed in the previous chapter) that the production of meat represents an unjustifiably extravagant use of natural resources. It is argued that the production of vegetable crops for direct human consumption avoids the energy losses involved in feeding livestock with products (like grains) which are suitable for meeting human nutritional needs. This kind of argument has both ecological and moral implications. In ecological terms, meat production is seen as a process which places an unnecessarily heavy load on the natural environment, which is exploited both extensively and intensively in order to maintain or increase the output of animal proteins. Particular attention has been focused on the destruction or degradation of natural habitats, like tropical rainforests, in order to extend the areas available for cattle ranching, and on the long-term environmental effects of overgrazing and overstocking, especially in arid or semi-arid areas. In this way, the concerns of the vegetarian become linked with those of the environmentalist, and vegetarianism is presented as a set of dietary options which involve food production patterns which have a lower environmental impact than modern farming methods and are ultimately more sustainable.

The moral dimension of the food production theme is not related to animal rights and interests (as in the first theme) but to the interests of humans. The argument here is that clear global inequalities in nutritional status are due, at least in part, to the diversion of resources towards the production of meat for the benefit of consumers in the most affluent economies. In this connection, vegetarianism is conceptualized as a way of reducing what is perceived as the distorting effects of meat production on the global food system, freeing crucial resources for the production of vegetable foods. Such increased production, it is then envisaged, could be used to alleviate hunger and malnutrition in those areas where food shortages are endemic.

The religious/spiritual theme

The religious or spiritual element in vegetarian ideologies is very ancient, and can be traced back, as we have seen, to doctrines relating to the transmigration of souls found in ancient Greek thought and in such major religions as Hinduism and Buddhism. In medieval thought, abstention from flesh foods was often associated with spirituality, purity and asceticism, since such foods were seen as embodying all that was carnal, worldly and corruptible. Meat was also associated with animal passions, and its avoidance was seen as enhancing the individual's control of his or her appetites and sexuality. Twigg (1979) maintains that in the context of contemporary vegetarianism similar ideas have persisted, but in a somewhat modified form, entailing what she terms a 'this-worldly form of mysticism' (Twigg 1979: 26). Concern is not for the wellbeing of some disembodied soul or spirit, but for the 'spiritual body' itself, the body as 'an immortal, youthful temple of the spirit' (Twigg 1979: 27). Such beliefs entail a kind of revulsion for the carnal and the physical, for the processes of digestion and elimination. The adoption of a vegetarian diet and the rejection of meat are characterized as key features of the quest for an ageless and uncorrupted body.

The 'New Order' theme

As well as discussing the spiritual element in contemporary vegetarianism, Twigg also seeks to demonstrate how vegetarian ideologies can embody a critique of what is regarded as the conventional social order, and a vision of a new, alternative mode of patterning social relationships. Thus, for example, vegetarian dishes commonly violate the highly structured form of conventional meals and are presented in a mixed, undifferentiated form. This repudiation of the structure of conventional eating can be seen as symbolic of a repudiation of wider patterns of hierarchy and power, in which the symbolism of meat carries such a positive potency. Nature itself, Twigg argues, is redefined and reconceptualized as a realm characterized not by conflict, competition and suffering, but by harmony and beneficence. This harmonized model of nature is then used as a yardstick against which to measure the deficiencies of contemporary human society, which is seen as having lost touch with the natural, becoming distorted and artificial (Twigg 1979: 22). The vegetarian diet, as a more 'natural' mode of eating, is seen as a device for restoring contact with harmonious nature. Even more ambitiously, however, vegetarian beliefs may entail a quest for a 'New Moral Order' (Twigg 1979: 29), and a vegetarian diet becomes a manifestation of a commitment to reform and social change. Indeed, a particularly radical example of such thinking can be found in the feminist arguments advanced by Adams (1990), for whom the practice of vegetarianism is advocated as a challenge to the male power symbolized by meat and as a means, ultimately, of achieving what she terms the 'destabilizing of patriarchal consumption' (Adams 1990: 186–90).

The health/physiological theme

Issues of health in vegetarian ideologies are closely related to concepts of disease-prevention. Non-vegetarian diets are seen, in effect, as pathogenic. The primary feature of this view is the idea that meat itself is hazardous as a foodstuff, replete with substances or agents, both naturally occurring and artificial, which pose threats to human health. The second, less specific, feature of this view is the idea that modern diets are inherently unhealthy in so far as they rely upon food items which are deficient in crucial nutritional properties as a result of excessive processing and refining. Additionally, such food items are seen as possibly contaminated with a whole range of synthesized additives whose purpose is commercial rather than nutritional, and which also pose potential health threats. In contrast, vegetarian diets, by eliminating meat products, avoid the hazards associated with them. What is more, the emphasis commonly laid upon the consumption of fresh fruits and vegetable products, subjected to minimal amounts of processing, is seen as a means of restoring the diet to a form more closely matching human nutritional needs and of avoiding the ingestion of dangerous substances. (There are clear parallels here with the health food beliefs discussed in Chapter 6.)

The conceptualization of meat as a hazardous food item may, in fact, be taken a stage further. A recurring theme in vegetarian discourse is the view that meat is not a 'natural' component of the human diet at all. It is argued that human physiology (e.g., dental and digestive) is quite unsuited to a carnivorous diet, and that meat eating, by implication, is likely to be deleterious rather than beneficial in health terms.

The aesthetic/gustatory theme

Revulsion in relation to the appearance, tactile properties and taste of meat also figures prominently in vegetarian concerns. Meat may be characterized as an object of disgust rather than as an object of appetite and gustatory enjoyment. The conventional positive symbolism of meat (particularly red meat), with its connotations of virility, strength and power, is rejected – and in its place a highly negative and pejorative symbolism occurs consisting of notions of violence, death and decay. In contrast, vegetable foods are described in highly positive language, not only in terms of their gustatory properties, but also as being charged with life, as opposed to the death associated with meat (Twigg 1979). What is more, underlying concepts of purity (vegetable foods) and contamination (flesh foods) form a highly emotive refrain in vegetarian beliefs.

The themes discussed above can in no sense claim to be exhaustive, although they do describe the main components of contemporary vegetarian ideologies. In fact, Maurer (1995) suggests that there is a deeper underlying rhetorical structure underpinning these themes. Drawing upon the work of Ibarra and Kitsuse (1993), she is able to identify two basic rhetorical idioms which are used to support the claims inherent in vegetarian discourse. The first of these idioms is that of 'entitlement', which emphasizes freedom, justice, choice and liberation, and which, in vegetarian rhetoric, can be applied to selected animal species as well as to humans. The second idiom is that of 'endangerment'. Here the emphasis is on health and the physical welfare of the body, and in vegetarian discourse the consumption of meat is construed as an irremediably 'endangering' activity.

Inevitably, of course, a whole range of much more personal or idiosyncratic motivations and justifications may figure in the experiences of particular individuals. For example, the adoption of vegetarianism may reflect a desire to conform with the expectations of those whom the individual concerned respects. Conversely, vegetarianism may be used as a means of demonstrating distance from individuals or groups towards whom there is a sense of antagonism or resentment. Or, perhaps more straightforwardly, a move towards vegetarianism may reflect simple curiosity and an attraction towards novelty. What is more, the motivations which an individual experiences or the justifications which he or she employs frequently combine and interact with one another. Although some individuals may identify a single dominant motive, others may be unwilling or unable to do so. Such variations will be discussed further when we consider a number of empirical studies of vegetarian beliefs, attitudes and practices.

The thematic strands of contemporary vegetarianism are not without their contradictions and tensions, however. Perhaps ultimately the most contentious of these themes is the moral one. Certainly, the argument that comprehensive moral considerations should be extended across the barrier between humans and other species inevitably involves both ethical and practical conundrums, which have been explored by such philosophers as Townsend (1979) and Frey (1983). Particular problems may arise when the argument shifts from a concern with animal welfare to a concern with animal rights. Whether animals can have rights, which animals should have rights and how those rights could be respected and protected, are issues which pose awkward questions for reflective vegetarians. In direct practical terms, for example, vegetarianism which entails the consumption of dairy products generates questions about the treatment of dairy cows and their fate when aged and unproductive, and about the disposal of unwanted male offspring. Indeed, in Western economies, the ready availability of reasonably priced cow's milk is bound up with the meat production industry. Similar problems are posed by the use of eggs in vegetarian diets, particularly the disposal of unproductive birds and unwanted males. Depending on their level of ethical sensitivity, some vegetarians may choose to ignore, or at least to set aside, such questions, whereas others may seek solutions. However, even veganism, with its more or less strict avoidance of animal products, does not provide a complete solution. The vast majority of the food items eaten by vegans are the products of farming, and farming itself inevitably entails the initial destruction of pristine ecological systems and their original plant and animal inhabitants. What is more, such processes as pest control, ploughing and harvesting inevitably involve the destruction of large numbers of small invertebrate and vertebrate animals, which have to be ruled outside the boundaries of moral consideration if food production is to continue. In this sense, the pursuit of what might be termed a 'blameless menu' looks to be a daunting task for the vegetarian and even the vegan.

Similarly, other pro-vegetarian arguments related to food production may present certain problems. The contention that the direct consumption of vegetable products by humans is a more efficient use of natural resources than using agricultural produce to feed livestock is not quite as straightforward as it appears. Vast areas of the earth's surface occupied by humans are quite unsuited to the growing of arable crops and can only be exploited by using browsing and grazing domesticated herbivores. In fact, the argument applies largely to the agricultural sectors of the developed economies, where intensively produced crops are fed to intensively reared food animals, and is, therefore, by no means universally applicable. What is more, we should be cautious about accepting the view that vegetarianism, were it to become the dominant dietary pattern in the developed economies, would automatically increase food availability in the Third World countries. As it stands, the argument does not address crucial problems of distribution. These problems refer not only to the practicalities involved in the transportation, storage and allocation of foodstuffs, but also to questions concerning the distribution of wealth and income. Those who suffer malnutrition and starvation tend to be those people who lack the resources to produce, or the purchasing power to buy, the food that they need. Such structural inequalities, and their political, economic and cultural roots are at least as significant as any notion of a global pool of foodstuffs that would be increased by vegetarian consumption patterns.

The spiritual dimensions of contemporary vegetarian ideologies also contain inherent tensions, for example, between a deep-seated asceticism on the one hand, and an emphasis on the care and cultivation of the body on the other. Even the vegetarian espousal of 'nature' and the 'natural' is fraught with difficulty, as the more brutal and ruthless manifestations of the interactions between individuals of the same or different species are masked with images of harmony and unity. Similarly, the radical or reformist dimensions of vegetarian thought may be said to suffer from a tension between, on the one hand, a stress on individual well-being and personal development and, on the other, a view of vegetarianism as a collective phenomenon, as a movement with broader political and moral aims.

However, despite such tensions, the underlying themes discussed above, in various forms, figure strongly in the pro-vegetarian literature (e.g., Amato and Partridge 1989) and in the thinking of practising vegetarians and vegans.

EMPIRICAL STUDIES OF CONTEMPORARY VEGETARIANSIM

Although there is an ever-lengthening list of books and articles advocating vegetarianism or providing advice and guidance for practising or aspiring vegetarians, there are comparatively few studies in this area carried out from a social scientific stand-point. In this section we will examine examples of such studies in order to gain some direct empirical insight into the everyday realities of vegetarian belief and practice.

Research published in the 1970s (Dwyer, Mayer, Dowd, Kandel and Mayer 1974) provided detailed information on the attitudes and dietary patterns of 100 young American adults who had converted to vegetarianism after maturity. Using a battery of interviews, questionnaires and dietary histories, the authors explore a range of issues, including reason for dietary change, attitudes to diet and health, abstinence patterns and religious, ecological and ethical views. The most frequently cited reason for conversion to vegetarianism was related to health, followed by ethical concerns. Spiritual or 'metaphysical' concerns were ranked next, followed by ecological issues, ranked equally with gustatory or aesthetic preferences linked to a distaste for meat. The authors make an important distinction between what they term 'joiners' (who had affiliated themselves to wider movements like macrobiotics, health foods and yoga) and 'loners' who were not affiliated in this way. They also distinguish between circumscribed avoidances (that is, where the diet excluded only quite a small range of items) and far-reaching avoidances (where the diet entailed the exclusion of a wide range of items). Some significant differences appeared to emerge on the basis of these distinctions. For example, the 'loners' with circumscribed avoidances tended to isolate their dietary patterns from other aspects of their daily lives, and many had gone to considerable lengths to devise a personal dietary system, often in the light of advice from health professionals. In contrast, the joiners with far-reaching avoidances tended to exhibit attitudes and practices similar to those found in extremist factions of sects or cults. These included rigidly observed abstinences, the performance of rituals and a sense of mission impelling them to seek to convert others (Dwyer, Mayer, Dowd, Kandel and Mayer 1974: 534).

A later study (Freeland-Graves, Greninger and Young 1986) attempts a direct comparison between vegetarians and non-vegetarians. The researchers studied a response group consisting of 150 vegetarians and 150 non-vegetarians living in Austin, Texas. The non-vegetarian group was created by matching each vegetarian respondent with a non-vegetarian respondent of the same sex and a similar age. While there were many overall similarities between the two groups, there were some interesting contrasts. Only 26 per cent of vegetarians were practising followers of traditional religions, as opposed to 59 per cent of non-vegetarians, and vegetarians' involvement in more exotic sects and non-Western religions was relatively low, leading the authors to suggest that the link between vegetarianism and 'cultism' is in decline. What is more, the vegetarians in the study showed a higher tendency to join clubs and organizations, went out more frequently with friends and entertained friends at home more frequently than did the non-vegetarians. There was evidence to indicate that vegetarians, and especially vegans, tended to form supportive networks of family and friends who were also vegetarian. In fact, 44 per cent of the vegetarian respondents reported that other family members also practised vegetarianism. Coupled with the fact that vegetarians tended to live in larger households (especially vegans), the findings suggest that collective social support may be an important component of the maintenance of vegetarian dietary practices for this particular set of respondents.

Strikingly, however, parental influence did not appear to have been a strong factor influencing the decision to become vegetarian. The authors argue that the choice of a vegetarian lifestyle may often involve the deliberate rejection of the meat-based dietary practices of parents. Indirect evidence for this proposition comes from the study's finding that, on average, vegetarians lived at greater distances from their parents and visited them less frequently than did non-vegetarians. It is perhaps ironic, then, that the majority of the vegetarian respondents (indeed, all the vegans) anticipated that their own children would remain vegetarian in adulthood, that is, would conform to parental expectations (Freeland-Graves, Greninger and Young 1986: 910).

Further information concerning the ideas and practices of American vegetarians is provided by Amato and Partridge (1989). Although their work is primarily concerned with making a case for vegetarianism and with providing guidance and support for existing or would-be vegetarians, the authors did engage in the collection of some pertinent data. Respondents were recruited by placing notices in the newsletters of vegetarian organizations, and 209 responses were received. A further sixty-one individuals were sent detailed questionnaires for completion. The authors accept that their response group, being essentially self-selected, cannot be regarded as in any sense statistically representative of all vegetarians in the USA; indeed, they admit, for example, that it is biased towards those holding professional or managerial positions in the occupational structure. Nevertheless, the authors argue that the group is sufficiently broadly based to provide valuable insights into the motives and experiences of vegetarians. The motivations of this group leaned heavily towards concerns about animal suffering or animal rights (mentioned by 67 per cent) and health concerns (which were mentioned by 38 per cent). Spiritual or religious factors were mentioned by 17 per cent of respondents, and aesthetic factors or dislike of meat by 12 per cent (Amato and Partridge 1989: 34). In fact, 43 per cent of respondents stressed a single reason for becoming vegetarian, whereas the remaining 57 per cent gave multiple reasons. The single-reason respondents were mainly those motivated by animal rights issues. What is more, motivations tended to change over time, with, for example, individuals who originally made the change for reasons based on self-interest (such as health concerns) gradually becoming aware of the ethical dimensions of vegetarianism. The authors also provide insights into the dynamics of the conversion process, describing how the decision may be influenced by friends, relatives, vegetarian literature or mass media coverage of the issues. They also give graphic accounts of instances where the individual's conversion was prompted by some dramatic and often distressing experience, for example, the witnessing of animal slaughter (Amato and Partridge 1989: 74–6). Less extreme instances may involve a sense of repulsion or disgust when the individual suddenly makes a previously unadmitted or suppressed connection between flesh food and the animal from which it came, particularly if that is an animal which would otherwise be accorded affection or regard.

The impact of the individual's conversion to vegetarianism upon his or her personal relationships is also analysed by Amato and Partridge. Parental reaction to the conversion of a son or daughter was reported by many respondents to be a very negative one. While this negative reaction was sometimes related to parents' concerns about the health and dietary implications of vegetarianism, it also appeared to emerge out of a sense that the rejection of the parents' eating patterns implied a rejection of the parents themselves and of their values and priorities. Conversely, however, some parents were approving and supportive. Most significantly, perhaps, the authors argue that the conversion to vegetarianism of a family member can lead to major changes in family relationships, which may be strengthened or, at the other extreme, may break down completely (Amato and Partridge 1989: 181–2). What is more, the stresses and strains which can be introduced into the family setting may be present in other forms in other settings. Workplace relationships, eating out and socializing with non-vegetarian friends may all become potential sources of tension or embarrassment with which the practising vegetarian has to learn to cope.

There are striking parallels between the findings presented by Amato and Partridge and a qualitative study of vegetarians, their motives and experiences carried out in the UK (Beardsworth and Keil 1992a). The UK study was based upon interviews with seventy-six respondents, recruited on a 'snowball' sample basis in the East Midlands region. The interviews themselves were open-ended and discursive in nature, in order to provide respondents with an opportunity to present their own accounts and experiences in their own terms as far as possible. All interviews were taped and fully transcribed, generating several hundred thousand words of transcript material, which was then analysed by being sorted into a series of emergent thematic categories. The response group generated showed a higher level of average educational attainment than the general population, and this is reflected in the fact that twenty-three out of the seventy-six respondents were in professional or managerial occupations. There was a roughly equal balance between the sexes, although the age distribution showed a marked clustering in the ranges 26–30 years and 31–5 years, and the majority of the respondents were without dependent children.

The motivations for conversion to vegetarianism (all but one of the respondents were converts; just one had been brought up vegan) were classified as moral, health-related, gustatory and ecological. A total of forty-three respondents maintained that, for them, moral motivations were primary; health-related motivations were reported as primary by thirteen respondents. Priority was allocated to gustatory factors by nine respondents, and only one indicated ecological concerns were paramount. However, from respondents' accounts it was clear that although primary motives could be readily identified in most cases, motives were interwoven and tended to support each other. What is more, the balance of motivations could change over time, with the emphasis shifting significantly. There were examples of individuals who had set out with primarily health-related concerns and who had subsequently moved towards a preoccupation with animal rights; there were also examples of individuals who had undergone the reverse of this process.

The actual conversion to vegetarianism also proved to be a decidedly variable experience. For example, some respondents described a protracted process of conversion, during which vague concerns and misgivings, which might reach back even as far as childhood, gradually came into focus and eventually prompted the progressive initiation of dietary changes. In contrast, some respondents reported undergoing a dramatic 'conversion experience' (Beardsworth and Keil 1992a: 257), which literally shocked them into an abrupt switch into vegetarianism. Such experiences could involve acute sensations of revulsion while eating meat (in which it is suddenly perceived as 'dead flesh', for example), being confronted with the sight of the remnants of slaughtered animals or even viewing a particularly powerful and disturbing television programme.

The implications of a move into vegetarianism for the individual's social and personal relationships drawn out by Amato and Partridge (1989) also came to the fore in the UK study. Significant contrasts emerged, for example, between situations where relatives (e.g., parents, siblings, in-laws) were reasonably approving and supportive of the convert and situations involving more or less severe disapproval. In the latter case, serious tensions could emerge, leading to the attenuation or even breakdown of the relationships in question.

The study also sought to analyse the powerful ideological currents present in vegetarian beliefs and priorities. Interestingly, for this group of respondents, at least, what might be termed the 'anti-meat theme' appeared to be more potent than the 'pro-vegetarian theme' (Beardsworth and Keil 1992a: 272–6). That is, anti-meat sentiments related to moral outrage, repulsion, disgust or to a sense of meat as wasteful of economic resources or as a food unsuitable or even dangerous for humans, seemed to dominate respondents' nutritional conceptualizations. Indeed, the vocabulary employed in expressing these ideas was often extreme and disturbing, conjuring up images of blood, slaughter and dismemberment. In contrast, respondents' discussions of the virtues of vegetarian dietary regimes were much more muted and less emphatic. In addition, the study also uncovered examples of respondents who were all too aware of the moral tensions involved in the vegetarian's use of dairy products or even of non-food products like leather. Vegan respondents tended to be critical of vegetarians in this respect, while often themselves acknowledging the difficulties involved in following a strictly vegan regime and the virtual impossibility of a totally harmless diet (Beardsworth and Keil 1992a: 282–3).

EXPLAINING THE RISE OF VEGETARIANISM

If we accept the contention that vegetarianism now represents an increasingly significant dietary option in countries like the UK and the USA, we are faced with the problem of trying to explain the rise in popularity of a dietary regime which was previously followed only by a tiny minority. In this chapter we have already examined the rhetoric of vegetarian ideologies, a rhetoric which permits the individual to think through his or her own priorities and concerns and to arrive at a decision as to whether or not to embrace vegetarian preferences and prohibitions. Of course, this is not to suggest that such a decision is necessarily a purely rational one, as a whole range of emotional and, indeed, gustatory factors may also be involved. Nevertheless, such rhetorical resources allow the decision to be formulated and, if necessary, described and justified to others.

However, merely citing such rhetorical themes does not in itself constitute a viable attempt to explain the rise of vegetarianism. What is required, in addition, is some grasp of the changes (sociological, cultural and economic) which have created the conditions in which vegetarian ideologies can thrive and can attract increasing numbers of adherents. In Chapter 9, the argument put forward by Fiddes (1991) to account for long-term falls in the consumption of red meat was described in some detail. It will be recalled that Fiddes maintains that the trend away from red meat is the result of an underlying cultural shift in that particular food item's symbolic significance. Whereas the production and consumption of red meat have traditionally acted as powerful expressions of the human ability to dominate and exploit the natural world, our collective perceptions of our relationship to that world have recently undergone a transformation. We no longer confidently celebrate our ascendancy over nature through a kind of triumphalist consumption of the flesh of large and powerful creatures. Rather, says Fiddes (1991: 219–23), an ideology of care and responsibility is replacing the doctrines of exploitation. In such a cultural climate, the adoption of a vegetarian diet and the avoidance of all meat can be construed as an expression of environmental concern and sensitivity, and thus perceived as having a clear logic behind it, a logic in tune with increasingly widely held values. In this sense, the contemporary increase in the popularity of vegetarianism is conceived of as but one component in a complex package of recent developments, which include the mounting salience of ecological and conservation issues, the emergence of environmentalist movements and the rise of 'green' politics and ethics. The implication of this view is that vegetarianism as a dietary option has, effectively, become more appealing because of its fit with deeper cultural trends.

The argument put forward by Fiddes that the reduction or avoidance of meat consumption, or the adoption of vegetarianism, are features of an underlying cultural shift is consistent with the concept of the 'civilizing of appetite' employed by Mennell (1985). This concept, which we have already encountered, refers to the process by which the celebration of gluttony and the indulgence of 'gargantuan' appetites characteristic of medieval culture, was progressively replaced by an emphasis on the refinement of taste and the exercise of self-restraint in relation to food consumption. Mennell (1985: 38–9) actually suggests that this cultural fixation on self-control in relation to appetite may well be implicated in eating disorders like *anorexia nervosa*, which formed a major theme in Chapter 8. However, it is also quite possible that it forms a component of vegetarian ideology. The symbolism of meat, as we have seen, is replete with the imagery of physical strength, animal nature, passion and power. All of these features are antithetical to notions of self-restraint and refinement. The vegetarian appetite, then, might be characterized as one strongly influenced by this civilizing process. Even where an affinity for 'nature' and the 'natural' is expressed, this is, as Twigg (1979) has pointed out, based on a conceptualization of nature which has been harmonized and sanitized, indeed, in a sense, civilized. The concept of an underlying civilizing process originates, of course, in the work of Elias. This author himself suggests that the advance of the civilizing process may also entail an advance in what he terms the 'threshold of repugnance' (Elias 1978a: 120). The culture of refinement and restraint means that individuals are less and less willing to confront the potentially disturbing and distasteful aspects of the production and processing of animal-derived foods. As a result, such features of the food system are increasingly concealed from public view. However, vegetarianism may represent an attempt to repudiate these features, at least partially, and veganism an attempt to repudiate them totally.

There also exists the distinct possibility that recent cultural and ideological changes which have begun to affect the balance of power in the realm of sexual politics may also have contributed to the emergence of a climate more congenial for vegetarianism. The arguments put forward by Adams (1990) concerning the complex symbolic and metaphorical associations between meat eating and male power over women (which were discussed in Chapter 9) lead her to exhort women to adopt a vegetarian diet as part of a challenge to male dominance. In fact, she sees vegetarianism, not only as historically associated with feminism but as a virtual obligation for the truly committed feminist. References to feminist values and priorities do not appear to figure significantly in the findings of the limited number of empirical studies of vegetarianism which are available, although this may be due in part to the original design and concerns of the studies in question. Certainly, the fact that what data we have suggest that rates of vegetarianism tend to be higher among women than among men, and especially among women in younger age groups, may provide some indirect support for the contention that the recent rise in the salience of feminist ideas could be a contributory factor in the increased popularity of this particular dietary option.

On the other hand, the empirical material does provide much more direct evidence that changing views of the links between diet and health have influenced the level and incidence of vegetarianism. Health concerns consistently appear in the accounts of vegetarian respondents, and some accord them overall priority. Health education messages and dietary guidelines promoted by government agencies, stressing the need to increase intakes of dietary fibre and fresh fruit and vegetables, can also be seen as contributing to a general climate more sympathetic to vegetarianism. In addition, given the continuing significance of common-sense conceptions of the connections between diet and health (see Chapter 6), vegetarianism may increasingly be seen as a strategy for the individual to exercise a degree of personal control over his or her health outcomes and physical well-being.

In a sense, this line of thought brings us back to the arguments developed in Chapter 7 concerning the ways in which the potential anxieties created by the underlying paradoxes of food and eating can be coped with or managed. Thus, vegetarianism may be one of the more significant emergent cultural devices for dealing, for example, with health-related food anxieties. Within the framework of vegetarian belief, the exclusion of meat from the diet is, in effect, the exclusion of a health-threatening substance. These threats to health are seen as arising from meat's supposed unsuitability for the human digestive system, its fat content, its proneness to bacterial infestation or its contamination by artificial additives and residues. Additionally, and even more obviously, vegetarianism can provide some sort of solution to the anxieties and the sense of guilt which may be generated by the killing of animals for food. As was suggested in Chapter 7, as traditional modes of coping with such concerns go into decline, their place is likely to be taken by alternative practices, conceptualizations and rhetorical devices. Thus, vegetarianism (and, perhaps to an even greater extent, veganism) is both a practice and a discourse well suited to the needs of the contemporary anxious eater. It is certainly significant that, in the transcript material reported in Beardsworth and Keil (1992a: 287), vegetarian respondents repeatedly stressed the idea that their dietary stance was, in part, an attempt to regain what they explicitly referred to as 'peace of mind'.

While it is perfectly feasible to itemize the kinds of factors which can be seen as making some contribution to the widening popularity of vegetarianism, it is far more difficult to try to rank them in order of importance. Indeed, any attempt to weight the relative contribution of any given factor is bound to be complicated by the possibility that these ideas may interact with each other in complex ways. Evidence for these interactions at the personal level is provided by the empirical studies discussed above, which show how respondents' own accounts interweave the various motivations they describe, and often portray them as supporting and confirming each other. At the social level, given the variety of themes and causes that can be accommodated beneath the vegetarian umbrella, it is open to question as to whether vegetarianism itself can be conceptualized as a reasonably coherent movement. Certainly, the findings in the empirical literature which point out an important distinction between 'join-ers' and 'loners' suggest that the adoption of vegetarianism does not necessarily entail a sense that the individual should become involved in collective attempts to promote its values or to convert others to its dietary practices. Yet, the distinct possibility exists that the emergence of vegetarianism as a dietary option with a following counted in millions may well be one manifestation of a broad spectrum of underlying cultural shifts and reassessments.

In fact, if we seek to assess the position of vegetarianism in the modern food system, it becomes apparent that this system actually facilitates a vegetarian regimen. The sheer range of vegetable-based foodstuffs now available to the affluent Western consumer, a range largely free from the restrictions of season and locality, makes feasible the creation of a vegetarian cuisine characterized by variety and novelty. Variety and enjoyment are features of food which many vegetarian respondents emphasize (Beardsworth and Keil 1992a). In contrast, adhering to a vegetarian diet in the context of a more localized and seasonal food supply would be an altogether less appealing prospect. For example, a vegetarian diet based solely on the produce of traditional northern European temperate agriculture could prove somewhat monotonous and restrictive.

If we accept the contention that the ideological levels of the food systems of Western societies are increasingly characterized by menu pluralism, there are clear implications for our understanding of contemporary vegetarianism. In a menu-pluralistic setting, the availability of a variety of menu principles (rational, moral, hedonistic, etc.), provides the individual with a good deal of flexibility (within certain social and economic constraints, of course) when it comes to the construction of his or her own personal dietary regimen. In such a climate, the adoption of vegetarianism is increasingly likely to be seen as just one more diet and lifestyle choice from among the many options on offer, and less likely to be construed as a form of dietary deviance or non-conformity. While this may actually render vegetarianism rather less attractive to those seeking ways of demonstrating difference or expressing protest, it will enhance its attractiveness to a wider range of potential converts.

This conclusion presents us with an interesting paradox, however. The rheto-ric of vegetarianism tends to place considerable emphasis on the idea of a challenge to conventional foodways. Such a challenge, as we have seen, may be couched in ethical terms, in nutritional terms, in terms of concepts of 'nature' and the 'natural', and so on. Yet it can be argued (Beardsworth and Keil 1993a) that this challenge to the conventional food system is, in practice, in the process of being re-incorporated into it. For a capitalist, market-based food system, vegetarian tastes and requirements present novel marketing and profit-making opportunities. Thus, specialized products and services aimed at vegetarian con-sumers are created to respond to the demands of a significant new minority niche. These developments are explicitly recognized by many respondents who have been vegetarian for some decades, as they comment on the improvements they have experienced in the availability of vegetarian dietary items, restaurants, etc. (Beardsworth and Keil 1992a). As vegetarianism is absorbed into the capitalist food system and converted into one more routinely available dietary option, its threshold of entry will effectively be lowered. In this way, the current following is likely to be maintained, or even significantly extended, as potential recruits are offered a progressively more straightforward process of conversion.

OVERVIEW

In this chapter we have traced the path which has led vegetarianism from its position as a long-established, but in a sense deviant, nutritional regimen to a position of being an increasingly popular dietary option among an array of other options on offer. The analysis of the shifting cultural, social and economic conditions behind this transformation might push us towards the conclusion that, in some senses at least, contemporary concerns, priorities and anxieties may be evolving in ways which are bringing them more and more into line with the preoccupations of vegetarianism. For these reasons, what was once a quintessential nutritional heresy is now becoming a kind of nutritional orthodoxy, with a substantial and expanding nucleus of adherents and a larger periphery of sympathizers and potential converts. This process is aided by the commercial dynamics of a food industry willing, indeed eager, to cater for novel forms of demand.

Predicting the future of vegetarianism in Western societies like the UK and the USA might seem to be a simple matter of extrapolating from existing trends. On this basis, it might even be anticipated that vegetarianism, at varying levels of strictness, would eventually become the dominant dietary pattern, with meat eating confined to a deviant and furtive minority. However, the data upon which we might base our views of overall trends in vegetarianism are currently far too fragmentary to generate much predictive confidence. What is more, these fragmentary data suggest that trends in meat consumption and meat avoidance are somewhat variable, even between the nations of Europe, for example. Even if clear trends could be established, their ultimate directions would still be shrouded in mystery. Could we expect vegetarianism to continue its inroads into conventional foodways on a steady basis? Would it, on the other hand, reach a kind of plateau, a level of penetration beyond which it could not extend? On the other hand, would it eventually begin to contract, losing ground to other priorities and nutritional ideologies as the cultural and economic frameworks of food production and consumption undergo changes as yet unforeseen? Or should the future of vegetarian cuisine simply be seen as one more culinary option which individuals can employ as and when they feel inclined?

While such questions are, for the time being, unanswerable, there is a pressing need for more empirical research in this area. More extensive and comprehensive survey data are needed to provide a clearer idea of the underlying trends. Survey work based on a comparative approach is also required to provide a clearer indication of the important contrasts which appear to exist between different, albeit neighbouring, societies. Additionally, as a complement to such data, more qualitative material is required, derived from small-scale, intensive studies, in order to enhance our insight into the subjective dimensions of vegetarianism. In particular, vegetarian biographies require attention, in order to reveal the ways in which motivations and accounts vary over time, as well as the patterns of conversion, adjustment and lapsing which commonly occur. Only through such work will we achieve the insights necessary to place the contemporary vegetarian phenomenon in its sociological and historical context.

11

SUGAR AND CONFECTIONERY
Sweetness in the human diet

James (1990) writes of the Baka of the Cameroons who, once a honey comb is located in the topmost branches of the rainforest canopy, spend time and effort in order to obtain it. 'They will quite literally go to enormous heights and put their lives at risk to obtain the honey' (James 1990: 632). She also draws our attention to a television advertisement in our own society which portrays a man undertaking a series of dangerous and acrobatic feats to deliver a box of chocolates to the woman he admires. What have these accounts in common? They are, argues James, just two examples of the extent to which sweet foods are valued. In each culture the source of sweetness may vary, as will the kinds of food, but the preference for sweet tastes remains a constant. There are many discussions about the biological basis and physiological functions of this preference for sweetness. However, for sociologists it raises questions about the social organization of the production, distribution and consumption of such highly valued foods and about the part which sweet foods play in society.

Any superficial account of the increase in the accessibility and consumption of such foods as sweets, confectionery and chocolate gives an impression that here is yet another success story involving human ingenuity in processing natural raw materials and, in relatively recent human history, the application of sophisticated technology to produce and distribute quantities of sweet foods on a scale unknown in previous historical periods. However, it is also relevant to recognize that, whichever aspect of the story of sweetness is considered, there are also contradictions and conflicts and a more complex account to be given. There are many examples, amongst the most revealing about social processes and relationships, of the consumer's ambivalence about a food which is, at the same time, both desirable and 'bad', and of the human as well as the economic price to be paid for the increase in the production of such sweet foods as sugar.

THE PHYSIOLOGICAL BASIS FOR THE PREFERENCE FOR SWEETNESS

Cultural analyses of food preference emphasize the fact that, of all the potentially edible foods available, human beings select relatively few and that these

242

choices are shaped by social experiences, each society building up a set of food resources appropriate to its physical and social environment. By way of contrast, the preference for sweetness is said to be innate. It is assumed to be linked to the fact that sweetness is the characteristic taste of many attractive energy sources, such as fruits (Rozin 1982: 228). Although we do not have a complete understanding of the biological function of the human preference for sweetness (Booth, Connor and Marie 1987: 156), there is agreement that 'Sweetness is the most neurally distinct of gustatory qualities' (Scott and Giza 1987: 28). The sensory receptors for detecting the chemicals associated with sugars appear to have emerged very early in primate evolution and to have persisted in modern primates including humans (Beidler 1982: 5). Human infants have been shown to prefer sweet solutions immediately after birth. As children grow up and become adult, the specific sweet foods chosen, together with their quantity and quality, are constrained by social and economic factors. Beauchamp and Cowart (1987: 136) review the available data on the development of sweet perception and draw the following conclusions. Newborn babies and young children demonstrate an avid taste for sweetness, which seems to be largely independent of the degree of early exposure to sweet tastes. However, the nature of dietary exposure to sweet tastes that the child experiences does appear to shape the expectations and the degree of acceptability of particular sweet foods. Strikingly, however, the taste for sweetness appears to decline with maturity, with adults judging lower levels of sweetness to be most pleasant as compared with the levels preferred by children.

This preference for sweetness is argued to be so powerful that, according to Rozin (1982: 228–9), it is in sharp contrast to many other foods in that it provides an example of one of the most straightforward links between biology, individual and culture. He suggests that there exists a relatively straightforward progression between the biological fact of the innate human liking for sweetness and the development of behaviour patterns designed to seek out sweet foods in the environment. Once such items are discovered, Rozin argues, they are readily incorporated into culture and, more specifically, into cuisine. Once incorporated, their presence provides the opportunity for further exposure to sweet tastes, thereby reinforcing their role in the human diet. Rozin sees these steps to the incorporation of sweet foods into culture as far simpler and more direct than the much more complex processes which may be involved in learning other flavour principles which are not so closely tied to any discernible physiologically innate taste preferences.

THE HISTORY OF SUGAR

Most of the historical studies of sweet foods (examples are Abbot 1990; Deerr 1949, 1950; Lees 1983; Mintz 1985; Toussaint-Samat 1992) tend to focus on the discovery and deliberate cultivation of plants, such as cane and beet, which produce sugar, with most attention on the development of sugar cane. However, these authors also give some insight into other sources of sweet foods. For example, Deerr (1949, 1950) in a two-volume history of sugar begins by indicating the importance of honey and fruits as sweet foods for 'primitive man' and reproduces a rock painting of neolithic honey gathering (Deerr 1949: 5). Sources such as honey and fruits have remained important but may have received less attention because they have never been the focus of the same level of sociopolitical intervention in their production and distribution as sugar cane and beet.

Although the large-scale consumption of sugar is relatively recent in Europe, there is evidence that sugar produced from cane on a commercial basis was widely available in India and China from ancient times. The cane is said to have originated in the south Pacific region and been transferred, first to India and later to China, into those areas where it was possible to find the right conditions for its growth: rich, moist soil for planting and great heat and ventilation for ripening (Toussaint-Samat 1992: 552–63). The ancestors of the Buddha were said to have come from 'the land of sugar', or Bengal, and Toussaint-Samat records a reference to a banquet in 1200 BC 'with tables laid with sweet things, syrup, canes to chew' (Toussaint-Samat 1992: 552). This fact, together with evidence of sugar prepared on a commercial basis for food preparation in China, is of particular interest in that it supports the notion that sugar was available in these societies as part of the general cuisine. This contrasts with evidence from other geographical areas and historical periods in Europe and the Middle East (for example in ancient Egypt and later amongst the Greeks and Romans) which suggests that sugar was only available in very small quantities and that its use was restricted to medicinal purposes. The Persians were said to have discovered the reed 'that gives honey without the aid of bees' (Toussaint-Samat 1992: 552) when they invaded the Indus valley, and it was they who first established the routes which brought sugar to Europe as part of the spice trade. In medieval Europe the crystallized sap of sugar cane was initially called 'Indian salt'. Its use gradually spread as it established itself as an exotic luxury food or medicinal substance available only to the wealthy. The large sums of money exchanged in the operation of the spice trade accounted for much of the prosperity of ports such as Venice during this period. However, sugar prices rose even higher as this precious commodity was distributed inland from the ports. Indeed, Toussaint-Samat illustrates the value placed on this substance by citing a thirteenth-century example from Burgundy in France, where sugar changed hands on the basis of its weight in silver (Toussaint-Samat 1992: 554).

The voyages of exploration of Christopher Columbus and others constituted the turning-point for sugar production and initiated its transformation from a medicine and a luxury into a more widely available and ultimately cheap food. These explorers discovered, in the 'New World' of the Americas, land that provided the particular conditions in which sugar cane would grow. Entire continents were claimed in the names of European sovereigns. For the first time, European societies such as Spain, Portugal, France, and later England and the Netherlands (in the East Indies), had access to sources of sugar over which they had political control. The plantations which were established continued the traditional, labour-intensive ways of growing cane, although the scale of production expanded. The main developments were in processing and it became the pattern to export unrefined sugar from the colonies for capital-intensive refinement in the European countries which controlled the plantations. Lees (1983) provides an account of the scientific (particularly chemical) and technological developments which made possible the wide range of sweets, chocolate and other confectionery, as well as refined sugar itself, which have been available to the British consumer since the middle of the nineteenth century. After an uncertain start and variable success, the Caribbean islands had become the world's leading producers and suppliers of sugar by the eighteenth century (Abbot 1990: 11), with production and trade expanding at a pace which accelerated in the nineteenth century, along with constant improvements in the reliability and predictability of supplies.

It is interesting to note that sugar cane production became so well established and the initial concerns about the security of supplies so diminished that there was little interest in exploiting knowledge of the high sugar content of a type of beet grown in Italy which had been documented as early as 1575 (Toussaint-Samat 1992: 560). That waited until the nineteenth century when countries such as France, when at war, could no longer be confident about supplies from their colonies. Compared with sugar cane, beet had the advantage that it could be planted as part of crop rotations and could be processed directly into refined sugar in on-site factories. These characteristics made sugar beet a highly profitable commodity and it was so successful that production continued when the political reasons for its development no longer obtained. Ironically, successful production of beet sugar in Europe contributed to uncertainty in the market overall. The proportions of cane and beet sugar have varied over time but cane sugar has remained at over half of the total supply (Abbot 1990: 12). By the 1970s the combination of sugar cane and beet production outstripped the demand for sugar as a foodstuff and experiments began for using sugar in other ways, for example, as a raw material for the production of fuel.

Any history of sugar which emphasizes the development of increasingly efficient production and the growth in consumption may give the impression that the history of sugar is merely one of the commercial and industrial adjustment between supply and demand. However, there is another story, that of the exploitative social relations involved in the use of sugar cane by Europeans who might not be able to grow the cane in their own temperate climate but who wielded power over both the peoples and the processes involved in sugar production in their colonies overseas. As Toussaint-Samat puts it dramatically: 'So many tears were shed for sugar that by rights it ought to have lost its sweetness' (Toussaint-Samat 1992: 560). According to Mintz (1985), an understanding of the history of sugar demands an analysis of power relationships between the 'Old' and the 'New' worlds.

The beginning of Mintz's account is familiar. As we have seen, the early status of sugar was as an expensive medicine, sold along with spices in apothecaries or pharmacies. It was regarded as beneficial but powerful, so that it was important not to eat it inappropriately (i.e., when not sick) or to excess. The production of sugar from cane grown in tropical or sub-tropical conditions in the Nile valley and some parts of the Mediterranean was highly labour-intensive, which explains the expense. However, Mintz argues that Columbus's second voyage to the New World in the late fifteenth century would transform the scale of sugar production when the explorer recognized the West Indies as offering the ideal conditions for growing sugar cane. However, in the newly established plantations the processing of the cane remained labour-intensive. It is in the provision of forced labour for the sugar plantations that power relations are revealed. Since a large proportion of the indigenous population of the West Indies had been taken to work the gold mines in South America, labour had to be imported. Since the aim was also to keep the cost of working the plantations as low as possible, already established links with the coastal peoples of West Africa were brought into play, as these peoples could provide slaves drawn from the African interior. The first of these were transported to the West Indies in 1505.

Other countries soon entered the competition for control over the New World, and the control of sugar became a political and military, as well as an economic, struggle. The first slaves reached an English colony in the West Indies in 1619 and, from then onwards, the English became the major and most successful players in the struggle. The sugar trade can be regarded as part of an economic investment where production and demand expanded together. The slaves themselves were rarely considered as human. They were treated as commodities in the two 'triangular trades' which hinged on sugar cane growing. The first of these trades involved the export of British finished goods to Africa, the transportation of slaves from Africa to the West Indies and the shipping of sugar from the West Indies to England. The other trade involved the export of New England rum to Africa, the transportation of slaves from Africa to the West Indies and the shipping of molasses from the West Indies to New England. These trading patterns were highly profitable activities from their beginnings, bringing at least three benefits to the home economy: firstly, returns on the initial investment; secondly, the export of machinery, cloth and even instruments of constraint and torture to plantations; thirdly, the import of a low-cost food for the labouring classes. The entire system of production was supported by the political and military strength of the British Empire, which shaped the asymmetrical power relationships between the home economy and the colonies. In such a context, it is easy to explain Britain's initial reluctance to abolish slavery and the fact that, even when West Indian slaves were given their freedom, their role continued to be limited to that of labourers in the sugar industry. Indeed, it was the government's deliberate policy to deny them the opportunity of becoming as rich as their previous masters from the production and export of sugar. Ironically, however, the exploitative conditions and relationships which characterized sugar production in the West Indies provided what can only be described as a bonanza of sweetness for the working classes in Britain.

Mintz (1985) argues that the pattern of consumption in Britain showed two characteristics: 'intensification' and 'extensification'. By intensification he means that the lower classes emulated the upper classes in the use of sugar, for example, in having elaborate wedding cakes which, until the availability of cheap sugar in the nineteenth century, had been unachievable luxuries even for the middle classes. By extensification, Mintz means that new ways of using sugar were developed, aimed at all social levels. Such products included condensed milk, chocolate, sherbert, sweets and biscuits, which meant that, increasingly, sugar was 'pumped into every crevice in the diet' (Mintz 1985: 188). The link between high levels of production and high levels of consumption in Britain is emphasized by contrast with the situation in France. The French too had colonially based sugar plantations but never exploited them to the same extent. As a consequence, sugar remained only a limited part of French cuisine and contemporary sugar consumption in France is only about one-tenth of that in Britain.

TRENDS IN SUGAR PRODUCTION AND CONSUMPTION

Focusing on the twentieth century in particular, Abbot (1990: 17–29) presents data on world sugar production and consumption. In discussing production he describes the ways in which the desire for self-sufficiency had the consequence of increasing the numbers of countries producing sugar. He calculates that by 1990 there were more than 120 sugar-producing countries. Production seems to follow a cycle which runs for between six and nine years and which is linked to fluctuations in demand and consequent prices on world markets. None the less, the pattern after a major expansion in the 1960s has been 'of alternating peaks followed by troughs with each peak higher than the last' (Abbot 1990: 17). The developing countries appear to be the major contributors to this overall rise in production (Abbott 1990: 17–20).

The figures for sugar consumption are also documented by Abbot. They show that the world consumption of sugar has increased almost fourfold in the first fifty years of the twentieth century, despite wide fluctuations in world prices. Abbot's detailed data are for the years 1972 to 1986 inclusive and document separately the consumption in what he defines as the 'developed', 'developing' and 'centrally planned' economies. The greatest increase in consumption was in the developing countries, whose share of world consumption rose from 34 per cent to approximately 45 per cent. However, there was a decrease in the total annual consumption in the developed countries, possibly because consumers in richer countries have become more calorie-conscious. However, the developed countries still consume the highest per capita quantities of sugar, for example, per capita consumption in Europe and North America is roughly twice the world average figure. In addition, there is evidence to suggest that any decline in sugar consumption in Western economies is not necessarily a decline in the overall demand for sweetness. A whole range of alternative sweeteners has been developed and the production and consumption of these is largely located in the developed world.

More refined data concerning per capita sugar consumption trends in the UK are available from the *Household and Food Consumption Expenditure Survey* which we have already encountered in Chapter 9 (Ministry of Agriculture, Fisheries and Food 1991). The data published here cover approximately five decades and document a steady rise in per capita sugar consumption from a level of 8.41 oz per person per week in 1942 to a peak of 18.49 oz per person per week in 1963. After this peak, a decline set in and by 1990 the level of consumption had fallen below the 1942 figure, having dropped to 6.04 oz per week. In parallel, certain other high-sugar foods also show this pattern of peak and decline, for example, preserves (including jams, honey and syrups) were consumed at the rate of 4.93 oz per person per week in 1942 and peaked in 1950 at 6.30 oz. Consumption of these foods then began to diminish consistently so that by 1990 only 1.69 oz per person per week were being consumed. Other sweet foods like cakes and pastries show a similar pattern of decline, although the consumption of biscuits, which peaked at 5.84 oz per person per week in 1958 has not fallen so markedly, the value in 1990 being still as high as 5.26 oz per person per week (Ministry of Agriculture, Fisheries and Food 1991: 96). However, the same source shows that within these figures there are wide variations by social class. For example, at the beginning of the period studied, the rationing of sugar resulted in very little difference in consumption levels by households in different income groups. However, over time, consumption in income groups 'A' and 'B' fell to below the average and that of groups 'D', 'E' and pensioners rose above it. Indeed, by 1990, pensioner households were consuming 82 per cent more sugar and preserves than the average, whereas group 'A' households were consuming 30 per cent less than the average (Ministry of Agriculture, Fisheries and Food 1991: 46).

In contemporary societies, the taste for sweetness can be satisfied by the consumption, not only of refined sugar, preserves, cakes and biscuits but also by the consumption of a very wide range of confectionery. Indeed, the demand for confectionery in the developed economies appears to be high and this is particularly true of the UK. For example, figures provided by James (1990: 668–9) indicate that the UK confectionery market in 1988 was worth £3,285 million, more than bread (£2,375 million) and cereals (£650 million). She adds that a 1990 survey indicated that about 95 per cent of the population ate chocolate confectionery at least once a day, with an average of 9.2 oz of confectionery being eaten per person per week in 1988. This is much higher than most other European countries, with only West Germany matching the British capacity for consuming confectionery (James 1990: 637). Sugar confectionery (that is, non-chocolate confectionery including boiled sweets, chewing-gum, liquorice and mints) is eaten vast in quantities in countries like the UK, whose consumption of such high-sugar items rose from 286,000 tonnes in 1987 to 302,000 tonnes in 1991 (Market Research Great Britain 1992: 83–101).

THE SYMBOLISM OF SWEETNESS

The data we have examined above demonstrate clearly the sheer scale of consumption of sweet foods in contemporary societies such as the UK. In one sense, this might be seen simply as a reflection of an innate human craving for sweetness which is indulged more and more frequently as sweet foods become increasingly available. However, in sociological terms, such an observation can only ever be a partial explanation. Just as we have had to consider the geopolitical background to historical increases in sugar production, we must also consider the cultural and symbolic context in which sweetness is consumed. For example, in spite of the cheapness and ready availability of sugar and other sweeteners in the Western world, Western cuisines rarely, if ever, contain sweet main courses. Since there is no nutritional reason why a main course could not be sweet, we are compelled to consider what kind of cultural or symbolic charges sweetness may carry which define this particular taste experience as one which is appropriate in some contexts and not in others.

The high intake of sugar in the British diet provides the main focus of the study by James (1990). She addresses the issue of why, in spite of what she terms the 'body technocrats' who warn us about the dangers of overindulgence, sugar and confectionery continue to play such a prominent part in our everyday eating. For James, the key lies in the place of confectionery in our system of food classification. In a sense, confectionery is regarded as both food and non-food. As such, it can take on meanings relevant to either identity and sometimes may even be assigned qualities which go beyond the properties of 'ordinary' food. She gives the example of Kendal Mint Cake, which is not in fact a cake but a mint-flavoured sugar bar, which has come to be regarded as an essential component of any mountaineer's survival kit (James 1990: 674). Culturally, confectionery itself is never regarded as part of a conventional meal, given its 'in-between' status as food and non-food. However, the flexibility created by this duality allows confectionery to take on a wide variety of social meanings. There are many examples: confectionery as a gift for mediating and repairing relationships between individuals; confectionery eaten on ritual occasions such as birthdays, Christmas and Easter. In addition, expensively packaged chocolates, presented as an extravagant gift within a framework of sentimentality and romanticism are seen as a particularly suitable gift for women (Barthel 1989). In other words, confectionery constitutes a kind of generalized symbolic currency acceptable to all. For most of us, to use 'ordinary' foods which do not have this dual status (for example, vegetables or cuts of meat) would seem inappropriate and even eccentric. However, there is also an element of ambivalence here, in that the pleasurable nature of chocolate and confectionery can become associated with self-indulgence and guilt. In contrast, 'goodness' and 'virtue' can become associated with 'dull' food. James illustrates this argument by pointing out the way in which parents may sometimes encourage children to eat 'dull/virtuous' foods by rewarding them with limited amounts of 'pleasurable/bad' foods like sweets and chocolate. In fact, she concludes that the symbolic significance of confectionery in the British diet is so powerful that it provides a serious challenge to attempts by officials and professionals to bring about an overall reduction in intake. As this author puts it: 'An apple a day may keep the doctor away but it does little to promote social relationships. That is the role of sweets, as a root symbol for all that is "naughty but nice" in the world of food' (James 1990: 685).

This moral ambivalence associated with sugar and confectionery is explored by Rozin (1987), who speculates about the relationship between sweetness, sensuality and sin. Rozin points out that, although refined sugar is one of the few chemically pure substances that are regularly consumed, and is an important source of gustatory pleasure, it has nevertheless become associated with 'sin' and 'danger'. He seeks to explain this association in a number of ways. The first of these explanations is based upon sugar's links with other self-indulgent substances, such as coffee, tea and sweetened alcohol. The second explanation relates to the set of 'Puritan values', which he sees as prevalent in the USA in particular, which suggests that anything that is extremely pleasurable must be bad. In some cases, he argues, this has reached the extreme that only the consumption of sugar-free food that is non-fattening and non-toxic can permit the consumer to occupy the moral high ground (Rozin 1987: 100). The third reason is that sugar is linked with obesity and, in a society where obesity is believed to be a moral failing, this may also contribute to the notion that sugar consumption is sinful. Rozin also speculates that the strength of feeling about sugar may be explained by the operation of powerful traditional beliefs, for example, that we are what we eat (so that by consuming sugar we become sinful) or that some foods, either on moral or health grounds, can simply 'taste too good to be good for you' (Rozin 1987: 101). Interestingly, in connection with the point made by James about the use of sweet things as a reward for eating 'dull' foods, Rozin argues that the outcome of such a strategy is somewhat unpredictable. In some instances, individuals rewarded with sweetness in this way come to develop an enhanced liking for the 'dull' food, whereas other individuals may experience a reduction in their liking for the food in question (Rozin 1987: 108). Thus, although the human taste for sweetness appears to be innate, the role of sweetness in particular dietary contexts can be complex and variable.

The increase in sugar consumption is also the focus for the analysis by Fischler (1987). As consumption increased, so reservations about the use of sugar began to appear, becoming, according to Fischler (1987: 86–7), ever stronger as the 'vulgarisation' of sugar occurred. It was almost as though sugar became more dangerous as it became more accessible to the lower classes. In a review of the literature on contemporary attitudes to sweetness, Fischler identifies what he terms 'saccarophobia' and illustrates this by citing studies which relate sugar consumption to a range of individual and social problems, including criminal behaviour, depression and divorce as well as diabetes, obesity and hyperactivity in children (Fischler 1987: 87–9). For Fischler, such condemnation has its origins in modern society's ambivalence about the social management of pleasure. Sweetness is, on the one hand, both gratifying and it makes for emotional security yet, on the other, it generates a sense of danger and feelings of undeserved gratification. This ambivalence is handled by socialized and ritualized consumption, which (in parallel with potential pleasures such as alcohol and sex) is more acceptable than individual, solitary use. To be socially acceptable, the consumption of sweet foods requires a clear social context and legitimization. If this is the case, Fischler argues, sweets and chocolates can only be given to children under supervision and if they behave well. There is some support for this contention from James (1982), who writes about the special category of children's sweets which are bought and eaten away from the supervision of adults. Such sweets are often considered 'rubbish' by adults and are eaten in ways which disobey adult rules, for example, they are not wrapped but are handled directly and they may be removed from the mouth and passed on to other children. In a sense, these violations of adult rules can be interpreted as a child's way of defining self and a rejection of the adult control which, Fischler argues, is so important for adults to exercise in this context.

The ambivalence of sugar and sweetness within culinary culture and within our gustatory experience is recognized by those responsible for marketing sweet food products. Whereas some of these products may make a direct and explicit appeal to our taste for sweetness (whether as nourishing snacks or as luxurious indulgences), other sweetened foods may be marketed in a more indirect way. For example, some products which tend to have a relatively high content of added sugar are not marketed explicitly in terms of their sweetness in order to avoid connotations of being highly calorific or unhealthy (Schutz and Judge 1987). Indeed, these authors also point out that in marketing foods for weight-conscious consumers, manufacturers may attempt to break the association between sweetness and high calorific content and may also distinguish between 'natural' sweetness and sweetness produced 'artificially' by the use of added sugar or synthetic sweeteners. In effect, food manufacturers and distributors are responding to the market opportunities generated by the powerful human preference for sweetness, sometimes through explicit appeals to our cravings and sometimes through the less publicized inclusion of sweetness in a wide range of everyday foods.

The fact that sweetness, particularly in the form of refined sugar, is so readily available and penetrates our culinary culture so pervasively raises an interesting question. What are the implications for individuals who, for health or social reasons, find themselves denied what most of us have come to regard as taken for granted, ready access to sugar and sweetness? Perhaps one of the most dramatic examples of the experience of sugar deprivation is the study by Posner (1983) which investigates the social dynamics of the management of the diabetic diet. Such a diet requires the avoidance of sugar no matter what foods it may be incorporated into (for example, sweets, jelly, ice-cream, biscuits, cake and chocolate). However, although the removal of such 'bad' foods from the diet might conventionally be construed as a move to a healthier pattern of eating, Posner makes the point that the consumption of such items is so deeply engrained in cultural terms that many diabetics may be reluctant wholly to give them up. Thus, in order for the diabetic to continue to be as 'normal' as possible and to have access to these symbolically significant items, a whole range of diabetic versions of sweet foods has been developed. In a sense, then, the consumption of synthetic sweetness permits the diabetic to attempt to hold on to the conventions and taste sensations of the sweetness culture.

Other kinds of consumer may also find it difficult to participate in the sweetness culture, but for very different reasons. This emerges strikingly in the study of low-income families carried out by Dobson and her colleagues which was discussed in Chapter 4 (Dobson, Beardsworth, Keil and Walker 1994). The study uncovered instances where mothers had gone to considerable lengths to manage a very tight family food budget in such a way that their children were still able to take chocolate bars or other sweet snacks to school. Superficially, this may appear to be an almost perverse use of very limited resources, particularly as food expenditure was one of the areas that these families had to control very rigorously. However, in sociological terms, the inclusion of such marginal or nutritionally dubious items in the family budget is not as puzzling as it might first appear. Given the cultural and symbolic power of these items, their significance is clearly much more than a merely nutritional one. Their consumption could allow an otherwise deprived child to retain a sense that he or she was still able to participate in the mainstream of consumer culture with its cornucopia of distinctively branded and heavily advertised products. What is more, such a child could also avoid any loss of face in the eyes of his or her peers that might arise from an inability to consume as others consume.

OVERVIEW

The consumption of sweet foods provides yet another example of the fascinating intersection of the biological, the psychological and the sociological dimensions of human activity. What appears to be an innate human preference has provided the foundation for the development of an enormous international apparatus for producing, manufacturing and distributing sweetness. Certainly, the special conditions required for the production of refined sugar (particularly from sugar cane) have meant that from the very beginning this has been an essentially delocalized crop which has been particularly susceptible to political control and manipulation. Consequently, sugar has been, historically, a particularly significant commodity within the emerging system of world trade. In this context it has also been associated with the extension of colonial domination and the exploitation of slave labour.

The pervasiveness of sweetness (based mainly on sucrose) is perhaps one of the most distinctive features of Western culinary culture. Yet, as we have seen, such sweetness is charged with ambivalence. Sweet foods are seen, on the one hand as delicious and attractive, and on the other as self-indulgent and potentially harmful. This good/bad duality is nowhere more apparent than in the case of chocolate and confectionery. Yet, in sociological terms, the ambivalence of those two items is of particular interest because they are seen both as foods and non-foods, and exist on the margin between the nutritious and the harmfully indulgent. But it is for this very reason that these products can be used as currency in patterns of gift giving which express a great variety of social relationships. Since they are in one sense non-foods and 'luxuries', they can be given by one individual to another without the implication that the recipient is in any way deprived or in need of the support of gifts of 'real' food. However, since, in another sense, they are also foods, they can be consumed by the recipient and will provide a degree of gustatory pleasure. The fact that such gifts are consumable may also be relevant since they do not accumulate and can be used to express relationships from the most permanent to the most ephemeral. It seems clear, therefore, that sweet foods in the multiplicity of manifestations in which they are available in Western society will continue to play a significant if controversial role in contemporary nutritional culture despite, or perhaps even because of, their symbolically paradoxical character.

EPILOGUE

In the course of the previous eleven chapters we have threaded our way through a maze of issues, studies and sources all related, directly or obliquely, to the search for a better understanding of the social and cultural dynamics of food and eating. At this point it is time to take stock, in order to attempt to provide some sort of overall appreciation of just what it is that emerges from this broad spread of material, and in order to begin to speculate about the possibilities for the future.

Of course, the core aim of this book, around which all the other aims laid out in the introduction revolve, is to introduce the reader to the main themes in the literature and to provide a reasonably full account of the ways in which these themes have been dealt with by the authors who have sought to address them. Inevitably, however, we have not necessarily been able to do full justice to the detailed arguments contained in our chosen sources, largely because we have been primarily concerned to extract the specifically sociological implications of the material. Furthermore, there are, inevitably, significant gaps in the existing literature, gaps produced by a lack of theoretical formulation, empirical research, or both. Thus, in a sense, the themes upon which this book is based are shaped as much by what *is not* available as by what *is* available in terms of knowledge. Drawing out the connections between the themes and the ways in which they are interwoven with each other is clearly important. Yet, the understandable desire to see some explicit, all-embracing framework within which these interconnections can be formalized in an integrated fashion is one which, at this stage in our knowledge, is likely to be only partially fulfilled. The very diversity of the material we have encountered is at the same time the source of its richness and a barrier to the creation of a single, authoritative synthesis.

Nevertheless, a brief recapitulation of the main themes we have encountered can serve to highlight deeper, underlying refrains which have expressed themselves repeatedly in the foregoing pages. The arguments discussed in Part I concerning the origins of human patterns of food production and consumption were, of necessity, somewhat speculative ones, given the difficulties of producing reliable data on the prehistory and early history of our species. In examining the emergence of the modern food system, however, we were on somewhat firmer

254

ground, with a much clearer and more highly developed historical perspective to hand. Certainly, two major transformations can be seen as of central importance to any understanding of human foodways: the emergence of domestication and agriculture, beginning up to 10,000 years ago, and the intensification, industrialization and globalization of food production, which began much more recently and which has proceeded so rapidly.

In Part II we examined food preparation and consumption in two contrasting settings: the private domain of the household and the public domain of the inn, restaurant or fast food outlet. Here again, the emphasis was on change. While the household setting may well continue to reflect relatively long-standing assumptions concerning age and gender differentiation, we noted that the distribution of household types is changing and that the social organization of eating within these various types is unlikely to remain static in the near future. Meanwhile, eating out, the consumption of food in the public domain, continues to expand and to form an increasingly important component of the experience of eating in contemporary Western society. In Part III the insistent refrain of change was also present, as we considered the ways in which conceptions of the links between diet and health have been strongly influenced by the processes of rationalization which are such central features of modern societies. Yet, running parallel with the increasing emphasis on the rational regulation of diet to promote the maintenance of health, we noted other, more sinister developments: the emergence of food-related anxieties, the periodic occurrence of major food scares, and Western culture's increasing 'fat phobia', plus an emphasis on the restriction of food intake in order to control weight, an emphasis which in extreme cases can take the form of a clinically recognized eating disorder. Finally, in Part IV, attention was directed towards two classes of food items (animal products and products characterized by high levels of sweetness) which are both, in some senses, problematical. It has been argued that humans may have some kind of 'innate' taste for both classes of foods, and yet both are loaded with powerful cultural and symbolic connotations which have potent negative as well as positive aspects.

Of course, the refrain of change is the one which reappears most frequently. Indeed, as was indicated in the Introduction, this refrain provides the central thread linking together the diverse contributions that make up the subject matter of this book. Changes in food production, food consumption and, indeed, in food symbolism, have all been linked to broader processes of change involving industrialization, rationalization, globalization, labour market restructuring, long-term modifications in gender roles and gender expectations, and far-reaching ideological and cultural shifts in the ways in which we view our relationships with other humans and with the natural world.

Yet, if the refrain of change is one whose importance was anticipated from the start, a second refrain emerged during the course of the writing of this book whose significance was not initially so clearly recognized: the refrain of ambivalence. For example, in Chapter 4 the essential ambivalence of women's

255

general responsibility for carrying out the preparation and presentation of food in the domestic setting emerged clearly. On the one hand, the successful completion of such tasks might conventionally be seen as an expression of the caring and nurturing aspects of feminine gender roles. However, on the other hand, the imposition of these responsibilities, which may well be perceived as unwelcome and onerous, might be construed as a component of the cultural apparatus which serves to perpetuate the subordination and control of women within a patriarchal context. The refrain of ambivalence is even more salient in relation to the questions of diet and health linkages which were raised in Chapter 6, in the sense that rational/medical models of healthy diet may be at odds with many individuals' gustatory habits and preferences. Thus, the following of what is prescribed as a healthy diet may come to involve a burdensome element of self-denial and self-discipline. A similar form of ambivalence concerning food intake figured significantly in Chapter 8. For many individuals, particularly women, food is seen both as a source of pleasure, gratification, reward or compensation and as an enemy, a threat to one's ability to achieve and maintain a desired weight or body shape.

Indeed, in Chapter 7 the concept of ambivalence took centre stage, as the fundamental paradoxes inherent in the very act of eating were subjected to detailed analysis. The fact that eating potentially provides both pleasure and discomfort, is both a source of sustenance and of danger, both maintains life and entails its destruction, generates deep-seated anxieties which, we have argued, require effective forms of masking and management. In this connection the ambivalence of meat as a source of nutrients was given particular attention (in Chapter 9), given its conflicting connotations of strength, power, vigour and masculinity on the one hand, and of suffering, death and decay on the other. Of course, the moral ambivalences that can be linked to the consumption of meat are not limited to concerns about the animals eaten but, as we saw in Chapter 10, may also extend to issues relating to global inequalities in nutritional standards and to the impact on the environment of what are seen as destructive or non-sustainable forms of animal husbandry. Even the human taste for sweetness, perhaps superficially to be viewed as a source of unalloyed pleasure, turns out to have ambivalent implications in the modern context of sucrose superabundance: sugar itself comes to be viewed as both desirable and dangerous, as a treat and a sinful indulgence, as a food and a nutritionally vacuous non-food.

Pondering on these two recurrent refrains of change and ambivalence leads almost inevitably to speculations about possible future trends in the context of the food system and of eating patterns. For example, are we likely to witness a continuing expansion in the range of choice of food items, dishes, flavour principles and menus available in contemporary Western societies, all located within an increasingly pluralistic framework within which variety and flexibility become the dominant values? Are we to anticipate the continuing expansion of the practice of eating out and will this necessarily be accompanied by a decline in long-established patterns of domestic eating and commensality? Does this, in turn, imply the continuing increase of the use of convenience foods in the domestic setting and will this lead to a decline in the culinary skills required for more 'traditional' forms of food preparation? Should we also anticipate fundamental changes in the gendered nature of foodwork as women's participation in the labour market changes and as the distributions of household types and life cycle patterns shift significantly? Can we expect to see the continuation of official attempts to set dietary targets and to promote current rational/ medical conceptions of healthy diets? Are such attempts likely to result in the establishment of a clear consensus and to continuing modifications of national dietary practices? Pursuing an alternative line of thought, we might ask whether the ethical dimensions of food and eating are set to rise in importance. Will there be a trend towards increasingly 'humane' diets, based upon foods produced in ways seen as minimizing animal suffering? Are vegetarianism and veganism established on a consistent upward trend or will they reach a plateau or go into decline in terms of numbers of adherents? Along similar lines, should we expect to see the emergence of 'ecologically sensitive' dietary patterns?

Of course, any attempt to make actual predictions would be foolhardy, which is why the preceeding paragraph is composed of questions rather than statements. However, beneath all these questions there is, perhaps, a deeper underlying question. Are we about to witness (or indeed, are we now witnessing) the emergence of what might loosely be termed a 'postmodern' food system and 'postmodern' eating patterns? Can we say that the monolith of the modern food system, with its emphasis on large-scale, intensive production and standardized manufacturing, on mass marketing and retailing, is in the process of giving ground to a more diversified and fragmented situation in which idiosyncratic, even 'playful', combinations of aesthetic, ethical, culinary and gustatory preferences can be assembled by individual consumers or groups of consumers? Or, are the foundations of the modern food system so deeply entrenched, and now so indispensable, that they must continue to underpin what are merely superficial fads and fashions?

The very fact that this book, in attempting to provide the reader with an overview of what we currently know about the social and cultural aspects of food and eating, leads us towards these types of questions is, in itself, highly significant. It provides a clear indication that a sociology of food is feasible, either through the application of established sociological concepts and perspectives or through the posing of novel questions about such biological and social processes. We are participating in the beginning of an important and distinctive sociological project which offers a wealth of opportunities for theoretical development and empirical research. Such opportunities include, for example, the design and implementation of effective longitudinal studies in order to document evolving trends in the domestic organization of eating and in domestic foodwork arrangements (particularly in respect of their gendered nature). Such a longitudinal approach would also be a valuable device for monitoring significant changes in patterns of food preference and avoidance, and for investigating the motivations behind them or the accounts, agendas and explanations provided by those whose diets exhibited such changes. Data generated in this way could potentially allow us to gain clearer insights into the ways in which such factors as health concerns, ideas of preferred body shape, ethical preoccupations and the drive for gustatory pleasure and novelty interact with each other and shift in terms of their relative weightings. Such an approach could be effectively complemented by studies focused more specifically on issues of food and identity. This particular focus would serve to extend our understanding of the ways in which such factors as class, ethnicity and gender shape our tastes while framing and constraining our experiences of eating.

In addition, there is enormous scope for the further development of the sociological analysis of the supply side of contemporary food systems. Supply side processes and institutions have not really attracted a great deal of attention from sociologists so far, and this fact is reflected in the structure and content of this book. Food production, processing, distribution and retailing are all areas of human activity which are worthy of a sustained effort to add a sociological perspective to complement those already offered by such disciplines as economics, agronomy, geography and history. Thus, the sociological gaze might be focused upon the multiplicity of occupations which make up the labour force of the food system – the farmer, the abattoir worker, the supermarket manager, the chef, the food technologist, the food co-operative organizer are just a few examples. At a quite different level, the globalization of the food supply has begun to generate food branding and marketing strategies which transcend local cultural differences, a process which is driven by the activities and interests of multinational corporations which contain extensive food producing, manufacturing or retailing divisions. These strategies, and the organizational and commercial ideologies which underpin them, also deserve the scrutiny of the sociologist.

The political dimensions of the food system also represent a fertile area for further sociological enquiry. The constantly evolving role of the state, and its various agencies, in the creation and elaboration of frameworks of regulation for the food industry is a topic of crucial interest. Similarly, the state's continuing attempts to set dietary targets for the general population and to achieve health improvements through the modification of eating patterns raise questions of direct sociological significance. Of course, the state is not the only player in this particular political arena, and the sociologist will also need to pay attention to the parts played by a plethora of commercial interests, pressure groups and professional bodies, each with its own goals and priorities.

Finally, there remains the challenge of extending and refining the theoretical apparatus through which we can apprehend and explain the cultural and symbolic levels of the food system. In a very real sense, these dimensions cross cut all aspects of this system, but equally they form an object of analysis in their own right. Describing the complex and changeable nuances of meaning in the realm of food symbolism promises a fascinating prospect for future sociological endeavour. This is particularly true in situations in which the availability of food, in abundance and in great variety, has become a taken-for-granted fact of life. In such settings the enjoyment of food may come to consist more and more of the consumption of images, representations and ideas of food, subtly crafted and 'fed' to us through advertisements, sumptuously illustrated cookbooks, newspaper features and a seemingly endless stream of television cookery programmes. We may need to ask whether, in such circumstances, we are quite literally eating ideas, experiencing gustatory pleasure directly with the mind, without the need for the participation of the mouth and the stomach!

The above paragraphs are intended to provide a guide to future possibilities, not an exhaustive list of topics for investigation or a definitive programme of research. Yet it is our hope that, in writing this book, we have provided, not only an insight into the present state of knowledge in the sociology of food but the stimulus to go further, to pose new and more searching questions. For the professional social scientist, we may have succeeded in encouraging him or her to make a direct contribution to this expanding area of scholarship. Equally importantly, we would like to think that we may have helped a much wider readership to begin to think critically about the apparently mundane and unremarkable act of eating and all that it entails. For when we do begin to think in this fashion, we find that on the intellectual menu there are insights, surprises, puzzles and paradoxes that all of us can savour.

BIBLIOGRAPHY

Abbot, G.C. (1990) *Sugar*, London: Routledge.

Adams, C.J. (1990) *The Sexual Politics of Meat: A Feminist-Vegetarian Critical Theory*, Cambridge: Polity Press.

Adburgham, A. (1989) *Shops and Shopping 1800–1914*, London: Barrie & Jenkins.

Adkins, L. (1995) *Gendered Work: Sexuality, Family and the Labour Market*, Buckingham: Open University Press.

Allaby, M. (1977) *World Food Resources, Actual and Potential*, London: Applied Science Publishers.

Amato, P.R. and Partridge, S.A. (1989) *The New Vegetarians: Promoting Health and Protecting Life*, New York: Plenum Press.

Anderson, K.N. (1993) *The International Dictionary of Food and Nutrition*, New York: Wiley.

Aron, J.P. (1975) *The Art of Eating in France: Manners and Menus in the Nineteenth Century*, London: Peter Owen.

Atkinson, P. (1979) 'From honey to vinegar: Lévi-Strauss in Vermont', in P. Morley and R. Wallis (eds) *Culture and Curing: Anthropological Perspectives on Traditional Medical Beliefs and Practices*, Pittsburgh, Pa.: University of Pittsburgh Press.

Atkinson, P. (1980) 'The symbolic significance of health foods', in M. Turner (ed.), *Nutrition and Lifestyles*, London: Applied Science Publishers.

Atkinson, P. (1983) 'Eating virtue', in A. Murcott (ed.) *The Sociology of Food and Eating*, Aldershot: Gower.

Bagwell, P. (1974) *The Transport Revolution from 1770*, London: Batsford.

Bansback, B. (1993) 'Meat demand economics', in *Meat Consumption in the European Community*, Luxembourg: Office for Official Publications of the European Communities.

Barkas, J. (1975) *The Vegetable Passion: A History of the Vegetarian State of Mind*, London: Routledge & Kegan Paul.

Barker, L.M. (1982) *The Psychobiology of Human Food Selection*, Chichester: Ellis Horwood.

Barthel, D. (1989) 'Modernism and marketism: the chocolate box revisited', *Theory, Culture and Society* 6: 429–38.

Barthes, R. (1979) 'Toward a psycho-sociology of contemporary food consumption', in R. Forster and O. Ranum (eds) *Food and Drink in History*, Baltimore, Md.: The Johns Hopkins University Press.

Baudrillard, J. (1988) *Selected Writings*, Cambridge: Polity Press.

Beardsworth, A.D. (1990) 'Trans-science and moral panics: understanding food scares', *British Food Journal* 92, 5: 11–6.

Beardsworth, A.D. and Keil, E.T. (1990) 'Putting the menu on the agenda', *Sociology* 24, 1: 139–51.

Beardsworth, A.D. and Keil, E.T. (1992a) 'The vegetarian option: varieties, conversions, motives and careers', *The Sociological Review* 40, 2: 253–93.

Beardsworth, A.D. and Keil, E.T. (1992b) 'Foodways in flux: from gastro-anomy to menu pluralism?', *British Food Journal* 94, 7: 20–5.

Beardsworth, A.D. and Keil, E.T. (1993a) 'Contemporary vegetarianism in the U.K.: challenge and incorporation?', *Appetite* 20: 229–34.

Beardsworth, A.D. and Keil, E.T. (1993b) 'Hungry for knowledge? The sociology of food and eating', *Sociology Review* (November). 11–5.

Beauchamp, G.K. and Cowart, B.J. (1987) 'Development of sweet taste', in J. Dobbing (ed.) *Sweetness: International Life Sciences Institute Symposium*, London: Springer-Verlag.

Beidler, L.M. (1982) 'Biological basis of food selection', in L.M. Barker (ed.) *The Psychobiology of Human Food Selection*, Chichester: Ellis Horwood.

Belasco, W.J. (1993) *Appetite for Change: How the Counterculture took on the Food Industry*, Ithaca, N.Y.: Cornell University Press.

Bennett, J. (1987) *The Hunger Machine: the Politics of Food*, Cambridge: Polity Press.

Binford, L.R. (1992) 'Subsistence – a key to the past', in S. Jones, R. Martin and D. Philbeam (eds) *The Cambridge Encyclopedia of Human Evolution*, Cambridge: Cambridge University Press.

Birch, G.G., Cameron, A.G. and Spencer, M. (1986) *Food Science*, Oxford: Pergamon Press.

Blaxter M. and Paterson E. (1983) 'The goodness is out of it: the meaning of food to two generations', in A. Murcott (ed.) *The Sociology of Food and Eating*, Aldershot: Gower.

Blaxter, K. (1986) *People, Food and Resources*, Cambridge: Cambridge University Press.

Bocock, R. (1993) *Consumption*, London: Routledge.

Booth, D.A., Conner, M.T. and Marie, S. (1987) 'Sweetness and food selection: measurement of sweeteners' effects on acceptance', in J. Dobbing (ed.) *Sweetness: International Life Sciences Institute Symposium*, London: Springer-Verlag.

Bordo, S. (1990) 'Reading the slender body', in M. Jacobus (ed.) *Body/Politics*, New York: Routledge.

Borgstrom, G. (1972) *The Hungry Planet: The Modern World at the Edge of Famine*, New York: Collier.

Bourdieu, P. (1979) 'Toward a psycho-sociology of contemporary food consumption', in R. Forster and O. Ranum (eds) *Food and Drink in History*, Baltimore, Md.: The Johns Hopkins University Press.

Bourdieu, P. (1984) *Distinction: A Social Critique of the Judgement of Taste*, London: Routledge & Kegan Paul.

Brown, C. and Jasper, K. (eds) (1993) *Consuming Passions: Feminist Approaches to Weight Preoccupation and Eating Disorders*, Toronto: Second Story Press.

Brownsell, V.L., Griffith, C.J. and Jones, E. (1989) *Applied Science for Food Studies*, Harlow: Longman.

Bruch, H. (1978) *The Golden Cage: The Enigma of Anorexia Nervosa*, London: Open Books.

Brumberg, J.J. (1988) *Fasting Girls: The Emergence of Anorexia Nervosa as a Modern Disease*, Cambridge, Mass.: Harvard University Press.

Buchanan, K.S. (1993) 'Creating beauty in blackness', in C. Brown and K. Jasper (eds) *Consuming Passions: Feminist Approaches to Weight Preoccupation and Eating Disorders*, Toronto: Second Story Press.

Burgoyne, J. and Clarke, D. (1983) 'You are what you eat: food and family reconstitution', in A. Murcott (ed.) *The Sociology of Food and Eating*, Aldershot: Gower.

Burnett, J. (1989) *Plenty and Want: A Social History of Food in England from 1815 to the present day*, third edition, London: Routledge.

Burt, J.V. and Hertzler, A.V. (1978) 'Parental influence on child's food preference', *Journal of Nutrition Education* 10: 123–34.

Cain, P.J. and Hopkins, A.G. (1993) *British Imperialism*, London: Longmans.

Calnan, M. and Cant, S. (1990) 'The social organization of food consumption. A comparison of middle class and working class households', *International Journal of Sociology and Social Policy* 10, 2: 53–79.

Carefoot, G.L. and Sprott, E.R. (1969) *Famine on the Wind: Plant Diseases and Human History*, London: Angus & Robertson.

Carlioro, B. (1994) '75 years: the odyssey of eating out', *Nation's Restaurant News* January: 11ff.

Cash, T.F. (1990) 'The psychology of physical appearance: aesthetics, attributes, and images', in T. Cash and T. Prusinsky (eds) *Body Images: Development, Deviance and Change*, New York: Guilford Press.

Cash, T.F. and Prusinsky, T. (eds) (1990) *Body Images: Development, Deviance and Change*, New York: Guilford Press.

Charles, N. and Kerr, M. (1986a) 'Eating properly, the family and state benefit', *Sociology* 20, 3: 412–29.

Charles, N. and Kerr, M. (1986b) 'Food for feminist thought', *Sociological Review* 34, 3: 537–72.

Charles, N. and Kerr, M. (1988) *Women, Food and Families*, Manchester: Manchester University Press.

Clark, S.R.L. (1984) *The Moral Status of Animals*, London: Oxford University Press.

Cline, S. (1990) *Just Desserts*, London: Andre Deutsch.

Clutton-Brock, J. (1987) *A Natural History of Domesticated Mammals*, Cambridge: Cambridge University Press/British Museum (Natural History).

Clutton-Brock, J. (1992) 'Domestication of animals', in S. Jones, R. Martin and D. Philbeam (eds) *The Cambridge Encyclopedia of Human Evolution*, Cambridge: Cambridge University Press.

Cohen, S. (1971) 'Mods, rockers and the rest: community reactions to juvenile delinquency', in W.G. Carson and P. Wiles (eds) *Crime and Delinquency in Britain*, London: Martin Robertson.

Cohen, S. (1973) *Folk Devils and Moral Panics: The Creation of the Mods and Rockers*, London: Paladin.

Coon, C.S. (1976) *The Hunting Peoples*, Harmondsworth: Penguin.

Copping, A.M. (1985) 'The founding fathers of the Nutrition Society', in D. Oddy and D. Miller (eds) *Diet and Health in Modern Britain*, London: Croom Helm.

Damas, D. (1972) 'The Copper Eskimo', in M.G. Bicchieri (ed.) *Hunters and Gatherers Today*, Prospect Heights, Ill.: Waveland Press.

David, E. (ed. J. Norman) (1994) *Harvest of the Cold Months: The Social History of Ice and Ices*, London: Michael Joseph.

Davis, D. (1966) *A History of Shopping*, London: Routledge & Kegan Paul.

Davis, K. (1966) *Human Society*, New York: Macmillan.

Deerr, N. (1949) *The History of Sugar: Volume One*, London: Chapman Hall.

Deerr, N. (1950) *The History of Sugar: Volume Two*, London: Chapman Hall.

Delahoyde, M. and Desperich, S.C. (1994) 'Creating meat-eaters: The child as advertising target', *Journal of Popular Culture* 28, 1: 135–49.

Delphy, C. (1979) 'Sharing the same table: consumption and the family' in C. Harris (ed.) *The Sociology of the Family*, Sociological Review Monograph Number 28.

Department of Health (1994) *Eat Well! An Action Plan from the Nutrition Task Force to Achieve the Health of the Nation Targets on Diet and Nutrition*, Heywood: BAPS, Health Publications Unit.

DeVault, M.L. (1991) *Feeding the Family: The Social Organization of Caring as Gendered Work*, Chicago: The University of Chicago Press.

Diamond, N. (1985) 'Thin is the feminist issue', *Feminist Review* 19, Spring: 45–67.

Dobash, R.E. and Dobash, R. (1980) *Violence Against Wives*, London: Open Books.

Dobbing, J. (ed.) (1987) *Sweetness: International Life Sciences Institute Symposium*, London: Springer-Verlag.

Dobson, B., Beardsworth, A.D., Keil, E.T. and Walker, R. (1994) *Diet, Choice and Poverty: Social, Cultural and Nutritional Aspects of Food Consumption among Low-Income Families*, London: Family Policy Studies Centre/Joseph Rowntree Foundation.

Dombrowski, D.A. (1985) *Vegetarianism: The Philosophy behind the Ethical Diet*, Wellingborough: Thorsons.

Douglas, M. (1966) *Purity and Danger: An Analysis of Concepts of Pollution and Taboo*, London: Allen & Unwin.

Douglas, M. (1975) 'Deciphering a meal', *Daedalus* 101, 1: 61–81.

Douglas, M. (1984) 'Standard social uses of food: introduction', in M. Douglas (ed.) *Food in the Social Order: Studies of Food and Festivities in Three American Communities*, New York: Russell Sage Foundation.

Driver, C. (1983) *The British at Table 1940–1980*, London: Chatto & Windus.

Durkheim, E. (1984) *The Division of Labour in Society*, Basingstoke: Macmillan.

Dwyer, J.T., Mayer, L.D.V.H., Dowd, K., Kandel R.F. and Mayer, J. (1974) 'The new vegetarians: the natural high?', *Journal of the American Dietetic Association* 65, November: 529–36.

Economist Intelligence Unit (1994) 'Slimming foods', *Retail Business* No.432: 48–58.

Ekström, M. (1991) 'Class and gender in the kitchen', in E.L. Fürst, R. Prättälä, M. Ekström, L. Holm, and U. Kjaernes (eds) *Palatable Worlds: Sociocultural Food Studies*, Oslo: Solum Forlag.

Elias, N. (1978a) *The Civilizing Process, Volume I: The History of Manners*. Oxford: Basil Blackwell.

Elias, N. (1978b) *What is Sociology?* London: Hutchinson.

Elias, N. (1982) *The Civilizing Process, Volume II: State Formation and Civilization*, Oxford: Basil Blackwell.

Ellis, R. (1983) 'The way to a man's heart: food in the violent home', in A. Murcott (ed.) *The Sociology of Food and Eating*, Aldershot: Gower.

Evans-Pritchard, E.E. (1967) *The Nuer: A Description of the Modes of Livelihood and Political Institutions of a Nilotic People*, Oxford: Clarendon Press.

Falk, P. (1991) 'The sweetness of forbidden fruit: towards an anthropology of taste', in E.L. Fürst, R. Prättälä, M. Ekström, L. Holm and U. Kjaernes (eds) *Palatable Worlds: Sociocultural Food Studies*, Oslo: Solum Forlag.

Fallon, A. (1990) 'Culture in the mirror: sociocultural determinants of body image', in T. Cash and T. Prusinsky (eds) *Body Images: Development, Deviance and Change*, New York: Guilford Press.

Farb, P. and Armelagos, G. (1980) *Consuming Passions: The Anthropology of Eating*, Boston, Mass.: Houghton Mifflin.

Featherstone, M. (1991) 'The body in consumer culture', in M. Featherstone, M. Hepworth and B.Turner (eds) *The Body: Social Processes and Cultural Theory*, London: Sage.

Featherstone, M., Hepworth, M. and Turner, B. (eds) (1991) *The Body: Social Process and Cultural Theory*, London: Sage.

Fiddes, N. (1991) *Meat: A Natural Symbol*, London: Routledge.

Fieldhouse, P. (1986) *Food and Nutrition: Customs and Culture*, London: Croom Helm.

Finkelstein, J. (1989) *Dining Out: A Sociology of Modern Manners*, Cambridge: Polity Press.

Fischler, C. (1980) 'Food habits, social change and the nature/culture dilemma', *Social Science Information* 19, 6: 937–53.

Fischler, C. (1986) 'Learned versus "spontaneous" dietetics: French mothers' views of what children should eat', *Social Science Information* 25, 4: 945–65.

Fischler, C. (1987) 'Attitudes towards sugar and sweetness in historical and social perspective', in J. Dobbing (ed.) *Sweetness: International Life Sciences Institute Symposium*, London: Springer-Verlag.

Fischler, C. (1988) 'Food, self and identity', *Social Science Information* 27, 2: 275–92.

Foley, R. (1988) 'Hominids, humans and hunter-gatherers: an evolutionary perspective', in T. Ingold, D. Riches and J. Woodburn (eds) *Hunters and Gatherers 1: History, Evolution and Social Change*, Oxford: Berg.

Foreman-Peck, J. (1993) *A History of the World Economy*, Hemel Hampstead: Harvester.

Fraser, W.H. (1981) *The Coming of the Mass Market 1850–1914*, London: Macmillan.

Freckleton, A.M., Gurr, M.I., Richardson, D.P., Rolls, B.A. and Walker, A.F. (1989) 'Public perception and understanding', in C.R.W. Spedding (ed.) *The Human Food Chain*, London: Elsevier Applied Science.

Freeland-Graves, J.H., Greninger, S.A. and Young, R.K. (1986) 'A demographic and social profile of age-and sex-matched vegetarians and nonvegetarians', *Journal of The American Dietetic Association* 86: 907–13.

Freeman, S. (1989) *Mutton and Oysters: The Victorians and Their Food*, London: Victor Gallancz Ltd.

Frey, R.G. (1983) *Rights, Killing and Suffering: Moral Vegetarianism and Applied Ethics*, Oxford: Blackwell.

Gabriel, Y. (1988) *Working Lives in Catering*, London: Routledge & Kegan Paul.

Gaman, P.M. and Sherrington, K.B. (1981) *The Science of Food: An Introduction to Food Science, Nutrition and Microbiology*, second edition, Oxford: Pergamon Press.

Garfinkel, P.E. and Garner, D.M. (1982) *Anorexia Nervosa: A Multidimensional Perspective*, New York: Brunner/Mazel.

Gilbert, G.N. and Mulkay, M. (1984) *Opening Pandora's Box: A Sociological Analysis of Scientists' Discourse*, Cambridge: Cambridge University Press.

Girouard, M. (1984) *Victorian Pubs*, New Haven, Conn. and London: Yale University Press.

Gofton, L. (1990) 'Food fears and time famines: some aspects of choosing and using food', *British Nutrition Foundation Bulletin* 15, 1: 78–95.

Goodman, D. and Redclift, M. (1991) *Refashioning Nature: Food, Ecology and Culture*, London: Routledge.

Goody, J. (1982) *Cooking, Cuisine and Class: A Study in Comparative Sociology*, Cambridge: Cambridge University Press.

Gordon, K.D. (1987) 'Evolutionary perspectives on human diet', in F.E. Johnston (ed.) *Nutritional Anthropology*, New York: Alan R. Liss.

Grigg, D. (1993) 'The role of livestock products in world food consumption', *Scottish Geographical Magazine* 109, 2: 66–74.

Grimble, A. (1952) *A Pattern of Islands*, London: John Murray.

Guenther, M. (1988) 'Animals in Bushman thought, myth and art', in T. Ingold, D. Riches, and J. Woodburn (eds) *Hunters and Gatherers 2: Property, Power and Ideology*, Oxford: Berg.

Hall, S., Critcher, C., Jefferson, T., Clarke, J. and Roberts, B. (1978) *Policing the Crisis: Mugging, the State and Law and Order*, London: Macmillan.

Halliday, M.A.K. (1961) 'Categories of the theory of grammar', *World Journal of the Linguistic Circle of New York* 17: 241–91.

Harris, M. (1978) *Cannibals and Kings: The Origins of Cultures*, London: Collins.

Harris, M. (1986) *Good to Eat: Riddles of Food and Culture*, London: Allen & Unwin.

Harrison, B. (1971) *Drink and the Victorians*, London: Faber & Faber.

Hartley, S.F. (1972) *Population: Quantity vs Quality*, New Jersey: Prentice Hall.

Hassall, A.H. (1876) *Food: Its Adulterations, and the Methods for Their Detection*, London: Longman, Green & Co.

Hilgartner, S. and Bosk, C.L. (1988) 'The rise and fall of social problems: a public arenas model', *American Journal of Sociology* 94, 1: 53–78.

Hobhouse, H. (1985) *Seeds of Change: Five Plants that Transformed Mankind*, London: Sidgwick & Jackson.

Hole, F. (1992) 'Origins of agriculture', in S. Jones, R. Martin and D. Philbeam (eds) *The Cambridge Encyclopedia of Human Evolution*, Cambridge: Cambridge University Press.

Hsu, L.K.G. (1990) *Eating Disorders*, New York: Guilford Press.

Hudson, P. (1992) *The Industrial Revolution*, London: Edward Arnold.

BIBLIOGRAPHY

Ibarra, P.R. and Kitsuse, J.I. (1993) 'Vernacular constituents of moral discourse: an interactionist proposal for the study of social problems', in G. Muller and J. A Holstein (eds) *Constructionist Controversies: Issues in Social Problems Theory*, New York: Aldine de Gruyter.

Jacobson, B., Smith, A. and Whitehead, M. (eds) (1991) *The Nation's Health: A Strategy for the 1990s*, London: King's Fund Centre.

James, A. (1982) 'Confections, concoctions and conceptions', in B. Waites, T. Bennett and G. Martin (eds) *Popular Culture: Past and Present*, London: Croom Helm/Open University Press.

James, A. (1990) 'The good, the bad and the delicious: the role of confectionery in British society', *Sociological Review* 33, 4: 666–88.

Jeffers, J.N.R. (1980), 'Ecological concepts and their relevance to human nutrition', in K. Blaxter (ed.) *Food Chains and Human Nutrition*, Barking: Applied Science Publishers.

Jelliffe, D.B. (1967) 'Parallel food classification in developing and industrialized countries', *American Journal of Clinical Nutrition* 20: 279–81.

Jones, P. (1985) 'Fast food operations in Britain', *Services Industries Journal* 5, 1: 55–63.

Jowell, R., Witherspoon, S. and Brook, L. (eds) (1990) *British Social Attitudes: 7th Report*, Aldershot: Gower.

Jukes, D.J. (1993) *Food Legislation of the U.K.: A Concise Guide*, third edition, Oxford: Butterworth Heinemann.

Jussaume, R.A. and Judson, D.H. (1992) 'Public perceptions about food safety in the United States and Japan', *Rural Sociology* 57, 2: 235–49.

Kandel, R.F. and Pelto, G.H. (1980) 'The health food movement: social revitalization or alternative health maintenance system?', in N.W. Jerome, R.F. Kandel and G.H. Pelto (eds) *Nutritional Anthropology: Contemporary Approaches to Diet and Culture*, New York: Redgrave.

Kerr, M. and Charles, N. (1986) 'Servers and providers: the distribution of food within the family', *The Sociological Review* 34, 1: 115–57.

Kuhn, T. (1964) *The Structure of Scientific Revolutions*, Chicago, Ill.: The University of Chicago Press.

Lalonde, M.P. (1992) 'Deciphering a meal again, or the anthropology of taste', *Social Science Information* 31, 1: 69–86.

Langford, P. (1989) *A Polite and Commercial People: England 1727–1783*, Oxford: Oxford University Press.

Laughlin, W.S. (1968) 'Hunting: an integrating biobehaviour system and its evolutionary importance', in R.B. Lee and I. Evore (eds) *Man the Hunter*, New York: Aldine Publishing.

Leclant, J. (1979) 'Coffee and cafés in Paris, 1644–1693', in R. Forster and O, Ranum (eds) *Food and Drink in History*, Baltimore, Md.: The Johns Hopkins University Press.

Lees, R. (1983) 'The sweet history of Britain', *New Scientist* 100: 873–7.

Leonard, W.R. and Robertson, M.L. (1994) 'Evolutionary perspectives on human nutrition: the influence of brain and body size on diet and metabolism', *American Journal of Human Biology*, 6: 77–88.

Levenstein, H. (1988) *Revolution at The Table: The Transformation of the American Diet*, New York: Oxford University Press.

Lévi-Strauss, C. (1963) *Structural Anthropology*, New York: Basic Books.

Lévi-Strauss, C. (1966a) *The Savage Mind*, London: Weidenfeld & Nicolson.

Lévi-Strauss, C. (1966b) 'The culinary triangle', *Partisan Review* 33: 586–95.

Lévi-Strauss, C. (1970) *The Raw and the Cooked*, London: Jonathan Cape.

Lowenberg, M.E., Todhunter, E.N., Wilson, E.D., Savage, J.R. and Lubowski, J.L. (1974) *Food and Man*, second edition, New York: John Wiley & Sons.

McCarthy, B. and Straus, K. (1992) 'Tastes of America 1992. Who in America eats out? Why do they? And what are they eating?', *Restaurants and Institutions* 102, Pt 29, December, 24–44.

McIntosh, W.A. and Zey, M. (1989) 'Women as gatekeepers of food consumption: a sociological critique', *Food and Foodways* 3, 4: 317–32.

McIntosh, W.A., Acuff, G.R., Christensen, L.B. and Hale, D. (1994) 'Public perceptions of food safety', *The Social Science Journal* 31, 3: 285–92.

MacSween, M. (1993) *Anorexic Bodies: A Feminist and Sociological Perspective on Anorexia Nervosa*, London: Routledge.

Malinowski, B. (1935) *Coral Gardens and their Magic*, New York: American Book Company.

Manderson, L. (1987) 'Hot–cold food and medical theories: overview and introduction', *Social Science and Medicine*, 25, 4: 329–30.

Market Research Great Britain (1992) *Market Focus Food: Sugar Confectionery*, London: Euromonitor.

Mars, G. (1982) *Cheats at Work: An Anthropology of Workplace Crime*, London: George Allen & Unwin.

Mass Observation (1987) *The Pub and the People*, London: Century Hutchinson Ltd.

Matthias, P. (1967) *Retailing Revolution*, London: Longmans.

Maurer, D. (1995) 'Meat as a social problem: rhetorical strategies in the contemporary vegetarian literature', in D. Maurer and S. Sobel (eds) *Eating Agendas: Food and Nutrition as Social Problems*, New York: Aldine de Gruyter.

Mazurkiewicz, R. (1983) 'Gender and social consumption', *Services Industries Journal* 3, 1: 49–62.

Meadow, R.M. and Weiss, L. (1992) *Women's Conflicts about Eating and Sexuality: The Relationship between Food and Sex*, New York: The Haworth Press.

Medlik, S. (1961) *The British Hotel and Catering Industry: An Economic and Statistical Survey*, London: Sir Isaac Pitman & Sons Ltd.

Mennell, S. (1985) *All Manners of Food: Eating and Taste in England and France from the Middle Ages to the Present*, Oxford: Blackwell.

Mennell, S. (1991) 'On the civilizing of appetite', in M. Featherstone, M. Hepworth and B. Turner (eds) *The Body: Social Process and Cultural Theory*, London: Sage.

Mennell, S. (1992) 'Indigestion 1800–1950: aspects of English taste and anxiety', paper presented to the inaugural meeting of the British Sociological Association Sociology of Food Study Group, BSA annual conference, University of Kent.

Mennell, S., Murcott, A. and Van Otterloo, A.H. (1992) *The Sociology of Food: Eating, Diet and Culture*, London: Sage.

Merton, R.K. (1957) *Social Theory and Social Structure*, New York: The Free Press.

Messer, E. (1987) 'The hot and cold in Mesoamerican indigenous and hispanicized thought', *Social Science and Medicine* 25, 4: 339–46.

Midgley, M. (1983) *Animals and Why They Matter*, Harmondsworth: Penguin.

Miller, D. and Reilly, J. (1995) 'Making an issue of food safety: the media, pressure groups, and the public sphere', in D. Maurer and J. Sobal (eds) *Eating Agendas: Food and Nutrition as Social Problems*, New York: Aldine de Gruyter.

Ministry of Agriculture, Fisheries and Food (1989) *Loaves and Fishes: An Illustrated History of the Ministry of Agriculture, Fisheries and Food*, London: HMSO.

Ministry of Agriculture, Fisheries and Food (1991) *Household Food Consumption and Expenditure 1990, with a Study of Trends over the Period 1940–1990*, London: HMSO.

Ministry of Agriculture, Fisheries and Food (1994) *National Food Survey 1993*, London: HMSO.

Mintz, S.W. (1985) *Sweetness and Power: The Place of Sugar in Modern History*, New York: Viking.

Mitchell, V.W. and Greatorex, M. (1990) 'Consumer perceived risk in the UK food market', *British Food Journal* 92, 2: 16–22.

Montanari, M. (1994) *The Culture of Food*, Oxford: Blackwell.

Muller, H.G. (1991) 'Industrial food preservation in the nineteenth and twentieth centuries', in C. Wilson (ed.) *Waste Not, Want Not: Food Preservation from Early Times to the Present Day*, Edinburgh: Edinburgh University Press.

266

Murcott, A. (1982) 'On the social significance of the "cooked dinner" in South Wales', *Social Science Information* 21, 4/5: 677–96.

Murcott, A. (1983) ' "It's a pleasure to cook for him": food, mealtimes and gender in some South Wales households', in E. Gamarnikow, E. Morgan, J. Purvis and D. Taylorson, (eds) *The Public and the Private*, London: Heinemann.

National Advisory Committee on Nutrition Education (1983) *A Discussion Paper on Proposals for Nutritional Guidelines for Health Education in Britain*, London: The Health Education Council.

National Research Council (1989) *Recommended Dietary Allowances*, tenth edition, Washington, D.C.: National Academy Press.

Nelson, M. (1993) 'Social-class trends in British diet, 1860–1980', in C. Geissler and D.J. Oddy (eds) *Food, Diet and Economic Change Past and Present*, Leicester: Leicester University Press.

Newby, H. (1983) 'Living from hand to mouth: the farmworker, food and agribusiness', in A. Murcott (ed.) *The Sociology of Food and Eating*, Aldershot: Gower.

Nicod, M. (1980) 'Gastronomically speaking: food studied as a medium of communication', in M.Turner (ed.) *Nutrition and Lifestyles*, London: Applied Science Publishers.

Oddy, D.J. (1990) 'Food, drink and nutrition', in F.M.L. Thompson (ed.) *The Cambridge History of Britain 1750 – 1950 Vol. 2 People and their Environment*, Cambridge: Cambridge University Press

Office of Population Censuses and Surveys – Social Survey Division (1993) *Health Survey for England 1991*, London: HMSO.

Orbach, S. (1988) *Fat is a Feminist Issue*, London: Hamlyn.

Parsons, T. (1951) *The Social System*, London: Routledge & Kegan Paul.

Paulos, J.A. (1988) *Innumeracy: Mathematical Illiteracy and its Consequences*, London: Viking.

Paulus, I.L.E. (1974) *The Search for Pure Food: A Sociology of Legislation in Britain*, London: Martin Robertson.

Payne, M. and Payne, B. (1993) *Eating Out in the UK: Market Structure, Consumer Attitudes and Prospects for the 1990s*, Economist Intelligence Unit Special Report No. 2169, London: Economist Intelligence Unit Ltd.

Pelto, G.H. and Pelto, P.J. (1985) 'Diet and delocalization: dietary changes since 1970', in R. Rotberg and T.K. Rabb (eds) *Hunger and History*, Cambridge: Cambridge University Press.

Pierce, J.T. (1990) *The Food Resource*, Harlow: Longman Scientific and Technical.

Pill, R. (1983) 'An apple a day...some reflections on working class mothers' views on food and health', in A. Murcott (ed.) *The Sociology of Food and Eating*, Aldershot: Gower.

Pillsbury, R. (1990) *From Boarding House to Bistro: The American Restaurant Then and Now*, Boston, Mass.: Unwin Hyman.

Posner, T. (1983) 'The sweet things in life: aspects of the management of diabetic diet', in A. Murcott (ed.) *The Sociology of Food and Eating*, Aldershot: Gower.

Prout, A. (1991) 'Review of Women, Food and Families', *The Sociological Review* 39, 2: 403–5.

Radcliffe-Brown, A.R. (1922) *The Andaman Islanders*, Cambridge: Cambridge University Press.

Read, B.E. (1982) *Chinese Materia Medica: Insect Drugs, Dragon and Snake Drugs, Fish Drugs*, Taipei, Republic of China: Southern Materials Center.

Realeat Survey Office (1993) *The Realeat Survey 1984–1993. Changing Attitudes to Meat Consumption*, 2 Trevelyan Gardens, London.

Realeat Survey Office (1995) *The Realeat Survey 1984–1995. Changing Attitudes to Meat Consumption*, 2 Trevelyan Gardens, London.

Reed, C.A. (1984) 'The beginnings of animal domestication', in I.L. Mason (ed.) *Evolution of Domesticated Animals*, London: Longman.

Regan, T. (1984) *The Case for Animal Rights*, London: Routledge.

Richards, A. (1932) *Hunger and Work in a Savage Tribe: A Functional Study of Nutrition among the Southern Bantu*, London: Routledge.

Richards, A. (1939) *Land, Labour and Diet in Northern Rhodesia*, Oxford: Oxford University Press.

Rindos, D. (1984) *The Origins of Agriculture: An Evolutionary Perspective*, Orlando, Fl.: Academic Press.

Rinzler, C.A. (1991) *Feed a Cold, Starve a Fever: A Dictionary of Medical Folklore*, New York: Facts on File.

Riska, E. (1993) 'The gendered character of professions in the field of nutrition' in U. Kjaernes, L. Holm, M. Ekström, E.L. Fürst and R. Prättälä (eds) *Regulating Markets, Regulating People: on Food and Nutrition Policy*, Oslo: Novus Vorlag.

Ritzer, G. (1993) *The McDonaldization of Society*, Newbury Park, Calif.: Pine Forge Press.

Roaf, M. (1990) *Cultural Atlas of Mesopotamia and the Ancient Near East*, Oxford: Equinox.

Roberts, G.K. (1989) 'Food' in C. Chant (ed.) *Science, Technology and Everyday Life*, London: Routledge/Open University.

Rosman, A. and Rubel, P.G. (1989) 'Stalking the wild pig: hunting and horticulture in Papua New Guinea', in S. Kent (ed.) *Farmers as Hunters: The Implications of Sedentism*, Cambridge: Cambridge University Press.

Rostow, W.W. (1990) *The Stages of Economic Growth*, third edition, Cambridge: Cambridge University Press.

Rotberg, R. and Rabb, T.K. (1985) *Hunger and History: The Impact of Changing Food Production and Consumption Patterns on Society*, Cambridge: Cambridge University Press.

Rowntree, B.S. (1901) *Poverty: A Study of Town Life*, London: Macmillan.

Rozin, E. and Rozin, P. (1981) 'Some surprisingly unique characteristics of human food preferences', in A. Fenton and T.M. Owen (eds) *Food in Perspective: Proceedings of the Third International Conference on Ethnological Food Research, Cardiff, Wales, 1977*, Edinburgh: John Donald.

Rozin, P. (1976) 'The selection of food by rats, humans and other animals' in J.S. Rosenblatt, R.A. Hinde, E. Shaw and C. Beer (eds) *Advances in the Study of Behaviour*, Vol. 6, London/New York: Academic Books.

Rozin, P. (1982) 'Human food selection: the interaction of biology, culture, and individual experience', in L.M. Barker (ed.) *The Psychobiology of Human Food Selection*, Chichester: Ellis Horwood.

Rozin, P. (1987) 'Sweetness, sensuality, sin, safety, and socialization: some speculations', in J. Dobbing (ed.) *Sweetness: International Life Sciences Institute Symposium*, London: Springer-Verlag.

Sahlins, M. (1974) *Stone Age Economics*, London: Tavistock Publications.

Salaman, R. (1985) *The History and Social Influence of the Potato*, Cambridge: Cambridge University Press.

Sapp, S.G. and Harrod, W.J. (1989) 'Social acceptability and intentions to eat beef: an expansion of the Fishbein–Ajzen model using reference group theory', *Rural Sociology* 54, 3: 420–38.

Saul, S.B. (1960) *Studies in British Overseas Trade*, Liverpool: Liverpool University Press.

Saussure, F. de (1960) *Course in General Linguistics*, London: Owen.

Schafer, E., Schafer, R.B., Bultena, G.L. and Hoiberg, E. (1993) 'Safety of the US food supply: consumer concerns and behaviour', *Journal of Consumer Studies and Home Economics* 17: 137–44.

Schutz, H.G. and Judge, D.S. (1987) 'Sweetness in marketing', in J. Dobbing (ed.) *Sweetness: International Life Sciences Institute Symposium*, London: Springer-Verlag.

Scola, R. (1992) *Feeding the Victorian City: The Food Supply of Manchester 1770–1870*, Manchester: Manchester University Press.

Scott, T.R. and Giza, B.K. (1987) 'Neurophysiological aspects of sweetness', in J. Dobbing (ed.) *Sweetness: International Life Sciences Institute Symposium*, London: Springer-Verlag.

Sellerberg, A.M. (1991) 'In food we trust? Vitally necessary confidence and unfamiliar ways of attaining it', in E.L. Fürst, R. Prättälä, M. Ekström, L. Holm and U. Kjaernes (eds) *Palatable Worlds: Sociocultural Food Studies*, Oslo: Solum Forlag.

Sharman, A. (1991) 'From generation to generation: resources, experience and orientation in the dietary patterns of selected urban American households', in A. Sharman, J. Theopano, K. Curtis, and E. Messer, (eds) *Diet and Domestic Life in Society*, Philadelphia, Pa.: Temple University Press.

Sharp, H.S. (1988) 'Dry meat and gender: the absence of Chipewyan ritual for the regulation of hunting and animal numbers' in T. Ingold, D.Riches and J. Woodburn (eds) *Hunters and Gatherers 2: Property, Power and Ideology*, Oxford: Berg.

Simmons, J. (1984) *The Victorian Hotel: The Sixth H.J. Dyos Memorial Lecture*, Leicester: University of Leicester, Victorian Studies Centre.

Simoons, F.J. (1961) *Eat Not This Flesh: Food Avoidances in the Old World*, Madison, Wisc.: University of Wisconsin Press.

Singer, P. (1976) *Animal Liberation*, London: Jonathan Cape.

Sjoberg, G. (1960) *The Preindustrial City*, New York: The Free Press.

Smith, M.J. (1991) 'From policy community to issue network: salmonella in eggs and the new politics of food', *Public Administration* 69, Summer: 235–55.

Snow, L.F. (1993) *Walkin' over Medicine*, Boulder, Colo.: Westview Press.

Solokov, R. (1991) *Why We Eat What We Eat: How The Encounter between the New World and the Old Changed the Way Everyone on the Planet Eats*, New York: Summit Books.

Spencer, C. (1993) *The Heretic's Feast: A History of Vegetarianism*, London: Fourth Estate.

Sponsel, L.E. (1989) 'Farming and foraging: a necessary complementarity in Amazonia?', in S. Kent (ed.) *Farmers as Hunters: The Implications of Sedentism*, Cambridge: Cambridge University Press.

Stahler, C. (1994) 'How many vegetarians are there?', *Vegetarian Journal* July/August: 6–9.

Sykes, J. D. (1981) 'Agricultural science', in G.E. Mingay (ed.) *The Victorian Countryside*, London: Routledge & Kegan Paul.

Tannahill, R. (1973) *Food in History*, first edition, London: Eyre Methuen.

Tannahill, R. (1988) *Food in History*, revised edition, Harmondsworth: Penguin.

Tansey, G. and Worsley, T. (1995) *The Food System: A Guide*, London: Earthscan Publications Limited.

Theopano, J. and Curtis, K. (1991) 'Sisters, mothers and daughters: food exchange and reciprocity in an Italian-American community', in A. Sharman, J. Theopano, K. Curtis, and E. Messer (eds) *Diet and Domestic Life in Society*, Philadelphia, Pa.: Temple Press.

Thomas, K. (1983) *Man and the Natural World: Changing Attitudes in England 1500–1800*, London: Allen Lane.

Thomas, M., Goddard, E., Hickman, M. and Hunter, P. (1994) *General Household Survey 1992*, London: HMSO.

Thomas, P.R. (ed.) (1991) *Improving America's Diet and Health, From Recommendations to Action: A Report of the Committee on Dietary Guidlines Implementation, Food and Nutrition Board, Institute of Medicine*, Washington, D.C.: National Academy Press.

Toussaint-Samat, M. (1992) *A History of Food*, Oxford: Blackwell.

Townsend, A. (1979) 'Radical vegetarians', *Australian Journal of Philosophy* 57, 1: 85–93.

Tracey, M.V. (1977) 'Human nutrition', in R. Duncan and M. Weston-Smith (eds) *The Encyclopaedia of Ignorance: Life Sciences and Earth Sciences*, Oxford: Pergamon Press.

Turner, B. (1982) 'The government of the body: medical regimens and the rationalization of diet', *The British Journal of Sociology* 33, 2: 254–69.

Turner, B.S. (1991) 'Recent developments in the theory of the body', in M. Featherstone, M. Hepworth and B. Turner (eds) *The Body: Social Processes and Cultural Theory*, London: Sage.

Turner, M. (1985) *Enclosures in Britain 1750–1830*, London: Macmillan.

Twigg, J. (1979) 'Food for thought: purity and vegetarianism', *Religion* 9, Spring: 13–35.

U.S. Bureau of the Census (1993) *Statistical Abstract of the United States*, Washington, D.C.: U.S. Government Printing Office.

Vegetarian Society, The (1991) *The 1991 Food Survey: Trends in Vegetarianism Amongst Adults and Young People*, Altrincham: The Vegetarian Society of the United Kingdom Limited.

Van der Merve, M.J. (1992) 'Reconstructing prehistoric diet', in S. Jones, R. Martin and D. Philbeam (eds) *The Cambridge Encyclopedia of Human Evolution*, Cambridge: Cambridge University Press.

Visser, M. (1986) *Much Depends on Dinner*, Harmondsworth: Penguin.

Visser, M. (1993) *The Rituals of Dinner: The Origins, Evolution, Eccentricities, and Meaning of Table Manners*, Harmondsworth: Penguin.

Waites, B., Bennett, T. and Martin, G. (eds) (1982) *Popular Culture: Past and Present*, London: Croom Helm/Open University Press.

Walton, J.K. (1992) *Fish and Chips and the British Working Class, 1870–1940*, Leicester: Leicester University Press.

Warde, A. (1991) 'Guacamole, stottie cake and thick double cream: elements of a theory of modern taste', paper presented to the British Association for the Advancement of Science annual conference, Polytechnic Southwest.

Warde, A. and Hetherington, K. (1994) 'English households and routine food practices: a research note', *The Sociological Review* 42, 4: 758–78.

Warnock, J.W. (1987) *The Politics of Hunger: The Global Food System*, New York: Methuen.

Washburn, W.L. and Lancaster, C.S. (1968) 'The evolution of hunting', in R.B. Lee and I. Devore (eds) *Man the Hunter*, New York: Aldine Publishing.

Weinberg, A.M. (1972) 'Science and trans-science', *Minerva* 10, 2: 209–22.

Whyte, W.F. (1948) *Human Relations in the Restaurant Industry*, New York: McGraw Hill.

Widdowson, J.D.A. (1981) 'Food and traditional verbal modes in the social control of children', in A. Fenton and T.M. Owen (eds) *Food in Perspective*, Edinburgh: John Donald.

Williams, B. (1994) *The Best Butter in the World: A History of Sainsbury's*, London: Ebury Press.

Wilson, C.S. (1981) 'Food in a medical system: prescriptions and proscriptions in health and illness among Malays', in A. Fenton and T.M. Owen (eds) *Food in Perspective*, Edinburgh: John Donald.

Wilson, C.A. (ed.) (1989) *Waste Not Want Not: Food Preservation from Early Times to the Present Day*, Edinburgh: Edinburgh University Press.

Wood, R. (1992) 'Dining out in the urban context', *British Food Journal* 94, 9: 3–5.

Wood, R.C. (1991) 'The shock of the new: a sociology of nouvelle cuisine', *Journal of Consumer Studies and Home Economics* 15, 4: 327–38.

Wood, R.C. (1992) *Working in Hotels and Catering*, London: Routledge.

Woodward, J. (1988) 'Consumer attitudes towards meat and meat products', *British Food Journal* 90, 3: 101–4.

Zeldin, T. (1983) Listener article, 15 April 1982, quoted in C. Driver, *The British at Table*, London: Chatto & Windus.

Zey, M. and McIntosh, W.A. (1992) 'Predicting intent to consume beef: normative versus attitudinal influences', *Rural Sociology* 57, 2: 250–65.

AUTHOR INDEX

SUBJECT INDEX

Comets, Popular Culture, and the Birth of Modern Cosmology

Comets, Popular Culture, and the Birth of Modern Cosmology

SARA SCHECHNER GENUTH

PRINCETON UNIVERSITY PRESS

PRINCETON, NEW JERSEY

Copyright © 1997 by Princeton University Press
Published by Princeton University Press, 41 William Street, Princeton, New Jersey 08540
In the United Kingdom: Princeton University Press, Chichester, West Sussex

Library of Congress Cataloging-in-Publication Data

Schechner Genuth, Sara, 1957–
Comets, popular culture, and the birth
of modern cosmology / Sara Schechner Genuth
p.   cm.
Includes bibliographical references and index.
ISBN 0-691-01150-8 (cloth)
1. Comets. 2. Cosmology. 3. Religion and
science. 4. Superstition. I. Title.
QB721.S367   1997
523.6—dc21   96-52186   CIP

This book has been composed in Sabon Typeface

Princeton University Press books are printed on acid-free paper and meet the guidelines for
permanence and durability of the Committee on Production Guidelines for Book
Longevity of the Council on Library Resources

Printed in the United States of America

1   2   3   4   5   6   7   8   9   10

FOR MIRIAM AND NAOMI

CONTENTS

ILLUSTRATIONS

ACKNOWLEDGMENTS

LIKE a tadpole growing into a frog, this book has undergone a number of transformations. My manuscript began life as a Harvard doctoral dissertation. In grateful appreciation for the help I received, I would like foremost to thank my academic advisers, Erwin Hiebert, I. Bernard Cohen, and Owen Gingerich. Their probing questions propelled me along, and to Owen goes the credit of steering my research into the history of astronomy. My training at Harvard and Cambridge in the history and philosophy of science had both breadth and depth, without which the interconnections in this book would not have been possible. I owe thanks to my teachers on both sides of the Atlantic and to my grad-school colleagues, especially Alnoor Dhanani and Elizabeth Knoll.

My manuscript grew legs during a fellowship at the Newberry Library in Chicago, when I turned my attention to the relationship of high and low culture. This was a wonderful year for me, and I am grateful to my companions-in-research—Kathleen Adams, Jane Tylus, Bill Klein, Julie Solomon, Sue Sheridan Walker, Jan Reiff, Eli Zaretsky, Jim Barrett, Bruce Calder, Fran Dolan, Mary Quinlan-McGrath, and O. C. Edwards—for providing intellectual stimulus and camaraderie.

Other institutions have also been a haven for research. I have benefited from the encouragement and support of the Adler Planetarium in Chicago, where I worked as a curator from 1983 until 1990. In recent years, the Committee on the History and Philosophy of Science at the University of Maryland at College Park has welcomed me. So has the Center for History of Physics at the American Institute of Physics. The rare book library of the Adler Planetarium's History of Astronomy Department is—thanks to the accessions of Roderick and Marjorie Webster—well stocked with cometary books and ephemera. It was my good fortune to have this library close to hand. Ten other collections provided many resources: Harvard's Houghton Library, the Special Collections of the Regenstein Library at the University of Chicago, the Newberry Library, the John Crerar Library, the Print and Drawing Study Room of the Art Institute of Chicago, the New York Public Library, the Folger Shakespeare Library, the Library of Congress, the National Library of Medicine, and the Dibner Library of the History of Science and Technology at the Smithsonian Institution. I must thank the staffs of each of these for their guidance and aid in locating unusual materials.

Three grants assisted my research and writing: The Herbert C. Pollock Award for Research in the History of Astronomy and Astrophysics, bestowed by the Dudley Observatory in Schenectady, New York, 1991–1992; a Newberry Library / National Endowment for the Humanities Fellowship, 1990–1991; and a National Science Foundation Graduate Fellowship,

1980–1983. I am pleased to acknowledge the generous support of my bene-factors and heartily thank them.

Still others have offered encouragement and advice along the way. Betty Krier, Susan Fisher, and Carolyn Robinowitz helped me to keep my balance while grappling with difficult problems. Mordechai Feingold, Ken Howell, Elizabeth Knoll, and Bruce Stephenson read early drafts and kept up my faith. In recent weeks, my daughters, Miriam and Naomi, joined me in gazing at Comet Hyakutake, and over the years they have decorated my office with brightly crayoned photocopies of comet broadsides. My hus-band, Joel Genuth, humored me in my quest to see Halley's comet in 1986 (accomplished at 5:00 A.M in the desert south of Santa Fe and north of the state penitentiary!). In fact, he saw it first. That was neither the first nor last odd time or place in which Joel contributed to my work or provided critical support. This book and my outlook on life are the better for his involvement.

Silver Spring, Maryland
June 1996

Comets, Popular Culture,
and the Birth of Modern Cosmology

INTRODUCTION

SHARED CULTURE, SEPARATE SPACES

A CENTURY separated the two statements whose outward contradictions
I aim to reconcile in this book. In the first, Edmond Halley celebrated the
new outlook engendered by Newton's masterful treatment of comets in the
Principia:

> . . . Now we know
> The sharply veering ways of comets, once
> A source of dread, nor longer do we quail
> Beneath appearances of bearded stars.[1]

In the second, Thomas Robert Malthus resurrected the very dread of
bearded stars to which Halley alluded. Referring to the French Revolution,
he wrote:

> Like a blazing comet, [it] seems destined either to inspire with fresh life and
> vigour, or to scorch up and destroy the shrinking inhabitants of the earth.[2]

Why did Malthus take this backward step? Had not Halley extolled the
passing of an era of entrenched superstitions concerning the malevolent effects of comets? By the end of the seventeenth century, astronomers had
agreed that comets were members of the solar system; and they had indeed
rejected as vulgar the notion that comets were miraculous signs sent by God
to sear the hearts of infidels or herald the demise of monarchs. As Halley
had understood, the practice of ascribing drought, floods, plague, or revolution to comets had come to be seen as a popular error. In this light, we
might be tempted to think that Malthus drew on antiquated notions for
rhetorical effect, but in fact, he was thoroughly up-to-date in his characteri-
zation of comets. In his day, comets were widely perceived as barges that
transported life-sustaining materials to the earth and fuel to the sun. Without the circulation of comets in the heavens, all life would cease. On the
other hand, it was also widely believed that comets had key roles to play in
the earth's Creation, Noachian Deluge, and ultimate destruction. The final
Conflagration would be ignited by a comet, many exegetes said, and natural
philosophers concurred that a blazing star could serve this function by im-
mersing the earth in its fiery tail, by dropping into the sun and causing a
solar flare, or by kicking the earth out of its orbit and transforming it into
a comet. Forced to travel in a much more elongated circuit around the sun,
the old earth would be scorched and frozen in turns; its denizens would
discover that they lived in hell! Therefore, widespread endorsement of the
new, periodic theory of comets had not mitigated the perception of comets
as agents of upheaval or renewal, nor indeed as tools God might use to

punish the wicked or save the elect. In fact, the cometary theory to which Malthus alluded was not counter to that of Newton and Halley (as commonly supposed) but derived directly from their studies. There was, it seems, a place for the "vulgar" in the recondite studies of astronomers.

The nature of this place and how vulgar seeds were sown there are the subjects of this book. My principal aim is not to demarcate the boundaries between so-called superstition and modern astrophysical science, but to break down the traditional intellectual fences of historians of cometary astronomy in order to examine shared discourse. In the pages that follow, I will show that the history of cometary science is a tale not of rigid borders, but of the fluid interplay of high and low beliefs about nature and religion.

When we tear down the fences, we discover that the traditional view of comets as divine signs—found alike in folk beliefs and theological texts—was not overturned by Newton and Halley's astronomical discoveries (as others have claimed), but was in fact embraced by scientists and used creatively in the development of their cosmological theories. Newton and Halley wished to see God's providence in nature, and to this end, they redescribed comet lore in natural philosophical terms. Their successors agreed that comets could be agents of world reform, and this hypothesis became a cornerstone of eighteenth-century cosmogonic theories.

The fact that comet lore survived in Newtonian cosmology leads us to reevaluate and challenge the received view that astronomical research and philosophical attacks were sufficient causes of the decline of cometary superstition and the rise of astronomical rationalism during the early modern period. Although these factors played their part, it appears that social factors perhaps played larger roles in influencing people to reject the crudest forms of prognostication, even though many—like Newton and Halley—continued to nurture other tenets of comet lore.

When Newton and Halley incorporated comet lore into their astrophysics, they drew on two principal traditions: one treated comets as signs, the other as causes. Having their roots in antiquity, these traditions evolved over a long period of time, were given voice by authors and artists of many different nationalities, and were heavily imbued with religious and political implications. Although the import ascribed to any given comet varied with the political commitments of the prognosticator, the methods and uses of divination varied little among forecasters. These tenets, methods, and uses of comet lore were funneled into seventeenth-century English works, whose authors frequently cited foreign and classical sources. To illuminate these references, I will trace the evolution of cometary beliefs and practices from antiquity to the early modern era and will draw on diverse Western sources.

In performing this task, I will depart from the trail blazed by other authors, who, for the most part, have either treated folk beliefs anecdotally or recorded them chronologically with minimal historical interpretation. More often than not, they have labeled old views as superstitious and described them with derision as a foil for modern convictions. By contrast, I will not

simply catalog comet lore but will also interpret, historicize, and thematically arrange it. I will distinguish between comets as signs and as causes, between local and global spheres of influence, and between religious and political subtexts. I will present new information, as well as a new structure for understanding it, when I treat comets in the context of monsters (and not simply astrology) and inquire into comets as physical agents.

Many learned and folk traditions set the stage for seventeenth-century cometography, and I will paint them in broad brush strokes in the opening, thematic sections of this book. A more detailed picture will be rendered of seventeenth-century customs and of English society in particular in the middle part. Here the intersections of high and low culture will be investigated at length as I examine the social contexts of English cometography and analyze the ways that vulgar comet lore was absorbed into the elite astronomical work of Newton and Halley. Newton's and Halley's thoughts on the functions of comets were greeted with enthusiasm by most natural philosophers in England and Europe during the eighteenth century, and their cometography in turn helped to propel the development of modern cosmological thought. To delineate the breadth of their influence and explore what it says about the tenacity of popular motifs, I will revert to a panoramic view in the book's closing section.

Generalizing about a phenomenon as multifaceted and diffuse as the rise and fall of beliefs in comets as signs and causes is difficult. The upper and lower rungs of society shared many beliefs, but the makeup of these social groups and the degree of their commitment varied with time and place. I will try to specify to whom I am referring at each step in my analysis. Despite the variety of constituents and endorsements, it is still useful to speak in terms of high and low audiences, elite and popular practices, in order to be mindful of the social differences as we study the way folklore and science were amalgamated.

HIGH AND LOW CULTURE

Since what constitutes high and low culture will be a recurrent theme of this book, a few definitions are in order here. By culture, I refer to attitudes and values expressed in performances (such as songs, stories, rituals, and plays) or embodied in artifacts (such as pictures, printed texts, and other material works).[3] By common people, I refer to those with little or no schooling who may or may not have been illiterate, to the unlearned in Latin, to those of poor or modest means who could not afford to buy more than a few books, to peasants and artisans. In upper-class parlance, I refer to the vulgar, the multitude, the mob, in contrast to the wealthy nobles and learned scholars who constituted the elite. As a starting point, popular culture may be defined in hierarchical terms as the culture of the subordinate classes. We know that popular culture included folk songs, folk dances, and folktales,

devotional images and mystery plays, street literature and chapbooks, sports such as bearbaiting and cockfighting, charivaris, and seasonal festivals. Popular culture embodied social control, as in shaming rituals like ridings and rough music deriding cuckolds beaten by their wives; and it gave voice to social protest or outlet to social tensions, as in Carnival plays that inverted the established social order. It was informally transmitted through oral as well as printed means, and was found in both public spaces (churches, taverns, markets) and more private places (barns, cottages, workshops). Learned culture, on the other hand, was cultivated in schools and universities; it embraced classical and medieval philosophy and the intellectual and artistic movements of the early modern era. Ideas were formally transmitted in Latin and other languages by texts and tutors.[4]

I said as a starting point above, because it is worth emphasizing that in early modern Europe, the two cultural traditions (popular and learned, "little" and "great") did not correspond symmetrically to the practices of the two main social groups (the common and elite). It first appears that learned culture was the restricted province of the educated elite, whereas popular culture was open to all. Artisans did not read Aristotle, but courtiers attended Carnival. During the course of the seventeenth and eighteenth centuries, the pattern changed. The elite gradually withdrew their participation from what came to be seen as vulgar activities, and engaged in a program to reform the manners of the common folk.[5]

But even this account is hard to sustain fully. A number of scholars in recent years have pointed out just how difficult it is to draw a line between high and low culture in terms of content and consumers.

One problem in identifying popular culture with the activities and artifacts of the subordinate classes is the extent to which these classes interacted with upper-class culture (fig. 1). Menocchio, a sixteenth-century Italian miller, read books and drew his own heretical conclusions from them.[6] Scattered fragments of ancient medical knowledge and natural history were found in popular thought, having been put into circulation by herbals and emblem books.[7] Popular forms of cultural expression were prepared not only by the people, but also for the people. The *bibliothèque bleue*, for example, the cheap booklets peddled to peasants in the French countryside in the seventeenth and eighteenth centuries, first circulated among the urban bourgeoisie and so were popular not in origin but ultimately in taste.[8] Some cultural products were shaped from below as well as imposed from above. Peasant lore was collected and published in works such as the *Calendrier des bergers*, thereby coming to the attention of learned professors like Antoine Mizaud, who decided to correct popular errors and instruct rustic audiences on useful subjects such as weather prediction.[9] English almanacs also reflected folklore but principally aimed to disseminate more academic views.[10] It is arguable as well that the efforts to reform popular practices and control the people at certain times and places might have been so total that popular culture became the creation of the ruling classes.[11]

Fig. 1. Broadsides, which catered to the common folk, mingled high and low elements. This broadside shows Halley's comet as it appeared over the Nuremberg observatory in 1682. The text (not shown) considers what the comet might portend. (WOP-19. Courtesy of Adler Planetarium & Astronomy Museum, Chicago, Illinois.)

By way of example, let me offer the circumscribed case of English civic pageantry and Lord Mayor's Shows in mid-seventeenth-century London. These were public spectacles that drew large crowds. In them, a procession made its way through the streets, stopping at one site or monument after another. At each stop, spectators were entertained by a dramatic performance. This was public theater, and its propaganda value was not lost on the government. Consequently, the elite did as much as they could to orchestrate the program and the public's participation in it. For instance, Charles II was the key actor in his coronation procession on 22 April 1661. As his cavalcade traveled from the Tower to Whitehall, many of his subjects had "their first glimpse of the returning monarch . . . as he threaded the narrow streets on that bright April morning, the principal character in a pageant whose brilliance outshone all else within living memory."[12] The tableaux in this pageant made court ideology manifest. Peace and prosperity, they declared, were fundamentally linked to the restoration of the monarchy and the return to the old order. Subsequent Lord Mayor's Day Shows tactfully reinforced this message, but after 1671 when Charles started to attend them regularly, these civic spectacles brazenly propagated the court's ideology.[13]

The traffic in high and low cultural elements flowed on a two-way street. If the common folk borrowed ideas from the learned, or were induced to accept the cultural hegemony of their social superiors, the elite were not above partaking of the culture of the masses. Bourgeois readers read the same almanacs and chapbooks as did the common people. Folk stories and motifs traveled up the social ladder and can be found embedded in scholarly texts. For example, visions of trips to heaven and hell, recorded in Latin by medieval monks, contained all the elements of folk accounts of journeys to the otherworld (albeit they were couched in a Christian framework).[14] To cite a case more central to this book, Ambroise Paré, the chief surgeon to two kings of France, took note of monsters, which were commonly thought to portend misfortune, and discussed their significance in a surgical work. Along with depictions of Siamese twins and fabulous animals, Paré published an image of a "celestial monster," identified as a "horrible blood-colored comet . . . that engendered such great terror in the common people that some of them died of fear over it"[15] (fig. 2). Such apparitions and wonders appealed to all groups in early modern society; they were interpreted not only in tabloid broadsheets but also in learned sermons, Latin prodigy books, and scientific treatises.

The foregoing examples suggest that popular culture, like elite culture, did not inhere in a specific set of texts, gestures, or beliefs. Here Roger Chartier's concept of "culture as appropriation" is helpful. Chartier emphasizes that "we must replace the study of cultural sets that were considered as socially pure with another point of view that recognizes each cultural form as a mixture, whose constituent elements meld together indissolubly."[16] "Popular" did not reside in specific artifacts or performances, but in how ordinary people appropriated and adapted those that interested them. Likewise, elite culture was constituted by the appropriation and alteration of many materials that did not initially belong to the upper crust.[17]

Good examples of the borrowing and blending of elements are seen in the case of religion and medicine. In England, the medieval Catholic Church assimilated many Anglo-Saxon folk rituals into authorized religious practice. The ancient worship of wells, for instance, became associated with a saint rather than a heathen spirit. The health-giving properties of a well were ascribed by the medieval church to the intercession of the saint with God, and later by early modern physicians to the medicinal powers of the spring water. Thus a folk belief was accommodated and adapted by different authoritarian segments of society. Lower on the social ladder, prayers were blurred in the popular mind with spells and incantations. Common folk thought that there was power in the mere repetition of holy words, and talismans inscribed with signs of the cross or verses of gospel were worn as preservatives against drowning, death in childbirth, and fever. Although theologians denied that the church could manipulate supernatural powers, at the parochial level many clergy shared the beliefs of their parishioners that holy water, relics, and consecrated wine and bread

Fig. 2. A grisly, "blood-colored comet" included among the "celestial monsters" discussed by Ambroise Paré in *Des monstres et prodiges*, 3d ed. (Paris, 1579). (Courtesy of the National Library of Medicine.)

had the power to heal the sick or perform other magical functions. When Protestant reformers rejected the magical elements they saw in Catholic rites and remedies, folk healers in the Tudor countryside continued the work of parish priests by dispensing holy charms and liturgical spells along with herbal remedies.[18]

Do the blurry boundaries between popular and learned culture threaten the usefulness of these terms? Not when one considers the act and patterns of consumption that create a cultural product in addition to the content and

structure of the product. Popular culture was shared by high and low, but evidence of this overlap should not obscure the distinctions of social space that separated the two groups. Take three examples: festivals, sporting events, and reading matter. In England, patricians and plebeians both attended Bartholomew Fair, May Day celebrations, and Lord Mayor's Shows in London. But the upper classes watched the Lord Mayor's Shows from balconies; the "blue apron" audience frolicked in the streets. The classical iconography of the pageants appealed to the learned, whereas simpler images such as Jack Straw appealed to members of the London trades. Sporting events also cut across but did not level class distinctions. Cockfights for gentlemen and poorer sorts took place on different days. When gentle and simple attended the same cockfight, there was often separate seating.[19] Almanacs were written by the educated for both high and low readers and so formed a bridge between them. Yet people did not always agree with what they read, and engaged at many levels with the texts before them. Chapbooks and broadsides amused upper-class children and sometimes their parents. But perhaps elite adults like Samuel Pepys were slumming when they collected these "penny merriments." They were, after all, viewed with curiosity and contempt by Sir William Cornwallis as early as 1600:

> Pamphlets, and lying stories and news, and two penny poets I would know them, but beware of being familiar with them: my custom is to read these, and presently to make use of them, for they lie in my privy.[20]

Being too familiar with popular material might be seen as evidence of having kept bad company, and elite reading matter quickly became déclassé once produced for the mass market. The chivalric romances and lurid tales that had appealed to aristocrats were disparaged as vulgar when coarsely printed in chapbooks.[21]

THE VERBAL AND VISUAL IN POPULAR CULTURE

Before we turn in this book to elements of popular culture that were embedded in elite scientific works, perhaps some justification is required for my heavy reliance on printed sources. Popular culture in early modern Europe was predominantly oral, but various forms of print culture reached segments of the common people nonetheless. The culture of print in France and England has been well studied. Between 1530 and 1660, a popular market for print culture was created in France and England, even though illiteracy remained high and book ownership low among the nonelite. Peddlers carried chapbooks, broadsheets, and prints in their packs. Evangelical Protestants introduced vernacular Bibles, Psalters, and Calvinist literature to the French countryside. With a higher literacy rate than peasants, urban artisans and tradesmen had greater opportunity for direct access to the contents of printed works, but because books were relatively expensive, they often

owned just one book at a time. Books circulated, however, being bought, lent, shared, and resold. In France, the most common volumes were books of hours, copies of the *Golden Legend*, Bibles, breviaries, missals, or technical works, such as a pattern book to be used in the workshop. The common folk in England indulged in the purchase of almanacs and street literature. As already noted, popular readers did not acquire books specific to their class; the same vernacular works were read by notables.[22]

The possession and private reading of books does not fully characterize the relationship of popular classes to print culture, however. Books were used collectively in workshops where apprentices and artisans consulted trade manuals and arithmetics, in Protestant assemblies where congregants sang psalms and heard the Scriptures read aloud, and in fraternal organizations where members circulated texts celebrating festive occasions.[23]

The oral and the printed interacted to a great degree, for reading was not a silent affair. French peasants might hear someone read aloud or translate a tale from French into the local dialect at a *veillée*, an evening gathering held especially during the winter months in rural communities.[24] Published news stories were talked about in English country alehouses, and broadside ballads were pinned to the back of doors and posted on the walls so that customers might entertain themselves. With pints in hand, farmers sat down with their neighbors to pore over the almanac's forecasts of weather and politics. In the marketplace, balladeers sang catchy tunes to encourage the sale of the printed sheets, and passersby who learned the words later sang the songs to the spinning wheel or chirped them beneath the cow to help her let down her milk. Political pamphlets were often written to be read aloud. Radicals during the English Revolution arranged for declarations to be announced by the town crier, or to be pinned to the market cross where they were audibly read by bystanders.[25]

Moreover, one cannot simply divide the world into oral and scribal, listeners and readers. There existed a spectrum of reading abilities between literacy and illiteracy, and a range of printed works that merged words with pictures.[26] Woodcuts and engravings were coupled with texts, not only in illustrated books but also in single printed sheets. The latter were designed for private or public use. They were stored in drawers or hung over the kitchen mantel, in the nursery, and on the parlor chimney; others were pasted on walls of the workshop, church, inn, and town.[27] Public display meant that the printed works reached audiences who could not read or afford to buy them. Broadsides made fascinating wallpaper, for they contained three elements: a bold title to be announced, a provocative image, and a short, explanatory text in prose or verse dealing with political events, sorcerers' misdeeds, monstrous births, or celestial wonders such as comets. Visual imagery was a link between print and oral culture.

In general, the impact of printing on people's lives depended on the literacy of those in their communities; the cost and availability of printed texts in a language that they knew; the existence of social occasions when books

could be read aloud or prints examined; the need or wish for information that they thought could be found more readily in printed than in oral sources; and the desire to use the press to tell someone else something. With the help of social networks at work, in the marketplace, in church, or in festive confraternities, the circulation of varied types of printed media—with pictures and texts—made the written word and the ideas it contained familiar to those who could not read.[28]

It must be noted that the culture of print did not supplant oral and folk art traditions, even though these traditions were sometimes found reflected in printed sources. There was a dynamic relationship between the printed and the oral, the verbal and the visual. Elucidating the oral components of popular culture from the surviving remains of material culture is a risky undertaking and is not the aim of this book.

THE CULTURE OF COMETS

What was the place of comets in popular culture? Setting aside elusive oral traditions, I draw my conclusions from artifacts and recorded performances, artwork and cheap tracts. These include ephemeral publications such as news-sheets, broadsides, almanacs, and chapbooks; ballads, plays, and sermons; paintings, woodcuts, and engravings. Here the feelings of terror and foreboding aroused by comets since antiquity are recalled (fig. 3). In folklore, comets heralded war, famine, plague, ill-luck, the downfall of kings, universal suffering, the end of the world, and yet sometimes good fortune.

High and low audiences shared certain beliefs about comets, and each audience appropriated learned and popular ideas. Stith Thompson's *Motif-Index of Folk-Literature* provides a starting point for the identification of popular elements that have appeared in folklore and may sometimes be found in erudite texts. The index contains detailed entries for many of the themes and subjects to be described in this book: the origin and condition of comets, meteors, stars, and planets; divination by means of the heavenly bodies and other celestial apparitions; omens and signs; prodigies; marvels of nature; monsters; world calamities and renewals. The specific entries are too numerous to mention here but will be cited as necessary in subsequent chapters.[29]

The study of high and low perceptions of comets supports the thesis that when popular and elite culture brushed up against each other, it was not a contact between "two juxtaposed and pre-existent worlds (one scholarly, the other popular)," but rather an encounter that "produced cultural or intellectual 'alloys,' the components of which were as solidly bound together as in metal alloys."[30] The alloys were always changing. I shall be analyzing their components in order to suggest that new patterns of idea consumption and amalgamation promoted both the decline of the interpre-

Fig. 3. Comet of 1577. Nuremberg broadside, detail. (Wickiana Collection. From the Department of Prints and Drawings of the Zentralbibliothek Zürich.)

tation of comets as portents and the rise of their interpretation as cosmological agents. The decline of prognostication in the seventeenth century was connected in part with the withdrawal of the elite from socially discredited and vulgar practices. The new, natural philosophical interpretation derived from the way Newton and Halley appropriated popular comet lore and melded it into their astrophysical thought.

Signs of the Times

Ancient Signs

CHANGES in weather and affairs of state—comets have imported these since ancient times. Babylonians, Greeks, and Romans laid the foundation for early modern ideas on the physical nature of comets, their capacity as portents, and the bearing their physical nature ostensibly had on their purpose. The ancients also provided models for the political use of cometary divination. I shall address these subjects here, reserving the early techniques of prognostication for discussion in chapter 3.[1]

PHYSICAL THEORIES OF COMETS

We know little of what people thought about comets before Aristotle, and most of what we know comes secondhand. From cuneiform astronomical tablets, and from works by Aristotle, Diodorus Siculus, Seneca, and one long attributed to Plutarch but now thought to be by Aëtius, we learn that ancient philosophers divided themselves into two main camps.[2] Some believed comets to be astronomical entities; others affirmed their meteorological nature. For convenience, I have cataloged philosophers according to their stand on this question in tables 1 and 2. The details of their thought, scant as they are, do not concern us here, but the ideas of Aristotle and Seneca, who endorsed opposing viewpoints, deserve a closer look.

Without a doubt, the most influential ancient theory of comets was that of Aristotle. In the *Meteorologica*, Aristotle judged that comets were sublunar meteors composed of hot, dry "windy" exhalations. They had two causes. The most common were formed when a condensed mass of volatile exhalations ascended from the earth into the upper atmosphere, where it was ignited by revolutions of the contiguous heavenly sphere. Comets were also formed when a star or planet gathered atmospheric exhalations into a stellar halo that appeared as the comet tail but was not attached to the star or planet. Unlike the first type of comet, which moved more slowly and erratically than the stellar sphere, the second type had the same motion as its generating star.[3]

Aristotle sorted comets according to their physical shape. When the fiery exhalations extended in all directions, a "long-haired" star or *astēr komētēs* (ἀστήρ κομήτης) was formed; from this we derive our modern word "comet." When the exhalations extended lengthwise, a "bearded" star (πωγωνίας—pogonias) was the result. This nomenclature was employed until the early modern era.[4]

TABLE 1
Classification of Ancient Theories of Comets as Celestial Objects

Planetary or Stellar Bodies	*Conjunctions*
Chaldaeans or Babylonians	

Pre-Socratics:

Pythagoreans (sixth–fifth centuries B.C.)	
Hippocrates of Chios (fl. 430 B.C.)	Anaxagoras (500–426 B.C.)
Aeschylus (student of Hippocrates)	Democritus (fl. 410 B.C.)
Diogenes of Apollonia (fl. 425 B.C.)	
Apollonius of Myndos (fourth century B.C., contemporary of Alexander the Great)	Artemidorus of Parium (n.d.)

Stoics:

Seneca (ca. 4 B.C.–A.D. 65)	Zeno of Citium (336–264 B.C.)

TABLE 2
Classification of Ancient Theories of Comets as Meteorological Objects

Enlightened or Inflamed Clouds (unclear whether optical or truly fiery effects)	*Ignited Exhalations*

Pre-Socratics:

Xenophanes of Colophon (fl. 520 B.C.)	
Metrodorus of Chios (early fourth century B.C., pupil of Democritus)	

Peripatetics:

Heraclides of Pontus (ca. 388–310 B.C., assoc. with Lyceum)	Aristotle (384–322 B.C.)
Strato of Lampsacus (fl. 290 B.C.)	Theophrastus (fl. 320 B.C.)
	Epigenes (fourth century B.C.?, contemporary of Apollonius?)

Stoics:

	Panaetius of Rhodes (185–ca. 110 B.C.)
	Posidonius (ca. 135–ca. 51 B.C., student of Panaetius)
	Boethus (second century B.C.)

Sources: Aristotle, Seneca, Aëtius.

Theophrastus and Ptolemy were among Aristotle's more notable follow-ers, but Seneca would have none of it.[5] "I do not think that a comet is just a sudden fire but that it is among the eternal works of nature," he declared.[6] Unlike fires, comets "move, preserve their continuity, and are uniform. . . . A comet has its own position and so is not quickly expelled but measures

out its own space. It is not extinguished but simply departs."[7] Seneca classified comets as mobile heavenly bodies but did not believe them to be planets as some of his predecessors did.[8] "To refute these theories is like exercising by throwing arm-length punches into the wind," he haughtily said.[9] It mattered not that comets moved outside of the zodiac, because it was more in keeping with the size and beauty of the universe for there to be diversity among the celestial wanderers and the routes in which they traveled.[10] Seneca acknowledged that men did not yet know whether comets ever reappeared according to pattern or sequence, but was inclined to think that they moved in eternal circuits.[11] He reminded his critics that nature did not often display comets. "Why, then, are we surprised that comets, such a rare spectacle in the universe, are not yet grasped by fixed laws and that their beginning and end are not known, when their return is at vast intervals?"

> The time will come when diligent research over very long periods will bring to light things which now lie hidden. A single lifetime, even though entirely devoted to the sky, would not be enough for the investigation of so vast a subject. . . . And so this knowledge will be unfolded only through long successive ages. There will come a time when our descendents will be amazed that we did not know things that are so plain to them.[12]

Seneca predicted that "some day there will be a man who will show in what regions comets have their orbit, why they travel so remote from other celestial bodies, how large they are and what sort they are."[13]

Seneca's universe was composed of many discordant yet eternal entities. Nature delighted in diversity and employed comets to lend glory to her works. "The appearance of comets is too beautiful for you to consider an accident, whether you examine their size or their brightness, which is greater and more brilliant than the other celestial bodies. In fact, their appearance has a kind of exceptional distinction. They are not bound and confined to a narrow spot but are let loose and freely cover the region of many celestial bodies," Seneca marveled.[14]

Such majesty was appropriate to things divine, and Seneca classified comets, stars, and planets among the sacred mysteries to be approached with reverence. In addressing astronomical matters, he said, we ought to draw in our togas modestly as if entering a temple, for in truth we strive to enter the temple of nature. As we examine heavenly matters, "we [may] believe that we are her [Nature's] initiates but we are only hanging around the forecourt," Seneca reminded. "Those secrets are not open to all indiscriminately. They are withdrawn and closed up in the inner sanctum." There is much we do not know. Indeed, "God has not made all things for man," nor are sacred things revealed all at once. "Our universe is a sorry little affair unless it has in it something for every age to investigate."[15]

Seneca's themes of the divine nature of comets and their mysterious purposes were repeated over the succeeding centuries.

TOKENS OF DOOM

What was the meaning of comets in the ancient world, and the natural link, if any, proposed to connect comets and portended events? Aristotle's and Seneca's investigations into the physical nature of comets were deeply rooted in each one's interpretation of their ominous significance. The physical theories of others, however, were oddly independent of their beliefs in the power of these bearded portents.

Aristotle's physical theory derived from his belief that comets were signs. He reasoned that comets must be fiery meteors because they heralded severe winds, drought, tidal waves, storms, earthquakes, and stones falling from the sky. Like comets, these terrible things appeared only when hot, dry exhalations were plentiful. These exhalations parched the air and disintegrated moist vapors, causing drought and windy weather. Severe winds heaved enormous stones into the air, churned the ocean, and heaped up tidal waves, whereas windy exhalations trapped within the earth rumbled below ground until they were vented in violent earthquakes.[16] Aristotle bolstered his theory with empirical data. The fall of the remarkable stone at Aegospotami in Thrace in 467 B.C. coincided with the apparition of a comet.[17] On the tail of the comet of 341/340 B.C. came a storm in Corinth. The great comet of 373–372 B.C. appeared during clear, frosty weather, ushering in an earthquake and tidal wave in Achaea, as well as a blustery, arid winter.[18] "So when comets appear frequently and in considerable numbers, the years are . . . notoriously dry and windy," Aristotle concluded.[19]

Thus Aristotle viewed comets as a barometer of the times. Their apparitions could be used to forecast drought, earthquakes, and prodigious rains. Comets were correlated to these calamities because all were symptoms of abundant amounts of hot, dry exhalations.

Theophrastus followed his master, Aristotle, in seeing comets as meteorological signs, but not causes, of wind, drought, and cold weather.[20] And Aratus of Soli, in his poem *Phaenomena*, offered a simple prayer: "May the stars above shine ever with due brightness; and may no comets, one nor two nor more, appear! for many comets herald a season of drought."[21] Pliny thought comets augured severe winds and heat, mentioning a horrible comet seen by Ethiopians and Egyptians, and named after Typhon, that "had a fiery appearance, . . . was twisted like a coil, and . . . very grim to behold."[22] The comet of A.D. 60 ushered in violent storms everywhere and earthquakes in Achaea and Macedonia in particular, Seneca reported. Like Aristotle, he found it noteworthy that the sea swallowed Buris and Helice at the appearance of the comet of 373–372 B.C.[23]

Again like Aristotle, Seneca drew his physical conclusions about comets from the fact that they were omens. But though his starting point was methodologically the same, his inferences were different.

> Aristotle says that comets indicate a storm and undue excess wind and rain. Well, what of it? Do you not judge that that which foretells the future is a celestial body? Indeed, a comet is not a sign of storm in the same way that there is a sign of coming rain when "The oil in the lamp sputters . . . ," or in the same way that it is a forecast of rough sea if "The sea-coots play on dry land . . . ," but in the way that the equinox is a sign of the year turning to hot or to cold, or as the things the Chaldaeans predict, the sorrow or joy that is established at people's birth by a star.[24]

A comet was a sign for the ensuing year just as a man's natal star determined the future course of his life. Unlike the sputtering lamp, a comet "has not drawn from its close neighbourhood the signs which it gives for the immediate future but . . . has them stored up and linked to the laws of the universe."[25] Divination from comets—like augury from sacrificial entrails, from birds, from lightning and thunder, and from the stars[26]—was permissible because events were prearranged by divine agency into a complex concatenated series.

> "But how do things indicate future events unless they are sent [by God] to do so?" In the same way as birds provide favourable or unfavourable auspices even though they are not, in this respect, moved in order to appear to us. . . . None the less, such things are carried out by divine agency, even if the wings of birds are not actually guided by god nor the viscera of cattle shaped under the very axe. The roll of fate [*fatorum series*] is unfolded on a different principle, sending ahead everywhere indications of what is to come, some familiar to us, others unknown.

"Whatever happens," Seneca concluded, "it is a sign of something that will happen."[27]

Pliny too seemed inclined to think this way. In noting that alarming disturbances followed the appearances of meteoric lights (e.g., the aurora borealis, falling stars, and rains of fire), Pliny remarked:

> My own view is that these [meteoric] occurrences take place at fixed dates owing to natural forces, like all other events, and not, as most people think, from the variety of causes invented by the cleverness of human intellects; it is true that they were the harbingers of enormous misfortunes, but I hold that those [misfortunes] did not happen because the marvellous [meteoric] occurrences took place but that these [meteors] took place because the misfortunes were going to occur, only the reason for their occurrence is concealed by their rarity, and consequently is not understood as are the risings and setting of the planets . . . and many other phenomena.[28]

For Pliny, there was a natural, albeit acausal, link between portentous meteors and civil disorders. The meteors did not cause the disorders. Rather, the physical conditions predisposed to foster the disorders also produced the meteors, or perhaps some divinity prearranged the natural sequence of events. Pliny's reasoning not only resonates with that of Seneca

but also here echoes Aristotle's treatment of cometary signs. Since Pliny's argument was fairly general, it is tempting to suggest that he perhaps applied it to cometary portents, which were commonly perceived to be meteors. Pliny, however, remained silent on this point.

With the exception of the terse confidences of Pliny and Seneca, Aristotle's *Meteorologica* alone advanced a theory of the natural relationship between comets and subsequent disasters. By the Roman period, authors did not much concern themselves with such details.

Marcus Manilius, a Stoic poet, set the tone and style. Although no doubt unoriginal in content, his poem *Astronomica* (composed between A.D. 9 and 15) transmitted classical views to the West and established the categories of cometary prognostication widely upheld in the Middle Ages and Renaissance.[29] Manilius subscribed to the Aristotelian theory of comets as inflammable terrestrial vapors but neglected Aristotle's reasoning on the role of exhalations in causing drought and death from natural disasters.[30] Instead Manilius insisted that God in pity sent comets as "tokens of impending doom,"[31] as portents of blighted crops and barren fields, grievous murrain among cattle, sickness among men, pestilence, plague, and death.

> For the fires wherewith the heavens blaze have never lacked significance, but farmers, cheated of their hopes, mourn over blighted fields, and amid barren furrows the weary ploughman vainly urges to the yoke his drooping team. Or else, when grievous sickness and a slow decline has gripped men's bodies, a mortal flame burns out the seat of life and sweeps away the stricken peoples; and the obsequies of the community fill whole cities with blazing pyres. Such was the plague which ravaged Erechtheus' folk and bore forth ancient Athens to an unwarlike grave, when, one after another, men collapsed upon the dead and died: no place was there for a doctor's skill, no prayers availed; duty fell a prey to sickness, and none were left to bury, none to weep the dead; the wearied fires sufficed not for their office, and limbs piled on limbs the corpses burnt: hardly was an heir to be found in that nation once so vast. Such are the disasters which the glowing comets oft proclaim.[32]

"Death comes with those celestial torches, which threaten earth with the blaze of pyres unceasing, since heaven and nature's self are stricken and seem doomed to share men's tomb."[33] From his words, one can almost feel nature's feverish shudder beneath the baneful streams of a comet.

In equating drought and disease with comets, Manilius was not far removed from Aristotle's work. Yet Manilius believed that the black shadow of death cast by comets extended beyond the realm of agriculture and public health into the political and social arena:

> Wars, too, the fires portend, and sudden insurrection, and arms uplifted in stealthy treachery; so of late in foreign parts, when, its oaths forsworn, barbarous Germany made away with our Commander Varus and stained the fields with three legions' blood, did menacing lights burn in every quarter of the skies; nature

herself waged war with fire, marshalling her forces against us and threatening our destruction. . . . Comets also presage civil discord and strife between kin. At no other time did heaven experience more conflagrations than when the sworn forces of the blood-stained conspirators filled with their ranks the plains of Philippi, and on sand scarcely yet dry of blood the Roman legionary took his stand on the bones of warriors and limbs mangled in former fighting; the empire's armed might engaged in conflict with itself, and Augustus, father of his country, marching in his father's steps, prevailed. Nor was this all: war at Actium was still to come.[34]

War, sudden insurrection, stealthy treachery, civil discord, strife between kin, conspiracy, murder, and nothing less were presaged by comets. Manilius underscored his point with the testimony of current events. He cited the military disaster of the Saltus Teutoburgiensis (A.D. 9), the conspiracy of Brutus and Cassius, the assassination of Julius Caesar (44 B.C.) and the subsequent civil war, and the defeat of Antony and Cleopatra's fleet in the naval battle at Actium (31 B.C.).

Prior to Manilius, similar views were expressed by Diodorus Siculus and Virgil, and may have originated with the Babylonians.[35] Cuneiform astronomical diaries that recorded apparitions of Halley's comet in 164 and 87 B.C. also contained contiguous notations on the death and accession of kings;[36] and Babylonian court astrologers may well have tied comets to changes of state many centuries earlier.[37] After Manilius, Ptolemy generically blamed wars and disturbed conditions on comets,[38] leaving Pliny, Seneca, and Lucan to be more specific in recalling how cometary portents appeared after the death of Demetrius Soter, king of Syria (151 B.C.) and shortly before the Achaean War; during the reign of Attalus III of Pergamum (who bequeathed his kingdom to Rome in 133 B.C.); at the start of the civil war between Pompey and Caesar (49–48 B.C.); after the assassination of Julius Caesar (44 B.C.) and during the civil disorder in the consulship of Octavius, later known as Augustus (43 B.C.); and during the tumultuous reigns of Augustus, Claudius, and Nero.[39] A comet during Nero's principate "took away the bad reputation of comets," Seneca ironically commented,[40] but Pliny wrote that it blazed "almost continuously and with a terrible glare."[41]

In general, a comet was viewed with dismay. "A terrifying star and not easily expiated," Pliny wrote, a comet announced no small effusion of blood.[42] And yet Pliny acknowledged that comets were not always horrific omens. The comet that appeared soon after the apotheosis of Julius Caesar was popularly regarded as a torch to light the new god's way into heaven. In the *Aeneid*, Virgil too regarded a cometary meteor as an appropriate vehicle to introduce a bittersweet message that in the midst of death, a great destiny may be established. Aeneas and his family welcomed the meteor as a divine sign that they should leave Troy, even though it still heralded the destruction of their home.[43] This theme, with overtones of sal-

vation through sacrifice, would reverberate in Christian cometary literature for centuries.

It might be noted here that this optimism with respect to occasional comets had very limited following. Chaeremon the Stoic (fl. A.D. 30–65), an Alexandrian scholar called to Rome to tutor the young Nero, was among the few to suggest that comets sometimes had heralded good events. He reputedly listed these exceptional comets in a book, *On Comets*, which has not survived.[44] It has been proposed that Chaeremon sought to flatter Nero, during whose reign two comets appeared (A.D. 60 and 64) that were widely regarded as evil omens.[45] A laudatory view of comets was the exception rather than the rule among high and low audiences alike. Indeed, from antiquity until the Renaissance, many repeated a story about Emperor Vespasian in order to prove that cometary optimism was nothing but foolhardy, false bravado. Of the comet of A.D. 79, Vespasian bravely declared, "This [hairy star] is an omen, not for me, but for the Parthian king; for he has long hair, whereas I am bald." Alas, Vespasian died shortly thereafter, vindicating folk beliefs.[46]

Vespasian was thought foolish to buck the trend. Common knowledge had it that "the hair of the baleful star . . . portends change to monarchs."[47] Even the garrulous, gossipy wife in Juvenal's satire noticed "the comet threatening the kings of Armenia and Parthia."[48]

Could the threat of comets be averted? Manilius implied that it could. "Wonder not at the grievous disasters which betide man and man's affairs, for the fault oft lies within us: We have not sense to trust heaven's message."[49] Indeed, a right understanding of the message led to a powerful political advantage.

POLITICAL MESSAGES AND MEANS

As already mentioned, the connection between comets and the downfall of princes may have originated with Babylonian astronomers, who practiced astrology as a vital part of statecraft. By the Roman period, astrology as a tool of government was well established, and the shrewd marshaled comets as political weapons. Remarkable was the use made of a comet that appeared shortly after the death of Julius Caesar and concurrent with some games dedicated to Venus Genetrix. The common people believed it signified that Caesar's soul had been received among the gods. In order to cater to public taste in this matter, and no doubt to exploit the showy celestial display so as to underscore the legitimacy and authority of the rule of the Julian house, Octavius—Caesar's adopted son who later appropriated the title Emperor Augustus—added a stellar emblem to the bust of Caesar placed in the Forum.[50] Between 30 B.C. and A.D. 14, Augustus also had minted commemorative silver coins, whose obverse showed his own bust with the inscription "AVGVSTVS CAESAR," while the reverse had an eight-

pointed star with a flaming tail and the words "DIVVS JVLIVS" (Divine Julius).[51] The comet even came to be worshiped in a Roman temple. Pliny revealed that Augustus privately rejoiced in the comet's appearance during games at the start of his rule and interpreted it as having been created more for his own sake than for Julius Caesar's. He deemed the comet most propitious to himself, and Pliny added, "to confess the truth, it did have a healthgiving influence over the world."[52]

Enthrallment with Caesar's comet aside, Roman nobility viewed bearded stars with much disquietude.[53] Comets were harbingers of the deaths of Cicero (43 B.C.) and Agrippa (12 B.C.).[54] Even Augustus, who had politically exploited the 44 B.C. comet, was made uneasy by apparitions of comets in A.D. 9 and 11. In order to quash rumors of his impending demise—circulated by astrologers to please their ambitious clients—and to check public restiveness, Augustus circumscribed the activities of all diviners in the empire. His edict in A.D. 11 prohibited calculations of a person's time of death and required all divinatory consultations to take place in the presence of a third party. To counter predictions that his own death was forthcoming, Augustus even dared to publish his horoscope. It seems, however, that mighty Augustus could not overrule the comets. His murder in A.D. 14 was heralded by a bloodred comet.[55] Forty years later, another comet rose and another emperor fell: Claudius succumbed to poison soon after a comet blazed in the Roman sky.[56]

The record of emperors and ambitious nobles surviving comets was not good, and Romans therefore expected more gore than glory from two notable comets during Nero's reign. Tacitus observed that in A.D. 60, "a comet blazed into view—in the opinion of the crowd, an apparition boding change to monarchies. Hence, as though Nero were already dethroned, men began to inquire on whom the next choice should fall."[57] Indeed, Nero was pleased neither by comets nor by the gossip that they engendered. Whereas Augustus had curtailed the astrologers, Nero listened to them and killed off his challengers on their advice. Suetonius reported:

> It chanced that a comet had begun to appear on several successive nights, a thing which is commonly believed to portend the death of great rulers. Worried by this, and learning from the astrologer Balbillus that kings usually averted such omens by the death of some distinguished man, thus turning them from themselves upon the heads of the nobles, he resolved on the death of all the eminent men of the State; but the more firmly, and with some semblance of justice, after the discovery of two conspiracies [of Piso and Vinicius].[58]

In reporting the apparition of A.D. 64, Tacitus noted that a comet was "a phenomenon to which Nero always made atonement in noble blood."[59] It is ironic that Seneca, who had formerly flattered Nero with an auspicious interpretation of the A.D. 60 comet, died in this purge.[60]

This suggests that the correlation between comets and noble demise was not purely coincidental. Nero sacrificed his political opponents in order to

secure his own safety, and it is possible that the conspirators in the deaths of Augustus and Claudius may have been encouraged by the knowledge that their deeds were foreordained by the heavens, and chose those propitious times to undertake their lethal political plots. Recognition that astrological forecasts could be self-fulfilling certainly seems to have motivated Augustus to enact his law against divination.

By ancient times, the signal nature of comets was well established not only among the learned elite but also among the common folk. People were interested in the origin of comets, their extraordinary behavior, and their meaning.[61] Folk beliefs were summed up in an image in the works of Hyginus. In describing the Greek mythology of the constellations, Hyginus likened a comet to a grief-stricken goddess, her long hair unbound and streaming.[62] Lamentation followed on her heels. His metaphor was apt for Roman contemporaries who thought that comets heralded blighted crops, sickness, civil discord, insurrection, war, and murder. In cataloging these horrors, Roman philosophers, historians, and poets went well beyond the agricultural and meteorological phenomena examined by Aristotle. Although most accepted Aristotle's theory of comet formation, they apparently cared little about finding an underlying cause for the correlation between comets and subsequent civil disorders, which were not readily explained by Aristotle's theory. Pliny and Seneca at least acknowledged the problem of cause. They conjectured the existence of an intricate web of cause and effect that operated behind the scenes of the natural world, but it remained an open question just how a comet, which was one strand in the web, could tug on or be tugged by such diverse strands as those of thunderclouds and political assassination. Aristotle alone of the ancient philosophers offered a consistent account of the way in which the underlying causes of comets produced the presaged events, but his account was limited.

Roman intellectuals emphasized the portentous character of comets, but with statesmen, they understood that comets could be more than tokens of impending doom. Bearded stars served political ends. Divination from comets legitimated the Julian house, flattered ambitious men, perhaps fortified conspirators, and justified political purges.

Thus classical interpretations of the nature and significance of comets had bearing in both philosophical and political quarters. The bipartite treatment of comets as natural and political signs lasted for centuries, for the philosophical authority of ancient authors was widely respected for the next sixteen hundred years, and the attempt to profit politically from the fears of one's fellows has always come naturally.

Monsters and the Messiah

> Can ye not discerne the signes of the times?
>
> —*Matt. 16:3*

FROM antiquity through the Renaissance, the classical view of cometary signs prevailed. Not only did Christian authors embrace the pagan viewpoint, but they colored it with their own beliefs and enlarged its scope. Comets became Christian signs of more than local disputes between secular and ecclesiastical powers, military engagements of consequence for the church, or a plague upon sinners. Comets were transformed into signs of the coming of the Messiah, the reformation of the church, and the final battle with the Antichrist. Comets too continued to be ciphers of political schemers, dissident groups, and millenarian visionaries who not only sought to foresee future changes in world affairs but also strived to enact reforms ushering in a golden age conducive to their respective goals.

In these capacities, comets were seen as monsters warning the public of the Lord's intentions. Most historical books on the subject of comets treat them only astrologically and overlook their importance as monsters and prodigies. Yet a thorough appreciation of this context is essential to an understanding of later developments in Christian iconography. It is therefore the aim of this chapter to locate comets in the canon of monstrosities; to describe the degree to which high and low audiences both respected comets as prodigies; and to note how pagan folklore was absorbed into Christian thought.

POPULAR AND PATRISTIC VIEWS OF COMETS

Both verbal and visual sources offer insight into the beliefs shared by the common folk and their social superiors. In 1066, Halley's comet made a dazzling appearance. Writing in Old English, some monks took special note of the omen in the *Anglo-Saxon Chronicles*, tying its appearance to power disputes, political intrigue, and the invasions of Harald Hardrada of Norway and William of Normandy.[1] Evidence that awe and alarm extended beyond scribal circles is to be found in the Bayeux Tapestry, commissioned by Queen Matilda, the wife of William the Conqueror, to commemorate her husband's victory (fig. 4). On one panel, awestruck En-

Fig. 4. Halley's comet as it appeared in 1066. Detail from the Bayeux Tapestry (1073–1083), Musée de la Tapisserie, Bayeux, France. (Giraudon/Art Resource, NY.)

glishmen point to the comet, which blazed in the sky several months before the Battle of Hastings. The embroidered legend reads, "Isti mirant stella[m]" (They marvel at the star). Seated to the right of the sky-gazers, King Harold of England learns of the evil omen, while beneath him, ghostly invasion ships foreshadow his defeat.[2]

Depictions in the *Anglo-Saxon Chronicles* and the Bayeux Tapestry were contemporaneous to the events recorded. Later historical works provide us with oblique but still useful reports of earlier public attitudes. According to the *Nuremberg Chronicle* (1493), for example, Halley's comet in 684 heralded three months of rain, thunder, and lightning, the death of men and flocks, withered grain, and plague on the heels of solar and lunar eclipses.[3] The chronicle also reports that during a hunt soon after the apparition of a comet in 1314, King Philippe IV was toppled from his horse by a wild boar and died from the injuries sustained.[4] Although the boar that forced itself between the horse's legs was more responsible for the monarch's demise, public interest centered on the comet. It, not the nasty boar, was illustrated in the chronicle (fig. 5).

Fables and folktales confirm that the common people had long connected extraordinary fires and lights in the heavens to the deaths of the great and small.[5] The *Nuremberg Chronicle* aimed a bit higher, however. Published with lavish illustrations in both Latin and German editions, the book was

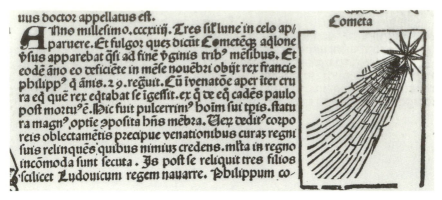

uus doctoz appellatus est.
Anno millesimo.ccccxiiij. Tres sit lune in celo apparuere. Et fulgoz quez dicut Cometecz adlone vsus apparebat qsi ad fine vginis trib' mesibus. Et eode ano eo deficiete in mese nouebzi obijt rex francie philipp' q anis.29.reguit. Cu ivenatoe aper iter cura eq que rex eqtabat se igessit.ex q de eq cades paulo post moztu'e. Hic fuit pulcerrim' boim sui tpis.statu ra magn',optie aposita bns mebza. Uex dedit'corpo reis oblectametis preapue venationibus curaz regni suis relinques quibus nimius credens.mlta in regno incomoda sunt secuta. Is post se reliquit tres filios salicet Ludouicum regem nauarre. Philippum co-

Fig. 5. Comet of 1314. Hartmann Schedel, *Liber cronicarum* (Nuremberg, 1493). Note that several woodcuts were used interchangeably for different comets in the German and Latin editions of this book. The images are of stylized comets, and they do not give any indication of how the comets appeared to contemporary spectators. (WOP-156e. Courtesy of Adler Planetarium & Astronomy Museum, Chicago, Illinois.)

addressed to a general, literate audience with money to spend. But it is not unusual to find popular elements embedded in texts of an elite character, and it would be wrong to presume that these elements were despised by most serious scholars.[6]

The early church fathers accepted comets as fatal omens, as had many Greco-Roman philosophers before them. Origen (ca. 185–254), the Greek theologian, exegete, and encyclopedist, scorned horoscope casting that precluded free will, but felt secure that comets portended dynastic changes, great wars, and terrestrial commotions.[7] Agreeing with Origen, Synesius of Cyrene (ca. 370–ca. 430)—the bishop of Ptolemais, a contemporary of Augustine, and friend of Hypatia—found the "hairiness" of comets offensive:

It is not even pious, in my opinion to call these [comets] stars, but if you wish to call them so, this much at least is clear, that hair is an evil, inasmuch as even in a star it produces a perishable form. And whenever these comets appear, they are an evil portent, which the diviners and the soothsayers appease. They assuredly foretell public disasters, enslavements of nations, desolations of cities, deaths of kings, nothing small or moderate, but everything that exceeds the disastrous.[8]

Isidore of Seville (ca. 560–636) and the Venerable Bede (673–735) similarly argued that comets were signs of war, political change, tempests, and pestilence.[9] These views were shared by many including John of Damascus (ca. 675–749), Peter Abelard (1079–1142), Robert Grosseteste (ca. 1168–1253), Albertus Magnus (ca. 1200–1280), Roger Bacon (ca. 1219–ca. 1292), Jean Buridan (ca. 1295–ca. 1358), and Nicole Oresme (ca. 1320–1382).[10]

The transformation of pagan cometary beliefs into a Christian form was really quite simple. Comets heralded the death of great churchmen as well as kings; they announced wars of religion and squabbles between ecclesiastical and political powers. For Bede and the monks compiling the *Anglo-Saxon Chronicles*, the comet of 678 portended the political quarrel between King Ecgferth and Bishop Wilfrid, resulting in the ousting of Wilfrid from his see. Comets in 729 augured the Easter-time deaths of the holy man Ecgbryht and King Osric of Northumbria, the rape of France by the Saracens, and the latter's ultimate comeuppance for their unbelief.[11] The death of Archbishop Sigeric was portended by the comet of 995.[12] And on its 1145 return, Halley's comet alarmed an English monk, who depicted it in a Latin Psalter beneath the text of Psalm 5, which mentions God's destruction of sinners and protection of the righteous.[13] Thus pagan elements of popular culture were readily Christianized.

But this was only the first step. In the ancient world, comets were sometimes seen as felicitous omens, even when they were grouped with foreboding monsters. In combining the monstrous and auspicious character of comets, Christian authors enlarged upon traditional beliefs as they incorporated them into their historical and eschatological views.

MONSTERS AND THEIR MESSAGES

From antiquity to the Renaissance people remarked how blazing stars belonged to a class of menacing and monstrous events. Comets did not just appear singly but often kept company with other prodigies and portents.[14] Pliny grouped comets with showers of milk, blood, flesh, iron, wool, baked bricks, and stones, with bizarre celestial spectacles of heavenly armies arrayed for battle, with disembodied noises of clanging armor and trumpet blasts heard echoing in the sky, and with inflamed clouds.[15] Comets were among the portents seen at the beginning of the war between Caesar and Pompey and at the time of Caesar's death, but other terrors filled earth, sea, and sky too. According to Lucan and Virgil, these included incessant lightning, meteoric javelins and torches, daytime stars, solar and lunar eclipses, volcanic eruptions, alpine avalanches, tidal waves, floods, and earthquakes. In the temples, fire disappeared from altars, and offerings suddenly fell from their places. Statues of the national deities wept tears, and those of the household gods perspired. Ominous entrails and unlucky birds and dogs boded ill. Howling wild beasts frequented the metropolis, and brutes spoke as men. There were monstrous births and groaning graves. The air was filled with crashing arms and the sounds of spectral armies; and pathless forests echoed eerily with disembodied voices and loud screams. Pale specters stalked in twilight, and wells disgorged blood. And in the midst of these horrors, "never so oft blazed fearful comets."[16] In the same tone, Tacitus reported:

At the close of the year [A.D. 64], report was busy with portents heralding disaster to come—lightning-flashes in numbers never exceeded, a comet . . . ; two-headed embryos, human or of the other animals, thrown out in public or discovered in the sacrifices where it is the rule to kill pregnant victims. Again, in the territory of Placentia, a calf was born close to the road with the head grown to a leg; and there followed an interpretation of the soothsayers, stating that another head was being prepared for the world; but it would be neither strong nor secret, as it had been repressed in the womb, and had been brought forth at the wayside.[17]

In classical sources like these, portents occurred in groups. The texts suggest that the gods spoke in a verbose manner, reiterating their displeasure by sending prodigy after prodigy in an effort to impress the situation's gravity on the most dense human souls.

Viewed as contrary to nature and auguring divine wrath, comets were a form of monster.[18] Literally, the Latin word *monstrum* means a significant supernatural event, a wonder, a portent. It etymologically derives from *monere*, to warn; whereas the verb *monstrare*, which was formed from *monstrum*, means to show, point out, teach, inform, or denounce. Augustine said that monsters were prodigies since they demonstrated God's will.[19] Prodigy books and broadsides interpreted the historical meanings of such wonders, and comets found a happy home there.[20] A seventeenth-century broadside exemplifies this literature by illustrating and recording in verse "A Lamentable List, of certaine Hidious, Frightfull, and Prodigious Signes, which have bin seene in the Aire, Earth, and Waters"[21] (figs. 6–8).

When a single comet appeared, it was viewed as a warning gun that God discharged over sinners' heads before his murdering weapons went off.[22] Monstrous and hideous, it announced no more than local misfortune. But when comets clustered together with other prodigies, general upheaval was in store. The ancients believed that constellations of prodigies augured major revolutions, and Christians came to see them as setting the stage for judgment of the wicked and vindication of the elect on a global scale.

MONSTROUS COMETS IN SCRIPTURE

A biblical passage in the Apocrypha echoed the classical prodigy literature. In 2 Esdras, the angel Uriel predicted the downfall of Babylon and announced the following signs to herald Israel's vindication:

The sun shall suddenly shine forth at night, and the moon during the day. Blood shall drip from wood, and the stone shall utter its voice; the peoples shall be troubled, and the stars shall fall. . . . And the birds shall fly away together; and the sea of Sodom shall cast up fish; and one whom the many do not know shall make his voice heard by night, and all shall hear his voice. There shall be chaos also in many places, and fire shall often break out, and the wild beasts shall roam beyond their haunts, and menstruous women shall bring forth monsters.[23]

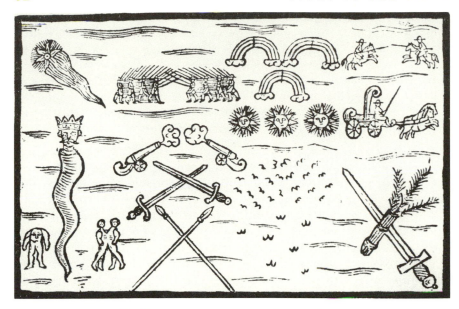

Fig. 6. "A Lamentable List, of certaine Hidious, Frightfull, and Prodigious Signes" (London, 1638). Broadside ballad. (From *The Pack of Autolycus*, edited by Hyder E. Rollins. Copyright © 1927 by the President and Fellows of Harvard College. Reprinted by permission of Harvard University Press.)

Although comets were not explicitly mentioned in this passage—there is only a reference to the stars' changing their courses—such passages were often cited in early modern times as tacit allusions to comets. Among these were the following verses in Joel:

> And I will give portents in the heavens and on the earth, blood and fire and columns of smoke. The sun shall be turned to darkness, and the moon to blood, before the great and terrible day of the Lord comes.[24]

Like the ten plagues in Exodus, these lamentable signs were apocalyptic. They were to herald redemption and judgment.

Another frequently cited, albeit equally ambiguous, reference to a comet appeared in 1 Chronicles, where God threatened to punish Jerusalem:

> And David lifted his eyes and saw the angel of the Lord standing between earth and heaven, and in his hand a drawn sword stretched out over Jerusalem.[25]

Writing in the first century A.D., the Jewish historian Flavius Josephus perhaps had this passage in mind when he recalled the monstrous signs auguring the siege and destruction of Jerusalem in A.D. 70. Among the portents was "a star, resembling a sword, [which] stood over the city, and a comet which continued for a year."[26] His remarks on the outstretched sword also echoed another biblical passage. When God chased Adam and

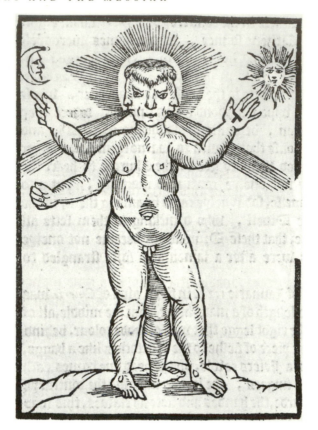

Fig. 7. Monstrous child born during the apparition of the 1577 comet. The child's head was surrounded by a cometary radiance, a bloody sun, and half-moon. It prophesied terrible times in 1588, then departed in a fiery blaze that scorched spectators. Plague followed. Stephen Bateman, *The Doome warning all men to the Judgemente* (London, 1581). (By permission of the Houghton Library, Harvard University.)

Eve from the Garden of Eden, "at the east of the Garden of Eden he placed the cherubim, and a flaming sword which turned every way, to guard the way to the tree of life."[27] This flaming sword barred entrance into the garden, and like that reputedly looming over Jerusalem in A.D. 66, it was a manifest sign of expulsion.

These two swords were portrayed as blazing comets by later Christian authors. In an influential poem, *La Seconde Sepmaine, ou Enfance du Monde* (1584), Du Bartas described the expulsion from Eden:

> Of our first *Parents*, out of *Eden* driven
> (of repeale hope-lesse) by the hand of Heaven;
> For the Almightie set before the dore

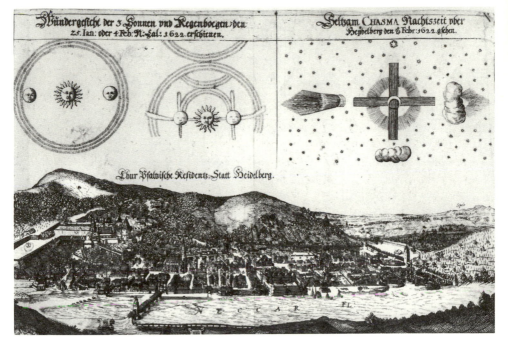

Fig. 8. Amazing sights over Heidelberg in 1622. The citizens were awed by the simultaneous appearance of three suns (parhelia), elaborate systems of rainbows, a curious aurora, images of a cross, and a comet. Broadside. (WOP-1. Courtesy of Adler Planetarium & Astronomy Museum, Chicago, Illinois.)

> Of th' holy Parke, a *Seraphin* that bore
> A waving sword, whose body shined bright,
> Like flaming Comet in the midst of night.[28]

John Milton, too, ended *Paradise Lost* (1667) with a fearsome comet:

> . . . For now too nigh
> Th' Archangel stood, and from the other Hill
> To thir fixt Station, all in bright array
> The Cherubim descended; . . .
> . . . High in Front advanc't,
> The brandisht Sword of God before them blaz'd
> Fierce as a Comet; which with torrid heat,
> And vapour as the *Libyan* Air adust,
> Began to parch that temperate Clime; whereat
> In either hand the hastning Angel caught
> Our lingring Parents, and to th' Eastern Gate
> Led them direct.[29]

Fig. 9. Sword-shaped comet appearing over Jerusalem (ca. A.D. 66–69) and fore-casting the city's destruction. Stephen Bateman, *The Doome warning all men to the Judgemente* (London, 1581). (By permission of the Houghton Library, Harvard University.)

When Adam and Eve looked back, they beheld a "flaming Brand" waving over the gate, now thronged with dreadful faces and fiery arms. Like-wise, the sword suspended over Jerusalem during the time of Josephus was illustrated as a comet in many sixteenth- and seventeenth-century works on comets, monsters, and other prodigies, including those by Stephen Bateman, Ambroise Paré, Stanislaw Lubieniecki, and Nathaniel Crouch (figs. 9–11).[30]

Josephus had written from the vantage point of a Jew who had witnessed the destruction of his capital, but Paré and others interpreted the ruin as divine vindication of the Christian religion and punishment of the Jews for their nonbelief:

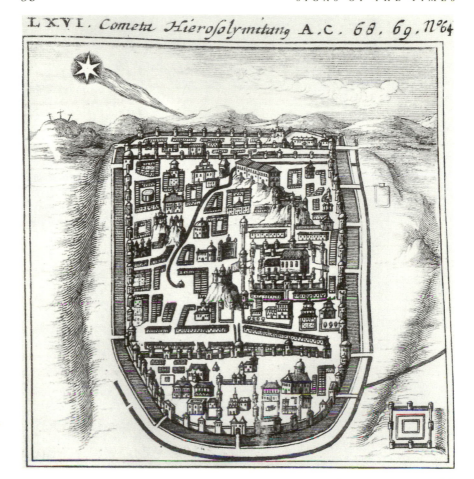

Fig. 10. Sword-shaped comet appearing over Jerusalem. Stanislaw Lubieniecki, *Theatrum cometicum* (Leiden, 1681). (Courtesy of Adler Planetarium & Astronomy Museum, Chicago, Illinois.)

> Josephus and Eusebius wrote that after the Passion of Jesus Christ, the wretched destruction of the city of Jerusalem was declared by several signs, and even, among others, a frightful comet in the form of a shining sword on fire, which appeared for easily the space of a year on the temple; as [if] demonstrating that divine ire wished to take vengeance over the Judaic nations, through fire, through blood, and through famine. Which [indeed] did happen.[31]

Thus auguries of local misfortunes could be transformed into signs of universal judgment. Texts in Josephus's *History*, the Old Testament, the Apocrypha, and the New Testament (to be discussed below) not only provided

The Dreadful Apparitions and Presages seen over the City of Ierusalem Page. 14

Fig. 11. Sword-shaped comet appearing over Jerusalem. Note the other monstrosities depicted: a cow giving birth to a lamb, and battling armies in the air. Nathaniel Crouch, comp., *Surprizing Miracles* (London, 1685). (By permission of the Houghton Library, Harvard University.)

fodder for a commonplace appetite for prodigies but also left room for provocative, if rather loose, interpretations. Over time, a tradition of ascribing cometary import to these passages was established. And in keeping with this tradition, some comets were thought to foreshadow landmark episodes in the sacred and natural history of the world.

STAR OF BETHLEHEM, HERALD OF JUDGMENT

In their adaptation of pagan cometary beliefs, some church fathers proposed that climactic moments in Christian history had been and would be marked by cometary exclamation points. This view gained new force in the writing of John of Damascus (ca. 675–748). In his *Exposition of the Orthodox Faith*, John argued that comets "are not any of the stars that were made in the beginning, but are formed at the same time by divine command and again dissolved."[32] Prior authors had viewed comets fundamentally as works of nature—either meteorological or astronomical—that cast an ominous shadow. John, however, was the first to state that comets were short-lived, special creations formed at God's discretion. John did not specify whether God generated comets by natural means or by miraculous ones, although most medieval authors believed that John suggested the latter. Nonetheless, it was clear that according to John, comets might well violate the natural order of stars as they fulfilled their divine ends.

The Star of Bethlehem was a similar starry object, being introduced in an extraordinary way by God after the Creation in order to herald the birth of Jesus. John examined it when he treated comets.[33] Although he did not explicitly state that the Magi's star was a comet, his text was open to this interpretation. Such a reading would certainly have been consistent with the ancient, folkloric view—for John, most recently expressed by Isidore of Seville—that comets could presage auspicious circumstances such as the birth of kings, heros, or holy persons.[34] Emperor Augustus, for example, had drawn on this tradition in a figurative sense when he interpreted the comet appearing at the start of his rule "as having been born for his own sake and as containing his own birth within it."[35]

Indeed, five centuries prior to this intimation by John of Damascus, Origen had boldly suggested that the Star of Bethlehem was a comet:

> The star that was seen in the east we consider to have been a new star, . . . partaking of the nature of those celestial bodies which appear at times, such as comets, or those meteors which resemble beams of wood, or beards, or wine jars. . . . We have read in the *Treatise on Comets* by Chaeremon the Stoic, that on some occasions also, when *good* was to happen, comets made their appearance. . . . If, then, at the commencement of new dynasties, . . . there arises a comet, . . . why should it be matter of wonder that at the birth of Him who was to introduce a new doctrine to the human race, . . . a [cometary] star should have arisen?[36]

Origen confessed that there was no prophecy that a comet would arise with respect to a particular kingdom, but he strove to bolster his interpretation by repeating a prophecy of Balaam in Numbers: "There shall step forth a star out of Jacob, and a sceptre [*shēvet*] shall rise out of Israel."[37] As in

Josephus's reference to a sword outstretched over Jerusalem, the combined allusions to a star and a spear or scepter (for *shēvet* means both) seemed pregnant with cometary import. Indeed, in the New English Bible, highly acclaimed for its translation, the verse reads: "A star shall come forth out of Jacob, a comet arise from Israel."

Later authors would variously take up this banner, although what the Magi saw has remained open to debate.[38] Thomas Aquinas (ca. 1225–1274), for instance, agreed that the Magi's star was newly created and moved by God's will. Although he placed it in the air near the earth, he rejected the notion that it was a comet, for comets, he insisted, "neither appear during the daytime nor vary their customary course." That is not to say, however, that the Star of Bethlehem had no cometary significance. Aquinas believed it acted like a comet in portending that Christ's heavenly kingdom would break apart and consume all earthly realms.[39] The cometary characteristics of the Star of Bethlehem were voiced as well by Jacobus de Voragine (1230–1298), archbishop of Genoa, in the *Golden Legend* (1275).[40] More widely owned by merchants and artisans than the Bible, printed editions of the *Golden Legend* may have popularized the idea in early modern Europe.[41] Visitors to the Scrovegni Chapel in Padua could also contemplate the Star of Bethlehem as a comet. The Florentine master artist Giotto di Bondone observed Halley's comet in 1301 and represented it as the Magi's star in a very moving fresco completed about 1304 (figs. 12–13).[42]

While the "comet of Bethlehem" augured for Christians the happy establishment of their kingdom on earth, Aquinas pointed out that comets presaged reform and salvation in another sense as well. Comets were apocalyptic monsters. He cited Saint Jerome's view that comets would be one of fifteen signs to precede the Day of Judgment: "On the *seventh* day all the stars, both planets and fixed stars, will throw out fiery tails like comets."[43]

Sixteenth-century artists such as Albrecht Dürer and Matthias Gerung drew on this tradition in their illustrations of the Book of Revelation. Dürer's best-known depiction of a comet was his engraving *Melencolia I* (1514), in which comets boding change and disaster were associated with Saturn, who ruled over the melancholy.[44] But this was not Dürer's first illustration of a comet. In 1498 and 1511 Dürer had examined the text in Revelation in which the sixth seal is opened:

> When he opened the sixth seal, I looked, and behold, there was a great earthquake; and the sun became black as sackcloth, the full moon became like blood, and the stars of the sky fell to the earth as the fig tree sheds its winter fruit when shaken by a gale.[45]

Dürer interpreted the falling stars as a shower of comets (fig. 14).[46] Cometary stars appeared in Gerung's Apocalypse series (1547) as well.[47] One woodcut (fig. 15) illustrated the verses:

Fig. 12. Giotto di Bondone, *Adoration of the Magi*, fresco in the Scrovegni Chapel, Padua, Italy. (Alinari/Art Resource, NY.)

> The third angel blew his trumpet, and a great star fell from heaven, blazing like a torch, and it fell on a third of the rivers and on the fountains of water. The name of the star is Wormwood.[48]

Another woodcut (fig. 16) depicted a cometary star bearing the key to the abyss:

> And the fifth angel blew his trumpet, and I saw a star fallen from heaven to earth, and he was given the key of the shaft of the bottomless pit; he opened the shaft of the bottomless pit, and from the shaft rose smoke like the smoke of a great furnace, and the sun and the air were darkened with the smoke from the shaft. Then from the smoke came locusts on the earth, and they were given power like the power of scorpions of the earth.[49]

Fig. 13. Star of Bethlehem as a comet. Stanislaw Lubieniecki, *Theatrum cometicum* (Leiden, 1681). (Courtesy of Adler Planetarium & Astronomy Museum, Chicago, Illinois.)

Texts in the Book of Revelation and the Gospels according to Matthew, Mark, and Luke resonate with both the classical prodigy literature and with folklore concerning the breakup of the heavens and disturbances to the earth at the end of the world. Common motifs that include the stars falling down or overtaking those in another constellation seem to suggest the appearance of comets.[50] It comes as no surprise, therefore, to find comets portrayed among the wonders of the last days in pictorial exegeses of verses in Revelation.[51]

Blazing stars as signs of the world's end are also to be found in manuscripts, tracts, and sermons in the early modern era. In England, some of the popular material, like the *Mirabilis Annus* pamphlets, was sensational street literature addressed to the disenfranchised.[52] On the learned, elite end

Fig. 14. Albrecht Dürer, German, 1471–1528, *The Opening of the Fifth and Sixth Seals*, from *The Apocalypse* (1498), engraving, 39.5 × 28.5 cm, Potter Palmer Collection, 1956.960. (Photograph © 1996, The Art Institute of Chicago. All Rights Reserved.)

Fig. 15. The Star Wormwood, described in Rev. 8:10–11. Matthias Gerung, *Apokalypse: Die Vision des 3. Engels* (1547), woodcut. (Kupferstichkabinett Staatliche Museen zu Berlin-Preußischer Kulturbesitz.)

Fig. 16. The star bearing the key to the bottomless pit, described in Rev. 9:1–3.
Matthias Gerung, *Apokalypse: Die Vision des 5. Engels* (1547), woodcut. (Kupferstichkabinett Staatliche Museen zu Berlin-Preußischer Kulturbesitz.)

of the scale was a discourse by Thomas Adams (fl. 1612–1653), the great Puritan preacher, and a sermon by William Strong (d. 1654), the independent divine whose congregation included many members of Parliament.[53] A self-described "country-ploughman" concluded, like Gerung, that the Star Wormwood was a comet, whereas Thomas Burnet (ca. 1635–1715) fell in line with Dürer's gloss of the stars falling at the opening of the sixth seal.[54] "I think this expression does chiefly refer to Comets," Burnet said, "And I am apt to think that Providence hath so contriv'd the periods of their motion, that there will be an unusual concourse of them at that time, within the view of the Earth, to be a prelude to this last and most Tragical Scene of the Sublunary World."[55] The latter days would be "dead and melancholy," with mountaintops smoking, earthquakes rumbling, and the sea sunken yet roaring, but the nights would offer more horrible specters "when the *Blazing-Stars* appear, like so many Furies, with their lighted Torches, threatning to set all on fire," Burnet declared.[56]

A hundred years prior to Burnet, Andreas Celichius, the Lutheran bishop of Altmark, also preached that the physical nature of comets made them appropriate heralds of the impending Day of Judgment. "Whoever would know the comet's real source and nature," Celichius admonished, "must not merely gape and stare at the scientific theory that it is an earthy, greasy, tough, and sticky vapour and mist, rising into the upper air and set ablaze by the celestial heat." The vapor might be mundane, and the fire celestial, but not in the Aristotelian sense. The vapor was "the thick smoke of human sins, rising every day, every hour, every moment, full of stench and horror, before the face of God, and becoming gradually so thick as to form a comet, with curled and plaited tresses, which at last is kindled by the hot and fiery anger of the Supreme Heavenly Judge." The supernatural ignition was accomplished so that mortals might witness and heed this blazing monument to human depravity.[57]

Celichius's unusual argument had a following as late as 1620 in the work of Conrad Dieterich, archdeacon of Marburg, professor of philosophy and director of studies at the University of Giessen, and Lutheran bishop in southwestern Germany.[58] Yet the "sin-theory" had its early critics too. In 1579, Andreas Dudith, a Hungarian divine and famous humanist, retorted that if comets were composed from the sins of mortals, they would never be absent from the sky.[59]

We have seen how many viewed comets as divine creations to herald the birth of Jesus or the Day of Judgment. Having ushered in the Christian faith on earth, comets would witness its denouement. What these events had in common was a general sense in which comets presaged world reformation and the salvation of the elect. In keeping with this perspective, comets were thought to punctuate other points along the sacred time line. Dieterich, for instance, insisted that the first comet in world history had appeared with Noah's Flood, and Edmond Halley and William Whiston would return to this theme at the end of the seventeenth century.[60]

TIME OF THE END

It was but a small step from a theoretical discussion of harbingers of the Second Coming to an effort to establish empirically, if perhaps only roughly, the time of the end. In 1522, Martin Luther (1483–1546) noted in a sermon on the Second Coming:

> We see the Sun to be darkened and the Moon, the Stars to Fall, men to be distressed, the winds and waters to make a noise, and whatever else is foretold of the Lord, all of them to come to pass as it were together. Besides, we have seen not a few Comets, having the form of the Cross, imprinted from heaven, both on the bodies and garments of men, new kinds of diseases, as the French Pox, and some others. How many other Signs also, and unusual impressions, have we seen in the Heavens, in the Sun, Moon, Stars, Rain-bows and strange Apparitions, in these last four years? Let us at least acknowledge these to be Signs, and Signs of some great and notable change.[61]

Events of the sixteenth century confirmed many in their belief that they lived in the last days. Ancient and modern prophecies were scrutinized, and their predictions were compared to recent and unexpected occurrences in the natural and political worlds.[62] Pregnant with meaning but typical in its vagueness was the reputedly ancient prophecy of the sibyl Tiburtina inscribed on a marble slab unearthed from a Swiss mountain in 1520.

> A Star shall arise in *Europe* over the *Iberians*, towards the great House of the North, whose Beams shall unexpectedly enlighten the whole World.
>
> This shall be in a most desired time, when Mortals wearied with Wars shall Unanimously desire Peace. They shall strive indeed by occasion of a Long-lasting *Interregnum*, with various studies which shall obtain the Reignes of Empire. But at last, the Offspring of the Antient Blood shall overcome, and proceed victoriously by force of Arms, until resisted by contrary Fates. For about the same time, this *Star* being set, another Coeval Light blazing with more Ardent Flames of War, shall spread his Empire even to the Coasts of the *Antipodes*.
>
> But first, *France* shall submit her Neck to his Yoak, and *Brittany* suppliant in Ships, shall cast her self at his Feet; *Italy* faintly breathing towards Scepters so high, shall stretch out to him her Languishing Hand. But this bright Beam before his time, shall, with the vast desire of men abscond himself in the Clouds of the Gods.
>
> Who being extinct, after direful and bloody Comets, and flashings of Fire seen in the Heavens, there shall remain nothing for the future safe or healthy amongst Men: The Firmament of Heaven shall be dissolved, and the Planets be opposed in contrary courses, the Sphears shall justle one amongst another, and the fixed Stars move faster than the Planets; The Seas swell as high as the Mountains, and nothing remain but Night, Destruction, Ruine, Damnation, and Eternal Misery.[63]

According to the sibyl, comets and a great northern star augured the end, and Cornelius Gemma, Tycho Brahe, and Tommaso Campanella were among those who pondered the figurative or literal meaning of the prophecy.[64] Awestruck and gladdened by the new star of 1572, the comet of 1577, and the return of the great conjunctions of Jupiter and Saturn to the sign of Aries, they looked forward to profound social changes and the start of a new golden age.

Sibylline oracles and ancient prophecies also attracted the attention of Paracelsus (1493–1541), for he believed that the dissolution of the present world would be foreshadowed by a constellation of prodigies—comets overhead and isolated uprisings, widespread wars, and floods below. The comet of 1531 heightened his expectations since it appeared when the neighborhood of Sankt Gallen had been blighted by poor harvests, epidemics, and political and economic turmoil. The Swiss Confederation was approaching war, and Sankt Gallen was caught up in the conflicts among Catholics, Anabaptists, and Zwinglians. Paracelcus thought the comet augured the final assault on the Antichrist. He set the date for the vindication of the elect as early as 1542 and believed that all prophecies would be fulfilled by 1560.[65]

Paracelsus sent his tract on the comet of 1531 to Ulrich Zwingli, the Swiss reformer, who likewise believed that the blazing star betokened disaster.[66] How were people expected to respond? Since the early sixteenth century, gloomy astrological predictions disseminated in pamphlets were intended as a call to the people to awake, repent, and reform.[67] Pamphleteers urged people not only to be more pious but to amend social practices and institutions. Indeed, this was an age when prophecies were marshaled by political opponents in order to validate their positions and attract new followers. It should therefore come as no surprise that cometary portents were among the arsenal of monstrous prodigies used in the polemical battles of the Protestant Reformation.

REFORMATION IN RELIGION

Martin Luther and Philip Melanchthon (1497–1560) helped to establish comets in this new propagandist role. In analyzing monstrous births in a 1523 pamphlet, they broke with tradition by interpreting two monsters as specific portents of the Roman Church's imminent ruin, rather than as signs of general political upheaval through war. Their influential pamphlet injected arguments about monsters and other prodigies into the heart of Protestant and Catholic debate.[68] Melanchthon's and Luther's views on comets were widely known, being reprinted as epigrams to German tracts on cometary prognostication. Luther at one time declared comets to be "harlot stars" (*Huren-Sternen*) and works of the devil, but mostly he stressed their divine purpose.[69] "Whatever moves in the heaven in an unusual way is cer-

tainly a sign of God's wrath," he wrote.[70] The heathen may ascribe natural causes to comets, he preached, but they were created by God to instill horror.[71] As already mentioned, Luther saw in comets signs of the latter days. In letters and lectures, Melanchthon likewise classified comets and monstrous births among the divine signs mentioned in Scripture.[72] He composed a poem on the comet of 1556, concluding that God would soon crush the blaspheming Turks and pope.[73]

English and Scottish reformers gave voice to similar polemical statements. Writing to Henry VIII from Germany during the transition period between the old and new church, Thomas Cranmer reported the apparition of a comet and other celestial prodigies in 1532. "What strange things these tokens do signify to come hereafter, God knoweth, for they do not lightly appear but against some great mutation; and it hath not be[en] seen (as I suppose) that so ma[ny] comets have appeared in so short [a] time."[74] John Knox in his chronicle of the Scottish Reformation also took notice of comets and monstrous births as signs from heaven and warnings of crafty enterprises and the "Fidelitie of Princes, gydit by Preistis, whensoevir they seik thair awin Affectiounis to be served."[75] In a similar tone, *The Complaynt of Scotlande* (1549) affirmed that when a comet is seen, "ther occurris haistily eftir it sum grit myscheif."[76]

Although the propagandist nature of cometary prognostications will be discussed at greater length below, a single example may help to illustrate just how tightly comets, astrology, and Reformation politics could be enmeshed. During February 1524, all planets were to be in conjunction in Pisces, and astrologers warned of a catastrophic flood, severe weather, social unrest, a revolt of peasants, and attempts to overthrow the established secular and religious order.[77] An eye-catching woodcut that adorned the title page of a prognosticative work by Leonhart Reynmann depicts the celestial bodies meeting in Pisces. From the belly of the fish, a shower of rain falls upon a town and drowns it. Steeples topple. As fife and drum strike the cadence, banner-carrying peasants confront the ecclesiastical authority under the sign of Pisces. Beneath the fish's tail, a comet (perhaps that of 1523) brazenly reinforces the somber forecast (fig. 17).[78] The fact that the peasants did revolt in Germany in 1525 was seen by some to confirm the powers of prognostication, but other authorities recognized that such pamphlets had a polemical edge, and prophecies of civil disorder were designed to be self-fulfilling.[79]

While reformers marshaled contemporary comets for their political ends, later Protestants retrospectively saw those comets as confirming the wisdom of the Reformation. John Bainbridge (1582–1643), Savilian professor of astronomy at Oxford, believed that God stamped his approval on the Reformation with five comets, which appeared during ten years of Luther's preaching.[80] Puritan divine and president of Harvard College Increase Mather (1639–1723) confessed that the comets appearing before Wycliffe, Hus, and Luther began to publish their opinions were happy omens.[81]

Fig. 17. Great conjunction in Pisces, with comet to reinforce the forecast. Leonhart Reynmann, *Practica uber die grossen und manigfeltigen Coniunction der Planeten* (Nuremberg, 1524). (Courtesy of the Library of Congress.)

Thus we have seen how many scholars followed John of Damascus and viewed comets as miraculous creations formed by God at his discretion in order to herald the renovation of the world. As monsters, comets presaged the birth of the Christian Messiah, the redemption of the chosen and the downfall of the wicked, the reformation of the church and the final battle with the Antichrist. When the world's days became numbered and the end drew near, comets would blaze in the heavenly vault as hellish torches for the damned and sacred beacons for the rejoicing saints. Such was the grand religious design in which comets participated. At a local, shortsighted level, bearded stars continued to presage imminent events like the death of princes, political or religious revolutions, plague, or bad harvests. Compared to the birth of the Messiah and the final judgment, these were paltry events, but they were seen as ways in which God took sinful man to task, chastised him, and reminded him of those more magnificent occasions.

Divination

> . . . These Blazeing Starrs!
>
> Threaten the World with Famine, Plague, & Warrs:
>
> To Princes, Death: to Kingdoms, many Crosses:
>
> To all Estates, inevitable Losses!
>
> To Herds-men, Rot; to Plowmen, haples Seasons:
>
> To Saylors, Storms; to Cittyes, Civil Treasons.
>
> Du Bartas[1]

ASTRONOMERS and churchmen throughout the early modern era advised the faithful to take heed of comets. "Such unnatural births in the heavens . . . always have had something great to deliver to this lower world," Tycho Brahe (1546–1601) remarked.[2] Yes, agreed William Green, a minister of the gospel. "When God intends to punish a Nation, Country, or City, he is first pleased to give them notice thereof by Apparitions or Prodigies; and there hath never been any notable Apparition or Prodigy seen in the Heavens, but it hath been attended in the Sequel with some more than ordinary Troubles."[3] Astrologer John Gadbury (1627–1704) concurred, "I ever did and yet do, look upon Comets to be like Beacons; whose use and office, is, to give warning to mankinde of approaching dangers."[4]

What skills were needed to see the rough waters ahead? What talents were required to sharpen and decode the terrible vision reflected in those "Looking-Glasses of Gods wrath"?[5] Astrology held out a grab bag of divinatory techniques from which each prognosticator was free to pluck the tools of his choice. Ten key factors could be studied—the comet's color, conjunction, zodiacal position, mundane house, direction of tail, site of nucleus, shape, motion, duration, and resemblance to comets of the past.

COLOR

According to the standard Renaissance theory derived from Aristotle, comets consisted of terrestrial exhalations full of metalline and mineral vapors not only thrust out of the earth's bowels by an internal heat from subterranean spirits, but also extracted from the earth by the external heat of celes-

tial bodies, especially the heat of the sun. Pushed and drawn upward, the "Fuliginous Smoak" hung in the upper atmosphere until it ignited. It was assumed that comets took their colors from whatever planets were responsible for extracting the exhalations from the earth.[6] The respective colors of the planets were:[7]

Saturn	dusky, leaden, pale
Jupiter	splendid, brilliant, clear
Mars	fiery, red
Sun	golden
Moon	silver
Venus	yellow
Mercury	changeable

Astrologically each planet had a different influence on the earth. By using color to link a comet to its ruling planet, the astrologer drew on planetary lore in predicting the outcome of a particular blazing star. If a comet changed color, he simply compounded the effects of each planet.

The comet of 1680–1681, for example, reportedly changed colors three times during the course of its apparition. William Knight prophesied that when pale and Saturnian, the comet portended nothing less than fear, trouble, vexation, murmuring, repining, exile and banishment, scarcity of food, penury, grievous sickness, plague, consumption, agues, lingering distempers, tempestuous winds, shipwrecks, inundations, frosts and snows, and the destruction of fruits by worms or caterpillars. When the comet turned bright, clear, and Jovial, things began to look up. It then signified not only struggles over religious matters, laws, and privileges, but also a plentiful, fertile period, pleasant salubrious air, and seasonable winds and showers. These fine, Jovial events were not to last, however, for the comet turned a Martial red. There would be excessive hot weather, pestiferous winds, terrible thunder and lightning, and tempests. Rivers and fountains would dry up, and agricultural products would become scarce. People would be stricken with violent fevers, and their houses would burn down. An abundance of thieves, robbers, and pirates would scour the land and coasts. Soon to follow were wars, quarrels, naval battles, shipwrecks, slaughters, bloodshed, tumults, massacres, and changes of governors and governments. But that was not all to be forecast. Since the comet took on various colors, it had to be Mercurial. Although this augured much wit and shrewd policy among men engaged in business affairs, many more—alas—would employ their wits in vile and treacherous affairs and afterward would pretend to be innocent of their deeds. A Mercurial comet also denoted the demise of great men, wars, sickness, and food shortages.[8]

Not only could a comet change color, it was possible for it to exhibit various hues simultaneously. Tycho Brahe thought the head of the comet of 1577 had an evil, pallid tone while its tail was fiery and dark. His prognostication, therefore, compounded the effects of Saturn and Mars.[9]

CONJUNCTIONS

Another factor in cometary prognostication was the comet's possible conjunction with any of the planets or the major stars like Antares or Regulus. Through conjunctions the comet would be influenced by the great heavenly bodies, and its significance would be derived from them.[10] When a comet in 1618 conjoined with Mercury—identified by classical mythology as the messenger of heaven and patron of arts and traffic—John Bainbridge optimistically fancied that the East Indies would present Britain with aromatic and wholesome spices, precious jewels, and oriental riches.[11] Bainbridge, who styled himself a "Doctor of Physicke, and lover of Mathematicks," was on his way to becoming the first Savilian professor of astronomy at Oxford, and his candidacy may have been helped by the unusually upbeat nature of his propagandist tract, which was dedicated to King James.[12] Most contemporaries, however, viewed the conjunction in a bleaker light but, like Bainbridge, thought it astrologically significant.

PASSAGE THROUGH ZODIAC AND PROMINENT CONSTELLATIONS

Passage through zodiacal figures or prominent constellations provided the astrologer with further insight into a comet's presumed significance (fig. 18). There were three main schemes of interpretation in use. First, every country was assigned a zodiacal constellation, and a comet threatened those ruled by the constellation in which it appeared.[13] William Lilly, the astrologer, reassured his English countrymen that the comet of 1678 appeared in Taurus and so affected Russia, Poland, Sweden, Norway, Sicily, Algiers, Lorraine, and Rome.[14] Since the 1680 comet traversed part of Scorpio and Sagittarius, John Hill predicted that the French, German, and Spanish were likely to engage in war, perhaps among themselves. The English were not to be too smug, however. Since the comet passed into Capricorn, which was a sign for northern Scotland, Hill warned that the Scots might rebel against England. Additionally, Sagittarius was opposite to London's ascendant, indicating that the comet augured infectious air for the metropolis, from which would spring "Raging Pestilentall Diseases, Rumours and Real Wars and home bred Divisions, poysoning, [and] open and private Murders."[15]

The second technique for interpreting the motion of a comet through a constellation was to examine the iconography of that particular set of stars. For example, if the comet cut across the arm in which Virgo held a sheaf of grain, it portended crop failure. If the comet traversed the genital region of an anthropomorphic constellation, it presaged immorality. If it burned in the head of the northern or southern serpents, it brought poisonings. If it blazed in Sagittarius, it punished those associated with equestrian pursuits, archery, and the armaments of war. Similarly, a comet in Taurus presaged

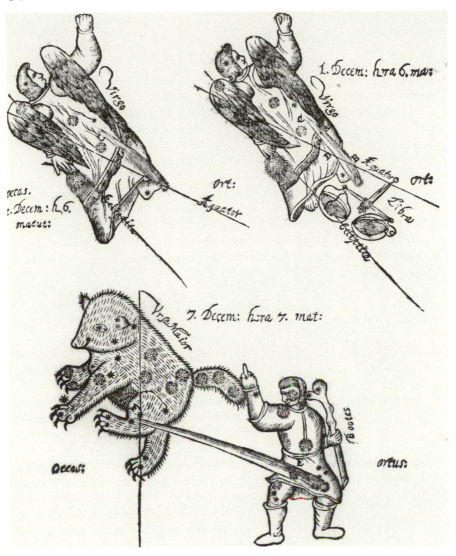

Fig. 18. Motion of the comet of December 1618 through the constellations, as observed by Cysat, with his telescope and sextant. Johann Baptista Cysat, *Mathemata astronomica de loco, motu, magnitudine, et causis cometae* (Ingolstadt, 1619). (Courtesy of Adler Planetarium & Astronomy Museum, Chicago, Illinois.)

the loss of cattle; in Aries, a sheep rot; in Pisces, a dearth of fish, and losses and crosses at sea. Such reasoning dated back to Pliny, who also considered the imagery formed by the alignment of a comet with respect to certain fixed stars. If a comet formed an equilateral triangle or rectangular quadrilateral with respect to other stars, the geometrical configuration presaged the birth of geniuses and a revival of learning.[16]

There was a lot of latitude in the iconographic technique, and the astrologer could put a positive spin on his predictions if he was so inclined. An optimist and propagandist, John Bainbridge claimed to deplore the illusory precepts of "vulgar Astrologie" but could not resist the temptation to interpret the comet of 1618 according to celestial pictograms of his own devising. Its tail pointing toward Virgo's flourishing spike, the comet had traveled from Libra toward Ariadne's Crown. For Bainbridge, the crown symbolized the imperial diadem of the whole British Isles. In reward for justice, the people would have a common throne and bountiful harvest. Passing near the eye of Ophiuchus's serpent, the comet reminded members of government to keep their eyes open lest they fall prey to plots like the "hellish gunpowder-treason" (i.e., the scheme associated with Guy Fawkes, to blow up the king and Parliament in 1605). When the comet cut across the spear of Arctophylax, it warned England to maintain its military discipline in times of peace. Bainbridge was worried by the deleterious effects of voluptuous living. "Muskets [had] turned into Tabacco pipes," he lamented, and English valor was going up in the smoke of the "outlandish weed." The comet of 1618 therefore called for reform, and despite his disclaimers, Bainbridge's gloss followed the astrological conventions of the second technique for interpreting the motion of a comet through the constellations.[17]

In the third technique, prognostication focused on the affairs traditionally designated by each zodiacal figure. According to common belief, comets in earthy signs portended barrenness due to drought, whereas comets in watery signs augured barrenness due to excessive rain. Comets in airy signs signified mighty winds, seditions, and pestilence, and those in fiery signs heralded ghastly wars and gruesome slaughter.[18]

William Knight kept more or less to this program in analyzing the passage of the comet of 1680–1681 through Scorpio, Sagittarius, Capricorn, Aquarius, Pisces, and Aries. For instance, Aquarius was an airy sign, despite its image as the Water-Bearer, and the comet's motion across it announced dark, obscure air, great winds, thunder and lightning, sweeping plague, cruelties, slaughter, and protracted war.[19] But more typically, astrologers used the scheme only as a starting point for their predictions. Lilly, for example, examined the 1678 comet's passage through Taurus, an earthy sign, and prophesied not only the loss of cattle and provisions one might expect from drought, but also the devastation of crops by caterpillars, bloodshed in battle, poverty, and numerous cold, wet calamities more in keeping with a watery sign: sea tempests, monstrous floods, strange thunder and hail, and particularly chronic and tedious diseases, such as consumption, long-enduring colds, violent coughs, agues, "griping in the Guts," and cold phlegmatic diseases that much afflicted children.[20]

As in the situation in which a comet changed color, a comet that traversed several zodiacal constellations heralded a fabric of interlocking disasters whose gory threads were dyed by the respective ruling signs of the zodiac.

ASTROLOGICAL HOUSES AND
CARDINAL ORIENTATIONS

Astrologers disagreed on the import of a comet that appeared in one of the cardinal directions, or that rose or set heliacally. Ptolemy emphasized the nearness of impending calamities. A comet in the Orient indicated rapidly approaching events; in the Occident, slowly approaching ones.[21] To Bede, the appearance of an eastern and western comet in 729 was more suggestive of the site and hour of affliction:

> For one went before the sun at his rising in the morning; the other followed the setting of the sun in the evening, both presaging as it were terrible destruction to the east as well as the west: or, if you will say, one was the forerunner of the coming of day, the other of night, to signify that at both times miseries were hanging over men's heads.[22]

Tycho concurred with Bede. Inasmuch as the 1577 comet "first let itself be seen with the setting of the sun," it presaged calamities for Europe west of Denmark.[23] Girolamo Cardano, however, stressed the nature of the augured event. A comet in the east signified the rise of an eminent law-giver, and a comet in midheaven, the rise of a very powerful king. A comet in the west, however, or in a succedent house seldom portended anything so illustrious.[24]

Cardano reminds us that when an astrologer referred to the cardinal points, what he had in mind may not have been points of the compass but rather a scheme of partitioning the sky. His horizon and meridian cut the zodiac, which revolved around him every twenty-four hours, and established a fixed reference frame for dividing the heavens. The simplest division was into four quadrants separated by four points known in Latin as *cardines*. The first point—the *horoscopus* or *ascendens*—marked the point of the ecliptic rising above the horizon at a given time. The second point was the *medium caeli* or midheaven, located where the astrologer's meridian crossed the ecliptic. The third point was the *occasus* or setting point of the ecliptic. The fourth point, the *imum caeli*, was below the horizon and diametrically opposite the midheaven point. These cardinal points also helped to establish the places of the twelve mundane houses, which, like the quadrants, served as a fixed framework within which the zodiac revolved. The houses did not contain equal numbers of degrees and their allocation was dependent on the degree of the ecliptic rising over the horizon at a given time and place.[25]

With respect to a comet, astrologers charted the houses at the time of the comet's "birth" or key moments in its "lifetime." Tycho, for instance, drew up two horoscopes for the 1585 comet—one for its nativity, which he con-

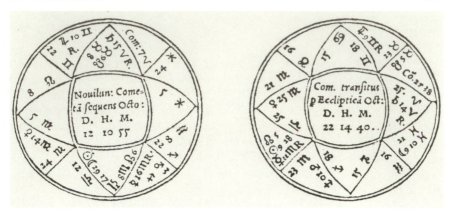

Fig. 19. Horoscopes of the 1585 comet drawn up by Tycho Brahe. Tycho Brahe, *De cometa seu stella crinita rotunda, quae anno antecedente in Octobri & Novembri apparuit* (Uraniburg, 1586). (Reproduced from *Tychonis Brahe Dani opera omnia* [Copenhagen, 1922], 4:404, 406.)

nected to the time of the new moon; and one for the moment when it crossed the ecliptic (fig. 19).[26]

The passage of a comet through different houses had special connotations. In the ninth house, a comet signaled religious scandal and hazards to the church. In the eighth, tenth, or twelfth houses, it announced pestilence or the spoil of corn. In the eleventh house, it heralded great slaughter and the destruction of noblemen. In the ninth or eleventh houses, a comet might also presage legal controversies or the dissolution of the law. A comet blazing in the cardinal signs, or in the tenth house, augured the demise of kings.[27] Thus when a comet first appeared after sunset on 11 November 1577, it was in the eighth house. This was the house of death, and Tycho predicted gruesome pestilence. A few evenings later, Tycho found the comet to be in the ninth house, which was associated with religion. He accordingly forecast the rise of new sects, his conviction being strengthened by his calculation that the comet had stood with Saturn in the fourth house at the moment of its first light (10 November, at one hour and twenty minutes past midnight).[28]

The importance of astrological houses for prognostication was supported by the *Centiloquium*, which circulated widely in medieval manuscripts and Renaissance printed texts. Although probably spurious, this work was attributed to Ptolemy and carried the full weight of his authority. According to the *Centiloquium*, if a comet was eleven signs from the sun, it portended the death of a prince in power. If the comet appeared in a succedent house, the treasury of the kingdom would thrive, but there would be a new governor. A comet appearing in a falling house boded sickness and sudden death.[29]

POINTING OF TAIL

Since the days of Ptolemy, the direction in which a comet's tail pointed was also a significant piece of evidence for the prognosticator.[30] "A Star with a Beard, or long Tayl . . . denotes the Death of Great and Noble Men, and Wars in those Countries unto which it points its Tayl," opined one astrologer.[31] Although the 1577 comet appeared in the west and principally menaced westward lands, Tycho observed that it would "also spew its venom" over the Muscovites and Tartars to the northeast, for its tail swept in their direction. Ivan the Terrible might even fall by 1583.[32] Analogously, an English pamphleteer predicted that popish power might be totally dissolved, because the 1680 comet's tail pointed southeast toward Rome.[33] Others correlated terrestrial locations with each constellation. If a comet tail pointed toward a given constellation, then the corresponding country would be influenced.

POSITION OF NUCLEUS

Just as the tail proved to be a signpost toward death and destruction, a comet nucleus overhead was no happy matter. The country directly beneath a comet was especially liable to malevolent influences.[34]

SHAPES AND SIZES

Ever since Ptolemy had correlated the size of comets and the number of visually discernible parts in their heads with the severity of ensuing winds, astrologers saw magnitude as an index of the vehemence of future events.[35]

   Comets were also seen to appear in multifarious and sometimes hideous shapes. Although Pliny mentioned a comet in the friendly shape of a flute, as well as comets formed like military instruments, early modern authors witnessed primarily fiery swords, daggers, torches, brooms, and monstrous faces (figs. 20–27).[36] The figures of comets were said to be mystical characters by which men might understand through analogy what good or evil accidents would befall them.[37] Pliny and Ptolemy were rather oblique on this point,[38] but others like Jacques Gaffarel, drawing on the work of Cornelius Gemma and sundry esteemed scholars, did not hesitate to enumerate general rules for reading these celestial hieroglyphics:

> If they [comets] are figured like a Columne, or Piller; they denote the Constancy of some Prince, or of some Great Saint, or else of some People, or Nation.
>   . . . When a Comet, or fiery Meteor, is Round, Cleare, Bright, and not Duskie at all, but lookes as it were, like another Sun; it may signifie the Birth of some Great Prince.

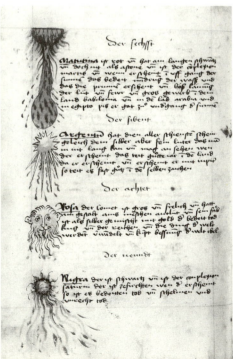

Figs. 20, 21, and 22. Comets known as Veru and Venaculus (*upper left*); Partica, Miles, and Ascone (*upper right*); and Matutina, Argentum, Rosa, and Nigra (*lower left*). *Book of Planets, Anatomical Treatise, Book of Synonyms*, probably Ulm, ca. 1450–1475, illumination on vellum. (83.MO.137, MS Ludwig XII 8, fols. 62^v–63^v. Collection of the J. Paul Getty Museum, Los Angeles, California.)

Fig. 23. Marvelous comet in fifth century. Hartmann Schedel, *Buch der Chroniken* (Nuremberg, 1493). (WOP-156d. Courtesy of Adler Planetarium & Astronomy Museum, Chicago, Illinois.)

. . . If they be of a Pyramidall Figure, we shall then suffer great Losses by Fire; and, by way of Analogy, may conclude, of some Tyranny approaching.

. . . If they be of much Extent, Waved, and Dissipated here and there, in the forme of Waters; they then denote Seditions in the People: seeing that among all the Hieroglyphical Characters, that signifie the People, This of *Water* is the Chiefest; according to that Vision of the Prophet: *Aquae multae, populi multi.* And it hath been very often observed, that after any Inundations, either of the Sea, or of Rivers; the People have presently also made Insurrections.

. . . If they be of the figure of a *Horne*, which is the *Hieroglyphicke of Power*; as may be observed out of the Scriptures, in very many places: they foreshew the Great strength of some Monarch, and an Absolute Power.

. . . If they beare the figure of a *Sword*, they presage Desolations, which shall be caused by the Sword. . . . If the Comet be figured like a Trumpet; it then also foretells of Wars: but if it be of the forme either of a Dart, or Arrow; or else of a Javelin, it denounceth both Warre, and Pestilence; the Effects whereof flye abroad, as swift as an Arrow.[39]

Less sanguine and perhaps less inventive than Gaffarel, many others alleged that comet shapes literally announced how God intended to punish sinners. A fiery sword implied war, a torch suggested a raging, hellish fire, and a broom presaged a general housecleaning in which God would sweep unclean spirits from the land.[40]

MOTION

Cometary motion with respect to the sun also indicated who would be affected and when. Speaking of the 1680 comet and no doubt alluding to the sun as the king of the solar system, Knight wrote, "That in regard from its first appearance, it took its progress towards the Sun, [and] its Effects will

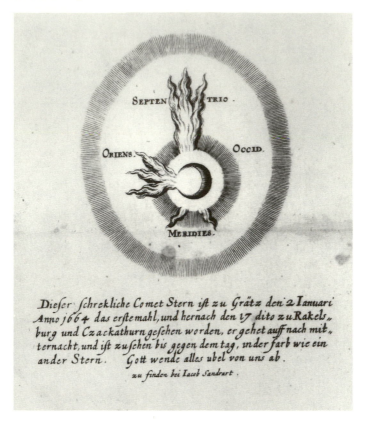

Fig. 24. A hideous, frightening comet that appeared in 1664. The caption piously exclaims, "May God divert all misfortunes from us." German broadside. (WOP-24. Courtesy of Adler Planetarium & Astronomy Museum, Chicago, Illinois.)

be manifested in a great measure on Eminent persons, and ineminent Actions."[41] In the time-honored tradition of the *Centiloquium*, foreign invasion was heralded by a comet that moved from west to east. A static comet signaled an indigenous enemy and seditious activities.[42] For Lilly, quick motions implied a mutation of empires. Retrograde motions, seen as uncommon, augured rare occurrences. The retrograde motion of a comet in 1618 foreshadowed the activities of "Retrograde Lords" whose domination of their subjects ended in rebellion.[43]

DURATION

There were no hard-and-fast rules concerning the duration of a comet's malevolent influence, although astrologers since Ptolemy had argued for a correlation between the term of the apparition and the interval of calamities.[44]

Fig. 25. Fiery swords, torches, and brooms. Comets in Alain Mallet, *Description de l'univers* (Paris, 1683). (WOP-150c. Courtesy of Adler Planetarium & Astronomy Museum, Chicago, Illinois.)

Lilly calculated a year of disaster for every day a comet was observed.[45] Another common measure was one half-year of influence for each day of cometary apparition.[46] Therefore, when a comet in 1618 appeared for twenty-eight days, it portended fourteen to twenty-eight years of affliction. A short-lived comet could be potent medicine for a sick society!

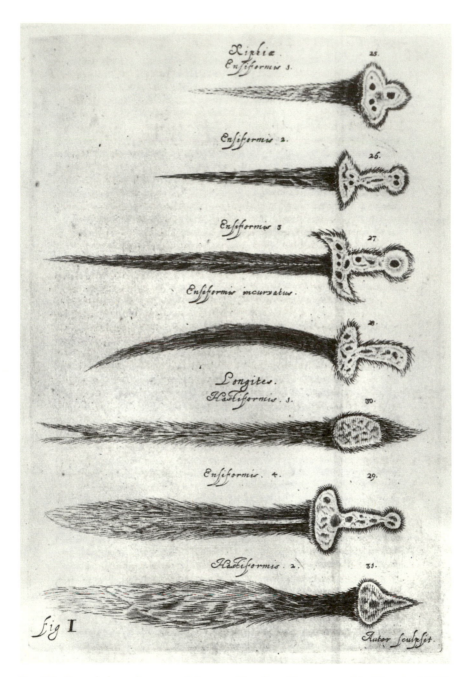

Fig. 26. Sword-shaped comets. Johannes Hevelius, *Cometographia* (Danzig, 1668). (Courtesy of Adler Planetarium & Astronomy Museum, Chicago, Illinois.)

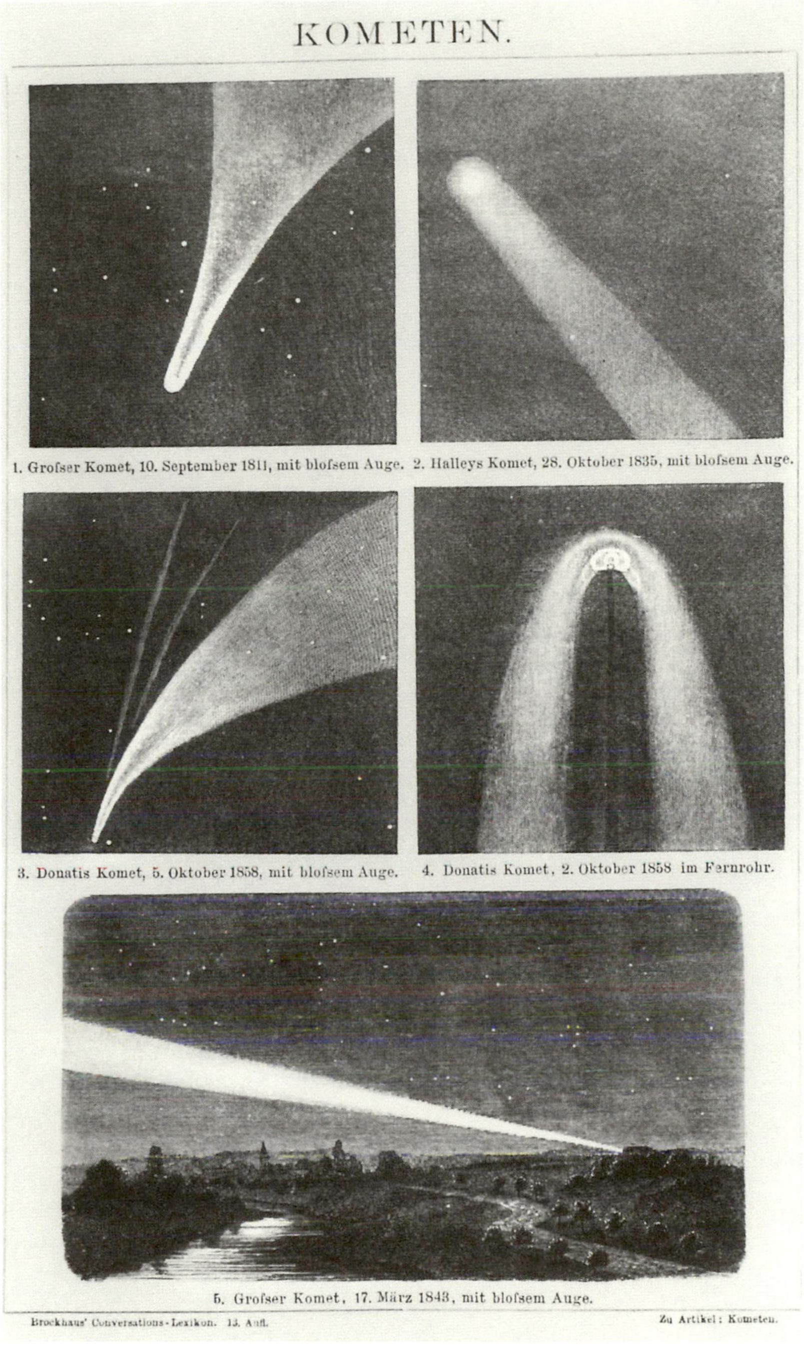

KOMETEN.

1. Grofser Komet, 10. September 1811, mit blofsem Auge.   2. Halleys Komet, 28. Oktober 1835, mit blofsem Auge.

3. Donatis Komet, 5. Oktober 1858, mit blofsem Auge.   4. Donatis Komet, 2. Oktober 1858 im Fernrohr.

5. Grofser Komet, 17. März 1843, mit blofsem Auge.

Brockhaus' Conversations-Lexikon. 13. Aufl.   Zu Artikel: Kometen.

Fig. 27. Realistic shapes of comets seen by the naked eye and by telescope. *Brockhaus' Conversations-Lexikon*, 13th ed. (Leipzig, 1882–1887), s.v. "Kometen." (WOP-183. Courtesy of Adler Planetarium & Astronomy Museum, Chicago, Illinois.)

HISTORICAL INDUCTION

Lastly, historical induction was a common tool of the prognosticator. The astrologer combed the historical records of past cometary horrors. If a present comet followed a path similar to any previous comet's, then the astrologer would confidently forecast a repetition of the misfortunes connected to the earlier comet.[47]

Perhaps based on historical evidence as much as on folklore were hypotheses that correlated future events to the timing of apparitions in the human life cycle. For instance, Cardano reasoned that when a comet appeared during the fourth or eighth month of pregnancy, the newborn child would prove to be prone to anger and quarrels. If the child was of "quality," his hot temper would be expressed in a public forum, and he would be prone to sedition.[48]

This canon of cometary divination offered much room for men to predict numerous and diverse disasters to attend comets. Of course, there were many examples of multiple and contradictory interpretations of the same comet. It remains to be asked just what was the engine behind all this prognostic activity. What satisfaction or power might one gain by consulting so inconsistent a prophet as the cometary astrologer? These questions must be asked if we are to understand the reasons for the seventeenth-century decline in cometary divination—a decline that I contend has been largely misunderstood[49]—and if we are to appreciate what aspects or metaphysical premises of the divinatory enterprise astronomers such as Tycho, Kepler, Newton, and Halley felt comfortable retaining.

Part of the answer is to be found in the realm of politics and people's desire to see providence manifest in both the social and natural worlds. In my discussion of Roman antiquity and the Reformation, I touched on the political and religious messages embedded in predictions from comets and chronicles about them. In the next chapter, I will analyze the social functions of prognostication and historical narration in depth. Although similar reports could be written for many early modern European countries, I will focus on England in order to provide background material essential to our understanding of Newton and Halley's cometography.

CHAPTER IV

Portents and Politics

> But if a true comet should appear in the heaven itself or an earth-
> quake should ensue, then it would be time for us astronomers
> along with the politicians to sharpen our pens.
>
> —Johannes Kepler, prognostic calendar for 1618

DIVERSE techniques of divination from comets often led to radically divergent and contradictory predictions. The plastic nature of the forecasts was
precisely what made comets of great interest to the populace. To understand the appeal, we must look at the types of prognosticative messages,
how they were transmitted, and to whom they were directed. I shall confine
my study to early modern England and will begin with a brief discussion of
popular literature and theater, for it is in works dear to the common people
that the social meanings of comets are most manifest.[1]

IN STREETS AND ALEHOUSES

In 1681, pamphleteer and preacher William Green and astrologer William
Knight offered an interpretation of recent comets without "any Cramp
words or Quaint Language, but in a homely and plain Stile" readily understood by common folk.[2] Just how common was their audience? One way to
gauge this is to examine the printed medium that conveyed their message.

Green and Knight's chapbook is an example of the vast quantity of
ephemeral texts aimed at the lowest levels of the literate in early modern
England, but not confined exclusively to that audience.[3] Between 1550 and
1700, 3,000 broadside ballads were registered with the Stationers' Company, but another 12,000 likely circulated. Almanacs sold at the staggering
rate of 400,000 copies per year in the 1660s: that is, two almanacs for every
five households. Add to this the distribution of chapbooks and cheap tracts.
The London bookseller George Thomason collected nearly 15,000 pamphlets and over 7,000 news-sheets published between 1641 and 1662. The
chapbook stock of a single publisher in 1664 was about 90,000 volumes.
These materials were not only plentiful but affordable. Broadsides sold
for a halfpenny or penny; almanacs for twopence; chapbooks three- to
sixpence. As many as 300 ballad-sellers hawked their sheets on London

street corners in 1641. By 1700, an estimated 10,000 petty chapmen worked England's roads.[4]

Many prosperous tradesmen, craftsmen, yeomen, and husbandmen parted with their pennies in order to learn the latest news or sing the newest songs. The middling sort who made up about 30–40 percent of the English population were the principal buyers of street literature. Pennies were real money for the lower sort, who were another 50–60 percent of the population. But these laborers and cottagers, milkmaids and fishwives, even though largely illiterate, could still indulge their taste for this escapist and edifying literature. Political pamphlets were recited in the marketplace, and ballads were sung on the commons and in the alehouses where they papered the walls.[5] Nor were the urban elite and gentry above partaking of this form of literature. Samuel Pepys was an avid collector.[6]

These popular texts entertained and educated. More than drinking songs or tales of love, ballads reported fires, floods, political events, and monstrous prodigies. Lurid accounts of crime and punishment, heavenly apparitions, and diabolical sorcery kept the balladeer in business. In the words of John Earle, the balladeer's

> frequent'st Workes goe out in single sheets, and are chanted from market to market, to a vile tune, and a worse throat; whilst the poore Country wench melts like her butter to heare them. And these are the Stories of some men of Tyburne, or a strange Monster out of Germany: or . . . Gods Judgements.[7]

Religion, which was largely absent from the oral ballad tradition, was emphasized in broadside ballads. Much of the religious content was partisan.[8] Chapbooks dealt with the same topics as ballads but also added riddles and jests, chivalric stories, and utilitarian information on diet, medicine, beauty care, and magic.[9] Almanacs were compendia of practical information about the calendar and festivals, times of sunrise and sunset, and planetary aspects. Health and gardening tips were dispensed along with religious instruction. Changes in the weather and in the affairs of state were both forecast.[10]

The authors of these texts included learned writers seeking to influence the common people, professional writers who may have written to please their publishers, and in some cases common folks who were uncommon in having published anything.[11] Balladeers were known to be actors, weavers, keepers of alehouses, and artisans.[12] John Earle described the ballad-writer as a drunken "pot-poet" scribbling in a bawdy house or alehouse.[13] Authors of almanacs, on the other hand, had a higher social standing, being ministers, physicians, surveyors, mathematical practitioners, and astrologers.[14]

Before 1640, ballads were more apt to contain political messages than were chapbooks, and Parliament suppressed the former between 1647 and 1656. During the Civil War, a new outlet for political expression was found in almanacs and cheap pamphlets.[15]

Political messages were also reinforced in theatrical works and street demonstrations. Plays were performed in streets and taverns, and at fairs. At the turn of the seventeenth century, a penny gained one admission to the public theaters. It is estimated that approximately 18,000 to 24,000 Londoners, including "Tailers, Tinkers, Cordwayners, [and] Saylers," went to the theater every week.[16] The repertoire of the public theaters included Shakespeare's plays, works that dramatized the grievances of Londoners against prerogative government, and plays based on historical events or classical mythology. In the streets, pageants and royal entries into London, coronation processions, bonfires, and Lord Mayor's Shows supported the monarchy and legitimated the established order. Opposition groups criticized political authorities in "pope burnings" and other forms of ritualized violence.[17]

As the foregoing suggests, popular culture did not consist solely of documents and artifacts, but also included performances and practices such as shaming rituals. Comets partook of both aspects of popular culture, for they were artifacts and events. As celestial phenomena, they were read as hieroglyphs and interpreted as visual signs. Printed images of comets served as emblems. On the other hand, the apparition of a comet was a "happening." Blazing stars caused a stir; they were the talk of the town.

In popular performance and literature, politics and prodigies went hand in hand. As prodigies, comets were seen as signs of the times. Their representations reveal not only popular interpretations but also the social functions of divination and the doctrine of providence.

GOD ON THEIR SIDE

"Stung I was with a bee on my nose, . . . [but] my face swelled not, thus divine providence reaches to the lowest things," confided Ralph Josselin, an Essex vicar, in his diary.[18] To the seventeenth-century mind, the hand of God was everywhere. No matter how fortuitous things appeared, nothing good or bad ever happened by chance. The successful man rejoiced in God's love and the propriety of his activities. The victim of misfortune consoled himself with the knowledge that his adversities were part of a divine scheme. If he was pious, he presumed that God was testing him. If he was dissolute, God was punishing him. Regional calamities were treated like personal misfortunes, as signs of the community's moral health. In the wake of famine, plague, fire, and flood, preachers and pamphleteers scrutinized the public's behavior and attempted to rout its vices.[19]

Yes, it was comforting to know that there was order in the rough and rugged ways of the world. But whose order was sanctioned by God? How could one distinguish the sorely tested from the utterly detested? Here the doctrine of providence had a self-confirming quality. Sectarians recorded

the judgments upon their enemies and mercies bestowed on their friends as proof of God's favor.[20]

Moral pressure could be exerted by the weight of such evidence. Stories of men drowned while bathing at sermon-time, or towns burnt to the ground after shops had remained open on Sunday, were intended to inhibit Sabbath breaking and reinforce canons of proper social conduct.[21] A similar didactic purpose was served in 1642 by the report of a comet that leveled a rapist:

> A Blazing Starre seene In The West At Totneis in Devonshire, on the foureteenth of this instant November, 1642. Wherin is manifested how Master Ralph Ashley, a deboyst Cavalier, attemted to ravish a young Virgin, the Daughter of Mr. Adam Fisher, inhabiting neare the said Towne. Also how at that instant, a fearefull Comet appeared, to the terrour and amazment of all the Country thereabouts. Likewise declaring how he persisting in his damnable attemt, was struck with a flaming Sword, which issued from the Comet, so that he dyed a fearefull example to al his fellow Cavaliers.[22]

A punishing fire plunging from heaven was a motif common to prodigy literature, folktales, and popular preaching.[23] The cavalier-killing comet fit right in, for in the popular mind, comets were respected as fiery signs of God's discipline—be this the stern yet fatherly chastisement depicted by Comenius in his emblem "Patience"[24] or the corporal punishment commemorated in a medal struck in 1666 (figs. 28–30).[25]

In addition to establishing moral codes of behavior, histories of signal acts of providence were used to keep people within the church or to gain converts to political causes. In keeping with a medieval tradition of reporting exemplary judgments befalling Sabbath-breakers, Catholics interpreted comets, plagues, and other disasters as divine displeasure with Protestantism. Protestants returned the favor in anti-Catholic tracts of their own. During the English Civil War, royalists and parliamentarians likewise traded volleys. The meaning of misfortune and good luck was debated until well after the Restoration.[26] When "Mens minds [are] disturbed with love or hatred . . . each party superstitiously interprets all accidents in favor of it self," John Spencer sardonically observed. "These Prodigies . . . (like mercenary soldiers) may be easily brought to fight on either side in any case."[27]

Comets, like other marvels, were exploited by polemicists in prodigy books. In 1661–1662, for example, radical English dissenters (perhaps Fifth Monarchists) published sensationalist reports of prodigies, including comets, which gloomily greeted the restoration of Charles II. These were interpreted as sermons from heaven, preached by the Lord against the "new conformists" and the Crown.[28] Even the pamphlet about the rapist struck down by a comet was steeped in political metaphor. Published in 1642 at the start of the Civil War, the pamphlet was a piece of parliamentarian

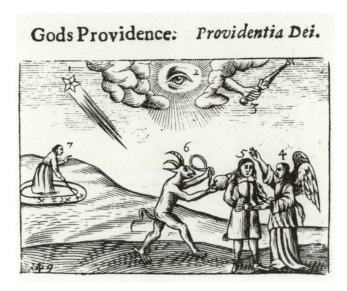

Fig. 28. Heavenly wonders—like comets—were signs of God's providence, as this emblem makes explicit. Johann Comenius, *Orbis sensualium pictus* (London, 1659), emblem 149, "God's Providence."

propaganda. The poor, vanquished maid was a Roundhead—i.e., a supporter of Parliament—whereas the diabolical scoundrel who assaulted her was a royalist Cavalier. The pamphlet thus intended to teach lessons of moral and political import. Let the court rape Parliament, if only it be ready to face God's wrath!

PROPHECIES AND PROPAGANDA

Let us now turn from the self-confirming character of these historical reports of divine retribution to the self-fulfilling nature of prophecies of future judgments. One social function of astrology was that it offered a person the prospect of greater freedom through knowledge of impending events. In 1556 Robert Recorde made the same point about comets and other heavenly marvels:

> But who that can skyll of their natures, and conjecture rightlye the effect of them and their menacynges, shall be able not only to avoide many inconveniences, but also to atchive many unlikelye attemptes: and in conclusion be a governoure and rulare of the stars accordynge to that vulgare sentence gathered of Ptolemye:
>
> > Sapiens dominabitur astris.
> > The wise by prudence, and good skyll,
> > Maye rule the starres to serve his will.[29]

Fig. 29. Johann Comenius, *Orbis sensualium pictus* (London, 1659), emblem 114, "Patience."

The person who could predict natural or political events might be able to profit from the good, avert the bad, or at least be prepared for them both. Knowledge was power.

Moreover, it was widely recognized in sixteenth- and seventeenth-century England that to be forewarned was not simply to be forearmed. Famine was blamed not only on poor weather but on the almanac's predictions of dearth. Upon hearing the forecasts, farmers sometimes refrained from planting all their fields or greedily hoarded their crop in order to produce scarcity and jack up prices.[30] Astrological prophecies had a tendency to come true simply because they were made public. They did more than create a state of preparedness; they galvanized men into action.

Consequently, political aspirations were often expressed in astrological language. Comets were an excellent point of departure for propaganda. They had long been associated with the deaths of princes, as William Shakespeare (1564–1616) instances:

> When beggars die there are no comets seen;
> The heavens themselves blaze forth the death of princes.[31]

It took only an apparition of a bearded star for dissident groups to busy themselves with forecasts of the deaths of unpopular rulers. As Shakespeare's audiences well knew, it was no secret that opposition groups wished their political prophecies to be self-fulfilling. In *Henry VI*, when the French tried to regain Rouen, the dauphin Charles remarked of a burning torch:

Fig. 30. English commemorative medal (1666) connecting the comets of 1664 and 1665, the London fire (1666), plague (1665), and Anglo-Dutch war (1665–1666). On either side of the divine eye in the heavens, we read "SIC PVNIT" (Thus he punishes). Augustus W. Franks and Herbert A. Grueber, eds., *Medallic Illustrations* (London, 1885), medal 173. (By permission of The British Library.)

> Now shine it like a comet of revenge,
> A prophet to the fall of all our foes![32]

And in the play's opening lines, the Duke of Bedford bewailed the death of his brother, Henry V:

> Hung be the heavens with black, yield day to night!
> Comets, importing change of times and states,
> Brandish your crystal tresses in the sky,
> And with them scourge the bad revolting stars
> That have consented unto Henry's death.[33]

Like military banners seen in the distance, menacing apparitions of comets were used by dissidents to announce the approach of forces striving to overthrow an established order.

There were no fewer than twenty-five apparitions visible in seventeenth-century Europe, and these comets made frequent appearances in the polemical broadsheets and chapbooks hawked in the marketplaces (figs. 31–33).[34] Loyal to the parliamentary cause, astrologer William Lilly (1602–1681)

Fig. 31. Death-Clock with grisly numerals marked by bones, daggers, guns, and whips, and with clock-hands depicted by the comets of 1680, 1682, and 1683. This Augsburg broadside (1683) describes comets as "divine torches of wrath." (WOP-3. Courtesy of Adler Planetarium & Astronomy Museum, Chicago, Illinois.)

Fig. 32. Five comets seen in England during 1664–1682. Nathaniel Crouch, comp., *Surprizing Miracles* (London, 1685). (By permission of the Houghton Library, Harvard University.)

fumed that the "unnatural" retrograde motion of the last comet of 1618 had foreshadowed the oppression of the English people by "Retrograde Lords" and "sinister Counsels." In 1644, he cheekily declared that the comet yet portended "sudden death to some great King or Prince," back-handedly adding, "God blesse His Majesty of England, &c. The Pope can

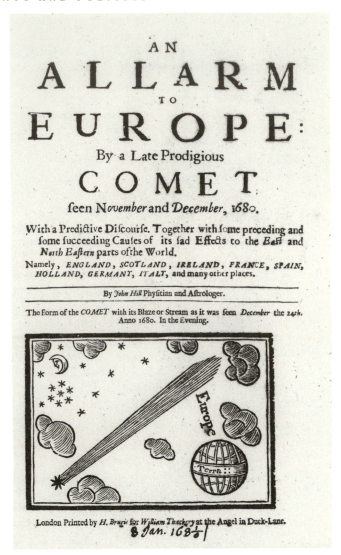

Fig. 33. Pamphlet with apocalyptic tone and pseudoscientific woodcut of the 1680 comet. The caption implies that this was the true form of the comet as it appeared in London on the evening of 24 December 1680. But the illustration is hardly as specific and objective as its legend purports! John Hill, *An Allarm to Europe* (London, 1680). (By permission of the Houghton Library, Harvard University.)

find no leasure to die."[35] No doubt, Charles I took little comfort in this prognostication. For other pamphleteers and balladeers, the comets of 1618 had augured plague among the New England Indians; the 1652 comet had presaged Cromwell's dissolution of the Rump Parliament and the spread of Quakerism; the 1661 comet had forecast "Black Bartholomew's Day" on

which nine hundred nonconformist clergymen were ejected from their bene-
fices according to the Act of Uniformity (1662); the comets of 1664 and
1665 had heralded the plague (1665), the great fire of London (1666), and
the Anglo-Dutch war (1665–1667); and the 1677 comet had ushered in the
Popish Plot (1678)—the fabrication of Titus Oates that Catholics planned
to kill Charles II, burn London, and massacre Protestants.[36]

A willing dupe of Titus Oates and his ally in "uncovering" the Popish
Plot, Ezerel Tonge exploited comets rhetorically in his *Northern Star*
(1680), a pro-Protestant, pro-English tract that he dedicated to Charles II.[37]
In November 1680, Tonge took part in the burning of a huge effigy of the
pope, in which cats and rats were imprisoned to represent devils.[38] Early in
the month, he might have seen the great comet that appeared in the morning
sky, but died soon after a second comet appeared in the evening sky in mid-
December. Others would gaze upon this comet until the end of March.
(These comets were later shown by Newton to have been a single comet.)
Tonge had little time to interpret the portents, but the comets reinforced the
message of his *Northern Star*. Brilliant and impressive, the comets of 1680–
1681 appeared in the middle of the Exclusion Crisis. Other Protestant polemicists lost no time in baiting Catholics and trying to force Parliament's
hand with their political predictions from the comets.[39] Reminding people
of the harrowing aftereffects of recent comets, not the least of which had
been the Popish Plot, ballad writers declared the downfall of Catholicism to
be foreordained. Lord Stafford was beheaded beneath the baneful streams
of the December comet for his reputed role in the conspiracy. On one
broadsheet, he rose from the grave (fig. 34) to intone:

> See the bright Star which o're your heads doth shine,
> I can as well as *Gadbury* Divine;
> What the bright stream of Radient Light doth mean,
> Which every Night so frequently is seen.
> Hear me, O *Rome*, though in your Cause I dy'd,
> Nigh is the setting of your Pomp and Pride:
> That *Star* doth shew, that *Day* is neer at hand,
> That *Rome* no longer shall the *World* command,
> And many years it hath not now to stand.

Why not speed up the process? balladeers asked. They recommended
the passage of the Exclusion Bill, barring James, duke of York, a Catholic,
from royal succession.[40] A pamphleteer, who styled himself Democritus,
agreed:

> This present Comet . . . is of a menacing Aspect, but if the *New Parliament* (for
> whose Convention so many good men pray) continue long to sit, I fear not but the
> STAR will lose its virulence and malignancy, or at least its portent be averted from
> this our Nation; which being the humble request to God of all good men, makes
> me thus entitle it, *A Petitioning-Comet*.[41]

Fig. 34. Lord Stafford's shrouded ghost interprets the comet of 1680–1681 as a divine warning to Catholics that the Millennium is not far off. [Christopher Ness], *The Lord Stafford's Ghost: Or, A Warning to Traitors, with His Prophesie Concerning the Blazing-Star* (London, [1681]). (Courtesy of the Newberry Library, Chicago.)

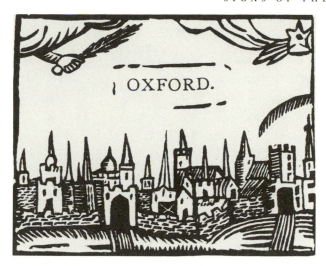

Fig. 35. The 1680–1681 comet hovering over Parliament, which was held in Oxford in March 1681. From a broadside ballad reprinted in *The Roxburghe Ballads* (Hertford, 1869–1901), 5:15.

The comet was to be dreaded "unless Providence grants that happy *Union of Protestants*, and *Exclusion of Papists*."[42] The same comet was shown hovering over Parliament in the woodcut on a broadside ballad (fig. 35).[43] Observing that it resembled a broom, Christopher Ness (1621–1705) prayed that God might use a "Parliamentary Besom" to sweep the unclean spirit of Babylon from the land.[44] There was a monster in the royal closet, and its name was popery. Left unchecked, it would chew up the privileges of Parliament and the liberty and properties of the people.[45]

There was widespread belief that the political power struggles were reflected in the disorderly course of nature. For Ness, the "Signs of the Times" included nothing less than a comet; the death of three Tower lions named Old Charles, Queen, and Duke; a female ghost bidding Charles II to keep Parliament in London; armies seen battling in the air; a fiery dart and flying bullet; the apparition of three suns; great hailstones; an earthquake that toppled churches in Malaga; the drying up of a Welsh river; a whale found inland in a river near Colchester; and a remarkable sea battle (fig. 36).[46] The report of prodigies like the death of three lions named after the king, queen, and duke of York was, if not outrightly treasonous, then verging on seditious.[47] Ness, a nonconformist excommunicated no fewer than four times, had to hide at least once from officers of the Crown who had a warrant to arrest him for his subversive publications.[48]

The politics in these cometary tracts was thinly veiled; the propaganda really rather crude—indeed, as crude as the woodcuts that adorned most. Yet many took serious notice of them. Even Edward Wetenhall (1636–1713), the Church of England bishop of Cork and Ross, who left astrologi-

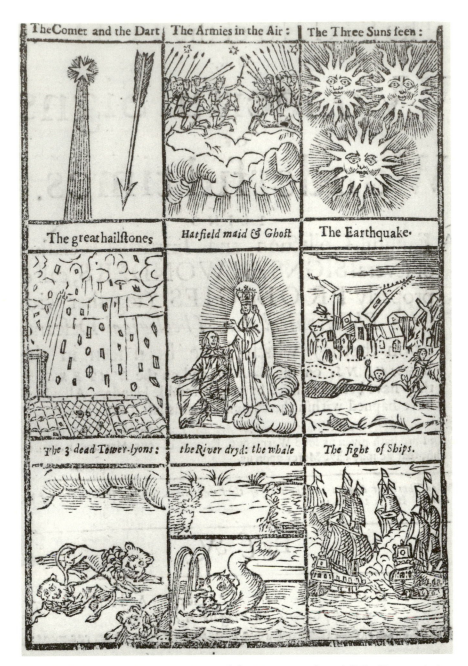

Fig. 36. Christopher Ness, *The Signs of the Times* (London, 1681). (By permission of the Houghton Library, Harvard University.)

cal judgments of the 1680 comet "to those incurable Cheats and Cheatees," felt it incumbent on him to assuage apprehensions that prophecies of an Irish plot to massacre Protestants would be self-fulfilling.[49] Perhaps he had good reasons to be worried about a plot, for one English pamphleteer warned the inhabitants of the northern isles that

> their *Murders*, their *Idolatries*, their *Blasphemies*, their Actions against God, The Laws of *Nations* and *Nature* enforces me to stile her the very Essence of *Antichrist*: and surely God hath a scourge in store for this *Monstrous Beast*; . . . let us not glory in the Ruine, but rather in the *Reformation* of our Enemies, *Protestant Christians* have offended, slighted, and committed sins against the God of Heaven that hath abounded in mercy towards them, therefore for the slighting of mercy, Judgment is near taking place.[50]

In a conspiratorial tone, the author further warned, "Let the inhabitants of *London* prepare for Death, for indeed a Plague is threatened, And God keep back the fury of bloody minded Men."[51]

All these outbursts were concerned with specific political quarrels. Some pamphleteers, however, raised themselves above the local rough water to examine a larger vista. They thought they saw a fast-approaching end to the world, and their works adopted an apocalyptic tone.[52] The comet of 1580 confirmed Francis Shakelton in his opinion that the Day of Judgment was near at hand. With urgency, he wrote a tract "to disswade the worlde, from freezing in the dregges of their synnes, by admonisheyng them of the finall dissolution of the Engine of this worlde, and seconde commyng of Christ in the cloudes, which by many manifest and inevitable reasons I gather, can not bee farre of[f]."[53] Although Regiomontanus and others agreed that 1588 would be a year of great revolutions and world mutations, Jesus had yet to reappear when William Lilly viewed the comets of 1664, 1665, and 1673 as tokens of the beginning of the end.[54] In comets like that of 1680, Ezerel Tonge, Christopher Ness, and others saw the great "northern star," the messianic herald of the last days predicted by the sibyl Tiburtina and Tycho Brahe.[55]

Panic and joy were heightened by the great conjunction of Jupiter and Saturn in the fiery trigon in 1682, which came on the heels of a comet's apparition (fig. 37).[56] While great conjunctions take place every twenty years, this one was part of an astrologically profound series of conjunctions that commenced with a climacteric (or "maximum") conjunction at the close of the sixteenth century. By definition, climacteric conjunctions occurred only every eight hundred years when the great conjunction of Jupiter and Saturn returned to the sign of Aries and to the fiery trigon (Aries, Sagittarius, Leo).[57] It was widely reported by the popular press that Tycho Brahe, Johannes Kepler, and Johann Heinrich Alsted (1588–1638) correlated historical periods with climacteric conjunctions[58] and believed that they portended great mutations and reformations of the spiritual and secular regimes.[59] Tycho Brahe reckoned that all odd-numbered maximum conjunctions were

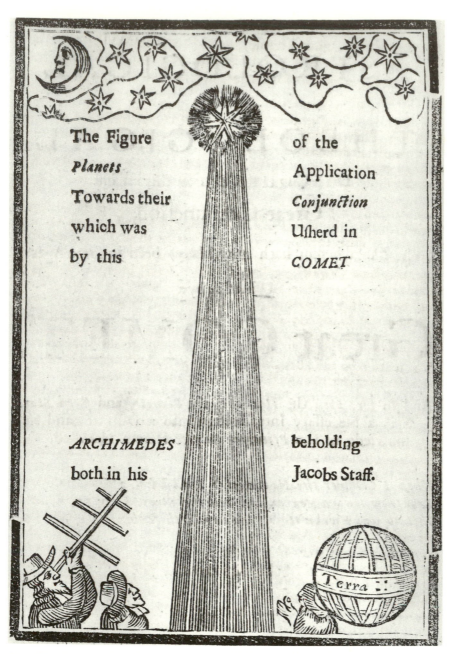

The Figure   of the
Planets   Application
Towards their   *Conjunction*
which was   Uſherd in
by this   COMET

ARCHIMEDES   beholding
both in his   Jacobs Staff.

Fig. 37. Great conjunction and comet, which excited astrologers in 1682. (Note that "Archimedes" is holding his Jacob's staff, or cross-staff, backwards.) Christopher Ness, *An Astrological and Theological Discourse Upon this present Great Conjunction . . . Usherd in by a Great Comet* (London, 1682). (By permission of the Houghton Library, Harvard University.)

auspicious, and urged people to look forward to the period of the sabbatical or seventh climacteric conjunction since the world's Creation, which he believed would follow the conjunction in Aries in 1583.[60] During the conjunction in Leo in October 1682, the planets allegedly would be in the same configuration as they had been at the beginning of the world.[61] Alsted believed this might be the last conjunction of the present world and publicly announced that the Millennium would commence in 1694.[62]

By itself, the great conjunction in the fiery trigon was a serious matter, but its power was corroborated by several other signs. Mars joined Jupiter and Saturn in 1682. There was a solar eclipse. But most critically, the great conjunction was ushered in by the comets of 1680 and 1682, and the former was said to have been unrivaled in eight hundred years. Many thought the comets augured the Apocalypse or Millennium, the end of the world or its renovation. In sensationalist street literature, radical pamphleteers took advantage of these comets. Not only did they encourage people to repent, they urged them to amend social institutions in preparation for a new world order. They observed that since the comets were Saturnine, Protestants would suffer at the hands of Saturnine sects—i.e., papists and Turks. There was danger that the Turks might invade England. The house of Austria, the empire of Germany, and the kingdom of France would soon lie in ashes. In the end, however, the Roman Church would be destroyed, the Turks converted, and the Jews called. With one flock under one shepherd, the world would be prepared for universal peace.[63]

Propagandist in intention and apocalyptic in tone, these tracts courted an unsophisticated audience. Yet it would be wrong to think that monarchs, courtiers, and governments despised them or ignored them. It was precisely because the tracts were propagandist works appealing to mass audiences that governments paid close attention to them. During the Civil War, George Wharton's almanacs openly defended the royalist cause, and in 1649, near the time of the regicide, he was arrested by order of Parliament. On the other side, William Lilly's prophetic tracts predicted victories for Cromwell's army and the permanent downfall of monarchy. His prognostications "kept up the Spirits both of the Soldiery, the honest People of this Nation, and many of us Parliament-men," praised one of his backers.[64] But as Lilly's zeal for Parliament waned, so did his favor with its members. At the Restoration, the Crown cracked down on the almanacs of Lilly and others, blaming them for fomenting insurrection and irreligion during the Civil War and Interregnum.[65]

Political authorities had long acknowledged the threats posed by prophecies to the social order, and laws dating back to 1402 had prohibited subversive prognostications.[66] Although the prophecies themselves were good for little more than "winter talk by the fireside, . . . the spreading or publishing of them is in no sort to be despised, for they have done much mischief," Lord Chancellor Bacon remarked.[67] Predictions of war, bloodshed,

or the imminent demise of the monarch had the potential to be self-fulfilling. Astrological forecasts fortified conspirators, heightened their courage,
and so made them more likely to succeed in their plots. Thus laws making
it a statutory felony to calculate the life expectancy of the ruling monarch
had to be enforced.[68] Astrologer John Gadbury confessed that he was asked
to cast Charles II's horoscope as part of a plot to murder the king, but denied any wrongdoing. Authorities were not fully convinced of his innocence. His report that the comet of 1521 presaged Henry VIII's condemnation of the papacy and his prophecy of "an eternal settlement in England of
the Romanists" helped to fuel allegations of his role in Catholic conspira-
cies and won him two trips to prison.[69] Astrological politicking from the
bottom up could be dangerous.

There also was astrological politicking from the top down. In addition to
trying to keep the prognosticative activities of dissident groups in check, the
ruling powers were interested in astrology and cometary portents as tools
they could themselves use for good government.[70] Niccolò Machiavelli
(1469–1527) observed, "Whence it comes I know not, but both ancient and
modern instances prove that no great events ever occur in any city or country that have not been predicted by soothsayers, revelations, or by portents
and other celestial signs."[71] It behooved a governor to take notice of celestial apparitions. In Tudor England, Henry VIII consulted John Robyns on
astrological matters and received a tract from Robyns on the meaning of
some recent comets.[72] Writing from Germany, Thomas Cranmer kept the
king informed about comets and perturbing political events abroad.[73] The
earl of Leicester invited John Dee to select an astrologically propitious day
for Queen Elizabeth's coronation, and Elizabeth I later invited Dee to offer
his opinions on the comet of 1577. Indeed, Elizabeth's interest in the comet
advanced her prestige. Her courtiers attempted to dissuade her from looking at the comet, but she boldly declared, "Iacta est alea" (The die is cast)
and approached the window. Curiously, her death was later said to have
been presaged by an apparition in 1602.[74] The court of James I was all agog
over the great blazing star of 1618–1619. The king quizzed Cambridge
mathematicians about its meaning. After his death it was reported that
James thought it portended the fall of the Stuarts and the Thirty Years War,
but in 1618 Sir Thomas Lorkin confided, "His majesty they say, swears it
is nothing but Venus with a firebrand in her ———."[75] Whatever ambivalence James may have had, the death of Queen Anne, his consort, was acknowledged by high and low to have been augured by the comet.[76]

The political utility of astrology was not lost on later Stuart monarchs.
During the reign of Charles II, celestial symbolism still played a governing
role. Astro-meteorological imagery figured in public rituals of the state,
such as the commemoration of Charles II's entry into London on his birthday (29 May 1660) and his coronation on Saint George's day (23 April
1661). Panegyrists compared Charles to the sun. Some described the ups

and downs of Charles's career metaphorically in terms of the alternation of sunny and cloudy days.[77] Others offered a favorable gloss on the weather during the Restoration year (loosely defined as the period between the above dates). It had rained prior to the coronation but was gloriously sunny for the festivities on 22 and 23 April. A great thunderstorm occurred at the end of the two-day celebration. Royalists proclaimed that the heavens had wept over the untimely deaths of Charles's brother and sister in late 1660. Then the rain had stopped so that the sun could honor the new king. The ominous fulminations at the close of the ceremonies were trickier to explain in terms that would legitimate the monarchy. Opponents of the Restoration argued that the thunder was a sign of God's displeasure, but supporters heard it as God's answer to their prayers.[78]

The sunny disposition of the weather during the coronation was seen as the fulfillment of a prophecy. In 1630, at the time of Charles's birth, a noon-day star or rival sun allegedly had appeared in the sky. Aurelian Cook in *Titus Britannicus* explained its import:

> As soon as Born, Heaven took notice of him, and ey'd him with a Star, appearing in defiance of the Sun at Noon-day, either to note, That his life shou'd be continu'd with Miracles, as it began with one; or that his Glory shou'd shine like a Star; or else to prove, That if it be question'd, whether Sovereigns be given us by chance, or by the hand of the Almighty, it is here manifest, that this Prince came from Heav'n, and that there is a World of difference put betwixt Kings supernaturally made by God, and those electively made by Man.[79]

For Cook, the extra sun announced that Charles ruled by divine right. Moreover, the timing of Charles's entry into London on his birthday was politically calculated to fulfill what had been portended at his birth. The point was grasped immediately by Abraham Cowley (1618–1667), poet, diplomat, and spy for the court during its exile:

> No *Star* amongst ye all did, I beleeve,
> Such vigorous assistance give,
> As that which thirty years ago,
> At *Charls* his *Birth*, did, in despight
> Of the proud *Sun's* Meridian Light,
> His future *Glories*, this *Year* foreshow.[80]

Edward Matthew devoted an entire book to the fulfillment of the prophecy, declaring Charles "ordained to be the most *Mighty Monarch* in the *Universe*" (fig. 38).[81]

Charles's return was seen as a rebirth for England and duly recorded by a special act in the statute book, which proclaimed that 29 May was "the most memorable Birth day not onely of his Majesty both as a man and Prince but likewise as an actual King, and of this and other His Majesties Kingdomes all in a great measure new borne and raised from the dead on

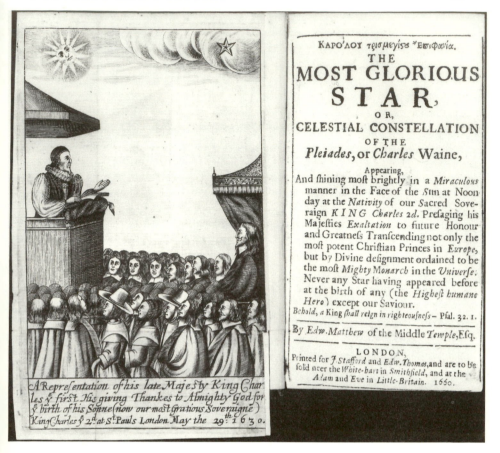

Fig. 38. Royalist propaganda interpreting the meaning of the daytime star that greeted the birth of Charles II. Edward Matthew, *Karolou trismegistou epiphania* (London, 1660). (By permission of the Houghton Library, Harvard University.)

this most joyfull day."[82] Viewing the Restoration as a resurrection reinforced the parallels also being drawn between Charles and Jesus, at whose birth a special star had likewise shone. In a speech delivered before the House of Lords, Dublin, Sir Audley Mervyn exclaimed:

> Astrologers have made Divinations from the fiery Trigon, and the conjunction of *Saturn* and *Iupiter* as to the Condition of Our King and his Kingdomes: bleer eyd men could you no[t] see when Our King was wrapt up in the swadling bands of Majesty, and after *Worcester* Fight laid in a Manger; Could you not see a Star over the place, the Wise men did see it, and did foretell that God had snatcht him as a Fire-brand out of the Fire, and designed him to be a Crown of Glory in the hand of the Lord, and a Royal Diadem in the hand of his God.[83]

Arise Evans, the Welsh prophet, went further, equating the Stuart Restoration with the establishment of Christ's kingdom on earth. In 1664, Evans announced that the star or comet which had shone at the king's nativity was the very same celestial body that the Magi had seen. Charles was to be God's viceroy. Evans predicted war with the Dutch, heaven-sent plague, the rise of the Jews under Charles, their ultimate conversion, the coming of Christ, and his reign with Charles by his side.[84] Edward Matthew reached similar conclusions, drawing on sources as varied as the Bible, the sibyl Tiburtina, and Tycho Brahe.[85] In other royalist literature, the eschatological language was muted but still present. Charles was a messiah, a savior, who would inaugurate a golden age. As Jesus had revived Lazarus, so Charles would restore England to life. It was in this sense that celestial and messianic symbolism came together in numerous poems about the coronation. For instance, the court poet Henry Bold compared Charles not only to Jesus but also to the sun on Easter Sunday. Other poets described Charles as the sun, imparting light and heat, bringing forth the spring, and reviving the dead.[86]

These leitmotivs were also prominent in the public spectacle of the coronation pageantry. On 22 April 1661, like a Roman hero, Charles II made his way from the Tower through the City, stopping at four triumphal arches. At the third arch, the figures of Concord, Love, and Truth sang to the king:

> Comes not here the King of Peace,
> > Who, the Stars so long fore-told,
> From all Woes should us release
> > Converting Iron-times to Gold?[87]

This message was reinforced by the design of the last arch—dedicated to Plenty—and the entertainment there:

> Great Sir, the Star, which at Your Happy Birth
> Joy'd with his Beams (at Noon) the wond'ring Earth,
> Did with auspicious lustre, then, presage
> The glitt'ring Plenty of this Golden Age.[88]

Here salvation and peace—foretold by Charles's natal star—were interpreted in mercantilist terms.[89]

John Dryden (1631–1700) would repeat this message in his poem *Annus Mirabilis* (1667), where he astrologically interpreted two comets appearing in 1664 and 1665. Although the comets had presaged London's plague and fire, one, he suggested, might yet have been "that bright companion of the Sun," the special star that purportedly had shone at the time of Charles's birth. Its return was benevolent, auguring the restoration of London and the establishment of a new golden age with Charles on the throne.[90]

In linking a comet to the daytime star that had announced Charles's birth, Dryden fell in line with those who believed the Magi's star had been

a comet. Daytime stars and comets were frequently connected in historical literature and associated with the births—real or metaphoric—of illustrious individuals, of whom Jesus was not the least. The comet of 44 B.C. was another well-known example. It had ushered in the reign of Augustus, and like the star at Charles's birth, it had been interpreted as a good omen and used to legitimate his ascendancy.[91] The analogy is striking because pageantry, literature, and medals struck in commemoration of Charles's coronation explicitly compared the careers of Augustus and Charles. Like Augustus, the new sovereign brought peace after civil war; he revived the state religion and the arts; and it was expected that he would pave the way for a glorious empire. The planners of the coronation procession clearly had Rome in mind when they erected the triumphal arches, which bore the legend "S.P.Q.L." (recalling the Roman "S.P.Q.R." and standing for *senatus populusque Londiniensis*). The first arch, moreover, carried the inscription *Adventus Augusti*.[92] To my knowledge, however, the panegyrists did not explicitly call attention to the fact that both Augustus and Charles thought a special star or comet had appeared on their behalf, nor did they call attention to the cunning ways in which each sovereign took advantage of his celestial show. Nevertheless, the historical and political parallels were there to be observed and indeed were made all the more manifest by the royalist propaganda that interpreted Charles's natal star as proof of his divine right. Despite their cheers for the restoration of an Augustan age, the polemicists were silent about their Augustan methods. Isaac Newton, however, recognized this aspect of Anglo-Augustan politics and was alarmed by it.

Thus in public displays and publications Charles II was compared to the sun, to the Messiah, and to Augustus. Astronomical imagery and astrological interpretations were embedded in these comparisons. The purpose of such comparisons was to draw political lessons: namely, the Restoration was foreordained; Charles ruled by divine right; and this was the dawning of a golden age of peace and prosperity. The point here is that members of the court and supporters of the established ecclesiastical polity were not above drawing on celestial symbolism when it suited their propagandist purposes. In Newton's day, astrological politicking was not limited to the vulgar or dissenting members of society.

From the castle to the marketplace, men surveyed the heavenly wonders with an eye to self-advancement. Competing political and religious factions, drawing on the doctrine of providence, offered their own "correct" judgments of the meaning of particular comets in order to validate their own beliefs, attract new followers, urge others to undertake moral or social reforms, and incite political action against their rivals. In the heat of the fray, narrow issues and local debates sometimes got couched in apocalyptic language. Indeed, there were those who truly believed that contemporary disputes fulfilled ancient prophecies, and the end of the world was near.

Cometary prognostications lent themselves well to the elevated plane of eschatological discourse, for there was a tradition of situating comets at the major turning points of Christian history. As I have described in chapter 2, many Christian thinkers held the Star of Bethlehem to have been a comet. Others thought church reforms and the assault on the Antichrist had been and would be announced by comets.

In millenarian pamphlets and political broadsheets, learned ideas put forward by Tycho, Kepler, and others were digested for the consumption of popular audiences. Ptolemaic methods of cometary prognostication were marshaled by polemicists in their cheap, propagandist works. Such sharing of ideas was not new. High and low audiences had long viewed comets with the same fearful spirit, and ideas had traveled up and down the social ladder since ancient times. In the early modern period, opinions of the educated and powerful, on one hand, reached the common sort through ballads and broadsheets, street theater and pageantry, almanacs and emblems. Folk beliefs, on the other hand, were embraced by the elite, who sometimes rationalized them but often blindly accepted them and frequently used them for social ends. In the mid–seventeenth century, however, this relationship was changing. The vulgarization of learned ideas in tawdry tracts coincided with the withdrawal of the elite from the popular culture they had long shared with the masses. For political and social reasons, to be described in chapter 6, the elite began to despise prodigy literature and astrological propaganda along with the popular and learned ideas they disseminated. Views once shared by high and low became socially unacceptable.

At the same time, the popular press spread the view that comets were forerunners of world mutations. The expansion of cometary import from a strictly local neighborhood to a universal domain was critical for theories later held by natural philosophers such as Isaac Newton and Edmond Halley. Like elite contemporaries, they rejected as vulgar the view that comets were portents of local war, plague, and famine, but in novel, astrophysical ways they embraced the popular religious idea that comets imported world reform.

PART TWO

Natural Causes

From Natural Signs to Proximate Causes

IN Part One of this book we saw that high and low audiences alike thought that comets prefigured calamity. Most individuals did not inquire how comets could augur the future, but simply accepted this as an article of their faith. For them, comets portended the future simply because God willed it so and had prearranged events to bring about this sequence.

A handful of medieval scholars, however, were not content to treat comets as celestial signs of the future. Robert Grosseteste, Albertus Magnus, and others to be discussed here believed that comets were caught up in a causal chain of events that produced the presaged disasters. This causal approach owed much to new attitudes toward nature in the late twelfth and early thirteenth centuries and the availability of texts by Aristotle and Ptolemy translated at that time.

NEW ATTITUDES TOWARD NATURE AND THE RECOVERY OF CLASSICAL SCIENCE

In the twelfth century, a number of scholars ceased to be satisfied with divine omnipotence as a complete explanation for natural occurrences and became interested in more immediate secondary causes. Although God was not swept from the scene—for he remained the author of all good things—he ceased to take center stage. The domain of the miraculous, preternatural, and occult shrank. William of Conches (ca. 1080–ca. 1154) and Adelard of Bath (fl. 1116–1142), for example, downplayed the marvelous, which their predecessors had deemed evidence of true providence, and turned their attention to the causes of the mundane and the routine; and John of Salisbury (ca. 1115–1180) attacked augury and judicial astrology as inconclusive and meaningless, however mindful he was that natural signs might be worthy of study.[1] Although these opinions were by no means universally held (or perhaps even consistently held by the above-mentioned individuals),[2] later medieval scholars became increasingly inclined to search for the natural causes of marvelous things.

Among the phenomena considered marvelous had been the relationship between cometary portents and foreshadowed events. John of Damascus had suggested that comets were special creations of God. Albertus Magnus (ca. 1200–1280) and Aegidius of Lessines (ca. 1235–1304) challenged this opinion on the grounds that divine creations were constant, whereas comets, like works of nature in general, were changing and corrupt.[3] Geoffrey

of Meaux (fl. 1310–post-1348) voiced a similar view,[4] and Jean Buridan (ca. 1295–ca. 1358) remarked: "There exists an opinion that comets are produced miraculously by God in the sky to presage the death of princes, in order to correct them, and then disappear in the same miraculous way. I believe firmly that God could well have done this and still can; but it appears to me absurd to think that God would make these comets."[5] The central question was this: Why should God dirty his hands in such paltry phenomena when he had no need to produce the effects miraculously? Nature would suffice.

This new attitude toward nature was bolstered by classical Greek and Arabic scientific sources that were made available at the time. The twelfth and thirteenth centuries were a great age of translation, and Aristotle's scientific works, including his *Meteorologica*, became available to medieval Latin scholars through the translations from Arabic to Latin by Gerard of Cremona (ca. 1114–1187) and the improved translations from the original Greek to Latin by William of Moerbeke (ca. 1215–ca. 1286).[6]

Prior to the "rediscovery" of Aristotle, Ptolemy, and other classical sources, there had been a steady decline in scientific understanding since the Roman era. The paucity of sources available in the early Middle Ages, and their continual adulteration and dilution in confused, inconsistent handbooks and encyclopedic works, had made for a meager scientific inheritance.[7] Cometary theory, like all else, had suffered. Encyclopedic authors such as Isidore of Seville and the Venerable Bede, for example, had reported little concerning the physical nature of comets and had been more interested in them as portents.[8] Therefore, the thirteenth-century scholars' fascination with underlying causes in cometary affairs represented a novel and radical departure from the tack of earlier centuries. Their causal approach must be seen as part of a larger program shared by others who were fervently committed to a natural account of the physical world. This new causal approach would not have been possible without the "new" scientific sources and the voracious appetites of medieval scholars for these treatises.

In the medieval writings to be discussed below, we shall find two key threads of reasoning that were sometimes intertwined. We may designate these "Aristotelian" and "Ptolemaic," even though they had been colored by Abū Maʿshar and others by the time they reached our medieval authors.[9]

ARISTOTLE AND TERRESTRIAL CORRUPTION

Aristotle had maintained that comets were nothing more than hot, dry exhalations burning below the moon. Emitted from the earth below, the exhalations ascended to the uppermost atmosphere where they were ignited by the motion of the contiguous celestial sphere. Sometimes the exhalations were gathered by a star or planet and followed that celestial body as a tail or halo. In both cases, comets were symptomatic of meteorological

conditions that generated plentiful supplies of exhalation. The same meteorological conditions that caused comets also caused winds, tidal waves,
and earthquakes.[10]

The Aristotelian position is apparent in the work of Robert Grosseteste
and Aegidius of Lessines, although neither slavishly followed Aristotle in
explaining why comets signaled deadly events.

At Oxford, Robert Grosseteste (ca. 1168–1253), himself an able translator of Greek learning, believed that all terrestrial bodies contained some
ethereal, fiery particles of a celestial nature.[11] In the generation of a comet,
these particles were released from matter and attracted by a star in the
manner that iron was drawn by a lodestone. To explain the significance of
comets, Grosseteste noted that the generation of a comet was but a sign of
a more general, widespread release of a spiritual nature from matter. As
spiritual particles were released, terrestrial bodies became corrupted. The
districts affected included those where the cometary fire had been sublimated, and those under the same planetary rule as the comet.[12] Grosseteste
guessed that one could identify these districts with places where men were
most alarmed by the comet.[13]

Grosseteste's account differed in detail from the standard Aristotelian
theory that comets were hot, dry exhalations, yet like Aristotle he affirmed
that comets were not proximate causes of local devastations but symptoms
of underlying natural conditions that promoted terrestrial corruption and
calamity. Comets indicated the corruption of earthly objects consequent
upon a general release of the spiritual from the gross.

Grosseteste's tract was known and cited by both contemporaries and later
authors, but his view of cometary significance had little following.[14] Among
those who chose to emulate Aristotle more closely was Aegidius (Giles) of
Lessines (ca. 1235–1304 or later), a Dominican residing in the Hainaut province of Belgium, and likely a former student of Albertus Magnus at Cologne
and Thomas Aquinas at Paris.[15] Aegidius had access to a formidable library
and drew heavily on Aristotle's *Meteorologica*, which he knew in the translation from the Greek made in 1260 by a fellow Dominican, William of
Moerbeke. An eyewitness to the comet of 1264, Aegidius argued that comets
were signs *per se*, *per consequens*, and *per accidens*.[16] As burning exhalations, comets *per se* signified an abundance of windy exhalations, the desiccation of the air, the consumption of subtle, humid vapors required for generation and nourishment, and the concentration and corruption of remaining
humidity. *Per consequens*, comets portended drought, the destruction of
agricultural produce, infection of the air, and pestilence among animals.
Earthquakes resulted from windy exhalations entrapped within the earth.
Comets *per accidens* signified events that at first glance seemed counter to
their natural hot, dry qualities but nonetheless were caused by concurrent
meteorological conditions. For example, floods, the submersion of cities beneath tidal waves, and tempests often struck after apparitions because violent, gale-force winds whipped up waves and gigantic storm clouds.[17]

PTOLEMY AND THE POWER OF MARS

Aristotle offered no reason for the observer to connect comets to political events, and in a commentary on the *Meteorologica* Albertus Magnus (ca. 1200–1280) asked why comets signified the death of magnates and forthcoming wars.[18] "The reason is not apparent," he asserted, "since vapor no more rises in a land where a pauper lives than where a rich man resides, whether he be king or someone else."[19] The way Albertus framed his question reveals a tacit rejection of the prevalent view that comets signified the death of potentates rather than peasants simply because God willed it so. In his answer, Albertus observed that a comet indicated the destruction of both rich and poor, "but the death of kings is noticed more because of their fame."[20] So what then was the natural connection between comets and the demise of men? Mars provided the link.

Here, like many scholars after him, Albertus conflated two aspects of Aristotle's theory. As mentioned above, Aristotle had distinguished two kinds of comets. In the most common type, the inflammable exhalations gathered independently in the atmosphere and moved freely as they burned. In the second type, exhalations in the form of a halo or coma accompanied a star or planet.[21] Although medieval scholars did not see comets as halos, they thought that the planets, and Mars in particular, generated comets when in certain aspects and conjunctions.

In emphasizing the role of Mars, they followed Ptolemy, from whom much of their prognostication scheme also derived. Ptolemy had written that comets "naturally produce the effects peculiar to Mars and to Mercury—wars, hot weather, disturbed conditions, and the accompaniments of these."[22] Although he never presented specific reasons why comets were predominantly Martial or Mercurial, his discussion of the power of those planets put this into focus. For example, Ptolemy remarked that "the nature of Mars is chiefly to dry and to burn, in conformity with his fiery colour and by reason of his nearness to the sun, for the sun's sphere lies just below him."[23] By means of its drying action, Mars wreaked havoc:

> Mars, when he assumes the rulership alone, is in general the cause of destruction through dryness and in particular, when the event concerns men, brings about wars, civil faction, capture, enslavement, uprisings, the wrath of leaders, and sudden deaths arising from such causes; moreover, fevers, tertian agues, raising of blood, swift and violent deaths, especially in the prime of life; similarly, violence, assaults, lawlessness, arson and murder, robbery and piracy. With regard to the condition of the air he causes hot weather, warm, pestilential, and withering winds, the loosing of lightning and hurricanes, and drought. Again, at sea he causes sudden shipwreck of fleets through changeable winds or lightning or the like; the failure of the water of rivers, the drying up of springs, and the tainting of potable waters. With reference to the necessities produced upon the

earth for human use, he causes a scarcity and loss of dumb animals and of things which grow from the earth, and the loss of crops by drying as the result of hot weather, or by locusts, or by the beating of the winds, or by burning in places of storage.[24]

Similar episodes proceeded from Mercury insofar as that planet was a desiccant by virtue of its longitudinal proximity to the sun. Also noted for its unstable character, Mercury caused changes in civil and religious customs and laws.[25]

That Mars foremost and Mercury secondarily denoted the meteorological conditions that produced comets did not escape the attention of medieval expositors. When Albertus Magnus, a Dominican named Gerard de Silteo, and Roger Bacon (ca. 1214–1294) surveyed the heavens for the planetary cause of comets in 1240 and 1264, they seized on Mars as the obvious first choice.[26] Comets were "of the character of Mars and so [were] from it as prime mover," penned Albertus,[27] and Bacon explained: "Then since the nature of Mars is fiery, whose nature is to increase jaundice, and consequently to excite men to anger, discord, and wars, therefore it happens that that [1264] comet portended angry passions, human discord, and wars, as learned astronomers teach us."[28] Aegidius of Lessines thought that Mercury was also to blame, yet his account of the political significance of comets differed little from that of Albertus Magnus and Roger Bacon.[29] Mercury and Mars aroused choler, inflamed blood, and thereby provoked anger in those individuals who had an abundance of these humors and were predisposed to such passions. Overindulgent nobles were especially susceptible, for habitual governing tended to ingrain their haughtiness and make them easily insulted. The agitation of hot-tempered princes inevitably led to the overturning of kingdoms, loss of armies, and public commotion. Thus political turmoil was presaged by comets through a chain of events that stemmed from the influence of Mars and Mercury.[30]

Following the lead of Abū Maʿshar, scholars also hailed the importance of conjunctions and aspects of the superior planets—Jupiter, Saturn, and Mars—in generating comets and establishing their significance. Conjunctions of Mars and Jupiter, reported Albertus Magnus, generated not only coruscations and running fires in the air, but also pestilential winds, corrupt air, and the horrors of plague.[31] He concurred with Bacon that revolutions of the superior planets were responsible for floods, earthquakes, pestilence, severe famine, comets, and fiery meteors.[32] Bacon also blamed conjunctions for subverting the laws of nature, fomenting rebellion, and inclining men to alter customs and laws, go to war, overturn dominions, and thwart princes.[33] And night-by-night observations of comets in 1315 and 1337 convinced Geoffrey of Meaux, a royal physician to Charles IV, that comets and their sequels—both civil and natural—were interrelated through the influence of conjunctions and aspects of the planets that drew terrestrial exhalations up into the atmosphere.[34]

What Geoffrey of Meaux had in common with Robert Grosseteste, Albertus Magnus, Gerard de Silteo, Roger Bacon, and Aegidius of Lessines was a commitment to discerning the natural causes underlying cometary significance. Whether subscribing to the "Aristotelian" theory that the sequels of comets were caused by the release of fiery exhalations or a spiritual principle from the earth, or to the "Ptolemaic" theory that the sequels were caused by the natural effects of Mars and other planets, these medieval authors ceased to see comets as divine tokens created by God outside the bounds of nature. Whatever God's intentions might be in hanging out these baneful banners in the heavens, the authors affirmed that God, in this case at least, worked through natural agents. Comets and their sequels were symptoms of some underlying natural disorder.

Stepping-Stones from Symptoms to Causes

Whereas Albertus and others saw comets and calamities as symptomatic of the operations of terrestrial exhalations and planets, authors in the fourteenth and fifteenth centuries began to hold comets and their constituent exhalations directly responsible for the cataclysmic events comets were thought to presignify. Indications of this shift in reasoning can be seen in a manuscript by Jean Buridan (ca. 1295–ca. 1358), the distinguished and influential teacher at the University of Paris. In his *Questions on the Meteora*, Buridan offered this causal account:

> It is said that comets announce great winds: that is, the comets and winds arise from the same matter, namely, from a smoky and dry exhalation. . . . They thus announce a state of dryness: that is, the abundant dry exhalations in the air dry out the air and absorb the humid vapours. They announce wars and rebellions: that is, the hot and dry exhalations dry out the air, and the constellations of hot and dry virtue, [thus] intensified, set into movement the bile—generator of choler, wars, rebellions, and quarrels. It is said that these announce the death of princes: that is, the latter are particularly harmed by these cholers, rebellions, and wars, in which many of them perish; and that, even if a great number of others also perish, we pay a greater attention to what befalls the great men.[35]

Buridan assigned a predominant role to the terrestrial exhalations that composed comets; they parched the air and instigated a chain of effects. Mars was notably absent from his account, but the constellations—presumably zodiacal—still had a share in the action. The parched air intensified the powers of the constellations to set bile in motion and incite hot passions. Buridan's acknowledgment that the death of princes attracted greater notice than that of paupers suggests he may have studied the work of Albertus Magnus.

Buridan's student Nicole Oresme (ca. 1320–1382), professor of arts and theology at the University of Paris, royal adviser to Charles V, and later

bishop of Lisieux, offered arguments similar to Buridan's natural explanation of cometary portents.[36] Oresme's contemporary at Paris, Henry of
Hesse (1325–1397), later professor of theology at the University of Vienna,
went further in claiming that one need not invoke any astrological powers
to explicate the aftereffects of comets when sublunar natural arguments
would suffice. Plague frequently followed comets but like them was simply
a symptom of unhealthy exhalations and pestilential vapors—such as those
that poisoned men who dug wells—rising from the earth's viscera. All ill-
effects that accompanied comets were by-products of their natural causes.[37]

Henry deplored the practice of ascribing dire consequences directly to the
influence of comets, arguing that comets existed in the upper atmosphere
and could have no effect on the air or earth below. Comets did not produce
violent winds, he claimed. Windy conditions more likely caused comets to
form. The theory Henry despised was held by another contemporary, John
of Legnano (d. 1383), a celebrated member of the faculty of law at Bologna,
who like Henry put pen to parchment soon after the apparition of a comet
in 1368. Although John did not attack astrology as wholeheartedly as did
Henry, he relegated astrological interpretations to the margins and endorsed a naturalistic technique of prognostication. All the standard sequels
to comets—gusting winds, earthquakes, sterility of the earth, inundations,
death of princes, and wars—could be explained, he said, as the natural and
direct effects of comets.[38]

John did not come to this conclusion easily, conceding that he had first
doubted these conditions to be true effects of comets:

> For in fact, it does not seem that they [comets] would signify a multitude of
> winds. For winds and comets are generated from the same material, as discussed
> above. Therefore, since much matter is consumed in the generation of a comet,
> from which [matter] winds could be generated, it appears that winds would not
> be generated. No indeed, winds would cease by their material being extinguished.
> Likewise, a comet does not seem to be able to signify a flood since it signifies
> dryness, which opposes [floods]. Likewise, it does not seem to signify the
> death of princes more than others, since preeminence naturally adds nothing
> more to the natural constitution [*complexio*] of men. Likewise, if the apparition
> of comets were signifying the death of princes, then all kings at once would be
> exterminated.[39]

Galileo gave voice to similar objections in 1619 when ghostwriting a piece
that bore the name of his disciple Mario Guiducci (1584–1646).[40] John of
Legnano, however, assuaged his doubts with "proof by natural reason."
Blazing stars parched the land and spoiled crops. As ignited exhalations
were elevated to form comets, intensely hot matter remained in the air, producing winds. Sometimes the exhalations were trapped within the earth by
the flow of cold external air into the earth's pores. With exits obstructed,
the exhalations struggled to escape their earthy confines, causing an earthquake. As they rumbled underground, headlands might crumble into the

sea, displacing the water, disrupting tides, and causing floods.[41] On agricultural and geophysical matters, John's reasoning was but a step away from Aristotle's, but he parted company with both Aristotle and Ptolemy when he considered the political relevance of comets. Whereas Albertus Magnus, Roger Bacon, and Aegidius of Lessines had contended that Mars aroused heat and wrath, and hence provoked animosity between hot-tempered individuals and ultimately instigated war, John shifted the political burden from Mars to the comets themselves. Burning cometary exhalations made men choleric and insane, and so disposed them to wage war, uproot the government, and overturn laws. Princes were more apt to die because their luxurious, dissipated, intoxicated lifestyles made them especially fractious, readily perturbed by comets, and prone to be murdered. And as principals in wars, they were placed in the line of fire, so to speak.[42]

The approach espoused by John of Legnano slowly gained support among those comfortable combining the natural scheme with traditional astrological precepts incorporating the influence of constellations, planets, and God's hand. Consider, for instance the outcome of the 1402 comet as predicted by Jacobus Angelus of Ulm, master of arts and licentiate in medicine, and physician to Leopold, duke of Austria and Styria. According to astrological conventions, Jacobus took note of the comet's conjunction with Mars in Aries and the direction its tail pointed, but did not stop there. Prior to the comet, he had observed fiery meteors, which indicated the elevation of exhalations throughout Swabia, and he concluded that the comet would especially affect this region. Moreover, the Swabians, like others who lived in the seventh clime—including the Franconians, Bohemians, Hungarians, Turks, Lombards, Italians, and French—were physically predisposed to be influenced by the comet. They were vengeful over injuries, constitutionally high-spirited, and easily provoked toward wrath and war. The comet's hot, dry nature would inflame their belligerent passions, but if it was strong enough to arouse more pacific men, then their wrath might prove more fierce than that of their war-prone neighbors, Jacobus averred.[43]

From the fifteenth to the seventeenth century, others joined Jacobus Angelus in professing that comets caused religious and political upheavals insofar as these changes were initiated by the minds and bodies of men, whose health depended upon their physical constitution, which in turn could be altered by comets. Of course, drought, sterility, and disease continued to be deemed subject to cometary jurisdiction. Comets contaminated the air with their hot, putrid vapors, and the results were devastating. Pamphlets, tracts, and treatises reveal that endorsement of the causal view cut across religious and political lines.[44]

Even more surprising, the theory continued to be embraced by astronomers who conceded for various reasons that comets were above the moon. Girolamo Cardano (1501–1576), the celebrated polymath who taught medicine at the University of Pavia, thought comets traveled beyond the moon

because they moved more slowly. Terrestrial vapors could neither ascend to sufficient heights to form comets nor supply enough fuel to feed their enduring fires. For him, comets were formed above the moon when star "light" or planetary "rays" collected into a round, translucent body.[45] Nevertheless, an apparition indicated that the air was extremely clear, dry, and "thin," whence followed the usual dire effects, including the death of princes unable to tolerate the tenuous air because they were weaklings who avoided exercise, supped on delicate meats, indulged in venereal pleasures, slept little, and were prone to be worried, old, and sick.[46] Cardano suggested that comets were responsible for thinning and dessicating the air, but how these celestial bodies did so was not clear from his text.[47] John Edwards (1637–1716), an esteemed Calvinist theologian in Cambridge[48] to whom the authorship of *Cometomantia* is attributed, placed comets above the moon because of their parallax but proposed that they operated on quasi-Aristotelian premises:

> If it once be admitted that Comets distemper and inflame the Air, and exhaust the *Succus* [i.e., juices] of the Earth, it will necessarily follow, that a barren Soil, and the corrupting and blasting of the fruits, must be the Products of them: And from these will naturally ensue Death, Scarcity and Famine. And, as the inevitable Effect of both, we must expect Sickness, Diseases, Mortality, and more especially the sudden Death of many Great Ones, because these are sooner and more easily hurt than others, for their delicate Feeding, and Luxurious course of Life, and sometimes their great Cares and Watchings, which weaken and infeeble their Bodies, render them more obnoxious than the vulgar sort of People. Hence it is that Comets may deservedly be said to presage the Death of mighty Monarchs and Princes, to be Funeral Torches to light Kings to their Tombs. And because by their noxious and infectious Irradiations, Mens Bloud is apt to be heightned into Fevers and Calentures, and all malignant Distempers, and even into the most contagious Diseases, the consequence of a Raging Pestilence from a Comet is very easie and natural, if not almost necessary.[49]

"It hath been proved by a large Induction of Experience and Observation," continued Edwards, that these conditions encouraged civil unrest too.[50] Distempered air inflamed human spirits, thereby producing tumults, brawls, confusions, seditions, wars, massacres, bloodshed, and mischiefs of all dimensions.[51]

CRITICS AND STRATEGIES

Although a vocal minority espoused the theory that comets were the proximate causes of catastrophic events, most authors in the fifteenth, sixteenth, and seventeenth centuries denied outright that comets were causal. For example, in 1578 Blaise de Vigenère (1523–1596), a French author and court

official,[52] rejected the theory that "comets menace great princes and kings with death because they live more delicately than other people; especially as the air is impregnated and thickened by a comet's impression, such that it is more harmful and dangerous to them than it would be to a laborer or scoundrel who lives on coarser food" because he observed that many people indulged their appetites for delicacies yet remained unharmed by comets.[53] In agreement was Thomas Erastus (1524–1583), professor of medicine at Heidelburg and physician and counselor to the elector Palatine Frederic III,[54] who authored a published letter concerning the 1577 comet, which was cited by Tycho Brahe. Erastus considered comets from the vantage point of his medical expertise. He argued that burning cometary exhalations would tend to purify rather than infect the air. Hence comets should not naturally cause pestilence.[55]

Criticism was also leveled at the natural scheme by those who rejected the premise that comets burned below the moon. As Johannes Kepler (1571–1630) and Jacques Gaffarel (1601–1681) observed, astronomers who placed comets in the heavens required another explanation of cause and effect that did not rely on burning exhalations.[56]

Kepler's strategy is worthy of comment. Although he first endorsed a material theory of comets similar to Cardano's,[57] he later declared them to be globular nebulae made of thick, fatty matter collected in the aether in the same way that purulent matter formed abscesses in the body. The formation of comets purified the aether, which would otherwise thicken and dim the light of the sun and stars.[58] As solar rays passed through the translucent body, they expelled gross matter, and this effluvium formed the tail. The continued effusion of matter eventually consumed the comet, "so that the tail represented the death of the head."[59] This cometary "physiology" set the stage for Kepler's views of cometary significance.[60]

Kepler believed that comets portended the future according to nature, sympathy, and pure signification.[61] He considered the danger posed should a comet graze the earth, or the earth somehow perforate an enormous, nebulous comet, or should a comet tail touch the globe directly or contact the plane of the ecliptic at a point intersecting the earth's annual orbit. In such cases, impure matter from the comet would taint the aether, defile our atmosphere, and thereby cause plague.[62] Plagues aside, Kepler utterly rejected the Aristotelian arguments that comets caused earthquakes, winds, floods, excessive humidity, parched farmland, sterility, and smoke-filled, pestilential air. Kepler called these arguments ridiculous and futile, for they relied on two false premises—that comets burned and that they were below the moon.[63]

Although Kepler repudiated the Aristotelian reasoning, he did not dismiss a natural connection between comets and the usual sequel of disasters. To explain the connection, Kepler called upon his doctrine of sympathy.[64] For Kepler, there was a sort of animal or vital faculty within the earth that

perceived celestial aspects and was stimulated when these struck sympathetic chords. When a comet appeared, this vital faculty caused those calamities that were customarily, yet wrongly, ascribed to the direct action of a remote comet:[65]

> When something unusual arises in the heaven, whether from strong constellations or from new hairy stars, then the whole of nature, and all living forces [i.e., faculties][66] of all natural things feel it and are horror stricken. This sympathy with the heaven particularly belongs to that living force which resides in the earth and regulates its inner works. If it is alarmed at one place it will, in accordance with its quality, drive up and perspire forth many damp vapors. From there arise long lasting rains and floods, and therewith (because we live by air) universal epidemics, headaches, dizziness, catarrh (as in the year 1582), and even pestilence (as in the year 1596).[67]

Innate human faculties, too, sensed and responded to cometary stimuli in the heavens:

> Man has such vivid and sensitive forces, attuned in a secret manner to heaven, that they would become disturbed and dismayed by the appearance of new comet stars even if he were blind and had never seen heaven. Thus disturbance causes not only unnatural movements of the blood and other humors and consequently illnesses but also strong emotions.[68]

Although Kepler found natural and sympathetic means adequate to illuminate the connection between comets and geophysical and medical effects, he felt that comets could not naturally or sympathetically influence political or religious circumstances. Yet the historical record convinced him that social woes followed comets.[69] How was the relationship between comets and these disturbances to be explained? Although he argued that the stars did not herald social change, he made a special exception for comets and novas.[70] Comets announced political and religious turmoil only because God specifically designed them to do so. According to Kepler, the basic rules of astrology were superstitious,[71] but God sometimes worked within men's silly conventions in order to convey particular messages. By divine decree, spiritual beings in the heavens steered comets into meaningful constellations and conjunctions.[72]

We can see the continuity between Kepler's ideas and those of medieval scholars, but there were epistemological breaks as well. Although he left room for comets as divine signs, he welcomed them as natural causes. His doctrine of sympathy cleverly explained the heavenly bodies' sublunar influence but had few followers. His theory that comet tails defiled the atmosphere was more traditional and had greater appeal. For instance, Increase Mather (1639–1723), a Puritan divine and president of Harvard College, wrote that contact with a comet tail brought drought, caterpillars, tempests, inundations, earthquakes, and disease.[73] And William Whiston (1667–

1752) saw every earthquake, volcanic eruption, stormy rain, meteor, conta-
gion, and pestilence as the pernicious and lasting effect of the atmosphere of
a comet that had brushed the earth at the time of the Deluge. Postdiluvian
lives were shorter than antediluvian ones, he said, because the comet had
corrupted the air and vegetables.[74] Even David Gregory (1661–1708)
thought cometary exhalations might be prejudicial to plants and animals.[75]
Newton, on the other hand, stood such theories on their heads, seeing cometary matter as beneficial and necessary for living things.[76]

As discussed in earlier chapters, there was a long tradition of folk belief
that comets might augur good as well as bad. Well before Newton, advocates of the causal view considered the good wrought by comets. In his
Danzig lectures, Bartholomaeus Keckermann (1571–1609) suggested that
God employed angels and demons to manipulate cometary exhalations in
order to cause happy or horrible effects.[77] Longomontanus (1562–1647),
formerly Tycho Brahe's assistant and then professor of mathematics at
Copenhagen, also saw a silver lining to the clouds of gloom and doom that
comets brought. He maintained that God and nature made nothing in vain
and so ordained the evil aftermath of comets to a wholesome end. Dearth
of agricultural produce and sterility allowed the earth to lie fallow so that
it could in the interim be refortified and prepared for a bountiful future
harvest. Tempests, which tossed and tumbled the air and water, effectively
purged them of dregs. Diseases, wars, and great mortality rooted out
wicked, ungodly men in order to renew the world. As divine agents, comets
served as purgatives and cathartics to cleanse the world.[78]

Taking an even wider view, Edwards also embraced the medical analogy:

> The very Rise and Production of them [comets] in those parts of the Heavenly
> Regions where they are generated is to good and excellent Purposes; for it is prob-
> able that the acute *Kepler* is in the right, who conceiveth a Comet to be a long
> Collection of corrupt and filthy matter, a kind of an Apostem in the Heavens, that
> as in Man's Body putrid Humours often gather into one part, so they do in the
> Heavenly ones. And these superfluous and excremental humours breaking out,
> the Aether (like the Body of Man) is thereby kept Sound and Hale, the un-
> wholesome matter is purged and drained away by these Catharticks. By this means
> the Heavens exonerate themselves of Noxious Qualities which had been long
> gathering, and would in time corrupt them. So that the evacuating of this matter
> is for the Preservation of the Heavens. The Sun and other Luminaries fare the
> better for the expulsion of this gross stuff which would otherwise over-run them
> with Thick *Maculae*.[79]

Whereas Longomontanus focused his attention on the earthly realm, Kepler
and Edwards considered the restoration of the heavens. Pierre Petit held a
similar view in 1665.[80] Although the details differed, comparable endorsements of the role of comets in preserving celestial order and cosmic health
began to appear only three years after Edwards's essay, in 1687, in the
works of Newton and his followers.

It was, however, in presenting the confused medley of ancient and modern opinions on comets that Edwards offered the clinching argument for comets as causes. He wryly commented: "Those that will not wholly grant the Efficacy and Operation of Comets, must, whether they will or no, confess their Influence in *This*, that they have caused grievous Wars and Feuds among Astronomers, who (we see) are engaged with great vigour against one another, and in the conclusion purchase nothing but Obscurity and Uncertainty."[81] No one could contest this. It was the last word on the local effects of comets.

The Decline of Cometary Divination

IN earlier chapters, we examined the scope of popular beliefs about comets and the way attitudes were shared by the learned elite and common folk. In the seventeenth century, this changed. The elite in England and Europe began to reject the pastimes and opinions of their social subordinates, and they consciously set themselves apart. By the end of the century, they scoffed at the old dread of comets. How this came about and the degree to which opinions changed has been little understood.

The conventional explanation has been that "superstitious" beliefs were successfully fought on two fronts. Philosophic and literary critics constituted one army whose mighty pens cut down superstitions with logical reasoning and witty discourse. On another side, a legion of astronomers bore down on the enemy with heavy scientific artillery developed by painstaking sweeps of the night sky. When clever arguments and observations proved that comets were not meteors but planetary bodies returning at regular intervals, traditional superstitions surrendered.[1]

In point of fact, this was not the case. Although there was some retrenchment, many clung tenaciously to traditional beliefs. Philosophical critiques and scientific discoveries may have helped to kill folk beliefs about comets, but they do not adequately explain the decline that occurred during the seventeenth century. This chapter will show why.

Beyond that, we must explore other reasons why comets lost their universal appeal as portents. An appreciation of these reasons will permit us to see how doors remained open for some old ideas; how shreds of folk beliefs could survive in Newton's cosmological thought; indeed, how a bridge could exist between vulgar prophecies and scientific inquiries.

ASTRONOMICAL REFORMS

Let us begin with the claim that astronomical discoveries made prognostication untenable. For two thousand years, philosophers had subscribed to Aristotle's theory that comets were burning meteors in the earth's atmosphere. In the Renaissance, new studies challenged this thesis.[2] Paolo Toscanelli (1397–1482) treated comets as if they were celestial bodies, and Georg Peurbach (1423–1461) and Regiomontanus (1436–1476) attempted to determine the distance of comets from the earth by measuring their parallax.[3] Although they were motivated by a desire to determine the shortest, not the longest, distance of a comet from the earth, their measurements of parallax

opened the door to debate, and in the next century, Girolamo Cardano (1501–1576), who was openly critical of Aristotle's theory, suggested using such measurements to decide whether comets were above or below the moon. Cardano never carried out this program but offered other arguments in support of the supralunar position.[4] Not until Tycho's careful study of the 1577 comet did most astronomers concede that comets were above, rather than below, the moon (fig. 39).[5]

Observations of comet tails were another nail in the coffin of Aristotelian theory. Although a student of Peurbach noted the reversal of the tail between the morning and evening appearances of the 1472 comet, he did not understand its significance.[6] In 1532 Peter Apian (1495–1552) pictorially represented the tails of the 1531 and 1532 comets as always directed away from the sun (fig. 40).[7] Although contemporaries credited him with first noting this feature of comets, he did not state it as a general rule until 1540, two years after Girolamo Fracastoro (ca. 1478–1553) had already published this important observation.[8] Although the direction of comet tails did not require comets to be above the moon, it did pose problems for the theory of burning exhalations. As Tycho Brahe recognized:

> Aristotle and all those who follow him cannot maintain their opinion, namely that the tail of a comet is a flame of the rare fattiness which is burning above the air, for if that were true, these flames would not have a relationship to the sun, and always turn themselves away from it, wheresoever it might be and howsoever the heavens might turn.[9]

In puzzling over this, Apian had suggested that comets might be translucent spheres through which sunbeams shone. The refracted sunlight produced the tail as an optical effect.[10] A similar theory was proposed by Girolamo Cardano, Jean Pena, Michael Maestlin, Tycho Brahe, Johannes Kepler, and John Bainbridge.[11]

Once comets were elevated into the celestial realm, astronomers considered their paths with greater care (fig. 41). For Aristotelians, any motion independent of the diurnal rotation of the heavens was simply due to a comet's following its source of fuel as flame travels along a wick. Non-Aristotelians, on the other hand, tended to treat comets as temporary planets and constructed "orbits" for them. Maestlin and Tycho believed the tracks to be pieces of great circles, but Kepler proposed rectilinear paths. The character of cometary paths was widely debated in the seventeenth century (fig. 42).[12]

Whether curved or straight, the motion of comets among the starry spaces and the opposition of tails to the sun made the Aristotelian-Ptolemaic system no longer tenable without modification. While some tried to argue that the curved appearance of comet paths proved that the earth moved around the sun, in general the motion and location of comets could only serve to discredit the Aristotelian-Ptolemaic theory.[13] It did not lend direct support to the Copernican theory.[14]

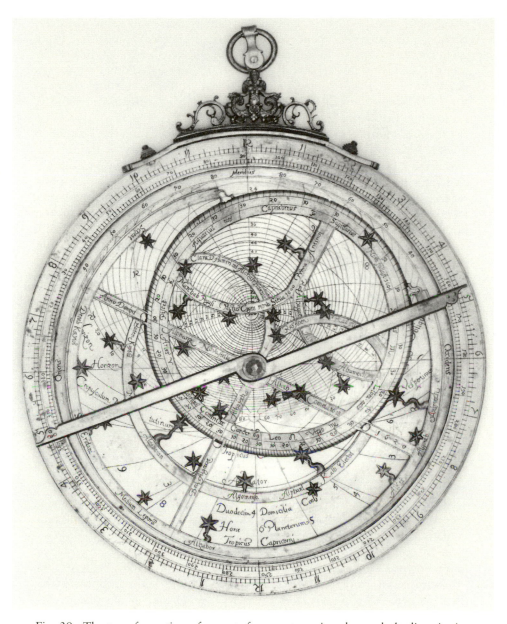

Fig. 39. The transformation of comets from meteors into heavenly bodies. An instrument maker decided that the bright 1618 comet and several novas were worthy of the company of the other fixed stars on the *rete* of this unusual copper astrolabe, dated 1620. The comet is right of center. (M-34. Courtesy of Adler Planetarium & Astronomy Museum, Chicago, Illinois.)

Practica auff dz·1532·Jar

Zu Eeren den Durchleuchtigen Hochgebornen Fürsten vnnd H. H. Herrn Wilhelmen vnd Herrn Ludwigen Pfaltzbey Rheyn Hertzogen in Obern vnd Nidern Bayrn ꝛc. Gebildere / Durch Petrum Apianum der löblichen Hohenn schül zu Ingelstat Mathematicum / nach rechter kunst vnd art der Astronomei Practicirt.

Auch wirdt nachuolgend von dem nechst erschinen Cometen / wie vnnd in was gestalt jn gemelter Apianus obseruirt hat: vn welche biß her / dero vil sindt / jn jrem schreiben jrrig gefunden / bewerlich angezaygt.

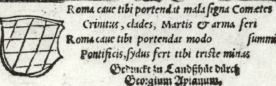

Roma caue tibi portendat mala signa Cometes
Crinitus, clades, Martis & arma feri
Roma caue tibi portendat modo summi
Pontificis, sydus fert tibi triste minas

Gedruckt zu Landßhut durch
Georgium Apianum.

Fig. 40. Comet tails pointing away from the sun. Peter Apian, *Practica auff dz. 1532. Jar* (Landshut, [1531]). (Crawford Library, Royal Observatory, Edinburgh.)

Fig. 41. An eyewitness draws a comet, with the aid of an assistant who holds a lantern and his tablet. Broadside printed by Peter Codicillus, *Von einem Schrecklichen und Wunderbarlichen Cometen* (Prague, 1577). (Wickiana Collection. From the Department of Prints and Drawings of the Zentralbibliothek Zürich.)

What ramifications did these debates have for augury? To begin, one could be a good Copernican and still see comets as tokens of God's displeasure. Some, such as Robert Recorde, joined Copernicus in placing comets below the moon and had no problem upholding the value of cometary prognostication. A man of affairs would do well to learn the meaning of recent comets before embarking on new ventures, Recorde said, for comets "ever were messangers of as wonderfull effectes, of newe innovations, straunge transmutations, and sometime utter subversions, not onlye of small provinces, but also of great kingdomes, yea and of many regions at ones."[15] Another Copernican, Thomas Digges (d. 1595), hinted that comets were supralunar, yet republished his father's claims that comets were signs and causes even though these were based on Aristotelian meteorology.[16]

New instruments also brought comets into sharper focus but did little to dissuade people of their import (fig. 43). When John Bainbridge, the future

Fig. 42. Debate over cometary paths. Aristotle on the left holds his diagram showing sublunar comets. Kepler, on the right, proposes that comets move in straight
lines. Hevelius, seated in the center, maintains that comets originate in the atmospheres of the outer planets and move in curved paths. Hevelius, *Cometographia*
(Danzig, 1668). (Courtesy of Adler Planetarium & Astronomy Museum, Chicago,
Illinois.)

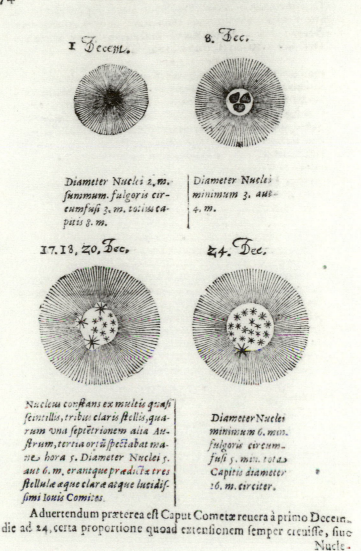

I Decem.

8. Dec.

Diameter Nuclei 2. m. summum. fulgoris circumfusi 3. m. totius capitis 8. m.

Diameter Nuclei minimum 3. aut 4. m.

17. 18, 20, Dec,

24. Dec.

Nucleus conftans ex multis quafi fcintillis, tribus claris ftellis, quarum vna feptetrionem alia Auftrum, tertia ortū fpectabat mane hora 5. Diameter Nuclei 5. aut 6. m. erantque prædictæ tres ftellulæ æque claræ atque lucidiffimi Iouis Comites.

Diameter Nuclei minimum 6. min. fulgoris circumfufi 5. min. totas Capitis diameter 16. m. circiter.

Aduertendum præterea eft Caput Cometæ reuera à primo Decem. die ad 24, certa proportione quoad extenfionem femper creuiffe, fiue

Nucle-

Fig. 43. Early telescopic observations of a comet's nucleus and its day-to-day changes. Johann Baptista Cysat, *Mathemata astronomica de loco, motu, magnitudine, et causis cometae* (Ingolstadt, 1619). (Courtesy of Adler Planetarium & Astronomy Museum, Chicago, Illinois.)

Savilian professor of astronomy at Oxford, trained his telescope and cross-staff on a comet in 1618, he saw evidence of divine providence.[17] The tools of the new astronomy mingled comfortably with old schemes of divination.

Whereas Copernicanism had little impact on popular and learned attitudes, we must ask whether more specific debates on the nature and locus of comets depreciated their value as portents. Parallactic observations of comets elevated them from the upper atmosphere into the realm of the planets. Once recognized to be so far away, they could not plausibly scorch the earth or poison the air. Yet one could still contend that they arose from terrestrial exhalations that had drifted into the heavenly regions, and so were both symptomatic of geological conditions fostering abundant exhalations below and significant of meteorological changes caused by these exhalations. Christopher Wren (1632–1723), as president of the Royal Society, mused along these lines in 1681 when he opined "that there might be some general constitution of the aether, that might be the cause as well of the earthquake as of the storm and comet."[18] The opposition of the tail to the sun countered the theory that comets were burning meteors no matter how high up, but left open the possibility that as heavenly bodies they might influence the earth in an astrological way. Many went down this road with Tycho, urging sinners to heed their message.[19] As "unnatural births in the heavens," comets were more portentous and powerful than the stars, Tycho exclaimed, and he even cast horoscopes for them.[20] Others chose to view comets as quasi-planets able to blast the earth with occult influences, radiate unhealthy light beams, or transmit noxious corpuscles.[21]

With only minor adjustments and ad hoc assertions, natural philosophers could accommodate the old ideas to each new piece of information on the nature of comets. Take, for example, Descartes's novel theory that comets were darkened suns, which, having been covered over with maculae, could no longer sustain their own stellar vortices and so were swept into neighboring vortices where they appeared as comets.[22] Whereas Descartes was silent on the significance of comets, Claude Mallement de Messange (1653–1723), a professor of philosophy at the Collège du Plessis, stepped in to posit that comets might draw off gross, pernicious matter from the edges of the vortex and push this uncongenial stuff toward the earth, thereby tainting our air and precipitating injury to crops and health (fig. 44).[23]

Even theories of the periodic return of comets—advocated unsuccessfuly by Ward, Cassini, Petit, and Bernoulli, and successfully by Newton and Halley—did not defeat cometary astrology.[24] In 1677, John Flamsteed (1646–1719) may have expressed his hope that the fearful predictions of astrologers would be undermined by demonstrations of comet periodicity, but periodicity was no threat to astrologers who had embraced the periodicity of great conjunctions as useful to their craft.[25] An omniscient God could synchronize the regular returns of comets with periods when he wished to bring sinners to their knees, observed Paul Fabricius in 1556 and William Whiston in 1696.[26] As late as 1789, Henry Adams reiterated in an almanac

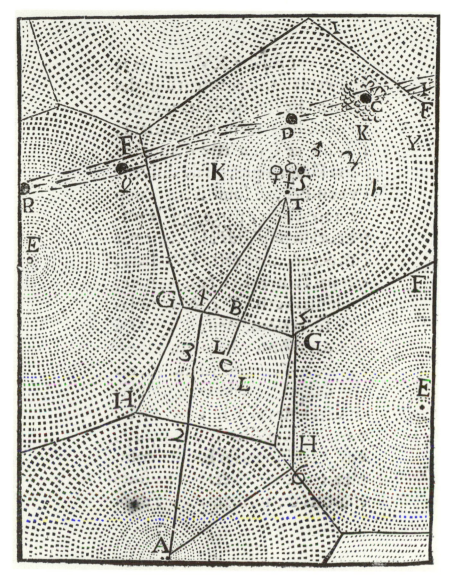

Fig. 44. Comet traveling from vortex to vortex (along path *R-Q-D-C*). Note the turbulent matter enveloping the comet (C), which the comet pushes from one vortex into the next. René Descartes, *Le monde* (Paris, 1664). (Courtesy of the National Library of Medicine.)

that the regular return of comets did not lessen their influence, since history revealed a cyclical pattern and the same causes may produce the same effects.[27] As we shall see in later chapters, Newton and Halley, too, did not find periodicity to eliminate the eschatological and prophetic functions of comets. Connections between comets and calamities could always be found by those who were eager to spell them out.

Thus natural and astrological arguments were left intact by the new discoveries. The learned questioned how comets acted, but not what they signified. Indeed, a celestial locus for comets enhanced traditional beliefs in cometary portents. As Seneca had long before pointed out, if comets were signs of the future, they ought to have a heavenly stature commensurate with the stars and planets.[28]

The downfall of cometary prognostication might then be tied to the general decline in astrological beliefs, because both were involved in interpreting the meaning and influence of moving bodies in the heavens. But astrology, too, was able to withstand the astronomical reformation initiated by Copernicus and abetted by Tycho, Kepler, Galileo, and Newton. The heliocentric theory set the earth in motion but did not preclude the earth's being swathed in celestial influences radiating from the stars and other planets. Observations of novas in 1572, 1600, and 1604 revealed the heavens to be mutable; Galileo's discoveries of Jupiter's satellites and countless Milky Way stars showed that numerous bodies dotted the celestial vault unbeknownst to us. As astronomers realized that much in the heavens was yet to be surveyed, the old anthropocentric universe gave way. But this did not make the task of astrologers impossible; astrological calculations simply became more complicated as one took the earth's motion and the new stars into account. Hence the part of astrology that treated the passage of comets through the constellations was still intact.

The destruction of the Aristotelian dichotomy between the celestial and sublunar regions posed a different problem for astrology. The dull, sluggish earth became a shining planet revolving rapidly on its axis and whirling about the sun. Observations of lunar mountains, sunspots, supralunar comets, and novas robbed the heavens of their eternal perfection; the celestial realm experienced corruption and change. "And now what of all this?" asked John Swan. "Nothing but onely thus: viz. If Comets be burnt, consumed and wasted in the starrie heavens, it seemeth that there is no great difference between them and things here below."[29] As the divorce between the heavens and earth was terminated, it became untenable to suppose that comets, stars, and planets exerted a unidirectional influence on the earth. This cut astrological theory to the quick, for even if one assumed an influence to radiate from planet Earth commensurate with those emanating from other celestial bodies, it made little sense to reason that conjunctions of Jupiter and Saturn exerted greater forces here on earth than the earth did itself. Nonetheless, this attack on the traditional mechanism of

astrological predictions was not insurmountable. Indeed, Kepler's theory of the sympathetic response of vital faculties within the earth and human bodies to those within the heavens circumvented this particular problem and reestablished astrological predictions on different grounds. When nasty planetary configurations or horrid comets troubled the heavens, earth and man naturally sensed the discord and were sympathetically thrown into consternation.

If astronomical reforms did not undermine astrology and strip comets of their portentous powers, perhaps philosophical criticism did.

EPISTEMOLOGICAL CRITICS

Pierre Gassendi (1592–1655) and Pierre Bayle (1647–1706) were not alone in rejecting the significance of comets, but their works appear to have been more widely read than those of Scaliger, Petit, and Bekker.[30] We can let their remarks serve as exemplars of common critiques.

Gassendi became an active astronomical observer after witnessing the greatest comet of 1618.[31] Although it inspired him to make some predictions, he soon rejected all forms of astrology, deviating from the path of Marin Mersenne (1588–1648), who had made an exception for comets and blamed the demise of princes on them.[32] Gassendi denied that comets were causal or signal,[33] and in his *Syntagma philosophicum* (posthumously published in 1658) he succinctly set forth his attack on traditional comet lore.[34]

Many of his views were later voiced by Bayle, who held the chair in philosophy at the Academy of Sedan when the 1680 comet appeared. It was in Sedan that Bayle drafted his famous, tract-length letter on comets. When Louis XIV closed the Protestant Academy in July 1681, Bayle left Sedan and obtained a professorship of philosophy and history at the Ecole Illustre in Rotterdam. Here in March 1682 he anonymously published the letter, which claimed to prove, contrary to popular wisdom, that comets did not presage disaster.[35] The following year, Bayle produced a second edition under a new title, and three other editions followed by 1708.[36] Despite the weight given to comets in the titles, Bayle used the subject of comets as a vehicle to discuss religious and moral questions, which were of greater interest to him. His treatment of these topics caused charges of atheism to be leveled against him, resulting ultimately in his ejection from his professorship in 1693.[37]

The strategy of the skeptics was simple. If comets were portents, Bayle and Gassendi reasoned, they had to be signs or efficient causes. One had only to prove that they were neither signs nor causes in order to show that they were not portents.[38]

Regarding causes, Bayle thought it absurd and heretical to maintain that comets caused wars, new religions, and other "plagues of human society," for these might occur a year or two later. He blamed social troubles on

human free will and fortuitous circumstances (such as sudden deaths, capricious sentiments, grudges, envy, avarice, pride, lust, and vanity).[39]

Bayle also judged that no physical theory could convincingly connect comets and calamities. Comets reflected their light from the sun. Their feeble rays could not carry off comet corpuscles, and comets were powerless to transmit their own matter over vast distances. Bayle was a Cartesian and argued, moreover, that any emanations would get caught up in the solar vortex and would recede centrifugally from the sun and earth. But what if comets stirred up eddies in the vortex and so drew off gross matter from the vortical extremities? Could this gross stuff form noxious clouds around comets and be pushed toward our purer region as the comets traveled through the solar system? Not really, Bayle said. Gross matter or cometary emanations would dissolve in the vortex and have inconsequential effects.[40]

Gassendi and Bayle both found a priori and a posteriori arguments to be defective. If comets produced anything, a priori, it might be beneficial rather than baleful. They chided people who falsely reasoned, "post hoc, ergo propter hoc," and mistook contiguous relationships for causal connections. The historical record, as they saw it, showed no more evils to occur after apparitions than before them.[41]

Causal arguments were also damned by the selective nature of misfortunes. On one hand, comets were thought to ravage any part of the earth over which they passed. Yet some kingdoms were spared while others were smitten. On the other hand, some effects were by tradition presumed to be restricted; comets were to kill kings but pass over peasants. Yet death left the palace and visited the hut. The choice of victim, Gassendi and Bayle inferred, had nothing to do with celestial configurations.[42]

Having dismissed all causal connections, Bayle and Gassendi mustered several reasons that comets could not be signs. First, they could not be natural signs, for there were no natural connections between comets and catastrophes. Nor were they instituted as divine signs (like the rainbow), because God had nowhere revealed that blazing stars would serve as warnings of extraordinary judgments.[43]

Contradictions appeared when one considered to whom these purported signs were directed. Were comets warnings to the wicked? No, those spared after the appearance of a comet were no more righteous or penitent than those punished.[44] Did comets single out certain countries? If so, why were they not imprinted with special characters by which one could interpret their meanings unambiguously? Could widely seen comets herald global judgments? Not likely. Earlier comets had not signified world reform, and God had not chastised the entire world or threatened universal judgment since the Flood.[45] Was astrology helpful in assessing comets? Sure, if one put faith in so nonsensical a system.[46]

Bayle believed in the periodic return of comets and thought it prevented them from being portents.[47] Even if comet returns had coincided initially with an independent cycle of terrestrial troubles, this correlation could not

last. Natural changes within the earth and a thousand fortuitous human actions would conspire eventually to desynchronize the tandem cycles.[48]

Indeed, comets were highly unsuited to serve as public beacons. On one hand, comets appeared too frequently to maintain their power as fearful warnings; men became inured to them. On the other hand, they were often shielded from our view by clouds and sunlight, or were too small to be seen by anyone except telescopically equipped astronomers, who seemed unlikely candidates to shoulder the responsibility of interpreting divine prodigies, preaching to the public, upholding moral standards, and exhorting people to reform.[49]

To conclude, Bayle suggested that religious arguments adduced on behalf of cometary portents were basically impious. Social troubles depended on free will. Thus for comets to portend evils, they must do so as miraculous signs.[50] But if God had miraculously formed comets in order to enjoin mankind to heed his injunctions, then God would in effect have prepared signs to confirm men in idolatrous practices, because pagans and other non-Christians startled by the fiery apparitions would offer prayers and sacrifices to false gods.[51] Indeed, Bayle exclaimed, it was wrong to think that God designed comets to prevent atheism, when at best they fostered idolatry. Comets themselves could not instill an appreciation of the true God into idol-worshipers who prayed to a pantheon of deities, or into atheists who believed that the natural order of the world proceeded from chance.[52]

Bayle decided that the commonplace opinion was derived not from divine revelation but from pagan superstitions carried over into Christianity. He believed that demons caused many natural effects like comets to be viewed as prodigies in order to propagate idolatry and superstition. Credulous men aided in this affair by willfully believing the poets, panegyrists, and flatterers who aggrandized the lives of their heros with prodigious circumstances. Politicians, too, manipulated the belief in order to intimidate or inspire the people to act in ways suitable to political ends.[53] Gassendi and Bayle urged people to open their eyes and to consider how unlikely it would be for God to waste his time using glorious prodigies to such paltry ends, as in announcing the less-than-surprising death of an old, infirm prince.[54]

These were stock criticisms of cometary portents.[55] While modern readers may find them persuasive, they must acknowledge that many contemporaries were unconvinced. John Edwards, the Calvinist theologian, for example, took time to rebut them.[56] A few examples are instructive in highlighting how a divine like Edwards remained unwavering in his faith. When Gassendi remarked that men were conceited to think that comets were prodigies prepared exclusively for them, Edwards responded that Gassendi aided "the Plot and Design of Atheistical Spirits, who would exclude God from the *Government* and *Care of the World*. . . . For by Comets God is pleased as by new Arguments to urge and inculcate his presence in the World, that when the ordinary course of Nature and Providence doth not move men, they may be rouzed by these Wondrous and Rare Objects."[57]

When Scaliger observed that many comets have been seen without subsequent mischief, and much mischief routinely occurred unannounced by comets, Edwards said that comets only conditionally signified dire events.[58] If men repented, God in his mercy might avert the planned punishment. Moreover, an apparition depended on God's free will, and God sometimes chose other natural signs to herald disasters. And when Bayle pooh-poohed the effects of comets, Edwards appealed to human experience. "We have felt the Effects of comets. . . . It hath been proved to us experimentally."[59] Edwards challenged the argument that prognostication was impious. "It is downright sottishness to think that these [comets] are set up for vain shews and useless sights," he declared. "It is unworthy of Providence to defend this."[60]

Beyond rebuttals, another factor to consider in evaluating the effectiveness of epistemological critiques is the issue of timing. Scholars, such as Scaliger, had in previous centuries attacked cometary divination with little effect. Why then, when similar arguments were offered by Gassendi and Bayle, were these lauded in learned circles? It seems that those who embraced them were already convinced or predisposed to be convinced. How could this be?

SHIFT IN PRIORITIES AND SIGNS OF DECLINE

Although vestiges of comet lore lingered in learned circles during the seventeenth century, they grew less robust as the century progressed. We catch a glimpse even in *Cometomantia*, when Edwards, sounding somewhat desperate, made a last-ditch appeal to skeptics. His pitch was a version of Pascal's wager:

> Lastly, If all that hath been said amounts not to a Demonstration . . . that Comets are Signs of impendent Evils, yet this ought to be remembered, that no Man can be certain that they *signifie Nothing*. . . . It will be best for us to look upon them as *such* [signs], and then, if we are mistaken, it will be on the *safest side*, and we shall err with the wisest and soberest Persons.[61]

While Edwards was right to suggest that many wise and sober persons perceived comets to be signs, there was an unmistakable shift in their attitudes. Many who examined the prospect and plausibility of cometary presages did so with an eye toward uncovering rules of nature rather than becoming prophets of future events.

The vituperative debate between Galileo Galilei (1564–1642) and the Jesuits at the Collegio Romano provides a good early example of this shift in interest.[62] The limited discussion of cometary signs and effects was aimed at ascertaining whether comets were burning objects. Galileo observed that if comets burned, they would consume arid, gusty matter and be followed by seasonable weather.[63] When Orazio Grassi (1583–1654) reported that a

large part of Italy had experienced unusually dry weather, mighty winds, and damaging earthquakes after the comets of 1618, Galileo felt confirmed in his opinion that comets did not burn. For him, they were nothing more than sunbeams refracted in misty vapors rising from the earth.[64]

Sir Francis Bacon (1561–1626) also explored tenets of cometary divination for philosophical rather than prognosticative reasons. Writing contemporaneously with Galileo, Bacon treated comets in various tracts associated with his *Instauratio magno* and proposed that a history of comets be prepared as part of the groundwork needed to establish a future philosophy.[65] He thought an understanding of the operations of comets would throw light on larger scientific problems. For instance, in investigating the form of heat in the *Novum organum* (1620), Bacon examined comets among the "instances in proximity where the nature of heat is absent." Although comets blazed overhead as the sun did, comet rays were not hot to touch; although comets were often followed by droughts, they did not increase seasonal temperatures in any constant manner.[66] How did comets promote drought without heating the air? Bacon did not know, but he was convinced of their efficacy and lamented that it was not more carefully analyzed:

> Comets . . . have . . . power and effect over the gross and mass of things; but they are rather gazed upon, and waited upon in their journey, than wisely observed in their effects; specially in their respective effects; that is, what kind of comet, for magnitude, colour, version of the beams, placing in the region of heaven, or lasting, produceth what kind of effects.[67]

Knowledge of comets' effects would prove useful to society, as would the development of an expurgated "sane astrology," among whose benefits Bacon listed the forecast of future comets.[68]

Like Galileo and Bacon, Sir Thomas Browne (1605–1682) approached comets with the goal of improving natural philosophy. As a schoolboy, Browne had seen the major comet of 1618,[69] and in his *Pseudodoxia Epidemica*, a catalog of popular errors, he examined the traditional correlation between comets and subsequent calamities. The only fault he found with the popular view was that it left no room for comets to augur good.[70] He also noted that comets, like rainbows, albeit part of the natural order, were signs. By the rainbow, God declared his convenant with Noah, and by blazing stars, he informed us that fire would ultimately destroy the world.[71]

In the foregoing examples, we detect a shift in the treatment of comets, but note that their potential to influence the earth was little questioned. Yet soon after the English Restoration and well before Bayle put pen to paper, comets had lost their prestige as portents among the English scientific elite. There was great talk about the 1664 and 1665 comets in the coffeehouses,[72] in Gresham College,[73] and at the Royal Society meetings,[74] but the character of that talk differed vastly from rumors in the marketplace. Samuel Pepys conversed with associates about these comets, which he himself had observed, but did not concern himself with their significance.[75] At Gresham

College, Robert Hooke (1635–1703) entertained Pepys among others with some "very curious" lectures on these comets. Hooke focused his attention on comet composition, dissolution, and possible periodicity; his later published remarks on comets were silent on their effects.[76] According to John Evelyn, Royal Society meetings revolved around "*Schemes* of the *Comets* progresse."[77] Henry Oldenburg engaged as intermediary in a two-year controversy between Hevelius and Auzout over the comets' paths, while various members of the Royal Society acted as astronomical referees. Cometary import never entered the discussion.[78] Stanislaw Lubieniecki was the only one to raise the subject with Oldenburg. The Polish author of a lavish catalog of past and present reports on comets,[79] Lubieniecki wrote in 1666 that he had received observations and divinatory judgments of a comet from various (unidentified) English mathematicians, and he later acknowledged his belief that the London fire was divinely instigated to chastise those worthy to be led into penitence.[80] Oldenburg responded courteously to Lubieniecki but did not take up the subject of God's retributive interference in natural affairs.[81]

Indeed the general tenor of the Royal Society can be gauged to an extent by the minutes of meetings recorded in Thomas Birch's history. Avidly discussed were observations and theories of motion, origin, destination, periodicity, substance, and duration.[82] When Cluverus shared two Italian treatises on the 1680 comet, they were found to consist primarily of astrological predictions and were scorned for containing "very little or nothing of considerable observation."[83] But cheap tracts continued to make their way into the Royal Society's rooms. For instance, Hooke presented an extract of Johann Heinrich Voigt's *Cometa matutinus et vespertinus*.[84] Voigt began his book with quotations from Luther on God's wrath revealed by comets and concluded with a prediction that the world would end in 1696. He labeled as atheist anyone who treated comets as less than prodigies. Minutes of the meeting, however, do not mention any of this. Although fellows of the Royal Society were exposed to vulgar ideas like Voigt's— plentiful enough in the marketplaces and alehouses—they apparently were more interested in astronomical observations than in prognostications.[85] John Evelyn and Ralph Thoresby still saw comets as warnings from God, but they were the exception.[86]

Across the Channel, a skeptical tone prevailed in the *Journal des sçavans*. In 1665, for instance, the journal reported a conference on comets held in the presence of royalty, prelates, and courtiers at the Jesuit Collège de Clermont in Paris. While the origin, substance, and motion of comets were debated, there is no evidence that prognostication was discussed or that the journal's editors entertained any interest in the subject.[87] Indeed, later that year, the journal took note of a satire of astrological tracts on comets, and in 1681 essays refuted beliefs in cometary portents.[88] Even so, the journal listed a treatise inquiring whether comets were not ruled by evil genii, and noticed that the 1682 comet had appeared five or six nights be-

fore the birth of the duc de Bourgogne.[89] Traditional beliefs were not eradicated overnight.

Reports of prodigious "comet eggs" caused quite a stir in Italy, France, and Germany during this period and deserve mention here. These marvelous eggs bore markings of comets, stars, and religious symbols. They were allegedly laid by fowl whose innate faculties resonated sympathetically with the menacing tones of the heavens.[90] Lubieniecki reported an egg laid by a Warsaw hen at the time of the 1665 comet.[91] This egg was marked with a sword, a flaming cross, a rod, and a drawn bow. Italian scholars vouched for the most famous egg, laid by a Roman hen ostensibly under the influence of the 1680 comet. Reports from Rome circulated in France and Germany where they reached the attention of academies of science as well as the general public. The egg, with its image of comet and stars, was featured on broadsides (fig. 45).[92] The editors of the *Journal des sçavans* felt it incumbent on them to report the natural wonder:

> As soon as we had received some letters from Rome touching the egg which has caused so much fuss everywhere, we treated this news as we had another report that was sent to us last year, touching an alleged monstrosity, which was found to be as false as we had judged at first. But since letters have been written about the egg to some persons of the first rank, such as Madame la Grand' Duchesse, and M. l'Internonce and several others have received a detailed account of it, we have thought that we should at least give the public the design of this prodigy, which was sent to them, together with the short account that follows.[93]

The report continued:

> Last Monday night, on 2 December, about eight o'clock (which corresponds to an hour after midnight according to our manner of reckoning) a hen, which had never before laid any eggs, after having cackled in an extraordinary manner following a great noise, laid an egg of an unusually large size, marked not with a comet, as the common people have believed, but with several stars, just as the figure represents it [fig. 46].
>
> If all that is quite true, it would not be the first prodigy of this nature that has appeared in Italy during eclipses or comets. For without speaking of crosses that appeared on linen in Calabria at the time of the comet of 1663, M. Cassini was formerly shown in the city of Bologna an eggshell on which was perfectly seen in relief a well-marked sun; and he was assured that this egg had been laid at the time of an eclipse.[94]

The story of the comet egg illustrates how far the learned elite had distanced themselves from vulgar beliefs and how far they had yet to go. The marked egg was treated with a healthy dose of skepticism but not dismissed outright as popular error. In part this was because aristocrats were giving it a hearing. Another reason was that scholars (such as the astronomer G. D. Cassini, then at the Paris Observatory) had treated such incidents seriously

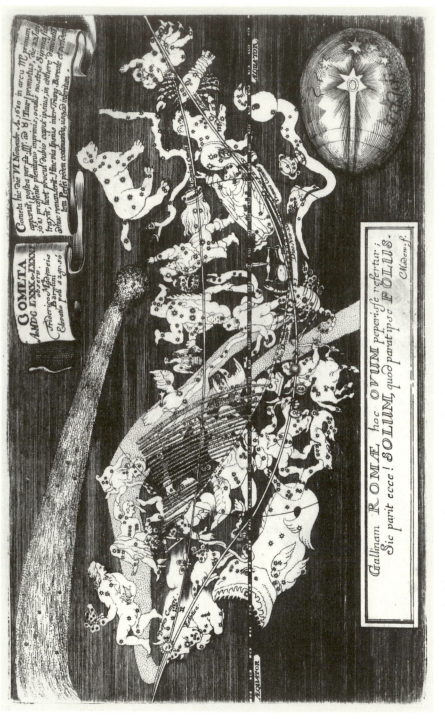

Fig. 45. Comet egg laid by a Roman hen in 1680. Broadside, Friedrich Madeweis, *Cometa Anno MDC LXXX et LXXXI* (Berlin, 1681). (WOP-205. Courtesy of Adler Planetarium & Astronomy Museum, Chicago, Illinois.)

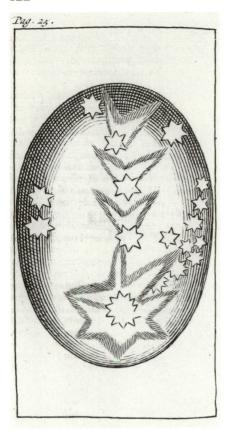

Fig. 46. Comet egg illustrated in *Journal des sçavans* (1681). (Courtesy of the Newberry Library, Chicago.)

in the past. In 1681, it seems that elite natural philosophers were interested not in whether the egg was a divine sign but in whether the heavens could influence terrestrial things.

But in general, skepticism reigned among most intellectuals of the day. Bernard le Bovier de Fontenelle drew comic inspiration from the 1680 comet and penned a humorous play, *La Comete*, which was performed during the end of January 1681 in Paris. In the play, Fontenelle caricatured and ridiculed popular fears of comets. In one scene, a countess was consulting her astrologer about the dreaded bearded star overhead when letters arrived from Rome bearing the awful news that a comet had been discovered *in* an egg![95] The countess, aghast, swore that she would eat no more eggs; she was seconded by her astrologer's valet, who dared not devour an "Omelette de[s] Cometes."[96]

Witty cynics like Fontenelle thus made public fun of cometary astrology, which was already being discredited in private circles, as revealed by a letter written as early as 1621 from a French ambassador to Spain: "It seems to me that the comet we joked about at Saint-Germain is no laughing matter,

since it has knocked down a pope, a grand duke, and a king of Spain in two months' time."[97] It remains to be asked what prompted these mocking remarks. As was shown in the earlier part of this chapter, basic astronomical reforms and critical remarks were by themselves insufficient to bring about this change in opinion even among the most erudite astronomers.

SOCIAL REASONS FOR THE DECLINE

By the time Bayle proffered serious refutations of the principles of cometary prognostication, these tenets had already lost their scientific prestige. English and French scientific circles were all but outrightly hostile to astrological predictions from comets. The subject had died a natural death, and as Keith Thomas has aptly observed with respect to astrology in general, "The clergy and the satirists chased it into its grave, but the scientists were unrepresented at the funeral."[98] What tarnished the reputation of traditional comet lore?

While I make no pretensions to offer a definitive answer to this question, which is as thorny as the reasons for the decline of magic and astrology, I would like to offer some tentative conclusions. I believe the answers are to be found in the social arena.

To begin, it is worth reviewing what functions were served by traditional comet lore. People consulted astrologers and clergymen about comets for many of the same reasons.[99] The past seemed chaotic, the future uncertain, and anxiety was high. Astrologers and clergymen offered reassurances, warned people of impending judgments, and tried to set them on the right track. Here comets were a helpful tool. Their timely appearances gave definition to an otherwise shapeless past. Historical periods of civil unrest, change in rulership, and epidemic illness were punctuated by comets. The victim of past misfortune could console himself with the knowledge that history was providential; his losses were part of a carefully worked out divine scheme—broadcast sometimes by comets—and not due to chance or the sovereignty of a capricious deity. With regard to the future, the astrologer who deciphered the meaning of comets offered clients greater freedom through advance knowledge of upcoming events. If war was threatened, or poor harvests foreseen, clients took precautions to avert personal hardship. Some fasted and prayed for deliverance. Others tried to profit from inside astronomical information. Governments, too, took stock of cometary predictions in formulating public policy. Divination from comets also helped folks make decisions in cases where, given the paucity of other useful information, they perhaps had no rational basis for choice. Was it a propitious time to plant or harvest a crop, to journey on business, to engage in battle, to assassinate a comet-struck monarch or overthrow the government? Questions such as these were posed and answered in the astrologer's consulting room and printed on broadsheets for all to learn.

The psychological appeal of cometary divination is undeniable. In providing a coherent explanation of historical circumstances, in consoling the star-crossed victim by shifting responsibility to God, comets, and one's sinful neighbors, in combating the notion that misfortune was random, in offering the prospect of control over future events, and in tendering answers to otherwise insoluble questions, divination from comets discharged many useful functions. Moreover, at the heart of interpretations of comets was the belief that the natural world reflected the moral order. This was a very satisfying belief indeed. It was said that a minister had no better text from which to preach repentance than a comet.[100]

While belief in the symmetry of the natural and moral worlds was deeply rooted in all levels of society, prognostication from comets became confined to inferior social groups during the seventeenth century. The elite chose to reject comets as omens, and this repudiation was part of a broader movement by which they set themselves apart from the common people.

The withdrawal of the upper classes occurred in stages, at different paces, and for different reasons in different parts of Europe, but its parameters can be summarized.[101] In 1500, popular culture was shared by all members of society, although it was a second culture for the educated, who kept one foot in academic traditions. By 1800, the nobility, clergy, and bourgeoisie—and their wives and daughters—had abandoned popular culture to the lower classes, from whom they were now divorced by enormous differences in worldview.

The withdrawal began earlier in England and France than in the rest of Europe. Ballads and chapbooks, for instance, which had appealed to artisans and aristocrats alike, came to be viewed as crass by French and English upper classes in the early seventeenth century but remained part of genteel culture in Denmark and Poland until the end of the seventeenth and the mid–eighteenth centuries respectively.[102]

Different members of society had their own reasons to become alienated from popular culture. Many clergy, for instance, withdrew as part of the Reformation and Counter-Reformation. In 1500, parish priests were of the same social class as their parishioners. They attended masquerades, danced on feast days, and told jokes from the pulpit. Reformers, however, soon demanded a more learned and solemn clergy. Protestant ministers were typically trained at university, and after the Council of Trent priests were increasingly graduates of seminaries. The new clergy were of higher social status, better educated, and more remote from their flocks. The clergy's alienation from the common people went beyond the mere fact of their social position. In popular practices, both Catholic and Protestant reformers saw traces of ancient paganism and overindulgence. Carnivals were compared to ancient Bacchanalia, and May Day celebrations to the Feasts of Flora. Festivals were seen as occasions for sin—drunkenness, lewd dancing, groping, disorderly behavior, blasphemy, and violence. The godly, therefore, made a systematic attempt to reform the culture of the common peo-

ple. Protestant and Catholic reformers did not have the same agenda, however. Both attempted to quash elements of popular religion, such as miracle and mystery plays and the public's devotion to charms, spells, and augury. But Protestants saw many Catholic rites as thinly disguised pagan ceremonies (Christmas taking the place of a solstitial festival, for instance), and they abhorred magical practices (like transubstantiation and exorcism) sanctioned by the Catholic Church.[103] The details of these reform efforts do not concern us here, but two things are relevant for this study of comets. First, the clergy were suspicious of astrology and attacked divination as illegitimate.[104] Second, pagan beliefs about comets were among the things the early church had accommodated in its efforts to gain converts. Respect for comets as divine signs was nothing more than folklorized Christianity and as such was subject to attacks leveled against pagan beliefs assimilated by the Catholic Church. Many of Bayle's arguments against divination come under this heading. But we should add that many ministers saw nothing impious or idolatrous in preaching from the "text" of a comet, and countercharges of atheism were sometimes brought against those like Bayle or Gassendi who claimed otherwise.[105]

The nobility seemed to differ from the clergy in their reasons for withdrawing from popular culture. Perhaps they wished to set themselves apart in order to justify their courtly privileges, now that they no longer had military obligations to the Crown. Whatever the case, in the Renaissance, nobles began to adopt more polished manners and a new, self-conscious style of behavior advocated by courtesy books, such as Castiglione's *Courtier*. They tried to be more dignified. Lords no longer sat elbow-to-elbow with their retainers in great halls; they took their meals in private dining rooms. They even shunned the local dialects used by peasants and craftsmen in favor of the language of the court. In southern France, French deposed Occitan; in Wales and Scotland, Celtic languages made way for English; in Bohemia, German replaced Czech. Scholars collected common proverbs, but use of them by the educated was seen as proof of having kept bad company.[106] Texts once shared came to be viewed by the elite as unworthy reading because they were so popular among the vulgar.[107] The upper classes also withdrew their support from popular festivals, which by the mid–seventeenth century they viewed as disorderly diversions. They began to work with the clergy in efforts to reform manners. In place of coarse recreations— such as bearbaiting, cockfighting, and smock races—they substituted more refined amusements. Dancing masters taught them formal dances that differed from country dances. They took refuge from the riffraff found in public theaters and attended plays in private auditoriums. Street theater was denounced as scurrilous and politically dangerous.[108] Their outlook on nature also changed. Magic was relegated to chapbooks, unworthy of noble hands. Their sick consulted physicians, not folk healers like charlatans, mountebanks, and cunning women. The prophecies of Mother Shipton and Merlin became the object of laughter. And belief in witchcraft, formerly

treated with respect and denounced as diabolical, came to be derided as superstitious. Such marked differences in worldview perhaps emerged because popular culture could not keep up with the rapid changes in learned culture during the period 1500–1800.[109]

As for the middling sort, many lawyers, officials, and prosperous merchants imitated the polished manners of their superiors, because they wanted to pass for noblemen.[110] In this sense, the worldview of the aristocracy and educated elite exerted hegemonic control over all but the lowest classes, for it must be said that popular culture strongly resisted the efforts to reform it.[111] And so, by the end of the seventeenth century in places like England and France, we can speak of two cultures—high and low—corresponding roughly to the practices and beliefs of the aristocracy, clergy, and "better sort" on one hand, and those of the great mass of laboring people (or "vulgar") on the other.[112]

While high and low culture were never hermetically sealed off from each other, there is no doubt that the gulf between them widened in the early modern period.[113] In the end, portentous comets made their home in the midst of low culture. The way comets lost the respect of the elite is illustrated in the pattern of their appearances in books codifying popular beliefs and correcting vulgar errors; for in these texts, the origin of the gulf between high and low can be glimpsed in part.

The sixteenth century witnessed the printing of many folk beliefs drawn from oral and written traditions, including vulgar regimens, secrets, and fortune-telling tools.[114]

Publications of popular lore brought it to the attention of learned individuals, such as Laurent Joubert, Sir Thomas Browne, and even John Flamsteed, who cataloged popular errors and attempted to correct them in other books. Authors of books of errors generally recognized that vulgar errors were shared by peasants and persons of higher rank, but their main goal was to change the views of the common people (even though their books circulated not among the people per se but among physicians, learned surgeons, and natural philosophers).[115] Folk beliefs about comets appeared in some of these books, but it was not clever logic that struck them down.[116] (Criticism in error books was no more sophisticated than the work already discussed.) More influential was the simple fact that comets were treated between the covers of these volumes. The books' effects were indirect.

Books of errors were part of the program of the elite to reform the manners of the common folk and distance themselves from amusements and opinions they had long shared with them. Learned observers of popular life described a sphere of culture they were making remote from themselves, and by demarcating it, they reinforced the new coherence and authority of their own culture. The social demarcation occurred in stages.[117] In the first stage, which spanned the late sixteenth and early seventeenth centuries, the learned observers were experts in the fields of medicine, astronomy, law, and religion.[118] In cataloging errors, they emphasized how premises were

dangerous or false with respect to established science or religion. Magic, for instance, was denounced as diabolical and Faustian. In the next stage, scholars pointed to the irrationality of folk beliefs and the reasonableness of academic truths. They attacked "ignorance" and denigrated magic as superstitious. In the final stage, whose hallmarks were apparent by the end of the seventeenth century, experts and nonexperts alike treated popular practices like the use of amulets as a distinct, sociocultural phenomenon. Magic, once taken seriously at court, was confined to the village.[119] To be denounced for such an error was to be socially discredited.

These stages can be seen in debates about the meaning and nature of comets. In the 1640s, Sir Thomas Browne challenged the folk view that comets augured evil but not good on technical, scientific grounds. Since comets were now found to be in the heavens instead of below the moon, they might hold favorable aspects with benevolent stars or planets. Since comets might arise from the effluvia of stars, they might retain the benignity of their sources. And since comets were colored, they should, like the stars, be influenced by planets of like color and so might portend good as well as bad.[120] Soon after, Gassendi argued that premises like Browne's were as false and vain as the astrology on which they were based. Stars and planets had no influence on the earth, and neither did comets. The contiguity of celestial and terrestrial events did not imply a causal connection. Gassendi, therefore, found cometary folk beliefs to be unreasonable.[121] In 1665, he was joined in spirit by Pierre Petit (1598–1677), the *intendant* of fortifications. Petit had been commissioned by Louis XIV to combat the credulous response of his people to a recent comet, a response Louis perhaps thought hindered the advance of his kingdom. Petit employed many of the arguments we have already discussed—some based on logic—but also introduced disparaging social demarcations when he wrote that the comet hysteria was barely worthy of "simple women and . . . little children." Reports that comets menaced kings or presaged wars were nothing more than "foolish tales to put children to sleep." To believe otherwise was the lot of "timid, simple folks who trusted in fables as if they were history." During the solar eclipse of 1654, the "ignorant people" in Europe had been struck with terror, believing that the end of the world was near at hand. The same level of ignorance and feeblemindedness was evident in the public's response to the recent comet, Petit complained.[122] As I have shown, these "ignorant people" would have included peasants and patricians, artisans and scholars fewer than fifty years before.[123] But so inclusive a definition of "ignorant" was clearly not what Petit had in mind. In particular, he did not include himself among the ignorant when he suggested that comets collected waste vapors and fumes near the sun and transported them elsewhere "for ends we will never know in this world."[124] That was a natural philosophical statement. Although teleologically it differed little from vulgar beliefs—and like them could still evoke fear—it was acceptable to Petit because it was framed in modern language and voiced by the better sort of person (namely,

himself). This attitude appears more clearly in 1680, when fear of the great comet was judged to be a "popular illness," and superstition was equated with erroneous beliefs of bygone eras.[125] After observing that ancient philosophers thought comets to be fiery meteors, indicative of disorder in the terrestrial sphere and hence of social revolutions, the *Journal des sçavans* continued, "But since we have learned that comets are celestial bodies, we have had our eyes opened to this error, which is nothing more than a popular error."[126] The message here is that adherence to archaic beliefs and practices was a marker of subservient status and perhaps justified a lower class position. In France, what had been denounced first in the name of accepted reason later became invalidated because it was labeled the product of an inferior social group.[127]

In England, folk beliefs about comets were also labeled with astrology as a component of an inferior political position.[128] With the collapse of official censorship in 1641, prognosticative tracts had flourished during the Civil War and Commonwealth.[129] Astrologers had a high profile. Their textbooks taught how to judge the permanency of a monarch, and their almanacs lent support to seditious activities and religious enthusiasm with claims that these were foretold by comets, eclipses, and conjunctions. Fifth Monarchists, Levellers, Ranters, Diggers—indeed radicals of all kinds—consulted astrologers, as did royalists and parliamentarians. The power of astrologers to incite the people was widely recognized. With the restoration of the Stuarts in 1660, the new government cracked down on astrologers and carefully censored their works.[130] Initially, the court encouraged astrological predictions in support of the Restoration, and celestial symbolism had a prominent place in public rituals of the state. But it appeared ever more evident that astrological politicking was a two-edged sword that censorship could not keep from being turned against the government. Prognostication from comets survived in popular culture, but political and religious authorities (and their social peers) began to eschew it as dangerous and enthusiastic. This low opinion was reinforced by the civil unrest contemporaneous with apparitions in the 1670s and 1680s.[131] Elite astronomers voiced similar objections during these same years. Lambasting astrology on both social and epistemological grounds, David Gregory wrote:

> It is hardly believable what great damage those predictions invented by Astrologers and ascribed to the stars have caused to our best kings, Charles I and II. . . . Therefore we prohibit Astrology to take a place in our Astronomy, since it is supported by no solid fundament, but stands on the utterly ridiculous opinions of certain people, opinions that are so framed as to promote the attempts of men tending to form factions.[132]

John Flamsteed also worried about "pernicious praedictions of the Weather, & State affaires" and "theire credit with the vulgar." In an ephemeris that remained unpublished, he attempted to correct popular errors and tried to rout astrology from the standard almanac.[133] By the end of

the century, as popular astrology became less politicized, the middling sort joined the gentry in shunning prognostication as vulgar and foolish. Divination was stigmatized and isolated in a plebeian ghetto. Polite society would not touch tenets of cometary astrology unless they were revamped by natural philosophy.

As we shall see, this revamping did occur to some degree in the work of Newton, Halley, and their contemporaries. Like Petit, even Gregory left room for comets to influence the earth by natural means. Let there be no misunderstanding, he warned his students:

> If the Tail of a Comet shou'd touch the Atmosphere of our Earth, (or if a Part of this Matter scatter'd and diffus'd about the Heavens shou'd fall into it) the Exhalations of it mix'd with our Atmosphere . . . may cause very sensible Changes in our Air, especially in Animals and Vegetables: For Vapours, . . . brought from strange and distant Regions, and excited by a very intense Heat, may be prejudicial to the Inhabitants or Products of the Earth; wherefore those things which have been observ'd by all Nations, and in all Ages, to follow the Apparition of Comets, may happen; and it is a thing unworthy a Philosopher to look upon them as false and ridiculous.[134]

Some ideas were just too compelling to abandon. And the first steps toward the appropriation of comet lore by natural philosophy had already been taken by medieval and Renaissance scholars who argued that comets were physical causes of future events.

To recap the argument of this chapter: During the early modern period, scientific and epistemological arguments were used to attack folk beliefs about comets, which were shared by all members of society. The attacks may have eroded traditional beliefs in learned circles, but many prominent astronomers and theologians continued to endorse the conventional view. By the mid–seventeenth century, the tide had turned. Augury from comets was attacked on social grounds and discredited as vulgar. It came to be shunned by those on the upper and middle rungs of society.

The rejection of comets as omens occurred earlier in England and France, later in Germany, Italy, and Poland.[135] This is why Henry Oldenburg, the secretary of the Royal Society, seemed to be talking past Stanislaw Lubieniecki, the Polish nobleman serving the king of Denmark, and why the tone of the learned academies in France and England seemed somewhat at odds with letters and tracts arriving from southern and eastern Europe. It is important to note this because the path taken by the new outlook across Europe paralleled the withdrawal of the upper classes from popular culture, and this fact lends support to a social explanation for the decline in prognostication.

World Reformation

Comets, Transmutations, and World Reform in Newton's Thought

IN THE late 1650s, a Lincolnshire schoolboy played a "philosophical" joke on his neighbors in Grantham:

> He first made lanterns of paper crimpled, which he used to go to school by, in winter mornings, with a candle, and tied them to the tails of the kites in a dark night, which at first affrighted the country people exceedingly, thinking they were comets.[1]

That boy was Isaac Newton (1642–1727), and his artificial comet "caus'd not a little discourse on market days, among the country people, when over their mugs of ale."[2]

We tend to think of Newton as living a life beyond the grasp of popular culture, but his kite-flying escapades tell us otherwise. Newton was a provincial boy, but his upbringing enabled him to engage in high and low activities. On one hand, he came from yeoman stock. His father was a prosperous husbandman who inherited the manor of Woolsthorpe, which had been purchased by Newton's grandfather. Although lord of the manor, Newton's father could not sign his own name, and his relatives were all illiterate. Their lives revolved around their sheep, cattle, and corn. Newton's mother, on the other hand, was the daughter of a gentleman and sister to an Anglican clergyman educated at Cambridge. She was barely literate. As it turned out, Newton's father died before he was born, and he was raised by his mother's family, who expected him to have at least a basic education.[3] At age twelve, he was sent to grammar school in Grantham, where he lodged with an apothecary. During this period, he read books, built sundials and mechanical contrivances, and learned about the composition of medicines. The apothecary's house stood on the High Street, next to an inn, exposing Newton to the popular culture of the village.[4] He took advantage of popular beliefs when he used his artificial comets to tease his neighbors.

Newton's mother had hoped that her son would return home to manage the family estate, but Newton had no patience with watching sheep and bringing produce to market. Ultimately, his uncle and his schoolmaster convinced her to send him to university. When Newton matriculated at Cambridge, he left rural life behind but not contact with popular culture. Throughout his life, this contact was both direct and indirect. Although Newton has been described as a solitary, somewhat dejected scholar, there is evidence that he continued to visit taverns from time to time.[5] On

one occasion, he disdained the chief room of a Temple Bar tavern and preferred to dine below-stairs with the common sort.[6] Sturbridge Fair—among
the greatest fairs in England—annually took place in late summer on a
common near Cambridge and was filled with "Coffee-Houses, Taverns,
Eating-Houses, Music Shops, Buildings for the Exhibition of Drolls, Puppet
Shews, Legerdemain, Mountebanks, Wild Beasts, Monsters, Giants, Rope
Dancers, etc."[7] There was also a Midsummer Fair in Cambridge. Newton
tells us that he attended these fairs, buying books and prisms in the mid-
1660s.[8] At least one of these books was about astrology, and Newton tried
to draw a chart around 1663.[9] Celestial wonders like comets caused a stir
at public gatherings whenever they appeared. Prognosticative broadsides
were pinned to the doors and walls of alehouses, and balladeers chanted the
latest forecasts on the commons and at fairs. When Newton took part in
the culture of taverns and fairs, he may well have been exposed to vulgar
beliefs about comets.

As for indirect contact with popular culture, Newton needed to go no
farther than his own library. Because popular culture was shared by all
members of society until the seventeenth century (even if it was a second
culture for the educated), Newton's library was stocked with books that
reported the conventional views on comets. A dozen classical authors described how comets augured blighted crops, sickness, terrestrial commotions, civil disorder, insurrection, war, and murder.[10] In other books, Jewish
and Christian scholars embraced the pagan views and gave them a new religious spin. Josephus and Eusebius, for example, wrote that a sword-shaped
comet had hovered over Jerusalem and announced its destruction in A.D.
70. Bede thought comets portended wars of religion and the deaths of holy
men. John of Damascus declared that comets fulfilled divine ends, and he
joined Origen in suggesting that the Star of Bethlehem was a comet.[11] The
Bethlehem apparition was pictured in Newton's copy of Lubieniecki's
Theatrum cometicum (1681), which like his edition of Origen shows signs
of being dog-eared.[12] Newton dog-eared another work that placed comets
within the context of sacred history: the *Telluris theoria sacra* (1681–1689)
by Thomas Burnet.[13] Burnet wrote that blazing stars would herald the last
days. In drafting the book, Burnet corresponded with Newton about cosmogony and the comet of 1680–1681.[14] His discussion of the world's end
no doubt caught Newton's eye, for the Book of Revelation and comets were
both dear to Newton's heart.[15]

At least one book offered advice on prognostication from comets. This
was Jacques Gaffarel's *Unheard-of Curiosities* (1650).[16] According to Gaffarel, a comet's shape could denote good things, such as constancy, the birth
of a great prince, or absolute power—or it could denote bad things, such as
losses by fire, tyranny, sedition, war, or pestilence. Some books debated the
power comets had over things. In his *Essays*, Francis Bacon argued that
comets were causes and worthy of study. Libertus Fromondus repeated
Kepler's doctrine of sympathy but rejected it, saying comets were divine

signs. Pierre Petit scorned the "ignorant people" who were terror-struck by comets, even as he asserted that comets cleaned the heavens of waste matter. The *Journal des sçavans* and Lubieniecki reported on famous comet eggs.[17]

Newton, therefore, was no stranger to popular culture or comet lore, even though his kite prank suggests that he viewed certain folk beliefs with detached interest. Although it would be presumptuous to say that Newton consciously rehabilitated folk beliefs in his physical studies of comets, they were nevertheless principal players, as this chapter will show.

CELESTIAL MECHANICS OF COMETS

In the field of cometography, Newton is best known for showing that comets were members of the solar system. "I am out in my judgment," he wrote, "if they are not a sort of planets revolving in orbits returning into themselves with a continual motion."[18] This remark led off Newton's masterful analysis of comets at the close of Book III of the *Principia*. This discussion was no mere afterthought. Newton's fascination with comets was lifelong. As a Cambridge scholar, Newton "sate up so often long in the year 1664 to observe a comet that appeared then, that he found himself much disordered," he later remembered.[19] When the 1665 comet appeared, he again lost sleep. His student notebook recorded his observations, sketches, reading notes, and queries.[20] Sixty years later, comets still held his interest when he had a famous fireside chat with John Conduitt, his nephew-in-law.[21] Between these dates, Newton returned again and again to the celestial mechanics and physics of comets.

In early November of 1680, a comet appeared before sunrise and was sighted heading toward the sun until the end of the month. In mid-December, another comet appeared in the evening sky, heading away from the sun. Its tail was immense, growing to be over seventy degrees long.[22] As we noted in earlier chapters, this comet stunned the common folk, who were showered with dire predictions about its political import. In England, it arrived on the heels of the Popish Plot and during the Exclusion Crisis, when paranoia about Catholics' coming to power reached a peak.

The comet not only interested radical pamphleteers but also commanded the attention of astronomers.[23] Newton observed it from December until March; kept a log of its tail; read works by Robert Hooke, Johann Hevelius, and Pierre Petit; and corresponded with John Flamsteed, the astronomer royal.[24] As early as 1677, Flamsteed had entertained the proposition that comets were periodic, and he believed that proof of periodicity would undermine seditious astrological prophecies.[25] Still clinging to this hope, Flamsteed proposed that the comets observed in November and December of 1680 were not two comets but rather one comet traveling in a highly bent line. Flamsteed treated the comet and sun magnetically, arguing that the sun first attracted one pole of the comet and then repelled the other.[26] Newton

had a lot of trouble with Flamsteed's astrophysical theory. He rejected Flamsteed's claim that hot bodies like the sun could retain their magnetism, and he opposed Flamsteed's claim that the comet had turned in front of the sun.[27] "To make ye Comets of November & December but one is to make that one paradoxical," he told Flamsteed as late as April 1681.[28]

Although Newton had already solved the dynamical problem of a planet circling the sun, in 1681 he did not apply the same method to these comets. He had not yet formulated his theory of universal gravitation. Like most astronomers, he saw comets as bodies foreign to the solar system and not governed by its laws. Comets were transient bodies. They moved in straight lines. In 1681, he attempted to find a rectilinear path for each comet moving at a uniform velocity. The results were not convincing. Later he learned that Edmond Halley too had failed to describe a rectilinear path from the observations.[29] Newton began to question the standard theory. Moreover, Flamsteed's idea of treating the comets dynamically had gotten under Newton's skin. In the spring of 1681, Newton began a letter to Flamsteed in which he discussed the nonlinear path a comet would describe under the influence of a magnetic force seated in the sun. The sun would pull the comet toward itself, but the comet's centrifugal force would overpower the attraction, carry the comet around the sun, and enable it to escape. Clearly, Newton had not yet fully articulated the theory that celestial motions were due to the combination of centripetal force and inertial motion in a straight line, but we see that he had privately begun to treat comets like the planets. It apparently was his first inclination to use the familiar if outmoded model that he had abandoned only recently for the planets, but it was a planetary model nonetheless.[30] Newton had taken a step toward his mature cosmological theory. But he suppressed this passage from the letter he eventually sent to Flamsteed. Publicly, he dug in his heels, insisting that the comets of November and December were distinct.[31]

Sometime between the spring of 1681 and the autumn of 1684, Newton changed his mind. As stubbornly as he had opposed Flamsteed's premise, he was now convinced that a single comet in November and December 1680 had rounded the sun in a tight, hairpin turn. Gravity, not magnetism, was the attractive force that had turned this comet from its rectilinear path. In a set of propositions composed before 1683, Newton remarked that all comets moved in curved paths, and some, like the planets, moved in closed orbits.[32] There were vestiges of Cartesian vortices in this document, but by 1684 Newton had broken free of them too. In *De motu*, a tract concerned with orbital mechanics, he outlined his theory of universal gravitation, asserting that the motions of comets and planets were governed by the same laws.[33] *De motu* laid the groundwork for the *Principia*, which was published three years later. As the revolutionary theory took shape, the comet of 1680–1681 became an important test case. Newton never gave Flamsteed credit for turning his attention to the influence of a central, attracting

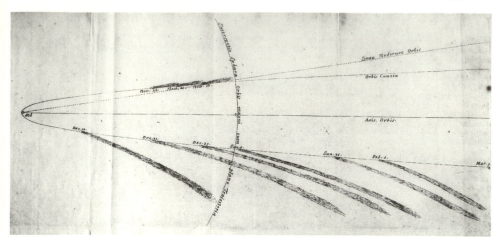

Fig. 47. The elliptical orbit of the 1680 comet approximated by a parabola in the vicinity of the sun. Isaac Newton, *Principia* (London, 1687). (Smithsonian Institution Libraries.)

force on a comet, and in 1685 Flamsteed was more than a bit vexed to learn of Newton's plans—using Flamsteed's data, no less—"to determin ye lines described by ye Comets of 1664 & 1680 according to ye principles of motion observed by ye Planets."[34]

To this end, Newton worked feverishly.[35] He struggled with diverse methods of computation, recognizing that it was impossible to distinguish the path of a comet from a parabola, but insisting that the true path was an ellipse (fig. 47).[36] His controversy with Hooke interfered, but Halley persuaded Newton not to suppress the *Principia*'s theory of comets because of Hooke's machinations.[37]

Once the first edition was printed, Newton never let the comet propositions rest but took them up again and again to revise the theory. According to David Gregory, Newton said "that this discussion about comets is the most difficult in the whole book."[38] Halley joined Newton in the hard work of computing elliptical comet orbits.[39] Newton incorporated the results into successive editions of the *Principia*.[40]

Much was invested in the comet theory. Not only did Newton wish to prove his comet theory by phenomena—that is, by showing that observations agreed with computed orbital positions—but he also took pride in the fact that the success of the comet theory was seen to confirm his theory of universal gravitation.[41] The comet theory also delivered a serious blow to the Cartesians.[42] Comet orbits evidenced more than the tenuity of the aether;[43] when retrograde, they were thoroughly inconsistent with vortices.[44] And if anyone should still have doubted the motion of the earth, the comet theory was thought to confirm that as well.[45]

But even more was at stake. In arguments from design, comet orbits were called upon to testify. Comets traveled about the sun in highly eccentric orbits inclined every which way to the ecliptic. This arrangement was not due to blind fate. Comets were carried quickly through the planetary regions with little time to disturb the motions of planets or other comets. At aphelion, where a comet's slow velocity and weak attraction to the sun might render it easily disturbed by other comets, the vast distance separating all comets from one another prevented disruptive interactions between them.[46] "Thus we always find, that what has, at first sight, the appearance of irregularity and confusion in nature, is discovered, on further enquiry, to be the best contrivance and the most wise conduct," reported Colin Maclaurin.[47] Wise conduct, indeed, for Newton perceived the behavior of comets to be goal-directed. During the course of his career, Newton observed again and again that comets were divine agents working to restore order in the cosmos. This chapter will spell out the manifold ways that celestial mechanics and natural philosophy reinforced and developed this belief. The bottom line, however, was Newton's faith in his theory's role in reestablishing true religion in an age of dangerous politics; and the first inkling appeared in a draft of the *Principia*.[48]

Pristine Truths and Political Corruption

By showing comets to be a sort of planet, Newton felt that he was returning comets to their rightful place in the heavens in accordance with ancient religion and Chaldaean astronomy. Although Newton never went public with this view, the strength of his conviction is apparent in the many surviving philosophical manuscripts in which he expressed it.[49] Of note is a suppressed draft for the third book of the *Principia*, written in the autumn of 1685 and known as "The System of the World."[50] Here Newton argued that ancient philosophers had understood: (1) the universe to be heliocentric; (2) comets to be a sort of planet traveling in eccentric orbits; and (3) celestial space to be devoid of matter (just as Newton's own system required). According to Newton, the ancients had encoded these doctrines in the design of their temples, at whose hearts perpetual fires burned. Within these buildings, sacred rites were meant to teach people that the natural world was the true temple of God. Unfortunately, true religion had been corrupted, and with it natural philosophy. "When the ancient philosophy began to decline," Newton wrote, Eudoxus and others had introduced the "whim of solid orbs." Comets were "thrust down below the Moon," where they epistemologically remained until recent work shattered the fictitious orbs and restored comets to their rightful place among the planets.[51] Thirty years later, Newton still held fast to this view, for in a draft preface to the third edition of the *Principia*, he remarked:

The Chaldaeans once believed that the planets revolved around the Sun in almost concentric orbits and the comets in very eccentric orbits. And the Pythagoreans introduced this philosophy into Greece.... This philosophy was discontinued (it was not propagated to us and gave way to the vulgar opinion of solid spheres). I did not discover this, but endeavoured to restore it to light by the power of demonstration.[52]

Newton's allegation that his doctrine had been anticipated by ancient mystical philosophers had theological and political ramifications.

To understand these ramifications, we must first recognize that the ideas in these philosophical extracts were connected to those in unpublished theological manuscripts: most notably, the "Philosophical Origins of Gentile Theology," begun by Newton in 1683–1684 and revised until the second decade of the eighteenth century.[53] In this text, Newton argued for the existence of a pristine natural-philosophical religion, which long ago had degenerated and spawned erroneous astronomical precepts and polytheistic customs. One of the early perversions had been the assignment of a soul to each solid heavenly sphere and the identification of the soul with the spirit of a dead hero or monarch. Newton reasoned that "the old heathens first commemorated their dead men then admired them, afterwards adored them as Gods then praised them . . . so as to make them Gods celestial."[54] This was an idolatrous practice, for it attributed false powers to natural objects; it led to the worship of heavenly bodies and the veneration of relics associated with the deceased. Newton had already begun to develop this theme at the time of the Popish Plot, when he attacked "monstrous Legends, fals miracles, veneration of reliques, charmes, ye doctrine of Ghosts or Daemons, & their intercession invocation & worship & such other heathen superstitions" that were brought into the Catholic Church by "that crafty politician Athanasius."[55] These idolatrous superstitions were particularly heinous insofar as corrupt individuals exploited natural signs in order to win allegiance or secure power. Newton explained that when the ancients mistook stars for deities, astrology and gentile theology reinforced each other. Cunning philosopher-priests promoted the study of the stars as a way to enhance their prestige. By claiming the right to interpret celestial signs, they had the means to control the lives of their followers.[56] Monarchs joined diviners in basing their power on this corrupt view of nature. Kings "called ye stars & elements by their names & caused them to be honoured with such solemnities & pompous ceremonies as soon created in the people a superstition towards them as Gods & by consequence a veneration of ye whole race of kings as descended from these Deities."[57] Princes then claimed to rule by divine right, and they "erect[ed] such a worship & such a priesthood as might awe the blinded & seduced people into such an obedience as they desired."[58] For Newton, divine-right monarchy and Catholicism were both to be condemned for institutionalizing distorted

views of nature as a means to grab and keep power. Astrology, the hand-maiden to idolatrous politicking, was to be condemned along with them.[59] The cure for these corruptions, Newton implied, was to restore Chaldaean cosmology. If comets were given free reign, they would sweep away all vestiges of the theory of solid spheres and with it the cult of priestcraft and divine-right politics.

These manuscripts are useful to our study, for they suggest Newton's frame of mind as he developed his comet theory. Newton wrote many of these papers during the period of the Popish Plot, the Exclusion Crisis, and the accession of the Catholic James II (1685), and the intensity of his writing suggests that he was worried about the Catholic "threat" and the doctrine of divine right. This view is supported by Newton's actions on two occasions. First, in the spring of 1687, Newton was upset about the king's efforts to catholicize Cambridge University; and he was among those to appear before the Court of Ecclesiastical Commission in order to defend the university's noncompliance with a royal mandate that would have admitted a Benedictine monk to the degree of master of arts. Second, in January 1689, after William had landed and James had fled, Newton was elected to represent the university in the parliamentary assembly convened to settle the terms of the Glorious Revolution.[60]

In their interconnectedness, Newton's political activities and astronomical projects likely brought him into contact with popular beliefs about comets. I have already mentioned Newton's direct contact with popular culture. Here we have further evidence—albeit circumstantial—of his contact with comet lore. Newton's political concerns reinforced his cometary work in a way that suggests his familiarity with English propaganda capitalizing on recent comets and viewing them as portents of the Stuart Restoration, the Popish Plot, the accession of James II, or the Second Coming. Such propaganda was disseminated by both the court and its adversaries, by both high and low members of society.[61] Although Newton did not directly refer to the modern tracts, his interpretation of ancient texts shows that he was sensitive to the existence of this sort of astrological politicking, especially when carried out from the top down. Indeed, his criticism of rulers' deifying their ancestors in order to aggrandize themselves brings to mind a well-known case of comet lore used for political gain: the case of Augustus and the comet of 44 B.C. Since Augustus was the chief symbol of the restored Stuart monarchy, this historical episode had immediate relevance for Newton and deserves a closer look.

Roman emperors encouraged the belief that the souls of their dead predecessors had become stars in the heavens. They gave the title "divus" (meaning "divine") to the deceased emperors and had them worshiped in temples. In this way, the political power of the current emperor was strengthened by the apotheosis of the former. Augustus appreciated this when a comet appeared soon after the death of Julius Caesar (44 B.C.). As Caesar's successor, Augustus exploited the common view that Caesar's soul

had been received among the gods, and used the comet to legitimate the power of the Julian line.[62]

This famous story—undoubtedly known to Newton—was not simply of antiquarian interest, for Augustan politics were alive and well in Restoration England. Just as Augustus had laid claim to the Julian comet, which appeared at the start of his rule, so Charles II took advantage of a star or comet that purportedly had blazed at midday on the occasion of his birth. It was a sign, royalists said, that Charles ruled by divine right. The Augustan message was reinforced in the pageantry of the coronation (1661), where allusions to ancient Rome abounded. Triumphal arches greeted the king's cavalcade as it traveled from the Tower to Whitehall. On the first arch were the words "ADVENTUS AUG[USTI]," identifying Charles II as a new Augustus. Statues of James I and Charles I flanked a tableau of Charles II driving Usurpation into the jaws of Hell. The monarchs were given the epithets "DIVO JACOBO" and "DIVO CAROLO" in emulation of the Roman practice and in affirmation of the view that Charles II ruled Britain by the grace of his divine ancestors.[63] When Charles II died in 1685, staunch supporters of the Stuart line in turn apotheosized him in order to legitimate his brother's reign. The dead monarch now ruled in the kingdom of heaven, they said, but his godlike perfection had been passed on to his successor, James II. It was time to "pay Religious Worship" to Charles by giving political allegiance to James.[64]

Newton did not support the rule of James II, and he opposed Anglo-Augustan politics. Such politicking had its roots in ancient Rome and in Augustus's exploitation of the comet of 44 B.C. Newton knew of this comet; he referred to it in the *Principia* and praised Halley for showing it to be the same as the 1680 comet.[65] In carrying out his program to reinstate comets in the heavens, Newton felt that he was rescuing comets from the hands of priests, astrologers, and rulers like Augustus, Charles, or James, who wrongly attributed God's powers to these bodies and connivingly used the apparitions to legitimate their own authority.

Newton was not alone in criticizing the political abuse of comets. Pierre Bayle, for one, had launched a similar attack in 1682.[66] In professing this view, Newton, like Bayle, revealed how much he scorned vulgar astrology, but this does not mean that Newton was uninfluenced by popular tenets concerning comets. This is apparent even in "The System of the World," where after his appeal for the restoration of Chaldaean cosmology, Newton described the splendor of comet tails in language that would have done any prodigy book proud. He quoted Justin's report that two comets "shined so bright that *the whole heaven seemed to be on fire*; and by their greatness filled up a fourth part of the heavens, and by their splendour exceeded that of the Sun." From Matthew Paris, he took "[In 1264] there appeared *a Comet so wonderful, that none then living had ever seen the like.*" From a historical source, he borrowed, "In the year 1401 or 1402, . . . there appeared in the west a bright and shining Comet, sending out a tail upwards,

in splendour like a flame of fire, and in form like a spear, darting its rays from west to east. When the Sun was sunk below the horizon, by the lustre of its own rays *it enlightned all the borders of the Earth*, not permitting the other Stars to shew their light, or the shades of night to darken the air, because its light exceeded that of the others, and extended it self to the upper part of the heavens." Lest we attribute these flourishes to the fancies of the sources quoted, here are Newton's own words: "In the year 1527, *Aug.* 11. about four in the morning," he wrote, "*there was seen almost throughout Europe*, a terrible Comet in *Leo*, which continued flaming an hour and a quarter every day. It rose from the east, and ascended to the south and west to a *prodigious length*. It was most conspicuous to the north, and *its cloud (that is its tail) was very terrible; having, according to the fancies of the vulgar, the form of an arm a little bent, holding a sword of a vast magnitude.*" Newton confided "*a rumour, that there appeared about Sun rising a bright beam*" in 1618; and he took note of a wondrous comet in 1668, whose "head was small, and scarcely discernible, but its tail extremely bright and refulgent, so that *the reflexion of it from the sea was easily seen by those who stood upon the shore.*"[67] These are the kinds of phrases one finds in prognosticative pamphlets, prodigy books, folktales, and broadsides.[68] To find them in the 1685 draft of Book III of the *Principia* is most fascinating. To learn that this language is excised from the published version (even though some references remain) is revealing.[69] It tells us that between 1685 and 1687, Newton was in the process of submerging comet lore into his astrophysics.

I say submerge, because Newton did not eradicate comet lore. Newton's analysis of cometary orbits repeatedly drew his attention to their divine offices. According to David Gregory, Newton remarked that "the great eccentricity in Comets in directions both different from and contrary to the planets indicates a divine hand: and implies that Comets are destined for a use other than that of the planets."[70] What was this special use? Or, as Newton himself raised the question, "To what end were comets framed?"[71] I shall argue that the ends Newton proposed differed little from the popular opinions retailed in vulgar street literature or the traditional beliefs codified in learned texts.

TRANSMUTATIONS AND PERPETUAL INTERCHANGE

While comet lore guided Newton in developing a teleological framework, matter theory explained how comets could fulfill their divine ends. Therefore, my account begins with Newton's views on the transmutation of matter.[72] In the 1687 *Principia*, Newton stated that any body could be transformed into another, and he held this doctrine throughout his career.[73] In published writings and private notes, he discussed how complex bodies

could be broken down into simpler parts by heat, and how components could be rearranged to form new substances: "If Gold could be brought once to ferment and putrefie, it might be turn'd into any other Body whatsoever," Newton observed in 1691/92. "And so of Tin, or any other Bodies; as common Nourishment is turn'd into the Bodies of Animals and Vegetables."[74] The problem was this: how could food be turned into the bodies of animals—or, to put it another way, how could passive particles organize themselves into living things—by mechanical impact alone? To solve this problem, Newton turned to a "vegetable spirit" or "fermental virtue." This was an alchemical agent responsible for reducing, revivifying, and generating new forms of matter.[75]

A premise of this chemical philosophy was the unity of matter, the existence of one universal substrate that could be wrought by nature into a plurality of forms. In 1675, Newton believed this catholic matter to be an aether, and he confided to Henry Oldenburg that "perhaps the whole frame of Nature may be nothing but aether condensed by a fermental principle." This aether was extremely rarefied, subtle, and elastic. Initially it had been uniform, but over time "various aethereall Spirits" and special effluvia had become entangled with the "maine flegmatic body of aether." Among these effluvia was a subtle spirit whose condensation resulted not only in gravitation but also in "humid active matter for the continuall uses of nature." Coagulating within the pores of the earth, this spirit became the "succus nutritious of ye earth or primary substance out of wch things generable grow." It was distinct, however, from a vital aerial spirit requisite for conserving flame and vital motions.[76] In Newton's aethereal cosmology, matter naturally circulated between the heavens and earth. In the 1660s and 1670s, Newton described this circulation in physiological terms:

> Thus this Earth resembles a great animall or rather inanimate vegetable, [and] draws in aethereall breath for its dayly refreshment & vital ferment & transpires again wth gross exhalations. . . . And thus perhaps a great p[ar]t if not all the moles of sensible matter is nothing but Aether congealed & interwoven into various textures.[77]

On other occasions, Newton described the circulation in more mechanical terms. The earth condensed the aether and forced it downward, carrying along any bodies in its path. Within the earth's core, subterraneous mineral fermentations concocted and coagulated the compressed aether into hard terrestrial bodies. With the addition of more heat, these compact bodies were readily transmuted into gross vapors, air, and exhalations.[78] "The vast body of the Earth . . . may be every where to the very center in perpetuall working."[79] The slow ascent of aerial matter out of the earth's bowels constituted the atmosphere. Continually buoyed up by new rising vapors, air eventually vanished into the heavens where it ultimately returned to its original aethereal form. This circulation of matter pleased nature immensely:

For nature is a perpetuall circulatory worker, generating fluids out of solids, and solids out of fluids, fixed things out of volatile, & volatile out of fixed, subtile out of gross, & gross out of subtile, Some things to ascend & make the upper terrestriall juices, Rivers and the Atmosphere; & by consequence others to descend for a Requitall to the former. And as the Earth, so perhaps may the Sun imbibe this Spirit copiously to conserve his Shineing, & keep the Planets from receding further from him. And they that will, may also suppose, that this Spirit affords or carryes with it thither the solarly fewell & materiall Principle of Light; And that the vast aethereall Spaces between us, & the stars are for a sufficient repository for this food of the Sunn & Planets.[80]

The versatile, plastic, spiritous aether fueled the sun and planets. Transmutations were performed on a cosmic scale.

Newton's aether had much in common with the universal spirit described by many alchemists and Neoplatonists.[81] Moreover, some Neoplatonists understood that the universal spirit was primarily seated in the sun, but its virtues were diffused throughout the universe. Certain earthly bodies were capable of drawing in this spirit in order to transmute it with the help of fermentation.[82] Newton drew on alchemical and Neoplatonic beliefs when he considered the role of heavenly bodies in supplying catholic matter, and the chain of earthly events that transformed that matter into diverse bodies.[83]

By 1687, however, Newton had cleared this aether from the heavenly spaces, fearful that it would impede the planets in their revolutions. He began to envision a cosmos filled with forces but devoid of much matter. To fill the aether's chemical role, Newton endorsed a watery fluid as a universal substrate. This fluid was porous and hence eminently transmutable:

Bodies of this kind [composed of a lattice structure] easily receive the motion of heat by means of the free vibrations of the elastic particles and they will conserve [heat] a long time through that motion if it is slow and long-lasting. Their particles coalesce in new ways and by means of the attractive forces of contiguous ones they come together more densely: for which reason that rare substance water can be transformed by continued fermentation into the more dense substances of animals, vegetables, salts, stones and various earths. And finally by the very long duration of the operation be coagulated into mineral and metallic substances. For the matter of all things is one and same, which is transmuted into countless forms by the operations of nature, and more subtle and rare bodies are by fermentation and the processes of growth [vegetation] commonly made thicker and more condensed.[84]

We can connect these ideas to Jean Baptiste van Helmont (1577–1644) and Robert Boyle (1627–1691), whose works Newton studied. In the mid-century, van Helmont published an account of his famous willow-tree experiment, which allegedly demonstrated that plants were little more than

transmuted water,[85] and Boyle reported the conversion of water into earth.[86] Indeed, this conversion of water into earth was one of the great established "facts" of Newton's age. It was not refuted until Antoine Lavoisier (1743–1794) performed his quantitative, three-month-long experiment with a "pelican" flask in 1768–1769.[87] Hence, it comes as no surprise to find Newton matter-of-factly recording that "Water by Frequent Distillations Changes into fix'd Earth, as Mr. *Boyle* has try'd."[88]

The transmutation of water into manifold forms of gross matter was apparently a unidirectional process. Water transmuted was water lost.

> . . . For all vegetables entirely derive their growths from fluids, and afterwards, in great measure, are turned into dry earth by putrefaction; and a sort of slime is always found to settle at the bottom of putrefied fluids; and hence it is that the bulk of the solid earth is continually increased; and the fluids, if they are not supplied from without, must be in a continual decrease, and quite fail at last.[89]

Without an extraterrestrial source of fluid, all planetary activity would cease. The magnificent earth would decay. This was not the case with the aethereal transmutations in Newton's earlier essays. Those transmutations were reversible, cyclical, and perpetual. Since Newton still believed that a cosmic circulation and transmutation of primal matter was requisite for the well-being of the cosmos, he looked for a new source of celestial nourishment. In the early 1680s, he had made extracts of Flamsteed's letters concerning the watery surfaces of comets, and as he prepared his *Principia*, he became impressed by the tenuous vapor tails of comets, which pointed away from the sun.[90]

> For all vapor in those free [celestial] spaces [he noted] is in a perpetual state of rarefaction and dilatation; and from hence it is that the tails of all comets are broader at their upper extremity than near their heads. And it is not unlikely but that the vapor, thus continually rarefied and dilated, may be at last dissipated and scattered through the whole heavens, and by little and little be attracted towards the planets by its gravity, and mixed with their atmosphere.[91]

If comet tails did mix with the atmosphere, then they could supply the vital fluid the system required.

> . . . For as seas are absolutely necessary to the constitution of our earth, . . . for watering of the earth, and for the production and nourishment of vegetables; . . . so for the conservation of the seas, and fluids of the planets, comets seem to be required, that, from their exhalations and vapors condensed, the wastes of the planetary fluids spent upon vegetation and putrefaction, and converted into dry earth, may be continually supplied and made up.[92]

Moreover, Newton suspected "that it is chiefly from the comets that spirit comes, which is indeed the smallest but the most subtle and useful part of our air, and so much required to sustain the life of all things with us."[93]

In a draft intended for a future edition of the *Principia*, and in subsequent editions of that book, Newton assigned salutary roles not only to comet tails but also to solar and stellar vapors.

> The vapors which arise from the sun, the fixed stars, and the tails of the comets, may meet at last with, and fall into, the atmospheres of the planets by their gravity, and there be condensed and turned into water and humid spirits; and from thence, by a slow heat, pass gradually into the form of salts, and sulphurs, and tinctures, and mud, and clay, and sand, and stones, and coral, and other terrestrial substances.[94]

In this way, a transmutation chain that began with comet tails ended in the concoction of animals, vegetables, and minerals. "Thus comes about the perpetual interchange of all things," Newton concluded, "and the Lord of all alone remains immutable, who by his own counsel and will disposes (through Ministers) all things in the best order."[95]

In fact, the "interchange of all things" described in the 1687 *Principia* was far from perpetual and complete. Nothing refueled the sun or stars.[96] As these bodies wasted away, comet tails increased the solid bulk of the planets.[97] Consequently, the solar system would gradually become unbalanced.[98] In the 1706 *Optice*, Newton further stressed that the mutual attraction of planets and comets would cause increasing perturbations in their respective orbits. Moreover, the quantity of motion in the world was evidently decreasing. Nature was unwinding and decaying without divine intervention. God's providence was essential to conserve motion and reform the cosmic system.[99]

For many years, Newton turned this problem of the unbalanced world over in his mind. For a time, he seems to have changed his opinion regarding the degree to which comet tails substantially increased the bulk of the planets. In the early 1680s, Newton had thought comet tails to be quite thick, but later concluded that they were extremely tenuous since stars could be seen through them.[100] He took Gregory aside in 1705 and told him that comets did not actually supply water to the earth along with vital spirits, as he had originally believed, but rather that they supplied a subtle, nonmechanical spirit capable of turning solids into fluids:

> When Mr. Newton says, in his Princip. Philos., that the Tails of the Comets may likely restore the Fluid to the Earth, so great a part of which is yearly turned into solids: This is not to be understood of the real fluid water so restored, . . . but of that subtle Spirit that does turn Solids into Fluids. A very small Aura or particle of this may be able to doe the business.[101]

One problem with accepting this change of heart is that Newton never put it in print. In drafts for the *Principia* and in all published editions, Newton repeated his conjecture that comet tails were condensed and converted into water and humid spirits.[102] A second problem is that the new interpretation was inconsistent with the increasing bulk of the planets,

which was independently deduced from astronomical measurements accepted by Newton.[103] If comets did not furnish water vapor but only an active spirit, comet tails would not augment the planets' bulk, because only a small "aura" of spirit was needed to reconvert solids back into fluids. Moreover, by maintaining a balance of solids and fluids, the spirit could curb the natural transmutation processes that tended to increase the bulk in the first place. But the role of comets in bulking up the planets was a point Newton made in all editions of the *Principia*; a point Flamsteed attributed to him as late as 1710; and, indeed, a point Gregory repeated in the 1726 edition of his textbook:

> It is to be believ'd that the Comets serve for the renewing of the Fluid of the Sun and Planets. . . . Hence will the Primary Planets be augmented; whence the satellite's Orbit . . . and Period will be contracted.[104]

Gregory referred here to the secular acceleration of the moon, which Newton and Halley attributed to the earth's gain in size.[105] If Gregory had any inside information, he certainly did not incorporate it into his textbook. The third problem in accepting Gregory's memorandum at face value is the fact that Newton's followers took the restoration of fluids quite literally. Although Gregory had noted, "its certain there are not such rains at or after a comet as this [water transfer] would inferr," William Whiston argued for increased rains—indeed, deluges—in the wake of close-approaching comets.[106] If Newton did change his mind in 1705, the new view may have been short-lived.[107] In the end, he may have reverted to the belief that comets transported vapors (which condensed and were converted into water and humid spirits) and a vital, active, nonmechanical spirit.

As for the unbalance produced by the diminution of stars, Newton informed readers of the 1713 edition of the *Principia* that God used comets to conserve the stellar bodies. Orbital calculations positioned the 1680 comet exceedingly close to the sun at perihelion. Indeed, the comet seemed to have passed through the solar atmosphere, where its motion would have been resisted and retarded. Every subsequent passage through the solar atmosphere would slow it further. Attractions by other comets would retard it also. Eventually, it would descend into the sun and would then rekindle that wasting star.

> So fixed stars, that have been gradually wasted by the light and vapors emitted from them for a long time, may be recruited by comets that fall upon them; and from this fresh supply of new fuel those old stars, acquiring new splendor, may pass for new stars.[108]

In 1713, Newton thus made public his belief that comets replenished the sun and stars, as well as the planets. Following the laws of universal gravitation, comets swept through the solar system with their beneficent supplies of a watery vapor and vital spirit. In this way, blazing stars helped to renovate the cosmos and preserve world order.

Fire, Water, and a Heavenly Physiology

This replenishment and renovation of the cosmos by comets had organic characteristics. Fire and water had long been connected with the maintenance of vital activities, and Newton's comets transported both fire and water about the universe—water in the form of vapors supplied to the planets (and sun!), and fire in the form of the subtle, nonmechanical, vital spirit.

Vital spirit was commonly associated with a philosophical fire interspersed throughout the atmosphere. The Paracelsians, for example, described a volatile, aerial niter and sulphur that sustained life and combustion. The niter and sulphur were composed of heavenly fire or astral emanations.[109] Where Newton discussed chemistry in the *Optice*, he did not mention a celestial source for an aerial sulphur and niter. He did, however, describe much in the Paracelsian vein how the fermentation of sulphureous steams and nitrous acids in the atmosphere promoted fiery meteors and other "Fermentations as appears by the rusting of Iron and Copper in it, the kindling of Fire by blowing, and the beating of the Heart by means of Respiration."[110] Thirty-five years earlier in an alchemical manuscript, Newton had also referred to a "subtil spirit . . . Natures universall agent, her secret fire, ye onely ferment & principle of all vegetation."[111] In these passages, Newton associated life with fire. This association was certainly an ancient opinion, given credence by the majority of Greek thinkers because of an innate heat evident in living things.[112]

On the other hand, since antiquity life had also been associated with water. Thales of Miletos (ca. 580 B.C.) and Hippo of Samos (ca. 475 B.C.) asserted water to be the ultimate substrate of all things. The Hippocratic authors further focused medical attention on four constituent humors in the body. Later Arabic and medieval thinkers supplemented these humors with "secondary humors," also called "humidities" or "moistures." The most venerable moisture was the "radical moisture," which accounted for the form and organization of living things. Without the radical moisture to assure the continuity of tissue organization, life would cease. The vicissitudes that the radical-moisture idea underwent during the medieval and early modern periods do not concern us here. We need only note that by Newton's day the theory had been recast into several distinct variants according to the predilections of its expositors. Although Descartes never mentioned it, and Bacon explicitly rejected it, the theory was alive and well in the work of Harvey, Gassendi, and van Helmont.[113]

Furthermore, Sendivogius, d'Espagnet, and Eirenaeus Philalethes (all authors studied by Newton) suggested that the radical moisture might be furnished by celestial means.[114] I think it is noteworthy that in 1675 Newton advanced a celestial, aethereal spirit that condensed into a "*humid* active matter for the continuall uses of nature" and was "the succus nutritious of ye earth or primary substance out of wch things generable grow."[115] I believe Newton may have had the radical moisture in mind.[116] When he later

rejected the cosmic circulation of this aethereal spirit, comet tails became responsible for transmitting the requisite moisture to earth. Within the atmosphere, the vapors of comet tails were "condensed and turned into water and humid spirits."[117]

While life had variously been associated with fire and water, a third Greek tradition emphasized the dynamic mixture of fire and water, and the interdependence of the body's innate heat and radical moisture. Not only could moisture be transformed into fire (or heat), it was a necessary fuel for fire.[118] Newton perhaps adopted this position, for he argued in 1675 that the aethereal spirit could condense into a humid active matter yet still be fit "food of the Sunn & Planets,"[119] and in 1725 that solar vapors "had their sediment as water."[120] In this Greek tradition, Newton's humid comets might indeed have refueled the fiery sun and stars, as well as have transported vital spirit and vapors to the planets. What Newton seemed to be describing was, in fact, a physiology of the heavens.

Some Neoplatonic and chemical authors, who compared the earth to an organism, also focused on the role of moisture in circulating fiery spirits.[121] Raindrops were key in drawing in the "universal spirit" from the heavenly bodies, or the celestial niter and sulphur from the atmosphere. "The earth can no more produce Vegetables, or Minerals without this connatural circulation, of water replenish'd with Celestial influences," one author concluded.[122] In Newton's comet theory, comets furnished the vital spirits along with an aqueous medium perhaps requisite for their diffusion.

The physiological tone (if not the details) of Newton's theory fell well within the bounds of folk traditions that saw comets as health-giving and restorative; and a handful of seventeenth-century mathematicians, theologians, and astrologers used medical analogies in delineating the wholesome effects of comets.[123] But whereas these authors focused on cleansing and purging, Newton paid attention to the roles of comets in enlivening matter and sustaining activity in the cosmos.

Comets served as divine agents that operated with regularity, but on occasion God gave them revolutionary roles. As the next section will show, Newton pondered the dramatic impact comets had on the sacred and natural history of the earth.

"REVOLUTIONS IN THE HEAVENLY BODIES"

What first caught Newton's notice was the apostle Peter's prophecy that on the Day of Judgment the earth would be consumed by fire and then be renewed:

> The heavens and earth that now exist have been stored up for fire, being kept until the day of judgment and destruction of ungodly men. . . . Then the heavens will pass away with a loud noise, and the elements will be dissolved with fire, and the earth and the works that are upon it will be burned up. . . . But

according to his promise we wait for new heavens and a new earth in which righteousness dwells.[124]

Newton made reference to these and related verses in his student notebook under the heading "Of Earth."[125] The end of the world thus held his interest at about the same time that he was observing the 1664 and 1665 comets. Later, as he observed the 1680–1681 comet, he turned his attention to the beginning of the world and entered into long discussions with Thomas Burnet.[126] Burnet was then preparing his *Sacred Theory of the Earth*, and Newton was sympathetic to the project.

From biblical sources, Newton was convinced that the physical state of the world paralleled the moral history of mankind. This conviction opened the door to cosmogonic speculations premised on Scripture and natural philosophy. Like Burnet, Newton attempted to provide physical accounts of the Creation, the Deluge, the Conflagration, and the rise of the newly purged earth after the Apocalypse; but as he warned Richard Bentley in 1693, "Ye growth of new systems out of old ones wthout ye mediation of a divine power seems to me apparently absurd."[127] What Newton's theory needed was a physical agent that operated routinely and nonmiraculously yet was capable of causing catastrophic change by divine design. In comets, he found what he required.

In private conversations held over the course of thirty years, Newton disclosed his daring thoughts to his closest disciples. It was on a Sunday night in March 1724/25 that Newton confided to Conduitt. He was eighty-three at the time and recovering from "a fit of the gout," but his mind was clear, and Conduitt asked him to divulge what he had often hinted before.

> He then repeated to me . . . that it was his conjecture (he would affirm nothing) that there was a sort of revolution in the heavenly bodies; that the vapours and light emitted by the sun, which had their sediment as water, and other matter had, gathered themselves by degrees, into a body, and attracted more matter from the planets; and at last made a secondary planet (viz. one of those that go round another planet), and then by gathering to them and attracting more matter, became a primary planet; and then by increasing still, became a comet, which after certain revolutions, by coming nearer and nearer to the sun, had all its volatile parts condensed, and became a matter fit to recruit, and replenish the sun (which must waste by the constant heat and light it emitted), as a faggot would this fire, if put into it (we were sitting by a wood fire), and that would probably be the effect of the comet of 1680 sooner or later.[128]

Thus Newton envisioned a self-charging, cyclical system. Solar vapors and celestial matter gathered to form moons, which grew into planets, and then into comets, which ultimately fell into the sun. From this fresh supply of comet fuel, an old star would acquire new brightness and would pass perhaps for a new star. The so-called novas that had puzzled Hipparchus, Tycho, and Kepler were probably old stars suddenly refueled by comets falling into them.[129]

This astonishing hypothesis tied together many loose ends of Newton's comet theory. In the *Principia*, he had discussed how comets increased the bulk of the planets with beneficent gifts of vapor and vital spirit. Nevertheless, he had not considered there the fate of an overgrown planet that no longer fit harmoniously within its orbit. While he had also suggested how comets replenished the stars, he had not mentioned any source for new comets. His readers could only presume that the comet supply was an exhaustible commodity.[130] In his fireside chat with Conduitt, however, all these components were fit neatly into a cyclical system.

Moreover, Newton suggested a mechanism that made possible the succession of worlds predicted in Scripture. Thirty years earlier, Gregory had reported Newton's disclosure that "the Satellites of Jupiter and Saturn can take the places of the Earth, Venus, Mars if they are destroyed, and be held in reserve for a new Creation."[131] Newton's conversation with Conduitt clarified how a satellite could become a planet fit for a new creation. Indeed, in this transformation, comets had dual roles. By naturally amassing the vapors from comet tails, the sun, stars, and even planets, a satellite grew to planetary proportions.[132] Moreover, as Gregory explained, a close-approaching comet not only could alter the orbit and period of a planet but "may also by its Attraction so disturb the Satellite, as to make it leave its Primary Planet, and itself become a Primary Planet about the Sun."[133] With the creation of new worlds explained, Newton explored how the present world would end. At first, he considered the impact of a comet. In 1703, Gregory noted, "The Comet whose Orbit Mr Newton determins may sometime impinge on the Earth. Origen relates the manner of destroying the Worlds by one falling on another."[134] Origen was a source to which Newton often turned in his studies of ancient natural philosophy, and I have shown that the former thought comets heralded religious reform.[135] Gregory's memorandum provides a clue to the connections Newton was making. But in the end, Newton found destruction by fire to be more in line with Scripture.[136] In 1725, he told Conduitt that when a comet fell into the sun, the newly stoked flames would sear the earth. In fact, Newton determined that the sun-grazing comet of 1680 was designed for that very end:

> He could not say when this comet would drop into the sun; it might perhaps have five or six revolutions more first; but whenever it did, it would so much increase the heat of the sun, that this earth would be burnt, and no animals in it could live.[137]

Fortunately, that gloomy prospect was comfortably far off, for Halley calculated the comet's period to be about 575 years.[138]

Given the roles comets might play in the Apocalypse, it is not surprising that Newton considered the role one might have played in the Flood. Gregory tersely recounted Newton's idea that "a comet passing near the Earth to the east has altered its course in perihelium just as the Moon by attracting the waters caused a deluge."[139] In the *Elements of Physical and Geometrical Astronomy*, Gregory reiterated this point, adding:

> Besides, it [the comet] may produce much greater Changes in the Globe of the Planet it self, not only by attracting the Fluid, if it has any, but also by other Qualities, as if, for Example, so vast a Body goes from the Sun's Neighbourhood, and being red-hot is carried near our Earth. But we have said enough of this Matter, especially since it does not belong to our present Purpose.[140]

Gregory may have been elliptical, but his readers would have readily connected these remarks to the work of two eminent Newtonians, Edmond Halley and William Whiston, who considered the dire effects of close-approaching comets. Halley and Whiston each thought comets had caused Noah's Flood, and expected them to play a part in the end of the world. Newton was in close touch with both men, and it is sometimes hard to distinguish with whom ideas originated.[141]

Newton regarded "these revolutions in the heavenly bodies" to be effected at the discretion of God. "He seemed to doubt whether there were not [i.e., suspect that there were] intelligent beings superior to us, who superintended these revolutions of the heavenly bodies, by the direction of the Supreme Being."[142] The earth and its inhabitants testified that the world had previously undergone dramatic reformations wrought by providentially directed comets for divine ends. No doubt it would undergo reformations in the future.

> He appeared also to be very clearly of the opinion, that the inhabitants of this world were of a short date, and alledged as one reason for that opinion, that all arts, as letters, ships, printing, needle, &c. were discovered within the memory of history; which could not have happened, if the world had been eternal; and that there were visible marks of ruin upon it, which could not be effected by a flood only. When I asked him how this earth could have been repeopled, if ever it had undergone the same fate it was threatened with hereafter by the comet of 1680; he answered, that required the power of a creator.[143]

Newton's theory implied a succession of earths, a series of creations and purgations. Historical periods were punctuated by comet catastrophes. When Conduitt asked Newton why he would not publish these ideas, Newton characteristically responded, "I do not deal in conjectures." He felt more secure in arguing that the distant fixed stars were revived by comets than that our sun would be revived too. In the former case, celestial reformations occurred far away from us. When it came to God's reconstituting the solar system here at home, Newton said "that concerned us more; and laughing, added that he had said enough [in the *Principia*] for people to know his meaning."[144]

Thus Newton did not dare make public the full extent of the "perpetual interchange" of matter he envisioned in the cosmos. If God could direct comets to refurbish the planets, he could also certainly destroy worlds with comets. Newton speculated about grand transformations and major revolutions in the heavenly bodies in which worlds were created and destroyed.

COMETS, TELEOLOGY, AND NEWTON'S APPROPRIATION OF COMET LORE

In his comet work, Newton brought together many aspects of his studies: His mathematics was instrumental in showing comets to be periodic, and celestial mechanics helped to establish their true functions. Wide-ranging in their orbits, comets were perfect agents to restore lost fluids and activate matter. They provided a chemical link between the heavens and earth. There was thus an intimate connection between Newton's matter theory and astronomy. Theological projects also entered in to the picture. Comets could serve as causes that brought the natural world into congruence with sacred history, especially at the end of time. They were thus natural instruments that accommodated "miraculous" events. Newton moreover believed that the restoration of the true philosophical meaning of comets led people a step closer to true religion.

To take this step, one had to see comets not only as stable members of the solar system but also as teleologically designed. Despite the brute characteristics comets shared with planets, there was no getting around two distinguishing attributes: comets had remarkable tails and traveled in eccentric orbits. This convinced Newton that comets were designed for purposes different from those the planets served. Newton's expositors repeatedly underscored this point and endorsed Newton's bold suggestion in the *Principia* that comets refurbished the planets, sun, and stars, and so contributed "to the renovation of the face of things."[145] Far from presaging God's wrath, comets witnessed God's benevolence toward mankind, for they showed how he preserved the world system. As Henry Pemberton marveled, Newton's speculations represented

> in the strongest light imaginable the extensive providence of the great author of nature, who, besides the furnishing [of] this globe of earth, and without doubt the rest of the planets, so abundantly with every thing necessary for the support and continuance of the numerous races of plants and animals, they are stocked with, has over and above provided a numerous train of comets, far exceeding the number of the planets, to rectify continually, and restore their gradual decay, which is our author's opinion concerning them.[146]

Nevertheless, this stocking of celestial cupboards was routine housework compared to the cataclysmic reformations Newton envisioned in private. To Gregory, Conduitt, and Halley, Newton intimated that comets were divine agents destined to reconstitute the entire solar system, to prepare sites for new creations, and to usher in the Millennium.[147]

Newton's views on the teleological design of comets has much in common with the traditional comet lore his celestial mechanics has been said to undermine.[148] On the most general level, folk wisdom held that comets augured good as well as bad. For Newton, comets sustained life as well as

destroyed worlds. The popular press depicted comets as monsters. For Newton, comets continued to demonstrate God's will. Religious traditions held comets to be signs of Noah's Flood, the birth of Jesus, the Protestant Reformation, and the Day of Judgment. Newton agreed that God sent comets to herald the punishment of the wicked, vindication of the elect, and reform of the world. Comets initiated the mutations recorded or prophesied in Scripture. They were key players in the beginning, deluge, and end of the world. In comparing Newton's comet theory to comet lore, we find parallels on more specific tenets too: Folklore taught that comets announced the deaths of princes, plague, poor weather, and bad crops. For Newton, comets affected health, weather, and agriculture, but in a positive way, being "absolutely necessary for [the] watering of the earth, and for the production and nourishment of vegetables."[149] Broadsides and pamphlets linked comets to civil disorder, social upheaval, and rebellion. Newton hinted that there was "a sort of revolution in the heavenly bodies" in which comets overturned the order of the solar system and set up new planetary hierarchies. Throughout Europe, clergymen preached that comets were sent by God to urge sinners to awake and repent; and in England, they said that comets presaged the downfall of Catholicism. For Newton, an understanding of the true nature of comets would lead people back to the principles of true religion and away from priestcraft.

By now it should be abundantly clear that Newton did not strip away the religious, political, and agricultural associations of comets but rather appropriated popular beliefs. Although comets were depicted as natural bodies following routine courses throughout the heavens, they remained apparitions of God's design. God used comets as a natural means to constitute, conserve, and renovate the cosmos. Even though Newton believed that his comet theory would overturn the kind of predictions found in street literature, there were only two tenets of his theory that truly differentiated it from the traditional lore: (1) that comets acted exclusively in a global theater; and (2) that laws of motion could be used to determine which comets were likely to wreck the earth. But this information was to be reserved for the scientific elite, rather than the pamphlet prognosticators, even though both desired to see the moral order reflected in the natural world.

In this sense, it is fascinating to take another look at the 1680 comet. As Newton pointed out in his *Principia*, Halley believed the 1680 comet to be a later apparition of the comet known as *Julium Sidus*. That comet had blazed shortly after the death of Julius Caesar, and common people had believed it signified his apotheosis. The comet had come to be worshiped in a Roman temple, and Augustus had turned it into political capital.[150] In 1680, on the occasion of that comet's purported return, many factions again tried to use the comet to push through their particular political programs. Some radicals saw it as a token of the last days and exhorted people to prepare for the Millennium.[151] These acts were just the kind of astrological politicking Newton hated: the type of divination and religious degrada-

tion he secretly hoped his comet theory would eradicate. How interesting it is that he should select this same comet as the judgment car, the vehicle God would use to refuel the sun and purge the earth in preparation for a new creation. In Newton's theory of the 1680 comet, we see the degree to which someone hostile to popular culture was willing to appropriate useful popular beliefs without their former labels. What Newton did was redescribe popular beliefs in sophisticated, natural philosophical terms.

We will never know if Newton consciously appropriated these ideas. We do know, however, that folklore was perceived by some early modern scholars to consist of degraded ancient knowledge.[152] Newton mined ancient philosophical texts for veins of pristine wisdom compatible with Scripture.[153] It may be that he thought he had found kernels of truth to be preserved in popular culture as well. If that is the case, Book III of the *Principia* can be read as a text in the tradition of books of errors, for here Newton subtly separated the wheat from the chaff and so corrected popular beliefs about comets.

Whether or not this was a conscious program of reform, Newton worked closely on this project with Edmond Halley. Halley's adaptation of comet lore will be considered next.

Halley's Comet Theory, Noah's Flood, and the End of the World

EDMOND HALLEY (1656–1742) is best remembered for his research on closed comet orbits and his successful prediction of the return of a comet that now bears his name. The new theory treated comets as the flotsam of the solar system. It challenged the ancient view that comets were unpredictable or miraculous signs sent by God to exhort sinners to reform. Historians of astronomy have argued that the old and new views were antithetical, that Halley's theory dispelled popular superstitions and paved the way for a more enlightened view. But closed orbits for comets were not incompatible with beliefs in their purposive nature. Like Isaac Newton, Halley continued to see comets as harbingers of cataclysmic events and world reform. And again like Newton, he took the privilege of defining the import of comets out of the hands of religious authorities, political pamphleteers, and astrologers and placed it squarely in the hands of the scientist. In the words of one eighteenth-century scientist, astronomers became the "authorized prophets." What distinguished Halley from Newton was the fact that he made these daring thoughts public and was censured by some politically conservative Anglicans who felt that their authority had been preempted and that arrogance like Halley's endangered the social order. They detested this turn of events and urged natural philosophers to restrict themselves to more secular matters.

Since celestial mechanics opened the door to this new, "offensive" arena of comet activity, Halley's investigation of cometary orbits will be outlined.[1]

INTEREST IN ORBITS

Comets first piqued Halley's interest at age twenty-four when he, en route between Calais and Paris, saw the Great Comet of 1680.[2] Once he arrived in Paris, he wrote Robert Hooke that "the generall talk of the virtuosi here is about the Comet, which now appears." Although cloudy weather made observations difficult, Halley promised to send Hooke whatever information he could glean about this bright comet, and he requested that Hooke keep him abreast of English observations.[3]

Wedded to Kepler's theory of rectilinear orbits, Halley struggled without success to represent the comet's positions by "an equable Motion in a right

line."[4] He was not ready to embrace Cassini's theory that the comet traveled in a great circle with a period of two and a half years, or that the comet of 1680 was identical with those of 1577 and 1665. Halley wrote Hooke, "I know you will with difficulty Embrace this Notion of his, but at the same tyme tis very remarkable that 3 Cometts should soe exactly trace the same path in the Heavens and with the same degrees of velocity."[5] Perhaps this was the seedling that germinated in Halley's mind and later bore the fruit we know as his *Astronomiae cometicae synopsis*. If it was, this seedling lay dormant in 1681, and Halley remained puzzled. "Your thoughts hereupon may serve to guide me in my Speculation," he told Hooke. "I am yet resolved to try one bout with it, and it will be with a great deale of regret that I shall be forced to give over [to Cassini's theory]."[6]

In August 1682, another comet blazed overhead, and Halley again briefly turned his attention to comets. He dutifully recorded his observations of this comet—today known as "Halley's comet"—but these were so crude, especially for someone who had served as Flamsteed's assistant and had proved his mettle in the southern hemisphere by cataloging stars, that when the comet later proved to be significant for him, he was forced to rely on the records of others.[7] To put it simply, Halley was preoccupied with non-cometary matters during this period.

Indeed, for the next ten years, there is only circumstantial evidence that Halley was interested in comet orbits. In letters to colleagues, Halley called attention to Newton's theory of comets as a major achievement of the forthcoming *Principia*, and he mustered all his diplomatic skills to keep Newton from repressing the cometary sections.[8] In 1690, he showed the Royal Society a copy of Gottfried Kirch's book on the 1680 comet,[9] and in 1693 Hooke noted that Halley discussed comets with him at home.[10]

It was not until August 1695 that Halley seriously got down to business calculating comet orbits in collaboration with Newton.[11] He first employed a "course [coarse] construction" to glean some sense of a comet's orbit and then "took the pains to examine and verifie it by an accurate Calculus."[12] From Newton's theory, he derived parabolic and elliptical orbits to fit observations by Flamsteed and others. Halley knew that Newton planned to revise the cometary propositions of the *Principia*, and he hoped to relieve Newton from the tedium of orbital computations. "It is no great trouble," he wrote Newton, "[for I am] desirous as far as you will permitt it, to ease you of as much of the drudging part of your work as I can, that you may be the better at leisure to prosecute your noble endeavours."[13] In subsequent letters Halley reported his cometary calculations and reminded Newton, "I have been hard at work to serve you."[14]

The exchange was not totally one-sided. In comparing the discrepancies between the observed and computed places for the 1680–1681 comet, Halley wrote Newton, "Perhaps Your sagacity may discover how to adjust the matter so as to remove the greatest part of those errours which upon severall attempts I found to[o] hard for me."[15] Newton responded with

emendations that enabled Halley to recompute the elliptical orbit.[16] They also conferred on Jupiter's and Saturn's perturbations of highly elliptical comet orbits.[17] When Flamsteed's animosity threatened the project, Halley asked Newton to intercede on his behalf.[18] "I must entreat you to procure for me of Mr. Flamsteed what he has observed of the Comett of 1682 particularly in the month of September," Halley wrote Newton, "for . . . he will not deny it you, though I know he will me."[19] Halley was especially eager to have these observations because he was "more and more confirmed that we have seen that Comett now three times, since ye Yeare 1531."[20]

By June 1696, Halley's calculations had firmly satisfied him that the apparitions of 1531, 1607, and 1682 were indeed the same comet. At a meeting of the Royal Society,

> Halley produced the Elements of the Calculation of the Motion of the two Comets that appear'd in the Years 1607 and 1682, which are in all respects alike, as to the place of their Nodes and Perihelia, their Inclinations to the plain of the Ecliptick and their distances from the Sun; whence he concluded it was highly probable not to say demonstrative, that these were but one and the same Comet, having a Period of about 75 years; and that it moves in an Elliptick Orb about the Sun, being when at its greatest distance, about 35 times as far off as the Sun from the Earth.[21]

This was a momentous finding, but Halley did not race to publish it. Instead, he continued to compute comet orbits.[22]

At first, he had hoped to construct the orbits of all observed comets but quickly learned that most observations were unsuitable for this task.[23] The reasons were clear. For centuries, Aristotle's opinion had prevailed, and astronomers had taken it for granted that comets were sublunary vapors or aery meteors. Consequently, "this most difficult Part of the Astronomical Science lay altogether neglected; for no Body thought it worth while to take Notice of, or write about, the Wandring uncertain Motions of what they esteemed Vapours floating in the *Aether*; whence it came to pass, that nothing certain, concerning the Motion of Comets, can be found transmitted from them to us."[24] Even Seneca had not seen fit to set down those observations of cometary motion by which he maintained his opinion that comets were celestial bodies.[25] "And indeed," Halley complained, "upon the Turning over very many Histories of Comets, I find nothing at all that can be of Service in this Affair, before, A.D. 1337. at which time *Nicephorus Gregoras*, a *Constantinopolitan Historian* and *Astronomer*, did pretty accurately describe the *Path* of a Comet amongst the Fix'd Stars, but was too laxe as to the Account of the *Time*; so that this most doubtful and uncertain Comet, only deserves to be inserted in our Catalogue, for the sake of its appearing near 400 years ago."[26]

As far as Halley was concerned, Tycho Brahe's study of the 1577 comet had ushered in a new era of precision, setting the stage for Cassini and Flamsteed, who observed the apparent motion of the 1680 comet with an

accuracy "perhaps as far as Humane Skill cou'd go." Their observations proved critical to cometary science. Making a sharp hairpin turn around the sun, this comet "by the very remarkable and peculiar Curvity of its Orbit (above all others) gave the fittest Occasion for investigating the *Theory of the Motion*."[27] Newton rose to the challenge and in the *Principia* subjugated the 1680 comet to his principle of universal gravitation and demonstrated a geometrical method of delineating comet orbits.

In 1705, Halley laid his own contribution to cometary science on Urania's altar. This offering was the *Astronomiae cometicae synopsis*.[28] Picking up where Newton left off, Halley explained his method of computing orbits and tabulated the orbital elements of twenty-four comets.

> Wherefore (following the Steps of so *Great a Man* [Newton]) I have attempted to bring the same Method to *Arithmetical Calculation*; and that with desired Success. For, having collected all the Observations of Comets I could, I fram'd this Table, the Result of a prodigious deal of Calculation, which, tho' but small in Bulk, will be no unacceptable Present to Astronomers. For these Numbers are capable of Representing all that has been yet observ'd about the Motion of Comets, by the Help only of the following *General Table*; in the making of which I spar'd no Labour, that it might come forth perfect, as a Thing consecrated to Posterity, and to last as long as *Astronomy* it self.[29]

Halley at first approximated cometary orbits with parabolas, but in later editions of the *Synopsis* he was able to offer a "ready Method" to compute elliptical orbits.[30] Indeed, the merit of Halley's table of orbital elements was premised on the reality of elliptical orbits. Halley presumed that the number of comets was determinate and perhaps not very great.[31] The orbital elements of each comet would then serve as its "fingerprint":

> The principal Use therefore of this Table of the Elements of their Motions, and that which induced me to construct it, is, That whenever a new Comet shall appear, we may be able to know, by comparing together the Elements, whether it be any of those which has appear'd before, and consequently to determine its Period, and the *Axis* of its Orbit, and to foretell its Return.[32]

Comparison of cometary orbits identified comets on their periodic returns. In surveying the parameters he had calculated, Halley suspected that the comets observed in 1531 by Apian, in 1607 by Kepler and Longomontanus, and in 1682 by himself were one and the same.[33] "Hence I dare venture to foretell, That it will return again in the Year 1758. And, if it should then return, we shall have no Reason to doubt but the rest must return too: Therefore Astronomers have a large Field to exercise themselves in for many Ages, before they will be able to know the Number of these many and great Bodies revolving about the common Center of the Sun; and reduce their Motions to certain Rules."[34] This was the program Halley set before astronomers, and he continued to compute orbits for many years to come (figs. 48–49).[35]

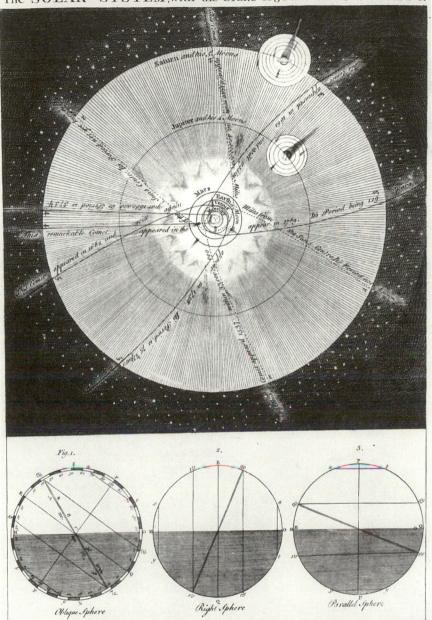

The SOLAR SYSTEM, with the Orbits of 5 remarkable COMETS.

Fig. 48. Betting on Halley's theory before it was proven in 1759. Textbooks depicted the orbits of comets whose periods Halley had computed. Emmanuel Bowen, *A complete system of geography . . . comprehending the history of the universe*, 2 vols. (London, 1744). (WOP-14. Courtesy of Adler Planetarium & Astronomy Museum, Chicago, Illinois.)

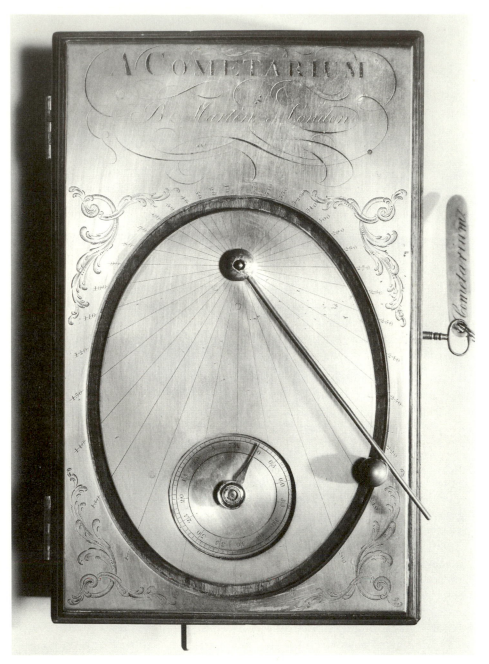

Fig. 49. Cometarium, an instrument manufactured and sold by London maker Benjamin Martin before the return of Halley's comet. It illustrated the elliptical orbit of the comet. (Courtesy of the Collection of Historical Scientific Instruments, Harvard University.)

Travel in closed orbits did not preclude comets' serving as divine agents. Just as Newton had noted that the wayward paths of comets made them well disposed to distribute vital matter throughout the heavens, careen into the sun, or alter the order of the solar system, Halley too seized on the possibilities. In comet collisions he thought he had found an explanatory device to account for major terrestrial upheavals. Comet collisions were completely compatible with closed comet orbits; indeed, Halley first publicly considered these catastrophes in 1687, when, in his capacity as midwife to Newton's *Principia*, he was busy reading Newton's page proofs on the periodicity of comets. At that time, Halley noted the possibility that long ago a comet might have struck the earth, altered its axis and orbit, and caused the biblical Flood.[36]

HALLEY'S THEORY OF THE DELUGE

Halley approached Scripture as an incomplete, often allegorical record.[37] Although Halley was impressed with certain details of the seventh chapter of Genesis, he maintained that its account of the Deluge seemed "much too imperfect to be the Result of a full Revelation from the Author of this dreadful Execution upon Mankind."[38] If God intended to reveal the secrets of nature, he would have spoken more clearly.

> This we may, however, be fully assured of, that such a Deluge has been; and by the many Signs of marine Bodies found far from and above the Sea, 'tis evident, that those Parts have been once under Water: or, either that the Sea has risen to them, or they have been raised from the Sea; to explicate either of which is a Matter of no small Difficulty, nor does the sacred Scripture afford any Light thereto.[39]

For Halley, the earth was littered with fossil evidence of the devastation God had wrought with the Flood;[40] the question was, how did God do it? Sacred Scripture did not provide the complete key.

With a firm belief that God acted through natural causes, Halley sought a physical cause for the Deluge. He stipulated, however, that the physical mechanism must be well understood and observable elsewhere. Any unprecedented physical cause would be just as miraculous as direct intervention by God.[41]

Consequently, Halley rejected the theories of Thomas Burnet and Robert Hooke. According to Burnet, the crust of the smooth, pristine earth had slowly dried in the constant heat of a perpetual summer. Because geophysics was divinely synchronized with human history, at a preappointed time coincident with unconscionable levels of sin, the crust had naturally fractured and vented subterranean waters.[42] Like most contemporaries, Halley found Burnet's theory "as jarring as much with the Physical Principles of Nature, as with the Holy Scriptures, which he has undertaken to reconcile."[43]

Nor did Halley find much to admire in Robert Hooke's theory.[44] Hooke had proposed that the Flood might have been caused by a gradual shifting of the poles within the body of the earth. As the earth spun on its axis, it became squashed at the poles and adopted the figure of an oblate spheroid.[45] The seas also took this figure and therefore bulged at the equator. As the poles supposedly shifted within the earth, dry landmasses would slip under the bulging water of the new equator. A shift in the poles implied by definition a shift in the latitudes of places. In 1687, Halley tested Hooke's theory by comparing modern observations of the latitude of Nuremburg with those made two hundred years before. Halley also compared a modern value for the latitude of Alexandria with that given by Ptolemy, Eratosthenes, Hipparchus, and Timocharis. He found little change and concluded that the motion of the poles was no more than a degree in twenty thousand years.[46]

Halley was willing to grant this slow alteration of the poles but noted that Hooke's theory implied an earth much more ancient than that established by traditional religious chronology.[47] This age did not particularly disturb Halley, except insofar as the time span required by the theory undermined the premise of a precipitous, cataclysmic, and universal Deluge.[48] In other words, it would require ages for the seas to cover the land, and "those Inundations could never be fatall to the Inhabitants, for that they would alwais give notice of their Coming, so that the People might provide for their safety."[49]

In contrast, Holy Scripture and pagan tradition unanimously concurred that the "last great Deluge" occurred suddenly, briefly, and without prior notice. If Hooke's hypothesis was to be reconciled with Scripture, there must have been a "great and sudden alteration in the Poles." No natural terrestrial cause seemed viable to effect this dramatic event. Halley suggested two possible causes that could provide the needed punch. The first, of course, was God's direct intervention. The second, and the one more favored by Halley, was a natural, if extraterrestrial, cause—"the casuall Choc of some transient body, such as a Comet or the like."[50]

In 1687, Halley confessed that such a collision of a comet with the earth implied changes in the earth's axis, diurnal rotation, the length of the year, and the eccentricity of the earth's orbit, "for which yet we have no sort of Authority."[51] In 1692, however, he hinted that a comet impact might explain the observed change of magnetic variation over time.[52] Perhaps this was sufficient authority for a reconsideration of the possibility that the Noachian Deluge had extraterrestrial causes. In 1694, he returned to this theme at a meeting of the Royal Society.[53]

Again he criticized Hooke's latest theory of the Deluge, which he said required a "preternatural *digitus Dei*" to compress the globe, squeeze out the flood waters, and then later restore its shape.[54] God worked through natural causes, Halley proclaimed, and the only viable cause of the Flood was the "casual *Choc* of a *Comet*, or other transient Body." The comet's

collision would have altered the poles and diurnal rotation instantly, thereby causing great confusion and reducing the earth into its "old Chaos." All elements would have been mixed into a heap. The dramatic force of the impact would have caused the sea and all other unconfined fluids to rush violently toward the site of the blow. Great waves would have recoiled back, furiously raking up the sea bottoms and burying marine life beneath the mountain chains that were heaped up where opposite waves clapped together. Present-day evidence of this comet shock included the craterlike depression of the Caspian Sea;[55] the unusually cold climate in North America (around Hudson Bay) near the unthawed, still icy site of the prediluvian North Pole;[56] the fossilized marine animals found on hilltops and deep underground; and the figure of the earth, which seemed "new made out of the Ruins of an old World."[57]

Halley remarked that the hypothesis of a comet's striking the earth might "render a probable Account of the strange Catastrophe we may be sure has at least once happened to the earth."[58] Here Halley intimated the possibility of recurrent comet strikes and a sequence of catastrophes. He broached this subject more explicitly a week later. After first presenting his theory to the Royal Society, he had remained puzzled about how Noah's ark could have survived the cataclysmic event.[59] On the advice of a person whose judgment he had great reason to respect (most likely Newton), Halley amended his theory. He suggested that this cometary impact more likely had happened before the Creation and had possibly reduced a former world into a Chaos out of whose ruins the present world was formed.[60]

This was no fleeting thought, for in 1697 Halley again regaled the Royal Society with his opinion on the effects "of a Collision of a great Body such as a Comet ag[st] the Globe of the Earth, which he described might be undisproved of times before Adam, wherein possibly that Earth might have been reduced to a Chaos, after having been for many years together such as now it is."[61] Halley held fast to his belief in a succession of former worlds, each destroyed by comet impacts; and this leads us to consider his view of the end of the present world.

THE END OF THE WORLD

In his famed *Astronomiae cometicae synopsis* (1705), where he made his well-known prediction of the return of the comet we now call Halley's comet, Halley once more raised the specter of a comet's striking the earth.[62] On the basis of orbital calculations, Halley noted that "some of these Comets have their Nodes so very near the Annual Orb of the Earth, . . . that the Earth [might] be found in the Parts of her Orb next [to] the Node of such a Comet, whilst the Comet passes by."[63] His explicit references to recently observed comets catapulted his discussion of comet collisions from the

misty realms of pre-Adamite history into the concrete realm of current physical possibility. Halley further underscored this distinction when he confided, "But hitherto none has threaten'd the Earth with a nearer Appulse, than that of 1680. For by Calculation I find, that [on] *Novemb.* 11°, 1ʰ, 6′, P.M. that Comet was not above the Semi-diameter of the[64] Sun to the Northwards of the Way of the Earth. At which Time, had the Earth been there, the Comet would have had a *Parallax* equal to that of the Moon, as I take it."[65] In other words, this comet had passed so near to a point in the earth's orbit that it would have been as close as the moon had the earth been there at the time. Then, as if with a sudden recognition of the possible explosive nature of these remarks, Halley quickly stepped back, and cautioned:

> This is spoken to Astronomers: But what might be the Consequences of so near an Appulse; or of a Contact; or, lastly, of a Shock of the Coelestial Bodies, (which is by no means impossible to come to pass) I leave to be discuss'd by the Studious of Physical Matters.[66]

And with these frightening words he closed his famous essay on comet periodicity.

If Halley in 1705 shied away from a full treatment of the earth's possible collision with the 1680 comet, he mustered more courage in the revised version of his *Synopsis* (posthumously published in 1752). For starters, a close, future approach of the comet could change the earth's orbit and the length of our year. Indeed, the earth had only narrowly escaped this calamity during the comet's last return in 1680, for

> it came so near the path of the *Earth*, that had it come towards the Sun thirty one days later than it did, it had scarce left our Globe one Semidiameter of the *Sun* towards the North: And without doubt by its centripetal force (which with the great *Newton* I suppose proportional to the bulk or quantity of matter in the Comet), it would have produced some change in the situation and species of the *Earth's* Orbit, and in the length of the year.[67]

The comet, too, would have paid a cost. "If by chance it had happened to meet any one of the Planets passing by, it must have produced very sensible effects [on them], and the motion of the Comet would have suffered the greatest disturbance."[68]

Should the 1680 comet on some future return smash into the earth, the present world would be at an end. Halley's readers need only have remembered his remarks on the devastating role of comets in punctuating a series of pre-Adamite worlds in order to shudder at this prospect of an imminent cometary end to the current world. This vision also struck Halley, who piously proclaimed, "But may the great good GOD avert a shock or contact of such great Bodies moving with such forces (which however is manifestly by no means impossible), lest this most beautiful order of things be intirely destroyed and reduced into its antient chaos. But of this by the bye."[69]

THE BENEFITS OF COMETS

Despite his disclaimer, "by the bye," a cometary end to the world was an event hardly to be treated incidentally and lightly.[70] Halley attempted to soften the blow by pointing out that even in their most destructive moments comets were wisely prearranged in their orbits for man's ultimate welfare. These catastrophic collisions, like near brushes with comets, were not without their salutary effects.

Halley deferred to Newton in discussions of the composition of comet tails and thus presumably subscribed to Newton's theory of the tails' replenishing roles.[71] Diffused throughout the solar system, the vapors from comet tails would eventually gravitate to the planetary atmospheres and there would condense into the vital fluids required to sustain terrestrial life.[72] The close approach of a comet might only enhance the earth's chances of capturing cometary vapor and having it mix with our atmosphere.

In 1694, Halley found a novel way to integrate the biological rewards of comets with their apocalyptic roles. Like Newton, Halley suggested that the surface materials of the earth would, over time, become hard and stony, unfit for vegetation and animal life. If a comet collided with the earth, these stony materials would be buried deep within the globe while a lighter, finer soil would settle on the surface:

> And perhaps, in due Periods of Time, such a Catastrophe may not be unnecessary for the well-being of the future World; to bury deep from the Surface those Parts, which by length of time are indurated into stony Substances, and become unapt for vegetable Production, by which all Animals are either immediately or mediately sustained: the ponderous Matter in such a Mixture subsiding first, and the lighter and finer Mould remaining for the latter Settling, to invest the exterior Surface of the New World.[73]

Although this collision would kill all inhabitants of the globe, it would be necessary to prepare the earth for future races and new creations.[74] Deadly in the short term, but healthful in the long run, comet collisions allowed for the succession of worlds.

Halley therefore used comets in accounts of the Flood, mass extinctions and the renewal of life, the origin of the present world, and its future end. Was this the same Halley who proclaimed that there was no reason for people to "quail beneath appearances of bearded stars"?[75] Indeed it was. On one hand, Halley wrote that "one of the principle Uses of the Mathematical Sciences . . . [was] to prevent the Superstition of the unskilful Vulgar; and by shewing the genuine Causes of rare Appearances, to deliver them from the vain apprehensions they are apt to entertain of what they call *Prodigies*; which sometimes, by the Artifices of designing Men, have been made use of to very evil purposes."[76] To this end, he published a broadside illustrating the path of a solar eclipse across England in order "that the suddain dark-

ness . . . may give no surprize to the People, who would, if unadvertized, be apt to look upon it as ominous."[77] The same sentiments were expressed by Halley in his ode to Newton's *Principia*: Now that "we know the sharply veering ways of comets," they no longer are a "source of dread."[78] On the other hand, it seems that the vulgar superstitions Halley kicked out his front door, he smuggled in his back door. In his work, comets were transformed from divine signs of calamitous local events into natural causes of global events. Where they had presaged revolution, religious reform, and agricultural change, Halley now made them active agents. Historical, sacred, and geological periods were punctuated by comet-induced discontinuities.

Halley may have thought that he was taking comets out of the hands of "designing Men," and that the world would be safer for it. Not all agreed. Halley's appropriation of comet lore into cosmology sparked lively comments from natural philosophers, men of letters, and ecclesiastical authorities.

THE SCIENTIFIC RESPONSE

Natural philosophers of the eighteenth century not only respected Halley's and Newton's comet theories but also expanded on them. Whiston, Buffon, Maupertuis, Wright, Kant, Herschel, and Laplace—to varying degrees—considered the roles of comets in the earth's Creation, the Deluge, the final Conflagration, and in major reorganizations of the celestial order. Many more proclaimed that comets refueled the sun and replenished the planets with vital fluids and spirits.[79]

In chapter 10, I will detail the cosmogonical ways in which eighteenth-century philosophers marshaled comets. Here I will make this point: In affirming a role for comets in the beginning and end of the world, natural philosophers derived a new sense of power. If comets were indeed divine tools for reforming the world, it became conceivably possible for astronomers to predict when certain scriptural prophecies might be fulfilled. In 1761, Johann Lambert (1728–1777) described this situation vividly:

> I was not far from looking at astronomers as authorized prophets and . . . from seeing in the invention of the telescope and in the rapid growth of astronomy the herald of an impending disaster. How could, I thought, a genie suggest to Copernicus the structure of the world, to Kepler its laws, and to Newton that terrible attraction and the doctrine about the course and impact of comets, so that everything might be available for the prediction of the calamity and the inhabitants of the earth might see to it that instead of having all come to an end[,] a seed for propagation might remain alive on the changed earth![80]

A number of ecclesiastical authorities were happy to take advantage of the new scientific approach to the end of the world. The Methodist evangelist John Wesley (1703–1791), for example, was content to see comets, like the

recent Lisbon earthquake, as part of God's arsenal in the war against sinners. In a sermon published in 1755 and 1756, he directed his congregants' attention to the imminent return of Halley's comet in 1758. Whether by mistake or by design, Wesley confused the near-approaching 1680 comet, whose return was not expected until 2255, with the 1682 comet, whose return was shortly expected, and cited Halley's orbital calculations to paint a vivid picture of the forthcoming blazing end to the world. Should men fail to repent, this fiery judgment would soon be at hand.[81]

Other churchmen were not so sanguine about the new role of comets or about the astronomer's role in forecasting the great world reformations that were heralded in Scripture. While they had no desire to return to the old view of comets as local signs of plague, poor harvests, and rebellion, which by this time had become socially discredited and labeled as superstitious, they could not tolerate the scientists' becoming arbiters of religious chronology and eschatology.

ECCLESIASTICAL CRITICISM

In treating Scripture as allegorical, and searching for a naturalistic explanation of the Deluge, Halley was not original. To varying degrees, Burnet, Ray, and Hooke had preceded him; Whiston and others would follow.[82] These theorists-of-the-earth argued that it was nobler for God to act through natural laws than for him to intervene directly in petty earthly affairs. While these men hardly advocated atheistic notions, their approach confirmed a widely held suspicion that the new natural philosophy was dangerous to religion.[83]

The dangers were manifold. When Burnet and Halley questioned the literal veracity of Scripture on the topic of Creation and Deluge, they opened the door to scriptural allegory elsewhere. This furnished the atheists with ammunition. As the eminent Newtonian John Keill (1671–1721) pointed out, "These contrivers of Deluges, have furnished the Atheist with an Argument, which upon their supposition is not so easily answer'd as their Theories are made."[84] Once divine miracles were precluded from the greatest episodes in terrestrial history, it was feared that all supernatural events would be totally submerged in the natural. God would be pushed from the world:

> Of all Philosophers, those have done Religion the least service, who have not only asserted, that the world was made by the laws of Mechanism, without the extraordinary concurrence of the Divine power, but also that all the great changes which have happened to it, such as the Deluge, and other great effects dilivered to us as miracles by the sacred writers, were the necessary consequences of natural causes, which they pretend to account for.[85]

So preached Keill, and others like Erasmus Warren said amen.[86]

Furthermore, in rendering the scriptural account physically intelligible and plausible, and by using scientific records to supply the purportedly missing data, the theorists seemed guilty of overstepping the boundaries of human reason and experience, and meddling with matters known only to God. Halley especially left himself open to this sort of criticism when he closed his 1694 comet paper with the following remarks. "What I have advanced," wrote Halley, "I desire may be taken for no more than the Contemplation of the Effects of such a *Choc* as might possibly, and not improbably, have befallen this Lump of Earth and Water in Times whereof we have no manner of Tradition, as being before the first Production of Man."[87] How could people know about a prehistoric comet catastrophe that prepared the earth for the generations of Adam? Halley contended that there were two ways: (1) by revelation; and (2) "*a posteriori* by Induction from a convenient Number of Experiments or Observations, arguing such an Agitation once, or oftner, to have befallen the Materials of this Globe."[88] In other words, the earth's present landscape and structure, disfigured and damaged, told us something about former worlds and pre-Adamite history, which were otherwise inaccessible through Genesis. Astronomical and geological records supplied the deficiencies of the Bible. Halley's empirical approach raised the eyebrows of Anglican authorities.[89] Halley was "sensible that he might have adventured *ultra crepidam*; and apprehensive least by some unguarded Expression he might incur the Censure of the Sacred Order."[90] For this reason, he withheld publication of his 1694 papers on the role of comets in the Deluge and world making until 1724, and ostensibly the papers were printed then only at the behest of the Royal Society from copies in its archives.[91]

Indeed, at about the time that Halley first ventured into naturalistic explanations of the Deluge, he found himself in trouble with Anglican authorities. The controversy revolved around his alleged belief in the eternity of the world. At stake was the Savilian chair of astronomy at Oxford.

In June 1691, the Savilian chair of astronomy had become vacant and Halley applied for the position with strong backing from his former college, Queen's at Oxford, and the Royal Society.[92] The chair's appointment was in the hands of two guardians of orthodoxy, John Tillotson (1630–1694), the archbishop of Canterbury, and Edward Stillingfleet (1635–1699), bishop of Worcester. In general, both clerics were fearful of atheism ushered in under the cloak of natural philosophy; in particular, they worried about atheism in the guise of the Peripatetic belief in the eternity of the world.[93] Halley shortly discovered that his access to the professorship was blocked by accusations of this Peripatetic heresy. He quickly penned a letter to Abraham Hill, comptroller to the archbishop, and asked him to intercede on his behalf with Tillotson in order to defer the election of the professorship for a short time. "But it must be done with expedition," Halley wrote,

"lest it be too late to speak. This time will give me an opportunity to clear myself in another matter, there being a caveat entered against me, till I can shew that I am not guilty of asserting the eternity of the world."[94]

Stillingfleet had also heard that Halley "was a Sceptick, and a Banterer of Religion, [and] he scrupled to be concern'd; till his Chaplain Mr. *Bentley* should talk with him about it; which he did."[95] According to reports, Halley's interviews with Stillingfleet and Bentley could not have been worse.

> Bishop Stillingfleet fell very foul upon the famous Dr. Halley too on the same account, who came to expostulate with him upon the occasion. The bishop began to ask him some questions. The Doctor told him, "My Lord, that is not the business I came about. I declare myself a Christian and hope to be treated as such."[96]

Thomas Hearne (1678–1735), the antiquary, also heard that Halley showed a definite want of tact. Hearne recorded that "Mr Hall[e]y went to Dr Stillingfleet, & y^t he told him y^t he bilievd a God & that was all."[97] According to William Whiston, when Bentley examined Halley, he found that "Mr. *Halley*, was so sincere in his Infidelity, that he would not so much as pretend to believe the Christian Religion, tho' he thereby was likely to lose a Professorship; which he did accordingly; and it was then given to Dr. *Gregory*."[98]

The authors of these reports were scarcely notable for their impartiality in the present case. Whiston in particular was jealous of Halley's ultimate success in gaining an Oxford chair in geometry in 1703 despite rumors of his irreligion.[99] Likewise, the ever morose Flamsteed, perhaps one source of the charges, continued acrimoniously to attack Halley by questioning his morals and alleging his turpitude.[100] At the time of the 1703 appointment, for example, Flamsteed acidly reported, "Dr Wallis is dead: Mr. Halley expects his place, who now talks, swears, and drinks brandy like a sea-captain."[101] Neither Whiston nor Flamsteed was of the disposition to enjoy Halley's raillery, and both rankled at his jocularity.[102] By no means the perfect saint, Halley, for instance, teased Whiston about his strict religious views. When Whiston refused a glass of wine because it was Wednesday or Friday, Halley asked him whether he "had a Pope in his Belly."[103] Halley's dubious reputation as "a *very* free thinker"[104] in part derived from his sallies and perhaps colorfully injudicious remarks, but accounts of his infidelity likely derived from the malice of others. There is little solid evidence to support their charges.

With regard to the original allegation of his belief in the eternity of the world, Halley took the charge seriously and strove to clear his name. He continued to argue for an antediluvian world of greater antiquity than accepted biblical chronology dictated,[105] but emphasized that his studies into the age of the world were "chiefly intended to refute the ancient Notion, some have of late entertained, of the Eternity of all Things; though perhaps by it the World may be found much older than many have hitherto imag-

ined."[106] In 1692 and 1693, Halley read astronomical papers to the Royal Society in which he endeavored to prove "the necessity of the worlds coming to an end, and consequently that it must have had a beginning."[107] Yet Halley confessed that "there still [was] wanting a valid argument to evince from what has been observed in nature that this Globe of the Earth ever did begin or ever shall have an end."[108] Therefore, even in these attempts to prove the end of the world, Halley never followed the rigidly orthodox line. He continued to challenge biblical chronology. In 1694, his arguments in favor of a cometary beginning and end to the present world were attached to reflections on a succession of pre-Adamite worlds.[109] And in 1715, he reiterated, "But whereas we are there [in Scripture] told that the Formation of *Man* was the last Act of the Creator, 'tis no where revealed in Scripture how long the *Earth* had existed before this last creation."[110] Whether or not these ideas were heretical, his whole approach to the issue was certainly heterodox, for Halley tried to establish his religious orthodoxy by invoking scientific arguments. He employed scientific criteria as arbiters in variant readings of sensitive scriptural passages and thereby trod into areas his critics contended were knowable only through revelation.

HALLEY'S ALLEGED FREETHINKING IN POLITICAL CONTEXT

With his abundant enthusiasm for the power of human reasoning and his extension of scientific approaches into religious domains, Halley appeared to contemporaries as a freethinker. In the political realm, reports of Halley's twisting political alignments painted him as an opportunist who gauged political situations by reason, rather than by some prearticulated principles. Such reliance on personal reason was subversive to the social order, according to contemporary Tory High Churchmen, because it led to the questioning of religious and political authority. They emphasized humility and obedience, not intellectual pride, as characteristics befitting the subjects of a stable government.

Within the nexus of this Tory High Church position, Halley's comet theory also came under attack. A brief sketch of the background to the eighteenth-century political and religious matrix is in order before we examine a select group of Tory High Churchmen and others of like mind who were among the most vocal critics of Halley and his comet theory.

Ever since the English Civil War, there had been a strong belief that religious nonconformity was firmly connected to revolution. In the words of one royalist, "Heresy is always the forerunner of rebellion."[111] Understandably, both were abhorred. With the Restoration, the Church of England had allied itself with the Crown and had advocated the twin doctrines of nonresistance to divine-right monarchy and the suppression of all nonconformity.[112] In exchange for its support, Charles II and his Parliament had granted the Anglican Church exclusive privileges. The Act of Uniformity, the Test

and Corporation Acts, and the Licensing Act had guaranteed the Anglican Church a monopoly of worship, of published religious opinions, and of political power.[113]

In 1688, however, the Glorious Revolution had eroded these safeguards. Tory High Churchmen had viewed William III as a usurper of power, and many, as nonjurors, had contemned the liaison between Low Churchmen and the Whig political establishment.[114] Moreover, the Toleration Act, the practice of occasional conformity, and the lapsing of the Licensing Act had opened the floodgates to anti-Anglican literature, dissenting academies, and other nonconformist activities.[115] Confronted with the advance of dissent and Whiggism, Tory High Churchmen rallied behind the cry, "Church in danger!"[116]

Under Anne, Tory High Churchmen had some success in stemming the tide of nonconformity with the Occasional Conformity Bill and the Schism Act.[117] But Tory power collapsed over the issue of the Hanoverian succession. Once again, the Whigs gained control and preferment passed to Low Churchmen. George I, who was advised of the Jacobite sympathies of the Tory High Churchmen, blocked the promotion of High Churchmen who questioned the legitimacy of his rule.[118]

Forbidden to vent their political frustrations in sermons or in the forum of convocation,[119] conservatives, such as Jonathan Swift (1667–1745), resorted to satire.[120] Halley may have been a tempting target as much for his suspected political leanings and religious beliefs as for the presumed social dangers stemming from his scientific exegesis of the Bible.

Although Halley professed to being a Tory and was accused of being a Whig, he can best be described as a member of the court interest. During the War of Spanish Succession, Queen Anne or her Tory ministry dispatched Halley to Vienna to advise the Austrian emperor Leopold on the fortification of northern Adriatic harbors. There is also some indication that in these missions, as well as in his survey of the English Channel, Halley performed some intelligence work for the Crown.[121]

Yet as soon as George I ascended the throne amidst the accolades of his Whig well-wishers, Halley quickly swore his allegiance. Tory nonjurors like Thomas Hearne were appalled:

> The said D^r. Halley defends taking all manner of Oaths, & as soon as ever King George came over, he went to Westminster & took ye Oaths publickly, & bragged of what he had done afterwards, in as publick a manner, particularly in the Coffee-Houses.[122]

Indeed, Halley's reputed chameleonic political character had drawn some notice after the 1688 Revolution too. It was rumored that he had continued openly to express his gratitude toward Charles II and the ousted James II. William III had been alarmed by Halley's disloyalty until he learned that Halley had no "particular dislike" for him.[123] In 1718, Halley justified his allegiance to Stuarts and Hanoverians alike. "For my part, says the D^r,

I am for the King in Possession. If I am protected, I am content. I am sure we pay dear enough for our Protection, & why should we not have the Benefit of it?"[124]

To Tories like Hearne, Halley's prostitution of the High Church principle of divine-right, hereditary succession to opportunist social ends was dangerous to both church and state. Hearne summarized, "Thus this Gentleman [Halley] is for Confusion, & if all were of his Mind, all Government would soon be at an end."[125] Moreover, Halley's suspected Whiggism was tantamount to irreligion. "The said Sir Isaac [Newton] is a great Whig. And so is D^r. Halley, tho' he pretends to be a Tory. In short, D^r. Halley hath little or no Religion."[126]

With the indignities of the Glorious Revolution and Hanoverian succession—not to mention the English Civil War—still fresh in their minds, Tories viewed freethinking in political and religious matters as destined to promote social upheaval. Rumors circulated that Halley was a great freethinker who judged issues by no higher authority than his own reason. Whatever truth there may be in these rumors is irrelevant. Once contemporaries gave them some credence, they viewed his scientific accomplishments through the veil of this gossip.

Halley seems to have understood this. As early as 1679, in the midst of the Popish Plot crisis, when John Aubrey had advised him to study astrology, he had responded that it was "a very ill time for it," given that "the Arch-Conjurer Gadbury"—a crypto-Catholic—was about to be hanged for it.[127] Halley did, however, go the library to consult the book on conjunctions Aubrey had recommended. Despite the risks, he wanted to judge for himself. No wonder he was considered a freethinker! During his quest for a Savilian chair, Halley became more sensitized to the political implications of his research and remained sensitized in the decades that followed. His political awareness did not hinder his work; rather, it seems to have encouraged him occasionally to use his scientific publications as a shield to protect himself from charges of political disloyalty and religious unorthodoxy. He certainly did this in the 1690s when accused of professing the eternity of the world, and again after 1713, when suspicions of his heresy resurfaced.[128] He also used this tactic in 1715—soon after the Hanoverian succession—when he published the path of a solar eclipse across England in order to enlighten people who would otherwise "Interpret it as portending evill to our Sovereign Lord King George and his Government, which God preserve."[129] This broadside not only assured Whigs of Halley's loyalty to the Crown but also threw down the gauntlet to Tory conservatives, because in effect Halley showed that his science was not subversive but served the state by quashing potentially dangerous, vulgar ideas. Perhaps emboldened by this thought and secure in his appointment as astronomer royal and Savilian professor of geometry, Halley finally agreed in 1724 to let the Royal Society publish the controversial Deluge paper he had written in 1694.

THE SATIRISTS' BARBS

In his forays into earth history, comet catastrophe, biblical exegesis, and perhaps politics, Halley displayed that pride and presumption of the modern scientist which never ceased to vex the conservative wits of the age. For Jonathan Swift, Alexander Pope, John Gay, John Arbuthnot, Thomas Parnell, and Robert Harley, earl of Oxford, all men with Tory or High Church leanings, it was more than folly for Halley and other scholars to present a naturalized account of the Creation, the Deluge, or the end of the world. It was potentially dangerous to the social order. An overemphasis of the power of science to dissect issues, both on earth and in heaven, led to an intellectual pride and arrogance that were incompatible with the proper subordination of personal belief to both religious and political authority. In short, pride in scientific virtuosity led directly to nonconformity in religion and revolution in politics. So boldly brandishing their pens, these satirists attempted to safeguard public security with the weapon of burlesque.[130] They lampooned Halley's theory and hoped thereby to ridicule the abuses of learning in order to promote the progress of true knowledge and preserve the fabric of society.

The Scriblerians baited Halley by attributing some of his research to their notorious pedant-hero, Martinus Scriblerus. Scriblerus was described as the "Prodigy of our Age; who may well be called *The Philosopher of Ultimate Causes*, since by a Sagacity peculiar to himself, he hath discover'd Effects in their very Cause; and without the trivial helps of Experiments, or Observations, hath been the Inventor of most of the modern Systems and Hypotheses."[131] Eighteenth-century readers would have recognized Halley's efforts among the "Discoveries and Works of the Great *Scriblerus*, made and to be made, written and to be written, known and unknown." There we find "all the new *Theories* of the *Deluge*," and "Tide-Tables, for a Comet, that is to approximate towards the Earth."[132]

Nor did Swift, in his *Gulliver's Travels* (1726), miss the chance to impute Halley's cometary calculations and apprehensions to the Laputans. The Laputans had forecast the earth's imminent destruction by the next comet's return, which they had calculated for "one and Thirty Years hence." This was a direct allusion to the predicted return of Halley's comet in 1758. Living under continual disquietude, Laputans daily inquired of each other "what hopes they have to avoid the stroak of the approaching Comet."[133] Elsewhere, Swift had written, "Old men and comets have been reverenced for the same reason; their long beards, and pretences to foretell events."[134] Swift ridiculed these old beliefs but found the contemporary dread of comets, which was deeply rooted in scientific discoveries, even more objectionable.

In the tradition of the Scriblerians, it was Henry Fielding (1707–1754), however, who published a full-scale parody of Halley's theory of the Deluge

that served as an indictment of the bloated pretensions of natural philosophy.[135] Fielding was a Whig magistrate and so did not write in defense of Tory or High Church causes. However, like Swift and the others, he found speculative natural philosophy to be both useless and dangerous. His attack on Halley may have been engendered by the suspicion that Halley's cometography was little more than folklore dressed up in mathematics.

Fielding began his narrative with a happy appraisal of a book on English ants that he admired for the moral lessons the author had drawn from natural history. In Fielding's essay, the moral utility of entomology was sharply contrasted with that of the overblown cosmogonies of his day. Indeed, Fielding set the tone for the satire with an epigraph from Horace: "Our Folly would look into Heaven."[136]

Reflections on the economy and sagacity of ants led Fielding to consider other similarities between insects and humans. He mused whether the ants "may possess many of our Sciences which we can never discover, as we do their Skill in Architecture, from the Effect; . . . because those Sciences among the Ants, as indeed among us, do end in nothing, and produce no Effect at all."[137] The sciences that Fielding had particularly in mind were the Baconian travails of the Royal Society:

> Such for Instance among us are the higher Branches of Natural Philosophy; that Philosophy, I mean, which is always prying into the Secrets of Nature, and lying in wait as it were to peep into her dressing Room to view her naked, and before she is drest in any Kind of Form. A bold Attempt, and for which the Philosophers have been often deprived of that little Share of Sense which they before possessed. Indeed, I am apt to think, that if a superior Being was to examine into the Ways of Man, with the same Curiosity with which my Author hath searched into those of Ants, he would not be able to make anything of this Philosopher, nor to discover what he was about when he was employed in his Lucubrations.[138]

For further entertainment, Fielding fancied a colony of natural-philosopher ants. In the midst of these musings, he fell asleep and dreamed about a Royal Society of Ants assembled to discuss the cause of a momentous and violent flood that had long ago submerged the whole anthill and swept away all but the queen and her court. One distinguished ant-philosopher, elevated by a podium of dirt, addressed the assembly on the inadequacies of past theories of the deluge. To the reader, it soon becomes evident that this paragon of insect-philosophers is Edmond Halley, for Fielding put Halley's "Considerations about the Cause of the universal Deluge" almost verbatim into the ant's mouth.[139] Following Halley's 1694 paper, the ant first rejected the theory of "that mighty Ant, Dr. Hook[e]":

> To repeat to you all that hath been advanced on this Subject, would be endless. None, I apprehend, have yet hit on the true Cause. As for that mighty Ant, Dr. Hook, who would account for this Deluge by a *Compression of the Earth*

into a prolate Spheroid, so as thereby to squeeze out the Waters of the Abyss, this would only drown the two extreme Zones of the Hill, whereas the middle Zone would thus be squeezed up instead of down, and so could never be immerged.[140]

But then the ant proceeded to reject Halley's own theory. Where Halley had first proposed the shock of a comet to explain the Flood but afterward bethought himself of Noah's implausible survival, the insect-scholar commented:

> And as for the egregious Ant who would have it [the Flood] to be occasioned by the Choc of a Comet, which instantly Changing the Poles and diurnal Rotations of the Globe, would occasion a Puddle of Water to recede from those Parts, towards which the Poles did approach, and to encrease upon and overflow those Parts wherefrom the Poles were departed; it is sufficient to observe, that the learned Ant himself did afterwards confess, he had forgot to consider the great Agitation such a Choc must necessarily occasion in the Puddle; and tho' he would not give up his Hypothesis (which no Ant ever did or will) he yet confesses it would be extreme[ly] difficult to conceive how her Majesty and her Court could be preserved alive in such a Convulsion.[141]

Halley's grand-scale account of oceanic convulsions was here reduced to some sloshing in a puddle.

The philosopher-ant now attempted his own improved theory of the deluge. First, like Halley, he cataloged the agreed preconditions of the flood. "The Air had been greatly obscured for a long Space of Time, and . . . violent Bellowings had been heard in it." An extraordinary low-hanging cloud covered the anthill, and then a torrent of water fell with precipitous violence.[142]

Now, at the beginning of the dream sequence, Fielding had confessed to the reader that his dream of an ant's preoccupation with the deluge was partly inspired by an accident he had witnessed the previous summer. Fielding had seen "a very large Cow discharge a vast Shower on an Ant-hill, which as I afterwards observed, had destroyed a great Number of the Inhabitants."[143] Readers of the satire would well remember the role of the huge cow in the anthill's deluge. But, of course, the philosopher-ant in the dream knew nothing of this. After he evinced all sorts of hydrostatic experiments and observations on the adhesion and coagulation, the evaporation and precipitation of water, the wise ant reached the thunderous, but wrong, conclusion that the deluge occurred because it had rained.[144]

"Here a violent Applause from the whole Assembly, put an End to my Sleep," Fielding continued. "I will here likewise put an End to this Paper, after having observed, that there are some Subjects on which a Wit and a Blockhead, a Man and an Ant, will exert themselves with the like Success."[145]

For Fielding, as for Swift, Arbuthnot, and the other Scriblerians, it mattered little whether a scholar had the stature of a Newton or a Halley, or of an ant, if that scholar proposed to examine revealed religious doctrine in the

light of unbridled human reason. At best, the enterprise was worthless. At worst, it was corrupting. Skepticism toward revealed scriptural truth undermined the authority of the church and opened a forum for free thought in other matters of church and state. Scientific arrogance promoted theological schism, political dissension, and sectarianism.

While the Tory and High Church critics of science found all forms of scientific pride ultimately subversive to the social order, comet theories like Halley's seemed especially dangerous. In the hands of Whiston, for example, the comet theories had a definite millenarian tone.[146] Millenarian prophecies foretold the downfall of the Antichrist and the rise of a new social order. During the English Civil War, radical sects, such as the Fifth Monarchists, who were eager to pave the way for the Second Coming, had used millenarian ideology to justify the destruction of a pernicious political order.[147] Comets were seen as signs that the time was right, and public pursuit of the Millennium had convulsive effects. In the charged political atmosphere of eighteenth-century England, in which religion and politics were tightly enmeshed, adventist expectations of the arrival of comets that were to reform the natural and political worlds seemed only too apt—once again—to fuel religious enthusiasm and justify rebellions as the fulfillment of biblical prophecy.[148]

Yet as I have argued, this new incendiary use of comets as agents in world reformations and revolutions had its roots in traditional comet lore. That lore saw comets as monstrous signs of divine wrath, as presages of political revolution and religious reformation. Halley was instrumental in transforming these monstrous signs into natural causes, by assimilating the traditional teleological roles of comets into his theory. In the naturalized scheme, comets engaged in the destruction, the renovation, and the transformation of celestial bodies; and during the course of the eighteenth century, they became ensconced as active agents in an array of evolutionary cosmogonies. In this way, the traditional comet lore, so often scoffed at as irrational and superstitious, and so often claimed to have died in the wake of Newton's and Halley's proof of comet periodicity, was in fact given new life by Halley's and Newton's theories.

Comet Lore and Cosmogony

A. Well, to end the Discourse of *Comets*, pray tell me in the last Place to what Use or Purpose they may serve?

B. Some conjecture they are appointed to demolish planetary old Worlds, and to supply Materials again for building them anew; others that they are so many Hells to punish the damned with perpetual Vicissitudes of intolerable Heat and Cold; but all is uncertain.

—Benjamin Martin, *The Philosophical Grammar: Being a View of the Present State of Experimented Physiology, or Natural Philosophy* (London, 1735)

Refueling the Sun and Planets

MANY eighteenth-century philosophers shared Halley's and Newton's penchant for giving comets teleological roles, both salutary and apocalyptic. This chapter will demonstrate the widespread belief in the refueling missions of comets, leaving the next to show support for comets as agents of world reform. The point here is to show that the comet lore which Newton and Halley redescribed in natural philosophical terms was not seen as an aberrant or idiosyncratic part of their philosophy but was energetically embraced and creatively deployed in the development of cosmological thought.

CIRCULATION OF VITAL MATTER

Citing Newton's hypotheses as authoritative, English natural philosophers affirmed that comets replenished the planetary fluids and humidity consumed by the processes of vegetation and putrefaction. Once attracted by the planets, cometary vapors condensed into water and humid spirits, and then were transformed by slow heat into salts, sulphurs, tinctures, mud and clay, sand and stones, coral, and other terrestrial substances. Newton's expositors also maintained that comet tails supplied the most subtle and active spirit in the air on which all life depended.[1]

In general, Newton's views were repeated verbatim in the early eighteenth century, but some were later modified according to current tastes in matter theory. In 1840, for example, the author of an American textbook disparaged Newton's theory of comets' refueling the sun and planets yet deemed it plausible that comets replenished the electrical fluid required by the planets.[2] (By electrical fluid, this author referred to one of the many forms of imponderable matter that natural philosophers had posited since the early eighteenth century in order to explain electrical effects.)[3]

This idea had been proposed decades before and derived from perceived similarities between the aurora borealis and comet tails.[4] Among the first to comment on the similarity was Edmond Halley. In 1716, he mused whether the aurora and comet tails might not both be the product of electrical or nebulous matter.[5] Implicit in comparisons of the earth's aurora and comet tails was the understanding that comets were a sort of planet, as Newton had argued. Jean Jacques d'Ortous de Mairan (1678–1771) made this clear when he declared a comet's tail to be its aurora borealis. For his part, Mairan rejected electrical explanations of the aurora, which were favored

by Georg Matthias Bose, Benjamin Franklin, William Watson, John Canton, and Giambatista Beccaria.[6] Joseph Priestley (1733–1804), however, argued that a comet's tail and the earth's aurora were both manifestations of electrical fluid interacting with their respective atmospheres.[7] In a commentary on Priestley's *History and Present State of Electricity* (1767), an anonymous author in the *Monthly Review* went one step further:

> Had we room or inclination to theorise on this subject; at the same time that, with other electricians, we allowed the electric fluid to be the cause of this last phenomenon [the aurora borealis], we should be for extending its connections still further, and attempt to shew the possibility, at least, of its near relation to, if not its identity with that luminous matter which forms the solar atmosphere, and produces the phenomenon called the *Zodiacal light*; which is thrown off principally, and to the greatest distance from the equatorial parts of the sun, in consequence of his rotation on his axis, extending visibly, in the form of a luminous pyramid, as far as the orbit of the earth; and which, according to Mons. de Mairan's ingenious, and, at least, plausible hypothesis, falling into the upper regions of our atmosphere, is collected chiefly towards the polar parts of the earth, in consequence of the diurnal revolution, where it forms the Aurora Borealis.[8]

The reviewer concluded:

> It would we think be no very bad hypothesis which should unite these two opinions [of Priestley and Mairan], by considering the sun as the fountain of the electric fluid; and the Zodiacal light, the tails of comets, the Aurora Borealis, lightning, and artificial electricity, as its various and not very dissimilar modifications.[9]

Anticipating Priestley by five years, Hugh Hamilton (1729–1805), F.R.S., professor of natural philosophy at the University of Dublin, also concluded that electric fluid was the key ingredient of comet tails and the aurora borealis, but he gave the theory a distinctly Newtonian twist. When electric fluid rose from the earth into the atmosphere, it formed the aurora, which an extraterrestrial spectator would see as the earth's tail. Subtle and fast-moving, this matter tended to diffuse throughout the planetary system, but comets, in their long excursions from the sun, could overtake it and attract it to themselves. Replete with electric fluid, they returned to the inner solar system where the sun's heat caused them to discharge the fluid and disperse it among the planets. Thus comets helped to circulate electric matter that Hamilton had reason to deem necessary for the solar system's health.[10] Claiming to have reached the same conclusions independent of Priestley and Hamilton, Charles Burney (1726–1814) wholeheartedly concurred, as did Samuel Vince (1749–1821), Plumian professor of astronomy and experimental philosophy at Cambridge.[11]

While proponents of a Newtonian view reported these felicitous uses of comets, Pierre de Maupertuis (1698–1759) observed that the task of conveying water and humid spirits to the planets might not be the most honor-

able employment for comets. Maupertuis added that the beneficial effects of cometary matter might be mitigated by its foreign nature. Alien cometary fluids might be too different from native moistures and so prove noxious. They might infect the air and water of a planet and be fatal to its inhabitants, even though they transported fluids necessary to the planet's long-term habitability. Nature often sacrificed small objects to the general good of the universe, Maupertuis observed.[12]

CRITICS

Maupertuis conceded some positive benefits from cometary matter, but others subscribed to a more traditional, non-Newtonian, pessimistic view. William Whiston argued that terrestrial life had become debilitated ever since the gross, chaotic atmosphere of a comet, close-approaching at the time of the Flood, had mingled with the earth's air and tainted it.[13] David Gregory remarked that it was unworthy of a philosopher to discredit as false or fabulous those changes reputedly observed by everyone to follow the apparitions of comets. If a comet tail touched our atmosphere, its exhalations might alter our air and harm animals and vegetables.[14] Cotton Mather (1663–1728) attributed a similar view to Cassini and himself upheld the more stringent position of Dr. George Cheyne (1671–1743) that these "Balls of Confusion" did not achieve the happy ends which Newton had described but rather fostered mischief and ruin.[15] Against Newton, Cheyne had argued:

> Some have thought it [a comet] design'd, to supply the Expence of Fluids in the *Sun* and the *Planets*. But as I have before hinted, this does not seem so very probable, because Nature always supplies constant and regular Expences after a constant and regular Manner. Now the Returns of these Bodies are so irregular and uncertain, and we so little feel the Effects of these Returns (which of necessity must be felt, if these frightful Bodies made the *Reimbursement* mention'd, since the *Sun* and *Planets* are recruited all at once, or in a very short time, of all the loss they have suffer'd in their Fluids for many Years before,) that I am afraid no such benign Influences, are to be expected from them. I readily grant, that there may be some Clouds of Vapours sweep'd off the *Tails* of these *Comets*, by the *Sun* and *Planets* as they approach them. But then it is uncertain of what Nature these Vapours are, for every Vapour will not become a Fluid, unless its Parts be of such a determin'd *Figure* and *Size* as the Nature of Fluids require. . . . Moreover its hardly accountable how the *Sun* shou'd draw from thence only the Fluid of Light, the Earth, that of Water, the other *Planets* their proper Fluids; or if they were suppos'd to draw all *promiscuously*, how these Effects can answer the Design, since Water in the *Sun*, which wanted only more of the Fluid of Light, wou'd be as improper a Guest, as Fire on the Earth, which wanted only more Water.[16]

Cheyne concluded, "I think it is more probable, that these frightful Bodies are the Ministers of *Divine Justice*, and in their Visits, lend us *Benign* or *Noxious* Vapours, according to the Designs of Providence."[17]

It is clear that Whiston, Gregory, Mather, and Cheyne were busy redescribing vulgar beliefs in natural philosophical terms. The transformation was not hard to accomplish or even consciously undertaken, given the tradition dating back to the Middle Ages of identifying comets as the causes of local calamities.[18] More interesting is the fact that natural philosophers who took pains to disagree with key features of Newton's comet theory continued to advocate naturalized, teleological roles for comets on a par with those advocated by Newton. Whether comets bestowed gifts of watery fluids, vital spirit, electrical effluvia, or other matter to the planets and stars, or menaced them with poisonous vapors, they did so on a global scale. However natural philosophers chose to bicker with Newton on the specific details of cometary effects, they debated within channels Newton had established. Newton, therefore, had set the agenda.

A striking example of Newton's general influence is found in the cosmogonic work of the comte de Buffon (1707–1788). Buffon never wrote about comets' supplying aerial spirits and fluids to the planets in the routine way described by Newton, but he argued that when the solar system was formed, a sun-grazing comet brought from the sun all "the volatile, aerial, and aqueous particles that today form the atmospheres and seas of the planets."[19]

Even more striking is the work of Thomas Wright (1711–1786) of Durham. Wright went far beyond Buffon, challenging the most fundamental premises of Newton's and Halley's theories, but this did not prevent him from endorsing the restorative roles of comets. In *An Original Theory or New Hypothesis of the Universe* (1750), Wright, like his contemporaries, had accepted Halley's theory of the return of comets,[20] but he later had "Second or Singular Thoughts upon the Theory of the Universe." In a manuscript composed about 1771, Wright rejected the periodic theory as "too preposterous."[21] In its place, Wright advanced his own theory of comets, which he deemed "more rational both of their origin, and laws of motion."[22]

In his extraordinary theory, he maintained that the heavens were constructed as concentric shells of fire, as a series of nested suns, with planets revolving between them.[23] The starry firmament was a solid orb whose visible interior surface was studded with celestial volcanoes. The fixed stars were nothing but perpetual eruptions of celestial lava; the Milky Way was a "vast chain of burning mountains forming a flood of fire"; and comets were combustible matter spewed out of the stellar volcanoes:

> The comets with great or rather inconcevable force being ejected from those vast erruptive vulcani, in all directions and some in hyperbolic trajectorys, and

returning again by their natural gravity or attraction, to the celestial & solid si-
derial concave, solve in the most obvious mañ[n]er all the several appearances of
those astronishing [*sic*] bodies.[24]

The comets that Halley alleged to be periodic, planetary bodies were
for Wright nothing more than periodic eruptions of the same star or its
neighboring stars.[25]

Nonetheless, Wright agreed that comets were "subject to some infinitely
wise purpose of the Divine Nature."[26] He noted that the free and uninterrupted passage of comets to and from the sun revealed a kind of perpetual
intercourse between the visible stellar regions and the planetary orbits, and
evidenced a natural connection between the whole universe and its component parts. This reminded him of circulation within biological organisms:

> As all animal & vegetative life exists by a regular circulation of material or
> mineral fluids, so, may universal nature be also sustained & preserv'd by a like
> circulation of a more refin'd & subtile celestial mater, and next to spirit.[27]

To comets Wright assigned the important task of circulating the preserving
celestial matter—a salutary, providential fire—throughout the universe:

> Thus by means of a multiplicity of comets in all mañ[n]er of directions a Prov-
> idential Fire is made to circulate thrô all the frame of Universal Nature and like
> the blood of animals which nurrishes and feeds all vital beings, purifies the eth-
> erial medium and probably supplies all its central suns with fuel.[28]

The concept of comets' circulating a nourishing spirit throughout the cosmos was distinctly Newtonian, but the notion of comets' purifying the
aether with fire echoed Kepler.

Supplying the concentric suns with fuel was equally important in preserving life, and Wright addressed this topic in several places. The "ignovomous
fountains of etherial fire" in the solid firmament were designed to eject
comets "to feed the numerous Sun and solar bodies with perpetual fuel."[29]
Sunspots perhaps were comets visibly dropping into the sun:

> [Since comets are] universal bodies and every where directed to ye Sun it is most
> probable that their sole or chief end is to supply the Sun with fresh and perpetual
> fuel, as many of them no doubt that reach his inflam'd atmosphere are torn to
> pieces there, and fall in to his ever burning lava. This manifestly appears from the
> many fragments of such dissipated bodies, visible to ye naked eye upon ye Sun
> disk, and flying round him in ye direction of his equatorial parts.[30]

Those comets that were ultimately "absorb'd in ye Suns body as a providential fuel ordain'd to fead his ever lasting or perpetual fire" preserved "in
full energy the fountain of light and heat, the visible prolific agent &
progenitor of all animal & vegitive life, the nurse of all nature, and pre-
server of creation."[31]

STOKING THE STELLAR FIRES

In addition to Wright, Immanuel Kant (1724–1804) believed that comets could stoke the solar fires, as did Maupertuis and Buffon.[32] Of course, Newton's mainstream expositors also asserted that comets refueled the sun and stars and so prevented these from wasting away.[33]

It must be noted, however, that some challenged the basic premises of this hypothesis. On one hand, William Whiston agreed that the stars dwindled away by emission of light and heat, but implied that comets offered an "intirely precarious or absolutely impossible" solution to the problem.[34] "These Suns and Systems are not of Permanent and Eternal Constitutions; but that, unless a miraculous Power interposes, they must all, in length of Time, decay and perish, and be rendred utterly incapable of those noble Uses for which at present they are so wonderfully adapted."[35] Leonhard Euler (1707–1783) and Benjamin Franklin (1706–1790), on the other hand, rejected the premise that the sun cannibalized itself and someday would be consumed. Euler wrote that so copious an emission of luminescent particles from the sun would not only visibly exhaust that star—and this was not verified by experience—but would fill up the aethereal regions with so much matter that the motions of planets and comets could not fail to be disturbed.[36] Franklin objected, "I am not satisfied with the doctrine that supposes particles of matter, called light, continually driven off from the sun's surface, with a swiftness so prodigious! . . . Must not the sun diminish exceedingly by such a waste of matter; and the planets, instead of drawing nearer to him, as some have feared, recede to greater distances through the lessened attraction[?]"[37] Franklin instead proposed that the sun reburned its fuel.[38] Like Euler, he resorted to an undulatory, rather than a particulate, explanation of light in order to explicate the sun's radiation.[39] John Michell (1724–1793) and Joseph Priestley retained the corpuscular view, but Priestley was able to use results from Michell's experiments on the momentum of light to compute the sun's loss to be only 670 pounds avoirdupois in 6,000 years. If solar matter was as dense as water, the sun's semidiameter would be shortened by merely 10 feet in that time.[40] Therefore, Priestley and Michell, Euler and Franklin had no recourse to comets to refuel the sun; there was no need in their respective theories.

Nor did William Herschel (1738–1822) see any flames to fuel, since he believed that the sun was a dark, habitable body with a luminous upper atmosphere. Yet it might be said that Herschel combined certain arguments of both Franklin and Priestley without rejecting the main tenets of Newton. Herschel reasoned that chemical decompositions of phosphoric, elastic fluids in the solar atmosphere emitted light. This light escaped, although all the other by-products of the decompositions returned to the sun and recirculated. Herschel reckoned that it would take ages for the luminous emission to sensibly diminish the solar body, but mused:

There may also be ways of restoration to compensate for what is lost by the emission of light; though the manner in which this can be brought about should not appear to us. Many of the operations of nature are carried on in her great laboratory, which we cannot comprehend; but now and then we see some of the tools with which she is at work. We need not wonder that their construction should be so singular as to induce us to confess our ignorance of the method of employing them, but we may rest assured that they are not a mere *lusus naturae*. I allude to the great number of small telescopic comets that have been observed; and to the far greater number still that are probably much too small for being noticed by our most diligent searchers after them.

Herschel commented that eleven comets which he and his sister Caroline had observed "had not the least appearance of any solid nucleus, and seemed to be mere collections of vapours condensed about a centre." He continued:

This throws a mystery over their destination, which seems to place them in the allegorical view of tools, probably designed for some salutary purposes to be wrought by them; and, whether the restoration of what is lost to the sun by the emission of light, the possibility of which we have been mentioning above, may not be one of these purposes, I shall not presume to determine.[41]

In this paper of 1795, Herschel hinted that comets served as tools to refurbish the sun. When observations of the 1807 and 1811 comets led him to change his mind about the construction of comets—now judged to have a solid core surrounded by a nebulous envelope—he held fast to the view that comets deposited their nebulous matter in the sun.[42]

Cometary matter was beneficial to more than the sun, Herschel also observed. Noting the general variety of cometary orbits and how much the orbit of a comet in 1770 had been perturbed by passing near the planets, he commented, "It appears clearly that they may be directed to carry their salutary influence to any part of the heavens."[43]

Thus the Newtonian hypothesis that comets circulated vital, renovating materials throughout the heavens and deposited fuel in the sun had adherents into the nineteenth century. Even those who clung to the ancient beliefs that comets poisoned or debilitated the air couched their opinions within a Newtonian framework of global causes; and speculative cosmologists like Wright and Herschel, whose worldviews bore little resemblance to Newton's on the structure and stability of the universe, still shared his belief in the usefulness of comets in refurbishing the heavens.

Revolution and Evolution within the Heavens

"By the Works of Creation," John Ray (1627–1705) wrote, "I mean the Works created by God at first, and by Him conserved to this Day in the same State and Condition in which they were first made."[1] Ray spoke for the majority of non-Cartesian philosophers. For them, the natural order of things was stable and fixed, and would last only as long as it pleased its creator. Creation and preservation of the world system were both acts of providence. "It's unphilosophical," Newton wrote, "to seek for any other Origin of the World, or to pretend that it might arise out of a Chaos by the mere Laws of Nature; though being once form'd, it may continue by those Laws for many Ages . . . till this System wants a Reformation."[2] Without divine intervention from time to time, the mutual gravitational interaction of comets and planets would eventually unbalance the solar system, but Newton felt sure that God would never let this happen. Indeed, God had taken some preparatory measures to prolong cosmic stability: "Lest the systems of the fixed stars should, by their gravity, fall on each other, he hath placed those systems at immense distances from one another," Newton wrote in the *Principia*.[3] In addition, God had wisely prearranged the orbits of comets in order to prevent one from crashing into a planet, unless he willed it.

Thus the world's stability was tied to its teleological design. Many agreed with Newton that "this most beautiful system of the sun, planets, and comets, could only proceed from the counsel and dominion of an intelligent and powerful Being."[4] Since Nature evidenced design and purpose, it ought to be unchanging, Ray had lectured. Constituted in order to sustain life and fulfill divine ends, the world should not be a momentary creation, but "ought to be firm, and stable and solid, and as much as is possible secured from all Ruins and Concussions."[5]

This static worldview, while remaining the majority opinion in the eighteenth century, was assaulted on two fronts—unintentionally from within and intentionally from without its corps of adherents. On one hand, the interpretation of sacred texts suggested that the earth had been and would be reformed. Although Newton, Halley, and Whiston were among those who believed that God closely supervised his creation, they unintentionally helped to undermine the static view, when in place of miraculous powers, they proposed various natural agents by which God could reform the earth and create a succession of worlds in time. On the other hand, critics of the steady-state view—such as Buffon, Herschel, and Laplace—overlooked, ignored, or rejected the role of God as chief superintendent of celestial

revolutions and focused all their attention on natural agents and transformations. Like Newton, Halley, and Whiston, they considered how the destruction of some celestial bodies contributed to the renovation of others, but they were not guided by comparisons of the Book of Nature with the Book of Scripture, nor were they interested in making a case for astrotheology and the argument from design. Thus it was not the subject matter that separated the practitioners of sacred astrophysics from the evolutionary cosmologists, but the approach; and the different approach led to different conclusions about the development of stellar and planetary systems. For the latter cosmologists, stability was not the result of divine fiat and the fixity of creation; rather, stability was connected to instances of dynamic equilibrium and the evolution of worlds. In the new cosmologies, the stable universe was one in a state of flux, with planetary systems evolving and decaying in endless cycles.[6]

Comets were the common denominator and the locus of transition between worldviews. Introduced as divine tools to create the earth, reconfigure its surface with water and fire, punish its sinners, and provide for its saints, comets retained their traditional roles as makers and destroyers of worlds within the new evolutionary cosmologies.

COME HELL OR HIGH WATER

Until the seventeenth century, comets were viewed as divine wonders that announced the punishment of the wicked and redemption of the elect. It was widely thought that comets had ushered in the Christian faith, had punctuated the Protestant Reformation, and would blaze forth at the Second Coming and final consummation of all things.[7] Newton and Halley borrowed and dressed up these popular beliefs, but it fell to William Whiston (1667–1752) to enunciate them in detail within the realm of Newtonian natural philosophy. In 1696, Whiston argued that the earth had been formed from a comet, that Noah's Flood had resulted from the near approach of a comet, and that the final Conflagration would be ignited by a return of the comet.

According to Whiston, comets satisfied all the conditions of the primordial chaos, for they had planet-sized, solid, compact, durable nuclei surrounded by enormous, confused atmospheres of gross exhalations. When God decided to create the earth, he rerouted a comet, transforming its elongated orbit into one concentric with the sun. As the great, churning coma subsided around the comet's hot core, its heterogeneous components settled according to their specific gravities in strata of dense fluids, earth, water, and air. The new earth had no diurnal rotation, but Eden enjoyed a perpetual equinox. After Adam's fall from grace, God cursed the primitive earth, tipped its axis, and subjected it to diurnal motions and seasonal variations.[8] Although in 1696 Whiston offered no insight into the way God had exacted

this penance, he later proposed a mechanism. A comet had obliquely smacked the earth. The impact tilted the axis and imparted diurnal rotation to the outer globe but less rotation to the earth's core. On behalf of this idea, Whiston cited Halley's theory of the variation of the compass.[9]

This was not all that Whiston apparently borrowed from Halley, for he too held a comet responsible for the Noachian Deluge. Whiston determined that at precisely 11:00 A.M. on Thursday, 27 November 2348 B.C., the earth had passed through the atmosphere and tail of a comet and was doused with vast amounts of vapors (fig. 50).[10] After the initial downpour, some vapors remained suspended in the earth's atmosphere and continued to shower the globe over the next forty days and nights. The comet's gravitational attraction had also caused an enormous tide to swell within the subterranean abyss, and these bulging waters distended the earth's crust into an ovoid shape. Under this enormous pressure, the crust cracked and fissured, thereby releasing the "fountains of the deep." The subterranean waters joined the torrents raining down from the "cataracts of heaven." After the comet's passage, life was never the same. The comet had transformed the planet's orbit from circular to elliptical, lengthened the period, and elongated the day. It had deposited so much water and matter on the planet that new oceans and continents were left in its wake. Its coma, moreover, had polluted the earth's air. Whiston held it responsible for the presence of earthquakes, volcanic eruptions, extremes of temperature, meteors, storms, contagions, pestilence, shortened life spans, and degenerate vegetables—in short, all the calamities commonly connected to apparitions since ancient times.[11]

Whiston was pleased with his "Account of the *Universal Deluge* from the Approach of a Comet in its descent towards the Sun," and decided that "it [would] not be difficult to account for the *General Conflagration* from the like Approach of a Comet in its ascent from the Sun."[12] There were two roles a comet might play. First, a large comet could perturb the earth's orbit and transform the planet into another comet:

> For 'tis evident . . . that in case a Comet pass'd behind the Earth, tho' it were in its Descent, yet if it came near enough, and were it self big enough, it wou'd so much retard the Earth's annual Motion, and oblige it to revolve in an *Ellipsis* so near to the Sun in its *Perihelion*, that the Sun it self wou'd scorch and burn, dissolve and destroy it in the most prodigious degree; and this Combustion being renew'd every Revolution, wou'd render the Earth a perfect *Chaos* again, and change it from a Planet to a Comet for ever after.[13]

Sufficient to burn the world, this mechanism was nonetheless rejected by Whiston as too violent. It would entirely ruin the globe and render it unfit for future habitation by the elect. Whiston would later reconsider this mechanism as a way to prepare a site for hell at the conclusion of the Millennium and after the Day of Judgment. To explain the Conflagration, Whiston was forced to consider a second theory. He proposed that a searing

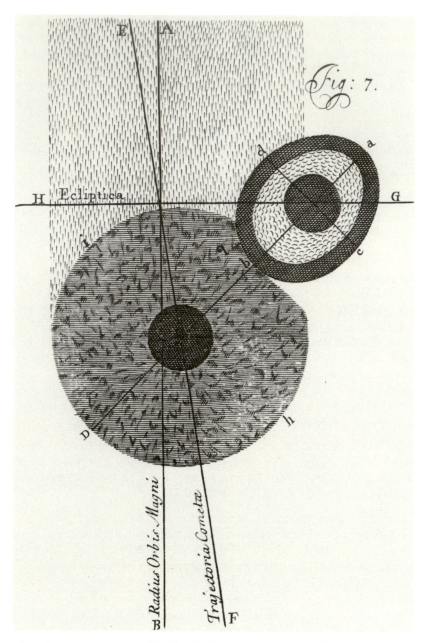

Fig. 50. A comet causes Noah's Flood. The enormous comet douses the contorted, egg-shaped earth with its tail and coma. William Whiston, *A New Theory of the Earth* (London, 1696). (Courtesy of the Library of Congress.)

comet, returning from the sun, might pass close by the earth and cause tidal fluctuations within the abyss. As during the Deluge, these tidal surges would open fissures in the distorted earthen crust, but on this occasion the vents would drain the oceans into the bowels of the earth. Once the landscape was emptied of cooling waters, the comet would scorch the earth with its burning torrents of melted matter. Backed up by eruptions of the earth's central heat, the comet would ignite the final Conflagration. The raging fire would reduce the upper earth and atmosphere into a primitive chaos, which would ultimately cool and subside into the form of the pristine, paradisiacal earth. This would be the site of the Millennium.[14]

In 1696, Whiston believed it quite probable that the very same comet which had caused the Deluge would also cause the Conflagration on its next return.[15] In 1714, Whiston thought he had found the Flood-maker, when he learned that Halley had computed a period of 575 years for the great comet of 1680. Whiston excitedly observed that the Noachian Flood had occurred 4,028 years before 1680, and since 4,028 was virtually divisible by 575, the 1680 comet could have made seven returns since the Flood.[16] Whiston decided, however, that the 1680 comet (like others in Halley's table) was unsuitable to cause the Conflagration and usher in the Millennium, as Newton and Halley were suggesting to their friends. "Therefore the Period or Time for that Conflagration, upon the Supposition that it is to be caused by a Comet, cannot now be discover'd by any natural Means; but must still remain, as formerly, only knowable from Divine Revelation."[17]

At the conclusion of the Millennium and Final Judgment, Whiston believed that the renovated earth would be consumed. Once again, a comet would serve as God's agent of destruction and reconstitution.

> If any Comet instead of passing by, or gently rubbing the Earth, hit directly against it, in its Course either towards or from the Sun, it must desert its ancient Station, and move in a quite different *Elliptick* Orbit; and so of a Planet become again a Comet, for the future Ages of the World.[18]

Thus from a comet the earth derived and to a comet it would revert.[19]

To be sure, many of these ideas did not originate with Whiston. The suggestion that comets played roles in the earth's Creation, Deluge, Conflagration, and consummation had been voiced privately by Newton and publicly by Halley. Whiston did not deny that he had close contact with both men. He acknowledged his indebtedness to Newton by dedicating his *New Theory* to him, and he later claimed that the manuscript had been "chiefly laid before Sir *Isaac Newton* himself, on whose Principles it depended, and who well approved of it."[20] For his part, Newton saw Whiston as his protégé and in 1701 named him as his successor in the Lucasian chair of mathematics at Cambridge.[21] But with Halley, Whiston never fully acknowledged his debt. This probably annoyed Halley, for in January 1707 Halley reminded the Royal Society of his priority, and when he published his papers on the Deluge and succession of worlds in 1724—thirty years after he had read

them to the Royal Society—he again took pains to note that his work had been presented a year and a half before Whiston published his *New Theory*.[22] Thus Halley insinuated that Whiston had stolen key ideas from him, even while Halley tried to dissociate himself from Whiston's unorthodox religious views.

Despite these debts—acknowledged or undisclosed—Whiston put his own stamp on the theory. This appears not only in the details of how comets brought world history in line with Scripture, but also in his extraordinary theory of hell. In his *Astronomical Principles of Religion* (1717), Whiston noted that "The external Regions of Comets, which by passing through such immense Heat when nearest, and such prodigious Cold when farthest off the Sun; and by the confused and Chaotick State of their Atmospheres, do evidently appear incapable of affording convenient Habitations for any Beings that have Bodies, or Corporeal Vehicles, whether visible or invisible to us."[23] If comets were not happy abodes, they could be places of punishment. Dr. George Cheyne may have been the first to observe this,[24] but Whiston was pleased to discover that the theory was compatible with Scripture:

I observe, that the Sacred Accounts of *Hell*, or of the Place and State of Punishment for wicked Men after the general Resurrection, is agreeable not only to the Remains of ancient profane Tradition, but to the true System of the World also. This sad State is in Scripture describ'd as a State of *Darkness*, of *outward Darkness*, of *blackness of Darkness*, of *Torment* and *Punishment for Ages, or for Ages of Ages*, *by Flame*, or *by Fire*, or *by Fire and Brimstone, with Weeping and Gnashing of Teeth*; where *the Smoak of the* Ungodly's *Torment ascends up for ever and ever*; where they are Tormented *in the Presence of the Holy Angels, and in the Presence of the Lamb; when the Holy Angels shall have separated the Wicked from among the Just, and have cast them into a Furnace of Fire*. Now this Description does in every Circumstance, so exactly agree with the Nature of a Comet, ascending from the Hot Regions near the Sun, and going into the Cold Regions beyond *Saturn*, with its long smoaking Tail arising up from it, through its several Ages or Periods of revolving, and this in the Sight of all the Inhabitants of our Air, and of the rest of the System; that I cannot but think the Surface or Atmosphere of such a Comet to be that *Place of Torment* so terribly described in Scripture, into which the Devil and his Angels, with wicked Men their Companions, when delivered out of their *Prison* in the Heart of the Earth, shall be cast for their utter *Perdition* or *second Death*; which will be indeed a terrible but a most useful Spectacle to the rest of God's rational Creatures; and will admonish them above all Things to preserve their Innocence and Obedience; and to *fear him who is* thus *able to destroy both Soul and Body in Hell*.[25]

This cometary hell was not located on just any comet, but on the old earth.[26] After the Millennium, it would be forced to travel through the heavens in a terrible blaze, leaving the blessed behind to watch the fearful spectacle from the vantage point of the earth's former orbit.[27]

In the chain of Creation, Deluge, Conflagration, and consummation, there were circumstances in which God directly interposed. Nonetheless, Whiston believed that by and large God had synchronized natural history and moral conduct: "Nature is God's Constitution, and ever subservient to him; and the state of the *Natural* is always accommodated to that of the *Moral* World."[28] One had only to look around to see that this was true, Whiston declared, for God had "previously adjusted and contemper'd the Moral and Natural World to one another, [so] that the Marks and Tokens of his Providence should be in all Ages legible and conspicuous, whatsoever the visible secondary Causes or Occasions might be."[29]

Such tokens were visible not only on the earth but throughout the solar system. Regular, uniform, and harmonious motions had prevailed among all the planets until sinful "changes in the Living and Rational, requir'd proportionable ones in the Inanimate and Corporeal World."[30] The disorderly eccentricities and aphelia of the planets revealed the degree to which their denizens had fallen from grace. Just as comets were the best agents for punishing the earth—"Seeing we know no other Natural Causes that can produce any great and general Changes in our Sublunary World, but such Bodies as can approach to the Earth, or, in other Words, . . . Comets"[31]— they were perfect for reforming the rest of the solar system:

> It being evident, that multitudes of Comets have pass'd through the Planetary System; that in such their passage they were sometimes capable of causing, nay, in very long periods must certainly, without a Miracle, have caused great alterations in the same; and that the nature and quantities of the present *Eccentricities* or Anomalies are no other than what must be expected from such Causes.[32]

In this way, comets were "fitted to cause the grand Mutations of Nature in the Planetary World; by bringing on *Deluges* in their Descent, and *Conflagrations* in their Ascent from the Sun,"[33] and "so seem capable of being the Instruments of Divine Vengeance upon the wicked Inhabitants of any of those Worlds; and of burning up, or perhaps, of purging the outward Regions of them in order to [bring about] a Renovation."[34]

Bearing in mind the natural role of comets and their significance as divine agents of reform and restitution, Whiston pondered the meaning of comets he himself had witnessed. Despite his disclaimer that the time of the end could not be predicted from the period of any known comet, he fervently hoped in 1736 that a recent comet portended the downfall of the Antichrist and the restoration of primitive Christianity in Europe.[35]

Whiston disseminated his views not only in print but also in lectures until the 1750s. Speaking on comets, religious chronology, and an imminent Millennium, he mesmerized audiences in the coffeehouses of London and in provincial towns.[36] The popularity of these performances, combined with the scandal of Whiston's Arianism, made some of his auditors uneasy about his social goals. In 1713, Alexander Pope (1688–1744) was among the

spellbound, but three years earlier he had referred to "the wicked Works of Whiston," and two months later he would organize the Scriblerus Club to satirize the false learning of Whiston, among others.[37] The presumed dangers of Whiston's philosophy made him the target of many wits.

This is not to say that Whiston had no supporters, even after his reputation was sullied by heresy. Although Voltaire (1694–1778) ridiculed Whiston's theory of the Deluge,[38] and Scriblerian John Gay (1685–1732) lampooned his forecast for the end of the world,[39] James Ferguson (1710–1776), John Hill, and Bartholomew Burges were among the many who embraced Whiston's theories.[40] With water and fire, comet tails could lash rogues on the earth and miscreants on other planets. It was satisfying to think that when comets "shall fall in the way of any of our planets, (the earth not excepted) in their descent toward the sun, they must, if they approach near enough to them, be the occasion of deluges; and, if they come too close to them in their ascent again from the sun, they must occasion universal conflagrations."[41] In this way, comets were "of infinite importance with respect to the other worlds in our system, being capable, in the hands of the Almighty, to produce strange changes and revolutions," John Hill declared.[42] Others took the correctional role of comets a step further and, like Whiston and Cheyne, seized on them as the site of hell. Cotton Mather and Mather Byles, writing from New England, thought that God set incorrigible planets ablaze and hurled these hells into cometary orbits.[43]

The return of Halley's comet in 1759 offered an occasion for the further broadcast and a possible test of these ideas. John Wesley, the Methodist evangelist, awaited the return with the fear that the comet would "set the earth on fire, and burn it to a coal, if it do not likewise strike it out of its course; in which case, (so far as we can judge,) it must drop down directly into the sun."[44] And Benjamin Martin (1704–1782), the instrument-maker and popularizer of science, warned that if the comet should pass through its descending node on 12 May 1758, "we should be in a dangerous Situation, as the denser Part of its blazing Tail would then envelope the Earth, which God forbid."[45] Wesley's sermons and pamphlets and Martin's broadsides and lectures did much to stir up the apprehensions of the English people. Henry Season, in his almanac for 1757, recalled that "the common People imagin'd the Comet was to fall on the Earth, which fill'd many with Astonishment and Horror."[46] In response, correspondents to the *Gentleman's Magazine* tried to calm the "many ignorant people, unskilled in the science of astronomy, and withal of timorous or rather very fearful dispositions," and critics like John Cowley, a London math teacher, reassured the public that God had wisely designed the universe to prevent such catastrophes.[47] This was a very common opinion and one to which Martin himself subscribed. But even though he assured his readers that they "need not be under any needless Terror" about the expected comet should it arrive be-

fore May 1758, he could not resist the temptation to point out that the possibility of a collision or tail immersion—albeit slim—still remained. "It will not be without Reason if our Fears and Apprehensions are considerably raised thereat," he said.[48]

Similar sentiments were voiced in America by Nathaniel Ames in his almanac for 1759,[49] and by John Winthrop (1714–1779), Hollis professor of mathematics and natural philosophy at Harvard College, in two special lectures celebrating the comet's return.[50] "It is not to be doubted," Winthrop said, "that the alwise AUTHOR of nature designed so remarkable a sort of bodies for important purposes, both *natural* and *moral*, in HIS creation."[51] On one side, Winthrop accepted Newton's theory that comets were designed to serve living things by restoring planetary fluids, vital spirits, and solar fuel. "On the other side," Winthrop confided, "it ought not to be concealed, that they seem fitted to be the ministers of divine justice as well as goodness, and capable of producing very great and destructive changes in the planetary worlds; some of them having their nodes situated not far from the orbits of the Planets."[52] If a massive comet passed near a planet, increased tidal fluxes could drown coastal communities. Should a planet pass through a comet tail, it would be drenched with aqueous vapors. Winthrop agreed with the "ingenious and learned Mr. Whiston" that a comet could have caused the biblical Deluge, and noted that another could destroy the earth by crashing into it, if God willed it. "Indeed, according to the laws of nature, particularly those of gravity, it is not possible but that the near approach of a Comet to a Planet, either in it's descent to the Sun or ascent from him, should draw after it a train of dangerous, if not fatal consequences."[53] Although Winthrop reminded his listeners that such disasters were rare, they understood his point. Comets were God's tools, and he could use them with devastating and dramatic effect.

And what could be more dramatic than a role for a comet in the Passion? Johannes Hevelius had suggested that the extraordinary darkness at the crucifixion of Jesus was due to the interposition of a comet between the earth and sun.[54] Increase Mather, the Puritan divine, and Nicolas Fréret (1688–1749), an academician, repeated this contention.[55] So did Roger Long (1680–1770), the master of Pembroke Hall, Cambridge, who observed that "this supposition does not detract from the miracle; the divine interposition would be as necessary to order that those two events should fall out exactly at the same time as it would be to cause such darkness by any other extraordinary means."[56]

Less sanguine about ad hoc visits from comets slyly coordinated with scriptural events, and remarking that Whiston's theory of the Deluge "essentially should be regarded as only a flippant conjecture," Jean d'Alembert (1717–1783) nonetheless observed in the *Encyclopédie* that this theory "contains nothing contrary in itself nor to the sound philosophy which teaches us (whatever system we follow) that the approach of such a comet is capable of upsetting the globe we inhabit" (fig. 51).[57] However one might

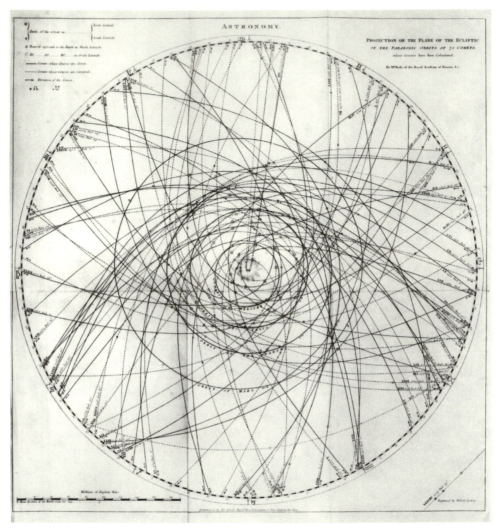

Fig. 51. Comet orbits and the risk to the planets. With such charts in hand, many scholars emphasized how wisely God had ordered the world system in order to prevent comets from colliding with the earth or with each other. Some natural philosophers were less sanguine about this messy arrangement and, like Halley, believed a comet collision with the earth was quite possible. Johann Elert Bode, *Projection on the Plane of the Ecliptic of the Parabolic Orbits of 72 Comets* (London, 1802). (WOP-27d. Courtesy of Adler Planetarium & Astronomy Museum, Chicago, Illinois.)

discredit the role of comets at critical epochs of the earth's sacred history—
that is, at its Creation, Deluge, and Conflagration—many natural philosophers of the eighteenth century, like d'Alembert, affirmed the power of comets to disrupt the order of the solar system, to create and destroy planetary
worlds, and to aid in the evolution of stellar systems.

From Creation to Cosmogony

"There is one error [that] runs through all these cosmogonists," Roger Long
of Cambridge remarked.

> [It is] that they seem to have too low and mean notions of the Divine Omnipo-
> tence, as if it were confined to act by human methods: a man going to build a new
> house, will perhaps, to save time and expence, pull down some other buildings,
> and make use of the materials: but are we therefore to imagin[e] that, when the
> Almighty Creator of all things is about to form a planet or an earth, for the habi-
> tation of men and other animals, he must cast about for a sun in decay, or take a
> comet out of its orbit whereof to compose a new world?[58]

Criticizing Descartes, Burnet, Whiston, and Buffon, Long advised natural
philosophers to confine themselves to the present constitution and nature of
the world. The Creation of the universe was the effect of a miraculous, infinite power setting a perfect world in place in an instant, Long insisted. It
was vain to imagine that we could solve any part of it by "mere mechanism,
matter and motion."[59]

Yet solutions downplaying God and emphasizing mechanism, matter,
and motion were attempted. Seven of these will be discussed in the rest of
this chapter: namely, the work of Buffon, Maupertuis, de Maillet, Kant,
Wright, Herschel, and Laplace. The cosmogonies I have selected are in-
credibly various, so various that my presentation may appear episodic. I
apologize for that. I also acknowledge that the social and political contexts
of each cosmogony could be laid out in detail in the way I have done for
the theories of Newton and Halley. This would be a worthwhile project,
but it is not my goal here. My goal is to hammer home the point that vulgar
beliefs absorbed by Newton and Halley continued to thrive in elite astronomy until the nineteenth century, and they advanced the development of
evolutionary thought. To make this point, I will focus on a leitmotiv that
runs through the work of the aforementioned scientists, one that appears all
the more striking against the panoply of views. This leitmotiv is the importance of comets as agents of change. With each recurrence of this theme,
we see how the popular lore appropriated by Newton and Halley endured,
became freed from its religious freight, and helped to shape modern cosmological thought.

Let us begin with Buffon, the *intendant* of the Jardin du Roi, Paris.
Whereas Whiston saw deviations in planetary orbits as evidence of falls

from grace and the "sad Effects of . . . Divine Malediction,"[60] Buffon was less impressed by irregularities in the solar system than by the enduring uniformity of planetary motions. It could hardly be accidental that the planets and satellites still revolved around the sun in one direction and in approximately the same plane, Buffon announced in his *Histoire naturelle* (1749).[61] Although Newton had ascribed the basic arrangement directly to God, Buffon sought a natural mechanism. The uniformity of the planetary motions indicated that their impulsive forces originated from one common cause, from one single stroke. Buffon thought that only a comet, dense and swift moving, was up to the task. He therefore proposed that a comet, in sideswiping the sun, had sheared off solar matter that, with the comet, had coalesced to form the planets and satellites. The obliquity of the comet stroke not only imparted a unidirectional motion to the solar pieces but also caused their diurnal rotation. As they spun on their axes, they threw off small quantities of matter, which formed the principal planetary satellites and Saturn's ring. Issuing from the sun in a state of liquid fire, a planet would burn for a while, "but, after cooling for some time, the rarified vapours, like those in the tail or atmosphere of a comet, would condense, and fall on the surface in the form of air and water."[62] Eventually, tidal fluctuations, ocean currents, and the action of winds and sun combined to furrow the earth, scoop out valleys, and elevate mountains.[63]

Thus Buffon affirmed that a comet played a role in the creation of the earth and solar system. He added that the near approach of a comet to the earth at a later date could also alter the earth's axis.[64] Although Buffon engaged comets as causal agents during some of the same epochs of earth history as Whiston did, Buffon's approach was not religiously motivated. Indeed, he scoffed that Whiston "treats this matter more like a polemical divine than an enlightened philosopher," and retorted that he "mistook passages of holy writ for physical facts, and for results of astronomical observations; and so strangely jumbled divinity with human science, that he has given birth to the most extraordinary system."[65] Buffon wanted to distinguish his own natural approach from Whiston's, but at the same time he tried to conceal his secular bent by observing that the sun-grazing comet had swept the planets from that star "at the time when God is said by Moses to have separated the light from the darkness. . . . On our supposition, there was a real physical separation; because the opaque bodies of the planets were detached from the luminous matter of which the sun is composed."[66] At the head of the section, a plate even showed God in the act of Creation, pitching a comet at the sun before an adoring crowd of angels (fig. 52). The image drew on comet lore and sacred astrophysics with its representation of comets as divine tools. But the verbal and pictorial tactics did not fool many folks. The strategy was seen as a limp gesture toward ecclesiastical critics, and Buffon was forced to retract his theory of the earth.[67] Nevertheless, he privately held fast to his theory, and in *Des époques de la nature* (1778), he again ventured to publish it in an expanded

Fig. 52. Opening Day and God hurls the first pitch. Buffon's illustration of the formation of the solar system from solar matter sheared off by a sun-grazing comet. Georges Louis Leclerc, comte de Buffon, *Histoire naturelle, générale et particulière*, vol. 1 (Paris, 1749). (Courtesy of the Library of Congress.)

form, declaring it "not impossible that someday new planets will be formed in this same way."[68]

At about the same time that Buffon first set forth his cometary cosmogony, Maupertuis was working along similar lines. Three years before his appointment as president of the Berlin Academy of Sciences, he joked in a letter addressed to the marchioness du Chatelet that "these stars, after having been so long the terror of the world, are suddenly fallen into such disrepute, that they are no longer held capable of producing any thing but colds."[69] There seems nonetheless to have been a nervous edge to Maupertuis's frivolity, for he went on to observe more soberly that "The course of Comets, once regulated, prevents our regarding them as supernatural presages [*presages particuliers*], or as flambeaux lighted up to menace the earth. But while our superior knowledge of Comets, compared with that of the ancients, exempts us from these fears; it informs us that they may be the physical cause of very extraordinary events."[70] Indeed, the extraordinary events envisioned by Maupertuis were no less menacing. Citing Halley and Whiston, Maupertuis did not preclude a comet's role in the Deluge and Conflagration.[71] The near approach of a comet might drown the earth in a torrent of vapors, surround it with exhalations, or, if the comet were especially hot, might submerge the earth in a burning river, or vitrify it. If the tail of the 1680 comet had brushed the earth, we would have died no better than a colony of ants doused with boiling water (Maupertuis offered this remark in a passage that prefigured Henry Fielding's satire on Halley).[72] Maupertuis deemed it possible for the sun to be disturbed by the attraction of an especially large comet. A comet could alter a planet's axis, kick the planet into a cometary orbit, or steal its moon. A planet could even be forced to become the satellite of a comet. Gravitational interactions with other comets might put a wayward planet back into its original orbit, or a comet might take the place of a "lost" planet or satellite. Comet impacts could also rearrange land masses, alter climate, or utterly smash the planet to pieces.[73] Indeed, the disfigured surface of the earth and extinction of species argued that the planet had been pummeled by comets in the past.[74]

Lest people be too quick to quake at the sight of a comet, Maupertuis pointed out that all these amazing actions need not produce morbid results. A comet might have felicitous uses. A little nudge of the earth's axis might fix the seasons into a continual spring. Our orbit could become more circular. Our old moon, perhaps itself a former comet, might gain a new companion satellite. Even if a small comet struck the earth and crushed a kingdom, Maupertuis chuckled, we might discover that the terrible heavenly body was made of gold and diamonds.[75] A comet tail, moreover, could wrap itself around a planet as a decorative ring. Maupertuis felt that this was the most probable origin of Saturn's ring.[76]

Maupertuis reasoned within the framework of Newtonian astronomy, with the caveat—and it was a big one—that providence did not protect the earth from being battered or enhanced by comets. Comets could be as de-

structive or profitable in Newton's theory, but they were divinely guided in their assignments. In Maupertuis's exposition, the teleological element was gone. In Maupertuis's world, people had good reason to worry about random acts of comets.

Similar opinions were voiced by the Cartesian naturalist and French diplomat Benoît de Maillet (1656–1738). De Maillet composed his unorthodox and materialistic cosmogonic work, *Telliamed*, between 1692 and 1718, but it was not published until 1748.[77] In it, he argued that plants and animals originated in the sea but became transformed into terrestrial creatures as the seas diminished during the course of billions of years. The diminution of the seas was part of a cosmological process. De Maillet believed that celestial bodies underwent endless vicissitudes, with alternating phases as fiery stars and dark planets. Solar rays perpetually brushed off dust and water from the inner planets and dumped this matter at the extremities of the vortex where it enriched the outer planets. The inner planets were continually denuded and desiccated, whereas the outer ones were covered with deposits of water and silt. When a sun was finally consumed, its dark husk was swept out of the vortex and into another. Then, the innermost, driest planet took its place and became inflamed. Thus de Maillet envisioned a cycle of renovation and dehydration.[78]

When an extinct sun was swept into neighboring vortices, it could carry off some planets. These transported planets and the debris of the extinct sun were comets. When the solar debris was broken into pieces and spread out in a long streak, the comet was perceived to have a long tail. Comets wandered between and through vortices until they passed near enough to another star to become thoroughly engaged in its vortex and compelled to revolve around it at a distance determined by their respective densities. If a comet penetrated a vortex near a smaller or larger globe, the comet was transformed into a planet or satellite respectively.[79] "Now in this process," de Maillet explained, "if such [cometary] bodies enter into this vortex in a place where another smaller opaque globe is already located, they drag it around themselves, whereas formerly it revolved around its own sun. On the contrary, one which enters into the particular vortex of a globe larger than itself is carried around that large body and, revolving around it, both are carried around the sun, which animates that vortex."[80] De Maillet believed that the earth had once been a comet that had compelled the moon, already in the sun's vortex, to become its satellite.

Drawing on the tradition of the Arcadians, who reported that their ancestors had inhabited the globe prior to the appearance of the present sun and moon, and on the biblical tradition that life spans were longer prior to the Flood, de Maillet argued that the biblical earth had revolved in sixty days around a star much smaller than our sun. At the time of the Deluge, the earth had left its original sun and entered the present solar system as a comet. Since the addition or diminution of waters on a planet depended on

its chance position within a star system, the migrant earth stopped losing waters and was again covered by them. This abrupt change was recorded as Noah's Flood.[81]

Therefore, in de Maillet's cosmology, planets and suns became comets, which were transformed first into planets or moons, and later into suns. The natural history of the earth and the Noachian Flood were explained in terms of the earth's having once been a comet. De Maillet added that Saturn's ring was perhaps formed by strewn debris from a broken sun—that is, by a comet tail—which was caught up in Saturn's particular vortex.[82]

A connection between comet tails and Saturn's ring also impressed Immanuel Kant in Königsberg, and he explained the connection in his *Universal Natural History and Theory of the Heavens* (1755). In this work, Kant offered a mechanical theory of the origin and evolution of the universe. According to Kant, in the beginning, all matter was diffused throughout space but soon began to take form as dense particles attracted lesser ones. In any given region, one great, central body predominated and ultimately became a sun. At the same time, repulsive forces gave rise to vortices by deflecting small particles that would otherwise have fallen toward the gravitational center. Within the vortices, bits of matter chemically and gravitationally collected together to form planets. Since attraction and repulsion were universal forces, Kant maintained that the universe was filled with stellar systems comparable to our solar system and hierarchically arranged into galaxies. Once set in motion, creation spread out from a central point into the region of chaos and animated the whole range of infinite space.[83]

In the outer reaches of the solar system, matter was lighter, less dense, and more sparsely distributed. Since it experienced less gravitational pull toward the sun and less resistance from neighboring particles, it tended to move with greater variations in direction and velocity than densely packed particles closer to the sun, which were more constrained to follow circular orbits. Kant attributed differences in the planets' eccentricities and inclinations to the combination of heterogeneous particles from which they were formed. Consequently, he believed that planetary eccentricity increased with distance from the sun.[84]

As eccentricity increased with distance, planetary orbits began to approximate cometary ones. Kant was persuaded that nature made no saltations but worked by insensible gradations. Reasoning that there was no essential difference between comets and planets except their orbital eccentricities, Kant declared, "It is not possible to regard the comets as a peculiar species of heavenly bodies entirely distinct from the race of planets." He thought that there might well be a continuous, graduated series of unknown planets beyond Saturn, each more eccentric than its interior neighbor, in which planets were gradually transformed into comets.[85]

This conclusion had several interesting consequences. First, Kant hesitated to accept the reality of retrograde comets and confessed that he would

like to regard them as optical illusions. Second, the "lawless freedom" of comet orbits increased with distance from the sun such that the most remote comets did not have closed orbits. Once formed they fell freely into the sun. This fact set a limit on the extension of the solar system. Third, Kant believed that deviations from circular orbits within the ecliptic plane derived from the initial conditions under which a comet or planet had been formed. Therefore, present-day orbits tell us where and how the celestial bodies originated.[86]

Furthermore, the distinguishing features of comets—their tails and comas—were merely the combined effects of their eccentric orbits and the sun's action upon the light, volatile matter from which such remote planetary bodies were formed. Kant reasoned that planets would have tails if they contained the same high percentage of light, fine, readily attenuated matter as comets did. Indeed, the earth's aurora borealis was formed in the same way as a comet's tail,[87] and Saturn's ring was evidence that the outlying planet had once been a comet toasted by the sun during earlier perihelion passages. After Saturn settled into its present orbit, it cooled and no longer emitted vapors suitable to replenish a coma or tail. Its old coma, however, was preserved in an atmosphere, which was compressed into the equatorial ring by consequence of the planet's axial rotation. The ring remained a stigma of Saturn's former cometary status.[88]

Kant conjectured that the earth too once had a watery cometary ring. Disrupted perhaps by a passing comet, the ring precipitated to cause the Flood. Along with the foreign and subtle vapors of this unnatural rain, the earth sucked in "that slow poison which brought all creatures nearer death and destruction."[89]

Kant troubled himself not only with explanations of the Noachian Flood but also with the end of the world. "All that is finite," he wrote, "whatever has a beginning and origin, has the mark of its limited nature in itself; it must perish and have an end."[90] When a world-system exhausted all the manifold variations that its structure could embrace, it perished in a violent conflagration fueled largely by comets dropping into its sun:[91]

> It is considered that after the final exhaustion of the revolving movements in the universe has precipitated all the planets and comets together into the sun, its glowing heat must obtain an immense increase by the commingling of so many and so great masses; especially as the distant globes [i.e., comets] of the Solar System . . . contain in themselves the lightest matter in all nature, and that which is most active on fire. This [solar] fire, thus put by new nourishment and the most volatile matter into the most violent conflagration, will undoubtedly not only resolve everything again into the smallest elements, but will also disperse and scatter these elements again in this way with a power of expansion proportional to the heat, and with a rapidity which is not weakened by any resistance in the intervening space; and they will thus be dissipated into the same wide regions of space which they had occupied before the first formation of nature.[92]

The conflagration dispersed all matter within the solar system and returned everything to the primordial chaos. Yet Kant believed that nature would truly be renovated by the fire. From the chaos, new creations would arise:

> After the violence of the central fire has been subdued by an almost total dispersion of its mass, the forces of attraction and repulsion will again combine to repeat the old creations and the systematically connected movements, with not less regularity than before, and to present a new universe.[93]

Just as creations had radiated out from a central point of the universe, so destructions would ripple through space; the world was bounded by the ruins of nature formerly destroyed and the chaos of nature as yet unformed.[94] At some period after individual planetary systems had undergone such destruction and renovation by fire, the galaxy too would be consumed. Kant thereby envisioned a "Phoenix of nature, which burns itself only in order to revive again in restored youth from its ashes, through all the infinity of times and spaces."[95]

Kant claimed to work within a Newtonian tradition with which Thomas Wright would have no truck. But even in his idiosyncratic theory, Wright joined Kant and Newton in believing that comets played key roles in the generation and dissolution of worlds. As fiery projectiles spewed forth from the celestial volcanoes, comets were occasional visitors to the planetary regions. Although Wright fundamentally believed that God kept a watchful eye on the earth such that it was in no danger from these erratic bodies, he maintained that they were "ordaind for some wise purpose of the Divine Nature as agents of his infinite power."[96] These uses included refueling the sun and circulating salutary fire throughout the system.[97] Moreover, comets awakened man to his duty to God and reminded him of the ultimate dissolution of nature.[98]

Comets reminded men of the end of the world in part because they could destroy planets by impact:

> That comets are capable of distroying such worlds as may chance to fall in their way, is, from their vast magnitude, velocity, firey substance, not at all to be doubted, and it is more than probable from the great and unoccupied distance betwixt ye planet Mars and Jupiter some world may have met with such a final dissolution.[99]

If a planet between Mars and Jupiter had met such a fate, even the earth might fall prey:

> If the motions of comets could be reduced to certainty & as solid and regualar bodies[,] the end of ye Earth might be as certainly predicted. For a point of time of course must be found in which some comet in its nodes might be so near ye Earth as to be attended with very alarming if not fatal consequences.[100]

If more concrete evidence were needed of the destructive capacity of comets, it was to be found in the different inclinations and obliquities of the planets' motions. Wright surmised that the near approach of great comets had disturbed planetary orbits. He even advised astronomers to delay computations whenever a new comet was in the vicinity, for the orbital parameters would need to be rectified.[101]

A connection between comets and the succession of worlds may also be seen in Wright's theory of the "generation and process of a world from its creation or prime embrio to its final catastrophy and desolution."[102] He suggested that a planetary world was first conceived in the atmosphere of the starry firmament when matter was ejected from a volcano on the circumorbent sun. As the new world slowly spiraled into the central sun, it successively experienced material conglobation, the origin of "terrafirma and of all the mineralization," the influence of solar light, heat, and vegetation, the development of animal and human life, evaporation and calcination near the sun's enflamed atmosphere, and, ultimately, conflagration and total consummation.

> Thus a perpetual succession of new created worlds is or may be continually flowing from ye celestial regions to ye Sun and as finally feeding its eternal fires, and at the same time connecting all the constituent parts of creation to gether in one congeres, or infinite unity. Thus also by successive seats of new life in destind states past, present or to come and all proportioned to ye sphere of glory in which they naturally exist, all beings are inbossomed in their divine creating God.
>
> This may be truly calld the great period of existence piculiar to evry world, and independent of each other, and in which light we may look upon ye planet Saturn in our system as not yet ariv'd at its prime perfection, the Earth to be upon its decline, and the planet Mercury to have passed its maturity so far as to be now tending to its final desolution.
>
> This great period of nature cannot be imagind to take up less time than a million of millions of years, in which . . . the atmospheres of evry world are continually condensing till all their respective fluids are absorbd and finally united in ye Sun.[103]

Although comets were not specifically mentioned by Wright in this theory of the birth and death of worlds, his depiction of planets had much in common with his portrayal of comets (his disclaimers to the contrary notwithstanding).[104] Like comets in Wright's system, the planetary worlds were spewed out from the firmament and designed to feed the solar fires. Both comets and planets interconnected the constituent parts of the creation. Additionally, Wright's conception of the desiccation of planetary bodies is reminiscent of Newton's public view of the loss of planetary moistures and his private view of planets' becoming fit fuel for the sun once transformed into comets.[105] It also harked back to *Telliamed*. What role Wright

intended for comets in the succession of worlds short of smashing into planets or disrupting their orbits is by no means clear, but the general structure of his argument was similar to contemporary evolutionary cosmogonies in which comets and planets were similar species capable of evolving into each other.

William Herschel, the discover of Uranus, joined Kant and Wright in pondering the development of stellar systems and the transformation of comets into planets.[106] Observations of the comets of 1807 and 1811 convinced Herschel that most comets contained a solid, condensed kernel and a self-luminous, nebulous coma and tail.[107] As a comet approached perihelion, solar rays expanded and decomposed the comet's nebulous matter, producing light, heat, chemical effects, and a tail. These effects would continue until all nebulous matter was exhausted.[108] Accordingly, Herschel believed that a long tail or bright coma depended not so much on the distance of the comet from the sun as on the quantity of nebulous matter it contained. He called this nebulous matter "unperihelioned matter," for every passage of a comet around the sun would extract and disperse it.[109] "The act of shining denotes a decomposition in which at least light is given out," he explained, "but . . . many other elastic volatile substances may escape at the same time, especially in so high a degree of rarefaction."[110] As light and volatile particles were emitted, the comet became more compact and less nebulous: "Then, since light certainly, and very likely other subtile fluids also escape in great abundance during a considerable time before and after a comet's nearest approach to the sun, I look upon a perihelion passage in some degree as an act of consolidation."[111] This process of consolidation gave Herschel the clue to explain why some comets appeared purely nebulous and others had well-defined planetary disks within them.[112]

In the 1790s, Herschel had boldly proposed that interstellar nebulae could gravitationally collapse to form stars,[113] but now his cometary studies convinced him that nebulae could also be transformed into comets and then into planets.

> Nay, from the complete resemblance of many comets to a number of nebulae I have seen, I think it not unlikely that the matter they contain is originally nebulous. It may therefore possibly happen that some of the nebulae, in which this matter is already in a high state of condensation, may be drawn towards the nearest celestial body of the nature of our sun; and after their first perihelion passage round it proceed, in a parabolic direction, towards some other similar body; and passing successively from one to another, may come into the regions of our sun, where at last we perceive them transformed into comets.[114]

Herschel suggested that small telescopic comets might have recently emerged from a nebulous condition and "in fact be such highly condensed nebulae."[115] As a comet traveled on a parabolic path through vast reaches of space, it passed through "extensive strata of nebulosity" and carried off

a portion of the nebulous matter. This unperihelioned matter would become consolidated when the comet spun round the nearest star. Since comets migrated from sun to sun—a hypothesis "rendered probable from our knowing as yet, with certainty, the return of only one comet among the great number that have been observed"[116]—their wide-ranging paths unavoidably and repeatedly intersected immense regions of nebulous matter. The continual accession of fresh nebulous matter enabled a comet, by means of the process of consolidation, to increase in bulk and "grow up to maturity" as a planet.[117]

Herschel noted that the observed construction of a comet informed us how lately the comet had emerged from a nebulous condition, how consolidated it was, how old, how planetary, and whether it had recently picked up fresh unperihelioned matter. "We may by observation of cometic phenomena arrange these celestial bodies into a certain order of consolidation, from which, in the end, a considerable insight into their nature and destination may be obtained."[118]

Moreover, in words that echoed Newton's (as reported by Conduitt), Herschel referred to "revolutions" in the heavenly bodies when he described the process by which nebulous comets became consolidated into planets.[119] In a fascinating letter, he connected these astronomical revolutions to geological revolutions:

> You mention Geology. . . . The subject seems every day more involved in obscurity by the numerous discoveries that prove the fact of many great revolutions. Astronomical observations however seem to throw a considerable light upon the subject of these revolutions. . . . For if we admit that Comets may gradually become planets, it cannot be wrong to surmise that Planets may have been Comets, and every perihelion passage will account for a revolution.[120]

In other words, a record of the astronomical revolutions to which the once cometary earth was subjected might be found in the terrestrial evidence of concomitant geological revolutions. In the strata, one read the story of the earth as a comet; and in comets rounding the sun, one saw geological beds being laid down on foreign worlds.

That astronomy shed light on geology was an opinion also voiced by Pierre-Simon Laplace (1749–1827). A French geologist, Déodat Dolomieu, reported in 1796:

> [Laplace] told me that among causes exterior to our globe, there were none which could sensibly change either the center of gravity nor the level of the seas and that all forces acting constantly on the earth concur to maintain it in its present state, but . . . *he thinks also that the possible shock of a comet may serve as a foundation for some geological systems.*[121]

And in 1813, when Laplace suggested that the earth's figure could be deduced from its primordial fluid state in accordance with his nebular hypothesis, he proclaimed:

This state of primitive fluidity, to which one is led by astronomical phenomena, should manifest itself in those things that natural history presents to us. . . . Geology, followed according to the point of view that connects it to Astronomy, will be able to acquire from it precision and certitude on a great many subjects.[122]

These two different tacks—catastrophic collisions and gradual formative causes—were developed by Laplace in various editions of his *Exposition du système du monde* (first published in 1796). Of relevance for our study of the submergence of comet lore into cosmogony are the ways that Laplace's opinions on the nature and effects of comets influenced his views on the relationship of astronomical events to the earth's natural history.[123]

In 1796, Laplace argued that there were no intermediary states between the nearly circular planetary orbits and the highly elongated, randomly inclined cometary orbits. This distribution was not due to chance, he contended, but must be the effect of some regular cause.[124] He sought an explanation in the origin of the solar system. Laplace believed that the sun's primal atmosphere had extended beyond the present planetary orbits and cometary perihelia. As it gradually contracted to its present limits, zones condensed into rings and slowly formed the planets. During this process, short-period comets, which had traversed the extended solar atmosphere, were reunited with the sun. The only comets to survive were the long-period, highly eccentric ones, which had been beyond the limits of the atmosphere at that time. Since the solar atmosphere exerted no control over their motions, these comets had random inclinations to the ecliptic.[125]

According to this theory, planets and comets were different species that shared certain traits. Reports that the 1744 comet had exhibited phases convinced Laplace that comets were opaque bodies like the planets, which borrowed their light from the sun.[126] In 1796, he also insisted that all nebulae were unresolvable groups of stars.[127] By 1808, Laplace began to have his doubts. He wrote that perhaps most nebulae were star clusters, and dropped the passage on the 1744 comet, implying that the observations were doubtful.[128] No phases had been seen in comets recently observed with the best telescopes. Since he now believed that the masses of comets were extremely small, he recognized that the diameter of a comet's disk must be insensible, and the so-called nucleus was only that part of the coma where the nebulosity was most dense. Its particles reflected sunlight in all directions, such that no phases could be seen. Laplace added that he presumed comets not to be self-luminous, and thought that astronomers should admit this "natural" supposition as long as possible.[129]

By 1813, Laplace had absorbed William Herschel's findings on the existence of true, celestial nebulosity (not resolvable into stars). He cited and embraced Herschel's observations that nebulous matter, distributed throughout the heavens, could condense into nuclei surrounded by atmospheres. Further condensation might transform these objects into "planetary nebulae," and then into stars. It was likely, therefore, that today's nebulae would eventually

become stars, whereas today's stars had a nebulous past. Laplace adapted Herschel's theory in order to back up his hypothesis that the sun once had a vast, nebulous atmosphere, which condensed to form the solar system.[130]

According to this new formulation, comets were viewed as strangers to the solar system. They were little nebulae formed by the condensation of nebulous matter scattered profusely here and there in the universe. Roaming from one solar system to another, they were forced to describe elliptical or hyperbolic orbits when they came within the sun's sphere of attraction. Since these outsiders were not formed within the sun's primordial atmosphere, all orbital directions, inclinations, and speeds were initially possible, but their motions were subject to planetary perturbations and resistance from the aether.[131]

Laplace also espoused Herschel's view of cometary consolidation. Since volatile substances would diminish at each return to perihelion, a comet would eventually display a fixed nucleus formed from the most dense strata or beds of nebulosity enveloping the comet's kernel. This should happen more quickly for short-period comets than for long-period ones. This hypothesis seemed to explain the mysterious disappearance of the 1770 comet and others. Perhaps their volatiles evaporated, leaving behind kernels too tiny to be visible. New answers, moreover, were now given to the question of phases. Laplace repeated that no phases had been recently seen with the strongest telescopes, but since Herschel had noted a bright spot within the nucleus of the 1811 comet, he conceded that the kernel could sometimes be seen. He also reported that Hevelius and de la Hire insisted they had seen phases in the 1682 comet. If one believed that comets became consolidated (or the nuclei "fixed," as Laplace phrased it), then one could conjecture that the 1682 comet—with its short period and alleged phases—approached this state of fixity.[132] "After several returns," Laplace concluded, "[a comet] should thus dissipate itself entirely or reduce itself to a fixed nucleus that will exhibit phases as the planets."[133]

With respect to comet tails, Laplace said we had nothing to fear. Although a tail extended "plusieurs millions de myriamètres," it was so rarefied that its mass was likely less than that of the smallest mountain. Indeed, it was possible that tails had enveloped the earth on several occasions without having been perceived.[134] Laplace praised "the light of science [that] has dissipated the vain terrors which comets, eclipses, and many other phenomena inspired in the ages of ignorance."[135]

Yet Laplace commented, "To the terrors which the apparition of comets then inspired, succeeded the fear, that of the great number which traverse the planetary system in all directions, one of them might overturn the earth." At first he downplayed the effects:

> They pass so rapidly by us, that the effects of their attraction are not to be apprehended. It is only by striking the earth that they can produce any disastrous effect [*funestes ravages*]. But this circumstance, though possible, is so little probable

in the course of a century, and it would require such an extraordinary combination of circumstances for two bodies, so small in comparison with the immense space they move in, to strike each other, that no reasonable apprehension can be entertained of such an event.

But Laplace added disquieting information:

Nevertheless, the small probability of this circumstance may, by accumulating during a long succession of ages, become very great. It is easy to represent the effect of such a shock upon the earth: the axis and motion of rotation changed, the waters abandoning their antient [sic] position, to precipitate themselves towards the new equator; the greater part of men and animals drowned in a universal deluge, or destroyed by the violence of the shock given to the terrestrial globe; whole species destroyed; all the monuments of human industry reversed: such are the disasters which a shock of a comet would produce.[136]

Like Halley and Newton before him, Laplace intimated that such a collision not only threatened the future but had disfigured the earth in the past:

We see then why the ocean has abandoned the highest mountains, on which it has left incontestible marks of its former abode: we see why the animals and plants of the south may have existed in the climates of the north, where their relics and impressions are still to be found: lastly, it explains the short period of the existence of the moral world, whose earliest monuments do not go much farther back than three thousand years.[137] The human race reduced to a small number of individuals, in the most deplorable state, occupied only with the immediate care for their subsistence, must necessarily have lost the remembrance of all sciences and of every art; and when the progress of civilization has again created new wants, every thing was to be done again, as if mankind had been just placed upon the earth. But whatever may be the cause assigned by philosophers to these phenomena, we may be perfectly at ease with respect to such a catastrophe during the short period of human life.[138]

These two passages are so similar to those in Halley's paper on the Deluge and Newton's thoughts as recorded by Conduitt that we might readily believe Laplace to have had those works in front of him.[139] A closer source was Joseph de Lalande (1732–1807), whose paper about the effects of close-approaching comets was much debated in the Académie des Sciences in the 1770s.[140] Whatever the source, it does not deter us from noting the enduring legacy of Newton and Halley. Nor does the similarity end with the connection of comets to mass extinctions, deluges, and altered land masses. Newton and Halley had scorned vulgar pamphleteers who interpreted comets as portents of ruin, even as they had authorized astronomers to investigate the earth-shattering and truly terrifying roles of comets. Laplace acted the same. On one hand, he admonished the common people who had mistaken a scientific discourse for a prophecy of impending doom and had become panicked in 1773 when Lalande considered the possibility (76,000 to 1) of "that great

revolution which for the human race will be the accomplishment of the centuries, the end of the world, or the beginning of a new order of things."[141] On the other hand, Laplace thought it important for future astronomers to investigate "the accidents, that the proximity, and even the shock of these bodies, may occasion in the planets, and in the satellites."[142]

These were Laplace's thoughts in 1796 and 1799, but by the time he prepared the 1808 edition of his *Système du monde*, he had become convinced that comets were not the massive, planet-sized bodies that eighteenth-century natural philosophers had envisioned. In a volume of the *Mécanique céleste* published in 1805, Laplace computed that the mass of the 1770 comet could be no more than one five-thousandth of the earth's mass.[143] Since comets suffered greater perturbations from the planets than they in turn inflicted on them or their satellites, these wandering bodies had to have a minuscule mass. This was further confirmed by the fact that the present motions of the planets did not seem to have been much altered by comets that statistically must have collided with them in the past. Laplace reasoned:

> It not only happens that the comets do not trouble the motions of the planets and satellites, by their attractions; but if, in the immensity of past ages, some of the comets have encountered them, which is very probable, it does not seem that the shock can have had much influence on the motions of the planets and satellites. It is difficult not to admit that the orbits of the planets and satellites were nearly circular at their origin, and that the smallness of their ellipticity, as well as their common direction from west to east, depend upon the primitive state of the planetary system. The action of the comets, and their impact upon those bodies, have not varied these phenomena; yet if one of them, with a mass equal to that of the moon, should encounter the moon, or a satellite of Jupiter, there is not the least doubt that it would render the orbit of the satellite very excentric. Astronomy also presents to us two other phenomena, which seem to date their origin from that of the planetary system, and which would have been altered by a very small shock. We here allude to the equality in the rotatory motions of the moon, and the librations of the three inner satellites of Jupiter. It is evident . . . that the shock of a comet, whose mass was only 1/1000 part of that of the moon, would be sufficient to give a very sensible value to the actual libration of the moon, and to that of the satellites. We may therefore rest assured relative to the influence of the comets, and astronomers have no reason to fear that their action can impair the accuracy of astronomical tables.[144]

Consequently, when Laplace prepared his next edition of the *Système du monde*, he altered the passages I have quoted above. He qualified his earlier assertions by noting that the specified disasters would be produced only if a comet had a mass comparable to the earth's; and he repeated his assurance that a cataclysmic event was most unlikely during the course of a human life, especially since the masses of comets were so small and their impacts capable of producing only "local revolutions."[145]

While nineteenth-century scholars might wonder what upheavals La-place envisioned when he referred to "local revolutions," none could seri-ously fear an earth-shattering collision from an average comet in light of Laplace's calculations. It was a safe bet that the earth was in no danger at the moment. Yet this did not mean that our planet or our solar system was divinely protected or providentially preserved. Laplace criticized Newton's view that the arrangement of the solar system revealed both a divine origin and some divine intervention to keep it running. First, the origin could be explained by laws of motion acting on clumps of nebulous matter scattered throughout space. Second, the solar system would not need a reformation for the reasons Newton supposed, because the gravitational interaction of planets and comets could not alter the system's stability. But this is not to say that Laplace deemed the system everlasting. He questioned Newton's premise that the solar system would be preserved by God (or Nature) over the long haul. "Should there be in space no other fluid but light, its resis-tance and the diminution of the sun's mass produced by its emission would in the long run destroy the arrangement of the planets. To maintain this, without a doubt, a reform would be necessary."[146] Yet, as Cuvier had shown with fossils, the most apparently fixed things in nature had a ten-dency to change. The majesty of the solar system would not exempt it from this general law. Just a speck in the universe at large, it too would change.

Laplace concluded with a discussion of final causes. Newton had written that we know God "only by his most wise and excellent contrivances of things, and final causes; . . . and a god without dominion, providence, and final causes, is nothing else but Fate and Nature."[147] Laplace responded that anyone who traced the history of human errors and the progress of the mind could see that final causes were constantly receding to the boundaries of knowledge. "The same causes that Newton transported to the limits of the solar system [to supervise comets] were not long before placed in the atmosphere to explain meteors [among which the ancients had classified comets]; they are thus, in the eyes of a philosopher, only an expression of our ignorance of the true causes."[148]

Without some conception of final causes, the argument from design lost its punch. It was in this context that David Hume (1711–1776) had raised the theory of comets to show that if one could not agree on the origin, na-ture, and purposive structure of the world, one could know nothing about the nature of God. One might choose to argue from a clockwork universe to the Clockmaker, but perhaps the origin of the universe might be more aptly ascribed to generation or vegetation than to reason or design:

> But how is it conceivable, said DEMEA, that the world can arise from any thing similar to vegetation or generation?
> Very easily, replied PHILO. In like manner as a tree sheds its seed into the neighbouring fields, and produces other trees; so the great vegetable, the world, or this planetary system, produces within itself certain seeds, which, being scat-

tered into the surrounding chaos, vegetate into new worlds. A comet, for instance, is the seed of a world; and after it has been fully ripened, by passing
from sun to sun, and star to star, it is at last tossed into the unformed elements,
which everywhere surround this universe, and immediately sprouts up into a
new system.

Or if, for the sake of variety (for I see no other advantage), we should suppose
this world to be an animal; a comet is the egg of this animal.[149]

This passage is notable not only for its vivid portrayal of the kind of cometary cosmogonies discussed in this chapter but also for its theological implications. Having no experience of the origin of worlds, we must argue
from analogy, but our analogies are indeterminate, and the argument from
design flawed. The argument survived Hume's critique, but as the cosmogonic hypotheses of Laplace and others gained wider acceptance, it became
harder to see convincing evidence of God's handiwork and superintendence
within astronomical systems. This was precisely what Laplace desired. Like
Lalande and Buffon, he wanted to unlink astrotheology from celestial mechanics and jettison it as dangerous cargo.

It seems, however, that final causes were not just pushed out of natural
philosophy but were also pushed within its theories. As God's direct agency
was chased to the limits of our understanding, secondary causes took his
place. Comets, which were first seen as celestial hieroglyphics of God's message and atmospheric threats of his future actions, came to be transformed
into natural agents manipulated by God to achieve his designs. At first these
agents acted locally, but in the works of Newton, Halley, Whiston, and others, they were invested with global powers. Final causes were still present,
for comets followed God's directions. Whiston was adamant on this point:

For though the Solutions here given are mechanical, and depend upon the known
Laws of Matter, Motion and Gravity; and the Calculations are strictly astronomical and geometrical; . . . Yet is all this no Impediment to the Interposition of God
and his Providence in this grand Catastrophe [of the Deluge or consummation],
but rather a sure Demonstration of the same.[150]

When comets were transformed into planets or planets into comets, when
comets created new earths or demolished old ones, when they conveyed
precious materials or dumped toxic loads, they did so according to God's
plan and with his supervision. "Thus," Dionis du Séjour observed with disdain, "the comets, after having been for a long time the signs of heavenly
anger, . . . have become in the eyes of some speculative philosophers
the agents that the Supreme Being uses to change the face of the universe."[151] In the cosmogonies of Kant and Wright, God was noticeably distant, and in those of Buffon, Maupertuis, de Maillet, Herschel, and Laplace,
God was evermore absent, but comets still retained their abilities to create
or destroy, reform or restore planetary systems. The teleology was gone;
Fate and Nature were cheered; and there was no expectation to find the

moral order reflected in the natural world. Nevertheless, the new cosmogonic roles for comets were not really new at all. They originated in folk beliefs and religious traditions that depicted comets as heavenly wonders fulfilling divine ends.

In the mid–eighteenth century, conjectures concerning the baleful effects of comets were labeled as "foolish fear or pious fraud."[152] Yet while Maupertuis scoffed from the high road that "our superior knowledge of Comets, compared to that of the ancients, exempts us from these [vulgar] fears," and Buffon railed against the Whistons who jumbled Holy Writ with physical facts, the potent role of comets in their cosmogonies declared the debt they owed to these sources.[153] Hence, in the evolutionary cosmologies described above, we see a creative end product of Newton's and Halley's appropriation of popular culture and comet lore. Vulgar beliefs—once redescribed in natural philosophical terms—were passed along to the evolutionary cosmologists by the practitioners of sacred astrophysics. Along with an appreciation of comets' destructive and restorative functions came a recognition of the possibility of both catastrophic change and progressive transformation of the earth and heavenly bodies over vast periods of time. The study of these natural changes was to become a distinguishing feature of modern cosmological thought. Its roots are to be found in the way Newton and Halley adopted comet lore.

CONCLUDING REMARKS

POPULAR CULTURE AND ELITE SCIENCE

IN ANTICIPATION of the return of Biela's comet in 1832, and perhaps in advance preparation for the return of Halley's comet in 1835, Dominique François Jean Arago (1786–1853) of the Paris Observatory wrote:

> The public mind has been much occupied with the Comet which is to reappear in 1832. Many journals have even announced that it would strike the earth and break it in pieces. The Board of Longitude has therefore judged it proper to publish, in the *Annuaire*, all the exact and indisputable results which science has made known upon this subject. To this object I at first intended to restrict myself, but soon the field enlarged before me, and I was induced to speak not only of the alleged dangers to be feared from the approaching comet, but also of the part which, according to some distinguished philosophers, other bodies of the same nature have formerly played in the great physical revolutions of which the earth has been the theatre.[1]

To this end, Arago devoted half of his tract to the following topics:

1. Is it possible for a Comet to strike the Earth or any other Planet?

2. Is there any Reason to suppose, from all that is known of Astronomical Phenomena, that Comets have ever fallen into the Sun or into Stars?

3. Can the Earth pass into the Tail of a Comet? What would be the Consequences of such an Event to our Globe? Were the Dry Fogs of 1783 and 1831 occasioned by the Tail of a Comet?

4. Was the Deluge occasioned by a Comet?

5. Has Siberia ever experienced a sudden Change of Climate, by the Influence of a Comet?

6. Is it necessary to have recourse to a Comet to explain the Severe Climate of North America?

7. Has the Depression of the Land in a great Part of Asia been occasioned by a Blow from a Comet?

8. Was the Moon ever a Comet?

9. Are Ceres, Pallas, Juno, and Vesta, Fragments of a large Planet broken in Pieces by a Blow from a Comet?[2]

Readers of this book will not be surprised by this list of queries, for I have shown that they were the concerns of Newton, Halley, Whiston, Buffon, Maupertuis, Laplace, and many other eighteenth-century natural philosophers.

It is my contention that the varied, but mainly affirmative, answers given to the above questions by astronomers prior to Arago reveal metaphysical

commitments rooted in traditional comet lore and show how that lore was assimilated into astrophysics. In this process, comets were transformed from monstrous signs of dire, local calamities into natural causes of global catastrophes and world reform.

It is appropriate here to review the steps of this transformation. Until the mid–seventeenth century, comets were interpreted by both the learned elite and common folk as portents of war, murder, civil discord, sickness, poor harvests, tidal waves, and earthquakes. The roots of these beliefs lay in ancient folklore and philosophy, but the young Catholic Church readily appropriated the pagan views. The clergy preached that comets were monsters, prodigies, and miraculous signs of God's wrath. Meanwhile, Origen, Aquinas, and other Fathers of the church enlarged the scope of cometary significance. According to the expanded interpretation, comets did more than presage the downfall of sinners; they demarcated critical periods in the sacred history of the world and church. It was said, for instance, that comets had augured the birth of Jesus, the inception of Christianity, and the reformation of the church. It was expected that they would blaze overhead as the Day of Judgment approached.

Religion went hand in hand with politics. As blazing swords, comets portended battles over belief as well as territory. Astrology, moreover, had been a vital part of statecraft since the Babylonian period, and during the Roman era cunning individuals marshaled comets as political weapons. The practice continued up to the early modern period, when prognosticators saw comets as signs of the times—that is, one way in which political power struggles were reflected in the disorderly course of nature. The popular press spread the self-serving predictions of dissidents, millenarian visionaries, and political schemers both in and outside the government. Often cometary propaganda was couched in apocalyptic language because dissidents believed that current affairs fulfilled ancient prophecies. In England, for example, the comets of the 1660s, 1670s, and 1680s were thought by some to augur the Apocalypse or Millennium, the end of the world or its renovation. Radical pamphleteers took advantage of such comets. Not only did they urge people to repent, they also urged them to amend social institutions in preparation for a new world order. The notion that comets were forerunners of world mutations—spread in sensational street literature and sermons—proved to be a resource for Newton's and Halley's theories of comets.

Another resource was the belief that comets could be physical causes. In the late Middle Ages, John of Legnano and others began to see comets not only as signs but also as the natural, proximate causes of cataclysmic—if localized—events. Strains of this belief were carried through to the seventeenth century and were expressed in popular fears that cometary exhalations parched or poisoned the air, or that contact with a comet tail resulted in tempests, floods, and earthquakes.

It is often said that Newton and Halley were instrumental in sweeping aside "superstitious" comet lore when they mathematically demonstrated

that comets traveled in closed orbits in our solar system. My own research challenges this assertion in two ways—first, by showing that neither scientific discoveries nor philosophical debates were sufficient causes for the decline in cometary divination; and second, by showing that Newton, Halley, and their followers continued to embrace key tenets of popular lore despite their hostility to vulgar astrological predictions. To be sure, Newton and Halley never linked comets with changes in church and state, and so never searched the heavens for divine messages pertaining to local affairs. Yet, like cometary prognosticators, they apparently desired to see the moral order reflected in the natural world and were led (unconsciously or otherwise) to rehabilitate comet lore by redescribing it in natural philosophical terms. Where comets had portended revolution, religious reform, and agricultural change, Halley and Newton now made them active agents. In their theories, historical, sacred, and geological periods were punctuated by cometary catastrophes.

Thus Newton and Halley drew on comet lore when they proposed that comets were involved in the renovation of the earth, Noah's Flood, the creation of new worlds, and perhaps the end of this one. Even though both men hoped that their comet theories would derail the practice of vulgar prognostication, there were only two elements truly differentiating their theories from the traditional lore: (1) that comets performed exclusively in a global arena; and (2) that celestial mechanics could be used to determine which comets might dash the earth. But this information was to be reserved for the scientific elite, rather than the common folk. Halley made this point explicitly. After confiding that the 1680 comet had come a little too close for comfort, he cautioned, "This is spoken to Astronomers: But what might be the Consequences of so near an Appulse; or of a Contact; or, lastly, of a Shock of the Coelestial Bodies, (which is by no means impossible to come to pass) I leave to be discuss'd by the Studious of Physical Matters."[3] As the scientist Johann Lambert would later acknowledge, astronomers were to be the "authorized prophets."[4]

In Newton's and Halley's discussion of comets, we see the degree to which people hostile to popular culture were willing to appropriate useful popular beliefs without their former labels. We will never know whether Newton or Halley consciously appropriated these ideas. We do know, however, that other natural philosophers followed their lead and explored the role of comets as God's agents in shaping the globe and the history of its inhabitants. Whiston, Buffon, Maupertuis, Wright, Kant, Herschel, and Laplace to varying degrees considered the role of comets in the earth's creation, deluge, and consummation, and in major changes in the celestial order.

Nevertheless, by the time Arago wrote his tract in 1832, it was less clear to him that comets had played roles in "the great physical revolutions of which the earth has been the theatre."

In my humble opinion [Arago wrote] they have had no part or lot in the matter;
I therefore apprize the reader beforehand, that he will find, in what I have to offer,
nothing to countenance such doctrines.

This tract is divided into two parts [Arago continued]. All the questions which
are discussed in the first would belong properly to a treatise on Astronomy; the
second is devoted to a detailed examination of certain hypotheses which I would
gladly have left in oblivion, if the approaching return of the comet, and the fears
occasioned by it, had not revived them.[5]

By Arago's day, statistical calculations had revealed how little probability
there was for a comet to strike the earth, even if it was likely for the earth
to intercept some matter diffused from a comet's tail. As to the latter, Arago
himself had compared meteorological records kept during apparitions of
comets in order to prove that comets did not affect the weather, and he
believed that their tails posed little danger. He rejected Whiston's theory of
the Deluge as gratuitous and argued that the comet impacts envisioned by
Halley would have been too precipitous and convulsive to explain the physical revolutions and ancient inundations studied by geologists. The fossil
record and the craggy figure of the earth's surface were better understood in
terms of the action of internal geological forces, which raised or depressed
parts of the surface. Since the moon lacked an atmosphere, Arago was convinced that it had never been a comet. The want of an observed atmosphere
on one of the four asteroids (discovered between 1801 and 1807) also
forced Arago to question the thesis that these were fragments of a planet
destroyed in a collision with a comet.

Arago's position contrasts sharply with those of Newton, Halley, and
many of the eighteenth-century cosmogonists discussed in this book. From
Arago's treatment, we recognize that catastrophism had gone out of style.
He supported gradual, slow processes of formation and development, and
praised the "ingenious hypotheses" of Laplace. Yet while the old cometary
catastrophism was dismissed, it must be observed that it had contributed to
the formulation of the dynamic, evolutionary cosmologies applauded by
Arago. Newton's and Halley's theories helped to wean people away from
views of a fixed, immutable creation and accustomed them to the idea of
birth and death in the heavens, the impact of one world on another, and the
transformation of one celestial body into another. Whereas their catastrophic theories focused attention on God's direct agency, the evolutionary
theories later advanced by Kant, Herschel, and Laplace tended to push God
to the margins and emphasized the interplay of natural forces. Stability once
maintained solely by divine fiat became connected to conditions of dynamic
equilibrium and gradual, cyclical change. In these manifold ways, modern
evolutionary cosmology drew something positive not only from the catastrophic cosmogonies in which comets were key players but also from the
popular beliefs that informed those cosmogonies.

A critical part of this story is the way that ideas traveled up and down the social ladder. When popular and elite culture brushed up against each other, their encounter did not simply juxtapose two independent worlds but produced cultural or intellectual alloys. High and low audiences shared certain beliefs about the natural world, and each audience appropriated ideas from the other. The borrowing and blending of ideas prior to the seventeenth century comes as no surprise, for during that period popular culture was a second culture for the better sort. With regard to comets, all members of society shared the belief that they were portents. In the seventeenth century, however, the learned and privileged began to withdraw from the untutored masses, and by the midcentury most consciously rejected what had come to be labeled as "popular errors" concerning comets. I will return in a moment to the reasons for this rejection, but here I want to point out that even though this distinction between high and low became sharper, in early modern England not only did learned, astronomical, and theological ideas continue to be vulgarized in street literature, theater, and ballads, but popular beliefs also continued to percolate up into the works of the learned and public rituals of the state. This suggests that popular cosmology did not inhere in a specific set of texts or beliefs but in what ordinary people borrowed and adapted for their own ends. Similarly, elite cosmology was constituted by the accommodation or appropriation of many ideas that did not initially or exclusively belong to the upper crust.

But beyond the shared beliefs, imprints and performances reveal the social uses to which beliefs were put. It is necessary to examine the social functions of astronomy in order to appreciate fully how high and low audiences inhabited different social spaces even though they shared cosmological beliefs. As I have pointed out, in early modern England competing political and religious factions offered their own judgments of the meaning of particular comets in order to validate their own beliefs, attract followers, urge others to undertake moral or social reforms, and incite political action against their rivals. Both high and low engaged in astrological politicking. Royalists, parliamentarians, and radicals of all kinds consulted astrologers, whose almanacs and texts issued uncensored from the presses during the Civil War and Commonwealth. With the Restoration of the Stuarts in 1660, the new government cracked down on astrologers, blaming them for having encouraged insurrection and irreligion during the war. Prognostication based on comets survived in popular culture and Restoration propaganda, but political and religious authorities concluded that it was dangerous and enthusiastic. Their low opinion was reinforced by the civil disorder contemporaneous with the cometary apparitions of the 1670s and 1680s. The connection between the Civil War and astrology also led elite English astronomers to reject astrological programs that they had revered prior to the Restoration. Thus it was the way ideas were used, rather than the ideas themselves, which ultimately led astronomers like David Gregory to conclude that their astronomy had been abused in street literature and demon-

strations. They began to distance themselves from these productions, labeling them first as seditious and then as the marker of an inferior social group. But even as they derided the tracts and rituals as dangerous and superstitious, they found some popular ideas too serviceable to give up. Hence social factors appear to have hastened the demise of the crudest forms of astrology in England, without mitigating the general wish of natural philosophers to see God's providence in nature.

In this book, changing perceptions about comets have been used to explore the interplay of high and low culture and the interfaces linking religious thought, political action, and natural worldviews. My method has been to compare ephemeral publications, artwork, performances, and other popular productions with scientific and philosophical treatises. This approach has exposed continuities of thought during periods of apparent change and stratification. It has revealed how popular and elite thought have enriched each other to a far greater degree than that indicated by earlier histories, which have focused exclusively on either the decline of astronomical superstitions or the development of astrophysics. If there is a message here, it is that we should widen our gaze and reconsider the boundaries between popular culture and modern science.

RECENT RESURGENCE OF COMETARY CATASTROPHISM

IN ONE of those curious twists that makes history so fascinating, cometary catastrophism has experienced a resurgence in recent years.[1] In puzzling over the death of the dinosaurs, the massive extinction at the end of the Cretaceous period sixty-five million years ago, and numerous smaller extinctions, Harold C. Urey in 1973 conjectured that these were caused by the collisions of comets with the earth.[2] In 1980, Luis and Walter Alvarez discovered an anomalous iridium layer at the Cretaceous/Tertiary (K/T) boundary and suggested that the impact of a comet or asteroid occurred at that time. The collision would have raised enough dust (rich in extraterrestrial iridium) to darken the planet, forestall photosynthesis, and promote mass extinction.[3] Even though a probable impact site was later identified at Chicxulub in the Yucatan, the Alvarez hypothesis has continued to be the subject of intense interdisciplinary debate.[4] In general, astronomers have embraced the theory while paleontologists have spurned it.[5]

In 1984, David Raup and John Sepkoski suggested that mass extinctions were periodic phenomena occurring roughly every twenty-six million years.[6] This hypothesis led others to explore the possible periodization of crater sites[7] and attempt to correlate these not only with the fossil record but also with the period of oscillation of the solar system above and below the plane of the Milky Way. Some argued that as the solar system bobbed up and down, it periodically met interstellar clouds of dust and gas. These clouds gravitationally perturbed the halo of comets (known as the Oort cloud) that encircles the solar system, thereby triggering showers of comets, which pelted the earth.[8] An alternative hypothesis proposed that the sun has a dim companion star revolving around it in an eccentric orbit. Every perihelion approach of "Nemesis" disturbed the sun's family of comets and induced a comet shower.[9] Others were mindful of the possibility of nonperiodic comet showers and said these might occur if the Oort cloud were perturbed by the close passage of neighboring stars.[10] The geological record, however, has yet to offer compelling evidence for a connection between comet impacts and mass extinctions other than the one at the K/T boundary.[11]

Deaths of the dinosaurs aside, Sir Fred Hoyle and Chandra Wickramasinghe have suggested that comets harbor microorganisms within warm, protected internal pools, and that they transport and dispense life throughout the universe. Hoyle and Wickramasinghe also believe that

comets have rained plague-causing microorganisms, viruses, and influenza upon the earth.[12]

Since the modern view of comets perceives them to be composed primarily of frozen water and as much as 10 percent organic molecules (including methane, ammonia, carbon dioxide, and hydrogen cyanide),[13] others have theorized that comets did not transmit life to earth but helped to seed the young planet with complex organic molecules from which life might arise. It is also argued that perhaps most of the earth's ocean water and atmosphere were deposited by comets, rather than by the outgassing of volatiles from the earth's interior.[14]

That comets could be both the agents of death and the conveyors of life's building blocks is not inconsistent, Kevin Zahnle and David Grinspoon have argued. Pointing to the heavy concentration of extraterrestrial amino acids that was recently detected in the rocks above and below the K/T boundary layer at Stevns Klint, Denmark, they suggested that these amino acids or their precursors were deposited on the earth as interplanetary dust. The source of this dust was a giant comet trapped in the inner solar system. Disintegration of the comet produced both the dust and the fragment that crashed to the earth sixty-five million years ago.[15]

The fragmentation of comet Shoemaker-Levy 9 as it passed by Jupiter in 1992 provided astronomers with a graphic demonstration of this breakup mechanism. When remnants of the comet crashed into Jupiter in 1994, they focused attention on the dangers posed to the earth by cometary collisions in the past and future.[16]

It is beyond the scope of this book to elucidate these latest theories or detail the heated debates that surround them. Nor do I wish to imply that modern scientists delved into the historical record to retrieve Newton's and Halley's all but forgotten theories of comets' furnishing water and life-sustaining materials to the planets, or their beliefs that comet impacts have caused mass extinctions. I rather suspect that modern scientists independently seized on comets for many of the same physical reasons that seventeenth- and eighteenth-century natural philosophers did. To explain certain episodes in the earth's geophysical and biological past, extraterrestrial causes seemed to be required. In comets, scientists found what they needed. The wayward paths and physical composition of comets made these heavenly visitors the most plausible natural agents to cause the dramatic extinctions or to prepare the terrestrial conditions so critical to the evolution of human life.

Plausibility, however, has meaning only in the context of scientific theory, and theories are colored by the cultures—high and low—in which scientists work. As I have shown, earlier scientists were not isolated from popular culture. Neither have all modern scientists remained apart from it (fig. 53). Comet lore has been particularly tenacious. I will not make the case that modern scientists have exploited popular eschatologies in their re-

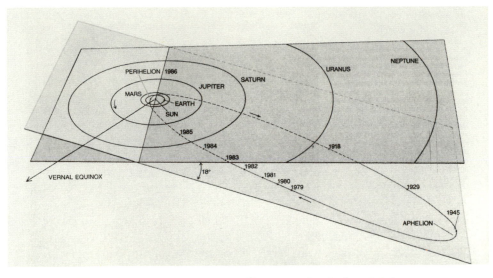

Fig. 53. The anthropocentric treatment of comets today. Perhaps it is human nature to correlate cometary periods with major historical events, but the choice of dates on this scientific diagram of the orbit of Halley's comet should give us pause. Do we really want to know where the comet was in 1918 (when World War I ended), 1929 (when the stock market crashed), or 1945 (when the United States dropped the atom bomb and ended World War II)?! Illustration by Dan Todd, from "Giotto's Portrait of Halley's Comet" by Roberta J. M. Olson. Copyright © 1979 Scientific American, Inc. All rights reserved.

search, but by the same token I believe that it is fair to challenge the myth that all modern science is bias-free and borrows nothing from the societies in which its practitioners live. What makes cometary catastrophism acceptable today, and the degree to which its current favor is driven by factors internal or external to the scientific enterprise, remain, for me, open and extremely interesting questions.

NOTES

INTRODUCTION

1. Edmond Halley, "Ode to Newton," trans. Leon J. Richardson, in Isaac Newton, *Sir Isaac Newton's Mathematical Principles of Natural Philosophy and His System of the World*, trans. Andrew Motte and rev. Florian Cajori (Berkeley and Los Angeles: University of California Press, 1962).

2. Thomas Robert Malthus, *An Essay on the Principle of Population* (London, 1798), 2.

3. My starting point has been Clifford Geertz, *The Interpretation of Cultures* (New York: Basic Books, 1973), 89; and Peter Burke, "Popular Culture in Seventeenth-Century London," *London Journal* 3 (1977): 143–162, esp. 143.

4. Burke, "Popular Culture in Seventeenth-Century London"; Peter Burke, *Popular Culture in Early Modern Europe* (New York: New York University Press, 1978); Natalie Zemon Davis, *Society and Culture in Early Modern France* (Stanford: Stanford University Press, 1975).

5. Burke, *Popular Culture*, chaps. 2, 9.

6. Carlo Ginzburg, *The Cheese and the Worms: The Cosmos of a Sixteenth-Century Miller*, trans. John and Anne Tedeschi (Baltimore: Johns Hopkins University Press, 1980).

7. Jacques Le Goff, "The Learned and Popular Dimensions of Journeys in the Otherworld in the Middle Ages," in *Understanding Popular Culture: Europe from the Middle Ages to the Nineteenth Century*, ed. Steven L. Kaplan (Berlin: Mouton Publishers, 1984), 19–37, esp. 20–21; and Keith Thomas, *Man and the Natural World* (London: Allen Lane, 1983), 76–77.

8. Davis, *Society and Culture*, chap. 7; Roger Chartier, "Culture as Appropriation: Popular Cultural Uses in Early Modern France," in Kaplan, *Understanding Popular Culture*, 229–253.

9. [Antoine Mizaud], *Les ephemerides perpetuelles de l'air: autrement l'astrologie des rustiques* (Paris, 1554); Davis, *Society and Culture*, 191, 197–199, 205. For English examples, see Burke, "Popular Culture in Seventeenth-Century London," 144, 155.

10. Bernard Capp, *English Almanacs 1500–1800: Astrology and the Popular Press* (Ithaca: Cornell University Press, 1979), 283, app. 1.

11. David Hall's introduction to Kaplan, *Understanding Popular Culture*, 5–18, see 11.

12. Eric Halfpenny, "The Citie's Loyalty Display'd," *Guildhall Miscellany* 10 (1959): 19–35, see 19; quoted in John Patrick Montaño, "The Quest for Consensus: The Lord Mayor's Day Shows in the 1670s," in *Culture and Society in the Stuart Restoration*, ed. Gerald Maclean (Cambridge: Cambridge University Press, 1995), 31–51, see 35.

13. Montaño, "Quest for Consensus." More will be said about the coronation pageant in chaps. 4 and 7 below.

14. Le Goff, "Learned and Popular Dimensions of Journeys."

15. Ambroise Paré, *Des monstres et prodiges*, which first appeared as part of his *Deux livres de chirurgie* (Paris, 1573), 365–580. Paré added a chapter on "celestial

monsters" in the third edition (1579) of *Des monstres* and augmented it in the fourth (1585) and fifth (1595) editions, which were issued in successive, revised editions of his collected works. The quotation is taken from *Des monstres et prodiges*, 3d ed. (Paris, 1579), which appeared in *Les oeuvres d'Ambroise Paré, conseiller, et premier chirurgien du roy. Divisees en vingt sept livres, avec les figures & portraicts, tant de l'anatomie que des instruments de chirurgie, & de plusieurs monstres*, rev. 2d ed. (Paris, 1579), IX.ʿXXII–X.ʿI, see IX.ʿXCVII–IX.ʿXCVIII; my translation. Paré's source for the image of the grisly comet was Pierre Boaistuau, *Histoires prodigieuses* (Paris, 1561). It also appeared in Conrad Lycosthenes, *Prodigiorum ac ostentorum chronicon* (Basel, 1557). Owen Gingerich has noted that this apparition was in fact an aurora over Westrie in 1528. See Owen Gingerich, review of *Fire and Ice: A History of Comets in Art*, by Roberta J. M. Olson, *Journal for the History of Astronomy* 17 (1986): 62–63; Ambroise Paré, *Des monstres et prodiges*, critical edition, ed. Jean Céard (Geneva: Librairie Droz, 1971); Ambroise Paré, *On Monsters and Marvels*, trans. Janis L. Pallister (Chicago: University of Chicago Press, 1982).

16. Chartier, "Culture as Appropriation," 233.

17. See also Roger Chartier, *Cultural History: Between Practices and Representations*, trans. Lydia G. Cochrane (Ithaca: Cornell University Press, 1988), 38–39; Le Goff, "Learned and Popular Dimensions of Journeys."

18. Keith Thomas, *Religion and the Decline of Magic* (New York: Charles Scribner's Sons, 1971), chaps. 2–3, 7–8. Cf. Mary R. O'Neil, "*Sacerdote ovvero strione*: Ecclesiastical and Superstitious Remedies in Sixteenth Century Italy," in Kaplan, *Understanding Popular Culture*, 53–83.

19. Barry Reay, "Popular Culture in Early Modern England," in *Popular Culture in Seventeenth-Century England*, ed. Barry Reay (London: Croom Helm, 1985), 1–30, esp. 15–17; Burke, "Popular Culture in Seventeenth-Century London," 151–152; Robert W. Malcolmson, *Popular Recreations in English Society, 1700–1850* (Cambridge: Cambridge University Press, 1973), 49–50; R. Ashton, "Popular Entertainment and Social Control in Later Elizabethan and Early Stuart London," *London Journal* 9 (1983): 3–19, esp. 9.

20. William Cornwallis, *Essays* (London, 1600), "Of the Observation and Use of Things"; quoted in Burke, *Popular Culture*, 277.

21. Capp, *English Almanacs*, 60, app. 1; Margaret Spufford, *Small Books and Pleasant Histories: Popular Fiction and Its Readership in Seventeenth-Century England* (London: Methuen, 1981; Athens: University of Georgia Press, 1982), 75; Hyder E. Rollins, "The Black-Letter Broadside Ballad," *Proceedings of the Modern Language Association* 34 (1919): 258–339; Keith Wrightson, *English Society, 1580–1680* (New Brunswick: Rutgers University Press, 1982), 197; Barry Reay, "Popular Literature in Seventeenth-Century England," *Journal of Peasant Studies* 10, no. 4 (1982–1983): 243–249; Davis, *Society and Culture*, 197–199, 208. On Pepys's collection, see Roger Thompson, ed., *Samuel Pepys' Penny Merriments* (New York: Columbia University Press, 1977); Roger Thompson, "Popular Reading and Humour in Restoration England," *Journal of Popular Culture* 9 (1975–1976): 653–671.

22. On France, see Chartier, "Culture as Appropriation"; Davis, *Society and Culture*, chap. 7. On England, see chap. 4 below.

23. Chartier, "Culture as Appropriation"; Davis, *Society and Culture*, chap. 7.

24. Davis, *Society and Culture*, 201–202.

25. Peter Clark, *The English Alehouse: A Social History, 1200–1830* (London: Longman, 1983), 155, 198; Rollins, "The Black-Letter Broadside Ballad," 328, 336–338; Bernard Capp, "Popular Literature," in Reay, *Popular Culture in Seventeenth-Century England*, 198–243, esp. 203–204; Reay, "Popular Culture in Early Modern England," 7.

26. On literacy, see, for example, David Cressy, *Literacy and the Social Order: Reading and Writing in Tudor and Stuart England* (Cambridge: Cambridge University Press, 1980).

27. Chartier, "Culture as Appropriation," 236–237; Clark, *The English Alehouse*, 198; Rollins, "The Black-Letter Broadside Ballad," 325–326, 336–338; Leslie Shepard, *The History of Street Literature* (Newton Abbot: David & Charles, 1973), 21–23.

28. Davis, *Society and Culture*, chap. 7; Chartier, "Culture as Appropriation."

29. Stith Thompson, *Motif-Index of Folk-Literature: A Classification of Narrative Elements in Folktales, Ballads, Myths, Fables, Mediaeval Romances, Exempla, Fabliaux, Jest-Books, and Local Legends*, rev. and enl. ed., 6 vols. (Bloomington: Indiana University Press, 1955–1958). Cf. *Standard Dictionary of Folklore, Mythology and Legend*, ed. Maria Leach, 2 vols. (New York: Funk & Wagnalls, 1949–1950), s.v. "comet."

30. Chartier, *Cultural History*, 39.

CHAPTER I
ANCIENT SIGNS

1. I do not aim to be comprehensive in retailing the viewpoint of every minor classical author. Please see subsequent notes for references to compendia of historical ideas. Here let me mention that many recent books celebrating the return of Halley's comet offer the reader long, uncritical lists of popular beliefs held in the past. Although the authors tend to deride out-of-date opinions, these works can be useful starting points for those who wish to gather up earlier theories, learn the latest scientific observations, and locate the modern-day border between science and superstition. See, for example, Nigel Calder, *The Comet is Coming! The Feverish Legacy of Mr. Halley* (New York: Viking Press, 1981); Richard Flaste et al., *The New York Times Guide to the Return of Halley's Comet* (New York: Times Books, 1985); Mark Littmann and Donald K. Yeomans, *Comet Halley: Once in a Lifetime* (Washington, D.C.: American Chemical Society, 1985); Patrick Moore and John Mason, *The Return of Halley's Comet* (New York: W. W. Norton & Company, 1984); Francis Reddy, *Halley's Comet!* ([Milwaukee]: AstroMedia, 1985); Carl Sagan and Ann Druyan, *Comet* (New York: Random House, 1985); Garry Stasiuk and Dwight Gruber, *The Comet Handbook* (Portland, Oreg.: Stasiuk Enterprises, 1984); Fred L. Whipple, *The Mystery of Comets* (Washington, D.C.: Smithsonian Institution Press, 1985); Donald K. Yeomans, *Comet Halley: Fact and Folly* (Santa Ana, Calif.: Gold Stein Press, 1985); Donald K. Yeomans, *Comets: A Chronological History of Observation, Science, Myth, and Folklore* (New York: Wiley Science Editions, 1991); M. E. Bailey, S.V.M. Clube, and W. M. Napier, *The Origin of Comets* (Oxford: Pergamon Press, 1990).

Asian observations of comets are an interesting study in themselves but are not relevant to my project. For those wishing to learn more, I recommend F. Richard Stephenson and Kevin K. C. Yau, "Far Eastern Observations of Halley's Comet: 240

BC to AD 1368," *Journal of the British Interplanetary Society* 38 (1985): 195–216; "Early Chinese Observations of Halley's Comet," in *Halley's Comet in History*, ed. F. Richard Stephenson and Christopher B. F. Walker (London: British Museum Publications, 1985), 41–51; Ho Peng Yoke [Ho Ping-Yü], "Ancient and Mediaeval Observations of Comets and Novae in Chinese Sources," *Vistas in Astronomy* 5 (1962): 127–225; Ho Peng Yoke [Ho Ping-Yü], *The Astronomical Chapters of the Chin Shu* [ca. A.D. 635] (Paris: Mouton & Co., 1966); Ichiro Hasegawa, "Catalogue of Ancient and Naked-Eye Comets," *Vistas in Astronomy* 24 (1980): 59–102; Xi Ze-zong, "The Cometary Atlas in the Silk Book of the Han Tomb [168 B.C.] at Mawangdui," *Chinese Astronomy and Astrophysics* 8 (1984): 1–7; Michael Loewe, "The Han View of Comets," *Östasiatiska museet. Bulletin* [Bulletin of the Museum of Far Eastern Antiquities, Stockholm] 52 (1980): 1–31; Edward H. Schafer, *Pacing the Void: T'ang Approaches to the Stars* (Berkeley and Los Angeles: University of California Press, 1977), 105–116; Joseph Needham, *Science and Civilization in China*, vol. 3, *Mathematics and the Sciences of the Heavens and the Earth* (Cambridge: Cambridge University Press, 1959); and, though much corrected by the above authors, John Williams, *Observations of Comets, from B.C. 611 to A.D. 1640. Extracted from the Chinese Annals* (London: For the author, 1871).

2. Aristotle, *Meteorologica* [ca. 356–ca. 340 B.C.], trans. H.D.P. Lee, Loeb Classical Library (Cambridge: Harvard University Press, 1978), 1.6; Lucius Annaeus Seneca, *Naturales quaestiones* [ca. A.D. 62–65], trans. Thomas H. Corcoran, 2 vols., Loeb Classical Library (Cambridge: Harvard University Press, 1971–1972), bk. 7; Diodorus Siculus [Diodorus of Sicily], *Library of History* [ca. 36–30 B.C.], trans. C. H. Oldfather et al., 12 vols., Loeb Classical Library (London: William Heinemann, 1933–1967), 1.81.5, 15.50.3; Aëtius [attributed author of work long ascribed to Plutarch], *De placitis philosophorum* 3.2. An English translation is [Aëtius], *Of Those Sentiments Concerning Nature with Which Philosophers were Delighted*, trans. John Dowel; available in *Plutarch's Morals*, ed. William W. Goodwin, 5 vols. (Boston: Little, Brown, and Company, 1871), 3:149–150.

For copies and translations of cuneiform texts that contain observations of comets, and for further information on Babylonian astronomy, see Stephenson and Walker, *Halley's Comet*; T. G. Pinches et al., *Late Babylonian Astronomical and Related Texts* (Providence: Brown University Press, 1955); F. Richard Stephenson, Kevin K. C. Yau, and Hermann Hunger, "Records of Halley's Comet on Babylonian Tablets," *Nature* 314 (1985): 587–592; F. Richard Stephenson, "The Babylonians Saw That Comet, Too," *Natural History* 94 (December 1985): 14–20; C.B.F. Walker, "Halley's Comet in Babylonia," *Nature* 314 (1985): 576–577; Otto Neugebauer, *The Exact Sciences in Antiquity*, 2d ed. (New York: Dover Publications, 1969), 100–101; Otto Neugebauer, *A History of Ancient Mathematical Astronomy*, 3 vols. (New York: Springer-Verlag, 1975), 1:347–555; Asger Aaboe, "Observation and Theory in Babylonian Astronomy," *Centaurus* 24 (1980): 14–35; A. J. Sachs, "A Classification of the Babylonian Astronomical Tablets of the Seleucid Period," *Journal of Cuneiform Studies* 2 (1948): 271–290; A. J. Sachs, "Babylonian Observational Astronomy," in *The Place of Astronomy in the Ancient World*, ed. F. R. Hodson (London: Oxford University Press for the British Academy, 1974), 43–50; also published in *Philosophical Transactions of the Royal Society*, ser. A, 276 (1974): 43–50; T. G. Cowling, "Astrology, Religion and Science," *Quarterly Journal of the Royal Astronomical Society* 23 (1982): 515–526.

Useful resources for concise accounts of ancient theories are Auguste Bouché-Leclercq, *L'Astrologie grecque* (Paris, 1899; reprint, Brussels: Culture et Civilisation, 1963), 357–362; C. Doris Hellman, *The Comet of 1577: Its Place in the History of Astronomy* (New York: Columbia University Press, 1944), chap. 1; and Jane L. Jervis, *Cometary Theory in Fifteenth-Century Europe* (Dordrecht: D. Reidel, 1985), chap. 1 (although I am not in complete agreement with her classification scheme on pp. 20–21). Further discussion is found in D. R. Dicks, *Early Greek Astronomy to Aristotle* (Ithaca: Cornell University Press, 1970), passim.

3. Aristotle, *Meteorologica* 1.4, 7.

4. Ibid. 1.7.

5. Theophrastus, *Concerning Weather Signs* [ca. 320 B.C.], 34, 57, in Theophrastus, *Enquiry into Plants and Minor Works on Odours and Weather Signs,* trans. Sir Arthur Hort, 2 vols., Loeb Classical Library (Cambridge: Harvard University Press, 1948–1949), 2:391–433.; Claudius Ptolemy, *Tetrabiblos* [or *Quadripartitum,* ca. A.D. 150–178], trans. F. E. Robbins, Loeb Classical Library (Cambridge: Harvard University Press, 1980), 2.13.102. See table 1 for other followers.

Pliny equivocated on the issue of the meteoric status of comets: "Some persons think that even comets are everlasting, and travel in a special circuit of their own, but are not visible except when the sun leaves them; there are others, however, who hold that they spring into existence out of chance moisture and fiery force, and consequently are dissolved." See Gaius Plinius Secundus [Pliny the Elder], *Natural History* [*Naturalis historia,* A.D. 77], trans. H. Rackham, W.H.S. Jones, and D. E. Eichholz, 10 vols., Loeb Classical Library (Cambridge: Harvard University Press, 1969–1986), 2.23.94.

6. Seneca, *Naturales quaestiones* 7.22.1.

7. Ibid. 7.23.2–3. Seneca presented four main arguments against Aristotle's theory: (1) Everything in the atmosphere is short-lived and constantly changing, whereas comets are durable. (2) Since fires cling to their fuel, those in the atmosphere should always descend into the region near the earth where the atmosphere is thicker. Comets never approach the ground. (3) Two recent comets moved in curved paths that were characteristic of the planets but not of fire, which moves either upward according to its nature or in the direction of its fuel. (4) With the exception of divine fires in the heavens, other fires are as fleeting as their temporary and accidental causes. Comets, however, are constant; they do not become larger or smaller on successive days in relation to the variable quantity of fuel at their disposal. (In fact, Aristotle and most astronomers did not accept this observation.) Ibid. 7.22.1–7.23.3.

In raising comets into the heavens, Seneca practiced a linguistic sleight of hand. He initially defined a comet vaguely as "an unusual star of strange appearance [that] is seen trailing fire streaming around it" (7.11.3). But he later narrowed his class of objects by setting aside as comets only celestial fires that were long-lived, stable, uniform and invariable in luster and size, and moving in a curved path. Fiery balls, torches, blazes, goats, barrels, beams, trumpets, and all erratic lights in the sky he deemed atmospheric meteors. Aristotle, Pliny, Manilius, and Ptolemy made no distinctions among these forms; all were varieties of comets, and comets were one class of meteors. Given their classification scheme, they argued that comets and other variable meteors could not be eternal, celestial bodies. See ibid. 1.1.2, 1.1.5–6, 1.15.1–5, 7.4.3–7.6.1, 7.21.1, 7.22–23.

8. Ibid. 7.13–15, 17–18. Seneca's key arguments against comets' being planets were: (1) Comets are largest when they first appear, and their size does not increase with their approach to the earth; (2) comets appear outside the zodiac; and (3) one can see stars through a comet's tail, but not through planets.

9. Ibid. 7.14.1.

10. Ibid. 7.24.1–3, 7.27.1–5.

11. Ibid. 7.3.1, 7.25.1–2.

12. Ibid. 7.25.3–5.

13. Ibid. 7.25.7.

14. Ibid. 7.27.6.

15. Ibid. 7.30.

16. Aristotle, *Meteorologica* 1.7.344b, 2.8. esp. 368a–b.

17. Ibid. 1.7.344b. Anaxagoras was alleged to have predicted this meteorite, which was reported to be the size of a wagon-load. Cf. Pliny, *Natural History* 2.59.149.

18. Aristotle, *Meteorologica* 1.6.343b, 1.7.344b–345a, 2.8.368b. Although Aristotle did not report explicitly how the towns of Buris and Helice were abruptly and forever submerged beneath the sea shortly after the great comet's apparition, many later authors would cite this event as evidence of the dreadful effects of comets.

19. Ibid. 1.7.344b.

20. Theophrastus, *Concerning Weather Signs*, 34, 57.

21. Aratus, *Phaenomena* [ca. 276 B.C.], trans. G. R. Mair, Loeb Classical Library (Cambridge: Harvard University Press, 1977), lines 1091–1093. For background, see Frederick H. Cramer, *Astrology in Roman Law and Politics* (Philadelphia: American Philosophical Society, 1954), 26–27.

The lines are tantalizing since they may provide a clue to one of Aristotle's sources. Aratus based his poem on an earlier astronomical treatise by Eudoxus of Cnidus (fl. 365 B.C.). It is unclear whether these verses reflect an opinion of Eudoxus, a view current at Plato's Academy (which Eudoxus joined about 367 B.C.), or one Aratus picked up later in Athens around the year 291 B.C., when he attended lectures by Aristotle's Peripatetic disciples. This last seems most likely, however, since the verses come from a section of the poem that treats weather signs and bears much similarity to the work of Theophrastus. Aratus eventually left the Peripatetic school to pursue the Stoic teachings of Zeno, who believed comets to be formed by the conjunction of starlight. We do not know whether Zeno taught Aratus to respect comets as heralds of drought, for there is little evidence of later Greek views on the significance of comets.

22. Pliny, *Natural History* 2.23.91.

23. Seneca, *Naturales quaestiones* 7.5.3–4, 7.16.2, 7.28.3.

24. Ibid. 7.28.1; quotations are from Virgil, *Georgics* 1.392 and 1.362, respectively.

25. Seneca, *Naturales quaestiones* 7.28.2.

26. Ibid. 2.31–50, 3.29; Cramer, *Astrology in Roman Law*, 117–121; Lynn Thorndike, *A History of Magic and Experimental Science*, 8 vols. (New York: Columbia University Press, 1923–1958), 1:103–104.

27. Seneca, *Naturales quaestiones* 2.32.3–4, see also 2.46.1.

28. Pliny, *Natural History* 2.25.96–2.26.97, quotation at 2.26.97.

29. Hellman, *Comet of 1577*, 34–35. Note the incunabular edition of Manilius

prepared by Regiomontanus, *M. Manilii Astronomicon* (Nuremberg: Johann Müller of Königsberg, 1474?).

30. Marcus Manilius, *Astronomica* [ca. A.D. 9–15], trans. G. P. Goold, Loeb Classical Library (Cambridge: Harvard University Press, 1977), 1.817–866.

31. "Seu deus instantis fati miseratus in orbem/signa per affectus caelique incendia mittit." Ibid. 1.874–875.

32. Ibid. 1.876–892.

33. Ibid. 1.893–895.

34. Ibid. 1.896–914.

35. Diodorus Siculus, *Library of History* 15.50.1–3; Publius Vergilius Maro [Virgil], *Georgics* [29 B.C.], trans. H. Rushton Fairclough, rev. ed., Loeb Classical Library (Cambridge: Harvard University Press, 1978), 1.464–490. Cf. Virgil, *Aeneid*, trans. H. Rushton Fairclough, rev. ed., 2 vols., Loeb Classical Library (Cambridge: Harvard University Press, 1978), 2.692–704, 10.272–273.

36. The cuneiform texts containing observations of the 164 and 87 B.C. apparitions are printed, transliterated, and translated in Stephenson and Walker, *Halley's Comet*, 17–40. Also see the references in n. 2 above.

37. The earliest references to comets are difficult to distinguish from meteorological annotations but begin to appear in astrological omen texts dating from the seventh or eighth century B.C. (Such a text from an Assyrian library at Nineveh is quoted in Stephenson and Walker, *Halley's Comet*, 17.) At about this time, Babylonians also began to keep diaries of astronomical observations of the planets, sun, and moon, along with records of the weather, earthquakes, the rise and fall of the Euphrates River at Babylon, the market prices of key commodities, and occasionally political events. Comets are mentioned in diaries preserved from 234 B.C. onward and may also have figured in tables like those that survive for eclipses. The compilation of such tables, if it occurred, would lend credibility to Diodorus Siculus's report that the Babylonians attempted to predict the occurrence of comets. By the way, the date 234 B.C. should not be confused with the date of the earliest reference to Halley's comet, which appears in Chinese observations from 240 B.C. The earliest extant Chinese record of a comet dates from 613 B.C. For more on Asian observations, see the references in n. 1 above.

38. Ptolemy, *Tetrabiblos* 2.9.90. Ptolemy's theory will be described at greater length in chap. 5.

39. Pliny, *Natural History* 2.23.92; Seneca, *Naturales qaestiones* 7.15.1–2, 7.17.2, 7.21.3–4; Marcus Annaeus Lucanus [Lucan], *The Civil War* [also called *The Pharsalia*, ca. A.D. 65], trans. J. D. Duff, Loeb Classical Library (Cambridge: Harvard University Press, 1977), 1.526–529. More will be said below on the comets that heralded the fatal poisonings of Augustus and Claudius, and the political purges in Nero's day.

It must be acknowledged that Seneca did not always elucidate the precise link between these comets and the ensuing civil disorders. Sometimes it seems that he employed changes of state and assorted disasters simply to date the comets for his readers. Nevertheless, there are ample grounds to argue that Seneca believed the associations to be more than coincidental, for he saw other extraordinary celestial phenomena to be prodigies, reporting, for example, how great meteoric balls of fire heralded the deaths of Augustus (A.D. 14) and Germanicus Caesar (A.D. 19), the condemnation of Sejanus (A.D. 31), and the Battle of Pynda (168 B.C.) (*Naturales quaestiones* 1.1.2–4). Whatever the case, his reports of comets in con-

junction with political and natural events certainly helped reinforce the popular belief in cometary signs.

40. Seneca, *Naturales quaestiones* 7.17.2; cf. 7.21.3.

41. Pliny, *Natural History* 2.23.92.

42. Ibid.

43. Virgil, *Aeneid* 2.692–704. There also is a cometary allusion to the destruction of Aeneas's enemies (*Aeneid* 10.272–273).

44. Origen, *Contra Celsum* 1.59. The fragment is also available in *Chaeremon:
Egyptian Priest and Stoic Philosopher. The Fragments Collected and Translated
with Explanatory Notes*, ed. Pieter Willem van der Horst (Leiden: E. J. Brill, 1984),
12, 13.

45. Van der Horst, *Chaeremon*, 53. For Roman opinions of these comets, see
Cornelius Tacitus, *The Annals* [*Annales*, A.D. 116], trans. John Jackson, 3 vols.,
Loeb Classical Library (Cambridge: Harvard University Press, 1951), 14.22, 15.47;
Gaius Suetonius Tranquillus [Suetonius], *The Lives of the Caesars* [A.D. 120], trans.
J. C. Rolfe, 2 vols., Loeb Classical Library (London: William Heinemann, 1914),
6.36; Pliny, *Natural History* 2.23.92.

46. Cassius Dio Cocceianus, *Dio's Roman History* [researched and composed
ca. A.D. 200–222, published ca. A.D. 229], trans. Earnest Cary, 9 vols., Loeb Classical Library (Cambridge: Harvard University Press, 1969–1980), epitome of bk. 66,
sec. 17 (for quotation, see 8:295 in Loeb ed.). Cf. Suetonius, *The Lives*, 8.23.

47. Lucan, *The Civil War* 1.528–529.

48. Decimus Junius Juvenalis [Juvenal], *Satires* [ca. A.D. 98–127], trans. G. G.
Ramsay, rev. ed., Loeb Classical Library (Cambridge: Harvard University Press,
1961), "The Ways of Women," 6.407–408. Juvenal found his humor in the comet
of A.D. 115.

49. Manilius, *Astronomica* 1.904–905.

50. Pliny, *Natural History* 2.23.93–94. Suetonius also reported this comet and
the star consequently placed on the crown of the head of Julius Caesar's statue.
Suetonius, *The Lives* 1.88. On the catasterism of Julius Caesar, see Cramer, *Astrology in Roman Law*, 78–80.

51. One comet coin is part of the Basserman-Jordan Collection at the Bayerisches
Nationalmuseum, Munich; it is illustrated in Roberta J. M. Olson, *Fire and Ice: A
History of Comets in Art* (New York: Walker & Company for the National Air and
Space Museum, Smithsonian Institution, 1985), 28. Another version of the coin is
illustrated in Littmann and Yeomans, *Comet Halley*, 6; and Yeomans, *Comets*, 13.
A similar cometary emblem graced a copper coin minted to commemorate the ruler
Mithradates, whose birth was heralded by a comet in 134 B.C. See Cramer, *Astrol-
ogy in Roman Law*, 118.

52. Pliny, *Natural History* 2.23.93–94.

53. Cramer, *Astrology in Roman Law*, 79–80.

54. Cassius Dio, *Roman History* 45.17.4, 54.29.8.

55. Ibid. 56.24.3–4, 56.25.5, 56.29.3; Cramer, *Astrology in Roman Law*, 99,
117–118.

56. Suetonius, *The Lives* 5.46; cf. Pliny, *Natural History* 2.23.92.

57. Tacitus, *Annals* 14.22.

58. Suetonius, *The Lives* 6.36. On the power of Balbillus and other court astrologers, see Cramer, *Astrology in Roman Law*, 81–145.

59. Tacitus, *Annals* 15.47.

60. Seneca, *Naturales quaestiones* 7.17.2, 7.21.3.

61. Related folk motifs are recorded in cultures as widely disparate as those of the Chinese, Tahitians, South American Indians, and the West. See Stith Thompson, *Motif-Index of Folk-Literature: A Classification of Narrative Elements in Folktales, Ballads, Myths, Fables, Mediaeval Romances, Exempla, Fabliaux, Jest-Books, and Local Legends*, rev. and enl. ed., 6 vols. (Bloomington: Indiana University Press, 1955–1958), A780, A786, D1311.6, D1812.5.1.6, F493.5.

62. Hyginus, *Poeticon astronomicon* [second century A.D.] (Venice: Erhard Ratdolt, 1482), sig. C2, "Taurus." A modern edition is *Hyginus Astronomus*, Scriptorum Romanorum quae extant omnia, nos. 255–256 (Pisa: Giardini, 1976), 60. Part of this work is available in *The Myths of Hyginus*, trans. and ed. Mary Grant (Lawrence: University of Kansas Press, 1960), see 211 for quotation. Also see Hyginus, *Fabulae*, CXCII. Hyas; translated in *Myths of Hyginus*, 149. For Latin text, see *Hygini Fabulae*, edited H. I. Rose (Leiden: A. W. Sythoff, 1933), 136–137. Hyginus's identity remains obscure, but scholars now believe that he was not C. Julius Hyginus, freedman of Augustus and director of the Palatine Library, nor Hyginus the Surveyor. (See Grant's introduction.)

CHAPTER II
MONSTERS AND THE MESSIAH

1. *The Anglo-Saxon Chronicles*, trans. and collated by Anne Savage (New York: Saint Martin's/Marek, 1983), year 1066 (p. 194). Also see the chronicles of Raoul Glaber, Guillaume de Nangis, William of Malmesbury (not to be confused with Oliver [Eilmer] of Malmesbury, whose remarks on the comet were reported by William), Florence of Worcester, Ordericus Vitalis, and Ingulph. For a survey, see Andrew Dickson White, *A History of the Warfare of Science with Theology in Christendom* 2 vols. (New York: D. Appleton and Company, 1930), 1:177; James Howard Robinson, *The Great Comet of 1680: A Study in the History of Rationalism* (Northfield, Minn.: Press of the Northfield News, 1916), 6; C. Doris Hellman, *The Comet of 1577: Its Place in the History of Astronomy* (New York: Columbia University Press, 1944), 47.

2. Bayeux Tapestry (1073–1083); first reproduction, drawn by Stothard, engraved by Basire, hand-colored from the original (London: The Society of Antiquaries, 1819).

3. Hartmann Schedel, *Buch der Chroniken* (Nuremberg: Anton Koberger, 1493), fol. 157^r; the German text is also available in a facsimile ed., *The Nuremberg Chronicle* (New York: Landmark Press, 1979). The Latin edition, which rearranged the woodcuts, is entitled *Liber cronicarum* (Nuremberg, 1493). For discussion of the illustrations, see R.J.M. Olson and J. M. Pasachoff, "Historical Comets over Bavaria: The *Nuremberg Chronicle* and Broadsides," in *Comets in the Post-Halley Era*, ed. R. L. Newburn, Jr., et al., 2 vols. (Dordrecht: Kluwer Academic Publishers, 1991), 2:1309–1341.

4. Schedel, *Liber cronicarum*, fol. 222^v; Schedel, *Buch der Chroniken*, fol. 222^v.

5. Stith Thompson, *Motif-Index of Folk-Literature: A Classification of Narrative Elements in Folktales, Ballads, Myths, Fables, Mediaeval Romances, Exempla, Fabliaux, Jest-Books, and Local Legends*, rev. and enl. ed., 6 vols. (Bloomington: Indiana University Press, 1955–1958), E741.1.1, F493.5, F797, F960, M356.2, Q552.13.

6. See, for example, Jacques Le Goff, "The Learned and Popular Dimensions of Journeys in the Otherworld in the Middle Ages," in *Understanding Popular Culture: Europe from the Middle Ages to the Nineteenth Century*, ed. Steven L. Kaplan (Berlin: Mouton Publishers, 1984), 19–37.

7. Origen, *Contra Celsum* [ca. A.D. 200–250] 1.59, 5.10–5.13; *Against Celsus*, trans. Frederick Crombie, in *The Ante-Nicene Fathers*, ed. Alexander Roberts and James Donaldson, 10 vols. (Grand Rapids: Wm. B. Eerdmans Publishing Company, 1980–1983), 4:422, 546–549. Also see Lynn Thorndike, *A History of Magic and Experimental Science*, 8 vols. (New York: Columbia University Press, 1923–1958), 1:456–458.

8. Synesius Cyrenaeus, *Praise of Baldness*, chap. 10, in *The Essays and Hymns of Synesius of Cyrene*, trans. Augustine FitzGerald, 2 vols. (London: Oxford University Press, 1930), 2:257. Thorndike, *History of Magic*, 1:540–543; Hellman, *Comet of 1577*, 42–43.

9. *Isidori Hispalensis episcopi etymologiarum sive originum libri XX*, ed. W. M. Lindsay, 2 vols. (Oxford: Clarendon Press, 1911), 3.71.16–17; an English translation of this section of Isidore's *Etymologies* can be found in Edward Grant, ed., *A Source Book in Medieval Science* (Cambridge: Harvard University Press, 1974), 16. *Isidori Hispalensis de natura rerum liber*, ed. Gustavus Becker (Amsterdam: Verlag Adolf M. Hakkert, 1967), 26.13. A slightly different version of Isidore's Latin text with a French translation is Isidore de Seville, *Traité de la nature*, ed. Jacques Fontaine (Bordeaux: Féret et Fils for the Centre National de la Recherche Scientifique, 1960), 26.13. See also Thorndike, *History of Magic*, 1:633.

Bede, *De natura rerum liber* [ca. 703], chap. 24; *De natura rerum liber*, ed. C. W. Jones and F. Lipp, in *Bedae Venerabilis Opera*, nos. 118A, 119, 119A–B, 120, 121–122, 123A–C (Turnhout, Belgium: Brepols, 1955–1983), 123A:173–234, see p. 216. Thorndike, *History of Magic*, 1:635; Theodore Otto Wedel, *The Mediaeval Attitude toward Astrology Particularly in England* (New Haven: Yale University Press, 1920), 29.

10. Others were John Laurentius Lydus (490–ca. 565), William of Conches (ca. 1080–ca. 1154), Michael Scot (ca. 1200–ca. 1250), William of Auvergne (fl. 1228–1249), Leopold of Austria (fl. 1275), Robert of York, who was known as Perscrutator (fl. 1350), Geoffrey of Meaux (fl. 1310–post 1348), John of Legnano (d. 1368). Hellman, *Comet of 1577*, 43–65; Thorndike, *History of Magic*, vols. 1–3, passim. John of Damascus will be discussed in this chapter, while Robert Grosseteste, Albertus Magnus, Roger Bacon, Geoffrey of Meaux, John of Legnano, Jean Buridan, and Nicole Oresme will be discussed in chap. 5.

11. Bede, *Ecclesiastical History of the English Nation* [ca. A.D. 730] 4.12, 5.23–24; available in *Baedae opera historica*, trans. J. E. King, 2 vols., Loeb Classical Library (London: William Heinemann, 1930); *Anglo-Saxon Chronicles*, years 678, 729 (pp. 53, 60).

12. *Anglo-Saxon Chronicles*, year 995 (p. 145).

13. Eadwine (Canterbury) Psalter, fol. 10^r, Cambridge, Trinity College Library. In Old English marginalia, the monk Eadwine noted, "Concerning the star called comet. A suchlike ray has the star known as Comet, and in English it is called 'the hairy star.' It appears seldom, after [periods of] many winters, and then for an omen." The folio is reproduced in Roberta J. M. Olson, *Fire and Ice: A History of Comets in Art* (New York: Walker & Company for the National Air and Space Museum, Smithsonian Institution, 1985), 15. The translation of Eadwine's text is in

F. Richard Stephenson and Christopher B. F. Walker, eds., *Halley's Comet in History* (London: British Museum Publications, 1985), 58.

14. For a study of changing attitudes toward monstrous phenomena, see Katharine Park and Lorraine J. Daston, "Unnatural Conceptions: The Study of Monsters in Sixteenth- and Seventeenth-Century France and England," *Past and Present* 92 (1981): 20–54; Harry Rusche, "Prophecies and Propaganda, 1641 to 1651," *English Historical Review* 84 (1969): 752–770.

15. Gaius Plinius Secundus [Pliny the Elder], *Natural History*, trans. H. Rackham, W.H.S. Jones, and D. E. Eichholz, 10 vols., Loeb Classical Library (Cambridge: Harvard University Press, 1969–1986), 2.57.147–2.59.150.

16. Publius Vergilius Maro [Virgil], *Georgics*, trans. H. Rushton Fairclough, rev. ed., Loeb Classical Library (Cambridge: Harvard University Press, 1978), 1.463–497, quotation at 1.488; Marcus Annaeus Lucanus [Lucan], *The Civil War*, trans. J. D. Duff, Loeb Classical Library (Cambridge: Harvard University Press, 1977), 1.522–583, 2.1–4.

17. Tacitus, *The Annals*, trans. John Jackson, 3 vols., Loeb Classical Library (Cambridge: Harvard University Press, 1951), 15.47.

18. Stated as early as Lucan, *The Civil War* 2.1–4.

19. Augustine, *De civitate Dei* 21.8; see *The City of God*, trans. Marcus Dods, in *A Select Library of the Nicene and Post-Nicene Fathers of the Christian Church*, ed. Philip Schaff, 1st ser., 14 vols. (Grand Rapids: Wm. B. Eerdmans Publishing Company, 1980–1983), 2:459–460. Cf. Isidore of Seville, *Etymologiarum* 11.3.

20. Prodigy books included Conrad Lycosthenes, *Prodigiorum ac ostentorum chronicon* (Basel, 1557); Pierre Boaistuau, *Histoires prodigieuses* (Paris, 1561); Stephen Bateman, *The Doome warning all men to the Judgemente* (London, 1581; S.T.C. 1582); and Ambroise Paré, *Des monstres et prodiges*, which first appeared as part of his *Deux livres de chirurgie* (Paris, 1573). Paré added a chapter on "celestial monsters" in the third edition (1579) and augmented it in the fourth (1585) and fifth (1595). See Ambroise Paré, *Des monstres et prodiges*, critical edition, ed. Jean Céard (Geneva: Librairie Droz, 1971); and Ambroise Paré, *On Monsters and Marvels*, trans. Janis L. Pallister (Chicago: University of Chicago Press, 1982). Town chronicles include Schedel, *Buch der Chroniken*, fol. 141ᵛ. Also Diebold Schilling, *Lucerne Chronicles* (ca. 1508–1513), MS in the Lucerne Zentralbibliothek, see fol. 61ᵛ for comet of 1456, fol. 77ʳ for the 1472 comet. The text and picture that illustrate the 1456 comet's effects focus on monstrous births (two-headed animals, children with Down's syndrome), earthquakes, illness, prodigious rains of blood. Illustrations can be found in Olson, *Fire and Ice*, 18, 36.

21. Hyder E. Rollins, ed., *The Pack of Autolycus, or Strange and Terrible News of Ghosts, Apparitions, Monstrous Births, Showers of Wheat, Judgments of God, and other Prodigious and Fearful Happenings as told in Broadside Ballads of the Years 1624–1693* (Cambridge: Harvard University Press, 1927), 21–25.

22. Increase Mather, *Heaven's Alarm to the World or a Sermon, wherein is shewed, that Fearful Sights And Signs in Heaven, are the Presages of the great Calamities at hand. Preached at the Lecture of Boston in New-England; January 20. 1680*, 2d ed. (Boston, 1682), 31.

23. 2 Esd. 5:4–8, revised standard version; cf. the translation given in the New English Bible.

24. Joel 2:30–31, revised standard version. Cf. Mark 13:24–25 and Rev. 6:12–13, which also mention stars falling from heaven.

25. 1 Chron. 21:16, revised standard version.

26. Flavius Josephus, *The Jewish War* [ca. A.D. 75–79], trans. H. St. J. Thackeray, 2 vols., Loeb Classical Library (London: William Heinemann, 1927–1928), bk. 6, chap. 5, sec. 3, line 289. Other portents included a midnight light around the altar, spontaneous opening of a temple gate, monstrous birth of a lamb to a cow, celestial apparitions of armies, and a voice in the temple.

27. Gen. 3:24, revised standard version.

28. *Bartas: His Devine Weekes and Workes*, trans. Joshua Sylvester (London, 1605; reprint, Gainesville, Fla.: Scholars' Facsimiles & Reprints, 1965), 322; cf. the French original in *The Works of Guillaume De Salluste Sieur Du Bartas*, ed. Urban Tigner Holmes, Jr., John Coriden Lyons, and Robert White Linker, 3 vols. (Chapel Hill: University of North Carolina Press, 1935–1940), 3:46.

29. John Milton, *Paradise Lost* (London, 1667), 10.1516–1530; John Milton, *Paradise Lost*, 2d ed. (London, 1674), 12.625–639, in *The Complete English Poetry of John Milton*, ed. John T. Shawcross (Garden City, N.Y.: Anchor Books, 1963), 489.

30. Bateman, *Doome warning all men*, 138. Paré, *Des monstres et prodiges*, 4th ed., published in *Les oeuvres d'Ambroise Paré, conseiller, et premier chirurgien du roy. Divisees en vingt sept livres, avec les figures & portraicts, tant de l'anatomie que des instruments de chirurgie, & de plusieurs monstres*, rev. 4th ed. (Paris, 1585), M.XCIII; Paré, *On Monsters and Marvels*, 153. Stanislaw Lubieniecki, *Theatrum cometicum*, 2d ed. (Leiden, 1681), "Historia universalis omnium cometarum," plate 64 opposite p. 48. Nathaniel Crouch, comp., R[obert] B[urton], [pseud.], *The Surprizing Miracles of Nature and Art. In Two Parts. Containing I. The Miracles of Nature, or the Strange Signs and Prodigious Aspects and Appearances in the Heavens, the Earth, and the Waters . . . with an Account of the most famous Comets, and other Prodigies, since the Birth of our Blessed Saviour, and the dreadful Effects of many of them: Also a particular Description of the five Blazing Stars seen in England, within Eighteen years last past, and abundance of other unaccountable Accidents and Productions of all kinds, till 1682. II. The Miracles of Art*, 2d ed. (London, 1685), 14–15.

31. Paré, *On Monsters and Marvels*, 152. For the Eusebius reference, see Eusebius, *The Ecclesiastical History* [ca. A.D. 311–323], trans. Kirsopp Lake, 2 vols., Loeb Classical Library (Cambridge: Harvard University Press, 1926–1932), 3.8.1–2. On Josephus, see above.

32. Saint John Damascene [John of Damascus], *De fide orthodoxa, Burgundionis versio*, ed. Eligius M. Buytaert (St. Bonaventure, N.Y.: The Franciscan Institute, 1955), 21.11 (p. 92). English translation taken from John of Damascus, *Exposition of the Orthodox Faith*, trans. S.D.F. Salmond, in *A Select Library of Nicene and Post-Nicene Fathers of the Christian Church*, ed. Philip Schaff and Henry Wace, 2d ser., 14 vols. (Grand Rapids: Wm. B. Eerdmans Publishing Company, 1982–1983), 9:24.

33. John of Damascus, *Exposition*, 9:24.

34. Isidore of Seville, *De natura rerum* 26.13; Thompson, *Motif-Index of Folk-Literature*, E741.1.2, F960.1–2, F961.2.1, V211.1.2.

35. Pliny, *Natural History* 2.23.94.

36. Origen, *Contra Celsum* 1.58–59; Origen, *Against Celsus*, trans. in *The Ante-Nicene Fathers*, 4:422.

37. Origen, *Contra Celsum* 1.59; Num. 24:17. I have used the translation from

the Hebrew given in the *Soncino Chumash*, which seems most accurate. *Shēvet* [שֵׁבֶט]
is a scepter, rod, staff, or lance.

38. See, for example, Ernest L. Martin, *The Birth of Christ Recalculated*, 2d ed.
(Pasadena: Foundation for Biblical Research, 1980); David W. Hughes, *The Star of
Bethlehem: An Astronomer's Confirmation* (New York: Pocket Books, 1980).

39. *The "Summa Theologica" of St. Thomas Aquinas* [1267–1273], trans.
Fathers of the English Dominican Province, 22 vols. (New York: Benziger Brothers,
1912–1925), pt. 3, quest. 36, art. 7 (16:142).

40. Jacobus de Voragine, *The Golden Legend or Lives of the Saints as Englished
by William Caxton* [1483], 7 vols. (London: J. M. Dent & Sons, 1922), 1:26–27,
41–49 (respectively, "The Nativity of Our Lord" and "The Feast of the Epiphany").

41. Roger Chartier, "Culture as Appropriation: Popular Cultural Uses in Early
Modern France," in *Understanding Popular Culture: Europe from the Middle Ages
to the Nineteenth Century*, ed. Steven L. Kaplan (Berlin: Mouton Publishers, 1984),
229–253, esp. 239; Natalie Zemon Davis, *Society and Culture in Early Modern
France* (Stanford: Stanford University Press, 1975), 132–133, 211.

42. Francesco Cessi, *Giotto: La Cappella degli Scrovegni* (Florence: Editoriale
Arsuna, 1978). Roberta J. M. Olson, "Giotto's Portrait of Halley's Comet," *Scientific American* 240 (May 1979): 160–170; reprinted in *Comets: Readings from Scientific American*, ed. John C. Brandt (San Francisco: W. H. Freeman and Company,
1981), 1–9. Although most scholars believe that Giotto's stunning image was inspired by the 1301 comet, David Hughes has suggested that Giotto may have seen
a December 1304 apparition of a long-period comet. David W. Hughes, "Halley's
Comet in Print," *Nature* 318 (1985): 132–134. Another image of the "comet of
Bethlehem" is to be found in Lubieniecki, *Theatrum cometicum*.

43. Aquinas, *Summa Theologica*, pt. 3 (supplement), quest. 73, art. 1 (20:88).
Aquinas also discussed comets in his commentary on Aristotle's *Meteorologica*;
see *Liber I Meteorologicorum*, lectiones 8, 9, 10; an English translation is available
in Lynn Thorndike, ed., *Latin Treatises on Comets between 1238 and 1368 A.D.*
(Chicago: University of Chicago Press, 1950), 77–86.

44. Saturn was traditionally associated with melancholy things, ruled over dogs
and bats, and was connected with woodworking, stonemasonry, and geometry (here
represented by workmen's tools, mathematical instruments, geometric solids, and a
sand glass, sundial, bell, scales, and dividers, which suggest measurement in time
and space, weight and number). Saturnine comets portended high seas and flooding,
as shown in the print. The magic square in which all columns and diagonals add up
to 34 (2 × 17) belonged to Jupiter, whose power was combined with Saturn's in
order to produce the melancholy yet brilliant philosopher, the unhappy genius. The
scales may also signify Libra, Saturn's exaltation. Unlike Panofsky and others,
Pingree believes that the celestial body in the engraving is not a comet but Saturn,
rising in its exaltation in conjunction with Jupiter, and so in the planet's most effective capacity to produce philosophers. For detailed discussion of the engraving's
iconography, see Erwin Panofsky, *The Life and Art of Albrecht Dürer* (Princeton:
Princeton University Press, 1955), 156–171; Raymond Klibansky, Erwin Panofsky,
and Fritz Saxl, *Saturn and Melancholy: Studies in the History of Natural Philosophy, Religion and Art* (London: Thomas Nelson & Sons, 1964); and David Pingree,
"A New Look at *Melencolia I*," *Journal of the Warburg and Courtauld Institutes* 43
(1980): 257–258.

45. Rev. 6:12–13, revised standard version.

46. Albrecht Dürer, *The Opening of the Fifth and Sixth Seals* (1511), woodcut; illustrated in Olson, *Fire and Ice*, 5, fig. 5. Cf. Simon Pauli (Lutheran professor of theology at Rostock), "Vom selben Cometen Erinnerung warnung und vermanu[n]g D. Simonis Pauli, so er in einer Intimation und etlichen Predigten gethan hat" (1577); cited in Hellman, *Comet of 1577*, 257–258.

47. Matthias Gerung, *Apocalypse Illustrations* (1547), woodcuts; illustrated in Olson, *Fire and Ice*, 39, figs. 32, 33.

48. Rev. 8:10–11, revised standard version.

49. Rev. 9:1–3, revised standard version.

50. Matt. 24:3–36; Mark 13:3–37; Luke 21:8–36; Thompson, *Motif-Index of Folk-Literature*, A1050–1053.1, A1060, M307.1.

51. In addition to these apocalyptic representations of comets, similar scriptural license was taken a century earlier by the Limbourg brothers. These artists prepared a magnificent illuminated book of hours for the duc de Berry. In their manuscript painting of the capture of Jesus in the garden of Gethsemane, three comets balefully streak across the night sky and prefigure his death. Limbourg brothers, "Jesus in the Garden of Gethsemane," *Les très riches heures de Duc de Berry* (1416), fol. 142^v, Musée Condé, Chantilly. A facsimile edition of the miniatures is *The Très Riches Heures of Jean, Duke of Berry, Musée Condé, Chantilly*, ed. Jean Longnon, Raymond Cazelles, and Millard Meiss (New York: George Braziller, 1969), pl. 107.

52. *Mirabilis Annus, Or the year of Prodigies and Wonders* (n.p., 1661); *Mirabilis Annus Secundus; Or, The Second Year of Prodigies* (n.p., 1662); *Mirabilis Annus Secundus: Or, The Second Part Of the Second Years Prodigies* (n.p., 1662).

53. Thomas Adams, *A Commentary or Exposition upon the Divine Second Epistle Generall, written by the Blessed Apostle St. Peter* (London, 1633), 1136; William Strong, *XXXI Select Sermons, Preached on Special Occasions* (London, 1656), 457; both quoted in Bryan W. Ball, *A Great Expectation: Eschatological Thought in English Protestantism to 1660* (Leiden: E. J. Brill, 1975), 110.

54. In keeping with the Geneva version of the Bible, the comet was to be metaphorically understood. *The Country-man's Festum festorum* (n.p., ca. 1736), 252; Newberry Library, Case MS 5A 30.

55. Thomas Burnet, *The Sacred Theory of the Earth*, ed. Basil Willey (London: Centaur Press, 1965), 298. This is a reprint of the 1690–1691 translation of Burnet's *Telluris theoria sacra*, 2 vols. (London, 1681–1689). An English translation of vol. 1 first appeared in 1684, again in 1691, and at later dates; the first appearance of the translation of vol. 2 was in 1690.

56. Burnet, *Sacred Theory*, 301.

57. The text is a sermon on the comet of 1577. Andreas Celichius, *Theologische erinnerung von dem newen Cometen* (Magdeburg, 1578); discussed in White, *History of the Warfare of Science*, 190–191, from whom I have borrowed my quotations from Celichius.

58. Conrad Dieterich, *Ulmische Cometen-Predigt, von dem Cometen, so nechst abgewischen 1618 Jahrs im Wintermonat erstenmahls in Schwaben sehen lassen* (Ulm, 1620); cited in White, *History of the Warfare of Science*, 191–193.

59. Andreas Dudith, *De cometarum significatione commentariolus* (Basel, 1579); cited in White, *History of the Warfare of Science*, 198.

60. Dieterich, *Ulmische Cometen-Predigt*; cited in White, *History of the Warfare of Science*, 191–193. On Halley and Whiston, see chaps. 8 and 10 below.

61. [Martin Luther], *The Signs of Christ's coming, and Of the last Day* (1522; reprint, London, 1661), 14, a sermon on Luke 21:25, 26; quoted in Ball, *A Great Expectation*, 114.

62. Richard H. Popkin, "Predicting, Prophecying, Divining and Foretelling from Nostradamus to Hume," *History of European Ideas* 5 (1984): 117–135.

63. English translation with Latin text in *Catastrophe Mundi: Or, Merlin Reviv'd, In a Discourse of Prophecies & Predictions, And their Remarkable Accomplishment. . . . As Also A Collection Of all the Antient (Reputed) Prophecies That are Extant, Touching the Grand Revolutions like to happen in these Latter Ages* (London, 1683), 86–89.

64. Cornelius Gemma, *De naturae divinis characterismis seu raris et admirandis spectaculis* (Antwerp, 1575); Tycho Brahe, *Astronomiae instauratae progymnasmatum pars tertia*, in *Tychonis Brahe Dani opera omnia*, ed. J.L.E. Dreyer, Joannes Raeder, and Eiler Nyström, 15 vols. (Copenhagen: Gyldendal, 1913–1929), 3:315–319; Tommaso Campanella, *Articuli prophetales* [1599], ed. Germana Ernst (Florence: La Nuova Italia Editrice, 1977), art. 7 (see pp. 75–76); Germana Ernst, "From the Watery Trigon to the Fiery Trigon: Celestial Signs, Prophecies and History," in *"Astrologi hallucinati": Stars and the End of the World in Luther's Time*, ed. Paola Zambelli (Berlin: Walter de Gruyter, 1986), 265–280; Bernard Capp, *English Almanacs 1500–1800: Astrology and the Popular Press* (Ithaca: Cornell University Press, 1979), 167–168.

65. Theophrast von Hohenheim [Paracelsus], *Usslegung des Commeten erschynen im hoch[ge]birg zu mitlem Augsten Anno 1531* (Zurich, 1531); in Paracelsus, *Sämtliche Werke: I Abteilung, Medizinische, naturwissenschaftliche und philosophische Schriften*, ed. Karl Sudhoff, 14 vols. (Munich: Otto Wilhelm Barth and R. Oldenbourg, 1922–1933), 9:371–393. Paracelsus, *Die Prognostikation auf 24 zukünftige Jahre* (1536), in *Sämtliche Werke*, 10:579–620. See Charles Webster, *From Paracelsus to Newton: Magic and the Making of Modern Science* (Cambridge: Cambridge University Press, 1982), 21–26. For other tracts dealing with cometary portents, see Paracelsus, *Sämtliche Werke*, 9:394–443; and Hellman, *Comet of 1577*, 100–103. For Paracelsus's opinion that guardian deities (*penates superi*) compounded comets from celestial matter in order to form these warning signs, see Tycho Brahe, "De cometa anni 1577" [1578, in German]; in *Tychonis Brahe Dani opera omnia*, 4:381–396; an English translation is available in J. R. Christianson, "Tycho Brahe's German Treatise on the Comet of 1577: A Study in Science and Politics," *Isis* 70 (1979): 110–140.

66. In fact, Zwingli perished that year at the battle of Kappel. White, *History of the Warfare of Science*, 1:182. Paracelsus also sent his tract to Leo Jud. See Webster, *From Paracelsus to Newton*, 26.

67. Hans-Joachim Köhler, "The *Flugschriften* and Their Importance in Religious Debate: A Quantitative Approach"; Dietrich Kurze, "Popular Astrology and Prophecy in the Fifteenth and Sixteenth Centuries: Johannes Lichtenberger"; and Paola Zambelli, "Many Ends for the World: Luca Gaurico Instigator of the Debate in Italy and in Germany"—all published in Zambelli, *"Astrologi hallucinati,"* 153–175, 177–193, 239–263, respectively.

68. Park and Daston, "Unnatural Conceptions."

69. Celichius, *Theologische erinnerung von dem newen Cometen*; cited in White, *History of the Warfare of Science*, 1:182.

70. White, *History of the Warfare of Science*, 1:182.

71. "Die Heyden schreiben: Der Comet enstehe natürlich; aber Gott schaffet keinen, der nicht ein gewiss-Unglück bedeute"; printed as epigrams in Adelarius Praetorius, *Ueber d. Cometstern* (Erfurt, 1580); and Johann Heinrich Voigt, *Cometa matutinus et vespertinus* (Hamburg, 1681). See also Luther's Kirch Postill for the second Sunday in Advent: "Du solt wissen, wann der Comet, der Schwantz-stern scheinet, dass gewisslich ein böss Zeichen das sehe, da ein Unfall nachkommen wird, dann also lehret die Erfahrung"; quoted in Johann Mayer, *Vorstellung des jüngsterschienenen Cometen* (Ulm, 1681), 33. "Wenn Gott will, so muss ein Comet brennen uns zum Schrecken"; quoted in Voigt, *Cometa matutinus et vesperinus*. See White, *History of the Warfare of Science*, 1:182; Robinson, *Great Comet of 1680*, 8–9.

72. White, *History of the Warfare of Science*, 1:182; Thorndike, *History of Magic*, 5:401; Stefano Caroti, "Melanchthon's Astrology," in Zambelli, "*Astrologi hallucinati*," 109–121.

73. For Melanchthon's Latin poem, see Lubieniecki, *Theatrum cometicum*, 352–353. Of note is the couplet, "Nulla aetas vidit flagrantem impune Cometen, / Non leve venturum nunciat ille malum" (No age saw a blazing comet with impunity; / It would announce no small future evil). One German author reversified this couplet as, "Wann ist doch ein Comet am Firmament gesehen, / Das Nicht viel ungemach bald in der Welt geschehen." *Unterschiedliche Beschreibung- und Bedeutungen, so wohl der Cometen ins Gemein, als insonderheit des ... Wunder-Cometen* (n.p., 1681), 16; quoted in Robinson, *Great Comet of 1680*, 8.

74. Thomas Cranmer to Henry VIII, 20 October 1532; printed in *The Remains of Thomas Cranmer*, ed. Henry Jenkyns, 4 vols. (Oxford: Oxford University Press, 1833), 1:13.

75. John Knox, *The Historie of the Reformatioun of Religioun within the Realm of Scotland* [1559–1571] (Edinburgh, 1732), 93.

76. Quoted in James R. Newman, review of *The Comets and Their Origins*, by R. A. Lyttleton, *Scientific American* 189 (July 1953): 88; reprinted in Brandt, *Comets*, 35.

77. Zambelli, "*Astrologi hallucinati*"; Thorndike, *History of Magic*, 5:178–233; Webster, *From Paracelsus to Newton*, 18–19. For the planetary positions, consult Bryant Tuckerman, *Planetary, Lunar, and Solar Positions A.D. 2 to A.D. 1649 at Five-day and Ten-day Intervals* (Philadelphia: American Philosophical Society, 1964).

78. Leonhart Reynmann, *Practica uber die grossen und manigfeltigen Coniunction der Planeten die im̃ jar M.D.XXiiii. erscheinen* (Nuremberg, 1524).

79. On predictions of doom intended as agents to change, see Helga Robinson Hammerstein, "The Battle of the Booklets: Prognostic Tradition and Proclamation of the Word in Early Sixteenth-Century Germany," and Köhler, "The *Flug-schriften*," pp. 129–151 and 153–175, respectively, in Zambelli, "*Astrologi halluci-nati*." Protestant preaching against traditional authority was one factor that stirred up the peasantry and helped them justify revolt against a feudal system. Other factors included overpopulation, overcrowding that was aggravated by aristocratic expropriation of common lands, new imperial taxes, poor harvests in 1523 and 1524, and the emperor's prolonged absence from the empire, which disquieted and emboldened the peasants. See Steven Ozment, *The Age of Reform (1250–1550)* (New Haven: Yale University Press, 1980), 272–285.

80. John Bainbridge, *An Astronomicall Description of the late Comet from the 18. of Novemb. 1618. to the 16. of December following. With certaine Morall Prognosticks or Applications drawne from the Comets motion and irradiation amongst the celestiall Hieroglyphicks* (London, 1619), 30–32.

81. Increase Mather, *ΚΟΜΗΤΟΓΡΑΦΙΑ [Kometographia]. Or a Discourse Concerning Comets* (Boston, 1683), 134 (hereafter cited by the transliterated Greek title, *Kometographia*). See also Christopher Ness, *A Philosophical and Divine Discourse Blazoning upon this Blazing Star* (London, 1681), 11–14.

CHAPTER III
DIVINATION

1. Version printed in John Gadbury, *De cometis: or, A Discourse of the Natures and Effects of Comets* (London, 1665), frontispiece, 54. I have used Gadbury's text because this was the most commonly quoted version of Du Bartas's verses. For example, see S[amuel] D[anforth], *An Astronomical Description of the Late Comet or Blazing Star, as it appeared in New-England in the 9th, 10th, 11th and in the beginning of the 12th moneth, 1664. Together with a brief Theological Application thereof* (Cambridge, 1665); and Increase Mather, *ΚΟΜΗΤΟΓΡΑΦΙΑ [Kometographia]. Or a Discourse Concerning Comets* (Boston, 1683), 143. Although Gadbury, Danforth, and Mather claimed that they used Sylvester's paraphrase and translation of Du Bartas, fol. 14, their text differed measurably from the standard edition of Sylvester, which read, "That hairie Commet, that long streaming Starre, / Which threatens Earth with Famine, Plague, & Warre." See *Bartas: His Devine Weekes and Workes*, trans. Joshua Sylvester (London, 1605), 60; for the original French, see *The Works of Guillaume De Salluste Sieur Du Bartas*, ed. Urban Tigner Holmes, Jr., John Coriden Lyons, and Robert White Linker, 3 vols. (Chapel Hill: University of North Carolina Press, 1935–1940), 2:253–254.

2. Tycho Brahe, "De cometa anni 1577" [MS in German, 1578], in *Tychonis Brahe Dani opera omnia*, ed. J.L.E. Dreyer, Joannes Raeder, and Eiler Nyström, 15 vols. (Copenhagen: Gyldendal, 1913–1929), 4:379–396; translated in J. R. Christianson, "Tycho Brahe's German Treatise on the Comet of 1577: A Study in Science and Politics," *Isis* 70 (1979): 110–140, quotation on 137. (This translation will hereafter be cited as Brahe, "German Treatise on the Comet.")

3. W[illiam] G[reen], *Memento's to the World; or, An Historical Collection of divers Wonderful Comets and Prodigious Signs in Heaven* (London, 1680/81), 26–27.

4. Gadbury, *De cometis*, advertisement to the reader.

5. Green, *Memento's to the World*, epistle dedicatory.

6. C[hristopher] N[ess], *A Full and True Account of the Late Blazing-Star: With some probable Prognosticks upon what may be its Effects* (London, 1680), 3; *A General Collection of Discourses of the Virtuosi of France, Upon Questions of all Sorts of Philosophy, and Other Natural Knowledg. Made in the Assembly of the Beaux Esprits at Paris, by the most Ingenious Persons of that Nation*, trans. G. Havers (London, 1664), 247–248. Compare the theory of William Fulke, first published in the mid–sixteenth century, that the sun drew cometary exhalations out of the earth but did not impart its color to comets. Color depended on the thickness of comet matter. Fulke thought comets were natural causes of dire events, and his

theory will be discussed in chap. 5 below. William Fulke, *Meteors: Or, A plain Description of all kinds of Meteors, as well Fiery and Ayrie, as Watry and Earthy: Briefly Manifesting the Causes of all Blazing-Stars, Shooting-Stars, Flames in the Aire, Thunder, Lightning, Earthquakes, Rain, Dew, Snow, Clouds, Springs, Stones, and Metalls* (London, 1654), 30–32.

7. Ness, *A Full and True Account of the Late Blazing-Star*, 4.

8. William Knight, *Stella Nova; Or, The New Star, Or, An Account of the Natural Signification of the Comet, or Blazing-Star, That hath so long been Visible in England, and other Countreys, and is yet hanging over our Heads* (London, 1680/81), 28–29.

9. Brahe, "German Treatise on the Comet," 138–139.

10. Gaius Plinius Secundus [Pliny the Elder], *Natural History*, trans. H. Rackham, W.H.S. Jones, and D. E. Eichholz, 10 vols., Loeb Classical Library (Cambridge: Harvard University Press, 1969–1986), 2.23.92; Brahe, "German Treatise on the Comet," 138.

11. John Bainbridge, *An Astronomicall Description of the late Comet from the 18. of Novemb. 1618. to the 16. of December following. With certaine Morall Prognosticks or Applications drawne from the Comets motion and irradiation amongst the celestiall Hieroglyphicks* (London, 1619), 33.

12. On Bainbridge's career, see Mordechai Feingold, *The Mathematicians' Apprenticeship: Science, Universities and Society in England, 1560–1640* (Cambridge: Cambridge University Press, 1984), 113–114, 143–148, 160–164.

13. Claudius Ptolemy, *Tetrabiblos*, trans. F. E. Robbins, Loeb Classical Library (Cambridge: Harvard University Press, 1980), 2.9.90; *A General Collection of Discourses*, 247–248; William Lilly, *Englands Propheticall Merline, Foretelling to all Nations of Europe untill 1663. the Actions depending upon the influence of the Conjunction of Saturn and Jupiter, 1642/3. The Progresse and motion of the Comet 1618. under whose effects we in England, and most Regions of Europe now suffer. What kingdomes must yet partake of the remainder of the influence, viz. of War, Plague, Famine, &c. When the English Common-wealth may expect Peace, and the City of London better times* (London, 1644), 44–45.

14. [William Lilly], *Lillies New Prophecy, Or, Strange and Wonderful Predictions, relating to the Year, 1678. As well from the late Blazing-Star* ([London], 1678), 3–4.

15. John Hill, *An Allarm to Europe: By a Late Prodigious Comet seen November and December, 1680. With a Predictive Discourse. Together with some preceding and some succeeding Causes of its sad Effects to the East and North Eastern parts of the World* (London, [1680]), 2. On the causal chain of cometary effects listed here, see chap. 5.

16. Pliny, *Natural History* 2.23.92–93; Brahe, "German Treatise on the Comet," 139; Lilly, *Lillies New Prophecy*, 3–4, 6; Knight, *Stella Nova*, 29–30.

17. Bainbridge, *An Astronomicall Description*, 33–40.

18. From the work of Girolamo Cardano paraphrased by William Lilly. William Lilly, *Anima Astrologiae: Or, a Guide for Astrologers. Being the considerations of the Famous Guido Bonatus Faithfully rendred into English. As also the Choicest Aphorisms of Cardans Seaven Segments* (London, 1676), 47.

19. Knight, *Stella Nova*, 29–30. Cf. Brahe, "German Treatise on the Comet," 138–139.

20. Lilly, *Lillies New Prophecy*, 3–4, 6. See also Lilly, *Englands Propheticall*

Merline, 44–48. Knight too goes beyond the scheme at times; see his forecast based on the comet's passage through Scorpio and Capricorn, in Knight, *Stella Nova*, 29–30.

21. Ptolemy, *Tetrabiblos* 2.9.91; *A General Collection of Discourses*, 247–248.

22. Bede, *Ecclesiastical History of the English Nation*, available in *Baedae opera historica*, trans. J. E. King, 2 vols., Loeb Classical Library (London: William Heinemann, 1930), 5.23–24. No doubt the two comets were the same comet before and after perihelion.

23. Brahe, "German Treatise on the Comet," 138–139.

24. Lilly, *Anima Astrologiae*, 45.

25. S. J. Tester, *A History of Western Astrology* (New York: Ballantine Books, 1989), 25–27, 36–37.

26. Tycho Brahe, *De cometa seu stella crinita rotunda, quae anno antecedente in Octobri & Novembri apparuit* (Uraniburg, 1586), in Brahe, *Opera*, 4:398–407.

27. Lilly, *Englands Propheticall Merline*, 34–36; Cardano cited in Lilly, *Anima Astrologiae*, 45.

Since the first house is just below the eastern horizon, and the twelfth is just above it, the most important houses for cometary astrology are all above the horizon. These houses rule the departments of life as follows: the eighth (*Mors*) governs death, inherited diseases, and accidents; the ninth (*Pietas*), religion, faith, wisdom, and travel; the tenth (*Regnum*), rule, career, ambitions, and practical arts; the eleventh (*Benefacta*), ideals, worthy causes, societies, fortune, and soul; and the twelfth (*Carcer*), restrictions, sorrow, illness, hidden enemies, deceivers, jealous persons, and large animals. For a brief synopsis of astrological principles, see Wayne Shumaker, *The Occult Sciences in the Renaissance: A Study in Intellectual Patterns* (Berkeley and Los Angeles: University of California Press, 1972), 1–17.

28. Brahe, "German Treatise on the Comet," 134, 138.

29. [Pseudo-Ptolemy], *Claudii Ptolemaei Alexa[n]drini astronomorum principis centum sententiae* [*Centiloquium*] (Rome, 1540), par. 100; *A General Collection of Discourses*, 247–248.

30. Ptolemy, *Tetrabiblos* 2.9.90; *A General Collection of Discourses*, 247–248; Lilly, *Englands Propheticall Merline*, 44.

31. Knight, *Stella Nova*, 30. Cf. Gadbury, *De cometis*, 52–53.

32. Brahe, "German Treatise on the Comet," 139.

33. Hill, *An Allarm to Europe*, 2.

34. This traditional belief was supported by the authority of Robert Grosseteste, *De cometis*. Lilly, *Englands Propheticall Merline*, 36–38. Cf. [John Edwards], *Cometomantia* (London, 1684), 148–165.

35. Ptolemy, *Tetrabiblos* 2.13.102; *A General Collection of Discourses*, 247–248.

36. Pliny cataloged ten basic types of comets: hairy stars, bearded stars, javelin stars, daggers, tub stars, horned stars, torch stars, horse stars, goat comets, and blindingly bright comets with silvery tresses and a man's countenance within them. Pliny, *Natural History* 2.22.89–2.23.93. Ptolemy referred to beams, trumpets, and jars. Ptolemy, *Tetrabiblos* 2.9.90. Later astrological writers were far more elaborate in their classification of comets, even giving them names such as Pertica and Veru. A manuscript at the J. Paul Getty Museum depicts nine such types (figs. 20–22). See *Book of Planets, Anatomical Treatise, Book of Synonyms*, probably Ulm, ca. 1450–1475, illumination on vellum, fols. 62ᵛ–63ᵛ (83.MO.137, MS Ludwig XII 8); the

manuscript is described in Anton von Euw and Joachim M. Plotzek, *Die Hand-schriften der Sammlung Ludwig* (Cologne: Schnütgen-Museum der Stadt Köln, 1982), 3:183ff. For other types and illustrations, see chap. 4 of *Liber de significatione cometarum*, an anonymous work composed in Spain about 1238 A.D., and published in Lynn Thorndike, ed., *Latin Treatises on Comets between 1238 and 1368 A.D.* (Chicago: University of Chicago Press, 1950), 25; Roberta J. M. Olson, *Fire and Ice: A History of Comets in Art* (New York: Walker & Company for the National Air and Space Museum, Smithsonian Institution, 1985), 40–41; C. Doris Hellman, *The Comet of 1577: Its Place in the History of Astronomy* (New York: Columbia University Press, 1944), 50, 231–232.

37. *A General Collection of Discourses*, 247–248.

38. Pliny remarked that javelin stars were atrocious omens, but did not say whether of war or something else. If a comet resembled a pair of flutes, it was a portent for the art of music. Pliny, *Natural History* 2.22.89–2.23.93. Ptolemy noted that the shape of the heads implied the kind of misfortune and class of people to be affected. Ptolemy, *Tetrabiblos* 2.9.90.

39. James [Jacques] Gaffarel, *Unheard-of Curiosities: Concerning the Talismanical Sculpture of the Persians; the Horoscope of the Patriarkes; And the Reading of the Stars*, trans. Edmund Chilmead (London, 1650), 364–368.

40. *The Wonderful Blazing Star: with the dreadful Apparition of two Armies in the Air* [broadside] (London: For Langley Curtiss, 1681); Ness, *A Full and True Account of the Late Blazing-Star*, 6; Edwards, *Cometomantia*, 73–79. The connection between comets and housecleaning is with us still in the scouring product Comet cleanser.

41. Knight, *Stella Nova*, 30.

42. *Centiloquium*, par. 100; Lilly, *Englands Propheticall Merline*, 34–36; Cardano cited by Lilly in *Anima Astrologiae*, 45; *A General Collection of Discourses*, 247–248.

43. Lilly, *Englands Propheticall Merline*, 36.

44. Ptolemy, *Tetrabiblos* 2.9.90–91.

45. Lilly, *Englands Propheticall Merline*, 34, 43–44.

46. James Howard Robinson, *The Great Comet of 1680: A Study in the History of Rationalism* (Northfield, Minn.: Press of the Northfield News, 1916), 15.

47. Edwards, *Cometomantia*, 121; cf. Mather, *Kometographia*, 24–142.

48. Lilly, *Anima Astrologiae*, 46.

49. This topic will be examined closely in chap. 6 below.

CHAPTER IV
PORTENTS AND POLITICS

1. Similar cases could be argued for other Western countries and the New World. On colonial New England, see Sara Schechner Genuth, "Blazing Stars, Open Minds, and Loosened Purse Strings: Astronomical Research and Its Early Cambridge Audience," *Journal for the History of Astronomy* 21 (1990): 9–20.

2. W[illiam] G[reen], *Memento's to the World; or, An Historical Collection of divers Wonderful Comets and Prodigious Signs in Heaven* (London, 1680/81); bound with William Knight, *Stella Nova; . . . Or, An Account of the Natural Signification of the Comet* (London, 1680/81), 27.

3. I refer to works simpler and cheaper than most described in Louis B. Wright,

Middle-Class Culture in Elizabethan England (Chapel Hill: University of North Carolina Press, 1935). For a general introduction to ephemeral literature, see Victor E. Neuburg, *Popular Literature: A History and Guide from the Beginning of Printing to the Year 1897* (Harmondsworth: Penguin Books, 1977); Leslie Shepard, *The History of Street Literature* (Newton Abbot: David & Charles, 1973); M. A. Shaaber, *Some Forerunners of the Newspaper in England, 1476–1622* (New York: Octagon Books, 1966); Bernard Capp, "Popular Literature," in *Popular Culture in Seventeenth-Century England*, ed. Barry Reay (London: Croom Helm, 1985), 198–243; Peter Burke, *Popular Culture in Early Modern Europe* (New York: New York University Press, 1978), chaps. 5, 6; Wright, *Middle-Class Culture*, chap. 12.

4. Hyder E. Rollins, "The Black-Letter Broadside Ballad," *Proceedings of the Modern Language Association* 34 (1919): 258–339, esp. 304; Margaret Spufford, *Small Books and Pleasant Histories: Popular Fiction and Its Readership in Seventeenth-Century England* (London: Methuen, 1981), chaps. 3, 4, 5; Barry Reay, "Popular Literature in Seventeenth-Century England," *Journal of Peasant Studies* 10, no. 4 (1982–1983): 243–249, esp. 245; Capp, "Popular Literature"; Shepard, *History of Street Literature*, 34; Neuburg, *Popular Literature*, 62; Bernard Capp, *English Almanacs 1500–1800: Astrology and the Popular Press* (Ithaca: Cornell University Press, 1979), 23, 44; Peter Burke, "Popular Culture in Seventeenth-Century London," *London Journal* 3 (1977): 143–162, esp. 154; Peter Burke, "Popular Culture in Seventeenth-Century London," in *Popular Culture in Seventeenth-Century England*, ed. Barry Reay (London: Croom Helm, 1985), 31–58, esp. 49–50 (this essay is an expanded and emended version of the foregoing work with the same title).

5. Barry Reay, "Popular Culture in Early Modern England," in *Popular Culture in Seventeenth-Century England*, ed. Barry Reay (London: Croom Helm, 1985), 1–30, esp. 1, 7; Rollins, "The Black-Letter Broadside Ballad," 325–329, 336–339; Peter Clark, *The English Alehouse: A Social History, 1200–1830* (London: Longman, 1983), 155, 198; Keith Wrightson, *English Society, 1580–1680* (New Brunswick: Rutgers University Press, 1982), chaps. 1, 7.

6. Roger Thompson, ed., *Samuel Pepys' Penny Merriments* (New York: Columbia University Press, 1977); Roger Thompson, "Popular Reading and Humour in Restoration England," *Journal of Popular Culture* 9 (1975–1976): 653–671; Hyder E. Rollins, ed., *The Pepys Ballads*, 8 vols. (Cambridge: Harvard University Press, 1929–1932); Rollins, "The Black-Letter Broadside Ballad," 332–339.

7. [John Earle], *Micro-cosmographie. Or, A Peece of the World Discovered; In Essayes and Characters* (London: W. S. for Ed. Blount, 1628), sig. F 2ᵛ, "A Pot-Poet."

8. Rollins, "The Black-Letter Broadside Ballad"; Hyder E. Rollins, comp., *An Analytical Index to the Ballad-Entries (1577–1709) in the Registers of the Company of Stationers of London* (Chapel Hill: University of North Carolina Press, 1924); Leslie Shepard, *The Broadside Ballad: A Study in Origins and Meaning* (London: Herbert Jenkins, 1962); Leslie Shepard, ed., *Street Literature: A Collection of 944 Whiteletter Broadside Ballads* (Hale, Altrincham: C. R. Johnson and C. P. Thiedeman, 1980); Shepard, *History of Street Literature*, 14–21, 160–186; Shaaber, *Some Forerunners of the Newspaper*, chap. 8. Some ballad collections include Joseph Lilly, ed., *A Collection of Seventy-Nine Black-Letter Ballads and Broadsides, Printed in the Reign of Queen Elizabeth, Between the Years 1559 and 1597* (London: Joseph Lilly, 1867); Rollins, *Pepys Ballads*; Hyder E. Rollins, ed., *The Pack of*

Autolycus, or Strange and Terrible News . . . as told in Broadside Ballads of the Years 1624–1693 (Cambridge: Harvard University Press, 1927); *The Roxburghe Ballads*, 8 vols. (Hertford: Stephen Austin and Sons for the Ballad Society, 1869–1901; reprint, New York: AMS Press, 1966).

9. Spufford, *Small Books*, chaps. 6–9; Thompson, *Samuel Pepys' Penny Merriments*; Capp, "Popular Literature." Cf. Jean-Pierre Séguin, *L'information en France avant le périodique: 517 canards imprimés entre 1529 et 1631* (Paris: Éditions G.-P. Maisonneuve et Larose, 1964); Roger Chartier, "Culture as Appropriation: Popular Cultural Uses in Early Modern France," in *Understanding Popular Culture: Europe from the Middle Ages to the Nineteenth Century*, ed. Steven L. Kaplan (Berlin: Mouton Publishers, 1984), 229–253.

10. Capp, *English Almanacs*, 29–31, 33, 283–286.

11. Burke, "Popular Culture in Seventeenth-Century London" (1977), 156; Shaaber, *Some Forerunners of the Newspaper*, chap. 10.

12. Rollins, "The Black-Letter Broadside Ballad," 303–304; Shepard, *Broadside Ballad*, 56.

13. Earle, *Micro-cosmographie*, sig. F 2ᵛ.

14. Capp, *English Almanacs*, 51–59, app. 1; Capp, "Popular Literature," 200; Natalie Zemon Davis, *Society and Culture in Early Modern France* (Stanford: Stanford University Press, 1975), chap. 7, "Printing and the People."

15. Shaaber, *Some Forerunners of the Newspaper*, chaps. 4–6, 8; Burke, "Popular Culture in Seventeenth-Century London" (1985), 49; Rollins, "The Black-Letter Broadside Ballad," 321, 335; Capp, *English Almanacs*, 72–88, 287–288; Capp, "Popular Literature," 226–228; Harry Rusche, "Merlini Anglici: Astrology and Propaganda from 1644 to 1651," *English Historical Review* 80 (1965): 322–333; Harry Rusche, "Prophecies and Propaganda, 1641 to 1651," *English Historical Review* 84 (1969): 752–770.

16. Burke, "Popular Culture in Seventeenth-Century London" (1985), 39; the quotation is from Stephen Gosson, a contemporary source.

17. Ibid., 39–41, 43–48; Burke, "Popular Culture in Seventeenth-Century London" (1977), 148–154; John Patrick Montaño, "The Quest for Consensus: The Lord Mayor's Day Shows in the 1670s," in *Culture and Society in the Stuart Restoration*, ed. Gerald Maclean (Cambridge: Cambridge University Press, 1995), 31–51; Gerard Reedy, "Mystical Politics: The Imagery of Charles II's Coronation," in *Studies in Change and Revolution: Aspects of English Intellectual History, 1640–1800*, ed. Paul J. Korshin (Menston, Yorkshire: Scolar Press, 1972), 19–42; Sheila Williams, "The Pope-Burning Processions of 1679, 1680 and 1681," *Journal of the Warburg and Courtauld Institutes* 21 (1958): 104–118; O. W. Furley, "The Pope-Burning Processions of the Late Seventeenth Century," *History* 44 (1959): 16–23.

18. Ralph Josselin, *The Diary of Ralph Josselin, 1616–1683*, ed. Alan Macfarlane (London: Oxford University Press for the British Academy, 1976), 19 (5 September 1644).

19. Keith Thomas, *Religion and the Decline of Magic* (New York: Charles Scribner's Sons, 1971), 78–89.

20. Ibid., 89–96, 104–106.

21. Ibid., 104.

22. *A Blazing Starre* (London, 1642); available in the series Reprints of English Books, 1475–1700, ed. Joseph Arnold Foster, no. 20 (Ingram, 1939).

23. On prodigy literature, see chap. 2 above. On folk tales, see Stith Thompson, *Motif-Index of Folk-Literature: A Classification of Narrative Elements in Folktales, Ballads, Myths, Fables, Mediaeval Romances, Exempla, Fabliaux, Jest-Books, and Local Legends*, rev. and enl. ed., 6 vols. (Bloomington: Indiana University Press, 1955–1958), F493.5, F797, F962.2, Q552.13. On popular preaching, see sermons and catechisms discussing the rain of fire and brimstone on Sodom and Gomorrah (Gen. 19:24).

24. Johann Amos Comenius, *Orbis sensualium pictus*, trans. Charles Hoole (London, 1659; facsimile ed., Menston, England: Scolar Press, 1970), emblems 114, 149.

25. Augustus W. Franks and Herbert A. Grueber, eds., with Edward Hawkins, comp., *Medallic Illustrations of the History of Great Britain and Ireland to the Death of George II*, 2 vols. (London: Trustees of the British Museum, 1885; reprint, London: Spink and Son, 1969), 1:525–526.

26. Rusche, "Prophecies and Propaganda"; Rusche, "Merlini Anglici"; Thomas, *Religion and the Decline of Magic*, 96, 104–105; Michael McKeon, *Politics and Poetry in Restoration England: The Case of Dryden's "Annus Mirabilis"* (Cambridge: Harvard University Press, 1975), chaps. 6–8.

27. John Spencer, *A Discourse concerning Prodigies: Wherein The Vanity of Presages by them is reprehended, and their true and proper Ends asserted and vindicated. . . . To which is added a short Treatise concerning Vulgar Prophecies*, 2d ed. (London, 1665), 15–16.

28. *Mirabilis Annus, Or the year of Prodigies and Wonders* (n.p., 1661); *Mirabilis Annus Secundus; Or, The Second Year of Prodigies* (n.p., 1662); *Mirabilis Annus Secundus: Or, The Second Part Of the Second Years Prodigies* (n.p., 1662); discussed in Thomas, *Religion and the Decline of Magic*, 95–96; McKeon, *Politics and Poetry*, 194–196; Bryan W. Ball, *A Great Expectation: Eschatological Thought in English Protestantism to 1660* (Leiden: E. J. Brill, 1975), 111–114; and John Redwood, *Reason, Ridicule and Religion: The Age of Enlightenment in England, 1660–1750* (Cambridge: Harvard University Press, 1976), 144.

29. Robert Recorde, *The Castle of Knowledge* (London, 1556), sig. a.v^v.

30. Thomas, *Religion and the Decline of Magic*, 341. Attempts to profit from astrological predictions are very ancient. See Pliny on clothing merchants in Rome who jacked up prices after forecasting a severe winter. Gaius Plinius Secundus [Pliny the Elder], *Natural History*, trans. H. Rackham, W.H.S. Jones, and D. E. Eichholz, 10 vols., Loeb Classical Library (Cambridge: Harvard University Press, 1969–1986), 18.60.225.

31. *Julius Caesar* 2.2.30–31; cf. *Hamlet* 1.1.117–118.

32. *1 Henry VI* 3.2.31–32.

33. Ibid. 1.1.1–5. For Shakespeare's astrological references, see Carroll Camden, Jr., "Astrology in Shakespeare's Day," *Isis* 19 (1933): 26–73.

34. Rollins, *Analytical Index to the Ballad-Entries*, nos. 22, 296, 807, 2630 are sixteenth-century examples of comet ballads. For illustrations and discussion of non-English comet broadsides, see J. Classen, *15 Kometenflugblätter des 17. und 18. Jahrhunderts* (Leipzig: Verlag Johann Ambrosius Barth, 1977); Gerhard Bott, ed., *Zeichen am Himmel: Flugblätter des 16. Jahrhunderts* (Nuremberg: Germanisches Nationalmuseum Nürnberg, 1982); R.J.M. Olson and J. M. Pasachoff, "Historical Comets over Bavaria: The *Nuremberg Chronicle* and Broadsides," in *Comets in the Post-Halley Era*, ed. R. L. Newburn, Jr., et al., 2 vols. (Dordrecht:

Kluwer Academic Publishers, 1991), 2:1309–1341; Owen Gingerich, "Tycho Brahe and the Great Comet of 1577," *Sky and Telescope* 54 (December 1977): 452–458; Séguin, *L'information en France*, 95–100, and plates 3, 6, 18, 19.

35. William Lilly, *Englands Propheticall Merline. Foretelling to all Nations of Europe untill 1663, the Actions depending upon the influence of the Conjunction of Saturn and Jupiter, 1642/3. The Progresse and motion of the Comet 1618. under whose effects we in England, and most Regions of Europe now suffer* (London, 1644), 36–48; W[illiam] L[illy], *Merlinus Anglicus Junior: The English Merlin revived: Or, His prediction upon the affaires of the English Common-wealth . . . this present Yeare, 1644* (London, 1644), sigs. A1^v, A3^r.

36. "The English-mans Advice" [1680], in Rollins, *The Pepys Ballads*, 3:47–50; Green, *Memento's to the World*, 23; C[hristopher] N[ess], *A Full and True Account of the Late Blazing-Star: With some probable Prognosticks upon what may be its Effects* (London, 1680), 5–6; Christopher Ness, *A Philosophical and Divine Discourse Blazoning upon this Blazing Star* (London, 1681), 15; *The Wonderful Blazing Star: with the dreadful Apparition of two Armies in the Air* [broadside] (London: For Langley Curtiss, 1681); Increase Mather, *КОМНТОГРАФІА [Kometographia]. Or a Discourse Concerning Comets* (Boston, 1683), 108–138.

37. E[zerel] T[onge], *The Northern Star: The British Monarchy: Or, The Northern the Fourth Universal Monarchy; Charles II, and his Successors, the Founders of the Northern, Last, Fourth, and most Happy Monarchy. Being a Collection of many choice Ancient and Modern Prophecies: Wherein also the Fates of the Roman, French, and Spanish Monarchies are occasionally set out* (London, 1680).

38. *Dictionary of National Biography*, s.v. "Tonge or Tongue, Israel or Ezerel," by Thomas Seccombe.

39. On anti-Catholic sentiment and popular politics, see Williams, "Pope-Burning Processions"; Furley, "Pope-Burning Processions"; Carol Z. Wiener, "The Beleaguered Isle: A Study of Elizabethan and Early Jacobean Anti-Catholicism," *Past and Present* 51 (1971): 27–62; Robin Clifton, "The Popular Fear of Catholics during the English Revolution," *Past and Present* 52 (1971): 23–55.

40. [Christopher Ness], *The Lord Stafford's Ghost: Or, A Warning to Traitors, with His Prophesie Concerning the Blazing-Star* (London, [1681]); *Merlin Reviv'd: Or, An Old Prophecy Found in a Manuscript in Pontefract Castle in York-shire* ([London, 1681]); *A New-Years-Gift for Plotters* (n.p., 1681); *England's Mournful Elegy For The Dissolving the Parliament* (London, [1681]). Cf. *The Country-mans Complaint, and Advice to the King* (n.p., 1681), which attacked the Crown's evidence for the Popish Plot with the verse: "In vain does Heaven her Fiery Comets light, / We stifle th' Evidence, and still grope in night." These balladsheets were collected by Narcissus Luttrell and bound together in a volume entitled *Poetry Longwaies 1678.79.80*, which is currently held by the Newberry Library (Vault, Case 6A 158). See nos. 50, 95, 96, 98, 100, 111; there are two versions of *Merlin Reviv'd*. See also "The English-mans Advice" [1680], in Rollins, *The Pepys Ballads*, 3:47–50.

41. Democritus [pseud.], *The Petitioning-Comet* (London, 1681), letter from author to the printer. Presumably the "New Parliament" was the Oxford Parliament of 21–28 March 1681, which considered the third Exclusion Bill.

42. Ibid., 11.

43. *The Roxburghe Ballads*, 5:15.

44. Ness, *A Full and True Account of the Late Blazing-Star*, 6. See also *Wonder-*

ful Blazing Star. As the language suggests, these authors saw the political turmoil of their day as signs of the Antichrist's last gasp. See the discussion below of apocalyptic tracts that deal with comets and the great conjunctions.

45. Christopher Ness, *The Signs of the Times* (London, 1681), 24–32.

46. Ibid., 37–81.

47. Cf. *The Lions Elegy, Or Verses on the Death of the three Lions in the Tower* (London, 1681), broadside no. 107 in Luttrell's collection, *Poetry Long-waies.* This broadside chides the "superstitious" and "spitefull [who] pervert Nature Laws, /And turn to poyson, every natural *Cause.*" The lions' death need not be seen as a sign of the Crown's downfall or pope's rise in power, but rather as an omen of the happy reconciliation of king and Parliament, and the defeat of Rome's religion.

48. *Dictionary of National Biography,* s.v. "Ness, Christopher," by Edward Walford.

49. [Edward Wetenhall], *A Judgement of the Comet Which became first Generally Visible To Us in Dublin December XIII. About 15 Minutes before 5 in the Evening Anno Dom. 1680. By a Person of Quality* (Dublin, 1682), "Stationer to the Reader," sig. a^r, and p. 1. *Dictionary of National Biography,* s.v. "Wetenhall, Edward," by Alexander Gordon.

50. John Hill, *An Allarm to Europe: By a Late Prodigious Comet seen November and December, 1680* (London, [1680]), sig. A2^r.

51. Ibid., sig. A2^v.

52. For background, see Christopher Hill, *Antichrist in Seventeenth-Century England,* rev. ed. (London: Verso, 1990); Ball, *A Great Expectation*; Richard Bauckham, *Tudor Apocalypse* (Appleford: Sutton Courtenay Press, 1978); Paul Christianson, *Reformers and Babylon: English Apocalyptic Visions from the Reformation to the Eve of the Civil War* (Toronto: University of Toronto Press, 1978); Katharine R. Firth, *The Apocalyptic Tradition in Reformation Britain, 1530–1645* (Oxford: Oxford University Press, 1979).

53. Francis Shakelton, *A blazyng Starre or burnyng Beacon, seene the 10. of October laste (and yet continewyng) set on fire by Gods providence, to call all sinners to earnest & speedie repentance* (London, 1580; S.T.C. 22272), sigs. a.ii^v–a.iij^r.

54. *Catastrophe Mundi* (London, 1683), 17–19, 113–114, which cites, among other sources, Lilly's almanac for 1677. See also *Mirabilis Annus* (1661); *Mirabilis Annus Secundus* (1662); *Mirabilis Annus Secundus: Or, The Second Part Of the Second Years Prodigies* (1662).

55. Tonge, *Northern Star*; [Ness], *Lord Stafford's Ghost*; Ness, *Signs of the Times*; *An Answer of a Letter From a Friend in the Country To a Friend in the City: Or some Remarks on the late Comet. Being a Relation of many Universal Accidents that will come to pass in the year, 1682 . . . with a Sober Caution to all, by speedy Repentance to avert the Judgments that are Impendent* (London, 1681).

56. In fact, Lilly predicted the 1682 comet on the strength of the upcoming conjunction. Lilly, *Almanack* (1677); quoted in *Catastrophe Mundi,* 113–119.

57. Jupiter and Saturn are in conjunction roughly every twenty years. If they meet first in Aries, they will next meet in Sagittarius, and then in Leo, before returning to Aries. This cycle repeats itself three more times in the fiery trigon. After that, the planets have conjunctions in other trigons—earthy, airy, and watery—before returning to Aries. This return to the fiery trigon is called a climacteric conjunction.

Taking precession into account, the whole cycle takes 786.4 years (i.e., roughly 800 years). Cf. the analyses given in Lilly, *Englands Propheticall Merline*, 52–58; Christopher Ness, *An Astrological and Theological Discourse Upon this present Great Conjunction . . . Usherd in by a Great Comet* (London, 1682); and C. Doris Hellman, *The Comet of 1577: Its Place in the History of Astronomy* (New York: Columbia University Press, 1944), 135–136n.37. For historical outlooks engendered by this view, see J. D. North, "Astrology and the Fortunes of Churches," *Centaurus* 24 (1980): 181–211; Eugenio Garin, *Astrology in the Renaissance: The Zodiac of Life*, trans. Carolyn Jackson and June Allen (London: Routledge & Kegan Paul, 1983), 15–29; Germana Ernst, "From the Watery Trigon to the Fiery Trigon: Celestial Signs, Prophecies and History," in *"Astrologi hallucinati": Stars and the End of the World in Luther's Time*, ed. Paola Zambelli (Berlin: Walter de Gruyter, 1986), 265–280.

58. Although the dates varied slightly, Tycho, Kepler, and Alsted correlated the following eras with climacteric conjunctions: (3975 B.C.) = Creation and Fall of Adam; (3182 B.C.) = Enoch; (2388 B.C.) = Noah's Flood; (1514 B.C.) = Moses, Exodus, giving of the Law; (794 B.C.) = Isaiah, servitude of Israelites in Media, loss of ten Tribes; (6 B.C.) = Jesus' coming; (A.D. 789) = Charlemagne; (A.D. 1583) = Stella Nova. See Tycho Brahe, *Astronomiae instauratae progymnasmata* (Prague, 1602), 805–806; in *Tychonis Brahe Dani opera omnia*, ed. J.L.E. Dreyer, Joannes Raeder, and Eiler Nyström, 15 vols. (Copenhagen: Gyldendal, 1913–1929), 3:312. Johannes Kepler, *De stella nova in pede Serpentarii, et qui sub eius exortum de novo iniit, trigono igneo* (Prague, 1606), 29–30; and Johannes Kepler, *Epitome astronomiae Copernicanae* (Linz and Frankfurt, 1618–1621), 6.5.6, "De coniunctionibus magnis et maximis" (854–856); in Kepler, *Gesammelte Werke*, ed. Walther von Dyck et al. (Munich: C. H. Beck, 1937–), 1:182–183, 7:488. Johann Heinrich Alsted, *Thesaurus chronologiae*, 4th ed. (Herborn in Nassau, 1650), 498–501, plus the pullout table, "Speculum Mundi," opposite 501.

59. Tycho Brahe, *De nova stella* (Copenhagen, 1573), sigs. D2ᵛ–E3ʳ; and Tycho Brahe, "De cometa anni 1577" (1578, in German); in Brahe, *Tychonis Brahe Dani opera omnia*, 1:30–34, 4:395 respectively. Kepler, *De stella nova*, chaps. 2–11, 29; and Kepler, *Epitome astronomiae Copernicanae*, 854–856; in Kepler, *Gesammelte Werke*, 1:165–208, 325–335, 7:487–488 respectively. Alsted, *Thesaurus chronologiae*, 498–503; and Johann Heinrich Alsted, *Encyclopaedia* (Herborn in Nassau, 1630), 1105. These works are cited in the popular tracts such as Ness, *Signs of the Times*, 38–39; Ness, *Astrological and Theological Discourse*; C[hristopher] N[ess], *A True Account of this Present Blasing-Star* (London, 1682); *Catastrophe Mundi*, 79–80.

60. Brahe, *Astronomiae instauratae progymnasmata*, 805ff.; in Brahe, *Tychonis Brahe Dani opera omnia*, 3:311ff. Cf. Brahe, "De cometa anni 1577;" in Brahe, *Tychonis Brahe Dani opera omnia*, 4:395.

61. Alsted, *Encyclopaedia*, liber II, p. 125; cited in Ness, *Signs of the Times*, 39; Ness, *Astrological and Theological Discourse*; and Ness, *True Account of this Present Blasing-Star*.

62. Johann Heinrich Alsted, *The Beloved City or, the Saints Reign on Earth a Thousand Yeares*, trans. William Burton (London, 1643), 13; Alsted, *Thesaurus chronologiae*, 501; and Alsted, *Encyclopaedia*, 1105. Reported in Ness, *Astrological and Theological Discourse*; *Catastrophe Mundi*, 80–81; and Mather, *Kometographia*, 136–138.

63. *The Mystery of Ambras Merlins. . . . With Sundry other Misterious Prophecys, both Ancient and Modern, . . . on the signification and portent of that prodigious Comet, seen by most part of the world Anno 1680 with the B[la]zing Star Anno 1682, and the conjunctions of Saturn and Jupiter in October following, and since, all which do purport many sad calamitys to befall most parts of the Europian continent in general before the year 1699. Some sooner then others. . . . Written by a lover of his country's Peace* (London, 1683). Also see Mather, *Kometographia*, 136–139; Ness, *Signs of the Times*; Ness, *Astrological and Theological Discourse*; and Ness, *True Account of this Present Blasing-Star*; Lilly, *Almanack* (1677), quoted in *Catastrophe Mundi*, 113–119.

64. William Lilly, *Mr. William Lilly's History of His Life and Times, From the Year 1602, to 1681*, 2d ed. (London, 1715), 71.

65. Rusche, "Merlini Anglici"; Rusche, "Prophecies and Propaganda"; Thomas, *Religion and the Decline of Magic*, 342–343, 345; McKeon, *Politics and Poetry*, 223–230; Derek Parker, *Familiar to All: William Lilly and Astrology in the Seventeenth Century* (London: Jonathan Cape, 1975).

66. Laws prohibiting the broadcasting of prophecies designed to arouse sedition and rebellion were enacted by Henry IV (1402 and 1406), Henry VIII (1541–1542), Edward VI (1549–1550 and 1552–1553), and Elizabeth (1562–1563 and 1580–1581). See *Rotuli Parliamentorum*, III, 508 and 583; *Statutes of the Realm*, 33 Hen. VIII c. 14; 3 and 4 Edw. VI c. 15; 7 Edw. VI c. 11; 5 Eliz. c. 15; 23 Eliz. c. 2. For further references see Rusche, "Prophecies and Propaganda," 753–754n.2.

67. Sir Francis Bacon, "Of Prophecies," in *The Essayes or Counsels, Civill and Morall* (London, 1625); reprinted in *The Works of Francis Bacon, Baron of Verulam, Viscount St. Alban, and Lord High Chancellor of England*, ed. James Spedding, Robert Leslie Ellis, and Douglas Denon Heath, new ed., 7 vols. (London: Longmans & Company, 1870–1875), 6:465, punctuation modernized. On the ability of prognostication to incite rebellion, insurrection, and dissension, see *Catastrophe Mundi*, sig. A2; and unpublished manuscripts of John Flamsteed (1674) and David Gregory (1686), quoted in Patrick Curry, *Prophecy and Power: Astrology in Early Modern England* (Princeton: Princeton University Press, 1989), 140–141, 144.

68. Thomas, *Religion and the Decline of Magic*, 343–345. Emperor Augustus had in 11 A.D. passed a comparable Roman law! See Frederick H. Cramer, *Astrology in Roman Law and Politics* (Philadelphia: American Philosophical Society, 1954), 99.

69. John Gadbury, *De cometis* (London, 1665), 42; John Gadbury, *Epistle to the Almanack* (1686); attack on Gadbury in Tonge, *Northern Star*, "Publisher's Admonition to the Reader"; *Dictionary of National Biography*, s.v. "Gadbury, John," by John W. Ebsworth.

70. Thomas, *Religion and the Decline of Magic*, 312–313, on astrology.

71. Niccolò Machiavelli, "Discourses on the First Ten Books of Titus Livius" 1.56; in *The Historical, Political, and Diplomatic Writings of Niccolò Machiavelli*, trans. Christian E. Detmold, 4 vols. (Boston: Houghton, Mifflin and Company, 1891), 2:212–213.

72. John Robyns, *De portentosis cometis*; MS described in Lynn Thorndike, *A History of Magic and Experimental Science*, 8 vols. (New York: Columbia University Press, 1923–1958), 5:320–321. See also Thomas, *Religion and the Decline of Magic*, 289.

73. Thomas Cranmer to Henry VIII, 20 October 1532; in *The Remains of Thomas Cranmer*, ed. Henry Jenkyns, 4 vols. (Oxford: Oxford University Press, 1833), 1:13.

74. Gadbury, *De cometis*, 43; Democritus, *Petitioning-Comet*, 3; and [John Edwards], *Cometomantia* (London, 1684), 167–168.

75. Thomas, *Religion and the Decline of Magic*, 290, 298–299; Mordechai Feingold, *The Mathematicians' Apprenticeship: Science, Universities and Society in England, 1560–1640* (Cambridge: Cambridge University Press, 1984), 160–164; Capp, *English Almanacs*, 287.

76. Arthur Wilson, *The History of Great Britain, Being the Life and Reign of King James the First, Relating to what passed from his first Accesse to the Crown, till his Death* (London, 1653), 128–129; Richard Shanne MS cited in Rollins, *Pack of Autolycus*, 21; Gadbury, *De cometis*, 43; Lilly, *Englands Propheticall Merline*, 45; George Wharton, *Calendarium Ecclesiasticum: Or, A New Almanack. . . . Attended on, by . . . Gesta Britannorum. or a Brief Chronologie for 57. years last past, viz. from the year 1600. (in which the late King Charls was born) untill the present 1658.* (London, 1658), sig. E^r; Ness, *Philosophical and Divine Discourse*, 15.

77. *An Ode on the Fair Weather that attended His Majesty on His Birth, To His Kingdom and His Crown* (London, 1661); Reedy, "Mystical Politics," 29.

78. Reedy, "Mystical Politics," 29–30, 33–37; McKeon, *Politics and Poetry*, 233–234.

79. Aurelian Cook, *Titus Britannicus: An Essay of History Royal: In the Life & Reign of His Late Sacred Majesty, Charles II. of Ever Blessed and Immortal Memory* (London, 1685), sig. [A8].

80. Abraham Cowley, "Ode, Upon His Majesties Restoration and Return" [31 May 1660], in *Verses Written Upon Several Occasions* (London, 1663), 22–37, see 22; *Dictionary of National Biography*, s.v. "Cowley, Abraham," by Leslie Stephen.

81. Edward Matthew, *ΚΑΡΟΛΟΥ τρισμεγίςγ ἔπιφανία [Karolou trismegistou epiphania]. The Most Glorious Star, or, Celestial Constellation of the Pleiades, or Charles Waine, Appearing, And shining most brightly in a Miraculous manner in the Face of the Sun at Noonday at the Nativity of our Sacred Soveraign King Charles 2d. Presaging his Majesties Exaltation to future Honour and Greatness Transcending not only the most potent Christian Princes in Europe, but by Divine designment ordained to be the most Mighty Monarch in the Universe: Never any Star having appeared before at the birth of any (the Highest humane Hero) except our Saviour* (London, 1660). Hereafter this work will be cited by the transliterated Greek title, *Karolou trismegistou epiphania*.

82. *An Act for a Perpetuall Anniversary Thanksgiving on the nine and twentyeth date of May*, 12 Car. 11 c. 14; quoted in Ronald Knowles, introduction to John Ogilby, *The Entertainment of His Most Excellent Majestie Charles II, in His Passage through the City of London to His Coronation* [London, 1662], facsimile edition (Binghamton, N.Y.: Center for Medieval and Early Renaissance Studies, SUNY Binghamton, 1988), 14.

83. Audley Mervyn, *A Speech Made by Sir Audley Mervyn his Majesties Prime Serjeant at Law in Ireland, the 11th. day of May in the House of Lords, when he was presented Speaker by the Commons* (Dublin, 1661), 7.

84. Arise Evans, *The Bloudy Vision of John Farly. . . . With Another Vision signifying peace and happiness. Both which Shew remarkable alterations speedily, to*

come to pass here in England, Also a Refutation of a Pamphlet, lately published by one Aspinwall: called a Brief discription of the fifth Monarchy. Shewing . . . that the fifth Monarchy will shortly be established in the Person of Charls Stevvart (London, 1653); Arise Evans, *Light for the Jews* [purportedly written in 1656] (London, 1664), 9–13, 27–28; McKeon, *Politics and Poetry*, 242–243.

85. Matthew, *Karolou trismegistou epiphania.*

86. Henry Bold, *St. Georges Day Sacred to the Coronation of His Most Excellent Majesty Charles the II* (London, 1661); reprinted in Henry Bold, *Poems Lyrique Macaronique Heroique, &c.* (London, 1664), 207–214; John Evelyn, *A Panegyric to Charles the Second, Presented To His Majestie The XXIII. [sic] of April, being the Day of His Coronation. MDCLXI.* (London, 1661); and others discussed in Reedy, "Mystical Politics," 20, 29–31; and Knowles, introduction, 29.

87. John Ogilby, *The Entertainment of His Most Excellent Majestie Charles II, in His Passage through the City of London to His Coronation* (London, 1662), 135.

88. Ibid., 165.

89. Reedy, "Mystical Politics," 31–32; Montaño, "Quest for Consensus," 35–37.

90. John Dryden, *Annus Mirabilis: The Year of Wonders, 1666* (London, 1667), stanzas 16–18, 291–292; reprinted in *The Poems of John Dryden*, ed. James Kinsley, 4 vols. (Oxford: Oxford University Press, 1958), 1:42–105, see 55, 103; discussed in McKeon, *Politics and Poetry*, 158, 166–167, 172–173, 180.

91. See chap, 1 above.

92. Ogilby, *Entertainment.* On Augustanism, see Knowles, introduction, 18–26; Reedy, "Mystical Politics," 22–23; Montaño, "Quest for Consensus."

CHAPTER V
FROM NATURAL SIGNS TO PROXIMATE CAUSES

1. John of Salisbury, *Policraticus, sive de nugis curialium et vestigiis philosophorum libri VIII* [1159], bk. 2; partially available in John of Salisbury, *Frivolities of Courtiers and Footprints of Philosophers*, trans. Joseph B. Pike (Minneapolis: University of Minnesota Press, 1938), 55–151; M. D. Chenu, "Nature and Man at the School of Chartres in the Twelfth Century," in *The Evolution of Science*, ed. Guy S. Metraux and François Crouzet (New York: New American Library, 1963), 220–235; Bert Hansen, *Nicole Oresme and the Marvels of Nature: A Study of His "De causis mirabilium" with Critical Edition, Translation, and Commentary* (Toronto: Pontifical Institute of Mediaeval Studies, 1985), 50–61.

2. For example, William of Conches held that comets were created by God's will in order to signal changes in empires. (Hansen, *Nicole Oresme*, 57.) John of Salisbury believed that comets were signs sent by God to warn men of the fall of thrones and the imminence of assemblies for the election of magistrates. (*Policraticus* 2.13; John of Salisbury, *Frivolities of Courtiers*, 74.)

3. Albertus Magnus, *De meteoris* [post-1240] 1.3.6; Aegidius of Lessines, *Incipit tractatus Fratris Egidii ordinis fratrum predicatorum de essentia, motu et significatione cometarum* [ca. 1264], chap. 4; see Lynn Thorndike, ed., *Latin Treatises on Comets between 1238 and 1368 A.D.* (Chicago: University of Chicago Press, 1950), 70–71, 120–121.

4. Geoffrey of Meaux, *De stellis comatis* [1315]; see Thorndike, *Latin Treatises*, 211.

5. Jean Buridan, *Questions on the Meteora* 1.12; translation prepared by Hansen, *Nicole Oresme*, 60. Hansen worked from the text given in Edmond Faral, "Jean Buridan: Maître ès Arts de l'Université de Paris," *Histoire littéraire de la France* 38 (1949): 462–605, see 554–555. I am indebted to Lorraine Daston for calling this reference to my attention.

6. For a list of their translations, see Edward Grant, ed., *A Source Book in Medieval Science* (Cambridge: Harvard University Press, 1974), 35–41.

7. Edward Grant, *Physical Science in the Middle Ages* (New York: John Wiley & Sons, 1971), chaps. 1, 2.

8. See discussion in chap. 2 above.

9. Jaʿfar ibn Muḥammad Abū Maʿshar al-Balkhī (Albumasar, Albumazar) lived between A.D. 787 and 886. This renowned astrologer was often cited in medieval comet tracts, including those by Albertus Magnus and Roger Bacon. His *Kitāb al-qirānāt* (Book of conjunctions) was written after 869 or perhaps 883. It was translated into Latin by John of Seville, and an incunabulum edition was published; see Albumasar, *De magnis coniunctionibus* (Augsburg: Erhard Ratdolt, 1489). *Dictionary of Scientific Biography*, s.v. "Abū Maʿshar al-Balkhī, Jaʿfar ibn Muḥammad," by David Pingree.

10. Aristotle, *Meteorologica*, trans. H.D.P. Lee, Loeb Classical Library (Cambridge: Harvard University Press, 1978), 1.4, 1.7; see chap. 1 above.

11. Robert Grosseteste, *Lynconiensis de cometis et causis ipsarum*. Based on different manuscripts, two versions of Grosseteste's tract appear in print. See S. Harrison Thomson, "The Text of Grosseteste's *De cometis*," *Isis* 19 (1933): 19–25; and *Die Philosophischen Werke des Robert Grosseteste, Bischofs von Lincoln*, ed. Ludwig Baur (Münster i. W.: Aschendorff, 1912), 36–41. Although it is difficult to date this manuscript, Grosseteste provided a clue when he said it was occasioned by a recent comet. During his lifetime, comets were observed in 1213, 1222 (Halley's), 1224, 1238, 1239, and 1240. In Thomson's edition of this tract, he suggested that it was Halley's comet (mistakenly reported as appearing in 1228) that prompted the essay, but there is little to confirm this. For accounts of contemporaneous comets, see Thorndike, *Latin Treatises*. For more on Grosseteste, see Gordon Leff, *Paris and Oxford Universities in the Thirteenth and Fourteenth Centuries* (Huntington, N.Y.: Robert E. Krieger Publishing Company, 1975).

12. Since every star was associated with a planet, each comet also had a ruling planet.

13. Grosseteste, *De cometis*; Lynn Thorndike, *A History of Magic and Experimental Science*, 8 vols. (New York: Columbia University Press, 1923–1958), 2: 446–447.

14. He is cited by Aegidius of Lessines, the anonymous author of a treatise on the 1338 comet, and Roger Bacon. See Thorndike, *Latin Treatises*; and *The Opus Majus of Roger Bacon*, trans. Robert Belle Burke, 2 vols. (Philadelphia: University of Pennsylvania Press, 1928), 1:400.

15. Aegidius of Lessines, *De essentia*; printed in Thorndike, *Latin Treatises*, 103–184. See Thorndike's helpful introduction (87–103); also Lynn Thorndike, "Aegidius of Lessines on Comets," in *Studies and Essays in the History of Science and Learning Offered in Homage to George Sarton*, ed. M. F. Ashley Montagu (New York: Henry Schuman, [1946]), 403–414; *Dictionary of Scientific Biography*, s.v. "Giles (Aegidius) of Lessines," by William A. Wallace.

16. Like Albertus Magnus, Aegidius reported his own observations on the 1264 comet and used them to impugn the theories of others. His observations were sufficiently good, in fact, to enable Richard Dunthorne in 1751 to compute an orbit from data contained in a manuscript of Aegidius's text found in Pembroke College. See Richard Dunthorne, "A Letter from Mr. Rich. Dunthorne to the Rev. Dr. Long, F.R.S., Master of Pembroke-Hall in Cambridge, and Lowndes's Professor of Astronomy and Geometry in that University, concerning Comets," *Philosophical Transactions* 47 (1753): 281–288.

17. Aegidius, *De essentia*, chap. 8; Thorndike, *Latin Treatises*, 157–158.

18. Albertus Magnus, *De meteoris*, bk. 1, tractatus 3, deals with comets; trans. and printed in Thorndike, *Latin Treatises*, 62–76; reprinted in Grant, *Source Book in Medieval Science*, 539–547. Albertus likely wrote the work soon after the 1240 comet, which he observed (*De meteoris* 1.3.5).

19. Albertus Magnus, *De meteoris* 1.3.11; Thorndike, *Latin Treatises*, 75.

20. Albertus Magnus, *De meteoris* 1.3.11; Thorndike, *Latin Treatises*, 76.

21. Aristotle, *Meteorologica* 1.7.

22. Claudius Ptolemy, *Tetrabiblos*, trans. F. E. Robbins, Loeb Classical Library (Cambridge: Harvard University Press, 1980), 2.9. For further information on Ptolemy's theory of comets, see chap. 1 above.

23. Ibid. 1.4. Ptolemy also detailed the powers of the other planets in this section. Note that the Ptolemaic order of the planets is Saturn, Jupiter, Mars, Sun, Venus, Mercury, and the Moon.

24. Ibid. 2.8.

25. Ibid. 1.4, 2.8. Although Ptolemy placed the sphere of Venus between the Sun and Mercury, Venus strayed farther from the Sun than Mercury did in terms of longitude.

26. Gerard de Silteo (Feltre?), *Summa de astris* [ca. 1291], pars 1, distinctio 23, capitula 1–4; printed in Thorndike, *Latin Treatises*, 185–195, with notes on Gerard's excerpts from Albertus Magnus. Bacon, *Opus majus*, 400. Bacon also discussed the 1264 comet in a manuscript, *De cometis*, and in the *Tractatus brevis* introducing his edition of the *Secretum secretorum*. See C. Doris Hellman, *The Comet of 1577: Its Place in the History of Astronomy* (New York: Columbia University Press, 1944), 53–54. Bacon adopted Grosseteste's metaphor that Mars attracted fiery vapors in a magnetic fashion, and upheld Grosseteste's belief that a comet consisted of sublimated fiery vapor assimilated to a celestial nature.

27. Albertus Magnus, *De meteoris* 1.3.11; Thorndike, *Latin Treatises*, 75. I have substituted "were" for "are" in the quotation.

28. Bacon, *Opus majus*, 400. For a comparable passage in the writings of Albertus Magnus, see *De meteoris* 1.3.11; Thorndike, *Latin Treatises*, 76.

29. Aegidius, *De essentia*, chaps. 5, 7; Thorndike, *Latin Treatises*, 121–122, 131–136.

30. Aegidius, *De essentia*, chap. 8; Thorndike, *Latin Treatises*, 159–160.

31. Albertus Magnus, *De meteoris* 1.3.11; Thorndike, *Latin Treatises*, 75. Albertus Magnus, *De causis et proprietatibus elementorum et planetarum* 2.2.1; Thorndike, *History of Magic*, 2:583. In this work, Albertus surprisingly did not connect comets explicitly with these fearful events in the same fashion in which he had elsewhere linked comets, through Mars, to the death of potentates and war. But what Albertus left unsaid, others like Roger Bacon proclaimed openly.

32. Albertus Magnus [attributed author], *Speculum astronomiae*; cited in Thorndike, *History of Magic*, 2:693–694, 700–701. Bacon, *Opus majus*, 400.

33. Bacon, *Opus majus*, 401.

34. Geoffrey of Meaux, *De stellis comatis* [1315]; and an untitled work opening, "Ad honorem illius sanctissimi astronomi qui solus numerat multitudinem stellarum propriis nominibus vocans eas . . . ," and closing ". . . poterit huiusmodi virtus. Et in hoc terminatur epistola magistri Gaufredi de pronosticatione comete" [1337]. Both are printed in Thorndike, *Latin Treatises*, 210–214, 221–225. Geoffrey of Meaux was a master of arts and medicine, and a lecturer perhaps at the University of Paris. For more on Geoffrey, see Thorndike, *History of Magic*, 3:281–283; Hellman, *Comet of 1577*, 57.

35. Buridan, *Questions* 1.13; Hansen, *Nicole Oresme*, 60; Faral, "Jean Buridan," 555.

36. In question 4 of "Sequuntur probleumata per modum tabule sine responsionibus ad ea," appended to his quodlibetal work, *De causis mirabilium* [ca. 1370], Nicole Oresme inquired whether any future events might be foreknown from the apparition of comets. His answer was yes. (See Hansen, *Nicole Oresme*, 60n.33, 366; I have not been able to examine the manuscript to which Hansen refers.) However, in *Le livre de divinacions* (written shortly after 1361), Oresme had stated that although wars, plagues, and death could sometimes be conjectured from comets, monsters, and the stars, these predictions were general and uncertain. See Nicole Oresme, *Le livre de divinacions* [ca. 1361–1365], chap. 11. The text of the manuscript, B.N. f. fr. 1350, is published with translation in G. W. Coopland, *Nicole Oresme and the Astrologers: A Study of His "Livre de Divinacions"* (Cambridge: Harvard University Press, 1952), see esp. 92.

37. Henry of Hesse, *Questio de cometa* [1368], in *Studien zu den astrologischen schriften des Heinrich von Langenstein*, ed. Hubert Pruckner (Berlin: B. G. Teubner, 1933), 89–138; see esp. chaps. 1–11, and the "conclusio prima" of the *Questio*, 89–119 of Pruckner's edition. For details on the manuscripts and on Henry's other work, see Thorndike, *History of Magic*, 3:472–510, and apps. 27, 30; Michael H. Shank, *"Unless You Believe, You Shall Not Understand": Logic, University, and Society in Late Medieval Vienna* (Princeton: Princeton University Press, 1988); Hellman, *Comet of 1577*, 62–63.

38. John of Legnano, *Tractatus de cometa compilatus per Ioannem de Lignano* [1368]; printed in Thorndike, *Latin Treatises*, 236–259. Also see Thorndike, *History of Magic*, 3:595. John was ambivalent about astrological interpretations of comets. He devoted considerable space to discussion of whether the 1368 comet came under the jurisdiction of Mars or Saturn, Taurus or Gemini, but then disowned his astrological sources and implored true Catholics to place little faith in these authorities. His belated admonition against astrology reads as little more than a pious convention.

39. John of Legnano, *Tractatus de cometa*; Thorndike, *Latin Treatises*, 247. My translation from the Latin.

40. Galileo urged astronomers to reject the theory that comets were burning exhalations on the grounds that the theory was inconsistent with the forecast of winds attendant upon comets; burning comets would consume arid, gusty matter and prohibit windy weather. Mario Guiducci, *Discorso delle comete di Mario Guiducci fatto da lui nell'Accademia Fiorentina nel suo medesimo consolato* (Florence, 1619), 17; trans. by Stillman Drake in *The Controversy on the Comets of 1618: Galileo*

Galilei, Horatio Grassi, Mario Guiducci, Johann Kepler, ed. Stillman Drake and C. D. O'Malley (Philadelphia: University of Pennsylvania Press, 1960), 21–65, esp. 35–36. Galileo's views are discussed further in chap. 6 below.

41. John of Legnano, *Tractatus de cometa*; Thorndike, *Latin Treatises*, 247–248. Cf. Aristotle, *Meteorologica* 2.7–8; and Seneca, *Naturales quaestiones*, bk. 6.

42. John of Legnano, *Tractatus de cometa*; Thorndike, *Latin Treatises*, 248–249.

43. Jacobus Angelus, *Tractatus de cometis* (1402), chaps. 5, 7. In addition to a manuscript preserved at Erfurt, an undated incunabulum edition was printed at Memmingen, Bavaria, in 1480 or 1490. A facsimile of the printed tract appears in Jane L. Jervis, *Cometary Theory in Fifteenth-Century Europe*, Studia Copernicana, no. 26 (Dordrecht: D. Reidel, 1985), 129–161. Jacobus Angelus is discussed by Jervis, 37–42; Thorndike, *History of Magic*, 4:80–87, 662–665; and Hellman, *Comet of 1577*, 66–71.

44. For example, see the works by Brother Matthew of Aquila, a professor of sacred theology of the order of Celestines, *De causis atque natura comete et terremotus* [manuscript, 1456]; Angelo Cato de Supino of Benevento, a self-styled "philosopher and physician," whose treatise on the comet of 1472 was printed at Naples by Sixtus Riessinger in 1472; and Jerome of Sancto Marcho, of the Order of the Friars Minor and a theology student at Paris, *Opusculum de universali mundi machina ac de metheoricis impressionibus* (London, 1505). Jerome of Sancto Marcho's work was possibly written in the fourteenth century. The three works are discussed in Thorndike, *History of Magic*, 4:416–417, 425–428, 703–707. See also William Fulke, *A goodly gallerye with a most pleasaunt prospect into the garden of naturall contemplation, to behold the naturall causes of all kynde of meteors* (London, 1563); reprinted under the title *Meteors: Or, A plain Description of all kinds of Meteors, as well Fiery and Ayrie, as Watry and Earthy: Briefly Manifesting the Causes of all Blazing-Stars, Shooting-Stars, Flames in the Aire, Thunder, Lightning, Earthquakes, Rain, Dew, Snow, Clouds, Springs, Stones, and Metalls* (London, 1654), 30–34. William Fulke, D.D. (1538–1589), the Puritan divine nicknamed "acerrimus Papamastix" for his role in several violent religious controversies, was a fellow of St. John's College and later master of Pembroke College, as well as the earl of Leicester's personal chaplain. See also the work of the radical nonconformist Christopher Ness, *A Philosophical and Divine Discourse Blazoning upon this Blazing Star* (London, 1681), 9–11. Cf. Georgius Busch, *Beschreibung von zugehörigen Eigenschafften und natürlicher Influentz des grossen und erschrecklichen Cometen welcher in diesem 1577. Jahr erschienen* (Erfurt, 1577); discussed in Hellman, *Comet of 1577*, 225–233; *A General Collection of Discourses of the Virtuosi of France, Upon Questions of all Sorts of Philosophy, and Other Natural Knowledg. Made in the Assembly of the Beaux Esprits at Paris, by the most Ingenious Persons of that Nation*, trans. G. Havers (London, 1664), 247; and *The Blazing Star: or, A discourse of comets, Their Natures and Effects: In a Letter from J. B. to T. C. concerning the late Comet seen on Sunday, December the 11. 1664. at Ibbesley in Hantshire* (London, 1665).

45. Hieronymus Cardanus [Girolamo Cardano], *De subtilitate liber XXI* (Nuremberg, 1550), bk. 4; Girolamo Cardano, *De rerum varietate libri XVII* (Basel, 1557), bk. 1, chap. 1; both works to be found in Girolamo Cardano, *Opera omnia*, 10 vols. (Lyons, 1663), see 3:420 and 3:2 respectively. See also Hellman, *Comet of*

1577, 91–96; James A. Ruffner, "The Background and Early Development of Newton's Theory of Comets" (Ph.D. diss., Indiana University, 1966), 40–41; C. Doris
Hellman, "The Role of Measurement in the Downfall of a System: Some Examples
from Sixteenth Century Comet and Nova Observations," *Vistas in Astronomy* 9
(1967): 43–52; Robert S. Westman, "The Comet and the Cosmos: Kepler, Mästlin
and the Copernican Hypothesis," *Studia Copernicana* 5 (1972): 7–30.

46. Cardano, *Opera omnia*, 3:2.

47. Sometimes he implies that comets could be seen only when the air was already dry and thin.

48. Educated at St. John's College, John Edwards received his B.A. in 1657,
M.A. in 1661, and became a fellow in 1658/59. In 1664 he became minister of
Trinity Church, Cambridge. He later had to resign his St. John's fellowship because
of his Calvinist views and soon after became minister of St. Sepulchre's, Cambridge.
In 1683 he received a benefice in Colchester, but in 1686, owing to ill health, he
retired from an active ministry and devoted himself to his publications. *Dictionary
of National Biography*, s.v. "Edwards, John," by Charles J. Robinson.

49. [John Edwards], *Cometomantia. A Discourse of Comets: Shewing their
Original, Substance, Place, Time, Magnitude, Motion, Number, Colour, Figure,
Kinds, Names, and, more especially, their Prognosticks, Significations and Presages.
Being a brief Resolution of a seasonable Query, viz. Whether the Apparition of
Comets be the Sign of approaching Evil? Where also is inserted an Essay of Judici-
ary Astrology, giving Satisfaction to this grand Question, Whether any certain Judg-
ments and Predictions concerning future Events, can be made from the Observation
of the Heavenly Bodies? Both occasioned by the Appearance of the late Comets in
England and other Places* (London, 1684), 65–66.

50. Ibid., 121.

51. Ibid., 61–73.

52. Blaise de Vigenère was described as "un homme très-docte, mais vicieux."
An author and translator of some repute, he served at court as an employee of the
office of the "premier secrétaire d'Etat." He accompanied the French envoy to the
Diet of Worms (1545). He later served as secretary to the duc de Nevers (1547) and
secretary to the ambassador at Rome (1566–1569). In 1584, Henri III gave him the
title of "secrétaire de la chambre." See *Biographie universelle ancienne et moderne*,
nouvelle édition [n.d.]; and *Nouvelle biographie générale depuis les temps les plus
reculés jusqu'à 1850–1860*, 1963 ed., s.v. "Vigenère (Blaise de)."

53. Blaise de Vigenère, *Traicté des cometes, ou estoilles chevelues, apparoissantes extraordinairement au ciel: Avec leurs causes & effects* (Paris, 1578), 95; my
translation. See also Hellman, *Comet of 1577*, 424–425; and Andrew Dickson
White, *A History of the Warfare of Science with Theology in Christendom*, 2 vols.
(New York: D. Appleton and Company, 1930), 1:198.

54. Author of both medical and theological works, Erastus articulated what later
came to be known as Erastian opinions—i.e., the view that the state should have
supreme authority in church matters. See *Biographie universelle*, s.v. "Eraste
(Thomas)"; and *New General Biographical Dictionary* (London, 1848), s.v. "Erastus (Thomas)."

55. Thomas Erastus, "De cometarum significationibus sententia" (1578), appended to Andreas Dudith, *De cometarum significatione commentariolus* (Basel,
1579). Also see Hellman, *Comet of 1577*, 120, 352–353; White, *History of the
Warfare of Science*, 1:198; Thorndike, *History of Magic*, 5:656–657.

56. Johannes Kepler, *De cometis libelli tres* (Augsburg, 1619), 104–105; James [Jacques] Gaffarel, *Unheard-of Curiosities* (London, 1650), 360–363.

57. In the *Astronomiae pars optica* (1604), Kepler suggested that a comet's tail might be formed by the refraction of sunlight passing through a transparent comet head, and he proposed an experimental model of a comet consisting of a glass globe (solid or water-filled) set up near a white wall in a darkened room. When a ray of sunlight intercepted the edge of the globe, a cometary image was projected onto the wall. Kepler later remarked that this model was inadequate to explain the true nature of comets. It required not only a crystalline comet but also very dense aether behind the comet to serve as the projection screen. The aether would also have to become increasingly condensed as one moved away from the comet so that refractions within it would increase with distance and produce the image of a bent comet tail. This did not make physical sense to Kepler. See Kepler, *Ad Vitellionem paralipomena, quibus astronomiae pars optica traditur* (Frankfurt, 1604), 264–267; Kepler, *Tychonis Brahei Dani hyperaspistes* (Frankfurt, 1625), 123, 192–193, 199; the appendix of the former work is translated by C. D. O'Malley, in Drake and O'Malley, *Controversy on the Comets*, 337–355, see 346–347, 353. Cf. Kepler to David Fabricius, 4 July 1603; in Kepler, *Gesammelte Werke*, ed. Walther von Dyck et al. (Munich: C. H. Beck, 1937–), 14:415–416.

58. It was the nova of 1604 that offered Kepler the opportunity to reconsider the origin of comets. See Kepler, *De stella nova in pede Serpentarii* (Prague, 1606), cap. 23; Kepler, *De cometis*, 99–100; cf. Kepler, *Ausführlicher Bericht von dem newlich im Monat Septembri und Octobri diss 1607. Jahrs erschienenen Haarstern oder Cometen und seinen Bedeutungen* (Halle in Saxony, 1608), sig. Aij^r; see Christian Frisch, ed., *Joannis Kepleri astronomi opera omnia*, 8 vols. in 9 (Frankfurt: Heyder & Zimmer, 1858–1871), 7:25; or *Gesammelte Werke*, 4:59. (Since the Frisch edition of this 1608 work is often easier to use, I will give references to its pages as well as to those in the *Gesammelte Werke*.) Michael W. Burke-Gaffney, *Kepler and the Jesuits* (Milwaukee: Bruce Publishing Company, 1944), 28–29.

59. Kepler, *Tychonis Brahei Dani hyperaspistes*, 193; Drake and O'Malley, *Controversy on the Comets*, 347. Cf. Kepler, *De cometis*, 100–101; and Kepler, *Ausführlicher Bericht*, sig. Aij^v–Aiij^r; Frisch, ed., *Opera omnia*, 7:26; Kepler, *Gesammelte Werke*, 4:60.

60. Kepler gave bk. 2 of his *De cometis* the title "Physicus, continens physiologiam cometarum novam." Although "physiologia" often meant natural philosophy, the strong medical and organic analogies in Kepler's theory make it tempting to translate "physiologia" as physiology.

61. Kepler, *De cometis*, 110.

62. Ibid., 103–104. On tail touching the earth, also see Kepler, *Astronomiae pars optica*, 267.

63. Kepler, *De cometis*, 104–105.

64. Thorndike, *History of Magic*, 7:20–21, 25–27.

65. Kepler, *De cometis*, 105.

66. The German text uses "lebhaffte Kräfften"; the Latin employs "facultates."

67. Kepler, *Ausführlicher Bericht*, sig. Aiiij^v–B^r; Frisch, ed., *Opera omnia*, 7:28; Kepler, *Gesammelte Werke*, 4:62. Cf. Kepler, *De cometis*, 105. I have used the translation given in Max Caspar, *Kepler*, trans. C. Doris Hellman (London: Abelard-Schuman, 1959), 302. Note that although Caspar appears to be discussing Kepler's *De cometis* (1619), his quotation and Hellman's translation

are taken from a very similar, yet slightly different, passage in *Ausführlicher Bericht* (1608).

68. Kepler, *Ausführlicher Bericht*, sig. B[r]; Frisch, ed., *Opera omnia*, 7:28; Kepler, *Gesammelte Werke*, 4:62. Cf. Kepler, *De cometis*, 105. Translation taken from Caspar, *Kepler*, 302.

69. Kepler, *Ausführlicher Bericht*, sig. Cij[r]; Frisch, ed., *Opera omnia*, 7:33; Kepler, *Gesammelte Werke*, 4:67. Cf. Kepler, *De cometis*, 111–112. Translation taken from Caspar, *Kepler*, 302–303.

70. Thorndike, *History of Magic*, 7:19, 23–25.

71. Edward Rosen, "Kepler's Attitude toward Astrology and Mysticism," in *Occult and Scientific Mentalities in the Renaissance*, ed. Brian Vickers (Cambridge: Cambridge University Press, 1984), 253–272.

72. Kepler, *Ausführlicher Bericht*, sig. Bij[r]–Bij[v]; Frisch, ed., *Opera omnia*, 7:29; Kepler, *Gesammelte Werke*, 4:64. Cf. Kepler, *De cometis*, 107, 111. Translation taken from Caspar, *Kepler*, 303.

73. Increase Mather, *ΚΟΜΗΤΟΓΡΑΦΙΑ [Kometographia]. Or a Discourse Concerning Comets* (Boston, 1683), 21–22, 132–134.

74. William Whiston, *A New Theory of the Earth, From its Original, to the Consummation of all Things* (London, 1696), 198–199, 336–339, 372; William Whiston, *A New Theory of the Earth. . . . To which is added, An Appendix, containing a New Theory of the Deluge*, 5th ed. rev. (London, 1737), 256–258, 359–363, 424, and app., 469–470 (referring to *New Theory* Phaenomena 38–44, 74).

75. David Gregory, *Astronomiae physicae & geometricae elementa* (Oxford, 1702), bk. 5, prop. 4, corollary 2 (p. 408).

76. See chap. 7 below.

77. Bartholomaeus Keckermann, *Systema physicum septem libris* (Danzig, 1610). See Thorndike, *History of Magic*, 7:378.

78. Christian Severin, known as Longomontanus, *Astronomia Danica*, 2d ed. (Amsterdam, 1640), "Astronomiae Danicae appendix de asscititiis coeli phaenomenis, nempe stellis novis et cometis," chap. 7. Cited in works such as John Gadbury, *De cometis* (London, 1665), 20.

79. Edwards, *Cometomantia*, 137–138.

80. Pierre Petit, *Dissertation sur la nature des cometes* (Paris, 1665), 288.

81. Edwards, *Cometomantia*, 51.

CHAPTER VI
THE DECLINE OF COMETARY DIVINATION

1. This stereotypical view has been held by, among others, Andrew Dickson White, *A History of the Warfare of Science with Theology in Christendom*, 2 vols. (New York: D. Appleton and Company, 1930), 1:201–204; James Howard Robinson, *The Great Comet of 1680: A Study in the History of Rationalism* (Northfield, Minn.: Press of the Northfield News, 1916); Stephen Toulmin and June Goodfield, *The Fabric of the Heavens: The Development of Astronomy and Dynamics* (1961; reprint, New York: Harper Torchbooks, 1965), 239; John C. Brandt and Robert D. Chapman, *Introduction to Comets* (Cambridge: Cambridge University Press, 1981), 19; Carl Sagan and Ann Druyan, *Comet* (New York: Random House, 1985), 59; Donald K. Yeomans, *Comet Halley: Fact and Folly* (Santa Ana: Gold Stein Press, 1985), 39–40; Donald K. Yeomans, *Comets: A Chronological History of Observa-*

tion, Science, Myth, and Folklore (New York: Wiley Science Editions, 1991), 106; Richard Flaste et al., *The New York Times Guide to the Return of Halley's Comet* (New York: Times Books, 1985), 42.

2. See esp. Jane L. Jervis, *Cometary Theory in Fifteenth-Century Europe* (Dordrecht: D. Reidel, 1985); Peter Barker and Bernard R. Goldstein, "The Role of Comets in the Copernican Revolution," *Studies in History and Philosophy of Science* 19 (1988): 299–319; James Alan Ruffner, "The Background and Early Development of Newton's Theory of Comets" (Ph.D. diss., Indiana University, 1966); C. Doris Hellman, *The Comet of 1577: Its Place in the History of Astronomy* (New York: Columbia University Press, 1944).

3. Peurbach and Regiomontanus had no intention of trying to test or discredit the Aristotelian system. Since they found enormously large values of parallax, they continued to place comets beneath the moon (which has a parallax of 1°).

4. He reasoned from another Aristotelian claim that the speeds of planets are inversely proportional to their distances (see *De caelo* 2.10). Since the 1532 comet moved more slowly than the moon, it had to be beyond it. He also thought that terrestrial vapors could not ascend high enough to form comets or supply sufficient fuel for them. Girolamo Cardano, *De subtilitate liber XXI* (1550), bk. 4; see Cardano, *Opera omnia*, 10 vols. (Lyons, 1663), 3:420. Also see Hellman, *Comet of 1577*, 91–96.

5. C. Doris Hellman, "The Role of Measurement in the Downfall of a System: Some Examples from Sixteenth Century Comet and Nova Observations," *Vistas in Astronomy* 9 (1967): 43–52; Robert S. Westman, "The Comet and the Cosmos: Kepler, Mästlin and the Copernican Hypothesis," *Studia Copernicana* 5 (1972): 7–30.

By dividing comets into two classes (above and below the moon), many accepted Tycho's findings without relinquishing the older view. See, for example, Fortunio Liceto of Genua (ordinary professor at Padua), *De novis astris et cometis libri sex* (Venice, 1623); Libert Froidmont (chief professor of philosophy at the College of the Falcon at Louvain), *Meteorologicorum libri sex* (Antwerp, 1627), bk. 3; Sir Francis Bacon, "Descriptio globi intellectualis" (1612), chaps. 4, 7; and "De fluxu et refluxu maris" (ca. 1616), first published in Sir Francis Bacon, *Scripta in naturali et universali philosophia* (Amsterdam, 1653); and Sir Francis Bacon, *Novum organum* (London, 1620), bk. 2, aphorisms 12, 35. Bacon's essays are conveniently printed in both Latin and English in *The Works of Francis Bacon, Baron of Verulam, Viscount St. Alban, and Lord High Chancellor of England*, ed. James Spedding, Robert Leslie Ellis, and Douglas Denon Heath, 7 vols., new ed. (London: Longmans & Co., 1870–1875), see esp. 1:241, 291; 3:53–54, 733, 751–752; 4:131, 178; 5:450, 509, 528. Lynn Thorndike, *A History of Magic and Experimental Science*, 8 vols. (New York: Columbia University Press, 1923–1958), 7:52–54.

6. *De cometis* (1472), attributed to Regiomontanus, but more likely written by a Zurich physician who was a member of Peurbach's school in Vienna. For Latin text and English translation, discussion of its attribution, and commentary on the tract, see Jervis, *Cometary Theory*, 114–120, 195–196.

7. Peter Apian, *Practica auff dz. 1532. Jar* (Landshut, 1531); Peter Apian, *Ein kurtzer bericht d'Observation unnd urtels des Jüngst erschinnen Cometen im weinmon un[d] wintermon dises XXXII. Jars* (Ingolstadt, 1532); A. Pogo, "Earliest Diagrams Showing the Axis of a Comet Tail Coinciding with the Radius Vector," *Isis* 20 (1933): 443–444.

8. Peter Apian, *Astronomicum caesareum* (Ingolstadt, 1540); Girolamo Fracastoro, *Homocentrica eiusdem de causis criticorum dierum per ea quae in nobis sunt* (Venice, 1538), fol. 44ʳ; Hellman, *Comet of 1577*, 86–88.

9. Tycho Brahe, "De cometa anni 1577" [MS in German, 1578]; printed in *Tychonis Brahe Dani opera omnia*, ed. J.L.E. Dreyer, Joannes Raeder, and Eiler Nyström, 15 vols. (Copenhagen: Gyldendal, 1913–1929), 4:379–396; translated in J. R. Christianson, "Tycho Brahe's German Treatise on the Comet of 1577: A Study in Science and Politics," *Isis* 70 (1979): 110–140, see 135.

10. Apian, *Astronomicum caesareum*, pt. 2, chap. 14, p. 5, col. 1.

11. Girolamo Cardano, *De rerum varietate libri XVII* (1557), bk. 1, chap. 1; Cardano, *De subtilitate* (1550), bk. 4; see Cardano, *Opera omnia* (1663), 3:2, 420. Jean Pena, *Euclides optica et catoptrica; praefatio de usu optices* (Paris, 1557); Brahe, "De cometa anni 1577"; Johannes Kepler, *Ad Vitellionem paralipomena, quibus astronomiae pars optica traditur* (Frankfurt, 1604), 264–267; Johannes Kepler, *Tychonis Brahei Dani hyperaspistes* (Frankfurt, 1625), 192–193; Michael Maestlin, *Observatio & demonstratio cometae aetherei qui anno 1577. et 1578 . . . apparuit* (Tübingen, 1578), chap. 1; John Bainbridge, *An Astronomicall Description of the late Comet from the 18. of Novemb. 1618. to the 16. of December following. With certaine Morall Prognosticks or Applications drawne from the Comets motion and irradiation amongst the celestiall Hieroglyphicks* (London, 1619), 3–6, 9–11, 23–25. Barker and Goldstein, "Role of Comets," 313–315; Thorndike, *History of Magic*, 6:71; Hellman, *Comet of 1577*, 127–128, 146–147, 309; Ruffner, "Background and Early Development," 57, 64.

12. J. A. Ruffner, "The Curved and the Straight: Cometary Theory from Kepler to Hevelius," *Journal for the History of Astronomy* 2 (1971): 178–194.

13. Johannes Kepler, *De cometis libelli tres* (Augsburg, 1619), 98. For others, see Ruffner, "Curved and the Straight."

14. Copernicus himself adopted the Aristotelian theory of sublunar comets and mentioned their motions in *De revolutionibus* only as evidence that the upper regions of the atmosphere were deprived of the earth's diurnal rotation, such that comets seemed to rise and set with the stars. Nicolaus Copernicus, *De revolutionibus orbium coelestium* (Nuremberg, 1543), 1.8.

15. Robert Recorde, *Castle of Knowledge* (London, 1556), sig. a.vᵛ; Francis R. Johnson, *Astronomical Thought in Renaissance England: A Study of the English Scientific Writings from 1500 to 1645* (Baltimore: Johns Hopkins Press, 1937; reprint, New York: Octagon Books, 1968), 126–128.

16. Leonard Digges, *A Prognostication of right good effect* (London, 1555), 5, 31; Thomas Digges, *Alae seu scalae mathematicae* (London, 1573), a work in which Digges associated the celestial nova of 1572 with comets; Thomas Digges, "A Perfit Description of the Caelestiall Orbes," a discusion of the Copernican system appended to Leonard Digges, *A Prognostication everlasting of ryghte good effecte* (London, 1576). See also Ruffner, "Background and Early Development," 48.

17. Bainbridge, *An Astronomicall Description*, 3, 19, and passim. Another to examine the 1618 comet with a telescope was Johann Baptista Cysat, *Mathemata astronomica de loco, motu, magnitudine, et causis cometae qui sub finem anni 1618. et initium anni 1619 in coelo fulsit* (Ingolstadt, 1619).

18. Thomas Birch, *The History of the Royal Society of London*, 4 vols. (London, 1756–1757), 4:63–64 (meeting held on 12 January 1681). On Wren's analysis of

comet paths in the 1660s, see J. A. Bennett, *The Mathematical Science of Christopher Wren* (Cambridge: Cambridge University Press, 1982), 65–69.

19. See Maestlin, *Observatio & demonstratio cometae aetherei*; Cornelius Gemma, *De prodigiosa specie, naturaq. cometae, qui nobis effulsit altior lunae sedibus* (Antwerp, 1578); Helisaeus Roeslin, *Theoria nova coelestium ΜΕΤΕΩΡΩΝ [meteoron]* ([Strasbourg], 1578), chaps. 6, 7; Paulus Fabricius, *Cometa visus mense Martio. LVI. anno* [a broadside with comet path illustrated and text] (Vienna, [1556]); Paulus Fabricius, *Judicium de cometa, qui anno Domini M.D.LXXVII. a 10. die Novemb: usque ad 22. diem Decemb: Viennae conspectus est. In quo varia de cometarum natura & forma in genera breviter tractantur* (Vienna, [1577]); Francis Shakelton, *A blazyng Starre or burnyng Beacon, seene the 10. of October laste (and yet continewyng) set on fire by Gods providence, to call all sinners to earnest & speedie repentance* (London, 1580), sigs. Diij–Diiij; Hellman, *Comet of 1577*, 106–107, 146–173, 182–183; Thorndike, *History of Magic*, 6:74–81; Westman, "Comet and the Cosmos"; Ruffner, "Background and Early Development," 49–57.

20. Brahe, "German Treatise on the Comet," 133, 137; Tycho Brahe, *De cometa seu stella crinita rotunda, quae anno antecedente in Octobri & Novembri apparuit* (Uraniburg, 1586); and a manuscript, unpublished in Tycho's lifetime, entitled "De crinita stella non caudata quae anno 1585 antecedente mense Octobri & Novembri apparuit" (1586). See Brahe, *Tychonis Brahe Dani opera omnia*, 4:397–414.

21. Increase Mather, *ΚΟΜΗΤΟΓΡΑΦΙΑ [Kometographia]. Or a Discourse Concerning Comets* (Boston, 1683), 21–22, 132–134. Cf. Kepler, *De cometis*, 103–104.

22. René Descartes, *Le Monde de M' Descartes, ou le traité de la lumiere* [ca. 1629–1633] (Paris, 1664), chap. 9; and René Descartes, *Principia philosophiae* (Amsterdam, 1644), pt. 3, secs. 115, 119, 126–129, 133–139.

23. Claude Mallement de Messange, *Dissertation sur les cometes à monsieur le procureur général du Grand Conseil* (Paris, 1681), 11–12, 15–17. Extracts from the work are reprinted in Pierre Bayle, *Pensées diverses sur la comète*, critical edition, ed. A. Prat, 2 vols. (Paris: Librairie E. Droz, 1939), 1:48–49, 363–364; and the essay is discussed in Thorndike, *History of Magic*, 8:340–341.

24. Seth Ward, *De cometis* (Oxford, 1653); Giovanni Domenico Cassini, *Hypothesis motus cometae novissimi*, MS transmitted to the Royal Society in February 1665, and printed in *The Correspondence of Henry Oldenburg*, ed. A. Rupert Hall and Marie Boas Hall, 13 vols. (vols. 1–9, Madison: University of Wisconsin Press, 1965–1973; vols. 10–11, London: Mansell, 1975–1977; vols. 12–13, London: Taylor & Francis, 1986), 2:363–367; Pierre Petit, *Dissertation sur la nature des cometes* (Paris, 1665); Jakob Bernoulli, *Conamen novi systematis cometarum, pro motu eorum sub calculum revocando & apparitionibus praedicendis adornatum* (Amsterdam, 1682); Ruffner, "Background and Early Development," 134–152. For Newton and Halley, see chaps. 7 and 8 below.

25. Flamsteed to Richard Towneley, 11 May 1677, Royal Society MS 243, no. 26; quoted in Patrick Curry, *Prophecy and Power: Astrology in Early Modern England* (Princeton: Princeton University Press, 1989), 141.

26. Fabricius, *Cometa visus mense Martio. LVI. anno*; William Whiston, *A New Theory of the Earth* (London, 1696).

27. Curry, *Prophecy and Power*, 141–142.

28. Lucius Annaeus Seneca, *Naturales quaestiones*, trans. Thomas H. Corcoran, 2 vols., Loeb Classical Library (Cambridge: Harvard University Press, 1971–1972),

7.28.1; cf. Brahe, "German Treatise on the Comet," 133; Sir Thomas Browne, *Pseudodoxia Epidemica* [1650 edition], ed. Robin Robbins, 2 vols. (Oxford: Clarendon Press, 1981), bk. 6, chap. 14 (1:535); Thorndike, *History of Magic*, 7:424.

29. John Swan, *Speculum Mundi: or A Glasse Representing the Face of the World* (Cambridge, 1635; S.T.C., 23516), 81; quoted in Johnson, *Astronomical Thought*, 276–277.

30. Julius Caesar Scaliger, *Exotericarum exercitationum liber quintus decimus, de subtilitate, ad Hieronymum Cardanum* (Paris, 1557), 79.2; Petit, *Dissertation sur la nature des cometes*; and Baltasar Bekker, *Ondersoek van de Betekeninge der Kometen* (Leuwarden, 1683; reprint, Amsterdam, 1692).

31. Pierre Gassendi, "Commentarii de rebus caelestibus," in *Opera omnia*, 6 vols. (Lyons, 1658), 4:77–79.

32. Thorndike, *History of Magic*, 7:436, 445.

33. Pierre Gassendi, *Viri illustris Nicolai Claudii Fabricii de Peiresc, Senatoris Aquisextiensis vita* (Paris, 1641), bk. 3, sec. 1618; in *Opera omnia*, 5:286b. Pierre Gassendi, *The Mirrour of True Nobility & Gentility. Being the Life of The Renowned Nicolaus Claudius Fabricius Lord of Peiresk, Senator of the Parliament of Aix*, trans. W. Rand (London, 1657), bk. 3, pp. 188–189.

34. Pierre Gassendi, *Syntagma philosophicum* [1658], "Physica," sec. 2, bk. 5, entitled "De cometis, et novis sideribus." See Gassendi, *Opera omnia*, 1:711b–712. His critique is also quoted at length in French translation in Alexandre Guy Pingré, *Cométographie, ou Traité Historique et Théorique des Comètes*, 2 vols. (Paris, 1783–1784), 1:100–101.

35. [Pierre Bayle], *Lettre à M.L.A.D.C. Docteur de Sorbonne. Où il est prouvé par plusieurs raisons tirées de la philosophie, & de la theologie, que les cometes ne sont point le présage d'aucun malheur. Avec plusieurs reflexions morales & politiques, & plusieurs observations historiques; & la refutation de quelques erreurs populaires* (Cologne [Rotterdam], 1682).

36. The second edition was entitled *Pensées diverses écrites à un Docteur de Sorbonne, à l'occasion de la Comète qui parut au mois de Décembre 1680.* Two more French editions appeared in Bayle's lifetime (1699, 1704), and an English edition appeared in 1708: Pierre Bayle, *Miscellaneous Reflections, Occasion'd by the Comet Which appear'd In December 1680. Chiefly tending to explode Popular Superstitions*, 2 vols. (London, 1708).

37. For background to the *Pensées* and subsequent disputes, see A. Prat's introduction to the critical edition of Bayle, *Pensées diverses* (1939); and Robinson, *Great Comet of 1680*, 91–106.

38. Gassendi, *Opera omnia*, 1:712; Bayle, *Pensées diverses*, sec. 263.

39. Bayle, *Pensées diverses*, secs. 235–246, 263.

40. Ibid., secs. 9–16, 263. See also sec. 13, which Bayle omitted from the second and subsequent editions of his book, but which can be found in vol. 1, app. 1 of the critical edition.

41. Ibid., secs. 16, 23–24, 29, 35–44, 263; Gassendi, *Opera omnia*, 1:712, 5286; Gassendi, *Mirrour of True Nobility*, bk. 3, p. 189.

42. Bayle, *Pensées diverses*, secs. 24, 263; Gassendi, *Opera omnia*, 1:712.

43. Bayle, *Pensées diverses*, secs. 72, 263; Gassendi, *Opera omnia*, 1:712, 5:286; Gassendi, *Mirrour of True Nobility*, bk. 3, p. 188.

44. Bayle, *Pensées diverses*, secs. 76–77.

45. Ibid., secs. 74, 263.

46. Ibid., secs. 17–22, 45–48, 74; Gassendi, *Syntagma philosophicum* (1658), "Physica," sec. 2, bks. 5, 6.

47. Bayle, *Pensées diverses*, secs. 33, 56, 263.

48. Ibid., secs. 33, 205–216.

49. Ibid., secs. 56, 263.

50. Ibid., secs. 58–59, 204, 216.

51. Ibid., secs. 57, 60, 263.

52. Ibid., secs. 103–104, 219–220.

53. Ibid., secs. 61–70, 73, 79, 81–84.

54. Ibid., sec. 57; Gassendi, *Opera omnia*, 1:712.

55. They were often repeated and discussed. See, for example, *A Dissertation on Comets. Extracted from the Writings of the most eminent modern Astronomers and Philosophers. In a Letter to a Reverend Professor. To which is prefixed, The Theory of a Comet, by Sir Isaac Newton* (London, [ca. 1720]).

56. [John Edwards], *Cometomantia. A Discourse of Comets: Shewing their Original, Substance, Place, Time, Magnitude, Motion, Number, Colour, Figure, Kinds, Names, and, more especially, their Prognosticks, Significations and Presages. Being a brief Resolution of a seasonable Query, viz. Whether the Apparition of Comets be the Sign of approaching Evil? Where also is inserted an Essay of Judiciary Astrology, giving Satisfaction to this grand Question, Whether any certain Judgments and Predictions concerning future Events, can be made from the Observation of the Heavenly Bodies? Both occasioned by the Appearance of the late Comets in England and other Places* (London, 1684), 132–179.

57. Ibid., 133–136; Gassendi, *Opera omnia*, 1:712. On similar grounds, Edwards also attacked John Spencer's sermon *A Discourse concerning Prodigies* ([Cambridge], 1663). Spencer saw God as an omniscient creator whose will was manifest in the regular laws of nature and the unfolding course of history. In contrast, Edwards emphasized God's power to intervene directly in the world in order to alter the course of human or natural history. For a comparative study of the historiography and cometography of Edwards and Spencer, see John Gascoigne, "'The Wisdom of the Egyptians' and the Secularisation of History in the Age of Newton," in *The Uses of Antiquity: The Scientific Revolution and the Classical Tradition*, ed. Stephen Gaukroger (Dordrecht: Kluwer Academic, 1991), 171–212.

58. Scaliger, *Exercitationes* 79.2.

59. Edwards, *Cometomantia*, 285.

60. Ibid., 90.

61. Ibid., 292–293.

62. The opening pitch was thrown by [Orazio Grassi], *De tribus cometis anni M.DC.XVIII. Disputatio astronomica publicè habita in Collegio Romano Societatis Jesu ab uno ex patribus eiusdem societatis* (Rome, 1619). Galileo's response appeared under the name of his disciple Mario Guiducci (1585–1646): Mario Guiducci, *Discorso delle comete di Mario Guiducci fatto da lui nell'Accademia Fiorentina nel suo medesimo consolato* (Florence, 1619). Greatly offended, Grassi prepared his rebuttal under the pseudonym of Lothario Sarsi of Siguenza (a defective anagram of Oratio Grassio Savonensi): Lothario Sarsi [Grassi], *Libra astronomica ac philosophica* (Perugia, 1619). While Galileo began to compose *The Assayer*, Guiducci himself replied in a letter (published in Florence, 1620), which he addressed to Father Tarquinio Galluzzi, a former professor of his at the Collegio Romano. After Galileo weighed Grassi's arguments, he published *Il saggiatore, nel*

quale con bilancia esquisita, e giusta si ponderano le cose contenute nella Libra astronomica, e filosofica, di Lotario Sarsi Sigensano, scritto in forma de lettera, all'illustrissimo, e reverendissimo monsig. d. Virginio Cesarini (Rome, 1623). In response, there appeared Lothario Sarsi [Grassi], *Ratio ponderum librae et simbellae: in qua quid e Lotharii Sarsii libra astronomica, quidque e Galilei Galilei simbellatore, de cometis statuendum sit* (Paris, 1626). With the exception of the latter work, translations of the above texts appear in Stillman Drake and C. D. O'Malley, eds., *The Controversy on the Comets of 1618: Galileo Galilei, Horatio Grassi, Mario Guiducci, Johann Kepler* (Philadelphia: University of Pennsylvania Press, 1960).

63. Guiducci [i.e., Galileo], *Discorso delle comete*, 17; Drake and O'Malley, *Controversy on the Comets*, 35–36.

64. Sarsi [Grassi], *Libra astronomica*, 70; Guiducci, *Discorso delle comete*; Galileo, *Il saggiatore*, 84–86, 91, 97, 105, 112–113, 126, 233–234; Drake and O'Malley, *Controversy on the Comets*, 21–65, 131–132, 229–230, 233, 237, 244–245, 250–251, 260, 334–335.

65. Bacon, "Descriptio globi intellectualis," chap. 4; Francis Bacon, "Catalogue of Particular Histories" appended to the *Preparative towards a Natural and Experimental History [Parasceve ad historiam naturalem et experimentalem]* (London, 1620); Bacon, *Works*, 1:405, 3:732–733, 4:265, 5:509.

66. Bacon, *Novum organum*, bk. 2, aphorism 12; Bacon, *Works*, 4:131.

67. Francis Bacon, *The Essayes or Counsels, Civill and Morall* (London, 1625), no. 58, "Of Vicissitude of Things"; Bacon, *Works*, 6:513.

68. Francis Bacon, *De augmentis scientiarum [The Advancement of Learning]* (London, 1623); Bacon, *Works*, 1:558, 4:353.

69. Sir Thomas Browne to Thomas Browne (his son), 1 January 1665; Sir Thomas Browne to Dr. Edward Browne (his son), 17 December 1680, 7 January 1681, and 12 January 1681; in *The Works of Sir Thomas Browne*, ed. Geoffrey Keynes, 4 vols. (Chicago: University of Chicago Press, 1964), 4:19, 175, 177–179.

70. Browne, *Pseudodoxia epidemica*, bk. 6, chap. 14 (1:535). Browne drew on a work by Niccolo Cabeo, *In quatuor libros meteorologicorum Aristotelis commentaria et quaestiones*, 4 vols. (Rome, 1646), liber 1, textus 37, quaestio 10 [reads "9" due to printer's error], which is found at 1:212–215. See Thorndike, *History of Magic*, 7:424.

71. Browne, *Pseudodoxia epidemica*, bk. 7, chap. 4 (1:546).

72. Samuel Pepys, *The Diary of Samuel Pepys*, ed. Robert Latham and William Matthews, 11 vols. (Berkeley and Los Angeles: University of California Press, 1970–1983), 15 December 1664 (5:346): "To the Coffee-house, where great talke of the Comett seen in several places and among our men at sea and by my Lord Sandwich, to whom I intend to write about it tonight."

73. Hooke delivered some lectures on the comet here.

74. The comets were discussed during at least seventeen meetings between 14 December 1664 and 21 June 1665, and publications pertaining to them were mentioned periodically at later dates. See Birch, *History of the Royal Society*, 1:508, 510–511, 2:1–63 passim; John Evelyn, *The Diary of John Evelyn*, ed. E. S. DeBeer, 6 vols. (Oxford: Clarendon Press, 1955), 3:392, 396–397; Bennett, *Mathematical Science of Christopher Wren*, 65–69. When the Royal Society recessed in June 1665 until February 1666 (for the duration of the plague), Henry Oldenburg corresponded with dispersed members about the comets; see Oldenburg, *Correspondence*, vols. 2, 3 passim.

75. Pepys, *Diary*, 15, 17, 21, 23, 24, 27 December 1664, 1 March 1665, and 6 April 1665 (5:346–357 passim, 6:48, 75). See also Marjorie Hope Nicolson, *Pepys' "Diary" and the New Science* (Charlottesville: University Press of Virginia, 1965), 36–37.

76. Robert Hooke, *Lectures and Collections Made by Robert Hooke, Secretary of the Royal Society. Cometa. . . . Microscopium* (London, 1678); reprinted in Hooke, *Lectiones Cutlerianae* (London, 1679); which is reprinted in R. T. Gunther, ed., *Early Science in Oxford*, vol. 8 (Oxford: For the editor, 1931). See also Pepys, *Diary*, 1 March 1665 (6:48); and Birch, *History of the Royal Society*, 2:19.

77. Evelyn, *Diary*, 3:392–393, 396–397.

78. Oldenburg, *Correspondence*, vols. 2–4 passim; and *Philosophical Transactions* 1 (1665–1666), passim.

79. Stanislaw Lubieniecki, *Theatrum cometicum* (Amsterdam, 1667; 2d ed., Leiden, 1681). Lubieniecki (1623–1675), a leader of the Socinian sect in northern Europe, was driven from Poland because of religious persecution but found employment under the king of Denmark. He reputedly was poisoned at Hamburg by religious enemies. On his work, see Robinson, *Great Comet of 1680*, 18–20.

80. Lubieniecki to Oldenburg, 10 July 1666 and 16 November 1666, Oldenburg, *Correspondence*, 3:179–181, 284–285.

81. Oldenburg, *Correspondence*, vol. 3, passim.

82. See esp. Birch, *History of the Royal Society*, 1:508–511, 2:1–63, 4:57–90, 162–167 passim.

83. Ibid., 4:66 (meeting held 19 January 1681).

84. Ibid., 74 (meeting on 16 March 1681).

85. J. H. Voigt, *Cometa matutinus et vespertinus* (Hamburg, 1681). The quotations from Luther are given above in chap. 2. On Voigt's various cometary discourses, see Robinson, *Great Comet of 1680*, 40–43.

86. Evelyn, *Diary*, 2:6–7; 3:392–393, 396–397, 477; 4:235; *The Diary of Ralph Thoresby, F.R.S.*, ed. Joseph Hunter, 2 vols. (London: Henry Colburn and Richard Bentley, 1830), 1:132.

87. *Journal des sçavans* 1 (1665–1666): 49–58. (I have used the Amsterdam edition of the *Journal*; vol. 1 was reprinted in 1684.) See also Thorndike, *History of Magic*, 8:324–325. Summaries of Cassini's observations, unvarnished by astrology, were often published too. E.g., *Journal des sçavans* 9 (1681): 157–168.

88. *Journal des sçavans* 1 (1665–1666): 163; *Journal des sçavans* 9 (1681): 14, 53–56; Thorndike, *History of Magic*, 8:325, 338; Robinson, *Great Comet of 1680*, 80–81.

89. *Journal des sçavans* 10 (1682): 86, 340; the work noted was Michael Praun, *Cometae malus genius, sive dissertatio singularis qua ad excitanda eruditorum ingenia, disquiritur an non cometae per malos genios regantur* (Frankfurt, 1681). Thorndike, *History of Magic*, 8:338.

90. On historical marked eggs, see Robinson, *Great Comet of 1680*, 27–28. As recently as 19 January 1985, the *Chicago Tribune* reported the discovery of a Halley's comet egg in Studley, England.

91. Lubieniecki, *Theatrum cometicum*, 16.

92. Friedrich Madeweis, *Cometa A[nn]o MDC LXXX et LXXXI* (Berlin, 1681). (For more on the author of this broadside, see Robinson, *Great Comet of 1680*, 47.) Other woodcuts of the egg are depicted in Mark Littmann and Donald K. Yeomans, *Comet Halley: Once in a Lifetime* (Washington, D.C.: American Chemical Society,

1985), 20; Roberta J. M. Olson, *Fire and Ice: A History of Comets in Art* (New York: Walker & Company for the National Air and Space Museum, Smithsonian Institution, 1985), 60; and Peter Lancaster Brown, *Comets, Meteorites and Men* (New York: Taplinger Publishing Company, 1974), pl. 34 following p. 174.

93. *Journal des sçavans* 9 (1681): 25–26, my translation.

94. Ibid., 26, my translation.

95. "Une Comete dans un Oeuf!" wrote Fontenelle.

96. Bernard le Bovier de Fontenelle, *La Comete. Comedie* (Paris, 1681), sc. 12, pp. 46–50, see 48 for quotations; reprinted in *Oeuvres de Monsieur de Fontenelle*, new ed., 12 vols. (Amsterdam, 1764), 10:187–220. Robinson, *Great Comet of 1680*, 83–85, describes the play at length.

97. M. de Bassompierre to M. de Luines, 1621, soon after the death of Philip III of Spain; quoted in Bayle, *Pensées diverses*, sec. 57, my translation.

98. Keith Thomas, *Religion and the Decline of Magic* (New York: Charles Scribner's Sons, 1971), 352.

99. Ibid., chaps. 11, 12.

100. Edwards, *Cometomantia*, 94.

101. Peter Burke, *Popular Culture in Early Modern Europe* (New York: New York University Press, 1978).

102. Ibid., 276–280.

103. Ibid., 207–243, 271; Thomas, *Religion and the Decline of Magic*, chaps. 2, 3, 9; Barry Reay, "Popular Religion," in *Popular Culture in Seventeenth-Century England*, ed. Barry Reay (London: Croom Helm, 1985), 91–128.

104. Browne, *Pseudodoxia epidemica*, bk. 1, chap. 10, discussed Satan's role in divination and astrology. For other worries, see Thomas, *Religion and the Decline of Magic*, chaps. 9, 12.

105. Robinson, *Great Comet of 1680*, 21, 105.

106. Burke, *Popular Culture*, 271–272, 278; cf. Natalie Zemon Davis, *Society and Culture in Early Modern France* (Stanford: Stanford University Press, 1975), 230–257.

107. Roger Chartier, "Culture as Appropriation: Popular Cultural Uses in Early Modern France," in *Understanding Popular Culture: Europe from the Middle Ages to the Nineteenth Century*, ed. Steven L. Kaplan (Berlin: Mouton Publishers, 1984), 229–253.

108. Burke, *Popular Culture*, 240–241, 272–273, 277; Robert W. Malcolmson, *Popular Recreations in English Society, 1700–1850* (Cambridge: Cambridge University Press, 1973); Davis, *Society and Culture*, 241–242; Peter Burke, "Popular Culture in Seventeenth-Century London," in *Popular Culture in Seventeenth-Century England*, ed. Barry Reay (London: Croom Helm, 1985), 31–58.

109. Burke, *Popular Culture*, 241–243, 273–281.

110. Ibid., 271–272.

111. On applications of Gramsci's concept of hegemony to studies of popular culture, see Barry Reay, "Popular Culture in Early Modern England," in *Popular Culture in Seventeenth-Century England*, ed. Barry Reay (London: Croom Helm, 1985), 1–30.

112. Harry C. Payne, "Elite versus Popular Mentality in the Eighteenth Century," *Studies in Eighteenth-Century Culture* 8 (1979): 3–32.

113. Roger Chartier, *Cultural History: Between Practices and Representations*, trans. Lydia G. Cochrane (Ithaca: Cornell University Press, 1988), 38–39; David

Hall, introduction, Jacques Le Goff, "The Learned and Popular Dimensions of Journeys in the Otherworld in the Middle Ages," and Chartier, "Culture as Appropriation," all in *Understanding Popular Culture*, ed. Steven L. Kaplan (Berlin: Mouton Publishers, 1984), 5–37, 229–253; Reay, "Popular Culture in Early Modern England"; Peter Burke, "Popular Culture in Seventeenth-Century London," *London Journal* 3 (1977): 143–162.

114. For example, Albertus Magnus, *The Book of Secrets of Albertus Magnus of the Virtues of Herbs, Stones and Certain Beasts. Also a Book of the Marvels of the World*, ed. Michael R. Best and Frank H. Brightman (Oxford: Oxford University Press, 1973); and works like those collected in Roger Thompson, ed., *Samuel Pepys' Penny Merriments* (New York: Columbia University Press, 1977). On such texts, see Bernard Capp, "Popular Literature," in *Popular Culture in Seventeenth-Century England*, ed. Barry Reay (London: Croom Helm, 1985), 198–243; Bernard Capp, *English Almanacs 1500–1800: Astrology and the Popular Press* (Ithaca: Cornell University Press, 1979); Davis, *Society and Culture*, 258–259.

115. Davis, *Society and Culture*, 205–208, 223–224, 258–264; Burke, *Popular Culture*, 273. Flamsteed's work, "Hecker: His large Ephemeris for the yeare 1674," was never published but fits the genre of books of errors in its attack on astrological conventions and the popularity of prognosticative almanacs among the common folk. It is printed with commentary in Michael Hunter, "Science and Astrology in Seventeenth-Century England: An Unpublished Polemic by John Flamsteed," in *Astrology, Science, and Society*, ed. Patrick Curry (Woodbridge, Suffolk: The Boydell Press, 1987), 260–300.

116. Browne, *Pseudodoxia epidemica*, bk. 6, chap. 14; Jean de Rostagny, *Traité de Primerose sur les erreurs vulgaires de la medicine, avec des additions très curieuses par M. de Rostagny* (Lyons, 1689), bk. 2, chap. 34, pp. 296–301.

117. Jacques Revel, "Forms of Expertise: Intellectuals and 'Popular' Culture in France (1650–1800)," in *Understanding Popular Culture: Europe from the Middle Ages to the Nineteenth Century*, ed. Steven L. Kaplan (Berlin: Mouton Publishers, 1984), 255–273.

118. They included Jesuit scholars who fixed the meaning of religious texts with orthodox glosses and emblems, and men such as Antoine Mizaud, natural philosopher, physician, and professor (1554), Laurent Joubert, chancellor of the Faculty of Medicine at the University of Montpellier (1578), Jacques Guillemau, royal surgeon (1609), René Choppin, jurist (1575), Antoine Loisel, lawyer-humanist (1607), and Jean-Baptiste Thiers, curé (1679). Their efforts to reform common practices are discussed by Davis, *Society and Culture*, 205–208, 222–225, 229, 242, 258–264.

119. On changing attitudes toward magic (and witchcraft), see Wayne Shumaker, *The Occult Sciences in the Renaissance: A Study of Intellectual Patterns* (Berkeley and Los Angeles: University of California Press, 1972); Brian Vickers, ed., *Occult and Scientific Mentalities in the Renaissance* (Cambridge: Cambridge University Press, 1984); Thomas, *Religion and the Decline of Magic*, chaps. 7–9, 14–18, 22; Burke, *Popular Culture*, 241–243, 274–275, 278.

120. Browne, *Pseudodoxia epidemica*, bk. 6, chap. 14.

121. Gassendi, *Opera omnia*, 1:711b–712.

122. Petit, *Dissertation sur la nature des cometes*, 77–147, quotations on 82, 113, 141, 143; my translation.

123. See chap. 2 above.

124. Petit, *Dissertation sur la nature des comets*, 288.

125. On the thesis that popular culture is composed of fragments of ancient, learned culture, see Le Goff, "Learned and Popular Dimensions of Journeys."

126. Quoted in Revel, "Forms of Expertise," 262.

127. Ibid.

128. On astrology, see *Prophecy and Power* by Patrick Curry, whose research corroborates my independent findings.

129. Harry Rusche, "Merlini Anglici: Astrology and Propaganda from 1644 to 1651," *English Historical Review* 80 (1965): 322–333; Harry Rusche, "Prophecies and Propaganda, 1641 to 1651," *English Historical Review* 84 (1969): 752–770; Capp, *English Almanacs*, 72–88, 287–288; Capp, "Popular Literature"; Curry, *Prophecy and Power*, 19–44.

130. Christopher Hill, *The World Turned Upside Down: Radical Ideas during the English Revolution* (Harmondsworth: Penguin Books, 1975), 89–91, 289–292; Curry, *Prophecy and Power*, 26–27, 46–50; Thomas, *Religion and the Decline of Magic*, 313, 342–345, 372–377.

131. See chap. 4 above.

132. David Gregory, unpublished MS dated 1686, Christ Church College (Oxford) MS 113, fols. 47–50; quoted in Curry, *Prophecy and Power*, 144.

133. Flamsteed, "Hecker: His large Ephemeris for the yeare 1674," printed in Hunter, "Science and Astrology," see 288 for quotations, and 291 for the dire social consequences of astrology.

134. David Gregory, *Astronomiae physicae & geometricae elementa* (Oxford, 1702), 408; translation taken from Gregory, *The Elements of Physical and Geometrical Astronomy*, 2d ed., rev. by Edmund Stone, 2 vols. (London, 1726), 2:716.

135. This regional pattern is clearly seen in the works discussed in Robinson, *Great Comet of 1680.*

CHAPTER VII
COMETS, TRANSMUTATIONS, AND WORLD REFORM
IN NEWTON'S THOUGHT

1. Dr. Stukeley to Dr. Mead, Grantham, 26 June 1727; printed in Edmund Turnor, *Collections for the History of the Town and Soke of Grantham containing Authentic Memoirs of Sir Isaac Newton* (London, 1806), 178.

2. William Stukeley, *Memoirs of Sir Isaac Newton's Life* [1752], ed. A. Hastings White (London: Taylor and Francis, 1936), 42. Stukeley claimed that Newton's escapades were commemorated by Samuel Butler in *Hudibras* (London, 1663–1664), 2.3.413–482, where Sidrophel mistakes a paper lantern on a kite for a comet. When the string broke and the lantern fell, he assumed the comet had fallen from the sky and the Day of Judgment was near at hand. A later edition of Butler's poem was in Newton's library. See John Harrison, *The Library of Isaac Newton* (Cambridge: Cambridge University Press, 1978), entry 319. I have consulted Samuel Butler, *Hudibras*, ed. John Wilders (Oxford: Clarendon Press, 1967).

3. Richard S. Westfall, *Never at Rest: A Biography of Isaac Newton* (Cambridge: Cambridge University Press, 1980), 40–55.

4. See Dr. Stukeley to Dr. Mead, 26 June 1727; printed in Turnor, *Collections*, 176. Stukeley, *Memoirs*, 37–43.

5. Westfall, *Never at Rest*, 79; Stukeley, *Memoirs*, 13–14.

6. The occasion was an annual feast to raise money for Lincolnshire charities; the date was 20 February 1720/21. Stukeley, *Memoirs*, 13–14.

7. Charles Caraccioli, *An Historical Account of Sturbridge, Bury, and the Most Famous Fairs in Europe and America* (Cambridge, 1773), 20–21; quoted in Robert W. Malcolmson, *Popular Recreations in English Society, 1700–1850* (Cambridge: Cambridge University Press, 1973), 20–21. A similar scene is described by Daniel Defoe in *A Tour Thro' the whole Island of Great Britain* [1724–1726], 2 vols. (London: Frank Cass & Company, 1968), 1:80–85.

8. Westfall, *Never at Rest*, 98, 157.

9. John Conduitt memorandum, 31 August 1726; and Abraham De Moivre memorandum, November 1727; cited in Westfall, *Never at Rest*, 88, 98.

10. These authors included Diodorus Siculus (517–518), Dion Cassius (521), Hyginus (825), Juvenalis (870–872), Lucanus (986), pseudo-Plutarch (1330–1331), Seneca (1486–1487), Suetonius Tranquillus (1577–1578), Tacitus (1590, 1592), Vergilius Maro (1676–1679). The numbers in parentheses refer to entries in Harrison's catalog. See Harrison, *Library of Isaac Newton*, for bibliographic details. Aristotle and Aratus should be added to this list, for Newton cites them in the *Principia* even though their works do not appear in Newton's library.

11. See Josephus (861–862), Eusebius Pamphili (589–590), Synesius (476), Beda (147), Origenes (1209, 1212), John of Damascus (854) in Harrison, *Library of Isaac Newton*.

12. See Lubieniecki (985) and Origenes (1209), in Harrison, *Library of Isaac Newton*. The work by Origen is a 1658 edition of *Contra Celsum*, and on the front Newton pasted a piece of paper inscribed, "Origenes est bonus Scripturarū Interpres, malus dogmatistes."

13. See Thomas Burnet (315–316) in Harrison, *Library of Isaac Newton*. Newton's copy of the first Latin edition was a gift of the author.

14. Newton to Thomas Burnet, 24 December 1680; Burnet to Newton, 13 January 1680/81; Newton to Burnet, January 1680/81; in *The Correspondence of Isaac Newton*, ed. H. W. Turnbull et al., 7 vols. (Cambridge: Cambridge University Press, 1959–1977), 2:319, 321–334 (hereafter cited as *Newton Correspondence*).

15. Newton's copy of the Holy Bible was dog-eared and annotated throughout, but especially so at the Books of Revelation and Daniel. See Harrison, *Library of Isaac Newton*, entry 188.

16. Harrison, *Library of Isaac Newton*, entry 647.

17. See Bacon (108–109), Fromondus (641), *Journal des sçavans* (863), Lubieniecki (985) in Harrison, *Library of Isaac Newton*. Petit's dissertation on comets (1665) does not appear in Newton's library but is cited in Newton manuscripts. See MS Add. 4004, fol. 103, University Library, Cambridge (hereafter cited as U.L.C.); cited in Westfall, *Never at Rest*, 393.

18. Isaac Newton, *Philosophiae naturalis principia mathematica* (London, 1687), bk. 3, lemma 4, corollary 3; quotation taken from Isaac Newton, *Sir Isaac Newton's Mathematical Principles of Natural Philosophy and His System of the World*, trans. Andrew Motte and rev. Florian Cajori (Berkeley and Los Angeles: University of California Press, 1962), 497 (hereafter cited as *Principia*, Motte-Cajori ed.).

19. John Conduitt memorandum, 31 August 1726; Kings College, Keynes MS 130.10, fol. 4^{v}; quoted in Westfall, *Never at Rest*, 104.

20. Newton, *Questiones quaedam philosophicae* (ca. 1664–1665), U.L.C. MS Add. 3996, fols. 93^v, 114^v–116^v, pp. 12, 54–58. This student notebook has been reprinted with commentary by J. E. McGuire and Martin Tamny, in *Certain Philosophical Questions: Newton's Trinity Notebook* (Cambridge: Cambridge University Press, 1983), see 356–358, 410–418, for the cometary notes. Further information about this notebook is found in A. Rupert Hall, "Sir Isaac Newton's Note-Book, 1661–65," *Cambridge Historical Journal* 9 (1948): 239–250; and Richard S. Westfall, "The Foundations of Newton's Philosophy of Nature," *British Journal for the History of Science* 1 (1962): 171–182.

21. John Conduitt memorandum, 7 March 1724/25; in Turnor, *Collections*, 172–173.

22. *Principia*, Motte-Cajori ed., 523.

23. Eric G. Forbes, "The Comet of 1680–1681," in *Standing on the Shoulders of Giants: A Longer View of Newton and Halley*, ed. Norman J. W. Thrower (Berkeley and Los Angeles: University of California Press, 1990), 312–323.

24. Westfall, *Never at Rest*, 391–397; James A. Ruffner, "The Background and Early Development of Newton's Theory of Comets" (Ph.D. diss., Indiana University, 1966).

25. Flamsteed to Richard Towneley, 11 May 1677, Royal Society Library, MS 243, no. 26, quoted at length in Michael Hunter, "Science and Astrology in Seventeenth-Century England: An Unpublished Polemic by John Flamsteed," in *Astrology, Science, and Society*, ed. Patrick Curry (Woodbridge, Suffolk: The Boydell Press, 1987), 260–300, see 285; and cited in Simon Schaffer, "Comets and Idols: Newton's Cosmology and Political Theology," in *Action and Reaction: Proceedings of a Symposium to Commemorate the Tercentenary of Newton's Principia*, ed. Paul Theerman and Adele F. Seeff (Newark: University of Delaware Press, 1993), 206–231, see 215.

26. Flamsteed to James Crompton for Newton, 15 December 1680; Flamsteed to Halley, 17 February 1680/81; Flamsteed to Crompton for Newton, 7 March 1680/81; in *Newton Correspondence*, 2:315–317, 336–340, 348–356; John Flamsteed, *The Gresham Lectures of John Flamsteed*, ed. Eric G. Forbes (London: Mansell, 1975), lecture 3 (11 May 1681), pp. 105–117.

27. Newton to Crompton for Flamsteed, 28 February, 1680/81; Newton to [Crompton?], [April 1681]; in *Newton Correspondence*, 2:340–347, 358–362.

28. Newton to Flamsteed, 16 April 1681, *Newton Correspondence*, 2:363–367, quotation on 364.

29. Westfall, *Never at Rest*, 393–394; Halley to Robert Hooke, 19/29 May 1681, in *Correspondence and Papers of Edmond Halley*, ed. Eugene Fairfield MacPike (Oxford: Clarendon Press, 1932; reprint, New York: Arno Press, 1975), 51.

30. In 1679 and 1680, Newton had offered similar arguments for planetary motion. See D. T. Whiteside, "Before the *Principia*: The Maturing of Newton's Thoughts on Dynamical Astronomy, 1664–1684," *Journal for the History of Astronomy* 1 (1970): 5–19.

31. *Newton Correspondence*, 2:361, 363–367.

32. See U.L.C. MS Add. 3965.14, fol. 613; discussed in Ruffner, "Background and Early Development," 310–313.

33. Newton, *De motu corporum in gyrum* (autumn 1684), U.L.C. MS Add. 3965.7, fols. 55^r–62^r, see problem 4, scholium on fol. 60^r; printed in facsimile in *The*

Preliminary Manuscripts for Isaac Newton's 1687 Principia, 1684–1685, ed. D. T. Whiteside (Cambridge: Cambridge University Press, 1989), 2–11; printed and trans. in John Herivel, *The Background to Newton's "Principia"* (Oxford: Oxford University Press, 1965), 257–292.

34. Newton to Flamsteed, 12 January 1684/85, *Newton Correspondence*, 2:413. See also Flamsteed to Newton, 5 January 1684/85, *Newton Correspondence*, 2:408. Flamsteed's bitterness is evident in the marginalia he attached to Newton to Flamsteed, 19 September 1685, *Newton Correspondence*, 2:421n.4.

35. Newton to Flamsteed, 19 September 1685 and 14 October 1685; Flamsteed to Newton, 26 September 1685 and 10 October 1685; in *Newton Correspondence*, 2:419–430.

36. Newton to Halley, 20 June 1686, *Newton Correspondence*, 2:437; Simon Schaffer, "Newton's Comets and the Transformation of Astrology," in *Astrology, Science, and Society*, ed. Patrick Curry (Woodbridge, Suffolk: The Boydell Press, 1987), 219–243, see 225–228.

37. "The third [book of the *Principia*] I now designe to suppress. Philosophy is such an impertinently litigious Lady that a man had as good be engaged in Law suits as have to do with her," Newton wrote Halley on 20 June 1686. In the same letter, he cataloged Hooke's scientific blunders. Halley responded on 29 June 1686. See *Newton Correspondence*, 2:435–443, quotation on 437.

38. David Gregory, "In the new Edition of Newton's Philosophy these things will be done by the Author," memoranda, ca. July 1694; in *Newton Correspondence*, 3:385. Newton's revisions of cometary theory are described further in David Gregory, memoranda, 5, 6, 7 May 1694; Roger Cotes to Newton, 20 July 1712 and 23 October 1712; Newton to Cotes, 14 October 1712 and 21 October 1712; Newton to Halley, 3 December 1724 and 1 March 1724/25; in *Newton Correspondence*, 3:327–329; 5:315, 347, 350–351; 7:294–295, 310–311.

39. Halley to Newton, 5 April 1687, 7 September 1695, 28 September 1695, 7 October 1695, 15 October 1695, and 21 October 1695; Newton to Halley, 17 October 1695 and late October 1695; Newton to Flamsteed, 14 September 1695; Flamsteed to Newton, 6 August 1695 and 19 September 1695; and Gregory memoranda, July 1698, 21 May 1701, and March 1702/3. In 1698, Gregory reported that this computational program led Newton to rethink his comet propositions and indeed to construct them "afresh." See *Newton Correspondence*, 2:473–474, 4:159, 165–185, 276–277, 355, 402–403.

40. Newton commented on his improved comet theory in the prefaces to both the second and third editions of the *Principia*; see *Principia*, Motte-Cajori ed., xix, xxxv. Also note the draft preface (autumn 1712), in *Newton Correspondence*, 5:113.

41. Flamsteed wrote Newton, "The impossibility of answering accurate observations of Comets by any Theorys that are not built on ye laws of gravity shews them all false[:] the near agreement of yours with them demonstrates its truth & confirmes the Theory of Gravity at ye same time." Flamsteed to Newton, 19 September 1695, *Newton Correspondence*, 4:171. For discussion of the comet theory proved by phenomena, consult Newton's draft preface to the *Principia* (autumn 1712), in *Newton Correspondence*, 5:113; Henry Pemberton, *A View of Sir Isaac Newton's Philosophy* (London, 1728), 231, 233; and Colin Maclaurin, *An Account of Sir Isaac Newton's Philosophical Discoveries* (London, 1748), 371.

42. "The Cartesians dont like this argument one bit, it makes so strong against

them; so that you see they endeavor to avoid it by denying matter of fact. For this reason I wish you ... would take some pains to prove the Theory of Comets so clearly from their own observations, that they may have no power to deny it." Brook Taylor to John Keill, 26 April 1719, *Newton Correspondence*, 7:37. Guerlac contends that the evidence of retrograde motion in the 1664 comet encouraged Newton to reject Descartes's vortices. See Henry Guerlac, *Newton on the Continent* (Ithaca: Cornell University Press, 1981), 39. Nevertheless, Newton still discussed the paths of comets through vortices at least as late as 1681. See Newton to Crompton for Flamsteed, 28 February 1680/81, *Newton Correspondence*, 2:340–347.

43. Newton, *De motu sphaericorum corporum in fluidis* (ca. December 1684), revised draft of *De motu corporum*, U.L.C. MS Add. 3965.7, fols. 40^r–54^r, see esp. fol. 50^r; printed in facsimile in *Preliminary Manuscripts for Isaac Newton's 1687 Principia*, 12–27; with translation in Herivel, *Background to Newton's "Principia,"* 294–303, see 298, 302; and in *Unpublished Scientific Papers of Isaac Newton: A Selection from the Portsmouth Collection in the University Library, Cambridge*, ed. A. R. Hall and M. B. Hall (Cambridge: Cambridge University Press, 1962), 243–292, see 261, 286. Draft addition to the *Principia*, bk. III, prop. VI, Corollaries 4, 5, U.L.C. MS Add. 4005, fols. 28–29 (1690s); in *Unpublished Scientific Papers*, 315–316. Newton to Leibniz, 16 October 1693, *Newton Correspondence*, 3:287. Isaac Newton, *Opticks or A Treatise of the Reflections, Refractions, Inflections & Colours of Light*, 4th ed. (London, 1730; reprint, New York: Dover, 1952), queries 22 and 28, pp. 352–353, 364–369.

44. Newton's notes on Leibniz's "Tentamen," *Acta Eruditorum* (1689); in *Newton Correspondence*, 6:116–122; David Gregory, *Astronomiae physicae & geometricae elementa* (Oxford, 1702), 99–104; David Gregory, *The Elements of Astronomy, Physical and Geometrical*, 2 vols. (London, 1715), 1:177–178; Isaac Newton, *Philosophiae naturalis principia mathematica*, 2d ed. (Cambridge, 1713), "Scholium generale," 481; *Principia*, Motte-Cajori ed., 543.

45. Maclaurin, *Account of Sir Isaac Newton's Philosophical Discoveries*, 369–370.

46. Newton to Richard Bentley, 10 December 1692, *Newton Correspondence*, 3:234–235; *Principia* (1713), "Scholium generale," 481–482; *Principia*, Motte-Cajori ed., 543–544; Pemberton, *View of Sir Isaac Newton's Philosophy*, 235; and Maclaurin, *Account of Sir Isaac Newton's Philosophical Discoveries*, 376–377.

47. Maclaurin, *Account of Sir Isaac Newton's Philosophical Discoveries*, 377.

48. Schaffer, "Newton's Comets"; and Schaffer, "Comets and Idols."

49. Newton argued this point in the "System of the World" (1685); in "classical scholia" written for the second edition of the *Principia* and discussed with Gregory in 1694; in drafts of queries for the *Optice* (1706); in footnotes to the "General Scholium" published in the second edition of the *Principia* (1713); and in a draft preface to the third edition of the *Principia*. See J. E. McGuire and P. M. Rattansi, "Newton and the 'Pipes of Pan,'" *Notes and Records of the Royal Society of London* 21 (1966): 108–143; Paolo Casini, "Newton: The Classical Scholia," *History of Science* 22 (1984): 1–58; Robert Iliffe, "'Is he like other men?' The Meaning of the *Principia Mathematica*, and the Author as Idol," in *Culture and Society in the Stuart Restoration*, ed. Gerald Maclean (Cambridge: Cambridge University Press, 1995), 159–176; John Gascoigne, "'The Wisdom of the Egyptians' and the Secularisation of History in the Age of Newton," in *The Uses of Antiquity: The Scientific Revolution and the Classical Tradition*, ed. Stephen Gaukroger (Dordrecht: Kluwer

Academic, 1991), 171–212; Schaffer, "Newton's Comets," 237–238; and Schaffer, "Comets and Idols," 220.

50. U.L.C. MS Add. 3990; posthumously published by John Conduitt as *De mundi systemate liber* (London, 1728), and then translated by Andrew Motte [?] and published as *A Treatise of the System of the World* (London, 1728). A modern edition is "The System of the World," appended to *Principia*, Motte-Cajori ed., 549–626.

51. Newton, *Treatise of the System of the World*, 1–4; cf. Newton, *De mundi systemate*, 1–2.

52. Draft preface, post 1716, U.L.C. MS Add. 3968.9, fol. 109; Latin text printed in *The Mathematical Papers of Isaac Newton*, ed. D. T. Whiteside, 8 vols. (Cambridge: Cambridge University Press, 1967–1981), 8:458–459n.49; translated in Schaffer, "Newton's Comets," 238.

53. Richard S. Westfall, "Newton's Theological Manuscripts," in *Contemporary Newtonian Research*, ed. Zev Bechler (Dordrecht: D. Reidel, 1982), 129–143; Richard S. Westfall, "Isaac Newton's *Theologiae Gentilis Origines Philosophicae*," in *The Secular Mind: Transformations of Faith in Modern Europe*, ed. W. Warren Wagar (New York: Holmes & Meier, 1982), 15–34.

54. Fragment on the history of the church (1680s), Yahuda MS 18, fol. 3^r, Jewish National and University Library, Jerusalem; quoted in Schaffer, "Newton's Comets," 242. See also Yahuda MS 41, fol. 9^v; quoted in Iliffe, "'Is he like other men?'" 168.

55. "Paradoxical Questions concerning the morals & actions of Athanasius & his followers" (late 1670s–early 1680s), Clark Library, Los Angeles; quoted in Westfall, *Never at Rest*, 344–345.

56. "Theologiae gentilis origines philosophicae" (drafts from the 1680s and early 1690s), Yahuda MS 17.3, fols. 9^r, 15^r, and MS 41, fol. 8^r; quoted in Schaffer, "Newton's Comets," 242; and Iliffe, "'Is he like other men?'" 169.

57. A chapter from the "Theologiae gentilis origines philosophicae" (early 1690s), Yahuda MS 41, fol. 11; quoted in Westfall, "Isaac Newton's *Theologiae Gentilis*," 26.

58. New College MS 361.3, fol. 32, Bodleian Library; quoted in Frank E. Manuel, *Isaac Newton, Historian* (Cambridge: Cambridge University Press, 1963), 115.

59. Yahuda MS 17.3, fol. 8^r; quoted in Iliffe, "'Is he like other men?'" 169. See also Yahuda MS 15.7, fol. 133^v; quoted in Schaffer, "Newton's Comets," 242–243: "Astrologers, augurs, auruspicers &c are such as pretend to ye art of divining . . . without being able to do what they pretend to . . . and to believe that man or woman can really divine . . . is of the same nature with believing that the Idols of the Gentiles were not vanities but had spirits really seated in them."

60. Westfall, *Never at Rest*, 473–483.

61. See chap. 4 above.

62. See chap. 1 above.

63. John Ogilby, *The Entertainment of His Most Excellent Majestie Charles II, in His Passage through the City of London to His Coronation* (London, 1662), 13–42. For further discussion of Charles II's natal star and Anglo-Augustanism, see chap. 4 above.

64. See, for example, Aurelian Cook, *Titus Britannicus: An Essay of History Royal: In the Life & Reign of His Late Sacred Majesty, Charles II. of Ever Blessed and Immortal Memory* (London, 1685), sigs. C^v–C2^v.

65. Isaac Newton, *Philosophiae naturalis principia mathematica*, 3d ed. (London, 1726), 501; *Principia*, Motte-Cajori ed., 515. Current theory no longer supports Halley's claim.

66. See chap. 6 above.

67. Newton, *Treatise of the System of the World*, 106–109; my italics. Cf. Newton, *De mundi systemate*, 72–75.

68. See chaps. 1–4 above; and Stith Thompson, *Motif-Index of Folk-Literature: A Classification of Narrative Elements in Folktales, Ballads, Myths, Fables, Mediaeval Romances, Exempla, Fabliaux, Jest-Books, and Local Legends*, rev. and enl. ed., 6 vols. (Bloomington: Indiana University Press, 1955–1958).

69. Cf. *Principia* (1687), 507–508; *Principia*, Motte-Cajori ed., 531–532.

70. David Gregory, "Annotations Physical, Mathematical, and Theological from Newton" (memoranda), 5, 6, 7 May 1694, in *Newton Correspondence*, 3:336.

71. "Quem in finem facti sunt Cometae?" query 20, *Optice sive de reflexionibus, refractionibus, inflexionibus & coloribus lucis libri tres* (London, 1706), 314.

72. The material in this section is treated in greater depth in Sara Schechner Genuth, "Comets, Teleology, and the Relationship of Chemistry to Cosmology in Newton's Thought," *Annali dell'Istituto e Museo di Storia della Scienza di Firenze* 10, pt. 2 (1985): 31–65. On transmutation in Newton's thought, see J. E. McGuire, "Transmutation and Immutability: Newton's Doctrine of Physical Qualities," *Ambix* 14 (1967): 69–95; P. M. Rattansi, "Newton's Alchemical Studies," in *Science, Medicine and Society in the Renaissance: Essays to Honor Walter Pagel*, ed. Allen G. Debus (New York: Science History Publications, 1972), 2:167–182; Betty Jo Teeter Dobbs, *The Foundations of Newton's Alchemy, or "The Hunting of the Greene Lyon"* (Cambridge: Cambridge University Press, 1975); Karin Figala, "Newton as Alchemist," *History of Science* 15 (1977): 102–137; Richard S. Westfall, "The Role of Alchemy in Newton's Career," and Marie Boas Hall, "Newton's Voyage in the Strange Seas of Alchemy," in *Reason, Experiment, and Mysticism in the Scientific Revolution*, ed. M. L. Righini Bonelli and William R. Shea (New York: Science History Publications, 1975), 189–232, 239–246.

73. *Principia* (1687), bk. 3, hypothesis 3. This hypothesis was suppressed in later editions. An excellent discussion is to be found in McGuire, "Transmutation and Immutability"; and Alexandre Koyré, "Newton's 'Regulae Philosophandi,'" in *Newtonian Studies* (Cambridge: Harvard University Press, 1965), 261–272.

74. "De natura acidorum" [composed 1691/92 and published in 1710], and "Some Thoughts about the Nature of Acids," in John Harris, *Lexicon technicum*, 1st ed., 2 vols. (London, 1704–1710), vol. 2, introduction; reprinted in *Newton's Papers and Letters on Natural Philosophy*, ed. I. Bernard Cohen, 2d ed. (Cambridge: Harvard University Press, 1978), 255–258, quotation on 258.

75. Betty Jo Teeter Dobbs, *The Janus Faces of Genius: The Role of Alchemy in Newton's Thought* (Cambridge: Cambridge University Press, 1991), 24–25.

76. Newton to Oldenburg, 7 December 1675; in *Newton Correspondence*, 1:364–365. Also see Newton to Boyle, 28 February 1678/79; printed in *The Works of the Honourable Robert Boyle*, ed. Thomas Birch, 5 vols. (London, 1744), 1:70–73; and reprinted in *Newton's Papers and Letters*, 250–253.

77. "Of natures obvious laws & processes in vegetation" [ca. 1672], Dibner MS 1031 B, fol. 3^v, Dibner Library of the History of Science and Technology, Smithsonian Institution. (Prior to 1976, this manuscript was in the collections of the Burndy Library, Norwalk, Conn., and referred to as the "Vegetation of Metals,"

Burndy MS 16.) The manuscript is printed in Dobbs, *Janus Faces*, app. A, see 264–265 for passage quoted. On the comparison of the earth to a living organism, see David Kubrin, "Newton's Inside Out! Magic, Class Struggle, and the Rise of Mechanism in the West," in *The Analytic Spirit: Essays in the History of Science in Honor of Henry Guerlac*, ed. Harry Woolf (Ithaca: Cornell University Press, 1981), 96–121, esp. 113–114; and Allen G. Debus, "The Chemical Debates of the Seventeenth Century: The Reaction to Robert Fludd and Jean Baptiste van Helmont," in *Reason, Experiment, and Mysticism in the Scientific Revolution*, ed. M. L. Righini Bonelli and William R. Shea (New York: Science History Publications, 1975), 18–47, see 22.

78. "Of Gravity & Levity," in Newton's *Questiones quaedam philosophicae* (ca. 1664–1665), U.L.C. MS Add. 3996, fols. 97^r, 121^r, pp. 19, 67; printed in McGuire and Tamny, *Certain Philosophical Questions*, 362–365, 426–427. Newton to Oldenburg, 7 December 1675, in *Newton Correspondence*, 1:365–366; Newton to Boyle, 28 February 1678/79, printed in *Works of Boyle*, 1:70–73; Rattansi, "Newton's Alchemical Studies," 176. Newton's view on mineral fermentations and the central heat of the earth can be found in his letter to Bentley, 10 December 1692, in *Newton Correspondence*, 3:235; and in Newton, *Optice*, query 23, 325–326; *Opticks* (1730), query 31, 379–380.

79. Newton to Oldenburg, 7 December 1675, in *Newton Correspondence*, 1:365–366.

80. Ibid., 366.

81. Newton's interest in these sources has been well documented. See Dobbs, *Foundations of Newton's Alchemy*; Westfall, "Role of Alchemy"; Hall, "Newton's Voyage"; McGuire, "Transmutation and Immutability"; Rattansi, "Newton's Alchemical Studies"; Richard S. Westfall, "Newton and the Hermetic Tradition," in *Science, Medicine and Society in the Renaissance: Essays to Honor Walter Pagel*, ed. Allen G. Debus (New York: Science History Publications, 1972), 2:183–198. The key difference between Newton and these Neoplatonists was that Newton's aethereal medium was material, even mechanical, whereas the Neoplatonist universal spirit and "air" were not. Moreover, Newton nowhere mentioned in his 1675 letter any "magnetick" bodies capable of drawing in this spirit in order to specificate it.

82. Dobbs, *Foundations of Newton's Alchemy*, 37–38.

83. Schechner Genuth, "Comets, Teleology."

84. Draft Conclusion to the *Principia* (spring 1687), U.L.C. MS Add. 4005, fols. 25–28, 30–37; printed in *Unpublished Scientific Papers*, 341.

85. Jean Baptiste van Helmont, *Ortus medicinae* (Amsterdam, 1648), 117, or in the English edition, *Oriatrike* (London, 1662), 109. Newton's notes reveal a close reading of van Helmont's *Opera omnia* (1667). See Keynes MS 16, King's College, Cambridge; Debus, "Chemical Debates," 18–47; and Allen G. Debus, *The Chemical Philosophy: Paracelsian Science and Medicine in the Sixteenth and Seventeenth Centuries*, 2 vols. (New York: Science History Publications, 1977), 2:532–535.

86. Robert Boyle, *The Origine of Formes and Qualities (According to the Corpuscular Philosophy) Illustrated by Considerations and Experiments, (Written formerly by way of Notes upon an Essay about Nitre)* (Oxford, 1666), experiment 9, pp. 387–420; *Works of Boyle*, 2:519–524. Boyle developed these ideas further in his *Sceptical Chemist* (1680). Michael T. Walton, "Boyle and Newton on the Transmutation of Water and Air, from the Root of Helmont's Tree," *Ambix* 27 (1980): 11–18.

87. Lavoisier concluded that continuous heat did not convert water into earth but that the glass walls of the flask interacted with the water and were responsible for the residual earth at the end of the experiment. Antoine Laurent Lavoisier, "Sur la nature de l'eau et sur les expériences par lesquelles on a prétendu prouver la possibilité de son changement en terre," *Mémoires de l'Académie des Sciences* (1770), 73ff.; reprinted in *Oeuvres de Lavoisier*, 7 vols. (Paris, 1862–1964), 2:1–28.

88. Query 22, *Optice* (1706), 319; query 30, *Opticks* (1730), 374.

89. *Principia* (1687), 506; *Principia*, Motte-Cajori ed., 530.

90. Extract made by Newton of a letter from Flamsteed to Crompton, 12 February 1680/81; Flamsteed to Halley, 17 February 1680/81, in *Newton Correspondence*, 2:336, 338. Flamsteed described comets as broken planets swamped by water.

91. *Principia* (1687), 506; *Principia*, Motte-Cajori ed., 529.

92. *Principia* (1687), 506; *Principia*, Motte-Cajori ed., 529–530.

93. *Principia* (1687), 506; *Principia*, Motte-Cajori ed., 530.

94. *Principia* (1713), 481; *Principia*, Motte-Cajori ed., 542. Cf. draft revision of prop. 41, bk. III, *Principia*, U.L.C. MS Add. 3965, fol. 152^v; quoted in I. Bernard Cohen, "Isaac Newton's *Principia*, the Scriptures, and the Divine Providence," in *Philosophy, Science, and Method: Essays in Honor of Ernest Nagel*, ed. Sidney Morgenbesser, Patrick Suppes, and Morton White (New York: St. Martin's Press, 1969), 523–548, see 531, 537.

95. Draft revision of prop. 41, bk. III, *Principia*, U.L.C. MS Add. 3965, fol. 152^v; quoted in Cohen, "Isaac Newton's *Principia*, the Scriptures, and the Divine Providence," 531, 537.

96. Stars were diminished in size by the constant emission of light and a very small quantity of vapors and exhalations. Newton, however, felt stellar heat was conserved, because the stars' gravitational attraction would condense most vapors and fumes as soon as they began to ascend from the stars, and their vast atmospheres contained and conserved the heat. Draft Conclusion to the *Principia* (spring 1687), U.L.C. MS Add. 4005, fols. 25–28, 30–37, printed in *Unpublished Scientific Papers*, 320–347, see 343; and Newton, *Opticks: Or, a Treatise of the Reflexions, Refractions, Inflexions and Colours of Light* (London, 1704), query 11, p. 135. See also the augmented version of query 11 in the 1717 *Opticks*; *Opticks* (1730), 343–344.

97. *Principia* (1687), 506.

98. By 1694, Newton had realized this, and Halley announced at a meeting of the Royal Society "that M^r. Newton had lately told him, That there was reason to Conclude That the bulk of the Earth did grow and increase . . . by the perpetuall Accession of New particles attracted out of the Ether by its Gravitating power, and he [Halley] Supposed . . . That this Encrese of the Moles of the Earth would occasion an Acceleration of the Moons Motion, she being at this time Attracted by a Stronger Vis Centripeta than in remote Ages." Journal Book of the Royal Society, 31 October 1694; quoted in David C. Kubrin, "Newton and the Cyclical Cosmos: Providence and the Mechanical Philosophy," *Journal of the History of Ideas* 28 (1967): 325–346, see 337; and in Turnor, *Collections*, 184. In the second edition of the *Principia* (1713), 481, Newton argued that the increasing mass of the earth and decreasing mass of the sun led, respectively, to an acceleration of the moon's motion and a deceleration of the planets'. He dropped this passage in the third edition of the *Principia* (1726). See Isaac Newton, *Philosophiae naturalis principia mathematica*, 3d edition with variant readings, ed. Alexandre Koyré and

I. Bernard Cohen, with Anne Whitman, 2 vols. (Cambridge: Harvard University Press, 1972), 758.

99. Query 23, *Optice* (1706), 343, 345–346; query 31, *Opticks* (1730), 399, 402. Kubrin discusses how the unwinding-world theory was effective in fending off various deist heresies that would banish God's voluntary activity from his creation, or worse, would show that the everlasting clockwork universe had required no creator at all. Kubrin, "Newton and the Cyclical Cosmos." For further discussion of the issues of voluntarism and immanence, see P. M. Heimann, "Voluntarism and Immanence: Conceptions of Nature in Eighteenth-Century Thought," *Journal of the History of Ideas* 39 (1978): 271–283. On God's providence in keeping the fixed stars fixed, see M. A. Hoskin, "Newton, Providence and the Universe of Stars," *Journal for the History of Astronomy* 8 (1977): 77–101.

100. In 1681, Newton guessed that in proportion to their solid bodies, the atmospheres of comets were much thicker and perhaps thousands of times more extended than those of planets. In 1687, however, Newton estimated that the solid kernel of a comet had a radius equal to only a ninth or tenth of its entire radius. Newton to Crompton for Flamsteed, 28 February 1680/81, *Newton Correspondence*, 2:345; *Principia* (1687), 498–499, 503; *Principia*, Motte-Cajori ed., 521, 526; Pemberton, *View of Sir Isaac Newton's Philosophy*, 236–238.

101. Walter G. Hiscock, ed., *David Gregory, Isaac Newton and Their Circle: Extracts from David Gregory's Memoranda 1677–1708* (Oxford: By the editor, 1937), 26.

102. *Principia*, variorum ed., 744–745, 758; draft revision of prop. 41, bk. III, *Principia*, U.L.C. MS Add. 3965, fol. 152ᵛ; quoted in Cohen, "Isaac Newton's *Principia*, the Scriptures, and the Divine Providence," 531, 537.

103. In the 1670s, Halley had drawn up some astronomical tables for Sir Jonas Moore (d. 1679) in which he determined Saturn's present motion to be twenty-six minutes slower than it had appeared a hundred years previously. Halley reasoned that a slower period implied that the planet must have increased its distance from the sun, which in turn indicated that the planet had increased in bulk and weight. Newton accepted this finding. See *Newton Correspondence*, 2:412n.4.

104. David Gregory, *The Elements of Physical and Geometrical Astronomy*, 2d ed., rev. Edmund Stone, 2 vols. (London, 1726), 852–853; *Principia*, variorum ed., 745, 758; Flamsteed to Abraham Sharp, 11 February 1709/10; reprinted in Francis Baily, *An Account of the Revd. John Flamsteed, the First Astronomer-Royal* (London, 1835), 274.

105. Journal Book of the Royal Society, 31 October 1694 (quoted in n. 93 above). Halley and Newton first published their opinion in 1695 in Edmond Halley, "Some Account of the Ancient State of the City of Palmyra, with short Remarks upon the Inscriptions found there," *Philosophical Transactions* 19 (1695–1697): 160–175, see 174–175; and later in the *Principia* (1713), 481. See also Pemberton, *View of Sir Isaac Newton's Philosophy*, 246–247.

106. Hiscock, *Gregory's Memoranda*, 26; William Whiston, *A New Theory of the Earth* (London, 1696), 300–315; William Whiston, *Astronomical Principles of Religion, Natural and Reveal'd* (London, 1717), 93.

107. For an alternative interpretation, see Dobbs, *Janus Faces*, 239; Schaffer, "Newton's Comets," 236; McGuire, "Transmutation and Immutability," 87.

108. *Principia* (1713), 480–481, quotation on 481; *Principia*, Motte-Cajori ed., 541.

109. Allen Debus, "The Paracelsian Aerial Niter," *Isis* 55 (1964): 43–61; Debus, "Chemical Debates," 25–26, 42, on Fludd's and van Helmont's advocacy of a vital aerial spirit.

110. Query 23, *Optice* (1706), 326; query 31, *Opticks* (1730), 380. Compare Newton's earlier opinion that the aerial vital spirit was not the "imaginary volatile saltpeter." Newton to Oldenburg, 7 December 1675, *Newton Correspondence*, 1:365.

111. "Of natures obvious laws & processes in vegetation," Dibner MS 1031 B, fol. 3ᵛ; printed in Dobbs, *Janus Faces*, 264–265.

112. Everett Mendelsohn, *Heat and Life: The Development of the Theory of Animal Heat* (Cambridge: Harvard University Press, 1964); Thomas S. Hall, *History of General Physiology: 600 B.C. to A.D. 1900*, 2 vols. (Chicago: University of Chicago Press, 1975), 1:13–40, 270.

113. Thomas S. Hall, "Life, Death and the Radical Moisture: A Study of Thematic Pattern in Medieval Medical Theory," *Clio Medica* 6 (1971): 3–23.

114. Dobbs, *Foundations of Newton's Alchemy*, 158, 199; Harrison, *Library of Isaac Newton*, 217, 236, 243.

115. Newton to Oldenburg, 7 December 1675, *Newton Correspondence*, 1:365. Italics added.

116. Newton had fifty-seven medical books in his working library. The radical moisture was too common a belief for him not to have read about it in one of these texts. Harrison, *Library of Isaac Newton*, 59, 63–64.

117. *Principia* (1713), 481; *Principia*, Motte-Cajori ed., 542.

118. Among the Greek authors who adopted this view were Heraclitus, the Hippocratic author of "On Regimen," Aristotle, and Theophrastus. See Hall, "Life, Death and the Radical Moisture." For a later view, see Nicolas le Fèvre, *A Compleat Body of Chymistry* (London, 1664), 15.

119. Newton to Oldenburg, 7 December 1675, *Newton Correspondence*, 1:366.

120. Conduitt memorandum, 7 March 1724/25; in Turnor, *Collections*, 172.

121. Debus, "Chemical Debates," 22.

122. William Simpson, *Hydrologia Chymica: or, the Chymical Anatomy of the Scarbrough, And other Spaws in York-Shire* (London, 1669), 283–338, quotation on 303; [Jean d'Espagnet], *Enchyridion physicae restitutae; or, The Summary of Physicks Recovered* (London, 1651), 99–100; quoted in Dobbs, *Foundations of Newton's Alchemy*, 39.

123. See the work of Kepler, Longomontanus, Petit, Edwards, and Gadbury in chap. 5 above.

124. 2 Pet. 3:7–13, revised standard version.

125. *Questiones quaedam philosophicae*, U.L.C. MS Add. 3996, fol. 101ʳ, p. 27; printed in McGuire and Tamny, *Certain Philosophical Questions*, 374–377. There Newton wrote:

OF EARTH

Its conflagration testified 2 peter 3ᵈ, vers 6, 7, 10, 11, 12. The wiked probably to be punished thereby 2 Pet: 3ᶜʰᵃᵖ: vers 7.

The succession of worlds, probable from Pet 3ᶜ. 13ᵛ. in wᶜʰ text an emphasis upon yᵉ word WEE is not countenanced by yᵉ Originall. Rev 21ᶜ. 1ᵛ. Isa: 65ᶜ, 17ᵛ. 66ᶜ, 22ᵛ. Days & nights after yᵉ Judgm Rev 20ᶜ, 10ᵛ.

126. Newton to Thomas Burnet, 24 December 1680 and January 1680/81; Burnet to Newton, 13 January 1680/81; in *Newton Correspondence*, 2:319, 321–334.

127. Newton to Bentley, 25 February 1692/93, *Newton Correspondence*, 3:253; see also Newton to Bentley, 10 December 1692, *Newton Correspondence*, 3:234.

128. Conduitt memorandum, 7 March 1724/25, in Turnor, *Collections*, 172.

129. Ibid.; *Principia* (1726), 525–526; *Principia*, Motte-Cajori, 541–542.

130. Maclaurin emphasized that the comet theory gave new force to arguments against the eternity of the world. Given a finite stock of comets, comet supplies would have been exhausted long ago if the world had existed from eternity. Maclaurin, *Account of Sir Isaac Newton's Philosophical Discoveries*, 375–376.

131. David Gregory, "Annotations Physical, Mathematical and Theological from Newton," memoranda, 5, 6, 7 May 1694, *Newton Correspondence*, 3:336.

132. *Principia* (1687), 506; *Principia* (1713), 481; *Principia*, Motte-Cajori ed., 529–530, 542; Conduitt memorandum, 7 March 1724/25, in Turnor, *Collections*, 172.

133. Gregory, *Astronomiae physicae & geometricae elementa*, 481; quotation taken from the second English edition, *Elements of Physical and Geometrical Astronomy*, 2:853.

134. Gregory memorandum, March 1702/3, *Newton Correspondence*, 4:402.

135. On Newton's interest in Origen, see Schaffer, "Newton's Comets," 232; on Origen's view of comets, see chap. 2 above.

136. Among the Stoics, Newton also encountered ideas about the final Conflagration and succession of worlds, and may have concluded that some pristine truth was preserved in Stoicism. Stoic thought may have reinforced his interest in the end of the world and encouraged him to find a pyrotechnical means to bring it about. B.J.T. Dobbs, "Newton and Stoicism," *Southern Journal of Philosophy* 23, supplement (1985): 109–123, see 111–114.

137. Conduitt memorandum, 7 March 1724/25, in Turnor, *Collections*, 172.

138. Edmond Halley, "A Synopsis of the Astronomy of Comets," appended to Gregory, *Elements of Astronomy* (1715), 2:881–905, see 901–903; *Principia* (1726), 501; *Principia*, Motte-Cajori ed., 515.

139. Gregory memoranda, ? July 1698, *Newton Correspondence*, 4:277.

140. Gregory, *Elements of Physical and Geometrical Astronomy*, 2:853–854.

141. See chaps. 8 and 9 below; and David Kubrin, "'Such an Impertinently Litigious Lady': Hooke's 'Great Pretending' vs. Newton's *Principia* and Newton's and Halley's Theory of Comets," in *Standing on the Shoulders of Giants: A Longer View of Newton and Halley*, ed. Norman J. W. Thrower (Berkeley and Los Angeles: University of California Press, 1990), 55–90, see 71–73.

142. Conduitt memorandum, 7 March 1724/25, in Turnor, *Collections*, 172. For this usage of "to doubt whether . . . not," consult the *Oxford English Dictionary*.

143. Conduitt memorandum, 7 March 1724/25, in Turnor, *Collections*, 172–173.

144. Ibid., 173.

145. Pemberton, *View of Sir Isaac Newton's Philosophy*, 243–246, quotation on 244; Maclaurin, *Account of Sir Isaac Newton's Philosophical Discoveries*, 374–375; Gregory, "Annotations Physical, Mathematical and Theological from Newton," memoranda, 5, 6, 7 May 1694, *Newton Correspondence*, 3:336.

146. Pemberton, *View of Sir Isaac Newton's Philosophy*, 244.

147. Maclaurin also recognized the potentially fatal future effects of the 1680 comet on the earth. Maclaurin, *Account of Sir Isaac Newton's Philosophical Discoveries*, 372.

148. See, for example, Andrew Dickson White, *A History of the Warfare of Science with Theology in Christendom*, 2 vols. (New York: D. Appleton and Company, 1930), 1:201–204; James Howard Robinson, *The Great Comet of 1680: A Study in the History of Rationalism* (Northfield, Minn.: Press of the Northfield News, 1916); Stephen Toulmin and June Goodfield, *The Fabric of the Heavens: The Development of Astronomy and Dynamics* (1961; reprint, New York: Harper Torchbooks, 1965), 239; John C. Brandt and Robert D. Chapman, *Introduction to Comets* (Cambridge: Cambridge University Press, 1981), 19; Richard Flaste et al., *The New York Times Guide to the Return of Halley's Comet* (New York: Times Books, 1985), 42; Carl Sagan and Ann Druyan, *Comet* (New York: Random House, 1985), 59; Donald K. Yeomans, *Comet Halley: Fact and Folly* (Santa Ana, Calif.: Gold Stein Press, 1985), 39–40; Donald K. Yeomans, *Comets: A Chronological History of Observation, Science, Myth, and Folklore* (New York: Wiley Science Editions, 1991), 106.

149. *Principia* (1687), 506; *Principia*, Motte-Cajori ed., 529–530.

150. See chap. 1 above.

151. See chap. 4 above.

152. See Jacques Le Goff, "The Learned and Popular Dimensions of Journeys in the Otherworld in the Middle Ages," and Jacques Revel, "Forms of Expertise: Intellectuals and 'Popular' Culture in France (1650–1800)," in *Understanding Popular Culture: Europe from the Middle Ages to the Nineteenth Century*, ed. Steven L. Kaplan (Berlin: Mouton Publishers, 1984), 19–37, 255–273.

153. McGuire and Rattansi, "Newton and the 'Pipes of Pan' "; Casini, "Newton: The Classical Scholia"; Dobbs, *Janus Faces*, passim.

CHAPTER VIII
HALLEY'S COMET THEORY, NOAH'S FLOOD,
AND THE END OF THE WORLD

1. It is not my intention to treat Halley's orbital theory in detail for this has been amply treated elsewhere. Two historical discussions of Halley's method of computing orbits are William Whiston, *Sir Isaac Newton's Mathematick Philosophy More Easily Demonstrated: With Dr. Halley's Account of Comets Illustrated* (London, 1716), 408–443; and Benjamin Martin, *The Theory of Comets, Illustrated, in Four Parts. I. An Essay on the Natural History and Philosophy of Comets; .... II. Tables, containing the Elements of the Theory of a Comet's Motion, (in a Parabola or an Ellipsis) with their Nature and Use explained. III. The Method of constructing the Orbit of any Comet, and computing its Place therein. ... IV. The Method of delineating the visible Path of a Comet in the Heavens, on the Surface of a Celestial Globe. ... The whole adapted to, and exemplified in the Orbit of the Comet of the Year 1682, whose Return is now near at Hand* (London, 1757). A modern discussion is Angus Armitage, *Edmond Halley* (London: Thomas Nelson and Sons, 1966), 164–165.

2. Martin Folkes [?], MS Memoir on Halley; Jean Jacques d'Ortous de Mairan, "Eloge de M. Halley," *Mémoires de l'Académie Royale des Sciences (Histoire)*,

Année 1742 (Paris, 1744–1745), 172–188; both reprinted in Eugene Fairfield MacPike, ed., *Correspondence and Papers of Edmond Halley* (Oxford: Clarendon Press, 1932; reprint, New York: Arno Press, 1975), 4–5, 18.

3. Halley to Hooke, 5/15 January 1680/81, in MacPike, *Correspondence and Papers*, 48.

4. Halley to Hooke, 19/29 May 1681, in MacPike, *Correspondence and Papers*, 51. On Kepler, see chap. 6 above, and J. A. Ruffner, "The Curved and the Straight: Cometary Theory from Kepler to Hevelius," *Journal for the History of Astronomy* 2 (1971): 178–194.

5. Halley to Hooke, 19/29 May 1681, in MacPike, *Correspondence and Papers*, 51.

6. Ibid.

7. David W. Hughes and Andrew Drummond, "Edmond Halley's Observations of Halley's Comet," *Journal for the History of Astronomy* 15 (1984): 189–197. As an Oxford student (matriculated 1673), Halley assisted Flamsteed during his summer vacation. Before receiving his degree, he traveled to Saint Helena in 1676 and charted southern stars under very difficult conditions. His work superseded all previous southern catalogs. On his return to England, Halley published a star chart (1678) and the *Catalogus stellarum Australium, sive supplementum catalogi Tychonici* (London, 1679). See Norman J. W. Thrower, "Edmond Halley: His Life and Scientific Achievements," *Studies in Eighteenth-Century Culture* 17 (1987): 3–15, see 5; Deborah J. Warner, *The Sky Explored: Celestial Cartography, 1500–1800* (New York: Alan R. Liss, 1979), 107–109.

8. Halley to John Wallis, 9 April 1687, in MacPike, *Correspondence and Papers*, 81; Newton to Halley, 20 June 1686, and Halley to Newton, 29 June 1686, in *The Correspondence of Isaac Newton*, ed. H. W. Turnbull et al., 7 vols. (Cambridge: Cambridge University Press, 1959–1977), 2:435–443 (hereafter cited as *Newton Correspondence*); I. Bernard Cohen, "Halley's Two Essays on Newton's *Principia*," in *Standing on the Shoulders of Giants: A Longer View of Newton and Halley*, ed. Norman J. W. Thrower (Berkeley and Los Angeles: University of California Press, 1990), 91–108.

9. Journal Book of the Royal Society, 15 October 1690, in MacPike, *Correspondence and Papers*, 219.

10. Extract from Hooke's diary, 22 March 1692/93, in MacPike, *Correspondence and Papers*, 186.

11. See Halley to Newton, 7 and 28 September, [7], 15 and 21 October 1695, and an undated letter written ca. 1695/96, printed in MacPike, *Correspondence and Papers*, 91–97; and *Newton Correspondence*, 4:165, 169, 171–179, 182–183, 190. In addition, see Newton to Flamsteed, 14 September 1695; Newton to Halley, 17 and late October 1695, *Newton Correspondence*, 4:169, 180–181, 184–185.

12. Halley to Newton, 7 September 1695, in MacPike, *Correspondence and Papers*, 91.

13. Ibid.

14. Halley to Newton, 28 September 1695, in MacPike, *Correspondence and Papers*, 91.

15. Halley to Newton, [7] October 1695, *Newton Correspondence*, 4:174; cf. MacPike, *Correspondence and Papers*, 94.

16. Halley to Newton, 21 October 1695, in MacPike, *Correspondence and Papers*, 95–96.

17. Halley to Newton, [7] October 1695, *Newton Correspondence*, 173.

18. Flamsteed's hatred of Halley is discussed below.

19. Halley to Newton, 28 September 1695, in MacPike, *Correspondence and Papers*, 92.

20. Ibid.

21. Journal Book of the Royal Society, 3 June 1696, in MacPike, *Correspondence and Papers*, 238.

22. He shared with the Royal Society some of his preliminary findings on the 1618 comet. Journal Book, 1 July 1696, in MacPike, *Correspondence and Papers*, 238.

23. Halley to Newton, 21 October 1695, in MacPike, *Correspondence and Papers*, 96.

24. Edmond Halley, "Astronomiae cometicae synopsis," *Philosophical Transactions* 24 (1704–1705): 1882–1899. English translations will be taken from "A Synopsis of the Astronomy of Comets," in *Miscellanea Curiosa*, ed. Edmond Halley, 3 vols. (London: 1705–1707), 2 (1706): 1–24 [separately paginated after p. 320], see 1–3, quotation on 2. Hereafter these editions will be cited as "Synopsis" (1705) and "Synopsis" (1706), respectively.

25. Halley, "Synopsis" (1706), 2.

26. Ibid., 2–3.

27. Ibid., 3–5, quotations on 5.

28. See n. 24 above, for the full citation. On the publishing history of the "Synopsis," consult Walter G. Hiscock, ed., *David Gregory, Isaac Newton and Their Circle: Extracts from David Gregory's Memoranda 1677–1708* (Oxford: By the editor, 1937), 26; Peter Broughton, "The First Predicted Return of Comet Halley," *Journal for the History of Astronomy* 16 (1985): 123–133; Michael Hoskin, "The First Edition of Halley's 'Synopsis,'" *Journal for the History of Astronomy* 16 (1985): 133; and Owen Gingerich, "Halley's Letter to Gregory Concerning the 'Synopsis,'" *Journal for the History of Astronomy* 16 (1985): 223–224.

29. Halley, "Synopsis" (1706), 6.

30. Ibid., 20–21. For remarks on elliptical orbits, see Halley, "A Synopsis of the Astronomy of Comets," reprinted with commentary in Whiston, *Sir Isaac Newton's Mathematick Philosophy. . . . With Dr. Halley's Account of Comets*, 409–443, see 442 (hereafter cited as "Synopsis," Whiston ed. [1716]); and the posthumous edition of the "Synopsis," appended to Edmond Halley, *Astronomical Tables with Precepts Both in English and Latin for Computing the Places of the Sun, Moon, Planets, and Comets* (London, 1752), Oooo3–Ssss[1].

31. Halley, "Synopsis" (1706), 20.

32. Ibid., 21.

33. Ibid. Here and in later editions, Halley noted that the comets of 1305, 1380, and 1456 were also likely to be earlier apparitions of the 1682 comet. In this, he was partly incorrect; the 1301 comet (not the 1305) and the 1378 comet (not the 1380) were earlier apparitions. His dates were slightly off, but given the paucity of historical resources at his disposal, he really did quite well. He certainly was on the right track here. He was less fortunate, however, in his other assertions. He suggested, with less conviction (and wrongly), that the 1532 and 1661 comets were the same. And in 1715, he began to argue that the 1680–1681 comet had a 575-year period and was the same as the comets of 44 B.C., A.D. 531, and A.D. 1106. His forceful (but wrong) reasoning convinced Newton, who incorporated Halley's results into

the 1726 edition of the *Principia*. See Halley, "Synopsis" (1706), 22; Halley, "A Synopsis of the Astronomy of Comets," appended to David Gregory, *The Elements of Astronomy, Physical and Geometrical*, 2 vols. (London, 1715), 2:881–905, see 901–903; "Synopsis," Whiston ed. (1716), 440–441; Halley, *Astronomical Tables*, Ooo o3, Ssss2–Tttt3.

34. Halley, "Synopsis" (1706), 22; cf. Halley, *Astronomical Tables*, Ssss[1].

35. For example, see Halley to Hans Sloane, 7 November 1722; and Halley to Newton, 16 February 1724/25, in MacPike, *Correspondence and Papers*, 131–132.

36. Edmond Halley, "An Account of some Observations lately made at Nurenburg by Mr. P. Wurtzelbaur, shewing that the Latitude of that Place has continued without sensible alteration for 200 years last past; as likewise the Obliquity of the Eclipktick; by comparing them with what was observed by Bernard Walther in the Year 1487," *Philosophical Transactions* 16 (1686–1687): 403–406, see 406.

37. Simon Schaffer, "Halley's Atheism and the End of the World," *Notes and Records of the Royal Society of London* 32 (1977): 17–40, see 27.

38. Edmond Halley, "Some Considerations about the Cause of the universal Deluge, laid before the Royal Society, on the 12th of December 1694," *Philosophical Transactions* 33 (1724–1725): 118–123, see 118. Curiously, the University of Chicago copy, which I examined, had "Revelation" inked to "Relation." Also see the Journal Book of the Royal Society, 12 December 1694, in MacPike, *Correspondence and Papers*, 234. As evidence that the account was incomplete, Halley referred to difficulties relating to the ark's construction, the reception and harmony of the animals, the ark's preservation in the midst of a violent sea whipped by the winds God sent to dry up the flood waters, and the ark's landing. Halley noted that time may have added as well as subtracted some notable circumstances. See Halley, "Some Considerations about the Cause of the universal Deluge," 118–119.

39. Halley, "Some Considerations about the Cause of the universal Deluge," 119; Armitage, *Edmond Halley*, 91.

40. For Halley's interest in the location of fossils, see the Journal Book of the Royal Society, 1 August 1688 and 12 December 1694, in MacPike, *Correspondence and Papers*, 213, 234.

41. Halley, "Some Considerations about the Cause of the universal Deluge," 121; Schaffer, "Halley's Atheism," 28.

42. Thomas Burnet, *Telluris theoria sacra*, 2 vols. (London, 1681–1689).

43. Halley, "Some Considerations about the Cause of the universal Deluge," 120. For more on Burnet, see M. C. Jacob and W. A. Lockwood, "Political Millenarianism and Burnet's *Sacred Theory*," *Science Studies* 2 (1972): 265–279; and Marjorie Hope Nicolson, *Mountain Gloom and Mountain Glory: The Development of the Aesthetics of the Infinite* (Ithaca: Cornell University Press, 1959).

44. Hooke presented his theory of the earth in a series of lectures to the Royal Society between 1686 and 1688. The lectures were later published along with related work carried out between 1667 and 1699. See Robert Hooke, "Lectures and Discourses of Earthquakes," in *The Posthumous Works of Robert Hooke*, ed. Richard Waller (London, 1705), 277–450; David Kubrin, "'Such an Impertinently Litigious Lady': Hooke's 'Great Pretending' vs. Newton's *Principia* and Newton's and Halley's Theory of Comets," in *Standing on the Shoulders of Giants: A Longer View of Newton and Halley*, ed. Norman J. W. Thrower (Berkeley and Los Angeles: University of California Press, 1990), 55–90, see 56–61, 70.

45. Hooke referred to a prolate spheroid, but his arguments all read as if he intended an oblate spheroid, according to the modern usage of the term with respect to the axis of rotation. Hooke, "Lectures and Discourses of Earthquakes," 351, 322, 346–362; Halley, "Account of some Observations lately made at Nurenburg," 405–406; Thomas Birch, *The History of the Royal Society of London*, 4 vols. (London, 1756–1757), 4:521–529.

46. Halley, "Account of some Observations lately made at Nurenburg," 405; Halley to Wallis, 9 April 1687, in MacPike, *Correspondence and Papers*, 81.

47. Halley, "Account of some Observations lately made at Nurenburg," 406.

48. Halley was prepared to accept an increased age of the earth, but not an eternal world. See discussion below, and Edmond Halley, "A short Account of the Cause of the Saltness of the Ocean, and of the several Lakes that emit no Rivers; with a Proposal, by help thereof, to discover the Age of the World," *Philosophical Transactions* 29 (1714–1716): 296–300.

49. Halley, "Account of some Observations lately made at Nurenburg," 406. Hooke also seemed to recognize this problem and argued that the slow polar shifts or other mutations of the globe and the resultant fossils might not be directly connected with the Flood. Hooke, "Lectures and Discourses of Earthquakes," 408–409.

50. Halley, "Account of some Observations lately made at Nurenburg," 406.

51. Ibid.

52. Halley believed the external parts of the earth to be a shell surrounding a series of concentric, hollow spheres, each with its own set of magnetic poles. He attributed magnetic variation to the relative rates of diurnal rotation of the inner and outer spheres, adding, "This I conceive to arise from the Impulse whereby this diurnal Motion was imprest on the Earth, being given to the external parts, and from thence in time communicated to the internal; but not so as perfectly to equal the Velocity of the first Motion impressed on, and still conserved by the superficial parts of the Globe." The implication here is that a comet smacking into the globe caused it to rotate. Edmond Halley, "An Account of the cause of the Change in the Variation of the Magnetic Needle. with an Hypothesis of the Structure of the Internal parts of the Earth," *Philosophical Transactions* 17 (1691–1693): 563–578, see 570.

53. Journal Book of the Royal Society, 12 December 1694, in MacPike, *Correspondence and Papers*, 234.

54. Halley, "Some Considerations about the Cause of the universal Deluge," 121; cf. Hooke, "Lectures and Discourses of Earthquakes," 412–416. Halley calculated what quantity of water would be sufficient to drown the globe, and what width an earthen shell must be to contain it. Journal Book of the Royal Society, 13 March 1694/95, in MacPike, *Correspondence and Papers*, 235.

55. Halley also suggested that other great lakes around the world might be the result of the comet blow, but focused on the Caspian Sea as the site of the primary impact.

56. Here Halley used comet impacts to explain the puzzling difference in climate between North America and Europe on the same latitude. Vestiges of the arctic climate remained in North America, because vast quantities of prediluvian polar ice chilled the air and prevented the sun's warmth from being felt there.

57. Halley; "Some Considerations about the Cause of the universal Deluge," 121–123, quotation on 122; Journal Book of the Royal Society, 12 December 1694, in MacPike, *Correspondence and Papers*, 234. On contemporary views of a postdiluvian world in ruins, see Nicolson, *Mountain Gloom*, chap. 6.

58. Halley, "Some Considerations about the Cause of the universal Deluge," 123.

59. Ibid., 122.

60. Edmond Halley, "Some farther Thoughts upon the same Subject [the universal Deluge], delivered on the 19th of the same Month [December 1694]," *Philosophical Transactions* 33 (1724–1725): 123–125. For Newton's views, see chap. 7 above, and the John Conduitt memorandum, 7 March 1724/25, printed in Edmund Turnor, *Collections for the History of the Town and Soke of Grantham containing Authentic Memoirs of Sir Isaac Newton* (London, 1806), 172–173.

61. British Library MS Add. 4478b, fols. 142–150; partly quoted in Margaret C. Jacob, *The Newtonians and the English Revolution 1689–1720* (Hassocks, Sussex: Harvester Press, 1976), 135–136.

62. Halley, "Synopsis" (1705), 1898–1899.

63. Halley, "Synopsis" (1706), 23.

64. Word repeated in original text.

65. Halley, "Synopsis" (1706), 24.

66. Ibid.

67. Halley, *Astronomical Tables*, Tttt4.

68. Ibid.

69. Ibid.

70. See definition of "by the bye" as "incidentally," in the *Oxford English Dictionary*.

71. Halley, *Astronomical Tables*, Ssss2.

72. Isaac Newton, *Philosophiae naturalis principia mathematica* (London, 1687), 506.

73. Halley, "Some farther Thoughts," 124.

74. A pioneer of vital statistics and political arithmetic, Halley had quite a sanguine attitude toward the whole matter. "This may, perhaps, be thought hard, to destroy the whole Race for the Benefit of those that are to succeed. But if we consider Death simply, and how that the Life of each Individual is but of a very small Duration, it will be found that as to those that die, it is indifferent whether they die in a Pestilence out of 100000 *per Ann* or ordinarily out of 25000 in this great City, the Pestilence only appearing terrible to those that survive to contemplate the Danger they have escaped. Besides, as Seneca has it, 'Vitae est avidus quisquis non vult/Mondo secum pereunte mori.'" Ibid.

75. Halley's Ode to Newton, which prefaced the first edition of Newton's *Principia* (1687), vii–viii, is here translated by Leon J. Richardson, in *Sir Isaac Newton's Mathematical Principles of Natural Philosophy and His System of the World*, trans. Andrew Motte and rev. Florian Cajori (Berkeley and Los Angeles: University of California Press, 1962), xiii–xv, see xiv (hereafter cited as *Principia*, Motte-Cajori ed.). For Latin text and English translation with discussion, see also W. R. Albury, "Halley's Ode on the *Principia* and the Epicurean Revival in England," *Journal of the History of Ideas* 39 (1978): 24–43.

76. Edmond Halley, "An Account of the Cause of the late remarkable Appear-

ance of the Planet Venus, seen this Summer, for many Days together, in the Day time," *Philosophical Transactions* 29 (1714–1716): 466–468, see 466.

77. Edmond Halley, *A Description of the Passage of the Shadow of the Moon, over England, In the Total Eclipse of the Sun, on the 22ᵈ. Day of April 1715 in the Morning* [broadside] (London, 1715); reproduced in Owen Gingerich, "Eighteenth-Century Eclipse Paths," in *The Great Copernicus Chase and Other Adventures in Astronomical History* (Cambridge, Mass.: Sky Publishing, 1992; Cambridge: Cambridge University Press, 1992), 152–159, see 153.

78. Halley's "Ode to Newton," in *Principia*, Motte-Cajori ed., xiv.

79. Sara Schechner Genuth, "Newton and the Ongoing Teleological Role of Comets," in *Standing on the Shoulders of Giants: A Longer View of Newton and Halley*, ed. Norman J. W. Thrower (Berkeley and Los Angeles: University of California Press, 1990), 299–311. See chaps. 9 and 10 below.

80. J. H. Lambert, *Cosmologische Briefe* (Augsburg, 1761), 19; trans. and reprinted in *Cosmological Letters on the Arrangement of the World-Edifice*, trans. Stanley L. Jaki (New York: Science History Publications, 1976), 63.

81. John Wesley, "Serious Thoughts Occasioned by the Late Earthquake at Lisbon" (1755), in *The Works of John Wesley*, 14 vols. (London: Wesleyan Conference Office, 1872; reprint, Grand Rapids, Mich.: Zondervan Publishing House, 1958), 11:1–13. Cf. Wesley's sermon, "The Great Assize" (10 March 1758); *Works*, 5:180. Also see Craig B. Waff, "Comet Halley's First Expected Return: English Public Apprehensions, 1755–58," *Journal for the History of Astronomy* 17 (1986): 1–37.

82. On their theories, see Katharine B. Collier, *Cosmogonies of Our Fathers: Some Theories of the Seventeenth and Eighteenth Centuries* (New York: Columbia University Press, 1934); Roy Porter, "Creation and Credence: The Career of Theories of the Earth in Britain, 1660–1820," in *Natural Order*, ed. Barry Barnes and Steven Shapin (Beverly Hills and London: Sage Publications, 1979), 97–123.

83. Schaffer, "Halley's Atheism"; Ernest Tuveson, "Swift and the World-Makers," *Journal of the History of Ideas* 11 (1950): 54–74.

84. John Keill, *An Examination of Dr. Burnet's Theory of the Earth. Together with Some Remarks on Mr. Whiston's New Theory of the Earth* (Oxford, 1698), 19–20.

85. Ibid., 19.

86. Erasmus Warren, *Geologia: or, a Discourse Concerning the Earth before the Deluge* (London, 1690), 29; Tuveson, "Swift and the World-Makers," 62.

87. Halley, "Some farther Thoughts," 123–124.

88. Ibid., 124.

89. Schaffer, "Halley's Atheism."

90. Halley, "Some farther Thoughts," 125.

91. Ibid.

92. Colin A. Ronan, *Edmond Halley: Genius in Eclipse* (Garden City, N.Y.: Doubleday & Company, 1969), 122; Journal Book of the Royal Society, 11 November 1691, in MacPike, *Correspondence and Papers*, 226.

93. Their views are discussed in Schaffer, "Halley's Atheism"; Richard H. Popkin, "The Philosophy of Bishop Stillingfleet," *Journal of the History of Philosophy* 9 (1971): 303–319; David Kubrin, "Providence and the Mechanical Philoso-

phy: The Creation and Dissolution of the World in Newtonian Thought. A Study of the Relations of Science and Religion in Seventeenth Century England" (Ph.D. diss., Cornell University, 1968), chap. 2.

94. Halley to Abraham Hill, 22 June 1691, in MacPike, *Correspondence and Papers*, 88. Jacob, *Newtonians and the English Revolution*, 30–31, suggests that Halley and Tillotson were on good terms in the early 1680s.

95. William Whiston, *Memoirs of the Life and Writings of Mr. William Whiston*, 2 vols. (London, 1749–1750), 1:123; the second edition of Whiston's *Memoirs* is quoted in MacPike, *Correspondence and Papers*, 264.

96. *Table-talk of Bishop Hough*, quoted in MacPike, *Correspondence and Papers*, 264.

97. Thomas Hearne, *Remarks and Collections of Thomas Hearne*, ed. C. E. Doble et al., 11 vols. (Oxford: Clarendon Press for the Oxford Historical Society, 1885–1921), 3:473; also quoted in MacPike, *Correspondence and Papers*, 264. In reply to Robert Nelson's arguments against atheism, Halley purportedly stated that he agreed with Nelson's proofs of God's existence, but added, "But by God if you think to bring me in for any more of the family, you are mistaken." See MS Rawlinson, J. 4°, fols. 103, 105, Bodleian Library; quoted in Eugene Fairfield MacPike, *Hevelius, Flamsteed, and Halley: Three Contemporary Astronomers and Their Mutual Relations* (London: Taylor and Francis, 1937), 72; and in Richard S. Westfall, *Science and Religion in Seventeenth-Century England* (New Haven: Yale University Press, 1958), 134.

98. Whiston, *Memoirs*, 1:123; second edition quoted in MacPike, *Correspondence and Papers*, 264. Gregory was hardly notable for his piety and probity. He was accused of drunkenness and sloth in teaching, and he refused to subscribe to the Test in 1690. A manuscript at the Bodleian Library also reports an incident in which a Scottish stranger sought Halley several times in a London coffeehouse. When asked what business he had with Halley, the Scotsman replied, "Why Sr (says he) I would fain see the man that has less religion than Dr. Gregory." MS Rawlinson, J. No. 4.2; quoted in MacPike, *Correspondence and Papers*, 264–265n.10. Also see Schaffer, "Halley's Atheism," 18.

99. Whiston himself had been ousted from the Lucasian chair at Cambridge for his heretical, Arian beliefs. Whiston, *Memoirs*, 1:123.

100. From the 1680s onward, Flamsteed accused Halley of withholding scientific methods, plagiarism, dishonesty, libertinism, disingenuous trickery, slander, incivility, and irreligion. For the juicy details, see MacPike, *Hevelius, Flamsteed, and Halley*, 90–94, 98–102.

101. Flamsteed to Abraham Sharp, 18 December 1703; Francis Baily, *An Account of the Revd. John Flamsteed, the First Astronomer-Royal* (London, 1835), 215.

102. On their animosity toward Halley, see MacPike, *Correspondence and Papers*, 262–264, 268; and MacPike, *Hevelius, Flamsteed, and Halley*, 72, 90–94, 98.

103. Whiston, *Memoir*, 1:243. (I have paraphrased Whiston's first-person report.) Whiston felt that he had suffered for his sincere faith, and retorted, "Had it not been for the Rise now and then of a *Luther*, and a *Whiston*, he [Halley] would himself have gone down on his Knees to St. *Winifrid* and St. *Bridget*." Whiston, *Memoirs*, 1:243. Also see Ronan, *Edmond Halley*, 120–121; Armitage, *Edmond Halley*, 123.

104. MS Rawlinson, J. 4°, fols. 103, 105, quoted in MacPike, *Hevelius, Flamsteed, and Halley*, 72.

105. For example, see Halley, "Account of some Observations lately made at Nurenburg"; and Halley, "Short Account of the Cause of the Saltness of the Ocean."

106. Halley, "Short Account of the Cause of the Saltness of the Ocean," 300. This paper was based on work done in the 1690s at Gresham College.

107. Journal Book of the Royal Society, 19 October 1692 and 18 October 1693, in MacPike, *Correspondence and Papers*, 229, 232, quotation on 232. Both papers are printed in full in Schaffer, "Halley's Atheism," 29–33. See also Kubrin, " 'Such an Impertinently Litigious Lady,' " 65–68, 73–74.

108. "Some Observations on the Motion of the Sun," 18 October 1693, Royal Society RBC7.364, printed in Schaffer, "Halley's Atheism," 32–33, quotation on 33.

109. It has been suggested that Halley's early Deluge studies, and possible previews to friends of his 1694 comet papers, contributed to the accusations of heresy. S. P. Rigaud, in *London and Edinburgh Philosophical Magazine* 8 (1836): 219–221; Sir David Brewster, *Memoirs of the Life, Writings and Discoveries of Sir Isaac Newton*, 2 vols. (Edinburgh, 1855), 2:164–166; both quoted in MacPike, *Correspondence and Papers*, 266–268. I do not agree with Rigaud that Halley would have previewed his notions of the pre-Adamite earth before 1694, since his second 1694 paper gives the impression that this is a very new idea.

110. Halley, "Short Account of the Cause of the Saltness of the Ocean," 296.

111. Beaufort MSS (H.M.C.), 23; quoted in Christopher Hill, *The World Turned Upside Down: Radical Ideas during the English Revolution* (Harmondsworth: Penguin Books, 1975), 34.

112. Gerald R. Cragg, *The Church and the Age of Reason 1648–1789* (Harmondsworth: Penguin Books, 1970), chap. 4; Norman Sykes, *Church and State in England in the Eighteenth Century* (Cambridge: Cambridge University Press, 1934), chap. 1.

113. The Act of Uniformity (1662) required all clergy to be episcopally ordained and authorized the sole use of the Common Prayer Book. The Corporation Act (1661) excluded nonconformists from both the government and borough corporations by requiring all office holders to swear oaths of allegiance and nonresistance to the king, to receive the sacraments according to the Anglican rites, and to repudiate the Solemn League and Covenant. The Test Act (1673) barred Catholics from public office. The Licensing Act (1662) prohibited the publication of religious works without the license of a bishop.

114. Cragg, *Church and the Age of Reason*, 60–61; Sykes, *Church and State in England*, 28–40; W. A. Speck, *Stability and Strife: England, 1714–1760* (Cambridge: Harvard University Press, 1977), 91–93.

115. The Toleration Act (1689) permitted dissenters to preach openly if they registered their places of worship, took oaths of allegiance, and subscribed to the doctrinal portion of the Thirty-Nine Articles of religion. Under the practice of occasional conformity, dissenters annually took communion in the Anglican Church but worshiped in their own conventicles for the rest of the year. Thereby complying with the letter, if not the spirit, of the Test and Corporation Acts, dissenters had access to public office.

116. Issues reached a feverish pitch with Dr. Henry Sacheverell's seditious sermon (1709) and subsequent trial. See Geoffrey Holmes, *The Trial of Doctor Sacheverell* (London: Eyre Methuen, 1973); James E. Force, *William Whiston: Honest Newtonian* (Cambridge: Cambridge University Press, 1985), 96–100.

117. The Occasional Conformity Bill (1711) outlawed the practice of occasional conformity; and the Schism Act (1714) prohibited dissenting academies. Both were repealed in 1719.

118. Speck, *Stability and Strife*, 92–93; Sykes, *Church and State in England*, 35–36.

119. In 1714, George I prohibited the preaching of political sermons, and in 1717 he suppressed convocation. Speck, *Stability and Strife*, 93–96.

120. Lemuel Gulliver [Jonathan Swift], "A Voyage to Lilliput," *Travels into Several Remote Nations of the World*, 2 vols. (London, 1726); and the Scriblerus Club [Jonathan Swift, Alexander Pope, John Gay, John Arbuthnot, Thomas Parnell, and Robert Harley, earl of Oxford], *Memoirs of the Extraordinary Life, Works, and Discoveries of Martinus Scriblerus* [1741], ed. Charles Kerby-Miller (New York: Russell & Russell, 1966), 137–142, 280–293.

121. Ronan, *Edmond Halley*, 182–185; MacPike, *Correspondence and Papers*, 248–250; Alan H. Cook, "Halley in Istria, 1703: Navigator and Military Engineer," *Journal of Navigation* 37 (1984): 1–23; Alan H. Cook, "Halley, Surveyor and Military Engineer: Istria, 1703," in *Standing on the Shoulders of Giants: A Longer View of Newton and Halley*, ed. Norman J. W. Thrower (Berkeley and Los Angeles: University of California Press, 1990), 157–170.

122. Hearne, *Remarks and Collections*, 6:132; quoted in MacPike, *Correspondence and Papers*, 269.

123. *Biographia Britannica*, 4:2507, note BB; quoted in MacPike, *Correspondence and Papers*, 269.

124. Hearne, *Remarks and Collections*, 6:139–140; quoted in MacPike, *Correspondence and Papers*, 269.

125. Hearne, *Remarks and Collections*, 6:140.

126. Ibid., 132.

127. Halley to John Aubrey, 16 November 1679, in MacPike, *Correspondence and Papers*, 47–48.

128. Kubrin, "'Such an Impertinently Litigious Lady,'" 73–74.

129. Halley, *A Description of . . . the Total Eclipse of the Sun*.

130. Richard Olson, "Tory-High Church Opposition to Science and Scientism in the Eighteenth Century: The Works of John Arbuthnot, Jonathan Swift, and Samuel Johnson," in *The Uses of Science in the Age of Newton*, ed. John G. Burke (Berkeley and Los Angeles: University of California Press, 1983), 171–204; G. S. Rousseau, "'Wicked Whiston' and the Scriblerians: Another Ancients-Modern Controversy," *Studies in Eighteenth-Century Culture* 17 (1987): 17–44; Force, *William Whiston*, 93–94, 110–112, 129–132; Tuveson, "Swift and the World-Makers"; Scriblerus Club, *Memoirs of . . . Martinus Scriblerus*, Kerby-Miller introduction, 100–101, 197–198.

131. Scriblerus Club, *Memoirs of . . . Martinus Scriblerus*, 166.

132. Ibid., 166–167. In the same stroke, the Scriblerians also ridiculed Whiston's views. I agree with Rousseau that Whiston was the chief butt of their jokes, but disagree that Halley was exempt. (Cf. Rousseau, "'Wicked Whiston,'" 24–27.) Halley's theory of the concentric spheres within the earth, the variation of the com-

pass, the parallax and proper motions of the fixed stars, and his efforts to determine the longitude were also ridiculed (*Memoirs of . . . Martinus Scriblerus*, 168).

133. Gulliver [Swift], "A Voyage to Laputa," *Travels into Several Remote Nations*, pt. 3, pp. 29–31, 43–44. Also see Marjorie Hope Nicolson and Nora M. Mohler, "The Scientific Background of Swift's *Voyage to Laputa*," *Annals of Science* 2 (1937): 299–334; reprinted in Marjorie Hope Nicolson, *Science and Imagination* (Ithaca: Cornell University Press, 1956; reprint, Hamden, Conn.: Archon Press, 1976), 110–154; Tuveson, "Swift and the World-Makers"; Olson, "Tory-High Church Opposition to Science."

134. *The Prose Works of Jonathan Swift, D.D.*, ed. Temple Scott, 12 vols. (London: George Bell and Sons, 1897–1908), 1:281.

135. *Covent-Garden Journal*, no. 70, Saturday, 11 November 1752; reprinted in Alexander Drawcansir [Henry Fielding], *The Covent-Garden Journal*, ed. Gerard Edward Jensen, 2 vols. (New Haven: Yale University Press, 1915), 2:130–136 (hereafter cited as Fielding, *Covent-Garden Journal*). See Bertrand A. Goldgar, "Fielding, the Flood Makers, and Natural Philosophy: *Covent-Garden Journal* No. 70," *Modern Philology* 80 (1982): 136–144.

136. Horace, *Odes* 1.3.38.

137. Fielding, *Covent-Garden Journal*, 2:131.

138. Ibid., 131–132.

139. Cf. Halley, "Some Considerations about the Cause of the universal Deluge"; and Halley, "Some farther Thoughts."

140. Fielding, *Covent-Garden Journal*, 2:134; cf. Halley, "Some Considerations about the Cause of the universal Deluge," 121.

141. Fielding, *Covent-Garden Journal*, 2:134.

142. Ibid.

143. Ibid., 132.

144. Ibid., 135–136.

145. Ibid., 136.

146. Gay satirized Whiston's millenarian speeches about a forthcoming cometary end of the world, and he commented upon the disastrous social effects of false prophecy. See [John Gay], "A True and Faithful Narrative of What pass'd in London during the general Consternation of all Ranks and Degrees of Mankind; On Tuesday, Wednesday, Thursday, and Friday last," in *Miscellanies: The Third Volume*, ed. Jonathan Swift and Alexander Pope (London, 1732), 239–260; and since it was once wrongly attributed to Swift, it can be found in *The Works of the Rev. Jonathan Swift, D.D., Dean of St. Patrick's, Dublin*, ed. Thomas Sheridan, rev. John Nichols, new ed., 19 vols. (London, 1801), 17:358–372; or in Swift, *Prose Works*, 4:273–285. See also Rousseau, " 'Wicked Whiston' "; Tuveson, "Swift and the World-Makers," 67–69; Waff, "Comet Halley's First Expected Return"; and Force, *William Whiston*, 129–131.

147. Hill, *World Turned Upside Down*, 33–34, 92–93, 96–98.

148. Whiston, for instance, believed that the Jacobite rebellions fulfilled prophecy and an English defeat of Louis XIV would bring the Millennium closer. He delivered lectures in London coffeehouses on comets and the end of the world. On Whiston in the context of eighteenth-century millenarianism, see Force, *William Whiston*, 48, 111, 113–119, 131; Jacob, *Newtonians and the English Revolution*, 130–132. On the perceived dangers of his lectures and writings, see the sources cited in n. 146 above.

CHAPTER IX
REFUELING THE SUN AND PLANETS

1. John Harris, *Lexicon technicum*, 2d ed., 2 vols. (London, 1708–1710), s.v. "comets"; William Whiston, *Sir Isaac Newton's Mathematick Philosophy More easily Demonstrated* (London, 1716), 403–404 (on restoring planetary moistures only); Henry Pemberton, *A View of Sir Isaac Newton's Philosophy* (London, 1728), 244–246; Colin Maclaurin, *An Account of Sir Isaac Newton's Philosophical Discoveries* (London, 1748), 374–375; James Ferguson, *An Idea of the Material Universe, Deduced from a Survey of the Solar System* (London, 1754), 27; James Ferguson, *Astronomy Explained upon Sir Isaac Newton's Principles*, 4th ed. (London, 1770), 39; Benjamin Martin, *The Theory of Comets* (London, 1757), 11–15; John Winthrop, *Two Lectures on Comets* (Boston, 1759), 41; Roger Long, *Astronomy, in Five Books*, 2 vols. (Cambridge, 1742–1784), 2:562–563; John Hill, *A New Astronomical Dictionary, Or, A Compleat View of the Heavens; Containing the Antient and Modern Astronomy* (London, 1768), s.v. "comets"; Bartholomew Burges, *A Short Account of the Solar System, and of Comets in General: Together with a Particular Account of the Comet that Will Appear in 1789* (Boston, 1789), 15.

2. Samuel D. M'Cullough, *Picture of the Heavens* (Lexington, Ky., 1840), 101.

3. See J. L. Heilbron, *Electricity in the Seventeenth and Eighteenth Centuries* (Berkeley and Los Angeles: University of California Press, 1979); and I. Bernard Cohen, *Franklin and Newton* (Philadelphia: American Philosophical Society, 1956).

4. I will focus on those who considered the possibility of electrical connections between the aurora and comet tails, but it should be noted that Euler, Kant, and Herschel compared the two phenomena in a nonelectrical way. See Leonhard Euler, "Recherches physiques sur la cause de la queue des comètes, de la lumière boréale, et de la lumière zodiacale," *Histoire de l'Académie Royale des Sciences MDCCXLVI* (Berlin, 1748), 117–140; Immanuel Kant, *Allgemeine Naturgeschichte und Theorie des Himmels* [Leipzig, 1755]; translated in *Kant's Cosmogony, as in His Essay on the Retardation of the Rotation of the Earth and His Natural History and Theory of the Heavens*, trans. W. Hastie, intro. Gerald Whitrow (New York: Johnson Reprint Corporation, 1970), 101–102; William Herschel, "Observations of a Comet, made with a View to investigate its Magnitude and the Nature of its Illumination," *Philosophical Transactions* 98 (1808): 145–163; reprinted in *The Scientific Papers of Sir William Herschel*, ed. J.L.E. Dreyer, 2 vols. (London: Royal Society and Royal Astronomical Society, 1912), 2:403–413, see 411. See also J. Morton Briggs, Jr., "Aurora and Enlightenment: Eighteenth-Century Explanations of the Aurora Borealis," *Isis* 58 (1967): 491–503.

5. Edmond Halley, "An Account of several Nebulae or lucid Spots like Clouds, lately discovered among the Fixt Stars by help of the Telescope" [1716] and "An Account of the late surprizing Appearance of the Lights seen in the Air, on the sixth of March last; with an Attempt to explain the Principal Phaenomena thereof" [1716] *Philosophical Transactions* 29 (1714–1719): 390–392 and 406–428. More specifically, Halley considered whether the aurora was due to magnetic effluvia whose friction in penetrating the earth produced electric sparks, or whether the aurora appeared when effluvia ushered luminous matter (which was comparable to nebulous matter in the heavens) out of an internal cavity within the earth. Halley took up the question of the cause of the aurora borealis as part of his discussion of

the possibility of habitable(!) concentric spheres within the earth. He first posited such spheres in 1691 as part of a hypothesis attempting to explain the variation of the magnetic compass. See Journal Book of the Royal Society, 25 November and 2 December 1691, 27 January, 18 May, 26 October 1692; extracts are printed in Eugene Fairfield MacPike, ed., *Correspondence and Papers of Edmond Halley* (Oxford: Clarendon Press, 1932; reprint, New York: Arno Press, 1975), 226–227, 229.

6. Jean Jacques d'Ortous de Mairan, *Traité physique et historique de l'aurore boréale* (Paris, 1733; rev. 2d ed., Paris, 1754), which contained articles culled from the *Mémoires de l'Académie des Sciences, Paris* (1731, 1732, 1747, 1751). The second edition discussed the new electrical theory of the aurora. *Benjamin Franklin's Experiments*, ed. I. Bernard Cohen (Cambridge: Harvard University Press, 1941), 209, 299, 324; Samuel Vince, *The Elements of Astronomy*, 4th ed. (Cambridge, 1816), 254. See also Edmund Newton Harvey, *A History of Luminescence from the Earliest Times until 1900* (Philadelphia: American Philosophical Society, 1959), 255–263; Briggs, "Aurora and Enlightenment."

7. Joseph Priestley, *The History and Present State of Electricity, with Original Experiments* (London, 1767), 352, 376–377, 497–498; Priestley to Andrew Oliver, 12 February 1775, *Proceedings of the Massachusetts Historical Society*, 2d ser., 3 (1886–1887): 13–14.

8. *Monthly Review* 37 (1767): 253.

9. Ibid. See also Adam Walker, *A System of Familiar Philosophy in Twelve Lectures* (London, 1799), 535–536.

10. Hugh Hamilton, *Philosophical Essays On the following Subjects: I. On the Ascent of Vapours, the Formation of Clouds, Rain and Dew, and on several other Phaenomena of Air and Water. II. Observations and Conjectures on the Nature of the Aurora Borealis, and the Tails of Comets. III. On the Principles of Mechanicks* (Dublin, 1766); reprinted in *The Works of the Right Rev. Hugh Hamilton, D.D., Late Bishop of Ossory*, ed. Alexander Hamilton, 2 vols. (London, 1809), 2:159–274, see esp. 213–247.

11. [Charles Burney], *An Essay towards a History of the Principal Comets That Have Appeared since the Year 1742. . . . To which is prefixed, by way of Introduction, A Letter upon Comets. Addressed to a Lady, by the Late M. de Maupertuis. Written in the Year 1742* (London, 1769), 82–86; Vince, *Elements of Astronomy*, 253–255. Cf. [John Perkins], *The True Nature and Cause of the Tails of Comets. Elucidated In a rationale agreeing with their several Phanomena* (Boston, 1772), 3–8.

12. Pierre Louis Moreau de Maupertuis, *Lettre sur la comète* ([Amsterdam?], 1742), 101–103. Philip Stewart distinguishes two separate editions of Maupertuis's *Lettre* printed in 1742 without a place of publication given. I have consulted an edition of x + 111 pages, which he labels "B." See Philip Stewart, "Science and Superstition: Comets and the French Public in the Eighteenth Century," *American Journal of Physics* 54, no. 1 (January 1986): 16–24, see n. 4.

13. William Whiston, *A New Theory of the Earth, From its Original, to the Consummation of all Things* (London, 1696), 181–184, 198–199, 289–294, 336–337, 372; William Whiston, *A New Theory of the Earth. . . . To which is added, An Appendix, containing a New Theory of the Deluge*, 5th ed. rev. (London, 1737), 469–470.

14. David Gregory, *Astronomiae physicae & geometricae elementa* (Oxford, 1702), 408.

15. [Cotton Mather], *An Essay on Comets, Their Nature, The Laws of their Motions, the Cause and Magnitude of their Atmosphere, and Tails; With a Conjecture of their Use and Design* (Boston, 1744), 3, 5–7. This tract is an enlarged version of the text printed in Cotton Mather, *The Christian Philosopher* (London, 1721), 41–45. Cf. Cotton Mather, *Manuductio ad ministerium. Directions for a Candidate of the Ministry* (Boston, 1726), 54–55.

16. George Cheyne, *Philosophical Principles of Natural Religion: Containing the Elements of Natural Philosophy, And the Proofs for Natural Religion, Arising from them* (London, 1705), 120–121. Without citing Newton by name, and well before Newton publicized his opinions in 1713, Cheyne criticized the Newtonian view that comets refueled the sun. But Cheyne was in touch with Newton, Gregory, Halley, Keill, and others, and I suspect that he heard of Newton's views through those channels. (See Walter G. Hiscock, ed., *David Gregory, Isaac Newton and Their Circle: Extracts from David Gregory's Memoranda, 1677–1708* [Oxford: By the editor, 1937]; Robert E. Schofield, *Mechanism and Materialism: British Natural Philosophy in an Age of Reason* [Princeton: Princeton University Press, 1970], 57–62.) After Newton published his views and others began to embrace them, it seems that Cheyne dared not reprint his critique. The second edition of his book omitted this passage and offered a less than enthusiastic endorsement of the Newtonian views. See George Cheyne, *Philosophical Principles of Religion: Natural and Reveal'd*, 2 vols. in 1 (London, 1715), 1:149–163, 216–221, 244–246.

17. Cheyne, *Philosophical Principles of Natural Religion*, 121–122.

18. See chaps. 5 and 6 above.

19. Georges Louis Leclerc, comte de Buffon, *Histoire naturelle, générale et particulière*, 45 vols. (Paris, 1749–1804), vol. 42 [= supplément, vol. 5 (Paris, 1778)], pp. 256–257, in the section, "Additions et corrections aux articles qui contiennent les preuves de la Théorie de la Terre." My translation.

20. Thomas Wright of Durham, *An Original Theory or New Hypothesis of the Universe, Founded upon the Laws of Nature, and Solving by Mathematical Principles the General Phaenomena of the Visible Creation; and Particularly the Via Lactea* (London, 1750), 21.

21. Thomas Wright, *Second or Singular Thoughts upon the Theory of the Universe* [MS ca. 1771], ed. M. A. Hoskin (London: Dawsons of Pall Mall, 1968), 77. His reasons for rejecting the theory were: (1) comets passed through intolerable degrees of heat and cold in their eccentric orbits; (2) their tails swept around the sun with incredible velocities; (3) comets appeared to be very different from the planets; and (4) Halley's prediction of the return of the 1682 comet was not fulfilled. In an editorial note, Michael Hoskin reported that Wright did not know of Clairaut's recalculation of the comet's return, taking planetary perturbations into account. Still, it seems rather incredible that Wright missed all the public hoopla anticipating and celebrating the return in 1759. On the public response, see Ruth Wallis, "The Glory of Gravity—Halley's Comet 1759," *Annals of Science* 41 (1984): 279–286; Craig Waff, "Comet Halley's First Expected Return: English Public Apprehensions, 1755–58," *Journal for the History of Astronomy* 17 (1986): 1–37; and Peter Broughton, "The First Predicted Return of Comet Halley," *Journal for the History of Astronomy* 16 (1985): 123–133.

22. Wright, *Second or Singular Thoughts*, 29–30.

23. Ibid. On Wright's cosmology, see M. A. Hoskin, "The Cosmology of Thomas Wright of Durham," *Journal for the History of Astronomy* 1 (1970): 44–

52; Simon Schaffer, "The Phoenix of Nature: Fire and Evolutionary Cosmology in Wright and Kant," *Journal for the History of Astronomy* 9 (1978): 180–200.

24. Wright, *Second or Singular Thoughts*, 27–29, 34–35, 38–39, 41, 77–79, quotations on 29 and 79.

25. Ibid., 31–32.

26. Ibid., 32.

27. Ibid., 45–46.

28. Ibid., 53.

29. Ibid., 76.

30. Ibid., 35–36, quotation on 43.

31. Ibid., 41.

32. *Kant's Cosmogony*, 99–100, 153; Buffon, *Histoire naturelle*, 1:135; Maupertuis, *Lettre sur la comète*, 103–105. These works will be discussed at greater length in chap. 10 below.

33. See n. 1 above.

34. William Whiston, *Astronomical Principles of Religion, Natural and Reveal'd* (London, 1717), 79. Here and elsewhere, Whiston is silent on Newton's hypothesis that comets would refuel the sun, although he repeated that they refurbished the planets with moisture and spirit.

35. Ibid., 89–90.

36. Leonhard Euler, *Nova theoria lucis et colorum* (1746); in *Leonhardi Euleri opera omnia*, 72 vols. expected (Berlin-Göttingen-Leipzig-Heidelberg: Societatis Scientiarum Naturalium Helveticae, 1911–), ser. 3, vol. 5, pp. 1–45; Leonhard Euler, *Lettres à une Princesse d'Allemagne sur divers sujets de physique & de philosophie*, 3 vols. (St. Petersburg, 1768–1772), see letters 17–18 for his critique of Newton, and letters 19–20 for his own theory; in Euler, *Opera omnia*, ser. 3, vols. 11–12. Euler's *Lettres* were published numerous times; see the bibliography at the back of this book for editions consulted. See also Joseph Priestley, *The History and Present State of Discoveries relating to Vision, Light, and Colours* (London, 1772), 357–358.

37. Benjamin Franklin to Cadwallader Colden, 23 April 1752, reprinted in *Benjamin Franklin's Experiments*, 325.

38. Ibid., 326–327: "If the sun is not wasted by expence of light, I can easily conceive that he shall otherwise always retain the same quantity of matter; though we should suppose him made of sulphur constantly flaming. The action of fire only *separates* the particles of matter, it does not *annihilate* them. . . . So we have only to suppose, that the parts of the sun's sulphur, separated by fire, rise into his atmosphere, and there being freed from the immediate action of the fire, they collect into cloudy masses, and growing, by degrees, too heavy to be longer supported, they descend to the sun, and are burnt over again."

39. David Speiser, "The Distance of the Fixed Stars and the Riddle of the Sun's Radiation," in *Mélanges Alexandre Koyré*, 2 vols. (Paris: Hermann, 1964), 1:541–551; Henry John Steffens, *The Development of Newtonian Optics in England* (New York: Science History Publications, 1977), 70, 102–105.

40. Priestley, *History and Present State of Discoveries relating to Vision*, 387–390; Russell McCormmach, "John Michell and Henry Cavendish: Weighing the Stars," *British Journal for the History of Science* 4 (1968): 126–155.

41. William Herschel, "On the Nature and Construction of the Sun and fixed Stars," *Philosophical Transactions* 85 (1795): 46–72; reprinted in Herschel, *Scien-*

tific Papers, 1:470–484, see 478. See also the draft of this paper, Royal Astronomical Society Herschel MS, W.4/10.1, 18–19; quoted in Simon Schaffer, " 'The Great Laboratories of the Universe': William Herschel on Matter Theory and Planetary Life," *Journal for the History of Astronomy* 11 (1980): 81–111, see 93–94. On Caroline Herschel's comet-seeking activities, see Michael Hoskin and Brian Warner, "Caroline Herschel's Comet Sweepers," *Journal for the History of Astronomy* 12 (1981): 27–34; and J. A. Bennett, " 'On the Power of Penetrating into Space': The Telescopes of William Herschel," *Journal for the History of Astronomy* 7 (1976): 75–108.

42. Herschel, "Observations of a Comet" (1808); and William Herschel, "Observations of a Comet, with Remarks on the Construction of its different Parts," and "Observations of a second Comet, with Remarks on its Construction," *Philosophical Transactions* 102 (1812): 115–143, 229–237; reprinted in Herschel, *Scientific Papers*, 2:403–413, 498–519.

43. Herschel, "On the Nature and Construction of the Sun"; Herschel, *Scientific Papers*, 1:478.

CHAPTER X
REVOLUTION AND EVOLUTION WITHIN THE HEAVENS

1. John Ray, *The Wisdom of God Manifested in the Works of the Creation*, 3d ed. (London, 1701), preface. Cf. John Ray, *Three Physico-Theological Discourses*, 2d ed. (London, 1693), 329–330.

2. Isaac Newton, *Opticks*, 4th ed. (London, 1730; reprint, New York: Dover, 1952), query 31, p. 402.

3. Isaac Newton, *Philosophiae naturalis principia mathematica*, 2d ed. (Cambridge, 1713), General Scholium; quotation taken from Isaac Newton, *Sir Isaac Newton's Mathematical Principles of Natural Philosophy and His System of the World*, trans. Andrew Motte and rev. Florian Cajori (Berkeley and Los Angeles: University of California Press, 1962), 544 (hereafter cited as *Principia*, Motte-Cajori edition).

4. Ibid.

5. John Ray, *The Wisdom of God Manifested in the Works of the Creation*, 1st ed. (London, 1691), 137.

6. For background, see John C. Greene, *The Death of Adam: Evolution and Its Impact on Western Thought* (Ames: Iowa State University Press, 1959); Stanley L. Jaki, *Planets and Planetarians: A History of Theories of the Origin of Planetary Systems* (New York: John Wiley & Sons, [1978]); David C. Kubrin, "Providence and the Mechanical Philosophy: The Creation and Dissolution of the World in Newtonian Thought. A Study of the Relations of Science and Religion in Seventeenth Century England" (Ph.D. diss., Cornell University, 1968); Stephen Jay Gould, *Time's Arrow, Time's Cycle: Myth and Metaphor in the Discovery of Geological Time* (Cambridge: Harvard University Press, 1987).

7. See chap. 2 above.

8. William Whiston, *A New Theory of the Earth* (London, 1696), 69–104, 217–279. In later editions, in response to criticism from John Keill, Whiston modified his views on the shape of the orbit before and after the Fall. According to his new view, the comet's orbit slowly changed from extremely eccentric to modestly elliptical as the earth was formed. After the Fall, the orbit became perfectly circular,

until the Deluge, when it once again became mildly elliptical. See John Keill, *An Examination of Dr. Burnet's Theory of the Earth. Together with Some Remarks on Mr. Whiston's New Theory of the Earth* (Oxford, 1698); William Whiston, *A Vindication of the New Theory of the Earth from the Exceptions of Mr. Keill and Others* (London, 1698); William Whiston, *A New Theory of the Earth*, 2d ed. rev. (London, 1708), 108–118, 192, 233–234, 289–290, 299; William Whiston, *A New Theory of the Earth. . . . To which is added, An Appendix, containing a New Theory of the Deluge*, 5th ed. rev. (London, 1737), 109–118, 207, 244–245, 298–299, 308; also discussed in Kubrin, "Providence and the Mechanical Philosophy," 276, 282, 284–286.

9. Whiston, *New Theory of the Earth* (1708), 108–112; Edmond Halley, "An Account of the cause of the Change in the Variation of the Magnetic Needle. with an Hypothesis of the Structure of the Internal parts of the Earth," *Philosophical Transactions* 17 (1691–1693): 563–578.

10. Whiston, *New Theory of the Earth* (1696), 123–125. Drawing on different chronologies, Whiston referred to several dates for the commencement of the Deluge. He said that it began on the seventeenth day of the second month after the autumnal equinox, which equaled Friday, 28 November 2348 B.C. according to a contemporary Hebrew chronology, or 2 December 2925 B.C., according to a "more accurate Chronology of the ancient *Hebrew*, in the Days of *Josephus*." See Whiston, *New Theory of the Earth* (1737), 142, 461.

11. Whiston, *New Theory of the Earth* (1696), 126–156, 181–208, 287–356, 372; Whiston, *New Theory of the Earth* (1737), 467–477.

12. Whiston, *New Theory of the Earth* (1696), 368.

13. Ibid.

14. Ibid., 209–215, 368–378.

15. Ibid., 374.

16. The Deluge allegedly occurred in 2348 B.C.; and 2348 + 1680 = 4028 years, and 4028 ÷ 7 = 575.4. See William Whiston, *The Cause of the Deluge Demonstrated: Wherein it is proved that the famous Comet of A.D. 1680. came by the Earth at the Deluge, and was the occasion of it. Being an Appendix to the Second Edition of the New Theory of the Earth*, 2d ed. rev. (London, 1714). There were two editions of this pamphlet published in 1714. I have also consulted the revised, third edition (London, 1716). See also William Whiston, *Astronomical Principles of Religion, Natural and Reveal'd* (London, 1717), 74–75; Whiston, *New Theory of the Earth* (1737), 186–197, 461–467.

17. Whiston, *Cause of the Deluge*, 11–12, quotation on 12; Whiston, *New Theory of the Earth* (1737), 196–197.

18. Whiston, *New Theory of the Earth* (1696), 378.

19. Whiston, *Astronomical Principles of Religion*, 151–154.

20. William Whiston, *Memoirs of the Life and Writings of Mr. William Whiston*, 3 vols. (London, 1749–1750), 1:43.

21. They had a falling out about ten years later. James E. Force, *William Whiston: Honest Newtonian* (Cambridge: Cambridge University Press, 1985), 14, 23–24.

22. Halley on Whiston, 8 January 1707, MS Rigaud 37, fol. 89, Bodleian Library; cited in Simon Schaffer, "Newton's Comets and the Transformation of Astrology," in *Astrology, Science, and Society*, ed. Patrick Curry (Woodbridge, Suffolk: The Boydell Press, 1987), 219–243, see 233. Edmond Halley, "Some far-

ther Thoughts upon the same Subject [the universal Deluge], delivered on the 19th of the same Month [December 1694]," *Philosophical Transactions* 33 (1724–1725): 123–125, see 125.

23. Whiston, *Astronomical Principles of Religion*, 92. On the possibility of life on comets—hellacious or otherwise—see Sara Schechner Genuth, "Devils' Hells and Astronomers' Heavens: Religion, Method, and Popular Culture in Speculations about Life on Comets," in *The Invention of Physical Science: Intersections of Mathematics, Theology and Natural Philosophy since the Seventeenth Century. Essays in Honor of Erwin N. Hiebert*, ed. Mary Jo Nye, Joan L. Richards, and Roger H. Stuewer (Dordrecht: Kluwer Academic Publishers, 1992), 3–26.

24. George Cheyne, *Philosophical Principles of Natural Religion* (London, 1705), 119–122, 151.

25. Whiston, *Astronomical Principles of Religion*, 155–156.

26. William Whiston, *The Eternity of Hell-Torments Considered* [1740], 2d ed. (London, 1752), 105; D. P. Walker, *The Decline of Hell* (Chicago: University of Chicago Press, 1964), 100–101.

27. Whiston, *Astronomical Principles of Religion*, 154–155.

28. Whiston, *New Theory of the Earth* (1696), 361.

29. Ibid., 217–219, quotation on 219.

30. Ibid., 116.

31. Ibid., 367.

32. Ibid., 116.

33. Whiston, *Astronomical Principles of Religion*, 93.

34. Ibid., 23.

35. William Whiston, *The Astronomical Year: Or, An Account of the many remarkable Celestial Phaenomena of the Great Year MDCCXXXVI. Particularly of the Late Comet, Which was foretold by Sir Isaac Newton, and appeared at its Conclusion* (London, 1737).

36. Force, *William Whiston*, 19–21.

37. G. S. Rousseau, " 'Wicked Whiston' and the Scriblerians: Another Ancients-Modern Controversy," *Studies in Eighteenth-Century Culture* 17 (1987): 17–44, esp. 22–24, 32–34.

38. François Marie Arouet de Voltaire, *Letters Concerning the English Nation*, trans. John Lockman (London, 1733), letter 15; the first French edition appeared as *Lettres philosophiques* (London, 1734); I have used *Philosophical Letters*, trans. Ernest Dilworth (Indianapolis: Bobbs-Merrill Educational Publishing, 1961), 72 (but note his misspelling of Whiston's name). See also Voltaire, *Elémens de la philosophie de Neuton* (Amsterdam, 1738), 369–383. For Voltaire's opinion on the cometary cosmogonies of Buffon and Lalande, see nn. 67 and 141 below. For Voltaire's literary allusions to and droll comments about comets, see Philip Stewart, "Science and Superstition: Comets and the French Public in the Eighteenth Century," *American Journal of Physics* 54, no. 1 (January 1986): 16–24.

39. [John Gay], "A True and Faithful Narrative of What pass'd in London during the general Consternation of all Ranks and Degrees of Mankind; On Tuesday, Wednesday, Thursday, and Friday last," in *Miscellanies: The Third Volume*, ed. Jonathan Swift and Alexander Pope (London, 1732). See Rousseau, " 'Wicked Whiston,' " 27–28; Craig Waff, "Comet Halley's First Expected Return: English Public Apprehensions, 1755–58," *Journal for the History of Astronomy* 17 (1986): 1–37, esp. 7–8.

40. James Ferguson, *An Idea of the Material Universe, Deduced from a Survey of the Solar System* (London, 1754), 27; John Hill, *An New Astronomical Dictionary* (London, 1768), s.v. "comets"; Bartholomew Burges, *A Short Account of the Solar System, and of Comets in General* (Boston, 1789), 14–15.

41. Hill, *An New Astronomical Dictionary*, s.v. "comets."

42. Ibid.

43. [Cotton Mather], *A Voice from Heaven. An Account of a Late Uncommon Appearance in the Heavens* (Boston, 1719), 8–11, 13–16; Cotton Mather, *An Essay on Comets, Their Nature, The Laws of their Motions, the Cause and Magnitude of their Atmosphere, and Tails; With a Conjecture of their Use and Design* (Boston, 1744), 7; Mather Byles, *The Comet: A Poem* (Boston, 1744). See Schechner Genuth, "Devils' Hells and Astronomers' Heavens," 6–9.

44. John Wesley, "Serious Thoughts Occasioned by the Late Earthquake at Lisbon" (1755), in *The Works of John Wesley*, 14 vols. (London: Wesleyan Conference Office, 1872; reprint, Grand Rapids, Mich.: Zondervan Publishing House, 1958), 11:1–13, quotation on 9. Wesley conflated the comets of 1680 and 1682.

45. Benjamin Martin, *A View of the Solar System and Orbit of the Comet, (with its proper Elevation,) which will next return; truly representing all its Appearances for any Part of the Year* [broadside] ([London], 1757); pictured and quoted in Waff, "Comet Halley's First Expected Return," 12.

46. Henry Season, *Speculum anni redivivum: or, an almanack for the year of our Lord 1757* (London, [1756]), sigs. C3ᵛ–C4ᵛ; quoted in Waff, "Comet Halley's First Expected Return," 9, see also 19–20.

47. Paul Gemsege, "Cruelty of terrifying weak Minds with groundless Pains," *Gentleman's Magazine* 26 (February 1756): 71–72, quotation on 72; John Lodge Cowley, *A Discourse on Comets* (London, 1757), 38–41; Waff, "Comet Halley's First Expected Return," 8–9, 14.

48. Benjamin Martin, *The Theory of Comets Illustrated. . . . The whole adapted to, and exemplified in the Orbit of the Comet of the Year 1682, whose Return is now near at Hand* (London, 1757), 13–14, quotations on 13. See also B[enjamin] M[artin], "Of the Visible Way of the present Comet among the Stars, &c.," in *Miscellaneous Correspondence, Containing a Variety of Subjects Relative to Natural and Civil History, Geography, Mathematics, Poetry, Memoirs of monthly Occurrences, Catalogues of new Books, &c.*, The General Magazine of Arts and Sciences, pt. 5, vols. 1–2 (London, 1759), 2:646–647 (issue for October 1757).

49. Nathaniel Ames, *An Astronomical Diary or, an Almanack for the Year of our Lord Christ 1759* (Boston, 1759).

50. John Winthrop, *Two Lectures on Comets* (Boston, 1759). For more on colonial American attitudes toward comets, see Sara Schechner Genuth, "Blazing Stars, Open Minds, and Loosened Purse Strings: Astronomical Research and Its Early Cambridge Audience," *Journal for the History of Astronomy* 21 (1990): 9–20; and Sara Schechner Genuth, "From Heaven's Alarm to Public Appeal: Comets and the Rise of Astronomy at Harvard," in *Science at Harvard University: Historical Perspectives*, ed. Clark A. Elliott and Margaret W. Rossiter (Bethlehem: Lehigh University Press, 1992; London: Associated University Presses, 1992), 28–54.

51. Winthrop, *Two Lectures on Comets*, 38. Cf. Winthrop's letter in the *Boston News-letter*, 9 August 1770.

52. Winthrop, *Two Lectures on Comets*, 39–42, quotation on 42.

53. Ibid., 42–43.

54. Johannes Hevelius, *Cometographia* (Danzig, 1668), 540.

55. Increase Mather, *ΚΟΜΗΤΟΓΡΑΦΙΑ [Kometographia]. Or a Discourse Concerning Comets* (Boston, 1683), 18; Nicolas Fréret, "Réflexions sur un ancien phénomène céleste, observé au temps d'Ogygès," in *Oeuvres Complètes de Fréret, Secrétaire de l'Académie des Inscriptions et Belles-Lettres*, 20 vols. (Paris, 1796), 16:286–331, see 329–330.

56. Roger Long, *Astronomy, in Five Books*, 2 vols. (Cambridge, 1742–1784), 2:553.

57. Denis Diderot and Jean le Rond d'Alembert, *Encyclopédie, ou dictionnaire raisonné des sciences, des arts et des métiers*, 28 vols. (Paris and Neufchâtel, 1751–1772), s.v. "Comete," 3 (1753): 677b; my translation.

58. Long, *Astronomy*, 2:594.

59. Ibid., 585–594, quotation on 594.

60. Whiston, *New Theory of the Earth* (1696), 102.

61. Georges Louis Leclerc, comte de Buffon, "Preuves de la Théorie de la Terre," article 1: "De la formation des Planètes," in *Histoire naturelle, générale et particulière*, 45 vols. (Paris, 1749–1804), 1:134 on the improbability of the planetary arrangement. Unless otherwise noted, English quotations will be taken from Georges Louis Leclerc, comte de Buffon, *Natural History, General and Particular*, trans. William Smellie, 3d ed., 9 vols. (London, 1791), 1:65–66.

62. Buffon, *Histoire naturelle*, 1:133–138, 147–152, quotation on 163; Buffon, *Natural History*, 1:64–69, 77–82, quotation on 93.

63. Buffon, *Histoire naturelle*, 1:123–124, 163–165.

64. Ibid., 166.

65. Ibid., 169, 179; Buffon, *Natural History*, 1:98, 108. The first quotation is my translation.

66. Buffon, *Histoire naturelle*, 1:133–134; Buffon, *Natural History*, 1:64–65.

67. For charges of heresy and Buffon's retraction in 1751, see *Histoire naturelle* (Paris, 1753), 4:v–xvi. On the reception of Buffon's theory, see John Lyon and Phillip R. Sloan, *From Natural History to the History of Nature: Readings from Buffon and His Critics* (Notre Dame: University of Notre Dame Press, 1981). For Voltaire's opinion, see François Marie Arouet de Voltaire, "Si la Terre a été formée par une Comete," in *Dialogues d'Evhémére* (London, 1777), 97–104.

68. Buffon, *Des époques de la nature*, in *Histoire naturelle* (Paris, 1778), vol. 42 [= supplément, vol. 5]: 40–70, quotation on 53. My translation.

69. Pierre Louis Moreau de Maupertuis, *Lettre sur la comète* ([Amsterdam?], 1742), 4; [Charles Burney], *An Essay towards a History of the Principle Comets That Have Appeared since the Year 1742. . . . To which is prefixed, by way of Introduction, A Letter upon Comets. Addressed to a Lady. by the Late M. de Maupertuis. Written in the Year 1742* (London, 1769), 9, from which work I will take all English translations of Maupertuis.

70. Maupertuis, *Lettre sur la comète*, 55–56; Burney, *Essay*, 21.

71. Maupertuis, *Lettre sur la comète*, 69–76, 83–86.

72. Ibid., 68–71. On Fielding, see chap. 8 above.

73. Maupertuis, *Lettre sur la comète*, 65–67, 79–90, 95–99.

74. Pierre Louis Moreau de Maupertuis, *Essai de cosmologie* (Leiden, 1751), 167–175; reprinted in *Oeuvres de Maupertuis*, 4 vols. (Lyons, 1768), 1:ix–78, see 71–74.

75. Maupertuis, *Lettre sur la comète*, 95–99.

76. Ibid., 99–101. Pierre Louis Moreau de Maupertuis, *Discours sur les différentes figures des astres; d'ou l'on tire des conjectures sur les étoiles qui paroissent changer de grandeur; & sur l'anneau de Saturne* (Paris, 1732), 78–83; reprinted in *Oeuvres de Maupertuis*, 1:79–170, see 154–160 on Saturn's ring. Here Maupertuis also touched on many of the topics discussed in the *Lettre*—e.g., comets becoming trapped by planets and transformed into satellites. Dionis du Séjour later challenged this theory. See Achille Pierre Dionis du Séjour, *Essai sur les comètes en général, et particulierement sur celles qui peuvent approcher de l'orbite de la terre* (Paris, 1775), 184–197.

77. Benoît de Maillet, *Telliamed, ou entretiens d'un philosophe Indien avec un missionnaire François sur la diminution de la mer, la formation de la terre, l'origine de l'homme, &c.* (Amsterdam, 1748). I will refer to an English edition prepared from manuscripts of the work: Benoît de Maillet, *Telliamed, or Conversations between an Indian Philosopher and a French Missionary on the Diminution of the Sea*, trans. and ed. Albert V. Carozzi (Urbana: University of Illinois Press, 1968).

78. De Maillet, *Telliamed*, 173–192.

79. Ibid., 168–169, 175, 182.

80. Ibid., 168.

81. Ibid., 169–173.

82. Ibid., 169.

83. Immanuel Kant, *Allgemeine Naturgeschichte und Theorie des Himmels oder Versuch von der Verfassung und dem mechanischen Ursprunge des ganzen Weltgebäudes nach Newtonischen Grundsätzen abgehandelt* [Leipzig, 1755]; translated in *Kant's Cosmogony, as in His Essay on the Retardation of the Rotation of the Earth and His Natural History and Theory of the Heavens*, trans. W. Hastie, introd. Gerald Whitrow (New York: Johnson Reprint Corporation, 1970), 53–64, 71–82, 91, 135–140, 144–146.

84. *Kant's Cosmogony*, 80–82, 95–98.

85. Ibid., 66–67, quotation on 95.

86. Ibid., 99–100.

87. Ibid., 67, 98, 101–102.

88. Ibid., 113–117.

89. Ibid., 129–131, quotation on 131.

90. Ibid., 149.

91. Ibid., 151–154.

92. Ibid., 153.

93. Ibid., 153–154.

94. Ibid., 144–152.

95. Ibid., 154. See Simon Schaffer, "The Phoenix of Nature: Fire and Evolutionary Cosmology in Wright and Kant," *Journal for the History of Astronomy* 9 (1978): 180–200.

96. Thomas Wright, *Second or Singular Thoughts upon the Theory of the Universe* [MS ca. 1771], ed. M. A. Hoskin (London: Dawsons of Pall Mall, 1968), 31–32, 41, 43, quotation on 41.

97. See chap. 9 above.

98. Wright, *Second or Singular Thoughts*, 41–42.

99. Ibid., 42.

100. Ibid., 32.

101. Ibid., 43–44. Cf. Pierre-Simon Laplace, *Traité de mécanique céleste*, 5 vols. (Paris, 1798–1825), vol. 4, bk. 9, chap. 3, discussed below.

102. Wright, *Second or Singular Thoughts*, 71.

103. Ibid., 72–73.

104. Ibid., 21–22, 37–38, where Wright itemized the differences between planets and comets.

105. Newton, *Principia*, Motte-Cajori ed., 529–530, 541–542; and John Conduitt memorandum, March 1724/25, printed in Edmund Turnor, *Collections for the History of the Town and Soke of Grantham containing Authentic Memoirs of Sir Isaac Newton* (London, 1806), 172–173. See chap. 7 above.

106. See Simon Schaffer, "'The Great Laboratories of the Universe': William Herschel on Matter Theory and Planetary Life," *Journal for the History of Astronomy* 11 (1980): 81–111; Simon Schaffer, "Herschel in Bedlam: Natural History and Stellar Astronomy," *British Journal for the History of Science* 13 (1980): 211–239; Simon Schaffer, "Uranus and the Establishment of Herschel's Astronomy," *Journal for the History of Astronomy* 12 (1981): 11–26; Michael A. Hoskin, *William Herschel and the Construction of the Heavens* (London: Oldbourne, 1963); Michael A. Hoskin, "William Herschel and the Making of Modern Astronomy," *Scientific American* 254 (February 1986): 106–112; B. Sticker, "Herschel's Cosmology," *History of Science* 3 (1964): 91–101; Constance Lubbock, *The Herschel Chronicle: The Life-Story of William Herschel and His Sister Caroline Herschel* (Cambridge: Cambridge University Press, 1933).

107. William Herschel, "Observations of a Comet, made with a View to investigate its Magnitude and the Nature of its Illumination," *Philosophical Transactions* 98 (1808): 145–163; reprinted in *The Scientific Papers of Sir William Herschel*, ed. J.L.E. Dreyer, 2 vols. (London: Royal Society and Royal Astronomical Society, 1912), 2:403–413, see esp. 408–411.

108. William Herschel, "Observations of a Comet, with Remarks on the Construction of its different Parts," *Philosophical Transactions* 102 (1812): 115–143; see Herschel, *Scientific Papers*, 2:500–512.

109. William Herschel, "Observations of a second Comet, with Remarks on its Construction," *Philosophical Transactions* 102 (1812): 229–237; see Herschel, *Scientific Papers*, 2:518–519.

110. Herschel, "Observations of a Comet" (1812); see Herschel, *Scientific Papers*, 2:512.

111. Herschel, "Observations of a Comet" (1812); see Herschel, *Scientific Papers*, 2:513.

112. Herschel compared the physical construction of diverse comets in the papers I have cited and in William Herschel, "Observations on the Nature of the new celestial Body discovered by Dr. Olbers, and of the Comet which was expected to appear last January in its return from the Sun," *Philosophical Transactions* 97 (1807): 260–266; see Herschel, *Scientific Papers*, 2:401.

113. William Herschel, "On Nebulous Stars, properly so called," *Philosophical Transactions* 81 (1791): 71–88; William Herschel, "Astronomical Observations relating to the Construction of the Heavens," *Philosophical Transactions* 101 (1811): 269–336; see Herschel, *Scientific Papers*, 1:415–425, 2:459–497. See also Michael Hoskin, "William Herschel's Early Investigations of Nebulae: A Reassessment," *Journal for the History of Astronomy* 10 (1979): 165–176.

114. Herschel, "Observations of a Comet" (1812); see Herschel, *Scientific Papers*, 2:513–514.

115. Herschel, "Astronomical Observations relating to the Construction of the Heavens"; see Herschel, *Scientific Papers*, 2:480.

116. Herschel, "Observations of a Comet" (1812); see Herschel, *Scientific Papers*, 2:513.

117. Herschel, "Observations of a Comet" (1812); see Herschel, *Scientific Papers*, 2:513–514.

118. Herschel, "Observations of a Comet" (1812); Herschel, "Observations of a second Comet"; see Herschel, *Scientific Papers*, 2:513–514, 517–519, quotation on 519.

119. Conduitt memorandum, March 1724/25, in Turnor, *Collections*, 172: "[Newton conjectured] that there was a sort of revolution in the heavenly bodies; that the vapours and light emitted by the sun . . . and other matter had, gathered themselves by degrees, into a body, and attracted more matter from the planets; and at last made a secondary planet . . . and then by gathering to them and attracting more matter, became a primary planet; and then by increasing still, became a comet, which after certain revolutions, by coming nearer and nearer to the sun, had all its volatile parts condensed, and became a matter fit to recruit, and replenish the sun."

120. William Herschel to Sir William Watson, 7 July 1817, Royal Astronomical Society, Herschel Papers, W 1/1, fols. 298–299.

121. Dolomieu to Pierre Picot, 19 December 1796; quoted in Greene, *Death of Adam*, 85. Italics added.

122. Pierre-Simon Laplace, *Exposition du système du monde*, 4th ed., rev. and augmented (Paris, 1813), 438–439, my translation.

123. For discussion of other changes made by Laplace from edition to edition, see Stanley L. Jaki, "The Five Forms of Laplace's Cosmogony," *American Journal of Physics* 44 (1976): 4–11; and Jaki, *Planets and Planetarians*, 122–134.

124. Pierre-Simon Laplace, *Exposition du système du monde*, 2 vols. (Paris: De l'Imprimerie du Cercle-Social, l'An IV de la République Française, [1796]), 2:297–298.

125. Ibid., 301–303. The same view was held in the second edition (1799) and augmented in the third (1808). See Pierre-Simon Laplace, *The System of the World*, trans. J. Pond, 2 vols. [based on the 2d ed.] (London, 1809), 2:363–365; and Pierre-Simon Laplace, *Exposition du système du monde*, 3d ed. (Paris, 1808), 391–392.

126. Laplace, *Exposition du système du monde* (1796), 1:86–87, 215; Laplace, *System of the World*, 1:97–98, 257.

127. Laplace, *Exposition du système du monde* (1796), 2:306–308; Laplace, *System of the World*, 2:369–371.

128. Laplace, *Exposition du système du monde* (1808), 395: "Il est donc probable que les nébuleuses sont, pour la plupart, des groupes d'étoiles, vus de très-loin." Cf. Laplace, *Exposition du système du monde* (1796), 2:306–307: "Il est donc vraisemblable que les nébuleuses sans étoiles, sont des grouppes d'étoiles, vus de très-loin."

129. Laplace, *Exposition du système du monde* (1808), 126–127.

130. Laplace, *Exposition du système du monde* (1813), 431–432. In the fifth (1824) and later editions, these remarks were split between bk. 5, chap. 6 and n. 7. See Laplace, *Exposition du système du monde*, 6th ed. (Paris, 1835); in *Oeuvres*

complètes de Laplace, 14 vols. (Paris: Gauthier-Villars, 1878–1912), 6:482–483, 500.

131. Laplace, *Exposition du système du monde* (1813), 436–438; and Laplace, *Exposition du système du monde* (1835), in Laplace, *Oeuvres*, 6:483, 504–506. See also Pierre-Simon Laplace, "Sur les comètes" [read November 1813], in *Connaissance des Temps* (1816); reprinted in Laplace, *Oeuvres*, 13:88–97.

132. Laplace, *Exposition du système du monde* (1813), 132–134.

133. Laplace, "Sur les comètes"; see Laplace, *Oeuvres*, 13:91, my translation.

134. Laplace, *Exposition du système du monde* (1813), 133–134; Laplace, "Sur les comètes," in Laplace, *Oeuvres*, 13:88.

135. Laplace, *Exposition du système du monde* (1796), 1:86; trans. taken from Laplace, *System of the World*, 1:97–98.

136. Laplace, *Exposition du système du monde* (1796), 2:60–62; trans. taken from Laplace, *System of the World*, 2:63–64.

137. Laplace revised this number in successive editions of his book. The 1796 and 1799 editions reported 3,000 years; the 1808 edition reported 4,000; the 1813 and later editions reported 5,000. See Laplace, *Exposition du système du monde* (1796), 2:62; Laplace, *Exposition du système du monde* (1808), 213; Laplace *Exposition du système du monde* (1813), 222.

138. Laplace *Exposition du système du monde* (1796), 2:62–63; trans. taken from Laplace, *System of the World*, 2:64–65.

139. Cf. Edmond Halley, "Some Considerations about the Cause of the universal Deluge, laid before the Royal Society, on the 12th of December 1694" [1724]. *Philosophical Transactions* 33 (1724–1725): 118–123, esp. 121–122; John Conduitt memorandum, 7 March 1724/25, in Turnor, *Collections*, 172–173.

140. Joseph Jérôme le Français de Lalande, *Réflexions sur les comètes qui peuvent approcher de la terre* (Paris, 1773); Simon Schaffer, "Authorized Prophets: Comets and Astronomers after 1759," *Studies in Eighteenth-Century Culture* 17 (1987): 45–74, see 56–60.

141. Lalande prepared a paper to be read at the Académie des Sciences in April 1773 on the *improbable* conditions under which a comet might collide with the earth. When his reading of the memoir was postponed, rumors began to circulate that discretion had prevented Lalande from making public the *likelihood* of an earth-shattering impact expected within weeks. People panicked and prayed, until Lalande rushed his paper into print. See Lalande, *Réflexions sur les comètes*, quotation on 11 (my translation), probability of a collision on 30, cf. 38–39. Voltaire ridiculed the entire debacle in "Lettre sur la prétendue comète," *Journal Encyclopédique* (1 June 1773); reprinted in *Oeuvres complètes de Voltaire*, new ed., 52 vols. (Paris: Garnier Frères, 1877–1885), 29:47–51; and Voltaire joked about it in a letter to William Hamilton, 17 June 1773, *Voltaire's Correspondence*, 107 vols. (Geneva: Institut et Musée Voltaire, 1953–1965), 85:136. The incident is described in Stewart, "Science and Superstition," 22–23; J. H. Robinson, *The Great Comet of 1680: A Study in the History of Rationalism* (Northfield, Minn.: Press of the Northfield News, 1916), 118; and Schaffer, "Authorized Prophets," 57–59.

142. Laplace, *Exposition du système du monde* (1796), 2:310; trans. taken from Laplace, *System of the World*, 2:372–373. This passage appeared with various modifications, additions, and deletions in successive editions. The passage quoted was deleted altogether in the third and later editions. See Laplace, *Exposition du système du monde* (1808), 397; Laplace, *Exposition du système du monde* (1813), 447;

Laplace, *Exposition du système du monde* (1835), reprinted in Laplace, *Oeuvres*, 6:485–486.

143. If the 1770 comet had been as massive as the earth, its near approach should have increased the sidereal year by 11,612 seconds (using Laplace's centesimal division of the day). However, an increase of no more than 3 seconds was noted. From this, Laplace computed the comet's mass to equal 1/5,000 of the earth's but believed it likely to be less since the comet had not troubled the Jovian satellites when it passed between them in 1767 and 1779. See Pierre-Simon Laplace, *Mécanique céleste*, trans. Nathaniel Bowditch, 4 vols. (Boston, 1829–1839; reprint, New York: Chelsea Publishing Company, 1966), bk. 9, chap. 3 (4:435–437). Laplace summarized this finding in the *Exposition du système du monde* (1808), 214–215, and in subsequent editions.

144. Laplace, *Mécanique céleste*, 4:437.

145. Laplace, *Exposition du système du monde* (1808), 213–214; Laplace, *Exposition du système du monde* (1813), 222–223; and later editions.

146. First expressed in Laplace, *Exposition du système du monde* (1813), 443–444, my translation.

147. Newton, *Principia*, Motte-Cajori ed., General Scholium, 546.

148. Laplace, *Exposition du système du monde* (1813), 444, my translation. For discussion of the eradication of final causes in cometary literature, see also Laplace, *Exposition du système du monde* (1796), 2:59–60; Laplace, *System of the World*, 2:62–63; Laplace, *Exposition du système du monde* (1808), 212; Laplace, *Exposition du système du monde* (1813), 221–222.

149. David Hume, *Dialogues Concerning Natural Religion* [1779], ed. Norman Kemp Smith (Indianapolis: Bobbs-Merrill Educational Publishing, 1947), pt. 7, p. 177.

150. Whiston, *New Theory of the Earth* (1737), 477.

151. Dionis du Séjour, *Essai sur les comètes*, iv, my translation.

152. Candidus [pseud.], "Halley and Newton on the Comet expected in 1758," *Gentleman's Magazine* 26 (January 1756): 24–27, quotation on 24.

153. Maupertuis, *Lettre sur la comète*, 55–56; Burney, *Essay*, 21; Buffon, *Histoire naturelle*, 1:179.

Concluding Remarks

1. Dominique François Jean Arago, "Des comètes en général, et en particulier de la comète qui doit reparaître en 1832 et dont la révolution est de 6 ans ¾," *Bureau des longitudes. Annuaire pour l'an 1832*, 2d ed. (Paris, 1832), 156–383. I have used Arago, *Tract on Comets; and Particularly on the Comet That Is To Intersect the Earth's Path in October, 1832*, trans. John Farrar (Boston: Hilliard, Gray, and Company, 1832), 3.

2. Queries taken from the table of contents of Arago, *Tract on Comets*.

3. Edmond Halley, "A Synopsis of the Astronomy of Comets," in *Miscellanea Curiosa*, ed. Edmond Halley, 3 vols. (London, 1705–1707), 2:24.

4. J. H. Lambert, *Cosmologische Briefe* (Augsburg, 1761), 19; trans. and reprinted in *Cosmological Letters on the Arrangement of the World-Edifice*, trans. Stanley L. Jaki (New York: Science History Publications, 1976), 63.

5. Arago, *Tract on Comets*, 3.

APPENDIX

1. For general background to contemporary debates, see for example, David M. Raup, *The Nemesis Affair: A Story of the Death of Dinosaurs and the Ways of Science* (New York: W. W. Norton, 1986); Elisabeth S. Clemens, "Of Asteroids and Dinosaurs: The Role of the Press in the Shaping of Scientific Debate," *Social Studies of Science* 16 (1986): 421–456; Fred L. Whipple, *The Mystery of Comets* (Washington, D.C.: Smithsonian Institution, 1985); John C. Brandt and Robert D. Chapman, *Introduction to Comets* (Cambridge: Cambridge University Press, 1981); Carl Sagan and Ann Druyan, *Comet* (New York: Random House, 1985); and Stephen Jay Gould, *The Flamingo's Smile* (New York: W. W. Norton, 1985), 415–450.

2. Harold C. Urey, "Cometary Collisions and Geological Periods," *Nature* 242 (1973): 32–33.

3. Luis W. Alvarez et al., "Extraterrestrial Cause for the Cretaceous-Tertiary Extinction," *Science* 208 (1980): 1095–1108; Luis W. Alvarez et al., "The End of the Cretaceous: Sharp Boundary or Gradual Transition?" *Science* 223 (1984): 1183–1186; Walter Alvarez et al., "Impact Theory of Mass Extinctions and the Invertebrate Fossil Record," *Science* 223 (1984): 1135–1141. See also the other articles on this topic in *Science* 223 (1984): 1174–1183.

4. Carl C. Swisher III, et al., "Coeval ^{40}Ar/^{39}Ar Ages of 65.0 Million Years Ago from Chicxulub Crater Melt Rock and Cretaceous-Tertiary Boundary Tektites," *Science* 257 (1992): 954–958.

5. N. C. Wickramasinghe and Max K. Wallis, "The Cometary Hypothesis of the K/T Mass Extinctions," *Monthly Notices of the Royal Astronomical Society* 270 (1994): 420–426; Sidney van den Bergh, "Astronomical Catastrophes in Earth History," *Publications of the Astronomical Society of the Pacific* 106 (1994): 689–695; Michael E. Williams, "Catastrophic versus Noncatastrophic Extinction of the Dinosaurs: Testing, Falsifiability, and the Burden of Proof," *Journal of Paleontology* 68 (1994): 183–190.

6. David M. Raup and J. John Sepkoski, Jr., "Periodicity of Extinctions in the Geologic Past," *Proceedings of the National Academy of Sciences* 81 (1984): 801–805.

7. Walter Alvarez and Richard A. Muller, "Evidence from Crater Ages for Periodic Impacts on the Earth," *Nature* 308 (1984): 718–720.

8. Michael R. Rampino and Richard B. Stothers, "Terrestrial Mass Extinctions, Cometary Impacts and the Sun's Motion Perpendicular to the Galactic Plane," *Nature* 308 (1984): 709–712; Michael R. Rampino and Richard B. Stothers, "Geological Rhythms and Cometary Impacts," *Science* 226 (1984): 1427–1431; Richard D. Schwartz and Philip B. James, "Periodic Mass Extinctions and the Sun's Oscillation about the Galactic Plane," *Nature* 308 (1984): 712–713; Patrick Thaddeus and Gary A. Chanan, "Cometary Impacts, Molecular Clouds, and the Motion of the Sun Perpendicular to the Galactic Plane," *Nature* 314 (1985): 73–75.

9. Marc Davis, Piet Hut, and Richard A. Muller, "Extinction of Species by Periodic Comet Showers," *Nature* 308 (1984): 715–717; Daniel P. Whitmire and Albert A. Jackson IV, "Are Periodic Mass Extinctions Driven by a Distant Solar Companion?" *Nature* 308 (1984): 713–715; J. G. Hills, "Comet Showers and the Steady-State Infall of Comets from the Oort Cloud," *Astronomical Journal* 86 (1981): 1730–1740; J. G. Hills, "Dynamical Constraints on the Mass and Perihelion

Distance of Nemesis and the Stability of Its Orbit," *Nature* 311 (1984): 636–638. See also Richard A. Kerr, "Periodic Impacts and Extinctions Reported," *Science* 223 (1984): 1277–1279.

10. Piet Hut et al., "Comet Showers as a Cause of Mass Extinctions," *Nature* 329 (1987): 118–126 (a good review article).

11. Van den Bergh, "Astronomical Catastrophes," 694.

12. Fred Hoyle and Chandra Wickramasinghe, *Lifecloud: The Origin of Life in the Universe* (New York: Harper & Row, 1978); Fred Hoyle and Chandra Wickramasinghe, "Influenza from Space?" *New Scientist* 79 (1978): 946–948; Fred Hoyle and Chandra Wickramasinghe, *Diseases from Space* (New York: Harper & Row, 1979); Fred Hoyle, "Comets—A Matter of Life and Death," *Vistas in Astronomy* 24 (1980): 123–139; Fred Hoyle, *Evolution from Space* (Hillside, N.J.: Enslow Publishers, 1982).

13. See Michael F. A'Hearn, "Chemistry of Comets," *Chemical and Engineering News* (28 May 1984): 32–49. *Nature* 321 (1986): 259–366 contains the first scientific results of the spacecraft encounters with comet Halley.

14. J. Oro, "Comets and the Formation of Biochemical Compounds on the Primitive Earth," *Nature* 190 (1961): 389–391; W. M. Irvine, S. B. Leschine, and F. P. Schloerb, "Thermal History, Chemical Composition and Relationship of Comets to the Origin of Life," *Nature* 283 (1980): 748–749; R. W. Hobbs and J. M. Hollis, "Probing the Presently Tenuous Link between Comets and the Origin of Life," *Origins of Life* 12 (1982): 125–132; Stephen L. Gillett, "The Rise and Fall of the Early Reducing Atmosphere," *Astronomy* (July 1985): 66–71.

15. Kevin Zahnle and David Grinspoon, "Comet Dust as a Source of Amino Acids at the Cretaceous/Tertiary Boundary," *Nature* 348 (1990): 157–160; cf. Christopher F. Chyba, "Extraterrestrial Amino Acids and Terrestrial Life," *Nature* 348 (1990): 113–114.

16. Clark R. Chapman and David Morrison, "Impacts on the Earth by Asteroids and Comets: Assessing the Hazard," *Nature* 367 (1994): 33–40; Tom Gehrels, *Hazards Due to Comets and Asteroids* (Tucson: University of Arizona Press, 1994).

Aaboe, Asger. "Observation and Theory in Babylonian Astronomy." *Centaurus* 24 (1980): 14–35.

Aegidius of Lessines. *Incipit tractatus Fratris Egidii ordinis fratrum predicatorum De essentia, motu et significatione cometarum* [ca. 1264]. *See* Thorndike, 1950.

[Aëtius, attributed author]. *De placitis philosophorum*. Translated by John Dowel, under the title *Of Those Sentiments Concerning Nature with Which Philosophers were Delighted*. In *Plutarch's Morals*, edited by William W. Goodwin, 5 vols., 3:104–193. Boston: Little, Brown, and Company, 1871.

Afbeeldinge en Beschrijvinge van de drie aenmerckens-waerdige Wonderen in den Jare 1664. t'Amsterdam en daer ontrent voorgevallen. [Broadside.] Amsterdam: Marcus Doornick, 1664.

A'Hearn, Michael F. "Chemistry of Comets." *Chemical and Engineering News* (28 May 1984): 32–49.

Albertus Magnus. *De meteoris*. Liber 1, tractatus 3, translated by Lynn Thorndike. *See* Thorndike, 1950.

———. *The Book of Secrets of Albertus Magnus of the Virtues of Herbs, Stones and Certain Beasts. Also a Book of the Marvels of the World*. Edited by Michael R. Best and Frank H. Brightman. Oxford: Oxford University Press, 1973.

Albury, W. R. "Halley's Ode on the *Principia* and the Epicurean Revival in England." *Journal of the History of Ideas* 39 (1978): 24–43.

Alexandre, J., and S. Debarbat. *La comète de Halley, hier, aujourd'hui, demain*. Paris: Observatoire de Paris, 1985.

Alsted, Johann Heinrich. *The Beloved City or, the Saints Reign on Earth a Thousand Yeares*. Translated by William Burton. London, 1643.

———. *Thesaurus chronologiae*. 4th ed. Herborn in Nassau, 1650.

Alvarez, Luis W., Walter Alvarez, Frank Asaro, and Helen V. Michel. "Extraterrestrial Cause for the Cretaceous-Tertiary Extinction." *Science* 208 (1980): 1095–1108.

———. "The End of the Cretaceous: Sharp Boundary or Gradual Transition?" *Science* 223 (1984): 1183–1186.

Alvarez, Walter, Erle G. Kauffman, Finn Surlyk, Luis W. Alvarez, Frank Asaro, and Helen V. Michel. "Impact Theory of Mass Extinctions and the Invertebrate Fossil Record." *Science* 223 (1984): 1135–1141.

Alvarez, Walter, and Richard A. Muller. "Evidence from Crater Ages for Periodic Impacts on the Earth." *Nature* 308 (1984): 718–720.

Ames, Nathaniel. *An Astronomical Diary or, an Almanack for the Year of our Lord Christ 1759*. Boston, [1759].

The Anglo-Saxon Chronicles. Translated and collated by Anne Savage. New York: Saint Martin's/Marek, 1983.

An Answer of a Letter From a Friend in the Country To a Friend in the City: Or some Remarks on the late Comet. Being a Relation of many Universal Accidents that will come to pass in the year, 1682. According to the Prognostications of the Celestial Bodies, which will happen beyond the seas; with a Sober

Caution to all, by speedy Repentance to avert the Judgments that are Impendent. London, 1681.

Apian, Peter. *Practica auff dz. 1532. Jar.* Landshut, 1531.

———. *Astronomicum caesareum.* Ingolstadt, 1540.

Arago, Dominique François Jean. *Tract on Comets; and Particularly on the Comet That Is To Intersect the Earth's Path in October, 1832.* Translated by John Farrar. Boston: Hilliard, Gray, and Company, 1832.

Aratus. *Phaenomena.* Translated by G. R. Mair. Loeb Classical Library. Cambridge: Harvard University Press, 1977.

Aristotle. *On the Heavens.* Translated by W.K.C. Guthrie. Loeb Classical Library. Cambridge: Harvard University Press, 1971.

———. *Meteorologica.* Translated by H.D.P. Lee. Loeb Classical Library. Cambridge: Harvard University Press, 1978.

Armitage, Angus. *Edmond Halley.* London: Thomas Nelson and Sons, 1966.

Ashmole, Elias. *Theatrum chemicum Britannicum.* London, 1652.

Ashton, R. "Popular Entertainment and Social Control in Later Elizabethan and Early Stuart London." *London Journal* 9 (1983): 3–19.

Augustine. *The City of God* [*De civitate Dei*]. Translated by Marcus Dods. In *A Select Library of the Nicene and Post-Nicene Fathers of the Christian Church,* vol. 2. *See* Schaff, 1980–1983.

Bacon, Francis. *Descriptio Globi Intellectualis* [*Description of the Intellectual Globe*] (1612). In *Works of Francis Bacon,* vols. 3 and 5. London, 1870.

———. *De fluxu et refluxu maris* [*On the Ebb and Flow of the Sea*] (ca. 1616). In *Works of Francis Bacon,* vols. 3 and 5. London, 1870.

———. *Novum organum* [*New Organon*] (1620). In *Works of Francis Bacon,* vols. 1 and 4. London, 1875.

———. *Parasceve ad historiam naturalem et experimentalem* [*Preparative towards a Natural and Experimental History*] (1620). In *Works of Francis Bacon,* vols. 1 and 4. London, 1875.

———. *De augmentis scientiarum* [*The Advancement of Learning*] (1623). In *Works of Francis Bacon,* vols. 1 and 4. London, 1875.

———. *The Essayes or Counsels, Civill and Morall* (1625). In *Works of Francis Bacon,* vol. 6. London, 1870.

———. *The Works of Francis Bacon, Baron of Verulam, Viscount St. Alban, and Lord High Chancellor of England.* Edited by James Spedding, Robert Leslie Ellis, and Douglas Denon Heath. New ed. 7 vols. London: Longmans & Company, 1870–1875.

Bacon, Roger. *The Opus Majus of Roger Bacon.* Translated by Robert Belle Burke. 2 vols. Philadelphia: University of Pennsylvania Press, 1928.

Bailey, M. E., S.V.M. Clube, and W. M. Napier. *The Origin of Comets.* Oxford: Pergamon Press, 1990.

Baily, Francis. *An Account of the Revd. John Flamsteed, the First Astronomer-Royal; compiled from His Own Manuscripts, and Other Authentic Documents, Never Before Published.* London, 1835.

Bainbridge, John. *An Astronomicall Description of the late Comet from the 18. of Novemb. 1618. to the 16. of December following. With certaine Morall Prognosticks or Applications drawne from the Comets motion and irradiation amongst the celestiall Hieroglyphicks.* London, 1619.

Ball, Bryan W. *A Great Expectation: Eschatological Thought in English Protestantism to 1660*. Studies in the History of Christian Thought, no. 12. Leiden: E. J. Brill, 1975.

Barker, Peter, and Bernard R. Goldstein. "The Role of Comets in the Copernican Revolution." *Studies in History and Philosophy of Science* 19 (1988): 299–319.

Bateman, Stephen. *The Doome warning all men to the Judgemente*. London, 1581; S.T.C. 1582.

Bauckham, Richard. *Tudor Apocalypse*. The Courtenay Library of Reformation Classics, no. 8. Appleford: Sutton Courtenay Press, 1978.

Baumgardt, Carola. *Johannes Kepler: Life and Letters*. New York: Philosophical Library, 1951.

Bayeux Tapestry. London: The Society of Antiquaries, 1819.

[Bayle, Pierre]. *Lettre à M.L.A.D.C. Docteur de Sorbonne. Où il est prouvé par plusieurs raisons tirées de la philosophie, & de la theologie, que les cometes ne sont point le présage d'aucun malheur. Avec plusieurs reflexions morales & politiques, & plusieurs observations historiques; & la refutation de quelques erreurs populaires*. Cologne [Rotterdam], 1682.

———. *Miscellaneous Reflections, Occasion'd by the Comet Which appear'd In December 1680. Chiefly tending to explode Popular Superstitions*. 2 vols. London, 1708.

———. *Pensées diverses sur la comète*. Critical ed. Edited by A. Prat. 2 vols. Paris: Librairie E. Droz, 1939.

Bede. *Ecclesiastical History of the English Nation*. In *Baedae opera historica*. Translated by J. E. King. 2 vols. Loeb Classical Library. London: William Heinemann, 1930.

———. *De natura rerum liber*. Edited by C. W. Jones and F. Lipp. In *Bedae Venerabilis Opera*, no. 123A. Corpus Christianorum, Series Latina, nos. 118A, 119, 119A–B, 120, 121–122, 123A–C. Turnhout, Belgium: Brepols, 1955–1983.

Bekker, Baltasar. *Ondersoek van de Betekeninge der Kometen*. Leuwarden. 1683. Reprint, Amsterdam, 1692.

Bennett, J. A. "'On the Power of Penetrating into Space': The Telescopes of William Herschel." *Journal for the History of Astronomy* 7 (1976): 75–108.

———. *The Mathematical Science of Christopher Wren*. Cambridge: Cambridge University Press, 1982.

Bentley, Richard. *A Confutation of Atheism from the Origin and Frame of the World*. London, 1693.

Bible. See *The Geneva Bible*, 1560; *The Holy Bible*, 1611; *New English Bible*, 1970; *New Oxford Annotated Bible*, 1977; and *Soncino Chumash*, 1947.

Bion, Nicolas. *L'usage des globes celeste et terrestre, et des spheres suivant les differens systemes du monde*. Paris, 1744.

Birch, Thomas. *The History of the Royal Society of London for Improving Natural Knowledge from Its First Rise*. 4 vols. London, 1756–1757.

The Blazing Star: or, A discourse of comets, Their Natures and Effects: In a Letter from J. B. to T. C. concerning the late Comet seen on Sunday, December the 11. 1664. at Ibbesley in Hantshire, and since at London and Westminster, and divers other places of this Kingdom. London, 1665.

A Blazing Starre seene In The West At Totneis in Devonshire, on the foureteenth of this instant November, 1642. Wherin is manifested how Master Ralph Ashley, a deboyst Cavalier, attemted to ravish a young Virgin, the Daughter of Mr. Adam

Fisher, inhabiting neare the said Towne. Also how at that instant, a fearefull Comet appeared, to the terrour and amazment of all the Country thereabouts. Likewise declaring how he persisting in his damnable attemt, was struck with a flaming Sword, which issued from the Comet, so that he dyed a fearefull example to al his fellow Cavaliers. London, 1642. Reprints of English Books, 1475–1700, edited by Joseph Arnold Foster, no. 20. Ingram, 1939.

Blazing Stars, Messengers of God's Wrath; in a few serious and solemn Meditations upon the late wonderful Comet: Which for some Time has flamed in our Horizon. Together with a Solemn Call to Sinners, and Counsel to Saints; how to behave themselves when God is in this wise speaking to them from Heaven. [Broadside.] [Boston, 1760].

Boaistuau, Pierre. *Histoires prodigieuses.* Paris, 1561.

———. *Histoires prodigieuses.* Lyons, 1598.

Bode, Johann Elert. *Projection on the Plane of the Ecliptic of the Parabolic Orbits of 72 Comets.* London, 1802.

Bold, Henry. *St. Georges Day Sacred to the Coronation of His Most Excellent Majesty Charles the II.* London, 1661.

———. *Poems Lyrique Macaronique Heroique, &c.* London, 1664.

Book of Planets, Anatomical Treatise, Book of Synonyms. Illuminated MS on vellum, probably from Ulm, ca. 1450–1475. [83.MO.137; MS Ludwig XII 8.] The J. Paul Getty Museum.

Boston News-letter. Boston, 1770.

Bott, Gerhard, ed. *Zeichen am Himmel: Flugblätter des 16. Jahrhunderts.* Nuremberg: Germanisches Nationalmuseum Nürnberg, 1982.

Bouché-Leclercq, Auguste. *L'Astrologie grecque.* Paris, 1899. Reprint, Brussels: Culture et Civilisation, 1963.

Bowen, Emmanuel. *A complete system of geography . . . comprehending the history of the universe.* 2 vols. London, 1744.

Boyle, Robert. *The Origine of Formes and Qualities (According to the Corpuscular Philosophy) Illustrated by Considerations and Experiments, (Written formerly by way of Notes upon an Essay about Nitre).* Oxford, 1666.

———. *The Works of the Honourable Robert Boyle.* Edited by Thomas Birch. 5 vols. London, 1744.

Brahe, Tycho. *De nova stella.* Copenhagen, 1573.

———. "De cometa anni 1577" [MS in German, 1578]. In *Tychonis Brahe Dani opera omnia*, edited by J.L.E. Dreyer, vol. 4. Copenhagen: Gyldendal, 1922.

———. "De cometa anni 1577" [1578]. Translated in "Tycho Brahe's German Treatise on the Comet of 1577." *See* Christianson, 1979.

———. *De cometa seu stella crinita rotunda, quae anno antecedente in Octobri & Novembri apparuit.* Uraniburg, 1586. In *Tychonis Brahe Dani opera omnia*, edited by J.L.E. Dreyer, vol. 4. Copenhagen: Gyldendal, 1922.

———. "De crinita stella non caudata quae anno 1585 antecedente mense Octobri & Novembri apparuit" [MS, 1586]. In *Tychonis Brahe Dani opera omnia*, edited by J.L.E. Dreyer, vol. 4. Copenhagen: Gyldendal, 1922.

———. *Astronomiae instauratae progymnasmata.* Prague, 1602.

———. *Tychonis Brahe Dani opera omnia.* Edited by J.L.E. Dreyer, Joannes Raeder, and Eiler Nyström. 15 vols. Copenhagen: Gyldendal, 1913–1929.

Brandt, John C., ed. *Comets: Readings from Scientific American.* San Francisco: W. H. Freeman and Company, 1981.

Brandt, John C., and Robert D. Chapman. *Introduction to Comets.* Cambridge: Cambridge University Press, 1981.

Briggs, J. Morton, Jr. "Aurora and Enlightenment: Eighteenth-Century Explanations of the Aurora Borealis." *Isis* 58 (1967): 491–503.

Brockhaus' Conversations-Lexikon. 13th ed. Leipzig, 1882–1887.

Broughton, Peter. "The First Predicted Return of Comet Halley." *Journal for the History of Astronomy* 16 (1985): 123–133.

Brown, Peter Lancaster. *Comets, Meteorites and Men.* New York: Taplinger Publishing Company, 1974.

Browne, Sir Thomas. *The Works of Sir Thomas Browne.* Edited by Geoffrey Keynes. 4 vols. Chicago: University of Chicago Press, 1964.

———. *Pseudodoxia Epidemica.* Critical ed. Edited by Robin Robbins. 2 vols. Oxford: Clarendon Press, 1981.

Buffon, Georges Louis Leclerc, comte de. *Histoire naturelle, générale et particulière.* 45 vols. Paris, 1749–1804.

———. "La Théorie de la Terre." In *Histoire naturelle,* vol. 1. Paris, 1749.

———. *Des époques de la nature.* In *Histoire naturelle, Supplément,* vol. 5 [= vol. 42]. Paris, 1778.

———. *Natural History, General and Particular.* Translated by William Smellie. 3d ed. 9 vols. London, 1791.

Bullard, Sir Edward. "Edmond Halley (1656–1741)." *Endeavour* 15 (October 1956): 189–199.

Burges, Bartholomew. *A Short Account of the Solar System, and of Comets in General: Together with a Particular Account of the Comet that Will Appear in 1789.* Boston, 1789.

Burke, John G., ed. *The Uses of Science in the Age of Newton.* Los Angeles: University of California Press, 1983.

Burke, Peter. "Popular Culture in Seventeenth-Century London." *London Journal* 3 (1977): 143–162.

———. *Popular Culture in Early Modern Europe.* New York: New York University Press, 1978.

———. "Popular Culture in Seventeenth-Century London." In *Popular Culture in Seventeenth-Century England,* edited by Barry Reay, 31–58. London: Croom Helm, 1985.

Burke-Gaffney, Michael W. *Kepler and the Jesuits.* Milwaukee: Bruce Publishing Company, 1944.

Burnet, Thomas. *Telluris theoria sacra.* 2 vols. London, 1681–1689.

———. *The Sacred Theory of the Earth.* Edited by Basil Willey. London: Centaur Press, 1965.

[Burney, Charles.] *An Essay towards a History of the Principal Comets That Have Appeared since the Year 1742. . . . To which is prefixed, by way of Introduction, A Letter upon Comets. Addressed to a Lady, by the Late M. de Maupertuis. Written in the Year 1742.* London, 1769.

Butler, Samuel. *Hudibras.* Edited by John Wilders. Oxford: Clarendon Press, 1967.

Byles, Mather. *The Comet: A Poem.* Boston, 1744.

Cabeo, Niccolo. *In quatuor libros meteorologicorum Aristotelis commentaria et quaestiones.* 4 vols. Rome, 1646.

Calder, Nigel. *The Comet is Coming! The Feverish Legacy of Mr. Halley.* New York: The Viking Press, 1981.

Camden, Carroll, Jr. "Astrology in Shakespeare's Day." *Isis* 19 (1933): 26–73.

Candidus [pseud.]. "Halley and Newton on the Comet expected in 1758." *Gentleman's Magazine* 26 (January 1756): 24–27.

Capp, Bernard. *English Almanacs 1500–1800: Astrology and the Popular Press.* Ithaca: Cornell University Press, 1979.

———. "Popular Literature." In *Popular Culture in Seventeenth-Century England*, edited by Barry Reay, 198–243. London: Croom Helm, 1985.

Cardano, Girolamo. *De subtilitate liber XXI.* Nuremberg, 1550.

———. *De rerum varietate libri XVII.* Basel, 1557.

———. *Opera omnia.* 10 vols. Lyons, 1663. Facsimile reprint, New York: Johnson Reprint Corporation, 1967.

Caroti, Stefano. "Melanchthon's Astrology." In *"Astrologi hallucinati": Stars and the End of the World in Luther's Time*, edited by Paola Zambelli, 109–121. Berlin: Walter de Gruyter, 1986.

Casini, Paolo. "Newton: The Classical Scholia." *History of Science* 22 (1984): 1–58.

Caspar, Max. *Kepler.* Translated by C. Doris Hellman. London: Abelard-Schuman, 1959.

Cassius Dio Cocceianus. *Dio's Roman History.* Translated by Earnest Cary. 9 vols. Loeb Classical Library. Cambridge: Harvard University Press, 1969–1980.

Catastrophe Mundi: Or, Merlin Reviv'd, In a Discourse of Prophecies & Predictions, And their Remarkable Accomplishment. With Mr. Lilly's Hieroglyphicks Exactly Cut; And Notes and Observations thereon. As Also A Collection Of all the Antient (Reputed) Prophecies That are Extant, Touching the Grand Revolutions like to happen in these Latter Ages. London, 1683.

Cessi, Francesco. *Giotto: La Cappella degli Scrovegni.* Florence: Editoriale Arsuna, 1978.

Chaeremon of Alexandria. *Chaeremon: Egyptian Priest and Stoic Philosopher. The Fragments Collected and Translated with Explanatory Notes.* Edited by Pieter Willem van der Horst. Etudes Préliminaires aux Religions Orientales dans l'Empire Romain, no. 101. Leiden: E. J. Brill, 1984.

Chapman, Clark R., and David Morrison. "Impacts on the Earth by Asteroids and Comets: Assessing the Hazard." *Nature* 367 (1994): 33–40.

Chartier, Roger. "Culture as Appropriation: Popular Cultural Uses in Early Modern France." In *Understanding Popular Culture: Europe from the Middle Ages to the Nineteenth Century*, edited by Steven L. Kaplan, 229–253. Berlin: Mouton Publishers, 1984.

———. *Cultural History: Between Practices and Representations.* Translated by Lydia G. Cochrane. Ithaca: Cornell University Press, 1988.

Chenu, M. D. "Nature and Man at the School of Chartres in the Twelfth Century." In *The Evolution of Science*, edited by Guy S. Metraux and François Crouzet, 220–235. New York: New American Library, 1963.

Cheyne, George. *Philosophical Principles of Natural Religion: Containing the Elements of Natural Philosophy, And the Proofs for Natural Religion, Arising from them.* London, 1705.

———. *Philosophical Principles of Religion: Natural and Reveal'd.* 2 vols. in 1. London, 1715.

Christianson, J. R. "Tycho Brahe's German Treatise on the Comet of 1577: A Study in Science and Politics." *Isis* 70 (1979): 110–140.

Christianson, Paul. *Reformers and Babylon: English Apocalyptic Visions from the Reformation to the Eve of the Civil War.* Toronto: University of Toronto Press, 1978.

Chyba, Christopher F. "Extraterrestrial Amino Acids and Terrestrial Life." *Nature* 348 (1990): 113–114.

Clark, Peter. *The English Alehouse: A Social History, 1200–1830.* London: Longman, 1983.

Classen, J. *15 Kometenflugblätter des 17. und 18. Jahrhunderts.* Veröffentlichungen der Sternwarte Pulsnitz, no. 11. Leipzig: Verlag Johann Ambrosius Barth, 1977.

Clemens, Elisabeth S. "Of Asteroids and Dinosaurs: The Role of the Press in the Shaping of Scientific Debate." *Social Studies of Science* 16 (1986): 421–456.

Clifton, Robin. "The Popular Fear of Catholics during the English Revolution." *Past and Present* 52 (1971): 23–55.

Cohen, I. Bernard. *Franklin and Newton.* Philadelphia: American Philosophical Society, 1956.

———. " 'Quantum in se est': Newton's Concept of Inertia in Relation to Descartes and Lucretius." *Notes and Records of the Royal Society of London* 19 (1964): 131–155.

———. "Hypotheses in Newton's Philosophy." *Physis* 8 (1966): 163–184.

———. *Some Early Tools of American Science: An Account of the Early Scientific Instruments and Mineralogical and Biological Collections in Harvard University.* Cambridge: Harvard University Press, 1950. Reprint, New York: Russell & Russell, 1967.

———. "Isaac Newton's *Principia*, the Scriptures, and the Divine Providence." In *Philosophy, Science, and Method: Essays in Honor of Ernest Nagel,* edited by Sidney Morgenbesser, Patrick Suppes, and Morton White, 523–548. New York: St. Martin's Press, 1969.

———. *Introduction to Newton's "Principia."* Cambridge: Harvard University Press, 1971.

———. *The Newtonian Revolution.* Cambridge: Cambridge University Press, 1980.

———. "The *Principia*, Universal Gravitation, and the 'Newtonian Style,' in Relation to the Newtonian Revolution in Science." In *Contemporary Newtonian Research,* edited by Zev Bechler, 21–108. Studies in the History of Modern Science, no. 9. Dordrecht: D. Reidel, 1982.

———. "Halley's Two Essays on Newton's *Principia*." In *Standing on the Shoulders of Giants: A Longer View of Newton and Halley,* edited by Norman J. W. Thrower, 91–108. Berkeley and Los Angeles: University of California Press, 1990.

———, ed. *Newton's Papers and Letters on Natural Philosophy.* 2d ed. Cambridge: Harvard University Press, 1978.

Collier, Katharine B. *Cosmogonies of Our Fathers: Some Theories of the Seventeenth and Eighteenth Centuries.* New York: Columbia University Press, 1934.

Comenius, Johann Amos. *Orbis sensualium pictus.* Translated by Charles Hoole. London, 1659. Facsimile reprint, Menston, England: Scolar Press, 1970.

Cook, Alan H. "Halley in Istria, 1703: Navigator and Military Engineer." *Journal of Navigation* 37 (1984): 1–23.

———. "Halley, Surveyor and Military Engineer: Istria, 1703." In *Standing on*

the Shoulders of Giants: A Longer View of Newton and Halley, edited by Norman J. W. Thrower, 157–170. Berkeley and Los Angeles: University of California Press, 1990.

Cook, Aurelian. *Titus Britannicus: An Essay of History Royal: In the Life & Reign of His Late Sacred Majesty, Charles II. of Ever Blessed and Immortal Memory*. London, 1685.

Cook, Chris, and John Wroughton. *English Historical Facts, 1603–1688*. Totowa, N.J.: Rowman and Littlefield, 1980.

Coopland, G. W. *Nicole Oresme and the Astrologers: A Study of His "Livre de Divinacions."* Cambridge: Harvard University Press, 1952.

Copernicus, Nicolaus. *De revolutionibus orbium coelestium*. Nuremberg, 1543.

Cotton, John. *Gods Mercie Mixed with His Justice*. London, 1641.

The Country-mans Complaint, and Advice to the King. N.p., 1681.

The Country-man's Festum festorum. N.p., ca. 1736. Newberry Library, Case MS 5A 30.

Cowley, Abraham. *Verses Written Upon Several Occasions*. London, 1663.

Cowling, T. G. "Astrology, Religion and Science." *Quarterly Journal of the Royal Astronomical Society* 23 (1982): 515–526.

Cragg, Gerald R. *The Church and the Age of Reason 1648–1789*. Harmondsworth: Penguin Books, 1970.

Cramer, Frederick H. *Astrology in Roman Law and Politics*. Philadelphia: American Philosophical Society, 1954.

Cranmer, Thomas. *The Remains of Thomas Cranmer*. Edited by Henry Jenkyns. 4 vols. Oxford: Oxford University Press, 1833.

Crouch, Nathaniel, comp. [Robert Burton, pseud.]. *The Surprizing Miracles of Nature and Art. In Two Parts. Containing I. The Miracles of Nature, or the Strange Signs and Prodigious Aspects and Appearances in the Heavens, the Earth, and the Waters . . . with an Account of the most famous Comets, and other Prodigies, since the Birth of our Blessed Saviour, and the dreadful Effects of many of them: Also a particular Description of the five Blazing Stars seen in England, within Eighteen years last past, and abundance of other unaccountable Accidents and Productions of all kinds, till 1682. II. The Miracles of Art. 2d ed.* London, 1685.

Crowe, Michael J. *The Extraterrestrial Life Debate, 1750–1900: The Idea of a Plurality of Worlds from Kant to Lowell*. Cambridge: Cambridge University Press, 1986.

Curry, Patrick. *Prophecy and Power: Astrology in Early Modern England*. Princeton: Princeton University Press, 1989.

———, ed. *Astrology, Science, and Society*. Woodbridge, Suffolk: The Boydell Press, 1987.

Cysat, Johann Baptista. *Mathemata astronomica de loco, motu, magnitudine, et causis cometae qui sub finem anni 1618. et initium anni 1619 in coelo fulsit*. Ingolstadt, 1619.

Dales, Richard C. *The Scientific Achievement of the Middle Ages*. Philadelphia: University of Pennsylvania Press, 1973.

D[anforth], S[amuel]. *An Astronomical Description of the Late Comet or Blazing Star, as it appeared in New-England in the 9th, 10th, 11th and in the beginning of the 12th moneth, 1664. Together with a brief Theological Application thereof*. Cambridge, 1665.

Davis, John, ed. *Two Lectures on Comets, by Professor Winthrop, also An Essay on Comets, by A. Oliver, Jun. Esq. With Sketches of the Lives of Professor Winthrop and Mr. Oliver. Likewise, a Supplement, Relative to the Present Comet of 1811.* Boston, 1811.

Davis, Marc, Piet Hut, and Richard A. Muller. "Extinction of Species by Periodic Comet Showers." *Nature* 308 (1984): 715–717.

Davis, Natalie Zemon. *Society and Culture in Early Modern France.* Stanford: Stanford University Press, 1975.

Debus, Allen G. "The Paracelsian Aerial Niter." *Isis* 55 (1964): 43–61.

———. "The Chemical Debates of the Seventeenth Century: The Reaction to Robert Fludd and Jean Baptiste van Helmont." In *Reason, Experiment, and Mysticism in the Scientific Revolution,* edited by M. L. Righini Bonelli and William R. Shea, 18–47, 291–298. New York: Science History Publications, 1975.

———. *The Chemical Philosophy: Paracelsian Science and Medicine in the Sixteenth and Seventeenth Centuries.* 2 vols. New York: Science History Publications, 1977.

———, ed. *Science, Medicine and Society in the Renaissance: Essays to Honor Walter Pagel.* New York: Science History Publications, 1972.

Defoe, Daniel. *A Tour Thro' the whole Island of Great Britain* [1724–1726]. 2 vols. London: Frank Cass & Company, 1968.

De Maillet, Benoît. *Telliamed, ou entretiens d'un philosophe Indien avec un missionnaire François sur la diminution de la mer, la formation de la terre, l'origine de l'homme, &c.* Amsterdam, 1748.

———. *Telliamed, or Conversations between an Indian Philosopher and a French Missionary on the Diminution of the Sea.* Translated and edited by Albert V. Carozzi. Urbana: University of Illinois Press, 1968.

Democritus [pseud.]. *The Petitioning-Comet: or, a Brief Chronology of all the Famous Comets, and their Events, That have happen'd from the Birth of Christ, to this very day. Together with a Modest Enquiry into this present Comet.* London, 1681.

Derham, William. *Astro-Theology: Or a Demonstration of the Being and Attributes of God, from a Survey of the Heavens.* 1st ed. London, 1715.

———. *Astro-Theology: Or a Demonstration of the Being and Attributes of God, from a Survey of the Heavens.* 2d ed., corrected. London, 1715.

Desaguliers, John Theophilus. *The Newtonian System of the World, The Best Model of Government: An Allegorical Poem. With a plain and intelligible Account of the System of the World, by Way of Annotations.* Westminster, [London], 1728.

Descartes, René. *Principia philosophiae.* Amsterdam, 1644.

———. *Le Monde de Mr Descartes, ou le traité de la lumiere.* Paris, 1664.

———. *Oeuvres de Descartes.* Edited by Charles Adam and Paul Tannery. 13 vols. Paris, 1897–1913. Rev. ed., Paris: Vrin/C.N.R.S., 1964–1974.

———. *Le Monde, ou Traité de la lumière.* Edited with English translation by Michael Sean Mahoney. The Janus Library, no. 2. New York: Abaris Books, 1979.

———. *Principles of Philosophy.* Translated by Valentine Rodger Miller and Reese P. Miller. Synthese Historical Library—Texts and Studies in the History of Logic and Philosophy, no. 24. Dordrecht: D. Reidel Publishing Company, 1983.

Dick, Steven J. *Plurality of Worlds: The Origins of the Extraterrestrial Life Debate from Democritus to Kant.* Cambridge: Cambridge University Press, 1982.

Dictionary of Scientific Biography. Sv. "Abū Maʿshar al-Balkhī, Jaʿfar ibn Muḥammad," by David Pingree; "Albertus Magnus, Saint," by William A. Wallace; "Bacon, Roger," by A. C. Crombie and J. D. North; "Buridan, Jean," by Ernest A. Moody; "Giles (Aegidius) of Lessines," by William A. Wallace; "Grosseteste, Robert," by A. C. Crombie; "Henry of Hesse," by H. L. L. Busard; "Oresme, Nicole," by Marshall Clagett.

Diderot, Denis, and Jean le Rond d'Alembert. *Encyclopédie, ou dictionnaire raisonné des sciences, des arts et des métiers.* 28 vols. Paris and Neufchâtel, 1751–1772.

Digges, Leonard. *A Prognostication of right good effect.* London, 1555.

———. *A Prognostication everlastinge of ryghte good effecte.* London, 1576.

Digges, Thomas. "A Perfit Description of the Caelestiall Orbes." Appended to *A Prognostication everlastinge of ryghte good effecte*, by Leonard Digges. London, 1576.

Dio. *See* Cassius Dio Cocceianus.

Diodorus Siculus [Diodorus of Sicily]. *Library of History.* Translated by C. H. Oldfather, Charles L. Sherman, C. Bradford Welles, Russel M. Geer, and Francis R. Walton. 12 vols. Loeb Classical Library. London: William Heinemann, 1933–1967.

Dionis du Séjour, Achille Pierre. *Essai sur les comètes en général, et particulierement sur celles qui peuvent approcher de l'orbite de la terre.* Paris, 1775.

A Dissertation on Comets. Extracted from the Writings of the most eminent modern Astronomers and Philosophers. In a Letter to a Reverend Professor. To which is prefixed, The Theory of a Comet, by Sir Isaac Newton. London, [ca. 1720].

Dissertations sur la théorie des comètes qui ont concouru au prix proposé par l'Académie Royale des Sciences et Belles Lettres de Prusse pour l'année 1777, & adjugé en 1778. Utrecht, 1780.

Dobbs, Betty Jo Teeter. *The Foundations of Newton's Alchemy, or "The Hunting of the Greene Lyon."* Cambridge: Cambridge University Press, 1975.

———. "Newton and Stoicism." *Southern Journal of Philosophy* 23, supplement (1985): 109–123.

———. *The Janus Faces of Genius: The Role of Alchemy in Newton's Thought.* Cambridge: Cambridge University Press, 1991.

Drake, Stillman, and C. D. O'Malley, eds. *The Controversy on the Comets of 1618: Galileo Galilei, Horatio Grassi, Mario Guiducci, Johann Kepler.* Philadelphia: University of Pennsylvania Press, 1960.

Dryden, John. *The Poems of John Dryden.* Edited by James Kinsley. 4 vols. Oxford: Oxford University Press, 1958.

Du Bartas, Guillaume de Salluste, seigneur. *Bartas: His Devine Weekes and Workes.* Translated by Joshua Sylvester. London, 1605. Facsimile reprint, edited by Francis C. Haber. Gainesville, Fla.: Scholars' Facsimiles & Reprints, 1965.

———. *The Works of Guillaume De Salluste Sieur Du Bartas.* Edited by Urban Tigner Holmes, Jr., John Coriden Lyons, and Robert White Linker. 3 vols. Chapel Hill: University of North Carolina Press, 1935–1940.

Dunthorne, Richard. "A Letter from Mr. Rich. Dunthorne to the Rev. Dr. Long, F.R.S., Master of Pembroke-Hall in Cambridge, and Lowndes's Professor of As-

tronomy and Geometry in that University, concerning Comets." *Philosophical Transactions* 47 (1753): 281–288.

[Earle, John.] *Micro-cosmographie. Or, A Peece of the World Discovered; In Essayes and Characters.* London: W. S. for Ed. Blount, 1628.

Edberg, Stephen J. *International Halley Watch Amateur Observers' Manual for Scientific Comet Studies.* Pasadena: National Aeronautics and Space Administration and the Jet Propulsion Laboratory of the California Institute of Technology, 1983. Reprint, Cambridge, Mass.: Sky Publishing Corporation, 1983.

[Edwards, John.] *Cometomantia. A Discourse of Comets: Shewing their Original, Substance, Place, Time, Magnitude, Motion, Number, Colour, Figure, Kinds, Names, and, more especially, their Prognosticks, Significations and Presages. Being a brief Resolution of a seasonable Query, viz. Whether the Apparition of Comets be the Sign of approaching Evil? Where also is inserted an Essay of Judiciary Astrology, giving Satisfaction to this grand Question, Whether any certain Judgments and Predictions concerning future Events, can be made from the Observation of the Heavenly Bodies? Both occasioned by the Appearance of the late Comets in England and other Places.* London, 1684.

Eigentliche Vorstellung des Neu-entstandenen Cometen-Liechts. [Broadside.] Nuremberg, 1682.

Encyclopedia of Philosophy. S.v. "Bacon, Roger," by Allan B. Wolter.

England's Mournful Elegy For The Dissolving the Parliament. London, [1681].

Englefield, Sir Henry. *Tables of the Apparent Places of the Comet of 1661, Whose Return Is Expected in 1789. To which is added, A new Method of using the Reticule Rhomboide.* London, 1788.

Ernst, Germana. "From the Watery Trigon to the Fiery Trigon: Celestial Signs, Prophecies and History." In *"Astrologi hallucinati": Stars and the End of the World in Luther's Time,* edited by Paola Zambelli, 265–280. Berlin: Walter de Gruyter, 1986.

Euler, Leonhard. "Recherches physiques sur la cause de la queue des comètes, de la lumière boréale, et de la lumière zodiacale." *Histoire de l'Académie Royale des Sciences MDCCXLVI* (Berlin, 1748): 117–140.

———. *Lettres à une Princesse d'Allemagne sur divers sujets de physique & de philosophie.* 3 vols. St. Petersburg, 1768–1772.

———. *Lettres de M. Euler à une Princesse d'Allemagne, sur différentes questions de physique et de philosophie.* New ed., with additions by MM. le Marquis de Condorcet and De la Croix. 3 vols. Paris, 1787–1789.

———. *Letters of Euler on Different Subjects in Natural Philosophy. Addressed to a German Princess.* Edited by David Brewster, with additional notes by John Griscom. 2 vols. New York, 1833.

———. *Leonhardi Euleri opera omnia.* 72 vols, expected. Berlin-Göttingen-Leipzig-Heidelberg: Societatis Scientiarum Naturalium Helveticae, 1911–.

Eusebius. *The Ecclesiastical History.* Translated by Kirsopp Lake. 2 vols. Loeb Classical Library. Cambridge: Harvard University Press, 1926–1932.

Euw, Anton von, and Joachim M. Plotzek. *Die Handschriften der Sammlung Ludwig.* Vol. 3. Cologne: Schnütgen-Museum der Stadt Köln, 1982.

Evans, Arise. *The Bloudy Vision of John Farly. . . . With Another Vision signifying peace and happiness. Both which Shew remarkable alterations speedily, to come to pass here in England, Also a Refutation of a Pamphlet, lately published by one*

Aspinwall: called a Brief discription of the fifth Monarchy. Shewing . . . that the fifth Monarchy will shortly be established in the Person of Charls Stevvart. London, 1653.

Evans, Arise. *Light for the Jews*. London, 1664.

Evelyn, John. *A Panegyric to Charles the Second, Presented To His Majestie The XXXIII. [sic] of April, being the Day of His Coronation. MDCLXI*. London, 1661.

———. *The Diary of John Evelyn*. Edited by E. S. DeBeer. 6 vols. Oxford: Clarendon Press, 1955.

Fabricius, Paulus. *Cometa visus mense Martio. LVI. anno*. [A broadside with comet path illustrated and text.] Vienna, [1556].

———. *Judicium de cometa, qui anno Domini M.D.LXXVII. a 10. die Novemb: usque ad 22. diem Decemb: Viennae conspectus est. In quo varia de cometarum natura & forma in genera breviter tractantur*. Vienna, [1577].

Faral, Edmond. "Jean Buridan: Maître ès Arts de l'Université de Paris." *Histoire littéraire de la France* 38 (1949): 462–605.

Feingold, Mordechai. *The Mathematicians' Apprenticeship: Science, Universities and Society in England, 1560–1640*. Cambridge: Cambridge University Press, 1984.

Ferguson, James. *An Idea of the Material Universe, Deduced from a Survey of the Solar System*. London, 1754.

———. *Astronomy Explained upon Sir Isaac Newton's Principles*. 4th ed. London, 1770.

Fèvre, Nicolas le [Nicasius Le Febure]. *A Compleat Body of Chymistry*. London, 1664.

Fielding, Henry [Sir Alexander Drawcansir, Knt. Censor of Great Britain, pseud.]. *The Covent-Garden Journal*. Edited by Gerard Edward Jensen. 2 vols. New Haven: Yale University Press, 1915.

Figala, Karin. "Newton as Alchemist." *History of Science* 15 (1977): 102–137.

Firth, Katharine R. *The Apocalyptic Tradition in Reformation Britain, 1530–1645*. Oxford: Oxford University Press, 1979.

Flamsteed, John. *The Gresham Lectures of John Flamsteed*. Edited by Eric G. Forbes. London: Mansell, 1975.

Flaste, Richard, Holcomb Noble, Walter Sullivan, and John Noble Wilford. *The New York Times Guide to the Return of Halley's Comet*. New York: Times Books, 1985.

Fleming, Donald. "The Judgment upon Copernicus in Puritan New England." In *Mélanges Alexandre Koyré*, 2:160–175. 2 vols. Paris: Hermann, 1964.

Fontenelle, Bernard le Bovier de. *La Comete. Comedie*. Paris, 1681.

———. *A Plurality of Worlds*. Translated by J. Glanvill. London, 1688.

———. *A Plurality of Worlds*. Translated by J. Glanvill. London, 1702.

———. *Oeuvres de Monsieur de Fontenelle*. New ed. 12 vols. Amsterdam, 1764.

———. *Entretiens sur la pluralité des mondes*. Critical ed. Edited by Alexandre Calame. Paris: Librairie Marcel Didier, 1966.

Forbes, Eric G. "The Comet of 1680–1681." In *Standing on the Shoulders of Giants: A Longer View of Newton and Halley*, edited by Norman J. W. Thrower, 312–323. Berkeley and Los Angeles: University of California Press, 1990.

Force, James E. *William Whiston: Honest Newtonian*. Cambridge: Cambridge University Press, 1985.

Fracastoro, Girolamo. *Homocentrica eiusdem de causis criticorum dierum per ea quae in nobis sunt.* Venice, 1538.

Franklin, Benjamin. *Benjamin Franklin's Experiments.* Edited by I. Bernard Cohen. Cambridge: Harvard University Press, 1941.

Franks, Augustus W., and Herbert A. Grueber, eds., with Edward Hawkins, comp. *Medallic Illustrations of the History of Great Britain and Ireland to the Death of George II.* 2 vols. London: Trustees of the British Museum, 1885. Reprint, London: Spink and Son, 1969.

Freitag, Ruth S. *Halley's Comet: A Bibliography.* Washington, D.C.: Library of Congress, 1984.

Fréret, Nicolas. "Réflexions sur un ancien phénomène céleste, observé au temps d'Ogygès." In *Oeuvres Complètes de Fréret*, 16:286–331. Paris, 1796.

———. *Oeuvres Complètes de Fréret, Secrétaire de l'Académie des Inscriptions et Belles-Lettres.* 20 vols. Paris, 1796.

Frisch, Christian, ed. *Joannis Kepleri astronomi opera omnia.* 8 vols. in 9. Frankfurt: Heyder & Zimmer, 1858–1871.

Froidment, Libert. *Meteorologicorum libri sex.* Antwerp, 1627.

Fulke, William. *A goodly gallerye with a most pleasaunt prospect into the garden of naturall contemplation, to behold the naturall causes of all kynde of meteors.* London, 1563.

———. *Meteors: Or, A plain Description of all kinds of Meteors, as well Fiery and Ayrie, as Watry and Earthy: Briefly Manifesting the Causes of all Blazing-Stars, Shooting-Stars, Flames in the Aire, Thunder, Lightning, Earthquakes, Rain, Dew, Snow, Clouds, Springs, Stones, and Metalls.* London, 1654.

A full and true Relation of a Comet or Blazing-Star, That lately appeared, and was seen by many who are Eye-witnesses thereof, in this City of London, on the 28th and 29th of July last; with many weighty Observations upon the Same. [London, 1679].

Furley, O. W. "The Pope-Burning Processions of the Late Seventeenth Century." *History* 44 (1959): 16–23.

Gadbury, John. *De cometis: or, A Discourse of the Natures and Effects of Comets, As they are Philosophically, Historically & Astrologically Considered. With a brief (yet full) Account of the III late Comets, or Blazing Stars, Visible to all Europe. And what (in a natural way of Judicature) they portend. Together with some Observations on the Nativity of the Grand Seignior.* London, 1665.

Gaffarel, James [Jacques]. *Unheard-of Curiosities: Concerning the Talismanical Sculpture of the Persians; the Horoscope of the Patriarkes; And the Reading of the Stars.* Translated by Edmund Chilmead. London, 1650.

Galilei, Galileo. *Il saggiatore, nel quale con bilancia esquisita, e giusta si ponderano le cose contenute nella Libra astronomica, e filosofica, di Lotario Sarsi Sigensano, scritto in forma de lettera, all'illustrissimo, e reverendissimo monsig. d. Virginio Cesarini.* Rome, 1623.

———. *The Assayer.* Edited and translated by Stillman Drake. *See* Drake and O'Malley, 1960.

Garin, Eugenio. *Astrology in the Renaissance: The Zodiac of Life.* Translated by Carolyn Jackson and June Allen. London: Routledge & Kegan Paul, 1983.

Gascoigne, John. "'The Wisdom of the Egyptians' and the Secularisation of History in the Age of Newton." In *The Uses of Antiquity: The Scientific Revolution and*

the Classical Tradition, edited by Stephen Gaukroger, 171–212. Dordrecht: Kluwer Academic, 1991.

Gassendi, Pierre. *Viri illustris Nicolai Claudii Fabricii de Peiresc, Senatoris Aquisextiensis vita*. Paris, 1641.

————. *The Mirrour of True Nobility & Gentility. Being the Life of The Renowned Nicolaus Claudius Fabricius Lord of Peiresk, Senator of the Parliament of Aix*. Translated by W. Rand. London, 1657.

————. *Opera omnia*. 6 vols. Lyons, 1658.

————. *Syntagma philosophicum*. In *Opera omnia*, vol. 1. Lyons, 1658.

[Gay, John.] "A True and Faithful Narrative of What pass'd in London during the general Consternation of all Ranks and Degrees of Mankind; On Tuesday, Wednesday, Thursday, and Friday last." In *Miscellanies: The Third Volume*, edited by Jonathan Swift and Alexander Pope, 239–260. London, 1732. *See* Swift and Pope, 1732–1733.

Geertz, Clifford. *The Interpretation of Cultures*. New York: Basic Books, 1973.

Gehrels, Tom. *Hazards Due to Comets and Asteroids*. Tuscon: University of Arizona Press, 1994.

Gemma, Cornelius. *De prodigiosa specie, naturaq. cometae, qui nobis effulsit altior lunae sedibus*. Antwerp, 1578.

Gemsege, Paul. "Cruelty of terrifying weak Minds with groundless Pains." *Gentleman's Magazine* 26 (February 1756): 71–72.

A General Collection of Discourses of the Virtuosi of France, Upon Questions of all Sorts of Philosophy, and Other Natural Knowledg. Made in the Assembly of the Beaux Esprits at Paris, by the most Ingenious Persons of that Nation. Translated by G. Havers. London, 1664.

The Geneva Bible. A Facsimile of the 1560 Edition. Introduction by Lloyd E. Berry. Madison: University of Wisconsin Press, 1969.

Geoffrey of Meaux. *De stellis comatis* [1315]. *See* Thorndike, 1950.

————. "Ad honorem illius sanctissimi astronomi qui solus numerat multitudinem stellarum propriis nominibus vocans eas. . . . Et in hoc terminatur epistola magistri Gaufredi de pronosticatione comete" [1337]. *See* Thorndike, 1950.

Gerard de Silteo [Feltre?]. *Summa de astris* [ca. 1291]. Pars 1, distinctio 23. *See* Thorndike, 1950.

Gillett, Stephen L. "The Rise and Fall of the Early Reducing Atmosphere." *Astronomy* (July 1985): 66–71.

Gingerich, Owen. "Tycho Brahe and the Great Comet of 1577." *Sky and Telescope* 54 (December 1977): 452–458.

————. "Halley's Letter to Gregory Concerning the 'Synopsis.'" *Journal for the History of Astronomy* 16 (1985): 223–224.

————. Review of *Fire and Ice: A History of Comets in Art*, by Roberta J. M. Olson. *Journal for the History of Astronomy* 17 (1986): 62–63.

————. *The Great Copernicus Chase and Other Adventures in Astronomical History*. Cambridge, Mass.: Sky Publishing; Cambridge: Cambridge University Press, 1992.

Ginzburg, Carlo. *The Cheese and the Worms: The Cosmos of a Sixteenth-Century Miller*. Translated by John and Anne Tedeschi. Baltimore: Johns Hopkins University Press, 1980.

Goad, John. *Astro-Meteorologica, or Aphorisms and Discourses of the Bodies Celestial, their Natures and Influences*. London, 1686.

Goldgar, Bertrand A. "Fielding, the Flood Makers, and Natural Philosophy: *Covent-Garden Journal* No. 70." *Modern Philology* 80 (1982): 136–144.

Gould, Stephen Jay. *The Flamingo's Smile*. New York: W. W. Norton, 1985.

———. *Time's Arrow, Time's Cycle: Myth and Metaphor in the Discovery of Geological Time*. Cambridge: Harvard University Press, 1987.

Grant, Edward. *Physical Science in the Middle Ages*. New York: John Wiley & Sons, 1971.

———, ed. *A Source Book in Medieval Science*. Cambridge: Harvard University Press, 1974.

[Grassi, Orazio.] *De tribus cometis anni M.DC.XVIII. Disputatio astronomica publicè habita in Collegio Romano Societatis Jesu ab uno ex patribus eiusdem societatis*. Rome, 1619.

——— [Lothario Sarsi of Siguenza, pseud.]. *Libra astronomica ac philosophica*. Perugia, 1619.

——— [Lothario Sarsi, pseud.]. *Ratio ponderum librae et simbellae: in qua quid e Lotharii Sarsii libra astronomica, quidque e Galilei Galilei simbellatore, de cometis statuendum sit, collatis utriusque rationum momentis, philosophorum arbitrio proponitur*. Paris, 1626.

———. *On the Three Comets of the Year 1618*. Translated by C. D. O'Malley. *See* Drake and O'Malley, 1960.

———. *The Astronomical Balance*. Translated by C. D. O'Malley. *See* Drake and O'Malley, 1960.

G[reen], W[illiam]. *Memento's to the World; or, An Historical Collection of divers Wonderful Comets and Prodigious Signs in Heaven, that have been seen, some long before the Birth of Christ, and many since that time in divers Countries, with their wonderful and dreadful Effects. Together, with ample Discourses, and profitable Observations, upon that admirable Star which appeared at the Birth of Christ, to the Eastern Magi. As also upon that Comet which appeared in the Constellation of Cassiopea, after the horrid Massacre of the French-Protestants, Anno 1572. And several other Comets, with their Effects to this present time*. London, 1680/81.

Greene, John C. *The Death of Adam: Evolution and Its Impact on Western Thought*. Ames: Iowa State University Press, 1959.

Gregory, David. *Astronomiae physicae & geometricae elementa*. Oxford, 1702.

———. *The Elements of Astronomy, Physical and Geometrical . . . To which is annex'd, Dr. Halley's Synopsis of the Astronomy of Comets*. 2 vols. London, 1715.

———. *Astronomiae physicae & geometricae elementa*. 2d ed., rev. and corrected. 2 vols. Geneva, 1726.

———. *The Elements of Physical and Geometrical Astronomy*. 2d ed., revised by Edmund Stone. 2 vols. London, 1726.

Grosseteste, Robert. *Die Philosophischen Werke des Robert Grosseteste, Bischofs von Lincoln*. Edited by Ludwig Baur. Beiträge zur Geschichte der Philosophie des Mittelalters, no. 9. Münster i. W.: Aschendorff, 1912.

———. *Lynconiensis de cometis et causis ipsarum. See* Thomson, 1933.

Guerlac, Henry. *Newton on the Continent*. Ithaca: Cornell University Press, 1981.

Guiducci, Mario. *Discorso delle comete di Mario Guiducci fatto da lui nell'-Accademia Fiorentina nel suo medesimo consolato*. Florence, 1619.

Guiducci, Mario. *Discourse on the Comets*. Translated by Stillman Drake. *See* Drake and O'Malley, 1960.

Gunther, R. T., ed. *Early Science in Oxford*. 15 vols. Oxford: For the editor, 1923–1967.

Hall, A. Rupert. "Sir Isaac Newton's Note-Book, 1661–65." *Cambridge Historical Journal* 9 (1948): 239–250.

Hall, A. Rupert, and Marie Boas Hall, eds. *Unpublished Scientific Papers of Isaac Newton: A Selection from the Portsmouth Collection in the University Library, Cambridge*. Cambridge: Cambridge University Press, 1962.

Hall, David. Introduction to *Understanding Popular Culture: Europe from the Middle Ages to the Nineteenth Century*, edited by Steven L. Kaplan, 5–18. Berlin: Mouton Publishers, 1984.

Hall, Marie Boas. "Newton's Voyage in the Strange Seas of Alchemy." In *Reason, Experiment, and Mysticism in the Scientific Revolution*, edited by M. L. Righini Bonelli and William R. Shea, 239–246. New York: Science History Publications, 1975.

Hall, Michael G. "The Introduction of Modern Science into Seventeenth-Century New England: Increase Mather." In *Proceedings of the Tenth International Congress of the History of Science, Ithaca, 26 VIII 1962–2 IX 1962*, 261–264. Paris, 1964.

———. "Renaissance Science in Puritan New England." In *Aspects of the Renaissance*, edited by Archibald R. Lewis, 123–136. Austin: University of Texas Press, 1967.

Hall, Thomas S. "Life, Death and the Radical Moisture: A Study of Thematic Pattern in Medieval Medical Theory." *Clio Medica* 6 (1971): 3–23.

———. *History of General Physiology: 600 B.C. to A.D. 1900*. 2 vols. Chicago: University of Chicago Press, 1975.

Halley, Edmond. "An Account of some Observations lately made at Nurenburg by Mr. P. Wurtzelbaur, shewing that the Latitude of that Place has continued without sensible alteration for 200 years last past; as likewise the Obliquity of the Ecliptick; by comparing them with what was observed by Bernard Walther in the Year 1487" [1687]. *Philosophical Transactions* 16 (1686–1687): 403–406.

———. "An Account of the cause of the Change in the Variation of the Magnetic Needle. with an Hypothesis of the Structure of the Internal parts of the Earth" [1692]. *Philosophical Transactions* 17 (1691–1693): 563–578.

———. "Some Account of the Ancient State of the City of Palmyra, with short Remarks upon the Inscriptions found there" [1695]. *Philosophical Transactions* 19 (1695–1697): 160–175.

———. "Astronomiae cometicae synopsis" [1705]. *Philosophical Transactions* 24 (1704–1705): 1882–1899.

———. "A Synopsis of the Astronomy of Comets" [1706]. In *Miscellanea Curiosa*, edited by Edmond Halley, 2:[321–344]. 3 vols. London, 1705–1707.

———. "An Account of several extraordinary Meteors or Lights in the Sky" [1714]. *Philosophical Transactions* 29 (1714–1716): 159–164.

———. "A short Account of the Cause of the Saltness of the Ocean, and of the several Lakes that emit no Rivers; with a Proposal, by help thereof, to discover the Age of the World" [1715]. *Philosophical Transactions* 29 (1714–1716): 296–300.

————. *A Description of the Passage of the Shadow of the Moon, over England, In the Total Eclipse of the Sun, on the 22^d. Day of April 1715 in the Morning.* [Broadside.] London, 1715.

————. "An Account of several Nebulae or lucid Spots like Clouds, lately discovered among the Fixt Stars by help of the Telescope" [1716]. *Philosophical Transactions* 29 (1714–1716): 390–392.

————. "An Account of the late surprizing Appearance of the Lights seen in the Air, on the sixth of March last; with an Attempt to explain the Principal Phaenomena thereof" [1716]. *Philosophical Transactions* 29 (1714–1716): 406–428.

————. "An Account of the Cause of the late remarkable Appearance of the Planet Venus, seen this Summer, for many Days together, in the Day time" [1716]. *Philosophical Transactions* 29 (1714–1716): 466–468.

————. "An Account of a small Telescopical Comet seen at London on the 10th of June 1717" [1717]. *Philosophical Transactions* 30 (1717–1719): 721–723.

————. "An Account of the Extraordinary Meteor seen all over England, on the 19th of March 1718/9. With a Demonstration of the uncommon Height thereof" [1719]. *Philosophical Transactions* 30 (1717–1719): 978–990.

————. "Some Considerations about the Cause of the universal Deluge, laid before the Royal Society, on the 12th of December 1694" [1724]. *Philosophical Transactions* 33 (1724–1725): 118–123.

————. "Some farther Thoughts upon the same Subject [the universal Deluge], delivered on the 19th of the same Month [December 1694]" [1724]. *Philosophical Transactions* 33 (1724–1725): 123–125.

————. *Astronomical Tables with Precepts Both in English and Latin for Computing the Places of the Sun, Moon, Planets, and Comets.* London, 1752.

————. *Tables astronomiques de M. Halley, pour les planetes et les cometes, réduites au nouveau stile & méridien de Paris, augmentées de plusieurs tables nouvelles de différens auteurs, pour les sattellites de Jupiter & les étoiles fixes, avec des explications détaillées. Et l'histoire de la comete de 1759. Par M. de Lalande.* Paris, 1759.

————. *Correspondence and Papers of Edmond Halley.* Edited by Eugene Fairfield MacPike. Oxford: Clarendon Press, 1932. Reprint, New York: Arno Press, 1975.

————, ed. *Miscellanea Curiosa. Being a Collection of some of the Principal Phaenomena in Nature, Accounted for by the Greatest Philosophers of this Age. Together with several Discourses read before the Royal Society, for the Advancement of Physical and Mathematical Knowledge.* 3 vols. London, 1705–1707.

Hamilton, Hugh. *Philosophical Essays On the following Subjects: I. On the Ascent of Vapours, the Formation of Clouds, Rain and Dew, and on several other Phaenomena of Air and Water. II. Observations and Conjectures on the Nature of the Aurora Borealis, and the Tails of Comets. III. On the Principles of Mechanicks.* Dublin, 1766.

————. *The Works of the Right Rev. Hugh Hamilton, D.D., Late Bishop of Ossory.* Edited by Alexander Hamilton. 2 vols. London, 1809.

Hammerstein, Helga Robinson. "The Battle of the Booklets: Prognostic Tradition and Proclamation of the Word in Early Sixteenth-Century Germany." In *"Astrologi hallucinati": Stars and the End of the World in Luther's Time*, edited by Paola Zambelli, 129–151. Berlin: Walter de Gruyter, 1986.

Hansen, Bert. *Nicole Oresme and the Marvels of Nature: A Study of His "De causis mirabilium" with Critical Edition, Translation, and Commentary.* Studies and Texts (Pontifical Institute of Mediaeval Studies), no. 68. Toronto: Pontifical Institute of Mediaeval Studies, 1985.

Harris, John. *Lexicon technicum.* 1st ed. 2 vols. London, 1704–1710.

———. *Lexicon technicum.* 2d ed. 2 vols. London, 1708–1710.

Harrison, John. *The Library of Isaac Newton.* Cambridge: Cambridge University Press, 1978.

Harvey, Edmund Newton. *A History of Luminescence from the Earliest Times until 1900.* Philadelphia: American Philosophical Society, 1959.

Hasegawa, Ichiro. "Catalogue of Ancient and Naked-Eye Comets." *Vistas in Astronomy* 24 (1980): 59–102.

Hawthorne, Nathaniel. *The Scarlet Letter.* Boston, 1850.

Hearne, Thomas. *Remarks and Collections of Thomas Hearne.* Edited by C. E. Doble, et al. 11 vols. Oxford: Clarendon Press for the Oxford Historical Society, 1885–1921.

Heilbron, J. L. *Electricity in the Seventeenth and Eighteenth Centuries.* Berkeley and Los Angeles: University of California Press, 1979.

Heimann, P. M. "Voluntarism and Immanence: Conceptions of Nature in Eighteenth-Century Thought." *Journal of the History of Ideas* 39 (1978): 271–283.

Hellman, C. Doris. *The Comet of 1577: Its Place in the History of Astronomy.* New York: Columbia University Press, 1944.

———. "The Role of Measurement in the Downfall of a System: Some Examples from Sixteenth Century Comet and Nova Observations." *Vistas in Astronomy* 9 (1967): 43–52.

———. "Kepler and Comets." *Vistas in Astronomy* 18 (1975): 789–796.

Helmont, Jean Baptiste van. *Ortus medicinae.* Amsterdam, 1648.

———. *Oriatrike.* London, 1662.

Henry of Hesse. *Questio de cometa magistri Henrici de Hassia.* In *Studien zu den astrologischen schriften des Heinrich von Langenstein,* edited by Hubert Pruckner, 89–138. Berlin: B. G. Teubner, 1933.

Herivel, John. *The Background to Newton's "Principia."* Oxford: Oxford University Press, 1965.

Herschel, William. Correspondence. [Microfilm.] Herschel Archive. Royal Astronomical Society, London.

———. "On Nebulous Stars, properly so called." *Philosophical Transactions* 81 (1791): 71–88.

———. "On the Nature and Construction of the Sun and fixed Stars." *Philosophical Transactions* 85 (1795): 46–72.

———. "Observations on the Nature of the new celestial Body discovered by Dr. Olbers, and of the Comet which was expected to appear last January in its return from the Sun." *Philosophical Transactions* 97 (1807): 260–266.

———. "Observations of a Comet, made with a View to investigate its Magnitude and the Nature of its Illumination." *Philosophical Transactions* 98 (1808): 145–163.

———. "Astronomical Observations relating to the Construction of the Heavens." *Philosophical Transactions* 101 (1811): 269–336.

———. "Observations of a Comet, with Remarks on the Construction of its different Parts." *Philosophical Transactions* 102 (1812): 115–143.

————. "Observations of a second Comet, with Remarks on its Construction." *Philosophical Transactions* 102 (1812): 229–237.

————. *The Scientific Papers of Sir William Herschel.* Edited by J.L.E. Dreyer. 2 vols. London: Royal Society and Royal Astronomical Society, 1912.

Hevelius, Johannes. *Cometographia, totam naturam cometarum; . . . exhibens. . . . Cumprimis verò, cometae anno 1652, 1661, 1664 & 1665 ab ipso auctore, summo studio observati, aliquantò prolixiùs, . . . exponuntur, expenduntur, atq; rigidissimo calculo subjiciuntur. Accessit, omnium cometarum, à mundo condito hucusquè ab historicis, philosophis, & astronomis annotatorum, historia.* Danzig, 1668.

Hill, Christopher. *The World Turned Upside Down: Radical Ideas during the English Revolution.* Harmondsworth: Penguin Books, 1975.

————. *Antichrist in Seventeenth-Century England.* Rev. ed. London: Verso, 1990.

Hill, John. *An Allarm to Europe: By a Late Prodigious Comet seen November and December, 1680. With a Predictive Discourse. Together with some preceding and some succeeding Causes of its sad Effects to the East and North Eastern parts of the World.* London, [1680].

Hill, John. *A New Astronomical Dictionary, Or, A Compleat View of the Heavens; Containing the Antient and Modern Astronomy.* London, 1768.

Hills, J. G. "Comet Showers and the Steady-State Infall of Comets from the Oort Cloud." *Astronomical Journal* 86 (1981): 1730–1740.

————. "Dynamical Constraints on the Mass and Perihelion Distance of Nemesis and the Stability of Its Orbit." *Nature* 311 (1984): 636–638.

Hindle, Brooke. *The Pursuit of Science in Revolutionary America, 1735–1789.* Chapel Hill: University of North Carolina Press, 1956.

Hiscock, Walter G., ed. *David Gregory, Isaac Newton and Their Circle: Extracts from David Gregory's Memoranda 1677–1708.* Oxford: By the editor, 1937.

Ho Peng Yoke [Ho Ping-Yü]. "Ancient and Mediaeval Observations of Comets and Novae in Chinese Sources." *Vistas in Astronomy* 5 (1962): 127–225.

————. *The Astronomical Chapters of the Chin Shu.* Ecole Pratique des Hautes Etudes, 6ᵉ section, Sciences Economiques et Sociales; Le Monde d'Outre-Mer Passé et Présent, 2ᵉ série, documents, IX. Paris: Mouton & Co., 1966.

Hobbs, R. W., and J. M. Hollis. "Probing the Presently Tenuous Link between Comets and the Origin of Life." *Origins of Life* 12 (1982): 125–132.

The Holy Bible. A facsimile in a reduced size of the Authorized Version published in the year 1611. Introduction by A. W. Pollard. Oxford: Oxford University Press, 1911.

Homer. *The Iliad of Homer.* Translated and edited by Alexander Pope. 6 vols. London, 1715–1720.

————. *The Iliad of Homer.* Translated by Richmond Lattimore. Chicago: University of Chicago Press, 1951.

————. *The Iliad.* Translated by Robert Fitzgerald. Garden City, N.Y.: Anchor Press/Doubleday, 1974.

————. *The Iliad.* Translated by A. T. Murray. 2 vols. Loeb Classical Library. Cambridge: Harvard University Press, 1978.

Hooke, Robert. *Lectures and Collections Made by Robert Hooke, Secretary of the Royal Society. Cometa. . . . Microscopium.* London, 1678.

Hooke, Robert. *Lectiones Cutlerianae, or a Collection of Lectures: Physical, Mechanical, Geographical, & Astronomical. Made before the Royal Society on several Occasions at Gresham Colledge.* London, 1679.

———. *The Posthumous Works of Robert Hooke.* Edited by Richard Waller. London, 1705.

Hornberger, Theodore. "Puritanism and Science: The Relationship Revealed in the Writings of John Cotton." *New England Quarterly* 10 (1937): 503–515.

———. *Scientific Thought in the American Colleges, 1638–1800.* Austin: University of Texas Press, 1945.

Hoskin, Michael A. *William Herschel and the Construction of the Heavens.* London: Oldbourne, 1963.

———. "The Cosmology of Thomas Wright of Durham." *Journal for the History of Astronomy* 1 (1970): 44–52.

———. "Newton, Providence and the Universe of Stars." *Journal for the History of Astronomy* 8 (1977): 77–101.

———. "Lambert's Cosmology." *Journal for the History of Astronomy* 9 (1978): 134–139.

———. "Lambert and Herschel." *Journal for the History of Astronomy* 9 (1978): 140–142.

———. "William Herschel's Early Investigations of Nebulae: A Reassessment." *Journal for the History of Astronomy* 10 (1979): 165–176.

———. "The First Edition of Halley's 'Synopsis.'" *Journal for the History of Astronomy* 16 (1985): 133.

———. "William Herschel and the Making of Modern Astronomy." *Scientific American* 254 (February 1986): 106–112.

Hoskin, Michael, and Brian Warner. "Caroline Herschel's Comet Sweepers." *Journal for the History of Astronomy* 12 (1981): 27–34.

Hoyle, Fred. "Comets—A Matter of Life and Death." *Vistas in Astronomy* 24 (1980): 123–139.

———. *Evolution from Space.* Hillside, N.J.: Enslow Publishers, 1982.

Hoyle, Fred, and Chandra Wickramasinghe. "Influenza from Space?" *New Scientist* 79 (1978): 946–948.

———. *Lifecloud: The Origin of Life in the Universe.* New York: Harper & Row, 1978.

———. *Diseases from Space.* New York: Harper & Row, 1979.

Hughes, David W. *The Star of Bethlehem: An Astronomer's Confirmation.* New York: Pocket Books, 1980.

———. "Halley's Comet in Print." *Nature* 318 (1985): 132–134.

———. "The *Principia* and Comets." In *Newton's Principia and Its Legacy*, edited by D. G. King-Hele and A. R. Hall, 53–74. London: The Royal Society, 1988.

———. "Edmond Halley: His Interest in Comets." In *Standing on the Shoulders of Giants: A Longer View of Newton and Halley*, edited by Norman J. W. Thrower, 324–372. Berkeley and Los Angeles: University of California Press, 1990.

Hughes, David W., and Andrew Drummond. "Edmond Halley's Observations of Halley's Comet." *Journal for the History of Astronomy* 15 (1984): 189–197.

Hughes, Edward, ed. "The Early Journal of Thomas Wright of Durham." *Annals of Science* 7 (1951): 1–24.

Hume, David. *Dialogues Concerning Natural Religion.* Edited by Norman Kemp Smith. Indianapolis: Bobbs-Merrill Educational Publishing, 1947.

Hunter, Michael. "Science and Astrology in Seventeenth-Century England: An Unpublished Polemic by John Flamsteed." In *Astrology, Science, and Society*, edited by Patrick Curry, 260–300. Woodbridge, Suffolk: The Boydell Press, 1987.

Hut, Piet, et al. "Comet Showers as a Cause of Mass Extinctions." *Nature* 329 (1987): 118–126.

Huxley, G. L. "The Mathematical Work of Edmond Halley." *Scripta Mathematica* 24 (1959): 265–273.

Huygens, Christiaan. *ΚΟΣΜΟΘΕΩΡΟΣ [Cosmotheoros], sive de terris coelestibus earumque ornatu conjecturae*. The Hague, 1698.

———. *The Celestial Worlds Discover'd: or, Conjectures Concerning the Inhabitants, Plants and Productions of the Worlds in the Planets*. London, 1698.

Hyginus. *Poeticon astronomicon*. Venice: Erhard Ratdolt, 1482.

———. *Hygini Fabulae*. Edited by H. I. Rose. Leiden: A. W. Sythoff, 1933.

———. *The Myths of Hyginus*. Translated and edited by Mary Grant. Lawrence: University of Kansas Press, 1960.

———. *Hyginus Astronomus*. Scriptorum Romanorum quae extant omnia, nos. 255–256. Pisa: Giardini, 1976.

Ihr Betrachter und Beobachter der täglich-neuen Welt-Begebenheiten Stehet Schauer und Erstaunet. [Broadside.] Augsburg: Johann Jacob Schönigk, 1683.

Iliffe, Robert. "'Is he like other men?' The Meaning of the *Principia Mathematica*, and the Author as Idol." In *Culture and Society in the Stuart Restoration*, edited by Gerald Maclean, 159–176. Cambridge: Cambridge University Press, 1995.

Irvine, W. M., S. B. Leschine, and F. P. Schloerb. "Thermal History, Chemical Composition and Relationship of Comets to the Origin of Life." *Nature* 283 (1980): 748–749.

Isidore of Seville. *Isidori Hispalensis episcopi etymologiarum sive originum libri xx*. Edited by W. M. Lindsay. 2 vols. Oxford: Clarendon Press, 1911.

———. *Traité de la nature*. French/Latin ed., edited by Jacques Fontaine. Bibliothèque de l'Ecole des Hautes Etudes Hispaniques, no. 28. Bordeaux: Féret et Fils for the Centre National de la Recherche Scientifique, 1960.

———. *Isidori Hispalensis de natura rerum liber*. Edited by Gustavus Becker. Amsterdam: Verlag Adolf M. Hakkert, 1967.

Jacob, Margaret C. "Millenarianism and Science in the Late Seventeenth Century." *Journal of the History of Ideas* 37 (1976): 335–341.

———. *The Newtonians and the English Revolution 1689–1720*. Hassocks, Sussex: Harvester Press, 1976.

Jacob, M. C., and W. A. Lockwood. "Political Millenarianism and Burnet's *Sacred Theory*." *Science Studies* 2 (1972): 265–279.

Jacobus de Voragine. *See* Voragine, Jacobus de.

Jaki, Stanley L. "The Five Forms of Laplace's Cosmogony." *American Journal of Physics* 44 (1976): 4–11.

———. "An English Translation of the Third Part of Kant's *Universal Natural History and Theory of the Heavens*." In *Cosmology, History, and Theology*, edited by Wolfgang Yourgrau and Allen D. Breck. New York: Plenum, 1977.

———. *Planets and Planetarians: A History of Theories of the Origin of Planetary Systems*. New York: John Wiley & Sons, [1978].

Jervis, Jane L. *Cometary Theory in Fifteenth-Century Europe*. Studia Copernicana, no. 26. Dordrecht: D. Reidel, 1985.

John of Damascus. *De fide orthodoxa.* Burgundionis versio. Edited by Eligius M. Buytaert. Franciscan Institute Publications Text Series, no. 8. St. Bonaventure, N.Y.: The Franciscan Institute, 1955.

———. *Exposition of the Orthodox Faith.* Translated by S.D.F. Salmond. In *A Select Library of Nicene and Post-Nicene Fathers of the Christian Church*, vol. 9. *See* Schaff and Wace, 1982–1983.

John of Legnano. *Tractatus de cometa compilatus per Ioannem de Lignano* [1368]. *See* Thorndike, 1950.

John of Salisbury. *Frivolities of Courtiers and Footprints of Philosophers* [*Policraticus, sive de nugis curialium et vestigiis philosophorum libri VIII*]. Translated by Joseph B. Pike. Minneapolis: University of Minnesota Press, 1938.

Johnson, Francis R. *Astronomical Thought in Renaissance England: A Study of the English Scientific Writings from 1500 to 1645.* Baltimore: Johns Hopkins Press, 1937. Reprint, New York: Octagon Books, 1968.

Josephus, Flavius. *The Jewish War.* Translated by H. St. J. Thackeray. 2 vols. Loeb Classical Library. London: William Heinemann, 1927–1928.

Josselin, Ralph. *The Diary of Ralph Josselin, 1616–1683.* Edited by Alan Macfarlane. Records of Social and Economic History, n.s., no. 3. London: Oxford University Press for the British Academy, 1976.

Le Journal des sçavans. Vols. 1–10. Amsterdam, 1665–1682.

Juvenal [Decimus Junius Juvenalis]. *Satires.* Translated by G. G. Ramsay. Rev. ed. Loeb Classical Library. Cambridge: Harvard University Press, 1961.

Kant, Immanuel. *Allgemeine Naturgeschichte und Theorie des Himmels oder Versuch von der Verfassung und dem mechanischen Ursprunge des ganzen Weltgebäudes nach Newtonischen Grundsätzen abgehandelt.* [Leipzig, 1755].

———. *Universal Natural History and Theory of the Heavens; or an Essay on the Constitution and Mechanical Origin of the Whole Universe Treated According to Newton's Principles.* Translated by W. Hastie. In *Kant's Cosmogony.* Glasgow, 1900.

———. *Kant's Cosmogony, as in His Essay on the Retardation of the Rotation of the Earth and His Natural History and Theory of the Heavens.* Translated by W. Hastie, with a new introduction by Gerald Whitrow. Sources of Science, no. 133. New York: Johnson Reprint Corporation, 1970.

———. "An English Translation of the Third Part of Kant's *Universal Natural History and Theory of the Heavens.*" *See* Jaki, 1977.

Kaplan, Steven L. *Understanding Popular Culture: Europe from the Middle Ages to the Nineteenth Century.* New Babylon: Studies in the Social Sciences, no. 40. Berlin, New York, and Amsterdam: Mouton Publishers, 1984.

Keill, John. *An Examination of Dr. Burnet's Theory of the Earth. Together with Some Remarks on Mr. Whiston's New Theory of the Earth.* Oxford, 1698.

Kepler, Johannes. *Mysterium cosmographicum.* 1st ed. Tübingen, 1596.

———. *Ad Vitellionem paralipomena, quibus astronomiae pars optica traditur.* Frankfurt, 1604.

———. *De stella nova in pede Serpentarii, et qui sub eius exortu de novo iniit, trigono igneo.* Prague, 1606.

———. *Aussführlicher Bericht von dem newlich im Monat Septembri und Octobri diss 1607. Jahrs erschienenen Haarstern oder Cometen und seinen Bedeutungen.* Halle in Saxony, 1608.

———. *Epitome astronomiae Copernicanae.* Linz and Frankfurt, 1618–1621.

————. *De cometis libelli tres. I. Astronomicus, theoremata continens de motu cometarum, ubi demonstratio apparentiarum & altitudinis cometarum qui annis 1607. & 1618. conspecti sunt. . . . II. Physicus, continens physiologiam cometarum novam. . . . III. Astrologicus, de significationibus cometarum annorum 1607. & 1618.* Augsburg, 1619.

————. *Mysterium cosmographicum.* 2d ed. Frankfurt, 1621.

————. *Tychonis Brahei Dani hyperaspistes, adversus Scipionis Claramontii . . . Anti-Tychonem, in aciem productus à Joanne Keplero . . . quo libro doctrina praestantissima de parallaxibus, deque novorum siderum in sublimi aethere discursionibus, repetitur, confirmatur, illustratur.* Frankfurt, 1625.

————. *Joannis Kepleri astronomi opera omnia.* Edited by Christian Frisch. 8 vols. in 9. Frankfurt: Heyder & Zimmer, 1858–1871.

————. *Gesammelte Werke.* Edited by Walther von Dyck, Max Caspar, Franz Hammer, and Martha List. Munich: C. H. Beck, 1937–.

————. "Appendix to the *Hyperaspistes* or Gleanings from the *Assayer* of Galileo." Translated by C. D. O'Malley. *See* Drake and O'Malley, 1960.

————. *Mysterium Cosmographicum.* 2d ed. Frankfurt, 1621. Facsimile ed. with English translation by A. M. Duncan, with introduction and commentary by E. J. Aiton, and a preface by I. Bernard Cohen. The Janus Library, no. 9. New York: Abaris Books, 1981.

Kerr, Richard A. "Periodic Impacts and Extinctions Reported." *Science* 223 (1984): 1277–1279.

Klibansky, Raymond, Erwin Panofsky, and Fritz Saxl. *Saturn and Melancholy: Studies in the History of Natural Philosophy, Religion and Art.* London: Thomas Nelson & Sons, 1964.

Knight, William. *Stella Nova; Or, The New Star, Or, An Account of the Natural Signification of the Comet, or Blazing-Star, That hath so long been Visible in England, and other Countreys, and is yet hanging over our Heads.* London, 1680/81.

Knowles, Ronald, ed. *The Entertainment of His Most Excellent Majestie Charles II, in His Passage through the City of London to His Coronation*, by John Ogilby [London, 1662]. Facsimile ed. Binghamton, N.Y.: Center for Medieval and Early Renaissance Studies, SUNY Binghamton, 1988.

Knox, John. *The Historie of the Reformatioun of Religioun within the Realm of Scotland.* Edinburgh, 1732.

Köhler, Hans-Joachim. "The *Flugschriften* and Their Importance in Religious Debate: A Quantitative Approach." In *"Astrologi hallucinati": Stars and the End of the World in Luther's Time*, edited by Paola Zambelli, 153–175. Berlin: Walter de Gruyter, 1986.

Koyré, Alexandre. *Newtonian Studies.* Cambridge: Harvard University Press, 1965.

Kubrin, David C. "Newton and the Cyclical Cosmos: Providence and the Mechanical Philosophy." *Journal of the History of Ideas* 28 (1967): 325–346.

————. "Providence and the Mechanical Philosophy: The Creation and Dissolution of the World in Newtonian Thought. A Study of the Relations of Science and Religion in Seventeenth Century England." Ph.D. diss., Cornell University, 1968.

————. "Newton's Inside Out! Magic, Class Struggle, and the Rise of Mechanism in the West." In *The Analytic Spirit: Essays in the History of Science in Honor of Henry Guerlac*, edited by Harry Woolf, 96–121. Ithaca: Cornell University Press, 1981.

Kubrin, David C. " 'Such an Impertinently Litigious Lady': Hooke's 'Great Pretend-ing' vs. Newton's *Principia* and Newton's and Halley's Theory of Comets." In *Standing on the Shoulders of Giants: A Longer View of Newton and Halley*, ed-ited by Norman J. W. Thrower, 55–90. Berkeley and Los Angeles: University of California Press, 1990.

Kurze, Dietrich. "Popular Astrology and Prophecy in the Fifteenth and Sixteenth Centuries: Johannes Lichtenberger." In *"Astrologi hallucinati": Stars and the End of the World in Luther's Time*, edited by Paola Zambelli, 177–193. Berlin: Walter de Gruyter, 1986.

Lalande, Joseph Jérôme le Français de. *Réflexions sur les comètes qui peuvent ap-procher de la terre*. Paris, 1773.

Lambert, J. H. *Cosmologische Briefe über die Einrichtung des Weltbaues*. Augsburg, 1761.

———. *Cosmological Letters on the Arrangement of the World-Edifice*. Translated by Stanley L. Jaki. New York: Science History Publications, 1976.

Laplace, Pierre-Simon. *Exposition du systême du monde*. 2 vols. Paris: De l'Im-primerie du Cercle-Social, l'An IV de la République Française, [1796].

———. *Traité de mécanique céleste*. 5 vols. Paris, 1798–1825.

———. *Exposition du système du monde*. 3d ed., rev. and augmented. Paris, 1808.

———. *The System of the World*. [2d ed., 1799]. Translated by J. Pond. 2 vols. London, 1809.

———. *Exposition du système du monde*. 4th ed., rev. and augmented. Paris, 1813.

———. "Sur les comètes" [read November 1813]. In *Connaissance des Temps* (1816). Reprinted in *Oeuvres complètes de Laplace*, 13:88–97. Paris, 1904.

———. *Exposition du système du monde*. 6th ed. [according to title page, but really a reprint of 5th ed.]. Brussels, 1827.

———. *Mécanique céleste*. Translated by Nathaniel Bowditch. 4 vols. Boston: 1829–1839. Reprint, New York: Chelsea Publishing Company, 1966.

———. *Exposition du système du monde*. 6th ed. Paris, 1835. In *Oeuvres complètes de Laplace*, vol. 6. Paris, 1884.

———. *Oeuvres complètes de Laplace*. 14 vols. Paris, Gauthier-Villars, 1878–1912.

Lavoisier, Antoine Laurent. "Sur la nature de l'eau et sur les expériences par lesquelles on a prétendu prouver la possibilité de son changement en terre." *Mémoires de l'Académie des Sciences* (1770), 73ff. In *Oeuvres de Lavoisier*, vol. 2. Paris, 1862.

———. *Oeuvres de Lavoisier*. 7 vols. Paris, 1862–1964.

Lavoisier, Antoine Laurent, and Pierre-Simon Laplace. *Mémoire sur la chaleur lû à l'Académie Royale des Sciences, le 28 Juin 1783*. Paris, 1783.

———. *Memoir on Heat Read to the Royal Academy of Sciences, 28 June 1783 by Messrs. Lavoisier & de la Place of the same Academy*. Translated by Henry Guerlac. New York: Neale Watson Academic Publications, 1982.

Leff, Gordon. *Paris and Oxford Universities in the Thirteenth and Fourteenth Cen-turies*. Huntington, N.Y.: Robert E. Krieger Publishing Company, 1975.

Le Goff, Jacques. "The Learned and Popular Dimensions of Journeys in the Other-world in the Middle Ages." In *Understanding Popular Culture: Europe from the Middle Ages to the Nineteenth Century*, edited by Steven L. Kaplan, 19–37. Berlin: Mouton Publishers, 1984.

The Leibniz-Clarke Correspondence. Edited by H. G. Alexander. Manchester: Manchester University Press, 1956.

Leventhal, Herbert. *In the Shadow of the Enlightenment: Occultism and Renaissance Science in Eighteenth-Century America.* New York: New York University Press, 1976.

Liceto, Fortunio. *De novis astris et cometis libri sex.* Venice, 1623.

Lilly, Joseph, ed. *A Collection of Seventy-Nine Black-Letter Ballads and Broadsides, Printed in the Reign of Queen Elizabeth, Between the Years 1559 and 1597.* London: Joseph Lilly, 1867.

Lilly, William. *Englands Propheticall Merline, Foretelling to all Nations of Europe untill 1663. the Actions depending upon the influence of the Conjunction of Saturn and Jupiter, 1642/3. The Progresse and motion of the Comet 1618. under whose effects we in England, and most Regions of Europe now suffer. What kingdomes must yet partake of the remainder of the influence, viz. of War, Plague, Famine, &c. When the English Common-wealth may expect Peace, and the City of London better times. The beginning, and end of the Watry Trygon: An entrance of the fiery Triplicity, 1603. The Nativities of some English Kings, and some horary Questions inserted: performed.* London, 1644.

L[illy], W[illiam]. *Merlinus Anglicus Junior: The English Merlin revived; Or, His prediction upon the affaires of the English Common-wealth, and of all or most Kingdomes of Christendome this present Yeare, 1644.* London, 1644.

———. *A Collection of Ancient and Moderne Prophesies Concerning these present Times, with Modest Observations thereon.* London, 1645.

———. *Anima Astrologiae: Or, a Guide for Astrologers. Being the considerations of the Famous Guido Bonatus Faithfully rendred into English. As also the Choicest Aphorisms of Cardans Seaven Segments.* London, 1676.

———. *Strange News from the East, or, A Sober Account of the Comet, or Blazing-Star That has been seen several Mornings of late.* London, 1677.

[Lilly, William.] *Lillies New Prophecy, Or, Strange and Wonderful Predictions, relating to the Year, 1678. As well from the late Blazing-Star; The great Conjunction of Saturn and Mars, and other Figures and Aspects of the Heavenly Bodies. Wherein the Future State and Condition of Nations, and the Flourishing Happiness of England and Holland is Foretold and Asserted. With Particular Considerations Concerning Quarrels and disagreements between Men and their Wives; Plenty and Scarcity of the Earth, when to be Feared or Expected the Issue of Wars, and hopes of a General Peace throughout Europe.* [London], 1678.

———. *Mr. William Lilly's History of His Life and Times, From the Year 1602, to 1681.* 2d ed. London, 1715.

Littmann, Mark, and Donald K. Yeomans. *Comet Halley: Once in a Lifetime.* Washington, D.C.: American Chemical Society, 1985.

Lockwood, Rose. "The Scientific Revolution in Seventeenth-Century New England." *New England Quarterly* 53 (1980): 76–95.

Loewe, Michael. "The Han View of Comets." *Östasiatiska museet. Bulletin* [Bulletin of the Museum of Far Eastern Antiquities, Stockholm] 52 (1980): 1–31.

Long, Roger. *Astronomy, in Five Books.* 2 vols. Cambridge, 1742–1784.

Longnon, Jean, Raymond Cazelles, and Millard Meiss, eds. *The Très Riches Heures of Jean, Duke of Berry, Musée Condé, Chantilly.* New York: George Braziller, 1969.

Longomontanus [Christian Severin]. *Astronomia Danica.* 2d ed. Amsterdam, 1640.

Lovejoy, Arthur O. *The Great Chain of Being.* Cambridge: Harvard University Press, 1964.

Lubbock, Constance. *The Herschel Chronicle: The Life-Story of William Herschel and His Sister Caroline Herschel.* Cambridge: Cambridge University Press, 1933.

Lubieniecki, Stanislaw. *Theatrum cometicum.* Amsterdam, 1667. 2d ed. Leiden, 1681.

Lucan [Marcus Annaeus Lucanus]. *The Civil War.* Translated by J. D. Duff. Loeb Classical Library. Cambridge: Harvard University Press, 1977.

Lycosthenes, Conrad. *Prodigiorum ac ostentorum chronicon.* Basel, 1557.

Lyon, John, and Phillip R. Sloan. *From Natural History to the History of Nature: Readings from Buffon and His Critics.* Notre Dame: University of Notre Dame Press, 1981.

McCormmach, Russell. "John Michell and Henry Cavendish: Weighing the Stars." *British Journal for the History of Science* 4 (1968): 126–155.

M'Cullough, Samuel D. *Picture of the Heavens, for the Use of Schools and Private Families; Being a Full and Distinct Explanation of the Different Celestial Phenomena, Divested of Mathematical Formulae; with Tables for Determining the Moon's Age, Calculating Eclipses, etc. etc. Adapted to the Comprehension of Young Persons.* Lexington, Ky., 1840.

McGuire, J. E. "Transmutation and Immutability: Newton's Doctrine of Physical Qualities." *Ambix* 14 (1967): 69–95.

McGuire, J. E., and P. M. Rattansi. "Newton and the 'Pipes of Pan.'" *Notes and Records of the Royal Society of London* 21 (1966): 108–143.

McGuire, J. E., and Martin Tamny, eds. *Certain Philosophical Questions: Newton's Trinity Notebook.* Cambridge: Cambridge University Press, 1983.

Machiavelli, Niccolò. *The Historical, Political, and Diplomatic Writings of Niccolò Machiavelli.* Translated by Christian E. Detmold. 4 vols. Boston: Houghton, Mifflin and Company, 1891.

McKeon, Michael. *Politics and Poetry in Restoration England: The Case of Dryden's "Annus Mirabilis."* Cambridge: Harvard University Press, 1975.

McLachlan, Herbert. *Religious Opinions of Milton, Locke, and Newton.* Theological Series, no. 6. Manchester: Manchester University Press, 1941.

————, ed. *Sir Isaac Newton: Theological Manuscripts.* Liverpool: Liverpool University Press, 1950.

Maclaurin, Colin. *An Account of Sir Isaac Newton's Philosophical Discoveries.* London, 1748.

Maclean, Gerald, ed. *Culture and Society in the Stuart Restoration.* Cambridge: Cambridge University Press, 1995.

MacPike, Eugene Fairfield. *Hevelius, Flamsteed, and Halley: Three Contemporary Astronomers and Their Mutual Relations.* London: Taylor and Francis, 1937.

————. *Dr. Edmond Halley (1656–1742): A Bibliographical Guide to His Life and Work Arranged Chronologically.* London: Taylor and Francis, 1939.

————, ed. *Correspondence and Papers of Edmond Halley.* Oxford: Clarendon Press, 1932. Reprint, New York: Arno Press, 1975.

Madeweis, Friedrich. *Cometa A[nn]o MDC LXXX et LXXXI.* Berlin, 1681.

Mairan, Jean Jacques d'Ortous de. *Traité physique et historique de l'aurore boréale.* Paris, 1733.

————. *Traité physique et historique de l'aurore boréale.* Rev. 2d ed. Paris, 1754.

Malcolmson, Robert W. *Popular Recreations in English Society, 1700–1850.* Cambridge: Cambridge University Press, 1973.

Mallement de Messange, Claude. *Dissertation sur les cometes à monsieur le procureur général du Grand Conseil.* Paris, 1681.

Mallet, Alain. *Description de l'univers.* Paris, 1683.

Malthus, Thomas Robert. *An Essay on the Principle of Population.* London, 1798.

Manilius, Marcus. *Astronomica.* Translated by G. P. Goold. Loeb Classical Library. Cambridge: Harvard University Press, 1977.

Manuel, Frank E. *Isaac Newton, Historian.* Cambridge: Cambridge University Press, 1963.

Marsden, Brian G. *Catalogue of Cometary Orbits.* 4th ed. Cambridge: Central Bureau for Astronomical Telegrams and Minor Planet Center of the International Astronomical Union, located at the Smithsonian Astrophysical Observatory, 1982.

Martin, Benjamin. *The Philosophical Grammar; Being a View of the Present State of Experimented Physiology, or Natural Philosophy.* London, 1735.

———. *The Wonders of the Cometary World displayed in Five New Views of the Mundane System; With a True Elevation of the Orbit of the Comet of the Year 1744.* [London], 1754.

———. *The Young Gentleman and Lady's Philosophy.* 2 vols. The General Magazine of Arts and Sciences, pt. 1. London, 1755–1763.

———. *The Theory of Comets, Illustrated, in Four Parts. I. An Essay on the Natural History and Philosophy of Comets; being the Substance of all that has been hitherto published on that Head. II. Tables, containing the Elements of the Theory of a Comet's Motion, (in a Parabola or an Ellipsis) with their Nature and Use explained. III. The Method of constructing the Orbit of any Comet, and computing its Place therein; its Latitude and Longitude, as seen from the Earth or Sun; its Distance, Velocity, Magnitude, Length of Tail, and other Particulars relative thereto. IV. The Method of delineating the visible Path of a Comet in the Heavens, on the Surface of a Celestial Globe; and for drawing the Trajectory by Protraction with Scale and Compasses. The whole adapted to, and exemplified in the Orbit of the Comet of the Year 1682, whose Return is now near at Hand.* London, 1757.

———. "Of the Visible Way of the present Comet among the Stars, &c." In *Miscellaneous Correspondence, Containing a Variety of Subjects Relative to Natural and Civil History, Geography, Mathematics, Poetry, Memoirs of monthly Occurrences, Catalogues of new Books, &c.,* 2:646–647. The General Magazine of Arts and Sciences, pt. 5, vols. 1–2. London, 1759.

Martin, Ernest L. *The Birth of Christ Recalculated.* 2d ed. Pasadena: Foundation for Biblical Research, 1980.

Mather, Cotton. *A Voice from Heaven. An Account of a Late Uncommon Appearance in the Heavens.* Boston, 1719.

———. *The Christian Philospher.* London, 1721.

———. *Manuductio ad ministerium. Directions for a Candidate of the Ministry.* Boston, 1726.

———. *An Essay on Comets, Their Nature, The Laws of their Motions, the Cause and Magnitude of their Atmosphere, and Tails; With a Conjecture of their Use and Design.* Boston, 1744.

Mather, Increase. *Heaven's Alarm to the World or a Sermon, wherein is shewed, that Fearful Sights And Signs in Heaven, are the Presages of great Calamities at*

hand. *Preached at the Lecture of Boston in New-England; January 20. 1680*. 2d ed. Boston, 1682.

Mather, Increase. *The Latter Sign Discoursed of, in a Sermon Preached at the Lecture of Boston in New-England August, 31. 1682. Wherein is shewed, that the Voice of God in Signal Providences, especially when repeated and Iterated, ought to be Hearkned unto*. Boston, 1682.

———. *ΚΟΜΗΤΟΓΡΑΦΙΑ [Kometographia]. Or a Discourse Concerning Comets; Wherein the Nature of Blazing Stars is Enquired into: With an Historical Account of all the Comets which have appeared from the Beginning of the World unto this present Year, M.DC.LXXXIII. Expressing The Place in the Heavens, where they were seen, Their Motion, Forms, Duration; and the Remarkable Events which have followed in the World, so far as they have been by Learned Men Observed. As also two Sermons Occasioned by the late Blazing Stars*. Boston, 1683.

"The Mather Papers." *Collections of the Massachusetts Historical Society*, 4th ser., 8 (1868).

Matthew, Edward. *ΚΑΡΟΛΟΥ τρισμεγίςγ ἔπιφανία [Karolou trismegistou epiphania]. The Most Glorious Star, or, Celestial Constellation of the Pleiades, or Charles Waine, Appearing, And shining most brightly in a Miraculous manner in the Face of the Sun at Noonday at the Nativity of our Sacred Soveraign King Charles 2d. Presaging his Majesties Exaltation to future Honour and Greatness Transcending not only the most potent Christian Princes in Europe, but by Divine designment ordained to be the most Mighty Monarch in the Universe: Never any Star having appeared before at the birth of any (the Highest humane Hero) except our Saviour*. London, 1660.

Maupertuis, Pierre Louis Moreau de. *Discours sur les differentes figures des astres; d'ou l'on tire des conjectures sur les étoiles qui paroissent changer de grandeur; & sur l'anneau de Saturne*. Paris, 1732.

———. *Lettre sur la comète*. [Amsterdam?], 1742.

———. *Essai de cosmologie*. Leiden, 1751.

———. *Oeuvres de Maupertuis*. 4 vols. Lyons, 1768.

Mendelsohn, Everett. *Heat and Life: The Development of the Theory of Animal Heat*. Cambridge: Harvard University Press, 1964.

Merlin Reviv'd: Or, An Old Prophecy Found in a Manuscript in Pontefract Castle in York-shire. [London, 1681].

Mervyn, Audley. *A Speech Made by Sir Audley Mervyn his Majesties Prime Serjeant at Law in Ireland, the 11th. day of May in the House of Lords, when he was presented Speaker by the Commons*. Dublin, 1661.

Miller, Perry. *Errand into the Wilderness*. Cambridge: Harvard University Press, 1956. Reprint, Cambridge: Belknap Press, 1981.

———. *The New England Mind: The Seventeenth Century*. Cambridge: Harvard University Press, 1954. Reprint, Cambridge: Belknap Press, 1982.

———. *The New England Mind: From Colony to Province*. Cambridge: Harvard University Press, 1953. Reprint, Cambridge: Belknap Press, 1983.

Miller, Perry, and Thomas H. Johnson, eds. *The Puritans: A Sourcebook of Their Writings*. Rev. ed. 2 vols. New York: Harper Torchbooks, 1963.

Miller, Valentine Rodger, and Reese P. Miller, eds. and trans. *See* Descartes, 1983.

Milton, John. *Paradise Lost*. London, 1667.

———. *Paradise Lost*. In *The Complete English Poetry of John Milton*, edited by

John T. Shawcross. Anchor Seventeenth-Century Series. Garden City, N.Y.: Anchor Books, 1963.

Mirabilis Annus, Or the year of Prodigies and Wonders. N.p., 1661.

Mirabilis Annus Secundus; Or, The Second Year of Prodigies. N.p., 1662.

Mirabilis Annus Secundus: Or, The Second Part Of the Second Years Prodigies. N.p., 1662.

Mr. Whiston's Scheme of the Solar System epitomiz'd. To wch is annex'd a translation of part of ye general scholium at ye end of ye second Edition of Sr. Isaac Newton's Principia. Concerning God. London, [ca. 1825?].

Montagu, M. F. Ashley, ed. *Studies and Essays in the History of Science and Learning Offered in Homage to George Sarton.* New York: Henry Schuman, [1946].

Montaño, John Patrick. "The Quest for Consensus: The Lord Mayor's Day Shows in the 1670s." In *Culture and Society in the Stuart Restoration,* edited by Gerald Maclean, 31–51. Cambridge: Cambridge University Press, 1995.

The Monthly Review 37 (1767).

The Mystery of Ambras Merlins, Standardbearer Wolf. and last Boar of Cornwal. With Sundry other Misterious Prophecys, both Ancient and Modern, plainly unfolded in the following treatise, on the signification and portent of that prodigious Comet, seen by most part of the world Anno 1680 with the B[la]zing Star Anno 1682, and the conjunctions of Saturn and Jupiter in October following, and since, all which do purport many sad calamitys to befall most parts of the Europian continent in general before the year 1699. Some sooner then others. . . . Written by a lover of his country's Peace. London, 1683.

Needham, Joseph. *Science and Civilization in China.* Vol. 3, *Mathematics and the Sciences of the Heavens and the Earth.* Cambridge: Cambridge University Press, 1959.

N[ess], C[hristopher]. *A Full and True Account of the Late Blazing-Star: With some probable Prognosticks upon what may be its Effects.* London, 1680.

———. *The Lord Stafford's Ghost: Or, A Warning to Traitors, with His Prophesie Concerning the Blazing-Star.* London, [1681].

———. *A Philosophical and Divine Discourse Blazoning upon this Blazing Star: Divided into Three Parts; The I. Treating on the Product, Form, Colour, Motion, Scituation, and Signification of Comets. II. Contains the Prognosticks of Comets in General, and of this in particular; together with a Chronology of all the Comets for the last 400 years. III. Consists of (1.) the Explication of the grand Concerns of this Comet by Astrological Precepts and Presidents. (2.) The Application of its probable Prognosticks Astrologically and Theologically.* London, 1681.

———. *The Signs of the Times: Or, Wonderful Signs of Wonderful Times. Being A Faithful Collection and Impartial Relation of several Signs and Wonders, call'd properly Prodigies, (together with some Philosophical and Theological Descants upon them) which have been seen in the Heavens, on the Earth, and on the Waters, as they have been Testifyed by very Credible Hands. All which have hapned within the compass of this last Year 1680. Which may well be called another Annus Mirabilis, or Wonderful Year, wherein the Lord hath given us Loud Warnings to Repent of our Sins and Return to him, that he may have Mercy upon us.* London, 1681.

———. *An Astrological and Theological Discourse Upon this present Great Conjunction (The like whereof hath not (likely) been in some Ages.) Usherd in by a Great Comet. And so far, upon the Heavens, the Planets, and fixed Stars as is a*

Necessary Introduction into a Distinct and full Knowledg of the Principal Subject Herein Handled. London, 1682.

N[ess], C[hristopher]. *A True Account of this Present Blasing-Star. Presenting itself to the View of the World. This August. 1682. with Sundry Considerable Remarks and Observations thereupon*. London, 1682.

Neuburg, Victor E. *Popular Literature: A History and Guide from the Beginning of Printing to the Year 1897*. Harmondsworth: Penguin Books, 1977.

Neugebauer, Otto. *The Exact Sciences in Antiquity*. 2d ed. New York: Dover Publications, 1969.

―――. *A History of Ancient Mathematical Astronomy*. 3 vols. New York: Springer-Verlag, 1975.

The New English Bible with the Apocrypha. New York: Oxford University Press, 1970.

The New Oxford Annotated Bible with the Apocrypha. Revised standard version. Edited by Herbert G. May and Bruce M. Metzger. New York: Oxford University Press, 1977.

Newman, James R. Review of *The Comets and Their Origins*, by R. A. Lyttleton. *Scientific American* 189 (July 1953): 88. Reprinted in *Comets: Readings from Scientific American*, 35–38. See Brandt, 1981.

Newton, Isaac. *Philosophiae naturalis principia mathematica*. London, 1687.

―――. *Opticks: Or, a Treatise of the Reflexions, Refractions, Inflexions and Colours of Light*. London, 1704.

―――. *Optice sive de reflexionibus, refractionibus, inflexionibus & coloribus lucis libri tres*. London, 1706.

―――. "De natura acidorum," and "Some Thoughts about the Nature of Acids" [1710]. In *Lexicon technicum*, vol. 2. See Harris, 1704–1710.

―――. *Philosophiae naturalis principia mathematica*. 2d ed. Cambridge, 1713.

―――. *Philosophiae naturalis principia mathematica*. 3d ed. London, 1726.

―――. *De mundi systemate liber*. London, 1728.

―――. *A Treatise of the System of the World*. London, 1728.

―――. *Theological Manuscripts*. Edited by Herbert McLachlan. Liverpool: Liverpool University Press, 1950.

―――. *Opticks or A Treatise of the Reflections, Refractions, Inflections & Colours of Light*. 4th ed. London, 1730. Reprint, New York: Dover, 1952.

―――. *The Correspondence of Isaac Newton*. Edited by H. W. Turnbull et al. 7 vols. Cambridge: Cambridge University Press, 1959–1977.

―――. *Sir Isaac Newton's Mathematical Principles of Natural Philosophy and His System of the World*. Translated by Andrew Motte in 1729 and revised by Florian Cajori. Berkeley and Los Angeles: University of California Press, 1962.

―――. *Unpublished Scientific Papers of Isaac Newton: A Selection from the Portsmouth Collection in the University Library, Cambridge*. Edited by A. R. Hall and M. B. Hall. Cambridge: Cambridge University Press, 1962.

―――. *The Mathematical Papers of Isaac Newton*. Edited by D. T. Whiteside. 8 vols. Cambridge: Cambridge University Press, 1967–1981.

―――. *Philosophiae naturalis principia mathematica*. 3d ed. with variant readings. Edited by Alexandre Koyré and I. Bernard Cohen, with the assistance of Anne Whitman. 2 vols. Cambridge: Harvard University Press, 1972.

―――. *Newton's Papers and Letters on Natural Philosophy*. Edited by I. Bernard Cohen. 2d ed. Cambridge: Harvard University Press, 1978.

————. *Certain Philosophical Questions: Newton's Trinity Notebook.* Edited by J. E. McGuire and Martin Tamny. Cambridge: Cambridge University Press, 1983.

————. *The Preliminary Manuscripts for Isaac Newton's 1687 Principia, 1684–1685.* Edited by D. T. Whiteside. Cambridge: Cambridge University Press, 1989.

A New-Years-Gift for Plotters. N.p., 1681.

Nicolson, Marjorie Hope. *Mountain Gloom and Mountain Glory: The Development of the Aesthetics of the Infinite.* Ithaca: Cornell University Press, 1959.

————. *Pepys' "Diary" and the New Science.* Charlottesville: University Press of Virginia, 1965.

————. *Science and Imagination.* Ithaca: Cornell University Press, 1956. Reprint, Hamden, Conn.: Archon Press, 1976.

Nicolson, Marjorie Hope, and Nora M. Mohler. "The Scientific Background of Swift's *Voyage to Laputa.*" *Annals of Science* 2 (1937): 299–334.

North, John D. "Astrology and the Fortunes of Churches." *Centaurus* 24 (1980): 181–211.

————. "Celestial Influence—The Major Premiss of Astrology." In *"Astrologi hallucinati": Stars and the End of the World in Luther's Time,* edited by Paola Zambelli, 45–100. Berlin: Walter de Gruyter, 1986.

Ogilby, John. *The Entertainment of His Most Excellent Majestie Charles II, in His Passage through the City of London to His Coronation.* London, 1662.

Oldenburg, Henry. *The Correspondence of Henry Oldenburg.* Edited by A. Rupert Hall and Marie Boas Hall. 13 vols. Vols. 1–9, Madison: University of Wisconsin Press, 1965–1973; vols. 10–11, London: Mansell, 1975–1977; vols. 12–13, London: Taylor & Francis, 1986.

Oliver, Andrew. *An Essay on Comets.* Salem, 1772.

Olson, Richard. "Tory-High Church Opposition to Science and Scientism in the Eighteenth Century: The Works of John Arbuthnot, Jonathan Swift, and Samuel Johnson." In *The Uses of Science in the Age of Newton,* edited by John G. Burke, 171–204. Berkeley and Los Angeles: University of California Press, 1983.

Olson, Roberta J. M. "Giotto's Portrait of Halley's Comet." *Scientific American* 240 (May 1979): 160–170. Reprinted in *Comets: Readings from Scientific American,* 1–9. *See* Brandt, 1981.

————. *Fire and Ice: A History of Comets in Art.* New York: Walker & Company for the National Air and Space Museum, Smithsonian Institution, 1985.

Olson, R.J.M., and J. M. Pasachoff. "Historical Comets over Bavaria: The *Nuremberg Chronicle* and Broadsides." In *Comets in the Post-Halley Era,* edited by R. L. Newburn, Jr., et al., 2:1309–1341. 2 vols. Dordrecht: Kluwer Academic Publishers, 1991.

O'Neil, Mary R. "*Sacerdote ovvero strione*: Ecclesiastical and Superstitious Remedies in Sixteenth Century Italy." In *Understanding Popular Culture: Europe from the Middle Ages to the Nineteenth Century,* edited by Steven L. Kaplan, 53–83. Berlin: Mouton Publishers, 1984.

Oresme, Nicole. *Le livre de divinacions. See* Coopland, 1952.

————. *De causis mirabilium.* Latin text with English translation by Bert Hansen. *See* Hansen, 1985.

Origen. *Against Celsus* [*Contra Celsum*]. Translated by Frederick Crombie. In *The Ante-Nicene Fathers,* vol. 4. *See* Roberts and Donaldson, 1980–1983.

Oro, J. "Comets and the Formation of Biochemical Compounds on the Primitive Earth." *Nature* 190 (1961): 389–391.

Ozment, Steven. *The Age of Reform (1250–1550)*. New Haven: Yale University Press, 1980.

Panofsky, Erwin. *The Life and Art of Albrecht Dürer*. Princeton: Princeton University Press, 1955.

Paracelsus [Theophrastus von Hohenheim]. *Usslegung des Commeten erschynen im hoch[ge]birg zu mitlem Augsten Anno 1531*. Zurich, 1531.

———. *Sämtliche Werke: I Abteilung, Medizinische, naturwissenschaftliche und philosophische Schriften*. Edited by Karl Sudhoff. 14 vols. Munich: Otto Wilhelm Barth and R. Oldenbourg, 1922–1933.

Paré, Ambroise. *Deux livres de chirurgie*. Paris, 1573.

———. *Les oeuvres d'Ambroise Paré, conseiller, et premier chirurgien du roy. Divisees en vingt sept livres, avec les figures & portraicts, tant de l'anatomie que des instruments de chirurgie, & de plusieurs monstres*. Rev. 2d ed. Paris, 1579.

———. *Les oeuvres d'Ambroise Paré, conseiller, et premier chirurgien du roy. Divisees en vingt huict livres, avec les figures & portraicts, tant de l'anatomie, que des instruments de chirurgie, & de plusieurs monstres*. Rev. 4th ed. Paris, 1585.

———. *Des monstres et prodiges*. Critical ed. Edited by Jean Céard. Travaux d'Humanisme et Renaissance, no. 115. Geneva: Librairie Droz, 1971.

———. *On Monsters and Marvels*. Translated by Janis L. Pallister. Chicago: University of Chicago Press, 1982.

Park, Katharine, and Lorraine J. Daston. "Unnatural Conceptions: The Study of Monsters in Sixteenth- and Seventeenth-Century France and England." *Past and Present* 92 (1981): 20–54.

Parker, Derek. *Familiar to All: William Lilly and Astrology in the Seventeenth Century*. London: Jonathan Cape, 1975.

Payne, Harry C. "Elite versus Popular Mentality in the Eighteenth Century." *Studies in Eighteenth-Century Culture* 8 (1979): 3–32.

Pemberton, Henry. *A View of Sir Isaac Newton's Philosophy*. London, 1728.

Pepys, Samuel. *The Diary of Samuel Pepys*. Edited by Robert Latham and William Matthews. 11 vols. Berkeley and Los Angeles: University of California Press, 1970–1983.

[Perkins, John.] *The True Nature and Cause of the Tails of Comets. Elucidated In a rationale agreeing with their several Phanomena*. Boston, 1772.

Petit, Pierre. *Dissertation sur la nature des cometes*. Paris, 1665.

Pinches, T. G., J. N. Strassmaier, A. J. Sachs, and J. N. Schaumberger. *Late Babylonian Astronomical and Related Texts*. Providence: Brown University Press, 1955.

Pingré, Alexandre Guy. *Cométographie, ou Traité Historique et Théorique des Comètes*. 2 vols. Paris, 1783–1784.

Pingree, David. "A New Look at *Melencolia I*." *Journal of the Warburg and Courtauld Institutes* 43 (1980): 257–258.

Pliny the Elder [Gaius Plinius Secundus]. *Natural History*. Translated by H. Rackham, W.H.S. Jones, and D. E. Eichholz. 10 vols. Loeb Classical Library. Cambridge: Harvard University Press, 1969–1986.

Plutarch. *Plutarch's Morals*. Edited by William W. Goodwin, with an introduction by Ralph Waldo Emerson. 5 vols. Boston: Little, Brown, and Company, 1871.

Plutarch, pseudo-. *See* Aëtius.

Pogo, A. "Earliest Diagrams Showing the Axis of a Comet Tail Coinciding with the Radius Vector." *Isis* 20 (1933): 443–444.

Pope, Alexander. *The Poems of Alexander Pope.* Twickenham Edition. Edited by John Butt et al. 11 vols. London: Methuen & Company, 1961–1969.

———, trans. *The Iliad of Homer.* Edited by Maynard Mack, Norman Callan, Robert Fagles, William Frost, and Douglas M. Knight. Vols. 7–8 of *The Poems of Alexander Pope,* Twickenham Edition. London: Methuen & Company, 1967.

Popkin, Richard H. "The Philosophy of Bishop Stillingfleet." *Journal of the History of Philosophy* 9 (1971): 303–319.

———. "Predicting, Prophecying, Divining and Foretelling from Nostradamus to Hume." *History of European Ideas* 5 (1984): 117–135.

Porter, Roy. "Creation and Credence: The Career of Theories of the Earth in Britain, 1660–1820." In *Natural Order,* edited by Barry Barnes and Steven Shapin, 97–123. Beverly Hills and London: Sage Publications, 1979.

Priestley, Joseph. *The History and Present State of Electricity, with Original Experiments.* London, 1767.

———. *The History and Present State of Discoveries relating to Vision, Light, and Colours.* London, 1772.

———. "Letters of Joseph Priestley." *Proceedings of the Massachusetts Historical Society,* 2d ser., 3 (1886–1887): 11–40.

Pruckner, Hubert, ed. *Studien zu den astrologischen schriften des Heinrich von Langenstein.* Berlin: B. G. Teubner, 1933.

Ptolemy, Claudius. *Tetrabiblos.* Translated by F. E. Robbins. Loeb Classical Library. Cambridge: Harvard University Press, 1980.

Ptolemy, pseudo-. *Claudii Ptolemaei Alexa[n]drini astronomorum principis centum sententiae [Centiloquium]. Interprete Georgio Trapezuntio Lucae Gaurici oratio de inventoribus, utilitate et laudibus astronomiae.* Rome, 1540.

Rampino, Michael R., and Richard B. Stothers. "Geological Rhythms and Cometary Impacts." *Science* 226 (1984): 1427–1431.

———. "Terrestrial Mass Extinctions, Cometary Impacts and the Sun's Motion Perpendicular to the Galactic Plane." *Nature* 308 (1984): 709–712.

Rattansi, P. M. "Newton's Alchemical Studies." In *Science, Medicine and Society in the Renaissance: Essays to Honor Walter Pagel,* edited by Allen G. Debus, 2: 167–182. New York: Science History Publications, 1972.

Raup, David M. *The Nemesis Affair: A Story of the Death of Dinosaurs and the Ways of Science.* New York: W. W. Norton, 1986.

Raup, David M., and J. John Sepkoski, Jr., "Periodicity of Extinctions in the Geologic Past." *Proceedings of the National Academy of Sciences* 81 (1984): 801–805.

Ray, John. *The Wisdom of God Manifested in the Works of the Creation.* 1st ed. London, 1691.

———. *Three Physico-Theological Discourses, concerning I. The Primitive Chaos, and Creation of the World. II. The General Deluge, its Causes and Effects. III. The Dissolution of the World, and Future Conflagration.* 2d ed. London, 1693.

———. *The Wisdom of God Manifested in the Works of the Creation.* 3d ed. London, 1701.

Reay, Barry. "Popular Literature in Seventeenth-Century England." *The Journal of Peasant Studies* 10, no. 4 (1982–1983): 243–249.

———. "Popular Culture in Early Modern England." In *Popular Culture in Seventeenth-Century England,* edited by Barry Reay, 1–30. London: Croom Helm, 1985.

Reay, Barry. "Popular Religion." In *Popular Culture in Seventeenth-Century England*, edited by Barry Reay, 91–128. London: Croom Helm, 1985.

———, ed. *Popular Culture in Seventeenth-Century England*. London: Croom Helm, 1985.

Recorde, Robert. *The Castle of Knowledge*. London, 1556.

Reddy, Francis. *Halley's Comet!* [Milwaukee]: AstroMedia, 1985.

Redwood, John. *Reason, Ridicule and Religion: The Age of Englightenment in England, 1660–1750*. Cambridge: Harvard University Press, 1976.

Reedy, Gerard. "Mystical Politics: The Imagery of Charles II's Coronation." In *Studies in Change and Revolution: Aspects of English Intellectual History, 1640–1800*, edited by Paul J. Korshin, 19–42. Menston, Yorkshire: Scolar Press, 1972.

Revel, Jacques. "Forms of Expertise: Intellectuals and 'Popular' Culture in France (1650–1800)." In *Understanding Popular Culture: Europe from the Middle Ages to the Nineteenth Century*, edited by Steven L. Kaplan, 255–273. Berlin: Mouton Publishers, 1984.

Reynmann, Leonhart. *Practica uber die grossen und manigfeltigen Coniunction der Planeten die iñ jar M.D.XXiiii. erscheinen*. Nuremberg, 1524.

Righini Bonelli, M. L., and William R. Shea, eds. *Reason, Experiment, and Mysticism in the Scientific Revolution*. New York: Science History Publications, 1975.

Roberts, Alexander, and James Donaldson, eds. *The Ante-Nicene Fathers*. 10 vols. Grand Rapids: Wm. B. Eerdmans Publishing Company, 1980–1983.

Robinson, James Howard. *The Great Comet of 1680: A Study in the History of Rationalism*. Northfield, Minn.: Press of the Northfield News, 1916.

Rollins, Hyder E. "The Black-Letter Broadside Ballad." *Proceedings of the Modern Language Association* 34 (1919): 258–339.

———, comp. *An Analytical Index to the Ballad-Entries (1577–1709) in the Registers of the Company of Stationers of London*. Chapel Hill: University of North Carolina Press, 1924.

———, ed. *The Pack of Autolycus, or Strange and Terrible News of Ghosts, Apparitions, Monstrous Births, Showers of Wheat, Judgments of God, and other Prodigious and Fearful Happenings as told in Broadside Ballads of the Years 1624–1693*. Cambridge: Harvard University Press, 1927.

———, ed. *The Pepys Ballads*. 8 vols. Cambridge: Harvard University Press, 1929–1932.

Ronan, Colin A. *Edmond Halley: Genius in Eclipse*. Garden City, N.Y.: Doubleday & Company, 1969.

Rosen, Edward. "Kepler's Attitude toward Astrology and Mysticism." In *Occult and Scientific Mentalities in the Renaissance*, ed. Brian Vickers, 253–272. Cambridge: Cambridge University Press, 1984.

Rostagny, Jean de. *Traité de Primerose sur les erreurs vulgaires de la medicine, avec des additions très curieuses par M. de Rostagny*. Lyons, 1689.

Rousseau, G. S. " 'Wicked Whiston' and the Scriblerians: Another Ancients-Modern Controversy." *Studies in Eighteenth-Century Culture* 17 (1987): 17–44.

The Roxburghe Ballads. 8 vols. Hertford: Stephen Austin and Sons for the Ballad Society, 1869–1901. Reprint, New York: AMS Press, 1966.

Ruffner, James A. "The Background and Early Development of Newton's Theory of Comets." Ph.D. diss., Indiana University, 1966.

———. "The Curved and the Straight: Cometary Theory from Kepler to Hevelius." *Journal for the History of Astronomy* 2 (1971): 178–194.

Rusche, Harry. "Merlini Anglici: Astrology and Propaganda from 1644 to 1651." *English Historical Review* 80 (1965): 322–333.

―――. "Prophecies and Propaganda, 1641 to 1651." *English Historical Review* 84 (1969): 752–770.

Sachs, A. J. "A Classification of the Babylonian Astronomical Tablets of the Seleucid Period." *Journal of Cuneiform Studies* 2 (1948): 271–290.

―――. "Babylonian Observational Astronomy." In *The Place of Astronomy in the Ancient World*, edited by F. R. Hodson, 43–50. London: Oxford University Press for the British Academy, 1974. Also published in *Philosophical Transactions of the Royal Society*, ser. A, 276 (1974): 43–50.

Sagan, Carl, and Ann Druyan. *Comet*. New York: Random House, 1985.

Sandrart, Jacob. *Dieser schrekliche Comet Stern ist zu Grätz den 2 Januari Anno 1664 . . . gesehen worden*. [N.p., 1664].

Sarsi, Lothario. *See* Grassi, Orazio.

Scaliger, Julius Caesar. *Exotericarum exercitationum liber quintus decimus, de subtilitate, ad Hieronymum Cardanum*. Paris, 1557.

Schafer, Edward H. *Pacing the Void: T'ang Approaches to the Stars*. Berkeley and Los Angeles: University of California Press, 1977.

Schaff, Philip, ed. *A Select Library of the Nicene and Post-Nicene Fathers of the Christian Church*. 1st ser. 14 vols. Grand Rapids: Wm. B. Eerdmans Publishing Company, 1980–1983.

Schaff, Philip, and Henry Wace, eds. *A Select Library of Nicene and Post-Nicene Fathers of the Christian Church*. 2d ser. 14 vols. Grand Rapids: Wm. B. Eerdmans Publishing Company, 1982–1983.

Schaffer, Simon. "Halley's Atheism and the End of the World." *Notes and Records of the Royal Society of London* 32 (1977): 17–40.

―――. "The Phoenix of Nature: Fire and Evolutionary Cosmology in Wright and Kant." *Journal for the History of Astronomy* 9 (1978): 180–200.

―――. "'The Great Laboratories of the Universe': William Herschel on Matter Theory and Planetary Life." *Journal for the History of Astronomy* 11 (1980): 81–111.

―――. "Herschel in Bedlam: Natural History and Stellar Astronomy." *British Journal for the History of Science* 13 (1980): 211–239.

―――. "Uranus and the Establishment of Herschel's Astronomy." *Journal for the History of Astronomy* 12 (1981): 11–26.

―――. "Authorized Prophets: Comets and Astronomers after 1759." *Studies in Eighteenth-Century Culture* 17 (1987): 45–74.

―――. "Newton's Comets and the Transformation of Astrology." In *Astrology, Science, and Society*, edited by Patrick Curry, 219–243. Woodbridge, Suffolk: The Boydell Press, 1987.

―――. "Halley, Delisle, and the Making of the Comet." In *Standing on the Shoulders of Giants: A Longer View of Newton and Halley*, edited by Norman J. W. Thrower, 254–298. Berkeley and Los Angeles: University of California Press, 1990.

―――. "Comets and Idols: Newton's Cosmology and Political Theology." In *Action and Reaction: Proceedings of a Symposium to Commemorate the Tercentenary of Newton's Principia*, edited by Paul Theerman and Adele F. Seeff, 206–231. Newark: University of Delaware Press, 1993.

Schechner Genuth, Sara. "The Teleological Role of Comets in Seventeenth and

Eighteenth Century Natural Philosophy." *Bulletin of the American Astronomical Society* 16, no. 2 (1984): 476–477.

Schechner Genuth, Sara. "Comets, Teleology, and the Relationship of Chemistry to Cosmology in Newton's Thought." *Annali dell'Istituto e Museo di Storia della Scienza di Firenze* 10, pt. 2 (1985): 31–65.

———. "From Monstrous Signs to Natural Causes: The Assimilation of Comet Lore into Natural Philosophy." Ph.D. diss., Harvard University, 1988.

———. "Blazing Stars, Open Minds, and Loosened Purse Strings: Astronomical Research and Its Early Cambridge Audience." *Journal for the History of Astronomy* 21 (1990): 9–20.

———. "Newton and the Ongoing Teleological Role of Comets." In *Standing on the Shoulders of Giants: A Longer View of Newton and Halley*, edited by Norman J. W. Thrower, 299–311. Berkeley and Los Angeles: University of California Press, 1990.

———. "Astronomical Imagery in a Passage of Homer." *Journal for the History of Astronomy* 23 (1992): 293–298.

———. "Devils' Hells and Astronomers' Heavens: Religion, Method, and Popular Culture in Speculations about Life on Comets." In *The Invention of Physical Science: Intersections of Mathematics, Theology and Natural Philosophy since the Seventeenth Century. Essays in Honor of Erwin N. Hiebert*, edited by Mary Jo Nye, Joan L. Richards, and Roger H. Stuewer, 3–26. Dordrecht: Kluwer Academic Publishers, 1992.

———. "From Heaven's Alarm to Public Appeal: Comets and the Rise of Astronomy at Harvard." In *Science at Harvard University: Historical Perspectives*, edited by Clark A. Elliott and Margaret W. Rossiter, 28–54. Bethlehem: Lehigh University Press, 1992; London: Associated University Presses, 1992.

Schedel, Hartmann. *Buch der Chroniken.* Nuremberg: Anton Koberger, 1493.

———. *Liber cronicarum.* Nuremberg, 1493.

———. *The Nuremberg Chronicle.* Facsimile reprint of the German ed. New York: Landmark Press, 1979.

Schofield, Robert E. *Mechanism and Materialism: British Natural Philosophy in an Age of Reason.* Princeton: Princeton University Press, 1970.

Schwartz, Richard D., and Philip B. James. "Periodic Mass Extinctions and the Sun's Oscillation about the Galactic Plane." *Nature* 308 (1984): 712–713.

The Scriblerus Club [Jonathan Swift, Alexander Pope, John Gay, John Arbuthnot, Thomas Parnell, and Robert Harley, earl of Oxford]. *Memoirs of the Extraordinary Life, Works, and Discoveries of Martinus Scriblerus* [1741]. Edited by Charles Kerby-Miller. New York: Russell & Russell, 1966.

Séguin, Jean-Pierre. *L'information en France avant le périodique: 517 canards imprimés entre 1529 et 1631.* Paris: Éditions G.-P. Maisonneuve et Larose, 1964.

Seneca, Lucius Annaeus. *Naturales quaestiones.* Translated by Thomas H. Corcoran. 2 vols. Loeb Classical Library. Cambridge: Harvard University Press, 1971–1972.

Severin, Christian. See Longomontanus.

Shaaber, M. A. *Some Forerunners of the Newspaper in England, 1476–1622.* New York: Octagon Books, 1966.

Shakelton, Francis. *A blazyng Starre or burnyng Beacon, seene the 10. of October laste (and yet continewyng) set on fire by Gods providence, to call all sinners to earnest & speedie repentance.* London; 1580; S.T.C. 22272.

Shakespeare, William. *The Riverside Shakespeare*. Edited by G. Blakemore Evans. Boston: Houghton Mifflin Company, 1974.

Shepard, Leslie. *The Broadside Ballad: A Study in Origins and Meaning*. London: Herbert Jenkins, 1962.

———. *The History of Street Literature*. Newton Abbot: David & Charles, 1973.

———, ed. *Street Literature: A Collection of 944 Whiteletter Broadside Ballads*. Hale, Altrincham: C. R. Johnson and C. P. Thiedeman, 1980.

Shumaker, Wayne. *The Occult Sciences in the Renaissance: A Study in Intellectual Patterns*. Berkeley and Los Angeles: University of California Press, 1972.

Sibley, John Langdon, and Clifford Kenyon Shipton. *Sibley's Harvard Graduates*. 17 vols. Cambridge and Boston, 1873–1975.

Silverman, Kenneth. *The Life and Times of Cotton Mather*. New York: Columbia University Press, 1985.

———, ed. *Selected Letters of Cotton Mather*. Baton Rouge: Louisiana State University Press, 1971.

Simpson, William. *Hydrologia Chymica: or, the Chymical Anatomy of the Scarbrough, And other Spaws in York-Shire*. London, 1669.

The Soncino Chumash: The Five Books of Moses with Haphtaroth. Hebrew text with English translation and commentary. Edited by A. Cohen. London: The Soncino Press, 1947.

Speck, W. A. *Stability and Strife: England, 1714–1760*. Cambridge: Harvard University Press, 1977.

Speiser, David. "The Distance of the Fixed Stars and the Riddle of the Sun's Radiation." In *Mélanges Alexandre Koyré*, 1:541–551. Paris: Hermann, 1964.

Spencer, John. *A Discourse concerning Prodigies: Wherein The Vanity of Presages by them is reprehended, and their true and proper Ends asserted and vindicated*. [Cambridge], 1663.

———. *A Discourse concerning Prodigies. . . . To which is added a short Treatise concerning Vulgar Prophecies*. 2d ed. London, 1665.

Spufford, Margaret. *Small Books and Pleasant Histories: Popular Fiction and Its Readership in Seventeenth-Century England*. London: Methuen, 1981; Athens: University of Georgia Press, 1982.

Standard Dictionary of Folklore, Mythology and Legend. Edited by Maria Leach. 2 vols. New York: Funk & Wagnalls, 1949–1950.

Stearns, Raymond Phineas. *Science in the British Colonies of America*. Urbana: University of Illinois Press, 1970.

Steffens, Henry John. *The Development of Newtonian Optics in England*. New York: Science History Publications, 1977.

Stephenson, F. Richard. "The Babylonians Saw That Comet, Too." *Natural History* 94 (December 1985): 14–20.

———. "The Ancient History of Halley's Comet." In *Standing on the Shoulders of Giants: A Longer View of Newton and Halley*, edited by Norman J. W. Thrower, 231–253. Berkeley and Los Angeles: University of California Press, 1990.

Stephenson, F. Richard, and Christopher B. F. Walker, eds. *Halley's Comet in History*. London: British Museum Publications, 1985.

Stephenson, F. Richard, and Kevin K. C. Yau. "Far Eastern Observations of Halley's Comet: 240 BC to AD 1368." *Journal of the British Interplanetary Society* 38 (1985): 195–216.

Stephenson, F. Richard, Kevin K. C. Yau, and Hermann Hunger. "Records of Halley's Comet on Babylonian Tablets." *Nature* 314 (1985): 587–592.

Stewart, Philip. "Science and Superstition: Comets and the French Public in the Eighteenth Century." *American Journal of Physics* 54, no. 1 (January 1986): 16–24.

Sticker, B. "Herschel's Cosmology." *History of Science* 3 (1964): 91–101.

Stukeley, William. *Memoirs of Sir Isaac Newton's Life*. Edited by A. Hastings White. London: Taylor and Francis, 1936.

Suetonius [Gaius Suetonius Tranquillus]. *The Lives of the Caesars*. Translated by J. C. Rolfe. 2 vols. Loeb Classical Library. London: William Heinemann, 1914.

Swan, John. *Speculum Mundi: or A Glasse Representing the Face of the World*. Cambridge, 1635.

Swift, Jonathan [Lemuel Gulliver, pseud.]. *Travels into Several Remote Nations of the World*. 2 vols. London, 1726.

———. *The Works of the Rev. Jonathan Swift, D.D., Dean of St. Patrick's, Dublin*. Edited by Thomas Sheridan. Revised by John Nichols. New ed. 19 vols. London, 1801.

———. *The Prose Works of Jonathan Swift, D.D.* Edited by Temple Scott. 12 vols. London: George Bell and Sons, 1897–1908.

Swift, Jonathan, and Alexander Pope. *Miscellanies*. 4 vols. London, 1732–1733.

Swinden, Tobias. *An Enquiry into the Nature and Place of Hell*. London, 1714.

Swisher, Carl C., III, et al. "Coeval ^{40}Ar/^{39}Ar Ages of 65.0 Million Years Ago from Chicxulub Crater Melt Rock and Cretaceous-Tertiary Boundary Tektites." *Science* 257 (1992): 954–958.

Sykes, Norman. *Church and State in England in the Eighteenth Century*. Cambridge: Cambridge University Press, 1934.

Synesius Cyrenaeus. *The Essays and Hymns of Synesius of Cyrene*. Translated by Augustine FitzGerald. 2 vols. London: Oxford University Press, 1930.

Tacitus, Cornelius. *The Annals*. Translated by John Jackson. 3 vols. Loeb Classical Library. Cambridge: Harvard University Press, 1951.

Tamny, Martin. "Newton, Creation, and Perception." *Isis* 70 (1979): 48–58.

Tanner, Benjamin. *Dictionary of Arts and Sciences*. Philadelphia, 1798.

Tasso, Torquato. *Godfrey of Bulloigne, or The Recoverie of Jerusalem. Done into English Heroicall verse, by Edward Fairefax Gent*. London, 1600.

———. *Jerusalem Delivered*. Translated by Joseph Tusiani. Rutherford, N.J.: Fairleigh Dickinson University Press, 1970.

———. *Opere*. Edited by Ettore Mazzali. 2 vols. Naples: Casa Editrice Fulvio Rossi, 1970.

Tester, S. J. *A History of Western Astrology*. New York: Ballantine Books, 1989.

Thackray, Arnold. "'Matter in a Nut-shell': Newton's *Opticks* and Eighteenth Century Chemistry." *Ambix* 15 (1968): 28–53.

———. *Atoms and Powers: An Essay on Newtonian Matter-Theory and the Development of Chemistry*. Cambridge: Harvard University Press, 1970.

Thaddeus, Patrick, and Gary A. Chanan. "Cometary Impacts, Molecular Clouds, and the Motion of the Sun Perpendicular to the Galactic Plane." *Nature* 314 (1985): 73–75.

Theophrastus. *Enquiry into Plants and Minor Works on Odours and Weather Signs*. Translated by Sir Arthur Hort. 2 vols. Loeb Classical Library. Cambridge: Harvard University Press, 1948–1949.

Thomas, Keith. *Religion and the Decline of Magic*. New York: Charles Scribner's Sons, 1971.

———. *Man and the Natural World*. London: Allen Lane, 1983.

Thomas Aquinas, Saint. *The "Summa Theologica" of St. Thomas Aquinas*. Translated by the Fathers of the English Dominican Province. 22 vols. New York: Benziger Brothers, 1912–1925.

———. "Commentary on Aristotle, Liber I Meteorologicorum, Lectiones VIII, IX, X." Translated by Lynn Thorndike. *See* Thorndike, 1950.

Thompson, Roger. "Popular Reading and Humour in Restoration England." *Journal of Popular Culture* 9 (1975–1976): 653–671.

———, ed. *Samuel Pepys' Penny Merriments*. New York: Columbia University Press, 1977.

Thompson, Stith. *Motif-Index of Folk-Literature: A Classification of Narrative Elements in Folktales, Ballads, Myths, Fables, Mediaeval Romances, Exempla, Fabliaux, Jest-Books, and Local Legends*. Rev. and enl. ed. 6 vols. Bloomington: Indiana University Press, 1955–1958.

Thomson, S. Harrison. "The Text of Grosseteste's *De cometis*." *Isis* 19 (1933): 19–25.

Thoresby, Ralph. *The Diary of Ralph Thoresby, F.R.S.* Edited by Joseph Hunter. 2 vols. London: Henry Colburn and Richard Bentley, 1830.

Thorndike, Lynn. *A History of Magic and Experimental Science*. 8 vols. New York: Columbia University Press, 1923–1958.

———. "Aegidius of Lessines on Comets." In *Studies and Essays in the History of Science and Learning Offered in Homage to George Sarton*, edited by M. F. Ashley Montagu, 403–414. New York: Henry Schuman, [1946].

———, ed. *Latin Treatises on Comets between 1238 and 1368* A.D. Chicago: University of Chicago Press, 1950.

Thrower, Norman J. W. "Edmond Halley: His Life and Scientific Achievements." *Studies in Eighteenth-Century Culture* 17 (1987): 3–15.

———, ed. *Standing on the Shoulders of Giants: A Longer View of Newton and Halley*. Berkeley and Los Angeles: University of California Press, 1990.

T[onge], E[zerel]. *The Northern Star: The British Monarchy: Or, The Northern the Fourth Universal Monarchy; Charles II, and his Successors, the Founders of the Northern, Last, Fourth, and most Happy Monarchy. Being a Collection of many choice Ancient and Modern Prophecies: Wherein also the Fates of the Roman, French, and Spanish Monarchies are occasionally set out*. London, 1680.

Toulmin, Stephen, and June Goodfield. *The Fabric of the Heavens: The Development of Astronomy and Dynamics*. 1961. Reprint, New York: Harper Torchbooks, 1965.

Tucker, Bruce. "Beyond Reason and Revelation: Perspectives on the Puritan Enlightenment." *Studies in Eighteenth-Century Culture* 10 (1981): 165–179.

Tuckerman, Bryant. *Planetary, Lunar, and Solar Positions* A.D. 2 to A.D. 1649 *at Five-day and Ten-day Intervals*. Philadelphia: American Philosophical Society, 1964.

Turnor, Edmund. *Collections for the History of the Town and Soke of Grantham containing Authentic Memoirs of Sir Isaac Newton*. London, 1806.

Tuveson, Ernest. "Swift and the World-Makers." *Journal of the History of Ideas* 11 (1950): 54–74.

Urey, Harold C. "Cometary Collisions and Geological Periods." *Nature* 242 (1973): 32–33.

Van den Bergh, Sidney. "Astronomical Catastrophes in Earth History." *Publications of the Astronomical Society of the Pacific* 106 (1994): 689–695.

Vickers, Brian, ed. *Occult and Scientific Mentalities in the Renaissance*. Cambridge: Cambridge University Press, 1984.

Vigenère, Blaise de. *Traicté des cometes, ou estoilles chevelues, apparoissantes extraordinairement au ciel: Avec leurs causes & effects*. Paris, 1578.

Vince, Samuel. *The Elements of Astronomy*. 4th ed. Cambridge, 1816.

Virgil [Publius Vergilius Maro]. *Aeneid*. Translated by H. Rushton Fairclough. Rev. ed. 2 vols. Loeb Classical Library. Cambridge: Harvard University Press, 1978.

———. *Georgics*. Translated by H. Rushton Fairclough. Rev. ed. Loeb Classical Library. Cambridge: Harvard University Press, 1978.

Voltaire, François Marie Arouet de. *Elémens de la philosophie de Neuton*. Amsterdam, 1738.

———. "Lettre sur la prétendue comète." In *Journal Encyclopédique* (1 June 1773). Reprinted in *Oeuvres complètes de Voltaire*, 29:47–51. Paris: Garnier Frères, 1879.

———. "Si la Terre a été formée par une Comete." In *Dialogues d'Evhémére*. London, 1777.

———. *Oeuvres complètes de Voltaire*. New ed. 52 vols. Paris: Garnier Frères, 1877–1885.

———. *Voltaire's Correspondence*. 107 vols. Geneva: Institut et Musée Voltaire, 1953–1965.

———. *Philosophical Letters*. Translated by Ernest Dilworth. Indianapolis: Bobbs-Merrill Educational Publishing, 1961.

Von einem Schrecklichen und Wunderbarlichen Cometen. [Broadside.] Prague: Peter Codicillus, 1577.

Voragine, Jacobus de. *The Golden Legend or Lives of the Saints as Englished by William Caxton*. 7 vols. London: J. M. Dent & Sons, 1922.

Waff, Craig B. "Comet Halley's First Expected Return: English Public Apprehensions, 1755–58." *Journal for the History of Astronomy* 17 (1986): 1–37.

———. "The First International Halley Watch: Guiding the Worldwide Search for Comet Halley, 1755–1759." In *Standing on the Shoulders of Giants: A Longer View of Newton and Halley*, edited by Norman J. W. Thrower, 373–411. Berkeley and Los Angeles: University of California Press, 1990.

Walker, Adam. *A System of Familiar Philosophy in Twelve Lectures*. London, 1799.

Walker, C.B.F. "Halley's Comet in Babylonia." *Nature* 314 (1985): 576–577.

Walker, D. P. *The Decline of Hell*. Chicago: University of Chicago Press, 1964.

Wallis, Ruth. "The Glory of Gravity—Halley's Comet 1759." *Annals of Science* 41 (1984): 279–286.

Walton, Michael T. "Boyle and Newton on the Transmutation of Water and Air, from the Root of Helmont's Tree." *Ambix* 27 (1980): 11–18.

Warner, Deborah J. *The Sky Explored: Celestial Cartography, 1500–1800*. New York: Alan R. Liss, 1979.

Warren, Erasmus. *Geologia: or, a Discourse Concerning the Earth before the Deluge*. London, 1690.

Webster, Charles. *From Paracelsus to Newton: Magic and the Making of Modern Science*. Cambridge: Cambridge University Press, 1982.

Wedel, Theodore Otto. *The Mediaeval Attitude toward Astrology Particularly in England*. Yale Studies in English, no. 60. New Haven: Yale University Press, 1920.

Wesley, John. *The Works of John Wesley*. 14 vols. London: Wesleyan Conference Office, 1872. Reprint, Grand Rapids, Mich.: Zondervan Publishing House, 1958.

Westfall, Richard S. *Science and Religion in Seventeenth-Century England*. New Haven: Yale University Press, 1958.

———. "The Foundations of Newton's Philosophy of Nature." *British Journal for the History of Science* 1 (1962): 171–182.

———. "Newton and the Hermetic Tradition." In *Science, Medicine and Society in the Renaissance: Essays to Honor Walter Pagel*, edited by Allen G. Debus, 2:183–198. New York: Science History Publications, 1972.

———. "The Role of Alchemy in Newton's Career." In *Reason, Experiment, and Mysticism in the Scientific Revolution*, edited by M. L. Righini Bonelli and William R. Shea, 189–232, 305–316. New York: Science History Publications, 1975.

———. *Never at Rest: A Biography of Isaac Newton*. Cambridge: Cambridge University Press, 1980.

———. "Isaac Newton's *Theologiae Gentilis Origines Philosophicae*." In *The Secular Mind: Transformations of Faith in Modern Europe*, edited by W. Warren Wagar, 15–34. New York: Holmes & Meier, 1982.

———. "Newton's Theological Manuscripts." In *Contemporary Newtonian Research*, edited by Zev Bechler, 129–143. Dordrecht: D. Reidel, 1982.

Westman, Robert S. "The Comet and the Cosmos: Kepler, Mästlin and the Copernican Hypothesis." *Studia Copernicana* 5 (1972): 7–30.

[Wetenhall, Edward.] *A Judgement of the Comet Which became first Generally Visible To Us in Dublin December XIII. About 15 Minutes before 5 in the Evening Anno Dom. 1680. By a Person of Quality*. Dublin, 1682.

Wharton, George. *Calendarium Ecclesiasticum: Or, A New Almanack After the Old Fashion. For the Commune Year of Man's Creation—5607. Redemption—1658. . . . Attended on, by I. A Summary account of the Festivals and Fasts, as well Jewish as Christian, with the Original and end of their Institution. II. Gesta Britannorum. or a Brief Chronologie for 57. years last past, viz. from the year 1600. (in which the late King Charls was born) untill the present 1658*. London, 1658.

Whipple, Fred L. *The Mystery of Comets*. Washington, D.C.: Smithsonian Institution Press, 1985.

Whiston, William. *A New Theory of the Earth, From its Original, to the Consummation of all Things. Wherein the Creation of the World in Six Days, The Universal Deluge, And the General Conflagration, As laid down in the Holy Scriptures, Are Shewn to be perfectly Agreeable to Reason and Philosophy. With a large Introductory Discourse concerning the genuine Nature, Stile, and Extent of the Mosaick History of the Creation*. London, 1696.

———. *A Vindication of the New Theory of the Earth from the Exceptions of Mr. Keill and Others*. London, 1698.

———. *A New Theory of the Earth*. 2d ed., rev. London, 1708.

———. *The Cause of the Deluge Demonstrated: Wherein it is proved that the famous Comet of* A.D. *1680. came by the Earth at the Deluge, and was the occasion*

of it. Being an Appendix to the Second Edition of the New Theory of the Earth. 2d ed., rev. London, 1714.

Whiston, William. *The Cause of the Deluge Demonstrated.* 3d ed., with additions. London, 1716.

————. *Sir Isaac Newton's Mathematick Philosophy More easily Demonstrated: With Dr. Halley's Account of Comets Illustrated. Being Forty Lectures Read in the Publick Schools at Cambridge.* London, 1716.

————. *Astronomical Principles of Religion, Natural and Reveal'd.* London, 1717.

————. *The Astronomical Year: Or, An Account of the many remarkable Celestial Phaenomena of the Great Year MDCCXXXVI. Particularly of the Late Comet, Which was foretold by Sir Isaac Newton, and appeared at its Conclusion.* London, 1737.

————. *A New Theory of the Earth. . . . To which is added, An Appendix, containing a New Theory of the Deluge.* 5th ed., rev. London, 1737.

————. *Memoirs of the Life and Writings of Mr. William Whiston.* 3 vols. London, 1749–1750.

————. *The Eternity of Hell-Torments Considered.* 2d ed. London, 1752.

White, Andrew Dickson. *A History of the Doctrine of Comets.* Papers of the American Historical Association, vol. 2, no. 2. New York: G. P. Putnam's Sons, 1887.

————. *A History of the Warfare of Science with Theology in Christendom.* 2 vols. New York: D. Appleton and Company, 1930.

Whiteside, D. T. "Before the *Principia*: The Maturing of Newton's Thoughts on Dynamical Astronomy, 1664–1684." *Journal for the History of Astronomy* 1 (1970): 5–19.

Whitmire, Daniel P., and Albert A. Jackson IV. "Are Periodic Mass Extinctions Driven by a Distant Solar Companion?" *Nature* 308 (1984): 713–715.

Wickramasinghe, N. C., and Max K. Wallis. "The Cometary Hypothesis of the K/T Mass Extinctions." *Monthly Notices of the Royal Astronomical Society* 270 (1994): 420–426.

Wiener, Carol Z. "The Beleaguered Isle: A Study of Elizabethan and Early Jacobean Anti-Catholicism." *Past and Present* 51 (1971): 27–62.

Williams, John. *Observations of Comets, from* B.C. *611 to* A.D. *1640. Extracted from the Chinese Annals.* London: For the author, 1871.

Williams, Michael E. "Catastrophic versus Noncatastrophic Extinction of the Dinosaurs: Testing, Falsifiability, and the Burden of Proof." *Journal of Paleontology* 68 (1994): 183–190.

Williams, Sheila. "The Pope-Burning Processions of 1679, 1680 and 1681." *Journal of the Warburg and Courtauld Institutes* 21 (1958): 104–118.

Williamson, Hugh. "An Essay on Comets, and an account of their luminous appearance; together with some conjectures concerning the origin of Heat." *Transactions of the American Philosophical Society* 1 (1771): appendix, 27–36.

Wilson, Arthur. *The History of Great Britain, Being the Life and Reign of King James the First, Relating to what passed from his first Accesse to the Crown, till his Death.* London, 1653.

Winthrop, John. *Two Lectures on Comets, Read in the Chapel of Harvard College, in Cambridge, New-England, in April 1759. On Occasion of the Comet which appear'd in that Month. With an Appendix, concerning the Revolutions of that Comet, and of some others.* Boston, 1759.

————. *Two Lectures on Comets.* 2d ed. *See* Davis, 1811.

The Wonderful Blazing Star: with the dreadful Apparition of two Armies in the Air. [Broadside.] London: For Langley Curtiss, 1681.

Wright, Louis B. *Middle-Class Culture in Elizabethan England.* Chapel Hill: University of North Carolina Press, 1935.

Wright, Peter. "Astrology and Science in Seventeenth-Century England." *Social Studies of Science* 5 (1975): 399–422.

Wright, Thomas, of Durham. *An Original Theory or New Hypothesis of the Universe, Founded upon the Laws of Nature, and Solving by Mathematical Principles the General Phaenomena of the Visible Creation; and Particularly the Via Lactea.* London, 1750.

———. *Second or Singular Thoughts upon the Theory of the Universe* [MS ca. 1771]. Edited by M. A. Hoskin. London: Dawsons of Pall Mall, 1968.

———. *An Original Theory or New Hypothesis of the Universe.* Facsimile reprint, edited by Michael A. Hoskin. London: Macdonald, 1971.

Wrightson, Keith. *English Society, 1580–1680.* New Brunswick: Rutgers University Press, 1982.

Wündergesicht der 3 Sonnen und Regenboegen. [Broadside.] Heidelberg, 1622.

Xi Ze-zong. "The Cometary Atlas in the Silk Book of the Han Tomb at Mawang-dui." *Chinese Astronomy and Astrophysics* 8 (1984): 1–7.

Yeomans, Donald K. "The Origin of North American Astronomy—Seventeenth Century." *Isis* 68 (1977): 414–425.

———. *Comet Halley: Fact and Folly.* Santa Ana, Calif.: Gold Stein Press, 1985.

———. *Comets: A Chronological History of Observation, Science, Myth, and Folklore.* New York: Wiley Science Editions, 1991.

Yeomans, Donald K., and Zdenek Sekanina. *The Comet Halley Handbook: An Observer's Guide.* 2d ed. Pasadena: National Aeronautics and Space Administration and the Jet Propulsion Laboratory of California Institute of Technology, 1983.

Yourgrau, Wolfgang, and Allen D. Breck. *Cosmology, History, and Theology.* New York: Plenum Press, 1977.

Zahnle, Kevin, and David Grinspoon. "Comet Dust as a Source of Amino Acids at the Cretaceous/Tertiary Boundary." *Nature* 348 (1990): 157–160.

Zambelli, Paola. "Many Ends for the World: Luca Gaurico Instigator of the Debate in Italy and in Germany." In *"Astrologi hallucinati": Stars and the End of the World in Luther's Time*, edited by Paola Zambelli, 239–263. Berlin: Walter de Gruyter, 1986.

———, ed. *"Astrologi hallucinati": Stars and the End of the World in Luther's Time.* Berlin: Walter de Gruyter, 1986.

About the Author

Sara Schechner Genuth is Resident Scholar at the Dibner Library of the History of Science and Technology at the Smithsonian Institution. For many years the Curator of the History of Astronomy Collection at the Adler Planetarium in Chicago, she is Editor of the Adler Planetarium's catalog of its scientific instrument collection.